# Advertising & Marketing Law:
# Cases and Materials

## Volume II

Fourth Edition · Summer 2018

Rebecca Tushnet
Harvard Law
&
Eric Goldman
Santa Clara University School of Law

# Table of Contents

# Preface to the Fourth Edition

To make this book as accessible and easy-to-use for readers as possible, we have deliberately priced this casebook low and provided a DRM-free e-book. If you think your friends and colleagues would like their own copies, we'd appreciate it if you encouraged them to buy their own low-cost copies rather than sharing your copy with them.

## About the Authors

Eric Goldman is a professor of law and Co-Director of the High Tech Law Institute at Santa Clara University School of Law. Before he became a full-time academic in 2002, he practiced Internet law for eight years in the Silicon Valley. His research and teaching focuses on Internet, intellectual property and advertising law topics, and he blogs on those topics at the Technology & Marketing Law Blog, http://blog.ericgoldman.org. Email: egoldman@gmail.com.

Rebecca Tushnet is a professor of law at Harvard Law School. She clerked for Associate Justice David H. Souter and worked on intellectual property and advertising litigation before beginning teaching. Her academic work focuses on copyright, trademark and advertising law. Her blog is at http://tushnet.blogspot.com. Email: rtushnet@law.harvard.edu.

## A Note to Professors

If you are adopting this book for your course, please email us. We can provide you with a variety of support materials, including our course notes and PowerPoint slide decks as well as access to a database of case-related props. We are also working on a teacher's manual.

## A Note to Students

If you are interested in more information, consider the following resources:

- Professor Tushnet's blog at http://tushnet.blogspot.com or Twitter account at http://twitter.com/rtushnet.
- Professor Goldman's blog at http://blog.ericgoldman.org and Twitter account at http://twitter.com/ericgoldman.
- The ABA Antitrust Section's Advertising Disputes & Litigation Committee (at http://www.abanet.org/dch/committee.cfm?com=AT311570) has a number of useful resources as well, including an email list. They also put on teleconferences about careers in advertising law.

You may also want to check out Professor Goldman's blog post on Pursuing a Career in Advertising Law, http://blog.ericgoldman.org/personal/archives/2012/07/careers_in_adve.html. The post includes course recommendations too.

We are slowly developing a complementary website for the book. Check out our in-process efforts at http://www.advertisinglawbook.com/.

Please email us with your corrections to this casebook and any suggestions for improvement!

**If You Bought a Hard Copy of the Book**

If you bought a hard copy of this book: While we've done our best to make the hard copy version of the book useful to you, the hard copy is missing some features, such as color images, clickable links and keyword searching. You may find a PDF version of the book helpful to complement your hard copy version. Please email Prof. Goldman (egoldman@gmail.com) your purchase receipt (showing which edition you bought) and he will happily email you a PDF at no extra cost to you.

**A Note about International Advertising Law**

On occasion, this book discusses international advertising laws and perspectives. However, we have deliberately chosen to focus on U.S. law. International advertising laws differ from U.S. law in many important ways, so it would be hard to address all of these major differences sufficiently. For more information about international advertising legal issues, you might check out the resources at http://www.galalaw.com/.

**Editing Practices**

Some notes about our editing practices:

- Textual omissions are noted with ellipses.
- Omitted footnotes are not indicated, but all footnote numbers are original.
- In-text citations are omitted without indication (including parenthetical explanations and some parallel citations).
- Although we usually preserved the original formatting (such as italics, bold and block quotes), some of this formatting may have changed or been lost in the conversion.

To improve readability, we have aggressively stripped out case citations and parenthetical explanations (more so than most casebooks). If you are interested in the case's/author's full text or intend to quote or cite any republished materials in the book, we *strongly* recommend that you obtain and reference a copy of the original materials.

To make the book more functional for you, we've liberally provided hyperlinks to underlying source materials throughout the book. You'll see these as blue text in the PDF. Not all sources are linked, and of course, links are likely to rot. Still, we hope you find them helpful.

## Acknowledgements

Thanks are due to many people, including students in Professor Goldman's and Professor Tushnet's respective classes who provided feedback on drafts. Tamara Piety of the University of Tulsa organized a 2011 conference on the casebook, and participants were thoughtful and generous in their responses. Special thanks to James Grimmelmann, Sam Halabi and Brant Harrell for their comments. The authors also would like to extend special thanks to Susanna McCrea, Georgetown Law's manuscript editor, for her work.

CHAPTER 9: OTHER BUSINESS TORTS

---

This chapter doesn't cover the full range of business torts. Instead, it focuses on those most closely connected to false advertising claims, primarily the common law claims of *defamation* and *disparagement*: saying nasty things about the competition or about the competition's goods or services. These claims implicate the First Amendment, and over time the jurisprudence has become more tolerant of critical remarks and comparative advertising.

The torts we'll consider in this chapter can be brought alongside Lanham Act and state consumer protection claims, or occasionally on their own when the plaintiff wouldn't have standing to bring those core claims. They mostly involve statements about competitors' products—not statements about an advertiser's own products. Tortious interference with existing or prospective economic advantage is a potential exception, though that is usually only alleged when there's some sort of comparative statement or solicitation being made.

## 1.     Defamation and Disparagement

Though the Lanham Act and state consumer protection laws generally offer commercial plaintiffs greater prospects of success than defamation and product disparagement, the latter claims are still regularly pled and litigated. As you review the sometimes bewildering variety of common law claims, often with state-by-state variations in the way elements are described, keep in mind that the core differences between the common law causes of action in this chapter and statutory claims under the Lanham Act, the FTCA, and state consumer protection laws revolve around (1) scienter (sufficient knowledge of falsity, usually called "malice" in disparagement cases), (2) intent to harm, and (3) circumstances in which harm to the plaintiff can be presumed for purposes of awarding damages.

In addition, the torts of defamation/disparagement cover all speech, not just commercial speech. Because the causes of action are available to anyone—not just government regulators, competitors or consumers—higher standards with respect to awareness of falsity, intent to harm and proof of damages limit the torts.

Thus, saying something mistaken and negative about a business doesn't automatically lead to liability. Consider, for example, a talk show host who runs a story about the hidden dangers of apples or beef; without heightened standards for knowing falsity and intent to harm, sellers could deter speech about important health issues.

Given the increased First Amendment constraints on the common law claims, it was only a matter of time before a plaintiff bringing both Lanham Act and defamation claims would face the argument that the First Amendment also barred liability without fault under the Lanham Act. As you read the following case, pay attention to the remaining differences between defamation (which targets the plaintiff) and disparagement (which targets the plaintiff's goods or services). Can you identify differences that will be important in practice?

**U.S. Healthcare, Inc. v. Blue Cross of Greater Philadelphia, 898 F.2d 914 (3d Cir. 1990)**

. . . FACTS AND PROCEDURAL HISTORY

These cross appeals arise from a comparative advertising war between giants of the health care industry in the Delaware Valley—U.S. Healthcare on the one side and Blue Cross/Blue Shield on the other. The thrust of these claims is that each side asserts the other's advertising misrepresented both parties' products.

For over fifty years, Blue Cross/Blue Shield operated as the largest health insurer in Southeastern Pennsylvania by offering "traditional" medical insurance coverage. Traditional insurance protects the subscriber from "major" medical expenses, with the insurer paying a negotiated amount based upon the services rendered, and the subscriber generally paying a deductible or some other amount. The subscriber has freedom in choosing hospitals and health care providers (i.e., doctors).

In the early 1970's, U.S. Healthcare began providing an alternative to traditional insurance in the form of a health maintenance organization, generically known as an "HMO." An HMO acts as both an insurer and a provider of specified services that are more comprehensive than those offered by traditional insurance. Generally, HMO subscribers choose a primary health care provider from the HMO network who coordinates their health care services and determines when hospital admission or treatment from a specialist is required. Usually, subscribers are not covered for services obtained without this permission or from providers outside this network. By 1986, U.S. Healthcare was the largest HMO in the area, claiming almost 600,000 members. During the same period, Blue Cross/Blue Shield experienced a loss in enrollment of over 1% per year, with a large number of those subscribers choosing HMO coverage over traditional insurance, and a majority of those defectors choosing a U.S. Healthcare company.

. . . In late 1985, in an admitted attempt to compete with HMO, Blue Cross/Blue Shield introduced a new product that it called "Personal Choice," known generically as a preferred provider organization or "PPO." PPO insurance provides subscribers with a "network" of health care providers and hospitals, and generally "covers" subscribers only for services obtained from the network providers and administered at the network hospitals. Subscribers must obtain permission to receive treatment from providers outside the network, and in such instances receive at most only partial coverage.

Thereafter, Blue Cross/Blue Shield consulted with two separate advertising agencies before arriving at a marketing strategy for its new product. In July 1986, Blue Cross/Blue Shield launched what it termed a deliberately "aggressive and provocative" comparative advertising campaign calculated "to introduce and increase the attractiveness of its products"—in particular, Personal Choice—at the expense of HMO products. Blue Cross/Blue Shield's campaign, which included direct mailings, as well as television, radio and print advertisements, ran for about six months at a total cost of approximately $2.175 million. According to a Blue Cross memorandum that purported to reflect the directions of Markson, the campaign was designed specifically to "reduce the attractiveness of [HMO]."

The Blue Cross/Blue Shield advertising campaign consisted of eight different advertisements for the print media, seven different advertisements for television, three different advertisements for radio, and a direct mailing including a folding brochure. . . . After describing HMO's referral procedure, . . . three of the eight print advertisements—as well as the brochure—say the following:

> You should also know that through a series of financial incentives, HMO encourages this doctor to handle as many patients as possible without referring to a specialist. When an HMO doctor does make a specialist referral, it could take money directly out of his pocket. Make too many referrals, and he could find himself in trouble with HMO.

One of the print advertisements and the brochure also feature a senior citizen under the banner heading "Your money or your life," juxtaposed with Blue Cross/Blue Shield's description of "The high cost of HMO Medicare."

Of the seven television advertisements run by Blue Cross/Blue Shield, four are innocuous, mentioning HMO only in the closing slogan common to all seven of the ads: "Personal Choice. Better than HMO. So good, it's Blue Cross and Blue Shield." The fifth features an indignant every man, who simply states "I resent having to ask my HMO doctor for permission to see a specialist," before a spokesperson extols the benefits of Personal Choice without reference to HMO until, again, the closing slogan. The sixth features a cab driver who says, "I don't like those HMO health plans. You get one doctor, no choice of hospitals," before a shopper tells him about the virtues of Personal Choice—again, without reference to HMO until the closing slogan. The seventh television advertisement used by Blue Cross/Blue Shield, while following the same general format, seems to us a dramatic departure from the others in that it appears consciously designed to play upon the fears of the consuming public. The commercial features a grief-stricken woman who says, "The hospital my HMO sent me to just wasn't enough. It's my fault." The implication of the advertisement is that some tragedy has befallen the woman because of her choice of health care.

. . . [U.S. Healthcare's] responsive advertising campaign, which began sometime after the Blue Cross/Blue Shield campaign and ran until late February 1987, cost $1.255 million. . . .

U.S. Healthcare's responsive campaign did not just highlight the positive characteristics in its own product, but also featured "anti-Blue Cross" advertisements. Of the three remaining print advertisements, one simply shows a comparative list of the features available under HMO and Personal Choice, with a banner heading that reads "It's your choice." The other two explain that under Personal Choice, the number of hospitals available to the subscriber is limited and, moreover, that many Personal Choice doctors do not have admitting privileges at even those few. One of these advertisements ran under a banner heading of "When it Comes to Being Admitted to a Hospital, There's Something Personal Choice May Not Be Willing to Admit"; the other ran under a banner heading of "If You Really Look Into 'Personal Choice,' You Might Have a Better Name For It."

. . . The final television commercial was U.S. Healthcare's own attempt to play upon the fears of the consuming public. As solemn music plays, the narrator lists the shortcomings of Personal Choice while the camera pans from a Personal Choice brochure resting on the pillow of a hospital bed to distraught family members standing at bedside. The advertisement closes with a pair of hands pulling a sheet over the Personal Choice brochure.

. . . After a fourteen-day trial, followed by eight days of deliberations, the jury announced it was deadlocked on all issues of liability and damages. . . .

The [district] court held that because the objects of the advertisements are "public figures," and because the matters in the advertisements are "community health issues of public concern," heightened constitutional protections attach to this speech. [The district court then held that, under the First Amendment, the Lanham Act claims as well as the commercial disparagement, defamation and tortious interference claims required proof by clear and convincing evidence of knowledge or reckless disregard of falsity, and that neither party could satisfy that standard.] . . .

II. The Actionable Claims and Counterclaims under Applicable Substantive Federal and State Law .
. .

A. Applicable Federal and Pennsylvania Common Law.

. . . 2. Defamation.

Under Pennsylvania law, a defamatory statement is one that " 'tends so to harm the reputation of another as to lower him in the estimation of the community or to deter third persons from associating or dealing with him.' " It is for the court to determine, in the first instance, whether the statement of which the plaintiff complained is capable of a defamatory meaning; if the court decides that it is capable of a defamatory meaning, then it is for the jury to decide if the statement was so understood by the reader or listener. To ascertain the meaning of an allegedly defamatory statement, the statement must be examined in context.

> The test is the effect the [statement] is fairly calculated to produce, the impression it would naturally engender, in the minds of the average persons among whom it is intended to circulate. The words must be given by judges and juries the same signification that other people are likely to attribute to them.

Opinion that fails to imply underlying defamatory facts cannot support the cause of action.

In an action for defamation, the plaintiff has the burden of proving 1) the defamatory character of the communication; 2) its publication by the defendant; 3) its application to the plaintiff; 4) an understanding by the reader or listener of its defamatory meaning; and 5) an understanding by the reader or listener of an intent by the defendant that the statement refer to the plaintiff. Additionally, in order to recover damages, the plaintiff must demonstrate that the statement results from fault, amounting at least to negligence, on the part of the defendant. Finally, the plaintiff has the burden of proving any special harm resulting from the statement. . . .

392

3. Commercial Disparagement.

A commercially disparaging statement—in contrast to a defamatory statement—is one "which is intended by its publisher to be understood or which is reasonably understood to cast doubt upon the existence or extent of another's property in land, chattels or intangible things, or upon their quality, . . . if the matter is so understood by its recipient." In order to maintain an action for disparagement, the plaintiff must prove 1) that the disparaging statement of fact is untrue or that the disparaging statement of opinion is incorrect; 2) that no privilege attaches to the statement; and 3) that the plaintiff suffered a direct pecuniary loss as the result of the disparagement.

The distinction between actions for defamation and disparagement turns on the harm towards which each is directed. An action for commercial disparagement is meant to compensate a vendor for pecuniary loss suffered because statements attacking the quality of his goods have reduced their marketability, while defamation is meant protect an entity's interest in character and reputation. . . .

Given the similar elements of the two torts, deciding which cause of action lies in a given situation can be difficult. The Court of Appeals for the Eighth Circuit gave the following time-honored explanation of when impugnation of the quality of goods crosses the line from disparagement of products to defamation of vendors:

> [W]here the publication on its face is directed against the goods or product of a corporate vendor or manufacturer, it will not be held libelous per se as to the corporation, unless by fair construction and without the aid of extrinsic evidence it imputes to the corporation fraud, deceit, dishonesty, or reprehensible conduct in its business in relation to said goods or product. . . .

B. The Actionable Construction of the Advertisements

. . . [W]e consider as a group the bulk of the advertisements, which either compare the competing health plans on one or more points, or simply criticize the competitor's health plan without detailed exposition of the advertiser's own competing plan. Because they may contain misrepresentations beyond puffing, a cause of action may lie under the Lanham Act, even for those advertisements that focus exclusively on the competitor's health plan. In addition, as these advertisements all make representations about the competitor's product, a cause of action may lie for commercial disparagement with respect to any of them. None of these, however, could be said to impute to the competitor by fair construction any "fraud, deceit, dishonesty, or reprehensible conduct." Consequently, no cause of action for defamation will lie with regard to these. . . .

We believe [certain] advertisements are capable of defamatory meaning. These include, first, the Blue Cross/Blue Shield advertisements that suggest HMO primary care physicians have a financial interest in not referring patients to specialists and, indeed, that HMO makes reprisals against those primary care physicians who make too many referrals. These advertisements imply that U.S. Healthcare, the people who run it, and the doctors who are employed by it, all place personal profit above adequate health care. Such an implication goes beyond the comparative quality of HMO

393

health care to suggest reprehensible conduct by U.S. Healthcare and its employees in the conduct of their business.

Also capable of defamatory meaning is Blue Cross/Blue Shield's "Distraught Woman" advertisement. Her statement that "The hospital my HMO sent me to just wasn't enough," matched with her grief-stricken demeanor, suggests she has suffered some tragedy because of HMO's substandard care. The suggestion that U.S. Healthcare chose to send her to a hospital that could not adequately treat her problem goes beyond the product itself to impute reprehensible conduct to the corporation. Indeed, the scare tactic is the point of the commercial.

Finally, we find U.S. Healthcare's "Critical Condition" television commercial to be capable of a defamatory construction as well. As a dirge plays, the narrator lists the shortcomings of Personal Choice while the camera pans from a Personal Choice brochure resting on the pillow of a hospital bed to distraught family members standing around the bed. At the end of the advertisement, a pair of hands pulls a sheet over the Personal Choice brochure. We do not believe the depiction of a distressing death scene in a health insurance commercial is an uncalculated association. Again, we believe a scare tactic was the intent and, more to the point, a jury could find the commercial suggests Blue Cross/Blue Shield knowingly provides health care so substandard as to be dangerous.

As to this final group of advertisements, no action for commercial disparagement will lie because the statements are directed at the vendor, not his goods. Nonetheless, Lanham Act claims may lie. . . .

## III. First Amendment Principles and the Standard of Proof in Claims Arising from a Comparative Advertising Campaign

Having determined that some of the advertisements may be actionable under federal and state law, we must now consider whether the First Amendment affects the standard of proof. . . . [The district court] rejected U.S. Healthcare's argument that the advertisements were commercial speech and thereby entitled to less constitutional protection. The district court viewed the comparative advertising campaign giving rise to this litigation as a "dispute . . . about how best to deal with spiraling medical costs," and concluded that, "[t]o characterize the advertisements in this case as mere commercial speech ignores the fact that, at their core, they are instruments in a debate between two providers of public health care 'intimately involved in the resolution of important public questions.' " . . .

### A. Background

Distinguishing the Supreme Court's First Amendment jurisprudence is an express intention to "lay down broad rules of general application," rather than to allow balancing between competing values on a case-by-case basis, an approach that the Court fears would "lead to unpredictable results and uncertain expectations, and . . . render [its] duty to supervise the lower courts unmanageable." In delineating the limits placed on state authority by the First Amendment, the Court has articulated two distinct lines of cases, one involving defamation and the other involving government regulation of commercial speech. We have found no decision by the Court considering a defamation action involving expression properly characterized as commercial speech.

Despite its intention to enunciate general rules, the Court has implicitly recognized the need for balancing when a novel issue arises. Given the unique issue presented here, we believe it is necessary to evaluate the competing state and First Amendment interests. In taking this approach, we are mindful of the Supreme Court's admonition that nothing in *Gertz* "indicated that [the] same balance would be struck regardless of the type of speech involved."

Our approach will proceed in light of the analytical framework of the defamation cases. We have found no comparable case, and the parties cite none. In what we believe is a matter of first impression, we are presented with the unique circumstance of allegedly defamatory statements made in the context of a comparative advertising campaign.

B. Rules and Conceptual Framework

. . . In evaluating these competing interests, the Court has determined that the state has only a "limited" interest in compensating public persons for injury to reputation by defamatory statements, but has a "strong and legitimate" interest in compensating private persons for the same injury. The Court has provided a two-fold explanation for the discrepancy in the extent of the state interests. First, because public officials and public figures enjoy "greater access to the channels of effective communication and hence have a more realistic opportunity to counteract false statements than private individuals," the states have a greater interest in protecting private persons whose relative lack of "self-help" remedies render them "more vulnerable to injury." Second, the state has a stronger interest in protecting the reputations of private individuals because, unlike public persons, they have not voluntarily placed themselves in the public eye.

On the other side of the coin, the "type of speech involved" also affects the way in which the "balance is struck," by varying the weight of the First Amendment interest. "[S]peech on 'matters of public concern' . . . is 'at the heart of the First Amendment's protection.' " The Court has determined that "speech of private concern," such as a credit report for business, is of less First Amendment importance, in the same way that utterances labeled "commercial speech" are "less central to the interests of the First Amendment."

C. Application of the Rules and Conceptual Framework

. . . We next turn to assessing the relative weight of the First Amendment interests in this case. We recognize that traditional defamation analysis usually begins with an examination of the status of the plaintiff. Because of the facts presented, however, we shall first consider the content of the speech involved. Nor do we believe that such inverted analysis is improper.

Similarly, traditional defamation analysis would have us consider the public or private nature of the speech in assessing the weight of the First Amendment interests. We believe, however, that the novel facts here require a different approach. Our appraisal of these interests depends on whether the speech at issue can properly be characterized as commercial speech. "There is no longer any room to doubt that what has come to be known as 'commercial speech' is entitled to the protection of the First Amendment, albeit to protection somewhat less extensive than that afforded 'noncommercial speech.'" If the speech here is commercial speech, then it likely does not mandate heightened constitutional protection.

We recognize that the Supreme Court cases creating the commercial speech doctrine all involve some form of government regulation of speech and that none involve defamation actions. Further, the focus in the commercial speech cases is on First Amendment protection itself, not the heightened protection afforded by the actual malice standard. However, we believe the subordinate valuation of commercial speech is not confined to the government regulation line of cases.

In *Dun & Bradstreet*, the Court held that speech on matters of private concern, such as a credit report for business, receives less First Amendment protection than speech on matters of public concern. More significantly for our purposes, the Court justified its decision to allow less protection for speech of private concern by drawing an analogy to the reduced First Amendment protection afforded commercial speech:

> This Court on many occasions has recognized that certain kinds of speech are less central to the interests of the First Amendment than others. . . . In the area of protected speech, the most prominent example of reduced protection for certain kinds of speech concerns commercial speech. Such speech, we have noted, occupies a "subordinate position in the scale of First Amendment values." It also is more easily verifiable and less likely to be deterred by proper regulation. Accordingly, it may be regulated in ways that might be impermissible in the realm of noncommercial expression.

. . . [T]he statements here are commercial in nature. First, there is no question that they are advertisements; they were disseminated as part of an expensive, professionally run promotional campaign. Second, the speech specifically refers to a product; it touts the relative merits of Personal Choice (or U.S. Healthcare's HMO) over competing products. Third, the desire for revenue motivated the speech; the record contains abundant evidence that Blue Cross/Blue Shield launched the promotional campaign in order to recoup its share of the health insurance market. . . . Similarly, protection of its new market share motivated U.S. Healthcare's speech. In short, "common sense" informs us that the statements here propose a commercial transaction, and thus differ from other types of speech.

Even more importantly, we find it significant that the advertisements have all of the characteristics that the Supreme Court has identified in the commercial speech cases as making speech durable, not susceptible to "chill." Consequently, they do not require the heightened protection we extend to our most valuable forms of speech. Because the thrust of all of the advertisements is to convince the consuming public to bring its business to one of these health care giants rather than the other, there is no doubt that the advertisements were motivated by economic self-interest. Furthermore, given the size of the health care market in the Delaware Valley—Blue Shield virtually shouts about the hundreds of millions of dollars at stake—we believe it would have to be a cold day before these corporations would be chilled from speaking about the comparative merits of their products. *Cf. Dun & Bradstreet*, 472 U.S. at 762–63 (because credit report was solely motivated by profit "any incremental 'chilling' effect of libel suits would be of decreased significance").

In addition, these are advertisements for products and services in markets in which U.S. Healthcare and Blue Cross/Blue Shield deal—and, presumably, know more about than anyone else. The facts upon which the advertisements are based—comparative price, procedures, and services offered—are readily objectifiable. These advertisements were precisely calculated, developed over time and published only when the corporate speakers were ready. Consequently, the advertisements were unusually verifiable.

Finally, while the speech here does discuss costs and consequences of competing health insurance and health care delivery programs, some of the advertisements capable of defamatory meaning here add little information and even fewer ideas to the marketplace of health care thought.[26] The expression in these advertisements "differs markedly from ideological expression because it is confined to the promotion of specific . . . services." *Cf. Zauderer*, 471 U.S. at 637 & n. 77 (advertisement containing information that, in another context would be fully protected, nonetheless commercial speech, as it proposed commercial transaction in advertiser's self-interest). And to the extent that the advertisements are false statements of fact, of course, the speech has no constitutional value at all. . . .

Despite these conclusive indications that the speech here is commercial in nature, Blue Cross/Blue Shield argues that the speech should be accorded heightened constitutional protection. Relying on *Bigelow v. Virginia*, 421 U.S. 809 (1975), it argues that speech which does more than "simply propose a commercial transaction" constitutes something more than commercial speech. Furthermore, it maintains that the "*Bigelow* standard" is applicable when the products are not merely linked to a public debate but are themselves "at the center of the public debate."[27] Blue Cross/Blue Shield concludes that its own advertisements "educate[d] the public about the substantial differences among the[ ] available means for financing and delivering health care, thereby ensuring informed purchasing decisions" and rendering the advertisements non-commercial.

. . . [T]he *Central Hudson* decision, in which the Supreme Court expressly rejected such attempts to "blur further the line the Court has sought to draw in commercial speech cases," represents the proper approach. *Central Hudson* prevents an advertiser from immunizing, in effect, otherwise defamatory speech—behind the actual malice standard afforded to core speech by the First Amendment—simply by reference to an issue of public concern.

---

[26] We believe one such advertisement implicates important health care concerns. This advertisement suggests that HMO primary care physicians have a financial incentive to deny referrals to specialists. On the other hand, we believe the other advertisements capable of defamatory meaning make no such contribution. One portrays a woman grieving that the hospital to which HMO sent her was inadequate. The second, a "death" scene, shows a pair of hands pulling a hospital sheet over a personal choice brochure as a dirge plays. "There is simply no credible argument that this type of [advertisement] requires special protection to ensure that 'debate on public issues [will] be uninhibited, robust, and wide-open.' "

[27] In *Bigelow*, a newspaper editor published an abortion clinic's advertisement, which the state court determined violated a state criminal statute prohibiting dissemination of publications encouraging the processing of an abortion. The Supreme Court struck down the statute on First Amendment grounds, stating that the advertisement could not be regulated as commercial speech because, "[v]iewed in its entirety, [it] conveyed information of potential interest and value to a diverse audience—not only to readers possibly in need of the services offered . . . ."

. . . Therefore, while the speech here is protected by the First Amendment, we hold that the First Amendment requires no higher standard of liability than that mandated by the substantive law for each claim. The heightened protection of the actual malice standard is not "necessary to give adequate 'breathing space' to the freedoms protected by the First Amendment."

. . . [T]raditional defamation analysis is not well suited to strike the proper balance between the state and federal interests and First Amendment values in the context of commercial speech.

In weighing the state interest, we must look to the status of the claimants. As we have noted, the Court has determined that the state has only a "limited" interest in compensating public persons for injury to reputation but has a "strong and legitimate" interest in compensating private persons for the same injury. Contending that the actual malice standard applies because a public figure is implicated, Blue Cross/Blue Shield argues that the following factors render U.S. Healthcare a "public figure": it has voluntarily exposed itself to public comment on the issues involved in this dispute; it is a contributor to the ongoing debate concerning health care insurance; it is among the nation's largest providers of HMO-type insurance coverage; it markets its products extensively and aggressively, and has a substantial annual advertising budget; and it frequently and consistently asserts the advantages of its method of health care financing and delivery, and has done so in advertisements, press releases, professional journals, newspapers, magazines and speeches before public assemblies. These activities, Blue Cross/Blue Shield submits, "constitute a voluntary effort to influence the consuming public." Similar statements can be made regarding Blue Cross/Blue Shield.

*Gertz* identified three classes of public figures: those who achieve such stature or notoriety that they are considered public figures in all contexts; those who become public figures involuntarily, but these are "exceedingly rare"; and those who are deemed public figures only within the context of a particular public dispute. The Court defined the last group, limited purpose public figures, as individuals who voluntarily "thrust themselves to the forefront of particular public controversies in order to influence the resolution of the issues involved."

. . . The first factor indicative of a claimant's status is his relative access to the media. Clearly, both parties have access to the media. Moreover, the magnitude of the advertising campaigns shows their ability to utilize it on a vast scale. While access to the media does not always make one a public figure for purposes of First Amendment analysis, the tremendous ability of these parties to advertise, indicating their lack of vulnerability, would support a finding that both are public figures.

The second factor is the manner in which the risk of defamation came upon them. Both companies, attempting to influence consumers' decisions, have thrust themselves into the controversy of who provides better value in health care delivery and insurance. Blue Cross/Blue Shield began the comparative advertising war with its pointed attacks on HMO. U.S. Healthcare, even before responding with its own comparative advertising, had used advertising to help establish itself as a leading provider of health care in the Delaware Valley. Consequently, by inviting comment and assuming the risk of unfair comment, both claimants resemble public figures. *See* Steaks Unlimited, Inc. v. Deaner, 623 F.2d 264, 274 (3d Cir. 1980) ("In short, through its advertising blitz, [the plaintiff corporation] invited public attention, comment and criticism.").

Under traditional defamation analysis, the parties' considerable access to the media and their voluntary entry into a controversy are strong indicia that they are limited purpose public figures. Indeed, inflexible application of these factors would warrant a finding of public figure status and facilitate a finding of heightened constitutional protection. Nonetheless, we hold that these corporations are not public figures for the limited purpose of commenting on health care in this case.

As noted, *Gertz* defines the limited purpose public figure as one who has "thrust [himself] to the forefront of particular public controversies in order to influence the resolution of the issues involved." Although some of the advertisements touch on matters of public concern, their central thrust is commercial. Thus, the parties have acted primarily to generate revenue by influencing customers, not to resolve "the issues involved."

While discerning motivations of the speaker is often difficult, we have a more fundamental reason for declining to find limited purpose public figure status in this case. The express analysis in *Gertz* is not helpful in the context of a comparative advertising war. Most products can be linked to a public issue. And most advertisers—including both claimants here—seek out the media. Thus, it will always be true that such advertisers have voluntarily placed themselves in the public eye. It will be equally true that such advertisers have access to the media. Therefore, under the *Gertz* rationale, speech of public concern that implicates corporate advertisers—i.e., typical comparative advertising—will always be insulated behind the actual malice standard. We believe a corporation must do more than the claimants have done here to become a limited purpose public figure under *Gertz*.

In summary, we conclude that the speech at issue does not receive heightened protection under the First Amendment. Because this speech is chill-resistant, the *New York Times* standard is not, as we have noted, "necessary to give adequate 'breathing space' to the freedoms protected by the First Amendment." Therefore, the standard of proof needed to establish the substantive claims is that applicable under federal and state law. . . .

*NOTES AND QUESTIONS*

*Revisiting Advertising Theory.* Consider the search/experience/credence qualities framework from Chapter 4. The quality of medical services is a classic credence attribute. How might that affect consumer reactions to claims that a competitor's medical services are inferior?

*Malice Is a Term of Art.* A speaker acts with "malice" if it knows of the falsity of a statement or acts with reckless disregard toward its truth or falsity. Some states are also permit a malice finding if the defendant acts with ill will or intent to interfere with the plaintiff's economic interest in an unprivileged fashion. The Restatement (Second) of Torts takes no position on whether such a rule is appropriate, in part because the First Amendment implications of such a rule are unclear.

*Kinetic Concepts, Inc. v. Bluesky Medical Corporation*, 2005 WL 3068209 (W.D. Tex. 2005), found a genuine issue of material fact on malice when the defendant "described his marketing plan . . . as an effort to 'contract[ ] the market from $400 million per year to $40 million per year and therefore sow[

] the seeds of chaos and contraction into the marketplace." The letter went on to state that the defendant wished to "reduce and change the profit vector of the competition from Black to a glowing deep red hue." That is, the defendant really wanted to harm the plaintiff. Does that indicate the defendant acted maliciously? Is it appropriate to find malice if the defendant was negligently mistaken, but not reckless in its disregard for the truth? What if the defendant was not negligent, but simply mistaken—should its ill will or intent to interfere with the plaintiff's economic interest still count as malice? Recall that modern consumer protection statutes often don't require negligence or any fault at all, nor does the Lanham Act.

*Convergence in the Torts*

As the *Blue Cross/Blue Shield* case indicates, First Amendment constraints on defamation have made it more similar to the product disparagement tort. The differences between the classic causes of action for product disparagement, trade libel, and defamation, though highly technical and subject to judicial nitpicking, are often not practically significant in the context of claims brought by commercial entities, especially claims against other commercial entities.

In fact, the Restatement (Second) of Torts §623A subsumes the concept of trade libel within injurious falsehood, which is why we haven't used the term "trade libel" here, though some states still have a tort with that name. The Restatement says that "[o]ne who publishes a false statement harmful to the interests of another is subject to liability for pecuniary loss resulting to the other if (a) he intends for publication of the statement to result in harm to interests of the other having a pecuniary value, or either recognizes or should recognize that it is likely to do so, and (b) he knows that the statement is false or acts in reckless disregard of its truth or falsity." Then §626, Disparagement of Quality—Trade Libel, says that the injurious falsehood rules apply to statements "disparaging the quality of another's land, chattels or intangible things." "Trade libel" is simply the old term for this type of injurious falsehood.

Defamation law is aimed at protecting the personal reputation of the plaintiff, while the injurious falsehood tort is designed to protect economic interests. Before *New York Times v. Sullivan*, the general rule was that damaging statements were presumed false in defamation cases, and liability for falsity was strict, neither of which were true for injurious falsehood. These differences between the torts have been swept away by modern First Amendment jurisprudence. Likewise, defamation used to allow presumptions of damage, while injurious falsehood always required proof. Presumptions of damage in defamation have been cut back substantially in many instances. However, the presumptions may still be significant in some cases, especially in allowing a claim to survive dismissal at the pleading stage, as we will discuss below.

*The Line between Defamation and Product Disparagement*

The *Blue Cross/Blue Shield* court applied the rule that only ads that impute "fraud, deceit, dishonesty, or reprehensible conduct" to the other party could be defamatory, while product disparagement (or "commercial disparagement") covered a broader range of statements.

The remaining significance of this distinction involves pleading or presuming harm. Product disparagement requires proof of special damages—that is, specific harms such as specific lost customers. Courts often require plaintiffs to plead the names of lost customers or potential customers. Pleading only "lost sales" is insufficient to survive a motion to dismiss.

As a plaintiff's attorney, how would you find evidence of special damages for disparagement in the case of a large-scale, widely disseminated ad campaign? Is the special damages requirement an indication that the tort is not appropriate as a means to govern large-scale advertising campaigns?

In defamation, by contrast, damages may generally be presumed if the statements are per se defamatory—if they're the kind of statements that naturally would be expected to injure a party's reputation.

In *Dorman Products, Inc. v. Dayco Products, LLC*, 749 F. Supp. 2d 630 (E.D. Mich. 2010), the court held that statements about the inferiority of Dorman's products weren't defamatory. Allegations of inferiority are "par for the course" and "the most innocuous kind of puffing," generally not capable of misleading the public. However, statements that arguably suggested that Dorman misrepresented product quality were actionable as defamation, not just as trade disparagement. The potentially actionable statements included suggestions that Dorman's products were defective and that Dorman misled the public into believing that its products conformed to industry standards. Asserting that Dorman infringed Dayco's trade dress, that the similarity was non-coincidental, and that Dorman misled consumers, "ha[d] the potential" to impute an intent to mislead to Dorman, which was enough to survive a motion to dismiss.

Given this result, when can an advertiser be confident that its negative statements about a competitor will be judged by trade disparagement standards and not defamation standards? *See also* Cohen v. Hansen, 2015 WL 3609689 (D. Nev. June 9, 2015) (statements alleging that executive had been convicted of fraud and the business was organized to perpetrate illegal activities constituted defamation per se, not business disparagement, so actual damages need not be proved).

*Procter & Gamble Co. v. Haugen*, 222 F. 3d 1262 (10th Cir. 2000), involved false claims by Amway distributors that P&G was a corporate agent of Satan.

[Procter & Gamble's old logo with critiques]

Though the court of appeals held that P&G alleged a violation of the Lanham Act's prohibition on false statements about "commercial activities," it affirmed dismissal of P&G's state-law defamation claims:

> With regard to summary judgment on P & G's state law claims, under Utah law the subject message would be actionable as slander per se if "the defamatory words fall into one of four categories: (1) charge of criminal conduct, (2) charge of a loathsome disease, (3) charge of conduct that is incompatible with the exercise of a lawful business, trade, profession or office; and (4) charge of the unchastity of a woman." Slander per se . . . permits a finding of liability without the need to prove special harm. On appeal, P & G challenges the district court's conclusion that the satanic rumor was "not incompatible with conducting a lawful business." It argues the representations that it "financially supports the Church of Satan and places the Devil's mark on its products are incompatible with P & G's lawful business of selling popular products for personal care and hygiene and for the home."
>
> The false statements contained in the subject message are not the kind of allegations that constitute slander per se. As P & G notes, the question is whether the alleged behavior is incompatible with its business of selling household consumer goods, not whether the alleged behavior is lawful. . . . P & G's business is clearly lawful. However, allegations that it directs a percentage of its profits to the church of Satan are not incompatible with that business in the manner necessary to be actionable as slander per se.
>
>> Disparaging words, to be actionable per se . . . must affect the plaintiff in some way that is peculiarly harmful to one engaged in [the plaintiff's] trade or profession. Disparagement of a general character, equally discreditable to all persons, is not enough unless the particular quality disparaged is of such a character that it is peculiarly valuable in the plaintiff's business or profession.
>
> For example, "charges against a clergyman of drunkenness and other moral misconduct affect his fitness for the performance of the duties of his profession, although the same charges against a business man or tradesman do not so affect him." Although offensive to many, an allegation of Devil worship, like drunkenness, is "[d]isparagement of a general character, equally discreditable to all persons" and does not pertain to a quality that is peculiarly valuable in plaintiffs' professional activities of manufacturing and selling household consumer goods. We therefore hold that the district court properly granted summary judgment as to this claim. . . .

Would a statement that a business was routinely late in paying its bills be "disparagement of a general character, equally discreditable to all persons"? Could an accusation that a company's products come from China, not from America, be defamatory? *See* AvePoint, Inc. v. Power Tools, Inc., 981 F. Supp. 2d 496 (W.D. Va. 2013) (party's allegedly false accusation that the other party's software was developed and maintained in China and India, not the U.S. as advertised, was appropriately the basis for a claim for defamation).

## 2.     Commercial Speech in an Age of Convergence

The Third Circuit assumed that ads were readily distinguishable from non-ads. But as advertising methods have changed and the lines between advertising and editorial content blur, can its distinction be preserved?

In *Edward B. Beharry & Co., Ltd. v. Bedessee Imports Inc.*, 95 U.S.P.Q.2d 1480 (E.D.N.Y. 2010), *The Caribbean New Yorker*, read by the parties' customer base, ran an article stating that Beharry's Special Madras Curry Powder posed a threat to the public, given that the FDA had rejected a June 2008 shipment because it was "filthy." "Contradicting Beharry's claim of pride in providing its customers with high quality products and services, its 'famous' Indi brand curry was denied entry to the United States." The article concluded that "[t]he West-Indian community must be made aware of repeated adverse FDA actions regarding Beharry's food products and any corollary health risks," and provided (broken) links to the FDA announcements.

Beharry sued for defamation, alleging that its competitor Bedessee "contributed to, authored, conceived, submitted and/or otherwise caused" the piece to be published. Beharry alleged that individual defendant Invor Bedessee circulated the full article by email to distributors and the customer base.

The court denied Bedessee's motion to dismiss. Bedessee's denial of any connection to the publication merely created a factual dispute. Beharry noted that the publication didn't contain a byline, and claimed that the piece was a paid ad rather than a news article.

What should the result be if Bedessee is "connected" to the article in the sense of convincing the magazine that it was a worthwhile story to run, but didn't pay for it to appear?

Beharry also claimed violation of the Lanham Act. Bedessee argued that the Lanham Act claim failed because the article wasn't commercial speech. The court agreed. "No named defendant appears anywhere in the publication, nor do any of defendants' products, prices, or business contacts. As the public would have no reason to associate the publication with defendants, it cannot possibly propose a commercial transaction between defendants and readers of *The Caribbean New Yorker*. Even if defendants paid to run the piece with a motivation toward indirectly influencing customers to buy their goods, such a motivation does not transform the piece into commercial speech."

Is attribution required for this article to be commercial speech? What is the best argument against the court's holding?   Is this holding consistent with its ruling on defamation?

Consider the following case of speech to an independent news organization. It was speech by a competitor, but not in a traditional advertising context. What standard should regulate it?

## Boulé v. Hutton, 328 F.3d 84 (2d Cir. 2003)

Plaintiffs-appellants René and Claude Boulé ("the Boulés") appeal from the decisions of the district court (1) granting partial summary judgment to defendants-appellees Ingrid Hutton ("Hutton"), the Leonard Hutton Galleries, Inc. ("the Gallery"), Mark Khidekel ("Mark") and Regina Khidekel ("Regina"), (2) finding for defendants on certain of plaintiffs' claims after a bench trial, and (3) denying plaintiffs' motion for relief from judgment under Fed. R. Civ. P. 60(b). For the reasons set forth below, we affirm in part, and vacate in part the decisions of the district court.

At its heart, this is a dispute about the authenticity of works of art (the "Paintings") owned by the Boulés. While the Boulés believe the Paintings to be early works of the Russian Suprematist artist Lazar Khidekel ("Lazar"), Lazar's son Mark and daughter-in-law Regina (collectively, "Khidekels") claim that they are not. The Khidekels are selling their own collection of Lazar's art through Hutton and her Gallery.

The Boulés brought suit under the Lanham Act and state law causes of action to recover for the damage to the value of the Paintings that they assert occurred because of statements made by the defendants. The Honorable Miriam Goldman Cedarbaum held, inter alia, that the Boulés had not carried their burden of showing that the Paintings were authentic, that is, painted by Lazar. On the other hand, she found that the Khidekels had falsely and in bad faith denied that Mark had given the Boulés certificates acknowledging that at least some of the Paintings were indeed his father's. Applying the special damage rules that pertain to the law of defamation, the district court awarded the Boulés nominal damages. Each of these rulings and others entered by Judge Cedarbaum in her three opinions have been challenged on appeal.

### BACKGROUND

Lazar was born in 1904 in Vitebsk, Russia, and joined the Suprematist school of Russian avant-garde artists in the years following the Russian Revolution. In his youth, Lazar studied with two of the better-known artists of the period, Marc Chagall and Kazmir Malevich, and later in life became a prominent architect. The artworks in his possession upon his death in 1986 became the property of Mark and Regina.

The Boulés are Parisian art collectors who own a number of works from the Russian avant-garde period; in addition, Claude has published a scholarly work on Russian Constructivism. By the late 1980s, the Boulés had acquired 176 works attributed to Lazar. As it was both illegal and dangerous to acquire Russian avant-garde art prior to the fall of the Soviet Union, the majority of the Boulé's pieces were acquired through non-traditional channels.

The Boulés and the Khidekels first encountered each other in Paris in 1988. Over the next few years, the Khidekels and the Boulés developed a friendship, as the Khidekels were pleased to find admirers of Lazar's work in the West, and the Boulés were happy to show their collection to them. They made (ultimately unrealized) plans to pool their collections of Lazar's work for an exhibition in Canada, and, in 1991, in exchange for approximately $8,000, Mark signed certificates of authenticity in Paris for sixteen of the Paintings he selected from the Boulés' collection. The certificates stated: "I, Mark

Khidekel, having examined the artwork shown to me . . . hereby confirm that it is the work of my father, Lazar Khidekel, and that it can be identified as a study."

During this period, although the Khidekels were surprised that a collection of Lazar's work existed in Paris, and told the Boulés that some of the pieces they owned were different from those of Lazar's works that the Khidekels possessed, Mark and Regina never expressed to the Boulés any reservations about the legitimacy of the collection. As the district court found at trial, "Mark noted some differences between the Boulés' collection and his collection, and commented that the bulk of the Boulés' collection was created when Lazar Khidekel was a very young student—possibly as early as 1920."

The Boulés exhibited the Paintings at the Joliette Museum of Art in Montreal, Canada in 1992, and galleries in Canada over the course of the months that followed. Although Mark expressed an interest in lecturing at the Joliette Museum in conjunction with the exhibition of the Paintings, the Khidekels ultimately did not participate.

The Khidekels began an association with Hutton in 1992, and moved to New York in 1993. Hutton is a prominent dealer of art of the Russian avant-garde, which has a small but global market. The Khidekels soon entered into a consignment agreement with Hutton to facilitate the sale of their collection of Lazar's work. In 1995, the Gallery exhibited works from the Khidekel's collection. The exhibition catalogue noted that it represented the first-ever display of Lazar's work, despite the earlier show at the Joliette Museum in Canada that had included works from the Boulés' collection. In late 1995 and early 1996, the Khidekels and Hutton sent a jointly-signed letter to at least twenty-five art galleries around the world (the "Repudiation Letter"), repudiating the Paintings that had been loaned by the Boulés and attributed to Lazar in the Canadian exhibition.

In 1996, after being approached by a reporter, Hutton arranged for the Khidekels to be interviewed for an article in *ARTnews*, a leading industry publication, entitled "The Betrayal of the Russian Avant-Garde." The article discussed the entry of "thousands" of fraudulent artworks into galleries, museums and private collections. The Khidekels were quoted in the article as stating that the Paintings were not Lazar's work, and as so advising the Boulés when they had initially viewed the Boulés' collection.[3] An article that appeared shortly thereafter in Le Devoir, a Montreal publication,

---

[3] The *ARTnews* article contained the following passages:

[Lazar] never had a solo show during his lifetime, nor did he or his family ever sell or part with any of his works, according to his son and daughter-in-law, Mark and Regina Khidekel. On this point, they were adamant. . . .

Mark and Regina say that they told the Boulés the works were not Khidekels. . . . What makes Mark and Regina most indignant is that the catalogue [for the Joliette Museum exhibition] gives the impression that they endorse the Boulé collection, which they most emphatically do not.

contained a quotation from Regina specifically denying that she or Mark had ever authenticated any portion of the Boulés' collection.[4]

The Boulés brought suit in 1997, alleging that defendants' statements in the Gallery catalogue, the Repudiation Letter, *ARTnews*, and in *Le Devoir*, and other statements to art dealers and journalists violated the Lanham Act. They further alleged that the statements violated the New York General Business Law, and state law causes of action against disparagement, defamation, tortious interference with business relationships, unfair competition, unjust enrichment and breach of contract.

A. The summary judgment rulings

. . . . The district court found that the statements in the Repudiation Letter were not actionable because they could not be considered a "representation of fact" within the meaning of the Lanham Act. The claim pertaining to the statements to *ARTnews* was dismissed because the district court held that a response to an unsolicited inquiry from a reporter on a topic of public concern—fraud in the Russian avant-garde art market—was not a statement made "in commercial advertising or promotion."

B. The trial

. . . . Judge Cedarbaum did find for plaintiffs on part of their defamation claim. The district court found that the statements published in *Le Devoir* to the effect that Mark had never signed the certificates of authenticity, and in *ARTnews* representing that Mark and Regina had told the Boulés that the Paintings were not authentic, were false and defamatory, but that plaintiffs had not proved special damages. The district court found, however, that the *ARTnews* statements constituted libel per se with regard to Claude Boulé in her capacity as an art historian, but declined to award any more than nominal damages. The plaintiffs also received judgment on their breach of contract claim, as the district court found that Mark had breached the implied covenant of good faith and fair dealing by repudiating the certificates. On this basis, plaintiffs were awarded restitution, but not expectation damages. The remaining state law causes of action were dismissed. . . .

DISCUSSION

[The court concluded that the plaintiffs could not bring Lanham Act claims based on the *ARTnews* statements because they were not commercial speech, and the Lanham Act covers only commercial speech.]

. . . ii. State law claims

---

[4] In the February 23, 1996 *Le Devoir* article, Regina is quoted as saying that "neither she nor her husband ever 'authenticated' anything and the fake certificates were forged."

The Boulés appeal from the denial at trial of their claims under Section 349 of New York's General Business Law and the New York common law of unfair competition by disparagement. The district court denied these claims based on its conclusion that the plaintiffs had failed to carry their burden to show that the Paintings were authentic. While most of the state law claims were based on statements about the authenticity of the Paintings, some were not. The *Le Devoir* and *ARTnews* statements addressed the certificates that Mark had provided to the Boulés and the conversations between the Boulés and Khidekels about the Paintings. As the district court held that plaintiffs proved by a preponderance of the evidence the falsity of the statements in *Le Devoir* and *ARTnews*, we remand for further proceedings to determine whether these false statements constitute a violation of Section 349 and the claim of unfair competition by disparagement. In addition, because Section 349 requires proof of a deceptive practice, and does not require proof that a statement is false, we remand for further proceedings on all of plaintiffs' claims under Section 349.

A few additional observations about these two causes of action may prove of assistance on remand. Section 349 prohibits "[d]eceptive acts or practices in the conduct of any business, trade or commerce." N.Y. Gen. Bus. Law § 349(a). To establish a claim under Section 349, the plaintiff must show "a material deceptive act or practice directed to consumers that caused actual harm." We have not yet decided whether false statements are likely to be deceptive. "Deceptive acts" are defined objectively, as acts "likely to mislead a reasonable consumer acting reasonably under the circumstances." Further, a deceptive practice "need not reach the level of common-law fraud to be actionable under section 349."

The district court expressed reservations as to whether plaintiffs are within the class of persons, namely, consumers, for whose protection Section 349 was enacted. Section 349, however, allows recovery not only by consumers, but also by competitors if there is "some harm to the public at large." Although a Section 349 plaintiff is not required to show justifiable reliance by consumers, "[a]n act is deceptive within the meaning of the New York statute only if it is likely to mislead a reasonable consumer."

On appeal, the Boulés describe their claim of "unfair competition by disparagement" as a claim for defamation of another's business.[8] Where a statement impugns "the basic integrity" of a business, an action for defamation per se lies, and general damages are presumed. Nonetheless, actual damages must be proved with competent evidence of the injury. . . .

CALABRESI, Circuit Judge, concurring.

. . . . Congress did not wish to extend federal Lanham Act liability to speech that is subject to broader general First Amendment protection than is commercial speech. Such noncommercial speech, however, may well remain the grounds of recovery under state laws. In other words, as the opinion notes, even noncommercial speech may, in appropriate cases, be actionable. Today's holding means

---

[8] . . . On appeal, [the Boulés] press only the claim for defamation of their business presumably because of the difference in the standard for an award of damages. A claim for defamation of another's business is distinct from a claim for product disparagement. Among other things, special damages must be proven for a product disparagement claim. . . .

only that Congress chose not to make that kind of speech federally actionable under the Lanham Act. It is for these reasons that the opinion is able to remand the speech here discussed for consideration of whether it (a) violates section 349 of New York's General Business Law or (b) may be the basis for recovery under the New York common law of unfair competition by disparagement.

*NOTES AND QUESTIONS*

Given the First Amendment, how far does New York's General Business Law go in making noncommercial speech actionable? As applied to commercial speech, the law clearly covers false speech even when made without fault, but how could it constitutionally apply the same rule to noncommercial speech? Should a court refuse to apply the GBL to such speech at all, or should it imply special constraints on a GBL cause of action against noncommercial speech?

*Opinion versus Fact.* Were the Khidekels' statements about authenticity statements of fact or statements of opinion? How can we tell?

Defamation law's treatment of opinion is roughly similar to false advertising law's approach. But because the kinds of things that can be defamatory are more limited than the infinite matters one might advertise falsely about, judgmental language is more often crucial to defamation cases. In Cuba's United Ready Mix, Inc. v. Bock Concrete Foundations, Inc., 785 S.W.2d 649 (Mo. Ct. App. 1990), the plaintiff sold concrete and the defendant was a contractor that used concrete in construction. The defendant allegedly told many people that the plaintiff "was delivering inferior material and that he would not be a part of the fraud." The key question was whether this was a statement of fact or opinion. The court quoted the standard rule: "[A] defamatory communication may consist of a statement in the form of an opinion, but a statement of this nature is actionable only if it implies the allegation of undisclosed defamatory facts as the basis for the opinion." In this case, the defendant's statement implied that he had knowledge of undisclosed defamatory facts and could be defamatory.

Consider: After *Lexmark*, could a Lanham Act claim have been brought against the defendant? A Lanham Act case involving *implied* defamatory facts would, as you recall, require extrinsic evidence of consumer deception, usually in the form of a survey. However, no such extrinsic evidence would be required under defamation law for a jury to find liability. (The stringent requirements for showing damage from defamation arguably perform the same function, however.)

Was it the defendant's position as a user of concrete that made it plausible to think that he had knowledge of undisclosed defamatory facts supporting his opinion? What if he'd posted the same statement as an anonymous comment on a blog about the plaintiff—would the statement still be potentially defamatory?

The *Bock* defendant's statements were of the kind one might expect an individual to make in the course of soliciting specific customers. Historically, the business torts developed to address that kind of situation. Consider how well these torts fit with a modern, mass advertising campaign. (Hint: maybe not that well?)

In *Verizon Directories Corp. v. Yellow Book USA, Inc.*, 309 F. Supp. 2d 401 (E.D.N.Y 2004), Verizon sued Yellow Book over TV ads that used humor to suggest that Yellow Book was superior. According to Verizon, the ads falsely represented that more people used the Yellow Book than Verizon's offering; the number of users is relevant to the prices a directory can command from advertisers. One ad, for example, showed a "Senior Focus Group" in which everyone claimed to use the Yellow Book and no one had heard of the alternative (Verizon). In another ad, a wind tunnel easily blew Verizon's directory away, while the Yellow Book proved more substantial because it had "the right stuff." Verizon alleged Lanham Act claims, violation of New York's statutory false advertising law (§§ 349–350, discussed above), and product disparagement.

Yellow Book argued that its ads were merely puffery. The court, applying the same analysis to the Lanham Act claims as to the state law claims, found that it could not determine puffery as a matter of law. Though the ads were literally "playful and absurd," in context, consumers might interpret the ads to mean that more people used the Yellow Book than the Verizon directory. The ads were "skillfully crafted and shown at great expense to subtly but firmly communicate an idea—that the Yellow Book is preferred by users to Verizon's book and that, more to the point, advertisers will reach more potential consumers if they put their names and money in the former rather than the latter." The judge's background was very different from ordinary viewers', and the judge declined to resolve the meaning of the ad to them, an issue requiring "surveys, expert testimony, and other evidence of what is happening in the real world of television watchers and advertisers in yellow pages."

In applying the Lanham Act puffery standards to the state law disparagement claims, was the *Verizon* court doing something different than what the court did in the *Bock* case with respect to the line between opinion and fact? Historically, defamation and product disparagement cases didn't involve expert testimony or consumer surveys—juries were left to their own interpretation of the accused materials. Is that still the right rule for a defamation/disparagement claim? Is there something different about mass media campaigns that would justify different treatment?

## 3. Why All These Negative Ads?: Public Policy and Comparative Advertising

Historically, comparative advertising was regarded with suspicion (and still is in the European Union; see Chapter 11). A few decades ago, however, impelled by concerns that advertising restrictions were suppressing competition and raising prices, the FTC made a major push to encourage such advertising.

### Federal Trade Commission, Statement of Policy Regarding Comparative Advertising, August 13, 1979

. . .(b) Policy Statement

The Federal Trade Commission has determined that it would be of benefit to advertisers, advertising agencies, broadcasters, and self-regulation entities to restate its current policy concerning comparative advertising.[1] Commission policy in the area of comparative advertising encourages the naming of, or reference to competitors, but requires clarity, and, if necessary, disclosure to avoid deception of the consumer. Additionally, the use of truthful comparative advertising should not be restrained by broadcasters or self-regulation entities.

(c) The Commission has supported the use of brand comparisons where the bases of comparison are clearly identified. Comparative advertising, when truthful and non-deceptive, is a source of important information to consumers and assists them in making rational purchase decisions. Comparative advertising encourages product improvement and innovation, and can lead to lower prices in the marketplace. For these reasons, the Commission will continue to scrutinize carefully restraints upon its use.

(1) Disparagement

Some industry codes which prohibit practices such as "disparagement," "disparagement of competitors," "improper disparagement," "unfairly attacking," "discrediting," may operate as a restriction on comparative advertising. The Commission has previously held that disparaging advertising is permissible so long as it is truthful and not deceptive. In *Carter Products, Inc.*, 323 F.2d 523 (5th Cir. 1963), the Commission narrowed an order recommended by the hearing examiner which would have prohibited respondents from disparaging competing products through the use of false or misleading pictures, depictions, or demonstrations, "or otherwise" disparaging such products. In explaining why it eliminated "or otherwise" from the final order, the Commission observed that the phrase would have prevented:

> respondents from making truthful and nondeceptive statements that a product has certain desirable properties or qualities which a competing product or products do not possess. Such a comparison may have the effect of disparaging the competing product, but we know of no rule of law which prevents a seller from honestly informing the public of the advantages of its products as opposed to those of competing products.

Industry codes which restrain comparative advertising in this manner are subject to challenge by the Federal Trade Commission.

(2) Substantiation

On occasion, a higher standard of substantiation by advertisers using comparative advertising has been required by self-regulation entities. . . . However, industry codes and interpretations that impose a higher standard of substantiation for comparative claims than for unilateral claims are inappropriate and should be revised.

---

[1] For purposes of this Policy Statement, comparative advertising is defined as advertising that compares alternative brands on objectively measurable attributes or price, and identifies the alternative brand by name, illustration or other distinctive information.

*Effect of the FTC Statement*

The FTC's statement focused on consumer information and antitrust concerns: an agreement to refrain from saying nasty things about the competition could have anticompetitive effects. Comparative advertising became quite widespread in the U.S. By some measures, one-third of U.S. ads are comparative, and comparative ads may be more persuasive and memorable than non-comparative ads. *See* Jenna D. Beller, Comment, *The Law of Comparative Advertising in the United States and Around the World: A Practical Guide for U.S. Lawyers and Their Clients*, 29 INT'L LAW. 917 (1995).

A separate question is raised by comparative advertising: what happens when an ad doesn't name the competition? *Kinetic Concepts, Inc. v. Bluesky Medical Corporation*, 2005 WL 3068209 (W.D. Tex. 2005), applied the general defamation rule that "it is not necessary that the individual referred to be named if those who knew and were acquainted with the plaintiff understand from reading the publication that it referred to the plaintiff." The plaintiff in *Kinetic* conducted a study showing that 33.3% of physicians and 95% of nurses in its sample believed that the relevant ads were comparing the parties' products. This created a genuine issue of material fact on the element that a defamatory statement must be "of and concerning" the plaintiff to be actionable.

### 4.    A Final Business Tort: Tortious Interference

Tortious interference with contract or with prospective contractual relations is often alleged alongside various other advertising-related torts. There are substantial state-law variations in the elements of the tort, which we will not detail. It rarely succeeds in the advertising and marketing law context. The following case against Google, which makes its money from advertisers who often bid against their competitors even for their own trademarks, illustrates that the tort is not well-suited for a modern, large-scale advertising practice.

### Google Inc. v. American Blind & Wallpaper Factory, Inc., 74 U.S.P.Q.2d 1385 (N.D. Cal. 2005)

[This is a keyword advertising case, as described in Chapter 11: Google sells the plaintiff's trademark and domain name as keywords in its AdWords program so that competitors' ads appear as sponsored links in response to a search for "American Blind." The court refused to dismiss American Blind's trademark claims for failure to state a claim.]

. . . C. Tortious Interference with Prospective Business Advantage

Defendants move to dismiss American Blind's state law claim of tortious interference with prospective business advantage.[31] The elements of tortious interference with prospective business

---

[31] American Blind alleges that (1) "[m]any" of its customers are "repeat customers" and "regularly" purchase products from its Web site, (2) it is probable that "such customers and others" will "continue to seek to visit" the Web site and purchase products and services "in the future," (3) Defendants were aware of American Blind's "reasonable expectation of future transactions" with its "returning customers," as well as with customers who

advantage are as follows: (1) an economic relationship between the plaintiff and some third party, with the probability of future economic benefit to the plaintiff, (2) the defendant's knowledge of the relationship, (3) intentional acts on the part of the defendant designed to disrupt the relationship, which acts are wrongful by some legal measure other than the fact of interference itself,[32] (4) actual disruption of the relationship, and (5) economic harm to the plaintiff proximately caused by the defendant's acts. Defendants argue that American Blind fails to allege an independently wrongful act, as required by the third element, or probability of future economic benefit from existing economic relationships, as required by the first element.

. . . . As American Blind's claims of trademark violations, unfair competition, false representation, and injury to business reputation will proceed past the motion-to-dismiss stage, so too can those claims serve, for present purposes, as allegations that satisfy the pleading requirements for the third element of tortious interference with prospective business advantage.

However, the Court agrees with Defendants that American Blind's allegations with respect to the first element of the claim are insufficient. The tort of interference with prospective business advantage applies to "interference with existing noncontractual relations which hold the promise of future economic advantage. In other words, it protects the expectation that the relationship eventually will yield the desired benefit, not necessarily the more speculative expectation that a potentially beneficial relationship will eventually arise." Allegations that amount to a mere "hope for an economic relationship and a desire for future benefit" are inadequate to satisfy the pleading requirements of the first element of the tort.

Even though American Blind has alleged relationships with "repeat customers" who "probabl[y]" will "continue to seek to visit" its Web site and purchase its goods and services, American Blind's alleged expectation of "future and prospective sales" to these customers, with which Defendants are alleged to have interfered, is too speculative to support this claim. It does not rise to the level of the requisite "promise of future economic advantage," instead expressing merely a "hope . . . and a desire" for unspecified future sales to unspecified returning customers, in the form of a legal conclusion. Moreover, it goes without saying that American Blind's even more speculative allegations regarding "new" customers with whom it cannot claim any past or present interactions, however insubstantial, also are inadequate to support this claim. American Blind has failed to point to any case law suggesting that its allegations regarding the probability of future economic benefit from its existing economic relationships with third parties are sufficient. Accordingly, Defendants' motions to dismiss American Blind's claim of tortious interference with prospective business advantage are GRANTED.

---

"may be attracted" to its goods and services because of its goodwill, advertising, and promotion, (4) "[a]bsent Defendants' intentional and improper interference through their deceptive and manipulated search engine 'results,' it is reasonably certain that American Blind would realize additional sales from existing customers and/or new customers," (5) Defendants "intentionally and improperly interfered with American Blind's future and prospective sales," and (6) American Blind has suffered and will continue to suffer irreparable injury as a result of Defendants' actions.

[32] An act is independently wrongful if it is "unlawful, that is, if it is proscribed by some constitutional, statutory, regulatory, common law, or other determinable legal standard."

Copyright in the United States protects original works of authorship fixed in a tangible medium of expression, whether they are published or unpublished. Among other things, copyright protects most books, movies, music and software as well as choreography and architectural works. Copyright does not protect facts, ideas, systems, or methods of operation.

Copyright protection applies to a work even if there is no copyright notice on the work and even if the author has not filed a registration. Prompt registration (before infringement begins or within three months of publication), however, provides the owner with several procedural benefits and the possibility of receiving statutory damages and attorneys' fees in a successful infringement suit. Statutory damages can be significant—up to $150,000 per work infringed in the case of willful infringement. Registration, even if not done promptly, is a prerequisite for filing suit for infringement of a U.S. work.

Copyright owners' exclusive rights include the right to control reproduction, distribution, public performance (though there is no general public performance right for sound recordings) and derivative works. Derivative works are works that, while based on the original copyrighted work, transform, adapt, translate or otherwise rework the original's creative expression, such as a movie adapted from a novel. A claim for copyright infringement requires that the plaintiff prove two things: (1) its ownership of the copyright in a particular work, and (2) the defendant copied, or made another unauthorized use, of the work or a substantial and legally protectable portion of it.

## 1.    What is Protectable?

The U.S. Constitution specifically authorizes Congress to enact a copyright statute. *See* U.S. CONST., art. I, § 8, cl. 8. In the early years of copyright, however, it was unclear whether advertisements qualified for copyright protection. Ads were not "literary" like books or articles, and advertisements do not clearly "promote the Progress of Science" as the Constitution contemplated. That uncertainty produced the following case.

### Bleistein v. Donaldson Lithographing Company, 188 U.S. 239 (1903)

. . . The alleged infringements consisted in the copying in reduced form of three chromolithographs prepared by employees of the plaintiffs for advertisements of a circus owned by one Wallace....The circuit court directed a verdict for the defendant on the ground that the chromolithographs were not within the protection of the copyright law, and this ruling was sustained by the circuit court of appeals.

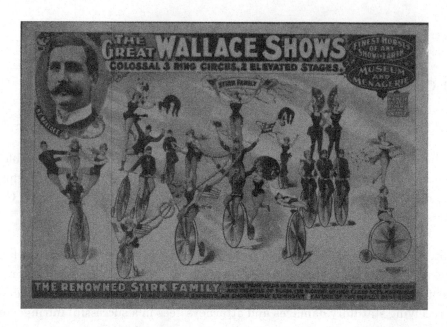

There was evidence warranting the inference that the designs belonged to the plaintiffs, they having been produced by persons employed and paid by the plaintiffs in their establishment to make those very things. . . .

It is obvious also that the plaintiff's case is not affected by the fact, if it be one, that the pictures represent actual groups—visible things. They seem from the testimony to have been composed from hints or description, not from sight of a performance. But even if they had been drawn from the life, that fact would not deprive them of protection. The opposite proposition would mean that a portrait by Velasquez or Whistler was common property because others might try their hand on the same face. Others are free to copy the original. They are not free to copy the copy. The copy is the personal reaction of an individual upon nature. Personality always contains something unique. It expresses its singularity even in handwriting, and a very modest grade of art has in it something irreducible which is one man's alone. That something he may copyright unless there is a restriction in the words of the act.

If there is a restriction, it is not to be found in the limited pretensions of these particular works. The least pretentious picture has more originality in it than directories and the like, which may be copyrighted. . . .

Certainly works are not the less connected with the fine arts because their pictorial quality attracts the crowd, and therefore gives them a real use—if use means to increase trade and to help to make money. A picture is nonetheless a picture, and nonetheless a subject of copyright, that it is used for an advertisement. And if pictures may be used to advertise soap, or the theater, or monthly magazines, as they are, they may be used to advertise a circus. Of course, the ballet is as legitimate a subject for illustration as any other. A rule cannot be laid down that would excommunicate the paintings of Degas.

. . . It would be a dangerous undertaking for persons trained only to the law to constitute themselves final judges of the worth of pictorial illustrations, outside of the narrowest and most obvious limits. At the one extreme, some works of genius would be sure to miss appreciation. Their very novelty would make them repulsive until the public had learned the new language in which their author spoke. It may be more than doubted, for instance, whether the etchings of Goya or the paintings of Manet would have been sure of protection when seen for the first time. At the other end, copyright would be denied to pictures which appealed to a public less educated than the judge. Yet if they command the interest of any public, they have a commercial value—it would be bold to say that they have not an aesthetic and educational value—and the taste of any public is not to be treated with contempt. It is an ultimate fact for the moment, whatever may be our hopes for a change. That these pictures had their worth and their success is sufficiently shown by the desire to reproduce them without regard to the plaintiffs' rights. We are of opinion that there was evidence that the plaintiffs have rights entitled to the protection of the law. . . .

HARLAN, dissenting:

Judges Lurton, Day, and Severens, of the circuit court of appeals, concurred in affirming the judgment of the district court. Their views were thus expressed in an opinion delivered by Judge Lurton:

> What we hold is this: that if a chromo, lithograph, or other print, engraving, or picture has no other use than that of a mere advertisement, and no value aside from this function, it would not be promotive of the useful arts within the meaning of the constitutional provision, to protect the 'author' in the exclusive use thereof, and the copyright statute should not be construed as including such a publication if any other construction is admissible.

> . . . No evidence, aside from the deductions which are to be drawn from the prints themselves, was offered to show that these designs had any original artistic qualities. The jury could not reasonably have found merit or value aside from the purely business object of advertising a show, and the instruction to find for the defendant was not error. . . .

I entirely concur in these views, and therefore dissent from the opinion and judgment of this Court. The clause of the Constitution giving Congress power to promote the progress of science and useful arts, by securing for limited terms to authors and inventors the exclusive right to their respective works and discoveries, does not, as I think, embrace a mere advertisement of a circus.

*NOTES AND QUESTIONS*

*Copyright's Non-Discrimination Principle. Bleistein* is the leading case supporting copyright law's general nondiscrimination principle: copyright protects all original creative works without judging their merit. Copyright equally protects major cultural contributions, advertising, and pornography.

Copyright law therefore protects works that would have been created without any protection from copyright law—such as ads, which do not require copyright's exclusion powers as an incentive to create them. For more on incentive arguments as applied to ads, *see* Lisa P. Ramsey, *Intellectual*

*Property Rights in Advertising*, 12 MICH. TELECOMM. & TECH. L. REV. 189 (2006); Alfred C. Yen, *Commercial Speech Jurisprudence and Copyright in Commercial Information Works*, 58 S.C. L. REV. 665 (2007); Note, *Rethinking Copyright for Advertisements*, 119 HARV. L. REV. 2486 (2006).

Other countries may impose higher standards for copyrightability that can exclude advertising. *See, e.g.*, Euro Depot, S.A. v. Bricolaje Bricoman, S.L., No. 64/2017 (Feb. 2, 2017) (Spanish Copyright Act didn't protect a commercial brochure, and copying it wasn't unfair competition because imitation is allowed in the absence of exclusive rights).

*Functional Ad Copy*. In *Webloyalty.com, Inc. v. Consumer Innovations, LLC*, 388 F. Supp. 2d 435 (D. Del. 2005), Webloyalty sued Consumer Innovations (CI) for copyright infringement, among other things. The parties competed in the market for membership discount programs. Webloyalty had registered copyrights in its "Sell Page" and "Special Offer Banner" that it used to entice consumers to subscribe to its programs when they visited websites with which Webloyalty had contracted. The Special Offer Banner read in part, "Click here to claim your Special Offer," and, if consumers clicked the Banner, they were directed to the Webloyalty Sell Page and could sign up for Webloyalty's program.

CI copied Webloyalty's Sell Page and Special Offer Banner with few changes, most related to the particular details of CI's rewards program, though CI's principal denied having done so under oath. This denial was not credible, in part because CI's draft sell page included Webloyalty's customer service phone number. CI also used a banner identical to the Webloyalty Banner except that "Reservation Rewards" was replaced by "Traveler Innovations."

The court set out the copyright infringement standard:

> In an action for copyright infringement under 17 U.S.C. § 501, the plaintiff must show by a preponderance of the evidence that its copyright registrations are valid and that the defendant copied the registered works. Copying is proven by showing that the defendant had access to the protected work and that there is a substantial similarity between the two works. The test for substantial similarity is subdivided into two considerations. The first consideration, actual copying, is established by showing the defendant's access to the copyrighted work coupled with "probative" similarity between the two works. The second consideration is whether the copying is actionable, which requires the fact finder to "determine whether a 'lay-observer' would believe that the copying was of protectable aspects of the copyrighted work."

CI challenged the validity of the copyrights on the ground that the material on the Sell Page and Special Offer Banner lacked sufficient originality.

The doctrine of "merger" applies when there is only one way, or are only a few ways, to express an unprotectable idea; to keep the idea free for use, the expression can't be protected. Usually when courts mention this doctrine, they only apply it to the extent that they construe the plaintiff's copyright as a "thin" one, meaning that only wholesale copying will infringe (as opposed to a "thick" copyright that is protected against somewhat more distant imitations).

The related concept of *scènes à faire* is similar: when, because of the genre of the works at issue, certain elements would naturally be expected—a training montage in a sports film, a gruff lieutenant in a police drama, and so on—similarity or even copying of those elements won't be enough to establish infringement.

The *Webloyalty* court rejected merger and *scènes à faire* as applied to the text. Other "sell pages" in the record established that there were other ways to express the same idea.

The court found infringement because an original visual arrangement of page elements, as well as other kinds of selection, coordination, and arrangement, can be copyrighted. The court further concluded the infringement was willful, which occurs when the defendant "actually knew it was infringing the plaintiff's copyrights or recklessly disregarded that possibility." Statutory damages were available; they are designed to compensate plaintiffs for damages that may be hard to prove and to deter and punish infringement. Webloyalty did lose business to CI, but that was not necessarily causally connected to the infringement; the lost business was at least in part the "inevitable" result of the client website's choice to test the two services head to head. As damages, the court awarded $25,000 per infringed work, 25 times CI's revenue from the infringing ads. The court also awarded attorneys' fees and costs of over $225,000 and an injunction.

If Webloyalty's ad copy did a better job than alternative ad copy at converting viewers into buyers than other ad copy, should the merger doctrine have barred copyright protection? Why did CI copy Webloyalty's ad copy instead of preparing its own text? Is what CI did any different from what attorneys and courts do when they begin with the briefs and opinions from earlier cases in forming their own arguments?

*Compare* Culver Franchising System, Inc. v. Steak N Shake Inc., 119 U.S.P.Q.2d 1808 (N.D. Ill. 2016), which rejected similarities in television ads for fast food chains promoting their beef burgers:

> Culver identifies the following common elements: (1) the commercial opens with a butcher in a white uniform in a butcher shop; (2) then, the company logo appears; (3) the butcher describes the beef's quality; (4) three different cuts of beef are shown as the butcher identifies the cuts and describes how they are "well-marbled"; (5) patties are grilled and flattened with a spatula as the griller describes how the cuts "come[] together," using the words "sear" and "seal"; (6) the burger is stacked and topped with cheese; and (7) the commercial ends with a close-up of the completed burger before the company's logo again appears. Culver maintains that the unique "combination of dialogue, pacing, sequence, background, and other visual and expressive elements" in its ad deserves copyright protection.

> ...the commercials are not substantially similar as a matter of law. Several of the seven common elements identified by Culver lack the necessary modicum of creativity to give rise to copyright protection. Regarding the second and seventh elements, there is nothing unique about a company displaying its logo and product at the beginning and/or end of a commercial. The same is true for the sixth element; at least as early as the iconic 1975 "Two all-beef patties, special sauce, lettuce, cheese, pickles, onions on a sesame-seed bun" McDonald's Big

Mac ad, burger commercials have regularly featured the grilling and/or assembling of a burger, followed by a view of the final product. The sequence of Culver's commercial is commonplace, as it would be nonsensical for a commercial to open with a cooked burger and then finish with a prolonged shot of a raw patty.

Regarding the fourth and fifth elements, pressing down on patties with a spatula and flipping them while they cook is standard grilling practice; adding cheese to a burger is not a stroke of originality; and it is common parlance to describe beef as "marbled," to speak of "searing" and "sealing" juices, and to discuss how flavors and ingredients "come together."...

As for the remaining common elements, both commercials take place in butcher shops and portray butchers wearing white aprons who show the three cuts of beef used to make the burgers in question. It is hardly original for an advertisement to describe the origins and quality of a meat product or to feature a butcher. The butchers function as stock characters—both don a white butcher coat and, unsurprisingly, work in a butcher shop. Indeed, Culver effectively concedes that the settings for the commercials are generic by describing each butcher shop as a "quintessential local butcher's shop." Because there is nothing distinctive about the expression of Culver's butcher, and because Culver cannot copyright the mere concept of a butcher talking about beef, Culver's butcher is not protected expression.

Moreover, the commercials differ in certain significant respects. While they both display images of raw beef, they do so differently; "Butcher-Quality Beef" displays the cuts simultaneously, while "The Original Steakburger" focuses on each cut individually. "ButcherQuality Beef" features a conversation between Craig Culver and Fritz, and twice uses a split screen to show three different images at once. In "The Original Steakburger," by contrast, an unnamed butcher speaks directly to the camera and the entire commercial consists of single images (i.e., it does not use split screens).

[From Culver's ad]

418

[From Steak n Shake's ad]

[From Culver's ad]

[From Steak N Shake's ad]

*Copyright and Advertiser Poaching. Webloyalty* applied the principle that copyright law can protect the ways that unprotectable elements are organized. Publishers of yellow pages directories have occasionally, though often unsuccessfully, invoked this rule to fight competing yellow pages directories making copies of ads, even though yellow page publishers usually don't own the copyright to any of the individual ads appearing in their directories. *See, e.g.*, Bellsouth Advert. & Pub'g Corp. v. Donnelley Info. Pub'g, Inc., 999 F.2d 1436 (11th Cir. 1993). (White pages, by contrast, are simply not copyrightable: they evince no protectable creative choice by listing entries in alphabetical order.) How should the doctrines of merger and *scènes à faire* apply to the selection, coordination, and arrangement of yellow pages directories?

## 2.    Who Owns Ad Copy?

When an advertiser creates an advertisement completely in-house using only its employees' labor, the advertiser will automatically own the copyright to the ad copy (unless it contracts with its employees otherwise).

In many cases, advertisers will rely on third-party help to prepare ad copy. It could be as simple as having a freelance designer help with ad layout or a photographer take photos of the advertised product. The advertiser might outsource the advertisement's development completely. For example, it may ask its ad agency to prepare the ad copy from scratch, subject only to the advertiser's approval.

Under default copyright law, independent third parties creating the copyrighted work own the copyright—even if the advertiser pays them to do custom work. This is counterintuitive. Advertisers unfamiliar with copyright law will insist, "I must own it because I paid for it!"

In theory, it's easy to avoid these unexpected outcomes or unwanted disputes: The parties' contract can spell out who owns what. A statute of frauds requires assignments or exclusive licenses of copyrighted works to be in writing, so **always get any copyright deals in writing**, and remember that **a deal involving the creation of ad content almost always involves the creation of copyrightable works**, even if the deal also serves other purposes.

Typically, advertisers prefer to specify that the third party's work be deemed a "work for hire," in which case copyright law automatically deems the commissioning party (here, the advertiser) the work's owner. When dealing with non-employees, however, a work for hire must be memorialized in writing and fit within one of nine content categories enumerated in the Copyright Act. The categories include motion pictures (which would include TV ads), compilations, and contributions to a collective work. For example, a photo intended to be paired with ad copy might be a contribution to a collective work or a compilation. However, not all ads obviously fall into one of the relevant categories, for example a standalone billboard entirely created by the contractor.

Unfortunately for advertisers, not all independent contractors will sign work-for-hire agreements or other agreements transferring ownership or granting an expansive license. Worse, a substantial number of ads are created without any contracts at all or with contracts that are silent about copyright ownership.

The following case shows how copyright issues can get complicated quickly. First, some products may themselves include copyrighted material such as labels. Second, representations of those products, such as standard "product shots" used in ads, may have their own copyright protection; they may also be derivative works of the original product. (A "derivative work" is "a work based upon one or more preexisting works"). Either way, if an advertiser is not very careful about contracting with a photographer, it can get into trouble later on. One way this can happen is if the advertiser hires a second photographer to take more product shots. If the second photographer's pictures closely resemble the first one's, are they infringing?

## Ets-Hokin v. Skyy Spirits, Inc., 225 F.3d 1068 (9th Cir. 2000)

This case requires us to apply copyright principles to stylized photographs of a vodka bottle. Specifically, we must decide whether professional photographer Joshua Ets-Hokin's commercial photographs, dubbed "product shots," of the Skyy Spirits vodka bottle merit copyright protection. Given the Copyright Act's low threshold for originality generally and the minimal amount of originality required to qualify a photograph in particular, we conclude that Ets-Hokin's photographs are entitled to copyright protection.

We also conclude that the district court erred in analyzing this case through the lens of derivative copyright. The photographs at issue cannot be derivative works because the vodka bottle—the alleged underlying work—is not itself subject to copyright protection. Accordingly, we reverse the grant of summary judgment for Skyy Spirits and remand for consideration of whether infringement has occurred.

### BACKGROUND

### I.     THE STORY

. . . Ets-Hokin is a professional photographer who maintains a studio in San Francisco. Maurice Kanbar, the president of Skyy Spirits, Inc. ("Skyy"), and Daniel Dadalt, an employee of the company, visited his studio in the summer of 1993. During this visit, Kanbar and Dadalt reviewed Ets-Hokin's photograph portfolio and subsequently hired him to photograph Skyy's vodka bottle. Ets-Hokin then shot a series of photographs and ultimately produced and delivered three photographs of the bottle. In all three photos, the bottle appears in front of a plain white or yellow backdrop, with back lighting. The bottle seems to be illuminated from the left (from the viewer's perspective), such that the right side of the bottle is slightly shadowed. The angle from which the photos were taken appears to be perpendicular to the side of the bottle, with the label centered, such that the viewer has a "straight on" perspective. In two of the photographs, only the bottle is pictured; in the third, a martini sits next to the bottle.

[Photos courtesy of Wesley Kinnear]

Under the terms of a confirmation of engagement, signed by Dadalt on Skyy's behalf, Ets-Hokin retained all rights to the photos and licensed limited rights to Skyy. The parties dispute the scope of the license, including whether Skyy was licensed to use the photographs in advertising or in publications distributed to the public. After the confirmation was executed, Ets-Hokin applied to the U.S. Copyright Office for a certificate of registration for his series of photos, and a certificate was issued effective on March 10, 1995. . . .

Skyy claims that it found Ets-Hokin's photographs unsatisfactory and thus hired other photographers to photograph the bottle. In dealing with these photographers, Skyy sought to purchase all rights to the photographs of the bottle, as opposed to the license arrangement it had

422

agreed to with Ets-Hokin. One photographer refused to sell his photograph outright, insisting on licensing. Two other photographers were apparently willing to sell all rights to their photographs.

Ets-Hokin brought suit against Skyy and three other defendants for copyright infringement, fraud, and negligent misrepresentation. He alleged that the company used his work in various advertisements, including in *Deneuve* magazine and the *San Francisco Examiner,* and on the side of a bus, without his permission and in violation of the limited license. He also alleged that Skyy used photographs taken by the other photographers that mimicked his own photos; specifically, he claimed that these photographers improperly used his photographs to produce virtually identical photos of the vodka bottle. . . .

I.       VALIDITY OF THE COPYRIGHT

Skyy argues, in a nutshell, that the commercial photographs of its vodka bottle are not worthy of copyright protection. We disagree. The essence of copyrightability is originality of artistic, creative expression. Given the low threshold for originality under the Copyright Act, as well as the longstanding and consistent body of case law holding that photographs generally satisfy this minimal standard, we conclude that Ets-Hokin's product shots of the Skyy vodka bottle are original works of authorship entitled to copyright protection. The district court erred in analyzing copyright protection under the rubric of derivative works. . . .

A.      History of Photography as Copyrightable Artistic Expression

It is well recognized that photography is a form of artistic expression, requiring numerous artistic judgments. As one photojournalist wrote,

> [u]p to and including the instant of exposure, the photographer is working in an undeniably subjective way. By his choice of technical approach (which is a tool of emotional control), by his selection of the subject matter to be held within the confines of his negative area, and by his decision as to the exact, climatic [*sic*] instant of exposure, he is blending the variables of interpretation into an emotional whole which will be a basis for the formation of opinions by the viewing public.

But these judgments are not the only ones. As the well-known photographer Edward Weston wrote,

> [b]y varying the position of his camera, his camera angle, or the focal length of his lens, the photographer can achieve an infinite number of varied compositions with a single, stationary subject. By changing the light on the subject, or by using a color filter, any or all of the values in the subject can be altered. By varying the length of exposure, the kind of emulsion, the method of developing, the photographer can vary the registering of relative values in the negative. And the relative values as registered in the negative can be further modified by allowing more or less light to affect certain parts of the image in printing. Thus, within the limits of his medium, without resorting to any method of control that is not photographic

423

(i.e., of an optical or chemical nature), the photographer can depart from literal recording to whatever extent he chooses.

. . . .

B.      Contemporary Standards for Copyright Protection of Photographs

[The registration was prima facie evidence of validity. Defendants therefore had the burden of proving invalidity.] This they have failed to do, primarily because the degree of originality required for copyrightability is minimal.

. . . Here there is no dispute over the independent creation of the photographs—they are the result of Ets-Hokin's work alone—so what we must decide is whether the photographs of Skyy's vodka bottle possess "at least some minimal degree of creativity."

*Feist,* which involved listings in a telephone directory, described the requisite degree of creativity as "extremely low; even a slight amount will suffice. The vast majority of works make the grade quite easily, as they possess some creative spark, 'no matter how crude, humble or obvious' it might be." When this articulation of the minimal threshold for copyright protection is combined with the minimal standard of originality required for photographic works, the result is that even the slightest artistic touch will meet the originality test for a photograph.

In assessing the "creative spark" of a photograph, we are reminded of Judge Learned Hand's comment that "no photograph, however simple, can be unaffected by the personal influence of the author." This approach, according to a leading treatise in the copyright area, "has become the prevailing view," and as a result, "almost any[ ] photograph may claim the necessary originality to support a copyright merely by virtue of the photographers' [*sic*] personal choice of subject matter, angle of photograph, lighting, and determination of the precise time when the photograph is to be taken." . . .

In view of the low threshold for the creativity element, and given that the types of decisions Ets-Hokin made about lighting, shading, angle, background, and so forth have been recognized as sufficient to convey copyright protection, we have no difficulty in concluding that the defendants have not met their burden of showing the invalidity of Ets-Hokin's copyright, and that Ets-Hokin's product shots are sufficiently creative, and thus sufficiently original, to merit copyright protection. Finally, although Ets-Hokin took photos that undoubtedly resemble many other product shots of the bottle—straight-on, centered, with back lighting so that the word "Skyy" on the bottle is clear—the potential for such similarity does not strip his work of the modicum of originality necessary for copyrightability. Indeed, the fact that two original photographs of the same object may appear similar does not eviscerate their originality or negate their copyrightability.

Having concluded that Ets-Hokin's photos are entitled to copyright protection, we leave to the district court the scope of Ets-Hokin's copyright in the photographs vis-à-vis the claimed infringement.

C. Derivative Copyright . . .

2. The Bottle Is Not Copyrightable

. . . . The district court treated the bottle as a whole as the underlying, "preexisting work," even though the bottle as a whole is a utilitarian object that cannot be copyrighted. [Useful articles such as bottles are not copyrightable unless there are features that are "separable" from the utilitarian features of the articles. While the law here is complex, the court concluded that this was an easy case of lack of separability. As an aside, the court noted that "[a] claim to copyright cannot be registered in a print or label consisting solely of trademark subject matter and lacking copyrightable matter." 37 C.F.R. § 202.10(b). Although a label's "graphical illustrations" are normally copyrightable, "textual matter" is not—at least not unless the text "aid[s] or augment[s]" an accompanying graphical illustration.]

. . . Because Ets-Hokin's product shots are shots of the bottle as a whole—a useful article not subject to copyright protection—and not shots merely, or even mainly, of its label, we hold that the bottle does not qualify as a "preexisting work" within the meaning of the Copyright Act. As such, the photos Ets-Hokin took of the bottle cannot be derivative works. The district court erred in so concluding.

## II.    INFRINGEMENT

. . . Ets-Hokin claims infringement with regard to Skyy's use of his product shots and with regard to solicitation and use of shots produced by other photographers who, Ets-Hokin contends, unlawfully mimicked his work. This issue, which the district court did not reach in view of its holding that Ets-Hokin failed to establish the validity of his copyright, should be addressed in the first instance by that court.

NELSON, dissenting:

The majority opinion errs in reversing the district court's summary judgment order because there is no way that Ets-Hokin can prove infringement given the low standard of originality for photographs. I agree with the majority opinion that under this standard that Ets-Hokin's photographs are original. By the same token, however, so are the other allegedly infringing photographs of Skyy's vodka bottle. These subsequent photographs are based on slightly different angles, different shadows, and different highlights of the bottle's gold label. Thus, even if the district court had applied the proper standard of originality, Ets-Hokin's lawsuit would not have survived summary judgment because the subsequent photographs also possess originality. Furthermore, as a matter of law, legal defenses such as *scènes à faire* and the merger doctrine prevent Ets-Hokin from prevailing on his copyright infringement claims. . . .

[Two of the challenged photos, taken by photographers other than Ets-Hokin.
Courtesy of Wesley Kinnear]

The dissent proved prophetic. The case soon returned to the Court of Appeals, and the court held that the defendant's photos, which differed in terms of angle, lighting, shadow, reflection, and background, did not infringe on the plaintiff's copyrights. Ets-Hokin v. Skyy Spirits, Inc., 323 F.3d 763, 765 (9th Cir. 2003) (*Skyy II*). Why? The only constant between the plaintiff's photographs and the defendant's photographs was the bottle itself, and an accurate portrayal of the unadorned bottle could not be infringing. Ets-Hokin had only a thin copyright offering protection perhaps only from verbatim reproduction of his photographs. His attempt to extend those copyrights to similar recreations of his work went too far, but it took a lot of courtroom time and attorneys' fees to reach that conclusion.

Compare *Skyy* to *Meshwerks, Inc. v. Toyota Motor Sales U.S.A., Inc.*, 528 F.3d 1258 (10th Cir. 2008), finding that digital wireframe models of Toyota vehicles, designed to be three-dimensional representations of the vehicles, were not copyrightable. Even though many decisions were required to figure out how best to create the 3-D models, the court found that they lacked originality, since the whole point of all the decisions was to replicate the cars as well as possible. Is there anything other than the shift from three to two dimensions that made Ets-Hokins' decisions copyrightable?

Consider this quote from *Feist*: "Assume that two poets, each ignorant of the other, compose identical poems. Neither work is novel, yet both are original and, hence, copyrightable." Is this a plausible scenario in the context of two ads showing the same product? Wouldn't the advertiser always have access to the first ad and thus have extreme difficulty showing independent creation? Maybe this is just a risk allocation issue: under *Ets-Hokin* and similar cases, advertisers must ensure that their contracts are airtight about the disposition of subsequent photos if their relationship with the photographer/other independent contractor sours, or else the photographer may be able to control subsequent ads. Is this the right result? Recall that not all advertisers are multimillion-dollar companies.

426

*Skyy* involved a photo of a product that was not itself copyrightable according to the court. What happens when the underlying product *is* copyrightable? In *Schrock v. Learning Curve International, Inc.*, 586 F.3d 513 (7th Cir. 2009), the plaintiff photographer took pictures of "Thomas & Friends" trains, which had their own copyrights, for use on Learning Curve's packaging. After defendant Learning Curve stopped giving Schrock work, he registered his photos and sued for infringement.

The district court granted summary judgment for the defendants, holding that Schrock had no copyright in the photos. The court classified the photos as "derivative works" of the Thomas & Friends characters. Though Schrock had permission to *make* the photos, the district court (relying on earlier precedent) held that he also needed permission to *copyright* them, which he did not have.

The Court of Appeals reversed, reasoning that it did not need to decide whether the photos were derivative works, only whether they contained sufficient new expression to be copyrightable, and the photos had that.

> [T]he photographs are accurate depictions of the three-dimensional "Thomas & Friends" toys, but Schrock's artistic and technical choices combine to create a two-dimensional image that is subtly but nonetheless sufficiently his own. This is confirmed by Schrock's deposition testimony describing his creative process in depicting the toys. Schrock explained how he used various camera and lighting techniques to make the toys look more "life like," "personable," and "friendly." He explained how he tried to give the toys "a little bit of

dimension" and that it was his goal to make the toys "a little bit better than what they look like when you actually see them on the shelf." The original expression in the representative sample is not particularly great (it was not meant to be), but it is enough under the applicable standard to warrant the limited copyright protection accorded derivative works under § 103(b).

Copyright then arose by operation of law, not by permission: "As long as he was authorized to make the photos (he was), he owned the copyright in the photos to the extent of their incremental original expression." The appeals court reasoned that this would not let Schrock hold up the creation of subsequent photos of the toys, because Schrock's copyright protected only his own original contributions. Is this sufficient to protect against lawsuits from photographers who may perceive their own works as especially influential on later ads? How would you write a contract between an advertiser and a photographer in light of this decision?

The Court of Appeals remanded for examination of the agreements between the parties to determine whether they agreed to alter the default rule of ownership or whether Learning Curve had an implied license to continue to use Schrock's photos.

*Schrock* is far from unusual. Advertisers often distribute photographs beyond what the photographer contends is the scope of any license granted. *See* Latimer v. Roaring Toyz, Inc., 601 F.3d 1224 (11th Cir. 2010). Why do you think this fact pattern repeats itself so regularly, despite the significant risks to advertisers?

*Photos of Third-Party Products.* May a retailer display photos of the goods it sells, including their copyrighted elements, without the photographer's permission?

*Fragrancenet.com, Inc. v. Fragrancex.com, Inc.*, 679 F. Supp. 2d 312 (E.D.N.Y. 2010), involved hundreds of photos of products allegedly copied by a competing retailer. The court refused to dismiss the claim because the photos could be original, even if minimally so.
However, "images of a third-party's intellectual property may receive less protection than a completely original work," protected only against "a precise re-creation or copying of the registrant's work." Given that the plaintiff asserted direct copying, it stated a claim despite the thinness of its copyright.

If the copyright in a basic photo of a product is so thin, what's the point of according it any protection at all?

What about the issue that plaintiff's photos featured third parties' perfume bottles, which might themselves contain copyrightable elements? Here, unlike in *Ets-Hokin* and *Schrock*, there doesn't seem to have been any implied license to create the photo. However, the court held the photographer's copyright derives from the photographer's original choices in subject selection, lighting, angle, and so on.

The court didn't mention the key reason that any copyright in the perfume bottles was irrelevant: In general, owning a copyrighted work doesn't give you the right to copy it, but 17 U.S.C. § 113(c) allows retailers and others to create product shots of useful articles for advertisements and commentaries:

> In the case of a work lawfully reproduced in useful articles that have been offered for sale or other distribution to the public, copyright does not include any right to prevent the making, distribution, or display of pictures or photographs of such articles in connection with advertisements or commentaries related to the distribution or display of such articles, or in connection with news reports.

Section 113(c) has some obvious limits. For example, books aren't useful articles, so they aren't covered by §113(c). Are photos of book covers infringing reproductions?

*Ad Agencies*. By default, the ad agency owns any ad copy the agency prepares for the advertiser, even if the advertiser paid for the work to be done. *See, e.g.*, Mkt. Masters-Legal, Inc. v. Parker Waichman Alonso LLP, 3:10-cv-40119-MAP (D. Mass. 2010) (ad agency got preliminary injunction against client law firm from using ad copy elements in other advertising). As a result, advertisers should address ownership issues in the ad agency contract.

Advertisers sometimes require ownership of materials that an ad agency prepares to pitch to acquire the advertiser's business, even before a full business relationship exists and the agency can be sure it will be paid. Not surprisingly, ad agencies don't like these requests. *See, e.g.*, Andrew McMains, *AutoZone Latest to Demand Ownership of Pitches*, ADWEEK, Oct. 31, 2010; American Association of Advertising Agencies, *Best Practice Guidance: Ownership of Agency Ideas, Plans And Work Developed During The New Business Process* (Jan. 26, 2007, as amended Oct. 2011).

*Website Designers*. Similar issues arise over copyright ownership of an advertiser's website designed by an independent contractor. For example, in *108 Degrees, LLC v. Merrimack Golf Club, Inc.*, 2010 DNH 054 (D.N.H. 2010), 108 Degrees sued Merrimack for refusing to pay for a website it commissioned, and it added a copyright infringement claim because Merrimack created a website that was nearly identical to the one 108 Degrees created. Defendants claimed, in response, that the website was a work for hire, thus making Merrimack, as the hiring party, the author by operation of law. But a work for hire not created by an employee requires a written agreement, and the court refused to grant summary judgment in favor of defendants on the copyright because it was unclear who owned the copyright. 108 Degrees claimed it had executed a promissory note with Merrimack stipulating that 108 Degrees would own the copyright until Merrimack paid.

If these allegations were true, 108 Degrees would gain substantial leverage in the underlying contract/payment dispute. If 108 Degrees timely registered the copyright, Merrimack was potentially liable for substantial damages, not to mention having to redesign the website until it no longer infringed (a tricky redesign effort).

Without a written contract specifying ownership or licensing terms, the website sponsor has to rely on an implied nonexclusive license to reuse the materials, which doesn't provide a lot of comfort. *See* Holtzbrinck Pub. Holdings, L.P. v. Vyne Commc'ns, Inc., 2000 WL 502860 (S.D.N.Y. 2000) (defendant, which created a website for plaintiff, granted at least an implied license to use its content, but that the license was in part revocable). *Holtzbrinck* also involved facts highlighting the vulnerability of a company to its website designer. When the dispute erupted between the parties, Vyne threatened to shut down the website in its entirety, obviously a great threat to any business (here, the magazine *Scientific American*). Copyright concerns may become secondary if a disgruntled business partner can cause the website files themselves to disappear.

*Copying Concepts*. Advertisements routinely appear to recycle concepts or memorable elements from prior ads. This type of apparent copying is almost never litigated, but it can be embarrassing. If litigated, the main question would be whether the concept or element is copyrightable expression or an uncopyrightable idea. Consider a few examples from http://adland.tv/badland/dupliclaims. Do any of them cross the line from copying idea to copying expression? We will revisit ownership of ideas in Chapter 12.

Ads also sometimes emulate or draw inspiration from artistic works. *See* Mia Fineman, *The Image Is Familiar; the Pitch Isn't*, N.Y. TIMES, July 13, 2008. How, if at all, should the analysis differ?

Consider the following. James Croak created a sculpture, "Pegasus, Some Loves Hurt More Than Others," a mixed-media, life-sized sculpture depicting "a winged, taxidermied horse that appears to be in the process of breaking through the roof of a sleek lowrider, as if about to take flight":

430

Toyota ran an ad campaign prominently featuring "a massive, pink stuffed animal–specifically, a hybrid of a unicorn and Pegasus–strapped to the roof of a Toyota RAV4." The voiceover narrates: "This is Lady. She's a unicorn. And a Pegasus. And why is she strapped to the roof of my RAV4? Well if you have kids, then you know why. Now the real question. Where's this going in the house? The RAV4. Toyota. Let's go places." The image also appeared in a print ad and a display featuring the stuffed animal at the 2015 Chicago Auto Show:

Is there substantial similarity between the Croak sculpture and the Toyota ads? *See* Croak v. Saatchi & Saatchi, North America, Inc., 174 F. Supp. 3d 829 (S.D.N.Y. 2016) (no).

*Overlapping Publicity Rights.* Even if the advertiser obtains all of the necessary copyright rights or permissions to include a copyrighted work in its advertising, the advertiser usually still needs separate permission to use the publicity/privacy rights of anyone depicted in the ad. (These issues are discussed more in later chapters.)

For example, Virgin Mobile downloaded a photo from the Internet for use in its ad campaign. The photo was distributed using a Creative Commons copyright license that allowed reuse in advertising. Nevertheless, the person in the photo sued the advertiser, alleging that she had been humiliated by the use. She also sued Creative Commons for allegedly failing to educate the photographer sufficiently about the license's scope. *See* _Lawsuit over Virgin Mobile's use of Flickr girl blames Creative Commons_, Sept. 25, 2007.

A related issue involves reuse of television ads online. Most radio and TV actors are members of the relevant guilds (SAG/AFTRA), and their standard contracts provide for extra payments if an ad is used in new contexts or after a certain time. What happens if a third party who likes an ad puts it up on YouTube after the campaign ends? The actors would like to be paid, but the advertiser often likes the free publicity and disclaims any responsibility for the new use. What should happen in such cases?

### 3.    Other Copyright Risks

#### A.    Depicting Everyday Life in Ads: Davis v. The Gap

Given the low standard for copyrightability, creators of ads have to be careful about every element contained in the final ad copy. Posters in the background, images on T-shirts, and anything else that might be copyrightable could potentially trigger a lawsuit.

In *Davis v. The Gap, Inc.*, 246 F.3d 152 (3d Cir. 2001), the plaintiff created Onoculii eyewear, "nonfunctional jewelry worn over the eyes in the manner of eyeglasses." As part of a campaign to show "people of all kinds" wearing Gap clothes, the Gap ran an ad described by the Court of Appeals as follows:

> [The ad] depicts a group of seven young people probably in their twenties, of Asian appearance, standing in a loose V formation staring at the camera with a sultry, pouty, provocative look. The group projects the image of funky intimates of a lively after-hours rock music club. They are dressed primarily in black, exhibiting bare arms and partly bare chests, goatees (accompanied in one case by bleached, streaked hair), large-brimmed, Western-style hats, and distinctive eye shades, worn either over their eyes, on their hats, or cocked over the top of their heads. The central figure, at the apex of the V formation, is wearing Davis's highly distinctive Onoculii eyewear; he peers over the metal disks directly into the camera lens.

[ad]

433

[closeup of Onoculii jewelry]

The people in the ad, who were not traditional models, were told to wear their own eyewear, wristwatches, earrings, nose-rings or other incidental items, thereby "permitting each person to project accurately his or her own personal image and appearance." Previous Onoculii designs had been seen on various entertainers, in runway shows, and in fashion magazines, though there was no indication in the reported facts that anyone at the Gap knew this. On one occasion, Davis received $50 from *Vibe* magazine for a photo showing the musician Sun Ra wearing an Onoculii piece.

The court first determined that the Gap's copying was not "de minimis," which covers unauthorized copying that is so trivial that the law refuses to impose liability. Here, "the infringing item is highly noticeable, in part because the design is "strikingly bizarre":

> [I]t is startling to see the wearer peering at us over his Onoculii. Because eyes are naturally a focal point of attention, and because the wearer is at the center of the group—the apex of the V formation—the viewer's gaze is powerfully drawn to Davis's creation. The impression created, furthermore, is that the models posing in the ad have been outfitted from top to bottom, including eyewear, with Gap merchandise. All this leads us to conclude that the Gap's use of Davis's jewelry cannot be considered a de minimis act of copying to which the law attaches no consequence.

Likewise, the court rejected the Gap's fair use defense. Fair use is a flexible, case-by-case defense to infringement. The Copyright Act, § 107, provides:

> [T]he fair use of a copyrighted work, including such use by reproduction in copies or phonorecords or by any other means specified by that section, for purposes such as criticism, comment, news reporting, teaching (including multiple copies for classroom use), scholarship, or research, is not an infringement of copyright. In determining whether the use made of a work in any particular case is a fair use the factors to be considered shall include—
>
> (1) the purpose and character of the use, including whether such use is of a commercial nature or is for nonprofit educational purposes;
>
> (2) the nature of the copyrighted work;

(3) the amount and substantiality of the portion used in relation to the copyrighted work as a whole; and

(4) the effect of the use upon the potential market for or value of the copyrighted work.

The fact that a work is unpublished shall not itself bar a finding of fair use if such finding is made upon consideration of all the above factors.

Courts often emphasize the first factor and fourth factors. In the first factor, current doctrine favors "transformative" uses—that is, a use that has a different purpose or adds new expression, meaning, or message, instead of substituting for the original.

The *Davis* court found nothing transformative about the Gap ad. "The ad shows Davis's Onoculii being worn as eye jewelry in the manner it was made to be worn—looking much like an ad Davis himself might have sponsored for his copyrighted design." In addition, the Gap's use was for an ad, which was the most extreme form of commerciality, weighing against fair use. *See* Campbell v. Acuff-Rose, Music, 510 U.S. 569 (1994) ("The use, for example, of a copyrighted work to advertise a product . . . will be entitled to less indulgence under the first factor . . . than the sale of [the new work] for its own sake.").

The second statutory factor, the nature of the copyrighted work, is rarely determinative. In theory, fair use should enable copying of factual works more freely than fictional/creative works, though empirical work does not confirm this. *See* Barton Beebe, *An Empirical Study of U.S. Copyright Fair Use Opinions, 1978–2005*, 156 U. PENN. L. REV. 549 (2008). In *Davis*, the court held that the plaintiff's work was an "artistic creation" close to the core of copyright's protective purpose.

The third factor, the "amount and substantiality of the portion used in relation to the copyrighted work as a whole," weighed against the Gap as well, because the ad presented "a head-on full view of Davis's piece, centered and prominently featured."

The final factor, "the effect of the use upon the potential market for or value of the copyrighted work," asks whether the accused work offers a market substitute for the original or harms its market through criticism or parody. Only the former kind of harm is cognizable in copyright. Here, the Gap's use was superseding. "By taking for free Davis's design for its ad, the Gap avoided paying 'the customary price' Davis was entitled to charge for the use of his design. Davis suffered market harm by losing the royalty revenue to which he was reasonably entitled in the circumstances, as well as through the diminution of his opportunity to license to others who might regard Davis's design as preempted by the Gap's ad."

Thus, all the fair use factors weighed in favor of Davis.

Because Davis didn't register until after the infringement began, he was only entitled to compensatory damages, which can include the infringer's profits from the infringement and the copyright owner's actual damages, but cannot provide a double recovery where the two overlap. In this case, however, it was impossible to figure out what percentage of the Gap's clothing sales was attributable to the appearance of Davis's jewelry in the Gap ad. Thus, there was no reasonable factual basis on which to award the infringer's profits. Davis also didn't show any lost sales. The Court of Appeals, however, held that Davis was entitled to a reasonable licensing fee for the use of his work in advertising.

*NOTES AND QUESTIONS*

Do you agree with the court's assessment of the prominence of Davis's design? Would the depiction have been excused if the wearer had been off-center?

The reasonable license fee Davis won was almost certainly less than his cost of litigating the case, so this ruling was almost certainly a financial loss for Davis. Was Davis' decision to litigate a good decision with a bad outcome, a bad decision with an expected bad outcome, or something else? If you had represented the Gap, how much would you have offered in settlement? Keep in mind that an appeal could easily cost several hundred thousand dollars in legal defense costs.

Davis probably achieved a financially dubious outcome, but Gap can't be too happy with the outcome. In addition to the many hassles of litigation, its legal defense costs alone reduced, and possibly exceeded, the overall profitability of the ad campaign. So, how could the Gap have avoided this problem in the first place? Be honest: if you were doing clearance on this ad, would you have identified the "nonfunctional eyewear" as a copyright risk? If not, how will you cope with potential risks like this when it's your responsibility?

Third party copyrighted material can creep into visual ads in countless ways. Even graffiti captured in the background of ordinary street scenes may become a problem. *See, e.g.*, Anasagasti v. American Eagle Outfitters, Inc., 1:14-cv-05618-ALC (S.D.N.Y. complaint filed July 23, 2014) (copyright lawsuit over American Eagle's inclusion of "street art" in ad copy). You must scrutinize every visual element in every ad to consider its potential copyright risk.

## B.     Characters and Parody

When copyrighted works are copied verbatim, it's straightforward to spot the infringement. But when less than the entire work is copied, the rules get more complicated. In the following case, the advertiser created its own ad but referenced a third party's copyrighted work for greater cultural relevance—to its peril.

*Metro-Goldwyn-Mayer, Inc. v. American Honda Motor Co., Inc., 900 F. Supp. 1287 (C.D. Cal. 1995)*

. . . This case arises out of Plaintiffs Metro-Goldwyn-Mayer's and Danjaq's claim that Defendants American Honda Motor Co. and its advertising agency Rubin Postaer and Associates, violated Plaintiffs' "copyrights to sixteen James Bond films and the exclusive intellectual property rights to the James Bond character and the James Bond films" through Defendants' recent commercial for its Honda del Sol automobile.

Premiering last October 1994, Defendants' "Escape" commercial features a young, well-dressed couple in a Honda del Sol being chased by a high-tech helicopter. A grotesque villain with metal-encased arms jumps out of the helicopter onto the car's roof, threatening harm. With a flirtatious turn to his companion, the male driver deftly releases the Honda's detachable roof (which Defendants claim is the main feature allegedly highlighted by the commercial), sending the villain into space and effecting the couple's speedy get-away. . . .

## II.      Factual Background

In 1992, Honda's advertising agency Rubin Postaer came up with a new concept to sell the Honda del Sol convertible with its detachable rooftop. . . . As the concept evolved into the helicopter chase scene, it acquired various project names, one of which was "James Bob," which Yoshida understood to be a play on words for James Bond. In addition, David Spyra, Honda's National Advertising Manager, testified the same way, gingerly agreeing that he understood "James Bob to be a pun on the name James Bond."

. . . [W]hen casting began on the project in the summer of 1994, the casting director specifically sent requests to talent agencies for "James Bond"-type actors and actresses to star in what conceptually could be "the next James Bond film."

With the assistance of the same special effects team that worked on Arnold Schwarzenegger's "True Lies," Defendants proceeded to create a sixty-and thirty-second version of the Honda del Sol commercial at issue: a fast-paced helicopter chase scene featuring a suave hero and an attractive heroine, as well as a menacing and grotesque villain. . . .

On January 15, 1995, in an effort to accommodate Plaintiffs' demands without purportedly conceding liability, Defendants changed their commercial by: (1) altering the protagonists' accents from British to American; and (2) by changing the music to make it less like the horn-driven James Bond theme. This version of the commercial was shown during the Superbowl, allegedly the most widely viewed TV event of the year. . . .

## III. Legal Analysis . . .

### b. What Elements Of Plaintiffs' Work Are Protectable Under Copyright Law

Plaintiffs contend that Defendants' commercial infringes in two independent ways: (1) by reflecting specific scenes from the 16 films; and (2) by the male protagonist's possessing James Bond's unique character traits as developed in the films.

Defendants respond that Plaintiffs are simply trying to gain a monopoly over the "action/spy/police hero" genre which is contrary to the purposes of copyright law. Specifically, Defendants argue that the allegedly infringed elements identified by Plaintiffs are not protectable because: (1) the helicopter chase scene in the Honda commercial is a common theme that naturally flows from most action genre films, and the woman and villain in the film are but stock characters that are not protectable; and (2) under the Ninth Circuit's *Sam Spade* decision, the James Bond character does not constitute the "story being told," but is rather an unprotected dramatic character.

## (1) Whether Film Scenes Are Copyrightable

In their opening brief, Plaintiffs contend that each of their sixteen films contains distinctive scenes that together comprise the classic James Bond adventure: "a high-thrill chase of the ultra-cool British charmer and his beautiful and alarming sidekick by a grotesque villain in which the hero escapes through wit aided by high-tech gadgetry." Defendants argue that these elements are naturally found in any action film and are therefore unprotected "scènes à faire."

. . . Plaintiffs' experts describe in a fair amount of detail how James Bond films are the source of a genre rather than imitators of a broad "action/spy film" genre as Defendants contend. Specifically, film historian Casper explains how the James Bond films represented a fresh and novel approach because they "hybridize[d] the spy thriller with the genres of adventure, comedy (particularly, social satire and slapstick), and fantasy. This amalgam . . . was also a departure from the series' literary source, namely writer Ian Fleming's novels." Casper also states: "I also believe that this distinct mélange of genres, which was also seminal . . . created a protagonist, antagonist, sexual consort, type of mission, type of exotic setting, type of mood, type of dialogue, type of music, etc. that was not there in the subtype of the spy thriller films of that ilk hitherto." . . .

Based on Plaintiffs' experts' greater familiarity with the James Bond films, as well as a review of Plaintiffs' James Bond montage and defense expert Needham's video montage of the "action/spy" genre films, it is clear that James Bond films are unique in their expression of the spy thriller idea. A filmmaker could produce a helicopter chase scene in practically an indefinite number of ways, but only James Bond films bring the various elements Casper describes together in a unique and original way.

Thus, the Court believes that Plaintiffs will likely succeed on their claim that their expression of the action film sequences in the James Bond films is copyrightable as a matter of law.[8]

## (2) Whether James Bond Character Is Copyrightable

.... Like Rocky, Sherlock Holmes, Tarzan, and Superman, James Bond has certain character traits that have been developed over time through the sixteen films in which he appears. Contrary to Defendants' assertions, because many actors can play Bond is a testament to the fact that Bond is a unique character whose specific qualities remain constant despite the change in actors. . . . A James Bond film without James Bond is not a James Bond film. . . .

Accordingly, the Court concludes that Plaintiffs will probably succeed on their claim that James Bond is a copyrightable character ....

---

[8] Of course, these film sequences would be only "scènes à faire" without James Bond. It is Bond that makes a James Bond film as the following section bears out.

c. Defendants' Alleged Infringement

. . . Viewing Plaintiffs' and Defendants' videotapes and examining the experts' statements, Plaintiffs will likely prevail on this issue because there is substantial similarity between the specific protected elements of the James Bond films and the Honda commercial: (1) the theme, plot, and sequence both involve the idea of a handsome hero who, along with a beautiful woman, lead a grotesque villain on a high-speed chase, the male appears calm and unruffled, there are hints of romance between the male and female, and the protagonists escape with the aid of intelligence and gadgetry; (2) the settings both involve the idea of a high-speed chase with the villain in hot pursuit; (3) the mood and pace of both works are fast-paced and involve hi-tech effects, with loud, exciting horn music in the background; (4) both the James Bond and Honda commercial dialogues are laced with dry wit and subtle humor; (5) the characters of Bond and the Honda man are very similar in the way they look and act—both heros [*sic*] are young, tuxedo-clad, British-looking men with beautiful women in tow and grotesque villains close at hand; moreover, both men exude uncanny calm under pressure, exhibit a dry sense of humor and wit, and are attracted to, and are attractive to, their female companions.

In addition, several specific aspects of the Honda commercial appear to have been lifted from the James Bond films:

(1) In "The Spy Who Loved Me," James Bond is in a white sports car, a beautiful woman passenger at his side, driving away down a deserted road from some almost deadly adventure, when he is suddenly attacked by a chasing helicopter whose bullets he narrowly avoids by skillfully weaving the car down the road at high speed. At the beginning of the Honda commercial, the Honda man turns to his companion and says, "That wasn't so bad"; to which the woman replies, "Well, I wouldn't congratulate yourself quite yet"—implying that they had just escaped some prior danger. Suddenly, a helicopter appears from out of nowhere and the adventure begins.

(2) In "Dr. No.," the villain has metal hands. In the Honda commercial, the villain uses his metal-encased hands to cling onto the roof of the car after he jumps onto it.

(3) In "Goldfinger," Bond's sports car has a roof which Bond can cause to detach with the flick of a lever. In the Honda commercial, the Honda del Sol has a detachable roof which the Honda man uses to eject the villain.

(4) In "Moonraker," the villainous henchman, Jaws, sporting a broad grin revealing metallic teeth and wearing a pair of oversized goggles, jumps out of an airplane. In the Honda commercial, the villain, wearing similar goggles and revealing metallic teeth, jumps out of a helicopter.

(5) In "The Spy Who Loved Me," Jaws assaults a vehicle in which Bond and his female sidekick are trying to make their escape. In the Honda commercial, the villain jumps onto the roof of the Honda del Sol and scrapes at the roof, attempting to hold on and possibly get inside the vehicle.

(6) In "You Only Live Twice," a chasing helicopter drops a magnetic line down to snag a speeding car. In the Honda commercial, the villain is dropped down to the moving car and is suspended from the helicopter by a cable.

In sum, the extrinsic ideas that are inherent parts of the James Bond films appear to be substantially similar to those in the Honda commercial. . . .

[The court rejected defendants' argument that the ad was independently created, and also rejected a fair use defense, focusing on its conclusions that the use was highly commercial and not transformative or commenting on the Bond films. In terms of the amount of the original taken, the court found that "the brevity of the infringing work when compared with the original does not excuse copying." As for market effect, the court accepted plaintiffs' argument that one of the most lucrative aspects of its copyrights was "their value as lending social cachet and upscale image to cars," and that association with a low-end Honda model would threaten the value of the franchise to future licensees.]

*NOTES AND QUESTIONS*

Honda argued that no character could be infringed in a 30-second commercial. What do you think of the claim that the amount of detail conveyed in such a short time almost necessarily must be an abstract idea or scènes à faire, rather than protectable expression? Does the court give MGM a de facto monopoly over a certain genre of video?

MGM argued that the economic harm it suffered was the risk the Honda ad posed to future license agreements with upscale advertisers who would engage in cross-promotion (paying for placement in a movie, supporting the movie with coordinated advertising, etc.). Should copyright extend to that kind of value?

Courts regularly do not give advertisers the benefit of the doubt in similar attempts at parody. *See* Tin Pan Apple, Inc. v. Miller Brewing Co., 737 F. Supp. 826, 832 (S.D.N.Y.1990) (beer commercial copying music video); D.C. Comics, Inc. v. Crazy Eddie, Inc., 205 U.S.P.Q. 1177 (S.D.N.Y. 1979) (commercial copying Superman).

## C.    Defendants Don't Always Lose! A Successful Parody

*Eveready Battery Co., Inc. v. Adolph Coors Co., 765 F. Supp. 440 (N.D. Ill. 1991)*

This case arises from a recently made (and not yet aired) beer commercial by defendant Adolph Coors Company ("Coors") which spoofs a popular series of Eveready battery commercials featuring a pink mechanical toy bunny (the "Energizer Bunny"). . . .

After airing the initial Energizer Bunny commercial, Eveready hired a new ad agency, Chiat/Day/Mojo Inc. Advertising ("Chiat/Day"), which developed an ad campaign revolving around the Energizer Bunny. The series of television commercials created by Chiat/Day as part of this campaign use the Eveready Bunny in a "commercial within a commercial" format. Each spot begins with what at first appears to be a typical television advertisement (which the viewer later realizes is for a fictitious product or service). At some point during the spot, an off-camera drum beat appears to distract the actors in the bogus commercial while the Energizer Bunny—which virtually always appears in its characteristic beach thongs and sunglasses—strolls onto screen beating his bass drum. The actors of the bogus commercial stare incredulously as the intruding mechanical toy bunny nonchalantly propels across the screen, beating the drum and often knocking over props from the fictitious commercial's set. In many of these Energizer commercials, the bunny spins around once and twirls his drum mallets before proceeding to propel out of the picture. Each of the commercials ends with a voice-over which states: "Still going. Nothing outlasts the Energizer. They keep going and going . . . [voice fades out]."

In the past two years, Eveready has produced approximately twenty Energizer Bunny commercials with the interruptive "commercial within a commercial" motif. Although these commercials have cost Eveready approximately $55,000,000 over the past two years (apparently a very modest sum by current advertising standards), they have become among the most popular television commercials in the country and are deemed "break through" ads among those in the advertising industry. . . .

Eveready has also obtained federal copyright registration for two of its Energizer Bunny interruptive format commercials—one for a bogus product called "Tres Cafe," an instant coffee, and the other for "Chug-A-Cherry," a fictional cherry flavored soda.

In late 1990, . . . Foote, Cone and Belding Communications, Inc. ("FCB"), the advertising [agency] for Coors, was given the job of creating a humorous commercial involving Leslie Nielsen, a well-known actor who has been featured in previous Coors Light commercials. . . .

The Coors commercial begins with a background voice, speaking over a classical music score, heartily describing the attributes of an unidentified beer. As the voice speaks, the visual shows an extreme close-up of beer pouring into a glass. The voice and music then grind to a halt as a drum beat is heard and Mr. Nielsen appears walking across the visual. Mr. Nielsen wears a conservative, dark business suit, fake white rabbit ears, fuzzy white tail and rabbit feet (which look like rectangular pink slippers). He carries a life-sized bass drum imprinted with the COORS LIGHT logo. After beating the drum several times, Mr. Nielsen spins rapidly seven or so times and, after recovering somewhat from his apparent dizziness, resumes walking. He says "thank you" before exiting off the screen. As Mr. Nielsen exits, another background voice states: "Coors Light, the official beer of the nineties, is the fastest growing light beer in America. It keeps growing and growing and growing . . . [voice fades out]." At the end of the spot, a visual appears depicting Coors' "Silver Bullet" logo—a horizontal Coors Light can—streaking across the bottom of the screen, leaving in its wake the mark "Coors Light." . . .

DISCUSSION

*. . . Copyright Infringement*

. . . In the present case, it is undisputed that the plaintiff has ownership of valid copyrights in its Energizer Bunny commercials. It is also undisputed that Coors had access to the Energizer spots and incorporated certain elements of those commercials into its commercial. In this sense, it is clear that Coors "copied" something from Eveready's commercials. Therefore, the court must determine whether the copied elements of the Energizer commercials constitute protectible [*sic*] original "expressions"—as opposed to unprotectible [*sic*] "ideas," *see* 17 U.S.C. § 102(b) (copyright protection does not extend to ideas underlying the author's expressions)[11]—and whether the extent of the copying was sufficient to constitute an improper appropriation.

---

[2] Ed. note: Ad at https://www.youtube.com/watch?v=gvfMd7Ydx4c.

[11] It is established that the copyrightable expressions of a television commercial may include: "individual artistic choices such as particular montage style, camera angle, framing, hairstyle [of actors/actresses], jewelry, decor, makeup and background. These choices express the concept behind any given commercial and distinguish its images and sounds from the otherwise infinite universe of commercials which might have been made."

. . . The court, however, finds it unnecessary to engage in a "substantial similarity" analysis here. Even assuming that Eveready can establish substantial similarity, it has not established a likelihood of success under the "fair use" provisions of the Copyright Act. . . .

Applying the statutory fair use factors to the Coors commercial, the court finds that Eveready cannot establish a likelihood of success on its position that the Nielsen commercial is an infringement of its copyrights. Although the first factor in the § 107 analysis—the purpose and character of Coors' use—weighs in Eveready's favor, none of the remaining three factors are similarly favorable.

The nature of the copyrighted work, like the character of the challenged work, is commercial. Indeed, the two works serve an identical purpose for their respective sponsors. Thus, Eveready cannot argue that its work is deserving of particularly strong protection. Thus, the second factor is at best neutral but certainly does not weigh in favor of Eveready.

Next, the court finds that the amount and substantiality of the portion used in relation to the copyrighted work as a whole is not sufficient to weigh in favor of Eveready. On this point, Eveready, quoting *Walt Disney Prods. v. Air Pirates*, 581 F.2d 751, 757 (9th Cir. 1978), asserts that: "One may lawfully parody copyrighted work *only* if he takes no more than is necessary to 'recall or conjure up the object of his satire.' " . . . This court, however, declines to adopt Eveready's rigid interpretation of the so called "conjure up" test. In *Fisher v. Dees,* the Ninth Circuit expressly stated that the "conjure up" test articulated in its *Air Pirates* opinion, was not meant to be interpreted rigidly "to limit the amount of permissible copying to that amount necessary to evoke only *initial* recognition" in the viewer. . . .

The court finds that the Coors spot did not borrow an impermissible amount of the Eveready commercials for the purposes of the fair use/parody analysis. As Coors points out, the Nielsen commercial is obviously not a verbatim copy of plaintiff's commercials. Rather, Coors' ad merely incorporates certain elements of those commercials necessary to conjure an image of the Eveready spots for humorous effect. Its imitation of the Energizer Bunny is far from excessive. Mr. Nielsen is not a toy (mechanical or otherwise), does not run on batteries, is not fifteen inches tall, is not predominantly pink, does not wear sunglasses or beach thongs, and would probably make a better babysitter than a children's gift. Although Mr. Nielsen dons rabbit ears, tail, and feet (thus imitating certain bunny-like features), he by no means copies the majority of the Energizer Bunny's "look." Indeed, the dissimilarities between the two far outweigh the similarities. Unlike the Energizer Bunny, Mr. Nielsen speaks; he does not disrupt actors in a fictional commercial; and he does not disturb any props on the "fictional" commercial's set. Also notable is the fact that the Coors commercial does not imitate any particular one of the Energizer spots. Instead, it imitates a few identifiable features, exaggerates some, and leaves out most others. Thus, the court finds that the "amount and substantiality" prong of the fair use analysis weighs against Eveready.

The fourth prong of the statutory fair use test—the effect of the use upon the potential market for or value of the copyrighted work—also weighs against Eveready. This factor has been described as "undoubtedly the single most important element of fair use." In the *Fisher* case, the Ninth Circuit discussed the standard applicable this factor when the use at issue is a parody, stating:

In assessing the economic effect of the parody, the parody's critical impact must be excluded. Through its critical function, a "parody may quite legitimately aim at garroting the original, destroying it commercially as well as artistically." Copyright law is not designed to stifle critics. . . . Accordingly, the economic effect of a parody with which we are concerned is not its potential to destroy or diminish the market for the original—any bad review can have that effect—but rather whether it *fulfills the demand* for the original. Biting criticism suppresses demand; copyright infringement usurps it. Thus, infringement occurs when a parody supplants the original in markets the original is aimed at, or in which the original is or has reasonable potential to become, commercially valuable.

. . . In the present case, there is no indication that the Coors commercial will supplant the market for the Eveready commercial. Viewers will not stop watching the Eveready commercials in order to watch the Coors commercial on another channel.[18] Thus, to the extent that the Coors commercial may have any effect on the market for the Energizer Bunny commercials, that effect would not be relevant to the copyright fair use analysis. For these reasons, the court finds that Eveready has not established a likelihood of success on its copyright claim. . . .

*NOTES AND QUESTIONS*

If the court had found it necessary to engage in a substantial similarity analysis, should it have found the commercials' expression to be substantially similar?

In *Leibovitz v. Paramount Pictures Corp.*, 137 F.3d 109 (2d Cir. 1998), the defendants' ad for the comic movie *Naked Gun 33 1/3: The Final Insult* copied Annie Leibovitz's famous photo of a pregnant, nude Demi Moore, except with star Leslie Nielsen's (again!) face on the body of a pregnant model:

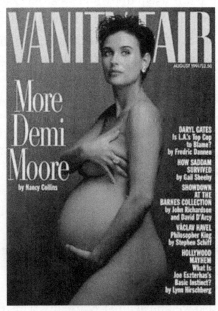

---

[18] The court also notes that because the Coors commercial may only be aired for a maximum of six weeks, it would have little opportunity to "supplant" the Energizer ads in any event.

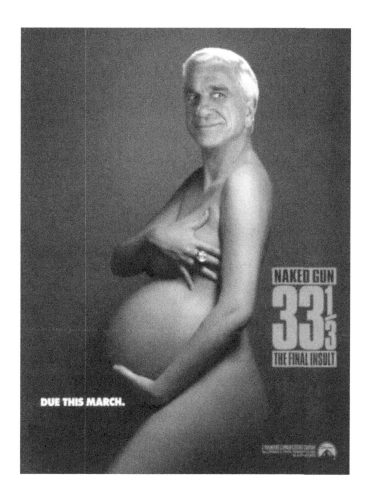

Unlike the *Eveready* case, the *Leibovitz* case came after the Supreme Court's 1994 decision in *Campbell v. Acuff-Rose*, in which the Supreme Court evinced special solicitude for parodies. Specifically, the Court favored "transformative" uses that "add[] something new, with a further purpose or different character, altering the first with new expression, meaning, or message." The Court also noted that commercial use is a factor weighing against fair use, and that the use of a copyrighted work to advertise a product is a context entitling the copying work to "less indulgence" than if it is marketed for its own worth. However, the Court also emphasized that each case must be decided on its own facts, and that commercial use is not fatal to fairness.

The critical question of transformativeness was whether the allegedly infringing use, at least in part, commented on the original's substance or style, though the Court warned against judging quality. The issue was "whether a parodic character may reasonably be perceived." When it comes to parodies, the "nature of the work" factor is not much help, because parodies almost always copy expressive works (rather than factual ones, which are otherwise considered fairer game). As to the amount copied, the Court required inquiry into both quantity and quality of what was taken, but pointed out that a parody must be allowed to "conjure up" at least enough of the original to make its point; the amount taken must be assessed for reasonability in light of whether the overriding purpose is parody or substitution for the original. Finally, the Court rejected any presumption of market harm from copying "involving something beyond mere duplication for commercial purposes."

Parodies and originals usually serve different markets, and harm to the original resulting from the critical sting of the parody is not cognizable harm. Only market substitution counts.

With this background, the *Leibovitz* court found that the ad could reasonably be perceived as commentary, at least in part, on the original photo. "Because the smirking face of Nielsen contrasts so strikingly with the serious expression on the face of Moore, the ad may reasonably be perceived as commenting on the seriousness, even the pretentiousness, of the original. The contrast achieves the effect of ridicule that the Court recognized in *Campbell* would serve as a sufficient 'comment' to tip the first factor in a parodist's favor." Though the court warned that differences aren't inevitably commentary on the original, this ad differed "in a way that may reasonably be perceived as commenting, through ridicule, on what a viewer might reasonably think is the undue self-importance conveyed by the subject of the Leibovitz photograph. A photographer posing a well-known actress in a manner that calls to mind a well-known painting must expect, or at least tolerate, a parodist's deflating ridicule." In addition, "the ad might also be reasonably perceived as interpreting the Leibovitz photograph to extol the beauty of the pregnant female body, and, rather unchivalrously, to express disagreement with this message." In the end, "the strong parodic nature of the ad tips the first factor significantly toward fair use, even after making some discount for the fact that it promotes a commercial product."

Because Leibovitz's photo was significantly creative, the second factor favored her, but its weight was minimal.

In terms of the amount taken, a parodist may be allowed to take the heart of the original, because that is its usual target. "The copying of these elements, carried out to an extreme degree by the technique of digital computer enhancement, took more of the Leibovitz photograph than was minimally necessary to conjure it up, but *Campbell* instructs that a parodist's copying of more of an original than is necessary to conjure it up will not necessarily tip the third factor against fair use." The third factor had "little, if any" weight against fair use as long as the first and fourth factors favored the parodist.

Leibovitz could not realistically contend that the Paramount ad interfered with any potential market for her photo or for derivative works based on it. Her only argument was that Paramount deprived her of a licensing fee. But she was not entitled to a licensing fee for a work that otherwise qualifies as a fair use. Leibovitz was concerned with the effect of the parody on her "special relationships" with the celebrities she photographed. But "like market harm caused by a negative book review, any lost revenue Leibovitz might experience due to celebrities' reluctance to be photographed for fear of enduring parodies is not cognizable harm under the fourth fair use factor. The possibility of criticism or comment—whether or not parodic—is a risk artists and their subjects must accept."

*Other Movie Ad Cases.* In *Columbia Pictures Industries, Inc. v. Miramax Films Corp.*, 11 F. Supp. 2d 1179 (C.D. Cal. 1998), the court held that Miramax's ads for Michael Moore's *The Big One*, which targeted large corporations, were not fair uses of the ads for the science fiction movie *Men in Black*. Miramax's ads drew on *Men in Black*, imitating its advertising slogan ("Protecting the Earth from the scum of the universe" became "Protecting the Earth from the scum of corporate America"), as well as creating both posters and trailers that were similar to the *Men in Black* poster and trailer.

The court rejected the defense that the ads parodied *Men in Black* by putting an average, out-of-shape documentarian in the hero's role. Do you agree? Can this case be reconciled with *Leibovitz*?

What about the following images (Saul Steinberg's famous "New Yorker's–eye view of the world" cover for *The New Yorker*, made into a popular poster, and a detail from the poster for *Moscow on the Hudson*, starring Robin Williams)? Is the extent of copying the same as it was in the *Leibovitz* case? What exactly is being copied? Should there be copyright protection for artistic style? *See* Steinberg v. Columbia Pictures Indus., 663 F. Supp. 706 (S.D.N.Y. 1987) (*Moscow on the Hudson* poster was infringing).

447

*Test Yourself: GoldieBlox.* GoldieBlox makes engineering toys for girls. For an ad showing off girls' creative construction skills, it copied the music and structure of the Beastie Boys' song "Girls," but changed the lyrics:

| Beastie Boys' original | GoldieBlox version |
| --- | --- |
| Girls—to do the dishes | Girls—to build the spaceship |
| Girls—to clean up my room | Girls—to code the new app |
| Girls—to do the laundry | Girls—to grow up knowing |
| Girls—and in the bathroom | That they can engineer that |
| Girls, that's all I really want is girls. | Girls. That's all we really need is girls. |

GoldieBlox argued that this was a parody, criticizing the sexist attitudes expressed by the original as part of its mission to promote equality. It filed a declaratory judgment against the Beastie Boys, seeking a fair use determination. The Beastie Boys responded that they didn't allow anyone to use their music in ads. *See* GoldieBlox, Inc. v. Island Def Jam Music Grp., No. 13-cv-05428 (N.D. Cal. complaint filed Nov. 21, 2013).

The case settled. GoldieBlox agreed to make annual payments of 1% of its gross revenue, until the total payments reached $1 million, to a charitable organization—chosen by the Beastie Boys and approved by GoldieBlox—that supports science, technology, engineering and/or mathematics education for girls. Beastie Boys v. Monster Energy Co., 1:12-cv-06065 (S.D.N.Y. 2014). If the litigation had continued, how should the court have ruled on fair use? Should GoldieBlox have had to pay anything? Does the settlement have any positive aspects for GoldieBlox?

### D.     Comparative Advertising

The use of others' copyrighted works in comparative advertising is often permitted when the works at issue are the comparison's subject.

In *Sony Computer Entertainment America, Inc. v. Bleem, LLC*, 214 F.3d 1022 (9th Cir. 2000), Bleem developed a software emulator that allowed consumers to play Sony PlayStation games on their computers. The emulator allowed consumers to skip purchasing a PlayStation console, which would have to be hooked up to a TV, and to play games on higher-resolution computer monitors. (At the time, consumers were more likely to have high-resolution monitors than high-resolution TV screens.)

The emulator itself wasn't infringing. Sony nevertheless argued that displaying screenshots from Sony's copyrighted games on the emulator's packaging infringed its rights. The screenshots compared what a game looked like on a Sony console and with the emulator and a speed-enhancing graphics card on a computer screen.

The court found that screenshots are ubiquitous on videogame packages because it is important to consumers to see "exactly what the game will look like on a screen when it is played."

On the first factor, the court concluded that Bleem's use of the screenshots constituted comparative advertising, which favored a finding of fair use. The court quoted the FTC's position that truthful and nondeceptive comparative advertising "is a source of important information to consumers and assists them in making rational purchase decisions. Comparative advertising encourages product improvement and innovation, and can lead to lower prices in the marketplace." The use here supported those goals:

> First, by seeing how the games' graphics look on a television when played on a console as compared to how they look on a computer screen when played with Bleem's emulator, consumers will be most able to make "rational purchase decisions." Sony argues that Bleem can advertise without the screen shots, which is certainly true, but no other way will allow for the clearest consumer decisionmaking. Indeed, Bleem's advertising in this fashion will almost certainly lead to product improvements as Sony responds to this competitive threat and as other emulator producers strive for even better performance.

> . . . Although Bleem is most certainly copying Sony's copyrighted material for the commercial purposes of increasing its own sales, such comparative advertising redounds greatly to the purchasing public's benefit with very little corresponding loss to the integrity of Sony's copyrighted material.

On the second factor, the nature of the work, the court reasoned that "although the copyrighted work is creative in nature generally, a screen shot is not necessarily. A screen shot is merely an inanimate sliver of the game," and found this factor generally worth "very little energy."

A screenshot, which was one of thirty frames per second, was temporally a small amount of the video game. Given that the games at issue had multi-hour plots, a screenshot was "of little substance to the overall copyrighted work."

Finally, on the fourth factor, which the court considered the most important, the relevant market was not the market for emulators or video games themselves, because the emulator did not infringe. Sony argued that Bleem's use of screenshots "impinges upon Sony's ability to use the screen shots for promotional purposes in the market. Bleem [responded] by contending that there is no *market* in screen shots. "Certainly screen shots are a standard device used in the industry to demonstrate video game graphics, but there is not a market for them, or at least not one in which Bleem may participate given Sony's refusal to license to it." Any market harm resulted from commercial competition with the underlying work, which is non-infringing. Thus, the court found fair use.

*Fair use of competitors' ads.* Courts have also favored copying competitors' ads for the purpose of explicit comparison. Miller UK Ltd. v. Caterpillar Inc., 2015 WL 6407223 (N.D. Ill. Oct. 21, 2015) (annotated copy of competitor's brochure was fair use; "[T]he commercial value to Miller and any resulting decline in the commercial value of the original work resulted not from the value of the original, but from the Miller additions. Such uses are not considered substitutes for the original work and are encouraged by the fair use doctrine.").

But if truthful comparative advertising is favored by fair use, does the analysis change if the ad at issue is false? In Ashley Furniture Industries, Inc. v. American Signature, Inc., 2014 WL 11320708 (S.D. Ohio June 25, 2014), the defendant copied the plaintiff's webpage to show it next to the defendant's furniture:

In other advertising, the defendant copied pictures of plaintiff's furniture in order to compare the parties' offerings:

The plaintiff, Ashley, argued that the comparisons were false and misleading for various reasons. The court rejected Ashley's argument that the falsity undermined fair use: "Very simply, copyright law protects Ashley's photographs, not Ashley's interest in selling the sofas depicted in the photos. As such, passing off in this context would entail Value City's sale of copies of Ashley's photographs as its own, which did not occur." Thus, "allegations that Value City's comparative advertisements did not disclose differences in the quality of the furniture, contained inaccuracies as to pricing, and led some consumers to believe that Value City was selling Ashley sofas are actionable, if at all, under the Lanham Act, not the Copyright Act." The copying was transformative fair use, and didn't harm the (nonexistent) market for photos of Ashley's furniture.

## 4. Adding Ads to Copyrighted Works

Ordinarily, a publisher displaying advertising adjacent to copyrighted material should not face copyright exposure because adjacencies don't implicate any of the exclusive rights of the copyright owner. For example, if newspapers want to show ads next to editorial content they license from others, newspapers don't need any separate permission to do so beyond the permission to publish the content. Similarly, movie theaters can show ads before a movie without requiring permission beyond the permission to exhibit the movie.

It would be great if we could categorically declare that placing ads around editorial content doesn't create copyright problems. Unfortunately, the case law is more equivocal.

A flagship case is *National Bank of Commerce v. Shaklee Corp.*, 503 F. Supp. 533 (W.D. Tex. 1980). The book at issue was called *All Around the House* by Heloise Bowles, author of a widely syndicated newspaper column called "Hints from Heloise." To boost her editorial integrity, Heloise never mentioned brand names in her column or endorsed any products.

Shaklee was a retailer of household goods sold via "independent distributors" typically via in-home sales (similar to Amway and Tupperware). Shaklee ordered 100,000 customized editions of the book that included Shaklee promotions on the front and rear covers and interspersed within the book's text.

[front and back covers]

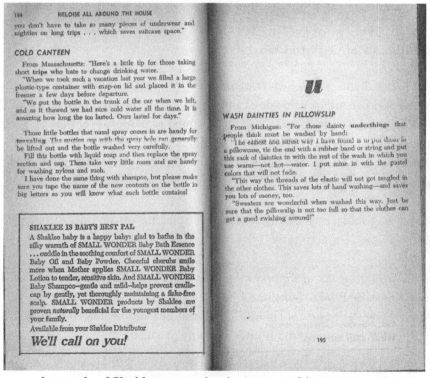

[example of Shaklee promotion interspersed into the book]

The court said Shaklee's additions were analogous to making unauthorized edits of a copyrighted work, so it held that the additions required the copyright owner's authorization, which hadn't been properly obtained.

Compare *Paramount Pictures Corp. v. Video Broadcasting Systems, Inc.*, 724 F. Supp. 808 (D. Kan. 1989). VBS added video advertisements (before the FBI warning) to cassettes rented or sold by video rental stores. Nevertheless, some VBS-inserted ads overlapped with the FBI warning or ads placed on the videocassettes by the copyright owner. With respect to its unauthorized editing, the court said:

> Paramount does not allege that defendants were granted certain rights in the motion pictures which they exceeded or abused. This is not a case where the substance of the protected work is significantly altered and its quality and integrity compromised by a licensee or grantee who oversteps his authority. This is not a case where the equities so obviously favor the copyright owner that the court must struggle with the notion of "moral rights." What . . . was applied in *Shaklee* . . . is the right to check distortion or truncation of a copyrighted work. This court is not satisfied that the result of defendants' addition is the distortion of plaintiff's motion picture.

The court said that "the mere addition of a commercial to the front of a videocassette" doesn't create a derivative work, and any distribution rights were exhausted by the cassette's first sale.

Can you reconcile these two results? Does the user's perception of whether the object at issue contains a single integrated work matter?

*NOTES AND QUESTIONS*

*Internet Issues.* Because each browser makes a copy (or copies) of the webpage a user visits, copyright law might be invoked when individual users attempt to control the appearance of their own computers—or when third-party advertisers help them do so.

In *Wells Fargo & Co. v. WhenU.com, Inc.*, 293 F. Supp. 2d 734 (E.D. Mich. 2003), the defendant engaged in "contextual marketing." That is, WhenU supplied a program to consumers, SaveNow, that generated pop-up and pop-under ads based on data about the websites that they visited, sometimes meaning that competitors' pop-ups obscured the website (at least until the consumer minimized or closed the pop-up). Plaintiffs sued for trademark and copyright infringement.

The court described the typical Windows user's experience of the "desktop," which mimics an actual physical desktop in certain respects, giving the impression of a three-dimensional space in which items can be on top of and underneath each other. The Windows environment allows users to have multiple browser windows open simultaneously, each displaying a different web page, and web pages can overlap on the screen. The court thus held that SaveNow ads didn't appear "on" the plaintiffs' websites. There was no interference with or change in the contents of those sites. Nor did they "modify" plaintiffs' sites. The user's computer's copy of the HTML code associated with the webpage was saved into the computer's RAM (random access memory); SaveNow ads didn't interfere with the stored code.

Computers also maintain a temporary form of memory called video memory, with a pixel-by-pixel snapshot of the screen at any given instant. As a result, plaintiffs argued, a SaveNow ad altered the content of video memory while plaintiffs' web pages were being displayed.

The court held that WhenU did not violate plaintiffs' exclusive right to prepare derivative works. WhenU did not incorporate the plaintiffs' sites into a new work. They merely provided a software product to computer users. As the court pointed out, this could only be actionable under a theory of contributory liability. Defendants who substantially and knowingly contribute to infringement can be held liable as infringers. The problem for plaintiffs, and probably why they did not assert secondary liability theories, is that contributory liability requires someone else to be the primary infringer, and in this case the only candidate was the ordinary browsing consumer.

Thus, the court considered whether SaveNow users infringed the right to prepare derivative works and concluded that they did not alter plaintiffs' websites, even though they altered the display of their screens. "The WhenU Window has no physical relationship to plaintiffs' websites, and does not modify the content displayed in any other open window." The mere presence of an overlapping window, without generating a fixed transferable copy of a work or a public retransmission of an altered version, could not create a derivative work. "Plaintiffs do not have any property interest in the content of a user's pixels, much less a copyright interest."

*Ad Subtraction.* Most broadcast television channels, as well as many cable television channels, are ad-supported. When third parties help consumers skip ads, does that create an infringing derivative work?

Replay, an early digital video recorder, was sued in part for creating a 30-second fast-forward button on its remote designed to allow easy ad skipping. This button is now available on various remotes, but Replay went out of business before the issue had been fully litigated. Under *Shaklee* and *Paramount Pictures*, what should the result have been? Does it matter that ads subsidize the production of creative broadcast works, and that ad skipping thus seems to attack the fundamental economic basis for offering free or cheap TV? *See* Fox Broad. Co. v. Dish Network LLC, 723 F.3d 1067 (9th Cir. 2013).

Brands are crucial business assets. According to a <u>2017 study by Kantar Millward Brown</u>, the top 100 global brands are worth a collective $3.6 trillion, and Google's brand is worth over $254 billion alone. Consumers can establish deep emotional responses to brands—favorite brands can lead to repeat patronage and good word-of-mouth, while disfavored brands can enter a death spiral.

Given these lofty stakes, it may not be surprising that companies look for ways to protect their brands against unwanted use. Trademark law is the principal legal tool for protecting brands.

Trademark protection is available for anything that signifies product source to consumers. This typically includes a company's brand names and logos. It can also include slogans, colors (e.g., the UPS's brown trucks), sounds (such as the trumpet fanfare preceding 20th Century Fox movies), unique product packaging and product features/attributes (the latter two are protected as "trade dress").

The contours of trademark law are notoriously amorphous for at least two structural reasons. First, trademark law attempts to govern cognitive associations that consumers make in their heads. We still do not completely understand the psychology or physiology of these mental processes, and even if we did, trademark doctrine rarely considers or incorporates the scientific lessons from other disciplines. Effectively, trademark doctrine reflects the guesses of a bunch of lawyers about what is going on in consumers' heads, with occasional assistance from marketing experts paid by one side or another. Not surprisingly, the resulting legal doctrines are confusing.

Second, trademark law lacks a single theoretical justification. Instead, several commonly proffered rationales explain trademark policy.

One common justification for trademark law is that it protects consumers by preventing them from being taken by imposter brands or having to invest in extra pre-purchase research to determine a product's quality. They can use the trademark as shorthand for at least some of the qualities of the product or service. In other words, trademark turns experience goods/attributes into easier-to-find search goods/attributes.

Another common justification for trademark law is that it rewards producers' investments in quality. Without trademark protection, competitive rivals would copy the branding of high-quality producers and offer lower-quality/cheaper knockoff products using the same brand. (This leads to the market for lemons, explored in Chapter 2.) The resulting price competition would negate the ability of producers to get an adequate return on their investments in producing high-quality products, discouraging those investments. Trademark law reverses that dynamic, encouraging those investments.

In some circumstances, such as undisclosed counterfeiting, these policy rationales (consumer protection and producer protection) align. When counterfeits fool consumers, consumers get unexpectedly inferior goods and producers lose sales to competitors who do not make equivalent quality investments. In those situations, both consumers and producers benefit from suppressing counterfeits.

In other circumstances, producer interests and consumer interests diverge, exposing the lack of consensus about why we protect trademarks in the first place. For example, when a competitor buys online keyword advertising triggered by a third-party trademark, consumers may find the presentation of competitive alternatives useful, but producers often resent the consumer's "diversion" away from their offerings. If trademark law is about protecting consumers, competitive keyword advertising may not be a problem; if trademark law is about protecting producers, it may be.*

As you review this chapter, consider how the tensions between the consumer protection and producer protection justifications for trademark law affect the doctrine and specific case results. The first half of the chapter gives the general framework of trademark law that applies to all advertising. The second half considers Internet-specific problems, which represent an ever-increasing share of advertising issues. Although the technological specifics of online advertising are likely to change, the way courts have dealt with new technologies provides guidance for the next innovation.

### 1.     Brief Overview of Trademark Law

Unlike patents and copyrights, the Constitution doesn't expressly authorize Congress to provide trademark protection. Instead, Congress has enacted trademark legislation pursuant to its Commerce Clause authority. Because of this, trademark law often reflects the murky boundaries of activity considered sufficiently commercial. This partially reflects Congress' need to stay within the Commerce Clause.

Trademarks are protected under both federal and state law. The main federal trademark law is the Lanham Act, enacted in 1946 and modified many times since then. There is a federal registration system for trademarks at the U.S. Patent & Trademark Office. Unregistered trademarks also are protectable.

States concurrently offer trademark protection. Many states have adopted a version of the Model State Trademark Bill, although the state adoptions aren't especially uniform. States may have their own registration system for state trademarks. Although state laws may deviate from the Lanham Act, judges often interpret federal and state trademark claims identically, with minor exceptions for dilution, which we will discuss shortly.

---

* Even knockoffs bought on street corners may satisfy consumers who are more interested in displaying the brand than in having the value of the product marked with the brand. In such cases, the trademark owner loses the cachet of exclusivity, and other consumers may suffer from that as well *if* consumers consider cachet is a benefit worth having.

There are many other trademark-like laws at both the federal and state level. For example, Congress has enacted trademark-like protection for the Olympics and related marks, and those protections differ from the Lanham Act in subtle but crucial ways.

Private entities may offer their own systems for resolving trademark complaints. For example, Google and other search engines have voluntarily adopted internal trademark policies for when they will accept ads referencing third-party trademarks; Amazon has brand policies that help owners of federally registered trademarks control sales on its platform; and the domain name system has its own extra-judicial adjudication process for trademark disputes over domain names. In practice, these private policies may have more influence on a brand owner's ability to resolve a problem than actual "law."

*Acquiring Trademark Rights*

Trademark owners acquire their trademark rights principally by making a "use in commerce" of the trademark. The Federal Lanham Act (15 U.S.C. § 1127) defines "use in commerce" as follows:

> The term "use in commerce" means the bona fide use of a mark in the ordinary course of trade, and not made merely to reserve a right in a mark. For purposes of this chapter, a mark shall be deemed to be in use in commerce—
> (1) on goods when—
>> (A) it is placed in any manner on the goods or their containers or the displays associated therewith or on the tags or labels affixed thereto, or if the nature of the goods makes such placement impracticable, then on documents associated with the goods or their sale, and
>> (B) the goods are sold or transported in commerce, and
> (2) on services when it is used or displayed in the sale or advertising of services and the services are rendered in commerce, or the services are rendered in more than one State or in the United States and a foreign country and the person rendering the services is engaged in commerce in connection with the services.

As this definition indicates, a trademark owner starts accruing protectable trademark rights by offering products or services for sale with the trademark displayed on the product or in advertising for the trademark—so long as the offering is actually available. *See* Couture v. Playdom, Inc., 778 F.3d 1379 (Fed. Cir. 2015). Advertising also plays an important role in establishing rights for products: advertising can strengthen consumers' recognition of the trademark, which can extend the geographic reach of the trademark rights or give the trademark owner extra leverage when evaluating consumer confusion (*see, e.g.,* the *Polaroid* factors discussed in the *MasterCard* case, to follow later).

In practice, most consumer brands federally register their trademarks. Typically, in advance of a new product rollout, a trademark owner will file an "intent-to-use" (ITU) application. The ITU application establishes the trademark owner's "priority" as the application date rather than the date of first use in commerce. This can be helpful when the vendor has selected a brand but has not begun using it; the ITU application reduces the fear that an interloper will emerge between product announcement and some subsequent date that qualifies as the first use in commerce.

An ITU application is merely a placeholder. Within the statutorily specified periods, the ITU applicant must file a statement that it has made a use in commerce; at that point, the application converts into a normal trademark registration but with the ITU application date as the trademark's priority date. The statutory period for showing use in commerce can, with the Trademark Office's permission, run up to three years after the office issued a "notice of allowance" that the mark otherwise qualifies for registration. If the ITU applicant doesn't make a qualifying use in commerce during the specified period, the ITU application expires. More than half of ITU applications never mature into valid trademarks. Barton Beebe, *Is the Trademark Office a Rubber Stamp?: Trademark Registration Rates at the PTO, 1981–2010*, 48 HOUS. L. REV. 752 (2012).

Even if a trademark owner doesn't file an ITU application before use, it typically will seek a federal registration of its trademarks at some point. Registration is not required to have enforceable trademark rights, but registration offers several advantages, including:

- The registration gives national priority to the trademark owner. Without this, a trademark owner's rights typically are limited only to the geographies where it has made a use in commerce. So, for example, if the trademark owner has sold its products only regionally, a copyist might replicate the trademark in a different region and obtain preemptive trademark rights in that region.
- The registration gives the trademark owner guaranteed access to federal courts and gives several procedural benefits in litigation, such as providing prima facie evidence of the trademark's validity, ownership and exclusive right to use the mark with associated goods.
- A federal registration provides eligibility for enhanced remedies in court, including potentially triple damages and attorneys' fees. As a practical matter, except when dealing with counterfeiters, the enhanced remedies are far less important than the registration's presumption of validity.

The stronger the trademark, the greater legal protection it gets. A trademark can gain strength from recognition in the marketplace. If it is widely recognized by consumers, courts will give the trademark greater protection. Trademark strength is also measured by a hierarchy of semantic distinctiveness (this focuses just on word marks; visual and aural marks are more complicated). From strongest to weakest:

- *Fanciful trademarks.* These are newly coined terms, such as Exxon and Oreo.
- *Arbitrary trademarks.* These are dictionary words being used for a novel meaning. For example, the word "Apple" had nothing to do with computers until Apple Inc. established that new meaning.
- *Suggestive trademarks.* These are dictionary words being used to suggest something about the associated product. For example, "Greyhound Bus" suggests something about the product's attributes (i.e., the bus service will be fast like greyhound dogs are).

458

- *Descriptive trademarks.* These are dictionary words being used in a way that describes the product's attributes. For example, it does not require consumers to do much mental work to figure out what offerings they might find at a retailer named Dress Barn. Personal names and geographic terms are also treated like descriptive trademarks.
- *Generic words.* These are words used for their dictionary meaning, such as the term "apple" to describe the associated fruit or "aspirin" to describe acetylsalicylic acid.

Despite the relative clarity of this semantic hierarchy, bright minds often disagree about where a particular trademark belongs on the hierarchy. Furthermore, while terms can start out as trademarkable, over time consumers may think of the term as the generic description for the class of goods, a phenomenon called "genericide." In that case, the trademark loses all protection no matter how hard the trademark owner tried to avoid that outcome. "Aspirin" is just one of many former trademarks that suffered genericide.

Fanciful, arbitrary and suggestive marks are called "inherently distinctive" trademarks. Inherently distinctive trademarks are eligible for trademark protection and registration immediately following their use in commerce. Generic words are never protectable as trademarks. Descriptive trademarks (including personal names and geographic terms being used as trademarks) can acquire distinctiveness and become protectable and registrable* only after they achieve "secondary meaning."

Secondary meaning occurs when consumers believe the descriptive term refers to only one producer in the marketplace. For example, the trademark "U-Haul" initially was descriptive, but eventually consumers became so familiar with the brand that they associated the term with one and only one marketplace participant. Once a sufficient number of consumers made the same cognitive association, U-Haul achieved secondary meaning and became a protectable trademark.

Although ordinarily a trademark owner needs to use the trademark in commerce itself to generate protectable rights, occasionally consumers will coin a nickname for a product that becomes so identified with the product that the trademark owner can enforce trademark rights in the nickname too. *Compare* Volkswagenwerk Aktiengesellschaft v. Rickard, 492 F.2d 474 (5th Cir. 1974) (Volkswagen can protect the nickname "Bug" for its Beetle cars) *with* Harley Davidson Inc. v. Grottanelli, 164 F.3d 806 (2d Cir. 1999) (Harley-Davidson cannot protect the term "Hog" for its motorcycles because "hog" describes large motorcycles generally). *See generally* Peter M. Brody, *What's in a Nickname? Or, Can Public Use Create Private Rights?*, 95 TRADEMARK REP. 1123 (2005).

---

* Descriptive trademarks are registrable on the principal registry only after they obtain secondary meaning. The U.S. also allows registration of descriptive trademarks on a supplemental registry, even if they haven't obtained secondary meaning. However, such registrations provide minimal rights for the registrant. The supplemental registry is mainly used for U.S. trademark owners who wish to seek international trademark registrations before they have achieved secondary meaning in the U.S. International standards for registering descriptive trademarks are more relaxed than the U.S.'s standards.

**2. Trademark Infringement**

A trademark infringement claim typically has the following prima facie elements:

(1) the plaintiff has valid and protectable trademark rights,

(2) the plaintiff's use in commerce date (determined either through usage or the ITU date) predates the defendant's, giving it "priority,"

(3) the defendant has used the trademark in commerce (as discussed shortly, not everyone agrees that this factor is part of the prima facie case), and

(4) the defendant's usage creates a likelihood of consumer confusion about the product's source, sponsorship or affiliation.

If the plaintiff establishes a prima facie case, the defendant can assert a number of possible defenses, such as nominative use.

**A. Consumer Confusion**

Consumer confusion is at the core of trademark law. If there's no confusion, there's no infringement (but dilution may still be possible). Likelihood of consumer confusion is typically evaluated using a multi-factor test, as illustrated by the following case.

*MasterCard International Inc. v. Nader 2000 Primary Committee, Inc., 2004 WL 434404 (S.D.N.Y. 2004)*

THERE ARE SOME THINGS MONEY CAN'T BUY. FOR EVERYTHING ELSE THERE'S MASTERCARD. . . .

BACKGROUND

MasterCard, a Delaware corporation with its principal place of business in New York, is a large financial institution that engages in the interchange of funds by credit and debit payment cards through over 23,000 banks and other foreign and domestic member financial institutions. Since Fall of 1997, MasterCard has commissioned the authorship of a series of advertisements that have come to be known as the "Priceless Advertisements." These advertisements feature the names and images of several goods and services purchased by individuals which, with voice overs and visual displays, convey to the viewer the price of each of these items. At the end of each of the Priceless Advertisements a phrase identifying some priceless intangible that cannot be purchased (such as "a day where all you have to do is breathe") is followed by the words or voice over: "Priceless. There are some things money can't buy, for everything else there's MasterCard."

In August 2000, MasterCard became aware that Ralph Nader and his presidential committee were broadcasting an allegedly similar advertisement on television that promoted the presidential candidacy of Ralph Nader in the 2000 presidential election. That political ad included a sequential display of a series of items showing the price of each ("grilled tenderloin for fundraiser: $1,000 a plate;" "campaign ads filled with half-truths: $10 million;" "promises to special interest groups: over $100 billion"). The advertisement ends with a phrase identifying a priceless intangible that cannot

460

be purchased ("finding out the truth: priceless. There are some things that money can't buy"). The resulting ad (the "Nader ad") was shown on television during a two-week period from August 6–17, during the 2000 presidential campaign, and also appeared on the defendants' web site throughout that campaign.[*] Plaintiff sent defendants a letter explaining its concern over the similarity of the commercials, and suggested that defendants broadcast a more "original" advertisement. When plaintiff contacted representatives of defendants a few days later, plaintiff MasterCard advised defendants to cease broadcasting their political advertisement due to its similarity with MasterCard's own commercial advertisement and resulting infringement liability. . . .

DISCUSSION . . .

1. Trademark Infringement

MasterCard's first count is based on Section 43(a) of the Trademark Act, 15 U.S.C. Section 1125(a). Plaintiff claims that defendants have used two of MasterCard's service marks—"THERE ARE SOME THINGS MONEY CAN'T BUY. FOR EVERYTHING ELSE THERE'S MASTERCARD," and "PRICELESS" to misrepresent that the 2000 presidential candidacy of Ralph Nader for the office of President of the United States was endorsed by MasterCard. Plaintiff's second count also pleads a claim for trademark infringement due to defendants' use of the two federally registered trademarks, ("THERE ARE SOME THINGS MONEY CAN'T BUY. FOR EVERYTHING ELSE THERE'S MASTERCARD," and "PRICELESS"), pursuant to Section 32(1) of the Trademark Act, 15 U.S.C. Section 1114(1).

In trademark infringement cases, the Court must apply the undisputed facts to the balancing test outlined in *Polaroid Corp. v. Polarad Elecs., Corp.*, 287 F.2d 492, 495 (2d Cir.1961), and may grant summary judgment where it finds, as a matter of law, that there is no likelihood of confusion to the public. In determining whether there is a likelihood of confusion between MasterCard's Priceless Advertisements and Ralph Nader's Political Ad, the Court weighs eight factors, as articulated in

---

[*] [Editor's note: you can watch the ad on YouTube at http://www.youtube.com/watch?v=mJOuPZKAspQ.]

*Polaroid*: (1) strength of the Plaintiff's mark; (2) degree of similarity between the two marks; (3) proximity of the products or services; (4) likelihood that the prior owner will "bridge the gap" into the newcomer's product or service line; (5) evidence of actual confusion between the marks; (6) whether the defendant adopted the mark in good faith; (7) the quality of defendants' products or services; and (8) sophistication of the parties' consumers.

In demonstrating the strength of the trademark, the plaintiff must establish either that the mark is inherently distinctive or alternatively, that the mark has acquired secondary meaning. MasterCard's marks, "PRICELESS" and "THERE ARE SOME THINGS MONEY CAN'T BUY, FOR EVERYTHING ELSE THERE'S MASTERCARD," are registered. MasterCard asserts that their marks have attained secondary meaning. Defendants concede that MasterCard's Priceless Advertisements are strong enough to have become a part of present-day American popular culture. The strength of MasterCard's trademarks is indisputable.

In determining the second factor, the similarity of the marks in issue, a court must consider whether the marks create the same overall commercial impression when viewed separately. A court may rely upon its own visual inspection in making this determination. In this instance, it is not necessary for the Court to do so, because once again, defendants do not dispute that the Nader Ad employs the word "priceless" in the same manner used by MasterCard in its television advertisements. The Nader Ad also employs the phrase "there are some things money can't buy," which is part of a MasterCard trademark. Defendants do not dispute that they employ that phrase in the same look, sound and commercial impression as employed by MasterCard.

The third and fourth factors, the proximity of the products or services and the likelihood that the prior user will bridge the gap, respectively, weigh in favor of defendants. There is little similarity between MasterCard's credit and debit card business and Ralph Nader's political candidacy. There is little likelihood and no evidence that MasterCard, a financial services company, would have any direct involvement in supporting a candidate in a political presidential campaign. Similarly, neither Ralph Nader nor his political campaign committee have expressed any desire or intent to enter the credit card business or offer the public any direct financial services.

Evidence of actual confusion, the fifth factor, also weighs in favor of defendants. This factor is perhaps the most significant when considering the overall likelihood of confusion by the public. "The best evidence of likelihood of confusion is the occurrence of actual confusion and mistakes." While it is not essential for a finding of trademark infringement to demonstrate actual confusion, "there can be no more positive proof of likelihood of confusion than evidence of actual confusion." . . . As evident by the present record, out of 452 e-mails to MasterCard regarding the Nader Ad, only two are relied upon as possibly reflecting confusion. This is certainly not enough to show actual confusion or that such confusion inflicted commercial injury to MasterCard. In support of its argument that actual confusion exists, MasterCard also relies on the written transcript of a broadcast of CNN's Late Edition, during which Connecticut Senator Christopher Dodd stated that he thought the Nader Advertisement was a credit card ad. A viewing of a tape of that program shows Senator Dodd laughing at his own joke, while speaking the words on which MasterCard relies to establish actual confusion. It is little or no evidence of actual confusion. Even if Senator Dodd had actually been confused, a few isolated instances of actual confusion are not sufficient to defeat a motion for summary judgment. The plaintiff should be able to demonstrate a reasonable likelihood that reasonable people will be confused.

The sixth factor regarding good faith adoption of the mark also favors defendants. The relevant intent in this inquiry is whether the alleged infringer intended "to palm off his products as those of another." In the present case, there is no evidence that defendants intended to confuse the public. There is no basis to argue that the Ralph Nader political ad which has the clear intent to criticize other political candidates who accept money from wealthy contributors, at the same time, attempts or intends to imply that he is a political candidate endorsed by MasterCard. There is uncontradicted testimony that neither Ralph Nader, nor his committees, had any such intent.

The seventh factor, the quality of defendants' products or services, is of insignificant weight in this case. There is no reasonable comparison to be made between the quality of the products and services provided by MasterCard and the value of defendants' politics. MasterCard provides a quality of financial services which can readily be compared to its commercial competitors. However, it is purely the public's subjective opinion of the appeal and attractiveness of a political candidate's ideas and record which determines whether the public will buy the politics any candidate for office is selling.

The eighth and final factor to be weighed is the level of consumer sophistication in either of the relevant markets for credit card services or for political candidates. Unless otherwise demonstrated, it is reasonable to conclude that the general American public is sophisticated enough to distinguish a Political Ad from a commercial advertisement. Rarely, if ever, is there a realistic opportunity to confuse the two. Indeed, as previously discussed, out of the 452 e-mails received by MasterCard regarding Ralph Nader's Political Ad, only 2–3 questioned MasterCard's involvement with Ralph Nader's campaign. This sampling of American consumers, which is the only proof offered on the record, is a sufficient indication that consumers are generally sophisticated enough to decipher between MasterCard's commercial purposes and Ralph Nader's political agenda.

When balancing the eight *Polaroid* factors, no one factor can determine the ultimate issue of likelihood of confusion to the consumer. To properly weigh these factors requires the court to view each factor in light of the totality of the evidence. Thus, after balancing the *Polaroid* factors, this Court finds that there is no genuine issue of material fact with regard to any likelihood of confusion between MasterCard's Priceless Advertisements and Ralph Nader's Political Ad which could constitute a violation of the Trademark Act. Defendants' summary judgment motion to dismiss Counts One and Two of plaintiff's complaint is therefore granted. . . .

*NOTES AND QUESTIONS*

*Tests for Likelihood of Confusion.* Most trademark infringement claims turn on the likelihood of consumer confusion. To measure this likelihood, courts typically use a multi-factor test. Each federal appellate circuit has its own test, although most of the tests include the same or similar factors. This court used the Second Circuit *Polaroid* test, and the *Polaroid* factors are representative of the factors found in other circuits' tests. Compare the First Circuit's *Pignons* test discussed in the *Venture Tape* opinion and the Ninth Circuit's *Sleekcraft* test discussed in the *Network Automation* opinion below.

*Copyright Claim.* The court rejected MasterCard's claim that Nader's ad infringed MasterCard's copyright, concluding: "The Nader Ad is a non-infringing fair use parody of MasterCard's Priceless Advertisements under Section 107 of the Copyright Act."

*A Humorless Legal System.* If we take our legal hats off, it was entirely clear to everyone that Nader's ad was a joke. Yet, trademark law (and the legal system generally) doesn't handle jokes very well. Instead, trademark owners are rarely amused when they feel that someone takes advantage of an asset they built at great expense, and judges often will apply the legal tests seriously rather than breezily dismiss an effort to shut down an obvious joke. For another example of a humorless trademark opinion, see the *Deere v. MTD* dilution case later in this chapter.

*Iconic Ad Campaigns.* Occasionally, advertising campaigns such as the MasterCard "Priceless" campaign are so massively successful with consumers that they become culturally iconic. Should trademark law protect secondary references to these iconic campaigns more or less aggressively? On the one hand, Nader clearly was trying to invoke the consumers' knowledge of MasterCard's campaign to tell his own story. On the other hand, precisely *because* the MasterCard campaign was so successful, consumers were more likely to remember MasterCard's original campaign and be able to recognize that invocations of MasterCard's campaign are coming from a different source. If so, this could lead to the possibly counterintuitive result that trademarks generated through culturally iconic campaigns might be *less* enforceable against some secondary uses than trademarks generated through less successful campaigns.

*The Relationship Between Trademark Infringement and False Advertising.* Assuming they qualify for both, plaintiffs will prefer to bring trademark infringement claims over false advertising claims, because trademark infringement applies to more activity than false advertising and has fewer doctrinal limits (such as the absence of a survey requirement for implicitly false claims and the absence of a materiality requirement). However, there may be reasons that a plaintiff can't bring a trademark claim—perhaps the term at issue is generic and not protectable as a trademark; perhaps the plaintiff is not using the mark at issue in commerce in the U.S. and thus can't claim rights of its own. Some courts will allow the plaintiff to bring a false advertising claim instead.

In *Belmora LLC v. Bayer Consumer Care AG*, 819 F.3d 697 (4th Cir. 2016), Bayer used the "FLANAX" mark in Mexico for analgesics.

In the U.S., Bayer used the brand name "Aleve" instead of FLANAX. Belmora registered FLANAX in the U.S. for analgesics and began selling the same type of analgesics under that mark in the U.S. Belmora's early packaging "closely mimicked" Bayer's Mexican FLANAX packaging in color scheme, font size, and typeface.

In addition, Belmora made statements to prospective distributors such as:

> For generations, Flanax has been a brand that Latinos have turned to for various common ailments. Now you too can profit from this highly recognized topselling brand among Latinos. Flanax is now made in the U.S. and continues to show record sales growth everywhere it is sold. Flanax acts as a powerful attraction for Latinos by providing them with products they know, trust and prefer.

Belmora ultimately revised the packaging, but there were still similarities to Mexican FLANAX.

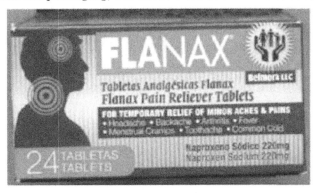

The Fourth Circuit allowed Bayer to proceed both on a claim under §43(a)(1)(A) for false association, based on its rights in Mexico, and on a false advertising claim under §43(a)(1)(B), based on its rights in Aleve in the United States. "If not for Belmora's statements that its FLANAX was the same one known and trusted in Mexico, some of its consumers could very well have instead purchased BHC's Aleve brand."

The court of appeals cautioned that Belmora owned Flanax as a mark in the US. "But trademark rights do not include using the mark to deceive customers as a form of unfair competition, as is alleged here." An appropriate remedy might allow Belmora to use the mark, but with measures to avoid confusion; "any remedy should take into account traditional trademark principles relating to Belmora's ownership of the mark," such as altering the font and color of the packaging, attaching the manufacturer's name to the brand name, or using a disclaimer. What do you think of this resolution?

### B.     Use in Commerce

We earlier suggested that the plaintiff's prima facie case may require it to show that the defendant used the plaintiff's trademark in commerce. This element is controversial for at least two reasons.

First, the federal statute defines the terms "commerce" and "use in commerce" in irreconcilable ways. The "use in commerce" definition suggests that plaintiffs must show that they used the plaintiff's trademark in ad copy or on product packaging as part of the plaintiff's prima facie case. The "commerce" definition simply requires the plaintiff to satisfy the Constitutional Commerce Clause requirements. This poor drafting creates an unresolvable ambiguity in the statute that may ultimately require congressional fixing. *See* Rescuecom Corp. v. Google Inc., 562 F. 3d 123 (2d Cir. 2009) (especially the appendix).

Second, and perhaps more importantly, courts often gloss over this element when the defendant clearly made a use in commerce of the plaintiff's trademark. For example, referencing the plaintiff's trademark in ad copy almost always will qualify as a use in commerce of the trademark. In those cases, courts are not very careful to acknowledge this prima facie element. For example, in *MasterCard*, the court simply raced past this element even though, as a political candidate, Nader did not make a "use in commerce" of MasterCard's trademarks in the traditional sense.

Sometimes, technological systems enable an advertiser to implicate a third-party trademark in a way that does not clearly constitute a use in commerce of the trademark. These circumstances force courts to tread more cautiously, and occasionally the defendant can win based on the absence of a use in commerce. We'll discuss two examples now and revisit this issue in the ambush marketing discussion later in this chapter.

*Keyword Advertising Triggering*

In *1-800 Contacts, Inc., v. WhenU.com, Inc.*, 414 F.3d 400 (2d Cir. 2005), WhenU operated "adware," software installed on users' computers that monitored their behavior and triggered "pop-up" advertisements when the software detected user behavior that matched one of the keywords purchased by advertisers. Advertisers had purchased keywords such as "contact lenses," and WhenU programmed its databases so that those advertisers would show in pop-up ads when users accessed the 1-800 Contacts website. The Second Circuit held that WhenU's behind-the-scenes association of the 1-800 Contacts domain name with advertising categories such as "contact lenses" did not constitute a trademark use in commerce.

Although the Second Circuit has not expressly overturned the *1-800 Contacts* ruling, the 2009 *Rescuecom* opinion substantially limits the case's holding. *See* Rescuecom Corp. v. Google Inc., 562 F. 3d 123 (2d Cir. 2009). We revisit keyword advertising later in this chapter.

*Billboards*

In *Howard Johnson International, Inc. v. Vraj Brig, LLC*, 2010 WL 215381 (D. N.J. 2010), Tucci owned a hotel building that Vraj Brig operated as a franchised Howard Johnson's hotel. Tucci stopped operating the building as a hotel, but he left up a billboard bearing the "Howard Johnson's" name. Howard Johnson sued Tucci for trademark violations. The court ruled in Tucci's favor:

Plaintiff has produced no evidence that Tucci ever did anything other than passively allow a preexisting billboard containing HJI's marks to remain standing on his property. Therefore, Tucci never "used" the protected marks within the meaning of that term as it appears in the Lanham Act. Furthermore, even if Tucci were held to have "used" HJI's marks, he never offered or provided any goods or services at the lodging facility in question. Therefore, his display of the marks does not satisfy the "in connection with goods or services" requirement either.

The court rejected Howard Johnson's argument even though the billboard might have frustrated consumers who exited the freeway looking for the hotel, only to be disappointed.

### C.    Defense: Descriptive Fair Use

Descriptive fair use occurs when a defendant uses the plaintiff's descriptive trademark to describe the defendant's own product. 15 U.S.C. § 1115(b)(4) provides a defense to trademark infringement when using "a term or device which is descriptive of and used fairly and in good faith only to describe the goods or services of such party." The descriptive fair use defense may only be invoked against descriptive trademarks; arbitrary, fanciful and suggestive trademarks are not subject to the defense.

For example, if a pump shoe manufacturer has developed a trademark in the slogan "Looks Like a Pump, Feels Like a Sneaker," a competitive shoe manufacturer may nevertheless advertise its own pump shoes with the following ad copy:

> "Think Of It As A Sneaker With No Strings Attached." The text of the ad includes the phrase, "And when we say it feels like a sneaker, we're not just stringing you along."

U.S. Shoe Corp. v. Brown Grp., Inc., 740 F. Supp. 196 (S.D.N.Y. 1990). Although the phrase "feels like a sneaker" appears in both the original slogan and the competitor's ad, the court found a descriptive fair use:

> In this case, the defendant uses the phrase "feels like a sneaker" in a descriptive sense, claiming a virtue of the product. It essentially restates the key selling claim of defendant's product—that the Townwalker shoe was designed specifically to incorporate the comfort of athletic shoes.

Two other descriptive fair use examples:

- Sunmark, Inc. v. Ocean Spray Cranberries, Inc., 64 F.3d 1055 (7th Cir. 1995). Sunmark makes SweeTARTS, a classic sweet-and-sour sugar candy. Ocean Spray subsequently decided to advertise its cranberry juice as having a "sweet-tart" flavor. The court held that Ocean Spray's use of "sweet-tart" qualified as a descriptive fair use.
- Cosmetically Sealed Indus., Inc. v. Chesebrough-Pond's USA Co., 125 F.3d 28 (2d Cir. 1997). The plaintiff marketed lip gloss under the registered trademark "Sealed with a Kiss." Chesebrough subsequently offered long-lasting lipstick in a counter display that included free postcards and an encouragement to mark the postcards with a lip-print, which ended

467

with the exhortation to "Seal it with a Kiss!!" (the "it" referring to the postcard). The court held that this display constituted descriptive fair use.

### D.        Defense: Comparative Advertising and Nominative Use

Advertisers often want to reference their competitors in ad copy to make comparative claims, e.g., "Acme is better than Bigco." If the comparative statements do not constitute false advertising, does trademark law nevertheless limit these comparative references?

That turns out to be an unexpectedly difficult question. Trademark law does not categorically permit the use of third-party trademarks in ad copy for comparative statements. Each ad copy reference must be independently analyzed under the applicable trademark doctrines.

Nominative use is a doctrine that facilitates some comparative references. Nominative use, sometimes called "nominative fair use," differs from descriptive fair use in how the defendant uses the plaintiff's trademark. In descriptive fair use, the defendant uses a word or symbol that is also a trademark to describe the *defendant's* product. In nominative use, the defendant uses the trademark to refer to the *plaintiff's* product. Unlike descriptive fair use, which is only applies to terms that are descriptive for the defendant's products or services, the nominative use defense can be invoked against all types of trademarks, even fanciful ones.

Each appellate circuit defines nominative use differently. The Ninth Circuit has the best-developed standards for nominative use, which requires three elements for a successful defense:

1.   The plaintiff's product is not readily identifiable without using the trademark.
2.   The defendant uses the plaintiff's trademark only as reasonably necessary to identify the plaintiff's product.
3.   The defendant's usage does not imply the plaintiff's sponsorship or endorsement.

These elements ought to permit many comparative advertising usages, but that doesn't mean comparative advertisers can confidently rely on the nominative use defense. First, because it is a defense, nominative use may be difficult to win at the early stages of litigation, thus imposing substantial litigation costs even for defendants who ultimately win in court. Second, the implied sponsorship/endorsement factor depends on consumer perceptions, which sets up a factual dispute that may be hard to predict. Third, not every circuit has embraced the nominative use defense; the Sixth Circuit has questioned whether the nominative use defense should be recognized, and the Second Circuit has held that the nominative fair use factors are simply to be added to the usual multifactor confusion test as additional considerations in appropriate cases.

The following case, a classic example of comparative advertising, was decided before the Ninth Circuit officially adopted the nominative use defense. Nevertheless, it provides a good example of how the analysis *should* go.

468

*Smith v. Chanel, Inc., 402 F.2d 562 (9th Cir. 1968)*

Appellant R. G. Smith, doing business as Ta'Ron, Inc., advertised a fragrance called "Second Chance" as a duplicate of appellees' "Chanel No. 5," at a fraction of the latter's price. Appellees were granted a preliminary injunction prohibiting any reference to Chanel No. 5 in the promotion or sale of appellants' product. This appeal followed.

The action rests upon a single advertisement published in "Specialty Salesmen,' a trade journal directed to wholesale purchasers. The advertisement offered "The Ta'Ron Line of Perfumes" for sale. It gave the seller's address as "Ta'Ron Inc., 26 Harbor Cove, Mill Valley, Calif." It stated that the Ta'Ron perfumes "duplicate 100% Perfect the exact scent of the world's finest and most expensive perfumes and colognes at prices that will zoom sales to volumes you have never before experienced." It repeated the claim of exact duplication in a variety of forms.

The advertisement suggested that a "Blindfold Test" be used "on skeptical prospects," challenging them to detect any difference between a well known fragrance and the Ta'Ron "duplicate." One suggested challenge was, "We dare you to try to detect any difference between Chanel #5 (25.00) and Ta'Ron's 2nd Chance, $7.00."

In an order blank printed as part of the advertisement each Ta'Ron fragrance was listed with the name of the well known fragrance which it purportedly duplicated immediately beneath. Below "Second Chance" appeared "*(Chanel #5)." The asterisk referred to a statement at the bottom of the form reading "Registered Trade Name of Original Fragrance House."

[Editor's note: the ad, followed by a close-up of "The Blindfold Test" and the order form:]

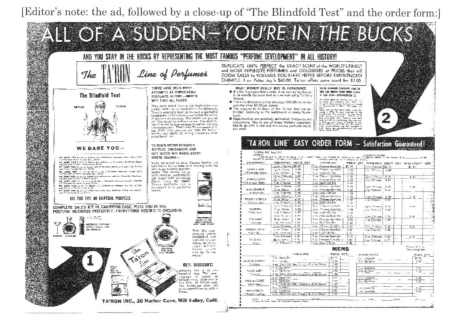

# The Blindfold Test

ARPEGE        TA'RON

# WE DARE YOU—

**WE DARE YOU** to try to detect any difference between White Shoulders (18.50) and Ta'ron's Love Lure, $7.00.

**WE DARE YOU** to try to detect any difference between Christmas Night (35.00) and Ta'ron's Persuasive, $7.00.

**WE DARE YOU** to try to detect any difference between Chanel #5 (25.00) and Ta'ron's 2nd Chance, $7.00.

**WE DARE YOU** to try to detect any difference between Youth Dew (22.50) and Ta'ron's Temptacious, $7.00.

**WE DARE YOU** to try to detect any difference between Guerlain Shalimar (25.00) and Ta'ron's Tahisia, $7.00.

**WE DARE YOU** to try to detect any difference between Lanvin Arpege (27.00) and Ta'ron's Volarie, $7.00.

**WE DARE YOU** to try to detect any difference between My Sin (27.00) and Ta'ron's Sweet Love, $7.00.

**WE DARE YOU** to try to detect any difference between Patou Joy (60.00) and Ta'ron's Al Di La, $7.00.

## USE THIS TEST ON SKEPTICAL PROSPECTS

## "TA'RON LINE" EASY ORDER FORM

TA'RON, INC. Dept. S-5
Gentlemen
I sure do want to "get in the bucks all of a sudden." Please rush Prepaid the following for payment is enclosed. ☐ Please send C.O.D. $_____ enclosed covering 1/3 — Balance

| FRAGRANCE | PERFUMES | PRICE | QTY | COLOGNES | PRICE |
|---|---|---|---|---|---|
| **LOVE LURE** *(White Shoulders) | ½ oz. Princess | $3.00 | | 2 oz. Princess Sprinkler | $2.75 |
| | ⅝ oz. Spray | 4.00 | | 4 oz. Princess Sprinkler | 4.00 |
| | 1 oz. Princess | 7.00 | | 4 oz. Gold Gift Set | 7.00 |
| **PERSUASIVE** *(Christmas Night) | ½ oz. Princess | 3.00 | | 2 oz. Princess Sprinkler | 2.75 |
| | ⅝ oz. Spray | 4.00 | | 4 oz. Princess Sprinkler | 4.00 |
| | 1 oz. Princess | 7.00 | | 4 oz. Gold Gift Set | 7.00 |
| **2nd CHANCE** *(Chanel #5) | ½ oz. Princess | 3.00 | | 2 oz. Princess Sprinkler | 2.75 |
| | ⅝ oz. Spray | 4.00 | | 4 oz. Princess Sprinkler | 4.00 |
| | 1 oz. Princess | 7.00 | | 4 oz. Gold Gift Set | 7.00 |

[portions magnified so they are easier to read]

Appellees conceded below and concede here that appellants "have the right to copy, if they can, the unpatented formula of appellees' product." Moreover, for the purposes of these proceedings, appellees assume that "the products manufactured and advertised by (appellants) are in fact equivalents of

470

those products manufactured by appellees." Finally, appellees disclaim any contention that the packaging or labeling of appellants' "Second Chance" is misleading or confusing.[4]

I

The principal question presented on this record is whether one who has copied an unpatented product sold under a trademark may use the trademark in his advertising to identify the product he has copied. We hold that he may, and that such advertising may not be enjoined under either the Lanham Act, 15 U.S.C. § 1125(a) (1964), or the common law of unfair competition, so long as it does not contain misrepresentations or create a reasonable likelihood that purchasers will be confused as to the source, identity, or sponsorship of the advertiser's product. . . .

In *Saxlehner* [216 U.S. 375 (1910)] the copied product was a "bitter water" drawn from certain privately owned natural springs. The plaintiff sold the natural water under the name "Hunyadi Janos," a valid trademark. The defendant was enjoined from using plaintiff's trademark to designate defendant's "artificial" water, but was permitted to use it to identify plaintiff's natural water as the product which defendant was copying.

Justice Holmes wrote:

> We see no reason for disturbing the finding of the courts below that there was no unfair competition and no fraud. The real intent of the plaintiff's bill, it seems to us, is to extend the monopoly of such trademark or tradename as she may have to a monopoly of her type of bitter water, by preventing manufacturers from telling the public in a way that will be understood, what they are copying and trying to sell. But the plaintiff has no patent for the water, and the defendants have a right to reproduce it as nearly as they can. They have a right to tell the public what they are doing, and to get whatever share they can in the popularity of the water by advertising that they are trying to make the same article, and think that they succeed. If they do not convey, but, on the contrary, exclude, the notion that they are selling the plaintiff's goods, it is a strong proposition that when the article has a well-known name they have not the right to explain by that name what they imitate. By doing so, they are not trying to get the good will of the name, but the good will of the goods. . . .

We have found no holdings by federal or California appellate courts contrary to the rule of these three cases. Moreover, the principle for which they stand—that use of another's trademark to identify the trademark owner's product in comparative advertising is not prohibited by either statutory or common law, absent misrepresentation regarding the products or confusion as to their source or sponsorship—is also generally approved by secondary authorities.

---

[4] Appellants' product was packaged differently from appellees', and the only words appearing on the outside of appellants' packages were "'Second Chance Perfume by Ta'Ron.'" The same words appeared on the front of appellants' bottles; the words "'Ta'Ron' trademark by International Fragrances, Inc., of Dallas and New York'York" appeared on the back.

The rule rests upon the traditionally accepted premise that the only legally relevant function of a trademark is to impart information as to the source or sponsorship of the product. Appellees argue that protection should also be extended to the trademark's commercially more important function of embodying consumer good will created through extensive, skillful, and costly advertising. The courts, however, have generally confined legal protection to the trademark's source identification function for reasons grounded in the public policy favoring a free, competitive economy. . . .

Since appellees' perfume was unpatented, appellants had a right to copy it, as appellees concede. There was a strong public interest in their doing so, "for imitation is the life blood of competition. It is the unimpeded availability of substantially equivalent units that permits the normal operation of supply and demand to yield the fair price society must pay for a given commodity." But this public benefit might be lost if appellants could not tell potential purchasers that appellants' product was the equivalent of appellees' product. "A competitor's chief weapon is his ability to represent his product as being equivalent and cheaper * * *." The most effective way (and, where complex chemical compositions sold under trade names are involved, often the only practical way) in which this can be done is to identify the copied article by its trademark or trade name. To prohibit use of a competitor's trademark for the sole purpose of identifying the competitor's product would bar effective communication of claims of equivalence. Assuming the equivalence of "Second Chance" and "Chanel No. 5," the public interest would not be served by a rule of law which would preclude sellers of "Second Chance" from advising consumers of the equivalence and thus effectively deprive consumers of knowledge that an identical product was being offered at one third the price.

As Justice Holmes wrote in *Saxlehner v. Wagner*, the practical effect of such a rule would be to extend the monopoly of the trademark to a monopoly of the product. The monopoly conferred by judicial protection of complete trademark exclusivity would not be preceded by examination and approval by a governmental body, as is the case with most other government-granted monopolies. Moreover, it would not be limited in time, but would be perpetual.

Against these considerations, two principal arguments are made for protection of trademark values other than source identification.

The first of these, as stated in the findings of the district court, is that the creation of the other values inherent in the trademark require "the expenditure of great effort, skill and ability," and that the competitor should not be permitted "to take a free ride" on the trademark owner's "widespread goodwill and reputation."

A large expenditure of money does not in itself create legally protectable rights. Appellees are not entitled to monopolize the public's desire for the unpatented product, even though they themselves created that desire at great effort and expense. As we have noted, the most effective way (and in some cases the only practical way) in which others may compete in satisfying the demand for the product is to produce it and tell the public they have done so, and if they could be barred from this effort appellees would have found a way to acquire a practical monopoly in the unpatented product to which they are not legally entitled.

Disapproval of the copyist's opportunism may be an understandable first reaction, "but this initial response to the problem has been curbed in deference to the greater public good." By taking his "free ride," the copyist, albeit unintentionally, serves an important public interest by offering comparable goods at lower prices. On the other hand, the trademark owner, perhaps equally without design, sacrifices public to personal interests by seeking immunity from the rigors of competition.

Moreover, appellees' reputation is not directly at stake. Appellants' advertisement makes it clear that the product they offer is their own. If it proves to be inferior, they, not appellees, will bear the burden of consumer disapproval.

The second major argument for extended trademark protection is that even in the absence of confusion as to source, use of the trademark of another "creates a serious threat to the uniqueness and distinctiveness" of the trademark, and "if continued would create a risk of making a generic or descriptive term of the words" of which the trademark is composed.

The contention has little weight in the context of this case. Appellants do not use appellees' trademark as a generic term. They employ it only to describe appellees' product, not to identify their own. They do not label their product "Ta'Ron's Chanel No. 5," as they might if appellees' trademark had come to be the common name for the product to which it is applied. Appellants' use does not challenge the distinctiveness of appellees' trademark, or appellees' exclusive right to employ that trademark to indicate source or sponsorship. For reasons already discussed, we think appellees are entitled to no more. The slight tendency to carry the mark into the common language which even this use may have is outweighed by the substantial value of such use in the maintenance of effective competition.

We are satisfied, therefore, that both authority and reason require a holding that in the absence of misrepresentation or confusion as to source or sponsorship a seller in promoting his own goods may use the trademark of another to identify the latter's goods. The district court's contrary conclusion cannot support the injunction. . . .

*NOTES AND QUESTIONS*

*Fact-Specific Inquiries.* Cases involving comparative advertising are often fact-specific. Consider the ad on the left below. The Bailey's ad includes part of Newport's logo (the remainder is covered by the plant) and contains an upper right box saying "Compare Bailey's with our competitor Newport Cigarettes." The upper white box and "compare" text was added to the original ad after Newport complained. Does this revised ad infringe Newport's trademark rights? (To help your evaluation, the image below on the right is one of Newport's own ads).

Could Bailey's have made its point without showing half of Newport's logo? Does the location of the half-logo at the top left of the page matter? *See* Lorillard Tobacco Co. v. S&M Brands, Inc., 616 F. Supp. 2d 581 (E.D. Va. 2009) (preliminary injunction granted against initial ad without large top right disclaimer, but denied against planned ad with disclaimer).

*Mentioning Noncompetitors.* Consumers Union, the publisher of *Consumer Reports*, engaged in a multi-year legal battle with Regina, a vacuum manufacturer, based on Regina's truthful quotes from a positive *Consumer Reports* review. *See* Consumers Union of United States, Inc. v. New Regina Corp., 664 F. Supp. 753 (S.D.N.Y. 1987). When Regina quoted *Consumer Reports*, at least some consumers perceived that *Consumer Reports* was affiliated with Regina, had been paid for the quote or for testing the Regina vacuum, or authorized the use of its name in the ad. The court held that Regina could not avoid a trial on likely confusion. Should the nominative use defense have applied?

Should it change the result if Regina used the same quotes but attributed them in a different manner? Say, "to a leading independent testing organization" or "a leading consumer review publication."

*Other Countries' Attitudes Toward Comparative Advertising.* The European Union does not tolerate comparative advertising nearly as much as the U.S. does. In general, comparative advertising is virtually banned in the European Union. *See* Directive 2006/114/EC. Comparative advertising is permitted only if all of the following are true:

1.  it is not misleading;
2.  it compares goods or services meeting the same needs or intended for the same purpose;
3.  it objectively compares one or more material, relevant, verifiable and representative features of those goods or services, which may include price;
4.  it does not create confusion in the marketplace between the advertiser and a competitor;

5. it does not discredit or denigrate the trademarks, trade names or other distinguishing signs of a competitor;

6. for products with a designation of origin, it relates to products with the same designation;

7. it does not take unfair advantage of the trademark or other distinguishing sign of a competitor;

8. it does not present goods or services as imitations or replicas of goods or services bearing a protected trademark or trade name.

As a practical matter, comparative advertisements in Europe require careful vetting. For example, the eighth requirement would preclude the ad at issue in the *Chanel* case.

India's approach resembles Europe's more than the U.S.'s. The Advertising Standards Council of India, a self-regulatory body, dictates that comparative ads must, among other things, make comparisons that are factual, accurate, and capable of being backed by substantial facts and evidence, and must not "make unjustifiable use" of the name or initials of any other entity, nor take unfair advantage of the goodwill attached to the trademark or symbol of another firm or its product or the goodwill acquired by its advertising campaign. In addition, a comparative ad must not be similar to another advertiser's ads in "general layout, copy, slogans, visual presentations, music or sound effects, so as to suggest plagiarism." Courts similarly require comparisons to be of material, relevant, verifiable and representative features, and as in Europe, comparisons may not compare a product with one designation of origin to another with a different designation of origin (e.g., no comparing Parmesan to Camembert). Havells India Ltd & Anr vs Amritanshu Khaitan & Ors DelHC CS(OS) 107/2015. However, Indian courts have allowed comparative puffery, such as claiming to be the "best" or "better" than competitors, as long as the claim doesn't rise to the level of defamation or disparagement. Colgate Palmolive Company & Anr. vs. Hindustan Unilever Ltd., 2014 (57) PTC 47 [Del](DB); Dabur India Ltd. vs. Colortek Meghalaya Pvt. Ltd. & Anr., 167 (2010) DLT 278 (DB).

*Contributory Trademark Infringement.* In an omitted part of the opinion, Chanel unsuccessfully argued that Smith should be responsible for any unsanctioned misrepresentations made by retailers who bought the knockoff from Smith. The current standard for contributory trademark liability comes from *Inwood Laboratories, Inc. v. Ives Laboratories, Inc.*, 456 U.S. 844 (1982):

> [I]f a manufacturer or distributor intentionally induces another to infringe a trademark, or if it continues to supply its product to one whom it knows or has reason to know is engaging in trademark infringement, the manufacturer or distributor is contributorily responsible for any harm done as a result of the deceit.

The standard for contributory infringement may differ for service providers (in contrast to manufacturers/retailers of chattels). The Ninth Circuit said that a service provider can be contributorily liable when it has "direct control and monitoring of the instrumentality used by a third party to infringe the plaintiff's mark." *See* Lockheed Martin Corp. v. Network Solutions, Inc., 194 F.3d 980 (9th Cir. 1999).

For example, if a web host is providing hosting services to a trademark infringer, it may have the requisite control over the hosted website to face contributory liability. *See* Louis Vuitton Malletier, S.A. v. Akanoc Sols., Inc., 591 F. Supp. 2d 1098 (N.D. Cal. 2008), *aff'd*, 658 F.3d 936 (9th Cir. 2011). In contrast, a domain name registrar who merely associates a domain name with the customer-specified IP address lacks the requisite control (*see Lockheed*).

Furthermore, contributory infringement requires that the secondary defendant have an appropriate level of scienter. Thus, the Second Circuit concluded that eBay lacked the requisite scienter for contributory infringement even though it had generalized knowledge that eBay's vendors were auctioning counterfeit Tiffany goods on the site. Tiffany (NJ) Inc. v. eBay Inc., 600 F.3d 93 (2d Cir. 2010). However, the court also held that Tiffany retained a viable false advertising claim if eBay's ads offering "Tiffany" products would have fooled reasonable consumers about the genuineness of the "Tiffany" products available on the site.

The federal trademark statute limits the remedies against publishers who publish ads that infringe trademarks. 15 U.S.C. § 1114(2)(B) states:

> Where the infringement or violation complained of is contained in or is part of paid advertising matter in a newspaper, magazine, or other similar periodical or in an electronic communication as defined in section 2510(12) of title 18, the remedies of the owner of the right infringed or person bringing the action under section 1125(a) of this title as against the publisher or distributor of such newspaper, magazine, or other similar periodical or electronic communication shall be limited to an injunction against the presentation of such advertising matter in future issues of such newspapers, magazines, or other similar periodicals or in future transmissions of such electronic communications. The limitations of this subparagraph shall apply only to innocent infringers and innocent violators.

We will revisit contributory liability principles in Chapter 16.

### 3.    Trademark Dilution

Federal trademark law provides extra protection for "famous" marks, defined as trademarks that are "widely recognized by the general consuming public of the United States as a designation of source of the goods or services of the mark's owner." These famous marks are protected against "dilution," which can occur in one of two ways: by "blurring," a use that "impairs the distinctiveness of the famous mark," and by tarnishment, a use that "harms the reputation of the famous mark." 15 U.S.C. § 1125(c).

Trademark dilution does not require any consumer confusion about product source. The availability of remedies, even when no consumer suffered any harm, makes dilution a controversial doctrine.

Trademark dilution traces its origins to Frank Schecter's seminal 1927 *Harvard Law Review* article, "The Rational Basis of Trademark Protection." In response to that article, a number of states enacted trademark dilution statutes over the years. Congress enacted federal dilution protection in 1995. The following case illustrates a state dilution lawsuit prior to the federal statute's enactment. As you read it, consider how dilution may affect comparative advertising.

### Deere & Co. v. MTD Products, Inc., 41 F.3d 39 (2d Cir. 1994)

This appeal in a trademark case presents a rarely litigated issue likely to recur with increasing frequency in this era of head-to-head comparative advertising. The precise issue, arising under the New York anti-dilution statute is whether an advertiser may depict an altered form of a competitor's trademark to identify the competitor's product in a comparative ad. . . .

Although a number of dilution cases in this Circuit have involved use of a trademark by a competitor to identify a competitor's products in comparative advertising, as well as use by a noncompetitor in a humorous variation of a trademark, we have not yet considered whether the use of an altered version of a distinctive trademark to identify a competitor's product and achieve a humorous effect can constitute trademark dilution. Though we find MTD's animated version of Deere's deer amusing, we agree with Judge McKenna that the television commercial is a likely violation of the anti-dilution statute. We therefore affirm the preliminary injunction.

### BACKGROUND

Deere, a Delaware corporation with its principal place of business in Illinois, is the world's largest supplier of agricultural equipment. For over one hundred years, Deere has used a deer design ("Deere Logo") as a trademark for identifying its products and services. Deere owns numerous trademark registrations for different versions of the Deere Logo. Although these versions vary slightly, all depict a static, two-dimensional silhouette of a leaping male deer in profile. The Deere Logo is widely recognizable and a valuable business asset.[3]

[Deere logo]

MTD, an Ohio company with its principal place of business in Ohio, manufactures and sells lawn tractors. In 1993, W.B. Doner & Company ("Doner"), MTD's advertising agency, decided to create and produce a commercial—the subject of this litigation—that would use the Deere Logo, without Deere's authorization, for the purpose of comparing Deere's line of lawn tractors to MTD's "Yard-Man" tractor. The intent was to identify Deere as the market leader and convey the message that Yard-Man was of comparable quality but less costly than a Deere lawn tractor.

---

[3] Deere's net sales of equipment bearing the Deere Logo for the fiscal year 1993 exceeded $6.4 billion, and Deere contends that revenues from its financial services and insurance operations, which also utilize the Deere Logo, exceeded $1.1 billion. Deere has spent a substantial amount of money using the Deere Logo to advertise its products and services.

Doner altered the Deere Logo in several respects. For example, as Judge McKenna found, the deer in the MTD version of the logo ("Commercial Logo") is "somewhat differently proportioned, particularly with respect to its width, than the deer in the Deere Logo." Doner also removed the name "John Deere" from the version of the logo used by Deere on the front of its lawn tractors, and made the logo frame more sharply rectangular.

More significantly, the deer in the Commercial Logo is animated and assumes various poses. Specifically, the MTD deer looks over its shoulder, jumps through the logo frame (which breaks into pieces and tumbles to the ground), hops to a pinging noise, and, as a two-dimensional cartoon, runs, in apparent fear, as it is pursued by the Yard-Man lawn tractor and a barking dog. Judge McKenna described the dog as "recognizable as a breed that is short in stature," and in the commercial the fleeing deer appears to be even smaller than the dog. Doner's interoffice documents reflect that the animated deer in the commercial was intended to appear "more playful and/or confused than distressed."

MTD submitted the commercial to ABC, NBC, and CBS for clearance prior to airing, together with substantiation of the various claims made regarding the Yard-Man lawn tractor's quality and cost relative to the corresponding Deere model. Each network ultimately approved the commercial, though ABC reserved the right to re-evaluate it "should there be [a] responsible complaint," and CBS demanded and received a letter of indemnity from Doner. The commercial ran from the week of March 7, 1994, through the week of May 23, 1994. . . .

On appeal, MTD argues that the anti-dilution statute does not prohibit commercial uses of a trademark that do not confuse consumers or result in a loss of the trademark's ability to identify a single manufacturer, or tarnish the trademark's positive connotations. Deere cross-appeals, contending that injunctive relief should not have been limited to New York State. We affirm both the finding of likely dilution and the scope of the injunction.

## DISCUSSION

Section 368-d, which has counterparts in more than twenty states, reads as follows:

> Likelihood of injury to business reputation or of dilution of the distinctive quality of a mark or trade name shall be a ground for injunctive relief in cases of infringement of a mark registered or not registered or in cases of unfair competition, notwithstanding the absence of competition between the parties or the absence of confusion as to the source of goods or services.

The anti-dilution statute applies to competitors as well as noncompetitors, and explicitly does not require a plaintiff to demonstrate a likelihood of consumer confusion.

In order to prevail on a section 368-d dilution claim, a plaintiff must prove, first, that its trademark either is of truly distinctive quality or has acquired secondary meaning, and, second, that there is a "likelihood of dilution." A third consideration, the predatory intent of the defendant, may not be precisely an element of the violation, but, as we discuss below, is of significance, especially in a case such as this, which involves poking fun at a competitor's trademark.

MTD does not dispute that the Deere Logo is a distinctive trademark that is capable of dilution and has acquired the requisite secondary meaning in the marketplace. Therefore, the primary question on appeal is whether Deere can establish a likelihood of dilution of this distinctive mark under section 368-d.

*Likelihood of Dilution.* Traditionally, this Court has defined dilution under section 368-d "as either the blurring of a mark's product identification or the tarnishment of the affirmative associations a mark has come to convey."

In previous cases, "blurring" has typically involved "the whittling away of an established trademark's selling power through its unauthorized use by others upon dissimilar products" [including such] " 'hypothetical anomalies' as 'DuPont shoes, Buick aspirin tablets, Schlitz varnish, Kodak pianos, Bulova gowns, and so forth.' " Thus, dilution by "blurring" may occur where the defendant uses or modifies the plaintiff's trademark to identify the defendant's goods and services, raising the possibility that the mark will lose its ability to serve as a unique identifier of the plaintiff's product.

"Tarnishment" generally arises when the plaintiff's trademark is linked to products of shoddy quality, or is portrayed in an unwholesome or unsavory context likely to evoke unflattering thoughts about the owner's product. In such situations, the trademark's reputation and commercial value might be diminished because the public will associate the lack of quality or lack of prestige in the defendant's goods with the plaintiff's unrelated goods, or because the defendant's use reduces the trademark's reputation and standing in the eyes of consumers as a wholesome identifier of the owner's products or services.

At the hearing on Deere's application for a temporary restraining order, the District Court initially suggested that there was neither blurring nor tarnishment as those terms have been used, and consequently no dilution of the Deere Logo. The Court observed that MTD's commercial "makes it clear that Deere is a distinct product coming from a different source than Yard-Man," and does not "bring the plaintiff's mark into disrepute." However, in its preliminary injunction ruling, the Court found that Deere would probably be able to establish a likelihood of dilution by blurring under section 368-d; tarnishment was not discussed.

The District Court noted that "the instant case [wa]s one of first impression" because it involved a defendant's use of a competitor's trademark to refer to the competitor's products rather than to identify the defendant's products. For this reason, the traditional six-factor test for determining whether there has been dilution through blurring of a trademark's product identification was not fully applicable. Focusing only on the alteration of the static Deere Logo resulting from MTD's animation, the Court concluded that MTD's version constituted dilution because it was likely to diminish the strength of identification between the original Deere symbol and Deere products, and to blur the distinction between the Deere Logo and other deer logos in the marketplace, including those in the insurance and financial markets. Although we agree with the District Court's finding of a likelihood of dilution, we believe that MTD's commercial does not fit within the concept of "blurring," but, as we explain below, nonetheless constitutes dilution.

The District Court's analysis endeavored to fit the MTD commercial into one of the two categories we have recognized for a section 368-d claim. However, the MTD commercial is not really a typical instance of blurring because it poses slight if any risk of impairing the identification of Deere's mark with its products. Nor is there tarnishment, which is usually found where a distinctive mark is depicted in a context of sexual activity, obscenity, or illegal activity. But the blurring/tarnishment dichotomy does not necessarily represent the full range of uses that can dilute a mark under New York law.

In giving content to dilution beyond the categories of blurring or tarnishment, however, we must be careful not to broaden section 368-d to prohibit all uses of a distinctive mark that the owner prefers not be made. Several different contexts may conveniently be identified. Sellers of commercial products may wish to use a competitor's mark to identify the competitor's product in comparative advertisements. As long as the mark is not altered, such use serves the beneficial purpose of imparting factual information about the relative merits of competing products and poses no risk of diluting the selling power of the competitor's mark. Satirists, selling no product other than the publication that contains their expression, may wish to parody a mark to make a point of social commentary, or perhaps both to comment and entertain. Such uses risk some dilution of the identifying or selling power of the mark, but that risk is generally tolerated in the interest of maintaining broad opportunities for expression.

Sellers of commercial products who wish to attract attention to their commercials or products and thereby increase sales by poking fun at widely recognized marks of noncompeting products risk diluting the selling power of the mark that is made fun of. When this occurs, not for worthy purposes of expression, but simply to sell products, that purpose can easily be achieved in other ways. The potentially diluting effect is even less deserving of protection when the object of the joke is the mark

480

of a directly competing product. The line-drawing in this area becomes especially difficult when a mark is parodied for the dual purposes of making a satiric comment and selling a somewhat competing product.

Whether the use of the mark is to identify a competing product in an informative comparative ad, to make a comment, or to spoof the mark to enliven the advertisement for a noncompeting or a competing product, the scope of protection under a dilution statute must take into account the degree to which the mark is altered and the nature of the alteration. Not every alteration will constitute dilution, and more leeway for alterations is appropriate in the context of satiric expression and humorous ads for noncompeting products. But some alterations have the potential to so lessen the selling power of a distinctive mark that they are appropriately proscribed by a dilution statute. Dilution of this sort is more likely to be found when the alterations are made by a competitor with both an incentive to diminish the favorable attributes of the mark and an ample opportunity to promote its products in ways that make no significant alteration.

We need not attempt to predict how New York will delineate the scope of its dilution statute in all of the various contexts in which an accurate depiction of a distinctive mark might be used, nor need we decide how variations of such a mark should be treated in different contexts. Some variations might well be de minimis, and the context in which even substantial variations occur may well have such meritorious purposes that any diminution in the identifying and selling power of the mark need not be condemned as dilution.

Wherever New York will ultimately draw the line, we can be reasonably confident that the MTD commercial challenged in this case crosses it. The commercial takes a static image of a graceful, full-size deer—symbolizing Deere's substance and strength—and portrays, in an animated version, a deer that appears smaller than a small dog and scampers away from the dog and a lawn tractor, looking over its shoulder in apparent fear. Alterations of that sort, accomplished for the sole purpose of promoting a competing product, are properly found to be within New York's concept of dilution because they risk the possibility that consumers will come to attribute unfavorable characteristics to a mark and ultimately associate the mark with inferior goods and services.

Significantly, the District Court did not enjoin accurate reproduction of the Deere Logo to identify Deere products in comparative advertisements. MTD remains free to deliver its message of alleged product superiority without altering and thereby diluting Deere's trademarks. The Court's order imposes no restriction on truthful advertising properly comparing specific products and their "objectively measurable attributes." In view of this, the District Court's finding of a likelihood of dilution was entirely appropriate, notwithstanding the fact that MTD's humorous depiction of the deer occurred in the context of a comparative advertisement. . . .

*NOTES AND QUESTIONS*

*Ad Redesign.* How would you redesign the ad to avoid diluting Deere's trademark? How do you think the court would analyze an ad where the advertiser removes the competitor's product name but the competitive product nevertheless has a recognizable profile/trade dress? Revisit the Bailey's cigarette ad example discussed after *Smith v. Chanel*. How would the *Deere* court analyze that ad for dilution purposes?

*Dilution and Nominative Use.* Interpreting both the federal Lanham Act and New York state law, the Second Circuit reached a different result in *Tiffany (NJ) Inc. v. eBay Inc.*, 600 F.3d 93 (2d Cir. 2010). Tiffany sued eBay because eBay had advertised that consumers could buy Tiffany items on eBay—a partially true statement, as eBay's auctions contained both legitimate and counterfeit Tiffany items. The Second Circuit rejected the dilution claims. The court said that because eBay had made a nominative use of the Tiffany mark, "[t]here is no second mark or product at issue here to blur with or to tarnish 'Tiffany.' "

The Lanham Act expressly mentions nominative use and comparative advertising as defenses to dilution. Dilution defenses include:

> [a]ny fair use, including a nominative or descriptive fair use, or facilitation of such fair use, of a famous mark by another person other than as a designation of source for the person's own goods or services, including use in connection with—
>
> (i) advertising or promotion that permits consumers to compare goods or services; or
>
> (ii) identifying and parodying, criticizing, or commenting upon the famous mark owner or the goods or services of the famous mark owner.

For unexplained reasons, the Second Circuit did not rely on this defense in its *Tiffany* ruling, instead concluding that no blurring or tarnishment had occurred.

If these defenses had been available to MTD, would the *Deere* case have come out differently?

Test yourself: does this law firm ad dilute the trademark of the nursing home?

McHugh Fuller Law Group, PLLC v. PruittHealth, Inc., S16A0655 (Ga. Sup. Ct. 2016) (no dilution under Georgia's state trademark law).

*MasterCard v. Nader.* The court rejected MasterCard's dilution claim because Nader's use was political and not commercial and also there was no evidence of any effect on the value of MasterCard's marks or on their capacity to distinguish MasterCard's services. Under current law, the trademark owner only needs to show "likely" dilution, though courts may consider the absence of evidence of an actual effect in their assessment of likelihood.

*Evidence of Dilution.* Apropos of the *Nader* case, what evidence persuasively demonstrates that dilution is occurring or likely to occur? Right now, no one has a clear understanding of how to prove—or disprove—dilution.

Some courts make it easy on plaintiffs by excusing them from marshaling any scientifically rigorous evidence of dilution. In *Visa International Service Ass'n v. JSL Corp.*, 610 F.3d 1088 (9th Cir. 2010), Judge Kozinski said "a plaintiff seeking to establish a likelihood of dilution is not required to go to the expense of producing expert testimony or market surveys; it may rely entirely on the characteristics of the marks at issue." Courts appear to be particularly lax about evidentiary requirements in cases involving tarnishment by association with sex. *See* V Secret Catalogue, Inc. v. Moseley, 605 F.3d 382 (6th Cir. 2010) (finding that tawdry Victor's Little Secret store, which sold lingerie and "adult toys," tarnished the classier Victoria's Secret mark).

*Dilution and the First Amendment. L.L. Bean v. Drake Publishers*, 811 F.2d 26 (1st Cir. 1987), involved a parody article published in *High Society*, an adult magazine, called "L.L. Beam's Back-To-School-Sex-Catalog." The district court granted L.L. Bean summary judgment under Maine's dilution law. The First Circuit reversed on First Amendment grounds:

> If the anti-dilution statute were construed as permitting a trademark owner to enjoin the use of his mark in a noncommercial context found to be negative or offensive, then a corporation could shield itself from criticism by forbidding the use of its name in commentaries critical of its conduct. The legitimate aim of the anti-dilution statute is to prohibit the unauthorized use of another's trademark in order to market incompatible products or services. The Constitution does not, however, permit the range of the anti-dilution statute to encompass the unauthorized use of a trademark in a noncommercial setting such as an editorial or artistic context.

However, courts generally are reluctant to apply the First Amendment to trademark claims, and it may be especially hard to convince a court to find First Amendment protection for a trademark claim against an advertisement.

*Louis Vuitton Malletier, S.A. v. Hyundai Motor America*, 2012 WL 1022247 (S.D.N.Y. 2012), illustrates this challenge. During the post-game show following the 2010 Super Bowl, Hyundai ran a 30-second commercial that its counsel later described as "a humorous, socio-economic commentary on luxury defined by a premium price tag, rather than by the value to the consumer." See the ad at http://www.youtube.com/watch?v=O7I4v7NYHrY. It consisted of brief vignettes that show "policemen eating caviar in a patrol car; large yachts parked beside modest homes; blue-collar workers eating lobster during their lunch break; a four-second scene of an inner-city basketball game played on a lavish marble court with a gold hoop; and a ten-second scene of the Sonata driving down a street lined with chandeliers and red-carpet crosswalks." The basketball game scene included a one-second shot of a basketball decorated with a pattern resembling Louis Vuitton's toile monogram "LV" on a chestnut-brown background. The LV was changed to LZ, and the proportions of the other designs were slightly altered.

[image from ad]

The court granted summary judgment to Louis Vuitton on trademark dilution. It rejected Hyundai's parody argument because there was no direct commentary on Louis Vuitton specifically; Hyundai was at most commenting on the concept of "luxury" generally, and thus didn't qualify for the statutory exception for "identifying and parodying, criticizing, or commenting upon the famous mark owner or the goods or services of the famous mark owner." The court also rejected a First Amendment defense because any commentary was too "subtle," and the "broader social critique" didn't justify use of Louis Vuitton's marks.

How does this square with the commercial speech doctrine you encountered in Chapter 2? For an argument that dilution law unconstitutionally regulates commercial speech, *see* Rebecca Tushnet, *Gone in Sixty Milliseconds: Trademark Law and Cognitive Science*, 86 TEX. L. REV. 507 (2008).

The *Hyundai* court's finding of dilution was surprising, and at least one court expressly declined to follow it because "the *Hyundai* Court blurred the distinction between association and dilution....[A]ssociation is a necessary, but not sufficient, condition for a finding of dilution by blurring." Louis Vuitton Malletier, S.A. v. My Other Bag, Inc., 156 F. Supp. 3d 425 (S.D.N.Y. 2016), *aff'd*, 674 Fed. Appx. 16 (2d Cir. 2016).

### 4.      Ambush Marketing

Some public events, such as major sporting events, are likely to attract substantial media hype and consumer interest. Think, for example, of the media coverage of the Olympics, the Super Bowl or the NCAA Men's Basketball tournament. The event organizers create and sell marketing opportunities to advertisers that allow them to capitalize on this media coverage and consumer interest, such as allowing the advertisers to call themselves "official sponsors" or to put up signage or other advertising displays at the event.

Advertising sponsorships might be "exclusive" among competitors, or sponsorship might be cost-prohibitive for some advertisers. For these and other reasons, advertisers have incentives to try to obtain the benefits of event sponsorship without paying the stated price. This is sometimes referred to as "ambush marketing." Examples of ambush marketing include running an advertising campaign while the Olympics are ongoing that shows athletes without explicit reference to the Olympics, or finding unauthorized ways to get advertising incorporated into photos or broadcasts of the events. *See generally* Simon Chadwick & Nicholas Burton, *Ambushed!*, WALL ST. J., Jan. 25, 2010 (defining a taxonomy of different types of ambush marketing).

For example, during the World Cup 2010, a South African discount airline, Kulula, ran print advertisements in which it called itself the "Unofficial National Carrier of the You-Know-What," promoting airfares for flights that presumably soccer fans would want to take to attend games. To reinforce the soccer theme, the ad displayed stadiums, vuvuzelas (plastic trumpets used by South African soccer fans), and national flags. *See FIFA Orders South African Airline to Drop 'Ambush' Ad*, BBC NEWS, March 19, 2010.

[initial ad]

FIFA, the organization that governs international soccer, objected to Kulula's ad as ambush marketing. As a result, Kulula created a second ad that had the same look and feel but replaced most soccer-related items with similar looking items. For example, the plastic trumpets were replaced with almost-identical-looking golf tees, and the soccer balls were replaced with other types of balls. *See* Herman Manson, *Kulula Answers FIFA with New Ad*, MARK LIVES, March 21, 2010.

[revised ad]

Ambush marketing is maddening to event organizers. It feels like the advertiser is free-riding on the event organizer's investments and intentionally drawing on consumers' goodwill towards the event, and it irritates the event organizer's customers (the sponsors) who pay huge sums only to see others obtain similar value for free.

Despite the temptation of characterizing ambush marketing as "free riding," ambush marketing typically is not legally actionable in the United States (in contrast, some other nations have various laws designed to stop it). For example, an advertiser can freely run a sports- or athlete-themed ad during the Olympics so long as the ad copy does not reference any Olympic trademarks (which are protected by a special statute, 36 U.S.C. § 220506) or make an unauthorized use of personality rights. This is true even though we all know what is going on—that the advertiser is trying to invoke and associate itself in consumers' minds with the Olympics.

However, event organizers are not completely defenseless. Even if they cannot bring an intellectual property claim, they can proactively use contracts with broadcasters and athletes to restrict these tactics. As a result, major events now often involve an arms race of sorts: event organizers seek to maximize their revenue and protect their sponsors' investments by anticipating and squelching ambush marketing efforts, and ambush marketers seek to get cheap advertising using innovative and unofficial techniques.

While the next case is not a classic "ambush marketing" case, it involves a similar situation where the advertiser tries to piggy-back on a competitor's marketing expenditures. Do you think the advertiser's actions unethical? If so, why?

**Heartland Recreational Vehicles, LLC. v. Forest River, Inc., 2009 WL 418079 (N.D. Ind. 2009)**

. . . III. Factual Background

On October 22 and 23, 2008, Forest River hosted a private (by invitation only) trade show and more than 700 guests were invited to attend, representing approximately 350 RV dealerships from across North America and as far away as Australia. A theme of this trade show was "Pick Your Partner," referring to the business relationships that can develop between an RV manufacturer and an RV dealer. One of the purposes of this event was to encourage sales of various Forest River products to new and existing RV dealers. To provide overnight accommodations for its guests, Forest River reserved several hotels in Mishawaka, Indiana, including the Hyatt Place, Country Inn & Suites, Residence Inn, Courtyard Marriott, Springhill Suites, Holiday Inn Express, Hampton Inn, and Varsity Club. Forest River created an internal business document, called a "Master List," identifying each guest who would be attending the private trade show and identifying the hotel where each guest would be staying. Forest River paid for its guests' accommodations at these hotels.

On Wednesday, October 22, at approximately 3:30 p.m., while most of Forest River's guests were in attendance at the private trade show, several of Heartland's employees ("Heartland employees") entered the hotels reserved by Forest River. The Heartland employees were carrying stacks of envelopes, each labeled with the name of a Forest River guest and an identification of which hotel that guest was staying [sic]. The Heartland employees went to the front desks of the hotels and then falsely stated and represented to the hotel attendants that they were "from Forest River" and that they had "important" envelopes which needed to be delivered to the Forest River guests "for a Forest River dealer meeting the next day." The Heartland employees induced the hotel attendants to immediately deliver the envelopes to the rooms of each named guest in their respective hotels, such as by slipping the envelopes under the guests' room doors. Security video cameras monitoring the front desks in at least two of these hotels recorded this event and the Heartland employees doing it.

The envelopes contained documents advertising Heartland's travel trailers and documents comparing several Flagstaff models of Forest River products with certain North Trail models of Heartland products. The envelopes also contained a specific invitation to visit Heartland's place of business in Elkhart that same week, while the guests were in the area attending Forest River's private trade show, including a map showing how to get there. Several of Forest River's guests, who were RV dealers, were induced by the contents of those envelopes to visit Heartland's place of business that same week and placed orders for Heartland travel trailers, causing lost sales by Forest River, a direct competitor of Heartland. Those actions (hereinafter referred to as "the hotel action"), resulted in "disruption and confusion among several of Forest River's guests because of the incongruity and surprising manner in which the envelopes were delivered . . . [and] adversely affect[ed] Forest River's good will with its dealers and adversely affected Forest River's sales of its products."

IV. Discussion . . .

In general, passing off, or palming off, arises when a producer misrepresents his own goods or services as someone else's goods or services. As best stated by Forest River's counsel during oral argument, the hotel action may have occurred in connection with goods, in that Heartland would not have been in the hotels if it was not for the purpose of selling RV's for a commercial purpose and possibly confusing people in connection with those goods. While this Court questions, and indeed doubts, whether Forest River has adequately pled a passing off violation under the Lanham Act, that doubt, combined with our standards for federal pleading under Rule 8(a) and for dismissal under Rule 12(b)(6), does not permit dismissal of Forest River's counterclaim at this time where relief is plausible. . . .

As pled, Heartland's intentionally deceptive conduct in the hotel action plausibly had the natural and probable tendency and effect of which was to deceive the public so as to pass off its goods or business as for that of Forest River. Moreover, the Court will not condone Heartland's actions as simply healthy competition. "Though trade warfare may be waged ruthlessly to the bitter end, there are certain rules of combat which must be observed. The trader has not a free lance. Fight he may, but as a soldier, not as a guerilla." Forest River, having identified a plausible legal basis for its counterclaim, precludes the finding that no viable cause of action exists upon which relief can be granted. . . .

*NOTES AND QUESTIONS*

*Fair vs. Unfair Competition.* What exactly did Heartland do wrong, and why does the court conclude that Heartland's behavior was not "simply healthy competition"?

Was the problem just Heartland's misrepresentations to the hotel employees, or was Heartland's broader scheme condemnable? Could Heartland employees have approached the hotel staff and identified themselves as being from "a local RV manufacturer"? Could Heartland have run radio ads during the weekend encouraging visiting dealers to come to Heartland's facility? Could Heartland have put moving billboards right outside the targeted hotels encouraging visiting dealers to come to Heartland's facility? Prior to the weekend, could Heartland have sent direct mail or email to Forest River's dealers saying "if you're coming to Mishawaka, come visit us"? *See* Martha C. White, *The Convention Crashers*, N.Y TIMES, Feb. 15, 2010 (discussing trade show efforts to suppress "outboarders," defined as "vendors who set up shop in a hotel suite near a trade show site to promote their products").

If Heartland got unauthorized possession of Forest River's "master list," would that constitute trade secret misappropriation (see Chapter 12)? How else could Heartland have figured out which Forest River dealers were in town and where they were staying?

*Are Sponsorship Deals a Good Deal?* In addition to the risk of ambush marketing, event sponsors face the constant risk that consumers will not give them full credit for their sponsorship. Consider the following chart showing who consumers thought sponsored Euro 2016, a major soccer event in Europe:

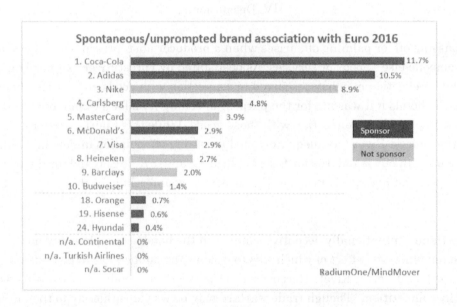

As you can see, consumers falsely assumed that several major consumer brands—including Nike, Mastercard, Visa and beer advertisers—were sponsors of Euro 2016. In other words, those brands got consumer goodwill for being event sponsors without paying a dime. How do you think the event sponsors feel about that?

## 5.    Online Advertising Issues

Online advertising raises many of the same issues addressed throughout this book, but online advertising can also raise some novel complications. This section explores some of these.

### A.    Domain Names

Every computer connected to the Internet has a unique numerical address associated with it, called an IP address. Because it can be hard to remember these long numerical strings, we typically identify Internet-connected computers by domain names, which act as mnemonics for the IP addresses.

Domain names have significant value independent of any trademark rights. We can see this from the lofty valuations attached to domain names that are unlikely to be eligible for trademark protection.

The Federal Circuit has declared that [noun].com domain names are generic, at least when the website offers goods or services having some relationship to the noun, and are therefore ineligible for trademark registration. *See In re* Hotels.com, 573 F.3d 1300 (Fed. Cir. 2009); *In re* 1800mattress.com IP, LLC, 586 F.3d 1359 (Fed. Cir. 2009).

Yet, even though these domain names lack any trademark protection, most of the domain names that have sold for a million dollars or more fit the [noun].com paradigm. *See* Jillian D'Onfro and Brandt Ranj, *Million-Dollar URLs: The Most Expensive Domain Names of All Time*, BUSINESS INSIDER, April 28, 2016.

Let's start by defining terms. Consider the following domain name:

> http://news.google.com/nwshp

This is the domain name for Google News's home page. In this domain name:

1.   .com is the "top level domain" (TLD)
2.   google is the "second level domain" (SLD)
3.   news is the "third level domain" which designates specific servers within the Google empire
4.   nwshp is called the "post-domain path"

Domain names are typically sold through a two-level distribution chain. Each TLD is operated by a "registry," the rough equivalent of the domain name manufacturer. Registries ensure that only one person registers each domain name within the TLD. ICANN (Internet Corporation for Assigned Names and Numbers), a nongovernmental organization, licenses the registries of many well-known TLDs. Registries license "registrars," the retailers, to sell domain names to "registrants," the customers.

In the early 1990s, domain names were freely registrable by anyone just for asking. A 1994 *Wired* article, *Billions Registered*, described how the author, Josh Quittner, registered McDonalds.com. This article sparked a gold rush as everyone started grabbing unregistered domain names.

In some cases, the registrants grabbed domain names containing third-party trademarks with the intent of ransoming the name back to the trademark owner, a process we now call "cybersquatting." In 1995, Congress enacted federal dilution protection in part to curb cybersquatting, but the new dilution law instead caused courts to overextend dilution protection to trademarks that did not deserve such heavy protection, and it did little to squelch the speculative bubble. Congress cracked down more successfully with the 1999 Anti-Cybersquatting Consumer Protection Act, discussed in more detail below.

In the 1990s, registrants believed that searchers might guess a domain name by adding .com to a generic word (i.e., pets.com) or a trademark (i.e., mercedes.com). Domain name owners call this "type-in traffic." Some domain name registrants even anticipate that searchers will make typographical errors when typing a domain name and register domain names containing logical typographical mistakes, a process sometimes called "typosquatting." While type-in traffic still exists, searchers rarely guess domain names any more because search engines are so easy to use, and mistyped or expired domain names can lead to pop-up ads, unexpected porn or malware.

Meanwhile, many web browsers have eliminated an "address bar" altogether. Most popular browsers use an "omnibox" that triggers searches for many entries into the "address bar," including some domain names. Given how many users begin their web sessions with a search, many marketers value a top result in organic or paid search results much more than the best domain name. The move to mobile apps has further degraded the value of domain names because the app connects directly with the online service without using domain names at all.

As a result, domain names are waning in importance and influence. Still, domain names remain a critical part of any online endeavor. New start-up companies, or existing companies seeking to launch a new brand, face a very crowded domain name space. Even if the company gets a relatively clean trademark search, it can be hard to find a desirable domain name for a new brand that is not already registered. Often, companies are forced to purchase their desired domain name from a domain name speculator.

Occasionally, domain name speculators will figure out a new company's intended domain name before it has been registered. Either there will be a public announcement of a new product launch before the domain name is secured, or speculators will make guesses (such as when a sports franchise considers moving to a new city or a corporate merger is imminent). In any of these cases, the domain name will be snatched up quickly by speculators if it is not secured before the publicity. The clear lesson: register or purchase any desired domain names before making any public announcements.

Some of the major legal regulations of domain names include the following:

### I. Trademark Infringement

Merely registering a domain name containing a third-party trademark is usually not trademark infringement because the defendant hasn't made a use in commerce. Doing anything else with the domain name, such as publishing a website using the domain name or offering the domain name for sale, might infringe.

Courts carefully scrutinize the exact domain name and how the defendant uses it. [Trademark].com often infringes the trademark owner's rights, but [trademark]sucks.com frequently does not. *See* Toyota Motor Sales, U.S.A., Inc. v. Tabari, 610 F.3d 1171 (9th Cir. 2010) (offering a taxonomy of presumptively legitimate and illegitimate domain names). The better-reasoned cases also will consider if the associated website contains a disclaimer or otherwise instantly clarifies the relationship between the domain name registrant and the trademark owner. However, other cases have found that the domain name standing alone creates "initial interest confusion" (discussed in more detail later) by including a third-party trademark, irrespective of the associated website's content.

## *II. Trademark Dilution*

As mentioned, in the 1990s, courts expanded dilution law to cover cybersquatting and other domain name misuses. In 2006, Congress amended the federal dilution law to, among other things, make it harder for marks to qualify as "famous marks." As a result, it is now harder to establish a dilution claim based on domain name misuse.

## *III. Anti-Cybersquatting Consumer Protection Act (ACPA)*

Passed in 1999 to curb cybersquatting, a successful ACPA claim requires the trademark owner to establish that the defendant:

(1) registers, traffics in, or uses a domain name that is identical or confusing similar to a trademark or dilutive of a famous mark,* and

(2) has a bad faith intent to profit from the trademark, which does not include situations where the registrant reasonably believed that it was making a fair or otherwise lawful use of the domain name.

These elements clearly ban 1990s-style cybersquatting registrations-for-ransom, and that activity has largely ceased. The elements also presumptively ban deliberate typosquatting on third-party trademarks. Although it was not clearly designed to do so, ACPA may apply to more recent domain name speculative activity, such as registering trademarked domain names to put up ads on the pages. *See, e.g.*, Verizon Cal., Inc. v. Navigation Catalyst Sys., Inc., 2008 WL 2651163 (C.D. Cal. 2008); Tex. Int'l Prop. Assocs. v. Hoerbiger Holding AG, 2009 U.S. Dist. LEXIS 40409 (N.D. Tex. May 12, 2009).

A successful ACPA plaintiff can get statutory damages of up to $100,000 per domain name, attorneys' fees, and the domain name either transferred to it or canceled. (Cancellation is not a common remedy because any canceled domain name almost certainly will be reregistered by other domain name speculators). Alternatively, ACPA allows trademark owners to sue to recover the

---

* ACPA also protects the Red Cross and Olympics (and related) trademarks.

domain name (an "in rem" action) in certain cases, such as when the domain name registrant is in a foreign jurisdiction.

ACPA also contains separate protection for domain names containing personal names that are registered for profitable resale (15 U.S.C. § 8131) and a safe harbor for domain name registrars.

### IV. Uniform Dispute Resolution Policy (UDRP)

Before Congress passed ACPA, ICANN was working on a self-regulatory process to curb cybersquatting. Congress ultimately felt that ICANN was taking too long, so Congress enacted ACPA. A few months later, ICANN launched the Uniform Domain-Name Dispute-Resolution Policy (UDRP), a private extra-judicial administrative proceeding to adjudicate domain name disputes. All domain name registrants in ICANN-operated TLDs (i.e., most major TLDs) agree to be bound to UDRP proceedings when they register the domain names.

Because they were designed to solve the same problem (cybersquatting) and were drafted around the same time (1999), the UDRP and ACPA have similar requirements. A UDRP complainant can succeed if it can show that the domain name registrant:

- has a domain name that "is identical or confusingly similar to a trademark or service mark in which the complainant has rights,"
- has "no rights or legitimate interests in respect of the domain name," and
- the "domain name has been registered and is being used in bad faith."

UDRP proceedings offer a number of advantages for trademark owners over judicial proceedings via ACPA or other legal doctrines. First, UDRP proceedings are fast and cheap; they can be done in a matter of months for typically less than $10,000, compared to judicial proceedings that take years and cost hundreds of thousands of dollars. Second, trademark owners win most UDRP proceedings. Trademark owners can select the UDRP vendor, so naturally they all select the vendors with the best batting average for complainants. Third, the UDRP's bad faith standards ("being used in bad faith") is broader than the ACPA's parallel standard ("bad faith intent to profit"), so it's possible to win UDRP proceedings where the registrant's motives are not clearly profit-oriented. Finally, because all registrants agree to be bound by the UDRP procedures, there are no problems with jurisdiction, service of process, etc.

UDRP proceedings have one obvious disadvantage compared to ACPA claims: because the UDRP is an extra-judicial administrative proceeding, the only remedy is to have the violating domain name transferred or canceled. Thus, complainants cannot get either damages or an injunction. Furthermore, a registrant can stop or overturn a UDRP proceeding by bringing a declaratory judgment action in court. As a result, trademark owners sometimes prefer to go to court for its finality and better remedies.

Nevertheless, the UDRP is more popular than the ACPA. More disputes are handled under the UDRP every year than in ten years of ACPA cases. Darryl C. Wilson, *Battle Galactica: Recent*

*Advances and Retreats in the Struggle for the Preservation of Trademark Rights on the Internet*, 12 J. HIGH TECH. L. 1 (2011).

For a more detailed comparison of ACPA and UDRP, see this comparison chart at INTA.

In addition to the UDRP, trademark owners have an even quicker dispute resolution option called the URS ("Uniform Rapid Suspension") System. The elements of a URS are similar to, but more stringent than, the elements of a UDRP. The URS process moves more quickly and has only a single remedy: suspension of the domain name for the remainder of its registration period.

ICANN has a variety of other dispute resolution procedures beyond UDRP and URS, especially with respect to new TLDs.

### *V. State Domain Name Laws*

State efforts to regulate Internet activities inherently raise dormant commerce clause issues, but a number of states have enacted domain name–specific laws nonetheless. A few examples:

- Utah SB 26, codified at Utah Code § 70-3a-309, which is structurally similar to the ACPA but has some extra benefits for trademark owners.
- California Business & Professions Code §§ 17525–17528.5, which gives ACPA-like rights to personal names.
- California Election Code §§ 18320–18323, the "California Political Cyberfraud Abatement Act," which restricts "a knowing and willful act concerning a political Web site that is committed with the intent to deny a person access to a political Web site, deny a person the opportunity to register a domain name for a political Web site, or cause a person reasonably to believe that a political Web site has been posted by a person other than the person who posted the Web site, and would cause a reasonable person, after reading the Web site, to believe the site actually represents the views of the proponent or opponent of a ballot measure."

### B.    Metatags

Every web page contains both a main page and a page of code that instructs the user's web browsing software how to display the web page. The code version of the page can also contain instructions for search engine robots about how they can gather information from the page. These instructions, sometimes called "metatags," are normally not visible to web users unless they look at the page's source code (you can find this version of the page typically by going to the "view source" option in your web browser).

There are hundreds of different types of metatags that website operators can use to accomplish different purposes. The three best-known metatags:

- The "title tag" causes the user's web browser to display the page's title when users visit the page. Search engines often display the page title as part of their search results for the page.
- The "description metatag" allows the website operator to propose language for the search engines to display in search results. Google sometimes uses the website's proposed language verbatim; other times, Google creates its own description for the website or uses a third party's description of the website.
- The "keyword metatag" allows the website operator to communicate index terms for the website. In theory, a website will pick some terms that summarize the website's content, and the search engines can choose to give extra credit to those self-selected index terms when determining how to rank its search results. In the 1990s, some unscrupulous websites would "stuff" the keyword metatags with irrelevant or duplicative information to try to fool the search engines. As a result of these efforts to game the search engines' algorithms, search engines—including Google—routinely ignore the keyword metatags altogether. *See* Matt Cutts, *Google Doesn't Use the Keywords Meta Tag in Web Search*, MATT CUTTS: GADGETS, GOOGLE, AND SEO, Sept. 21, 2009. Nor do keyword metatags show up when users view the page.

Courts have struggled with the legal implications of metatags. First, courts do not understand the different types of metatags. Second, courts do not understand that search engines handle metatags in different ways. Third, and most crucially, courts incorrectly assume that including a third-party trademark in keyword metatags will cause the page to rank high in searches on that trademark, even though the keyword metatag almost certainly has no effect on search results.

Because of this misimpression, courts often apply a de facto rule that including a third-party trademark in keyword metatags is per se trademark infringement, as the following case illustrates:

*Venture Tape Corp. v. McGills Glass Warehouse, 540 F.3d 56 (1st Cir. 2008)*

McGills Glass Warehouse ("McGills"), an internet-based retailer of stained-glass supplies, and its owner Donald Gallagher, appeal from a district court judgment finding them liable for infringement of the registered trademarks "Venture Tape" and "Venture Foil," and awarding the marks' owner, Venture Tape Corporation ("Venture"), an equitable share of McGills' profits, as well as costs and attorney's fees. We affirm.

I.

In 1990, Venture, a manufacturer of specialty adhesive tapes and foils used in the stained-glass industry, procured two federal trademark registrations (Nos. 1,579,001 and 1,583,644) for products called "Venture Tape" and "Venture Foil," respectively. Over the next fifteen years, Venture expended hundreds of thousands of dollars to promote the two marks in both print and internet advertising. Consequently, its products gained considerable popularity, prestige, and good will in the world-wide stained glass market.

Through its internet website, McGills also sells adhesive tapes and foils which directly compete with "Venture Tape" and "Venture Foil." Beginning in 2000, and without obtaining Venture's permission or paying it any compensation, McGills' owner Donald Gallagher intentionally "embedded" the Venture marks in the McGills website, both by including the marks in the website's metatags—a component of a webpage's programming that contains descriptive information about the webpage which is typically not observed when the webpage is displayed in a web browser—and in white lettering on a white background screen, similarly invisible to persons viewing the webpage. Gallagher, fully aware that the McGills website did not sell these two Venture products, admittedly took these actions because he had heard that Venture's marks would attract people using internet search engines to the McGills website.

Because the marks were hidden from view, Venture did not discover McGills' unauthorized use of its marks until 2003. . . .

Although Venture adduced evidence that McGills generated almost $1.9 million in gross sales during the period of its infringement from 2000–2003, Venture eventually requested only $230,339.17, the amount that it estimated to be McGills' net profits. Citing McGills' willful infringement and alleging McGills engaged in obstructionist discovery tactics, Venture sought $188,583.06 in attorney's fees and $7,564.75 in costs. After a hearing on Venture's motion, the district court granted Venture's requested recovery. . . .

II.

A. Lanham Act Liability . . .

"The purpose of a trademark is to identify and distinguish the goods of one party from those of another. To the purchasing public, a trademark 'signi[fies] that all goods bearing the trademark' originated from the same source and that 'all goods bearing the trademark are of an equal level of quality.' " To establish trademark infringement under the Lanham Act, Venture was required to prove that: (1) it owns and uses the "Venture Tape" and "Venture Foil" marks; (2) McGills used the same or similar marks without Venture's permission; and (3) McGills' use of the Venture marks likely confused internet consumers, thereby causing Venture harm (e.g., lost sales). The parties agree that no genuine factual dispute exists concerning the first two elements of proof.[5]

Our focus then becomes the "likelihood of confusion" among internet consumers. This inquiry requires us to assess eight criteria: (1) the similarity of Venture's and McGills' marks; (2) the similarity of their goods; (3) the relationship between their channels of trade (e.g., internet-based commerce); (4) the relationship between their advertising; (5) the classes of their prospective purchasers; (6) any evidence of actual confusion of internet consumers; (7) McGills' subjective intent in using Venture's marks; and (8) the overall strength of Venture's marks [hereinafter "*Pignons*

---

[5] Venture's registration of the two marks, when coupled with its continuous use of them from 1990 to 1995, is incontestible evidence of Venture's exclusive right to use the marks. Further, McGills concedes that, without Venture's permission, Gallagher embedded the marks verbatim on the McGills website.

factors" or "*Pignons* analysis"]. No single criterion is necessarily dispositive in this circumstantial inquiry.

By the conduct of its case below, McGills effectively admitted seven of the eight elements of the *Pignons* analysis. The record contains numerous admissions that meta tags and invisible background text on McGills' website incorporated Venture's exact marks. In his deposition, Gallagher admitted that the parties are direct competitors in the stained glass industry and that both companies use websites to promote and market their products. Gallagher even admitted that he intentionally used Venture Tape's marks on McGills' website for the express purpose of attracting customers to McGills' website and that he chose "Venture Tape" because of its strong reputation in the stained glass industry. These admissions illustrate the similarity (indeed, identity) of the marks used, the similarity of the goods, the close relationship between the channels of trade and advertising, and the similarity in the classes of prospective purchasers. They also support the conclusions that McGills acted with a subjective intent to trade on Venture's reputation and that Venture's mark is strong. Accordingly, only the sixth factor—evidence of actual consumer confusion—is potentially in dispute.

On appeal, McGills argues that Gallagher had no way of knowing whether or not his use of the Venture marks on the McGills website had been successful, i.e., whether the marks actually lured any internet consumer to the website. Thus, the company contends that summary judgment in Venture's favor was improper because there was no evidence of actual confusion. However, McGills' various protestations below and on appeal that there is no direct evidence of actual consumer confusion, even if accepted as true, are ultimately beside the point.

Although Venture might have attempted to adduce evidence of actual consumer confusion (e.g., internet user market surveys) in support of a favorable *Pignons* determination, the absence of such proof is not dispositive of the *Pignons* analysis. "[A] trademark holder's burden is to show likelihood of confusion, not actual confusion. While evidence of actual confusion is 'often deemed the best evidence of possible future confusion, proof of actual confusion is not essential to finding likelihood of confusion.' "

McGills' admissions regarding the other seven *Pignons* factors, particularly Gallagher's admission that his purpose in using the Venture marks was to lure customers to his site, permit us to conclude that no genuine dispute exists regarding the likelihood of confusion. As a result, Venture was entitled to summary judgment on the liability issue.

B. Award of Profits under the Lanham Act

[The court upheld an award of $230,339.17, McGills' net profits for the three-and-a-half-year period of infringement, holding that the district court's finding of willfulness was not clearly erroneous. Gallagher's "admittedly intentional use" was enough even though he didn't know this use was illegal. His "intentional concealment" of the marks by displaying them in the same color as the webpage background provided strong circumstantial evidence of "willfulness." Venture didn't have to show any harm to its own business. The court also upheld an attorney's fee award of $188,583.06, for similar reasons.]

*NOTES AND QUESTIONS*

*White-on-White Text.* White-on-white text was a trick that some website operators used around 2000 to include third-party trademarks into their website without showing those trademarks to users. Because it was an effort to game the search engine algorithms, many search engines reconfigured their algorithms to ignore white-on-white text. As a result, McGills' white-on-white text was probably as effective as the keyword metatags—that is to say, not at all. It's also not a good idea from a legal standpoint. *See* Agdia, Inc. v. Xia, 2017 WL 3438174 (N.D. Ind. 2017).

*Willfulness and Diversion.* McGills admitted that it was trying to get its web pages to show up when users searched for Venture Tape's trademarks. It seems clear that the court morally objected to McGills' behavior. But why?

Assume McGills succeeded in getting the search engines to index it for Venture Tape's trademarks. McGills apparently is a legitimate competitor of Venture Tape, and McGills's goal is to let Venture Tape's potential buyers of stained glass adhesive tape know that McGills can fulfill their needs as well, perhaps at a lower cost or with better quality. Are such efforts to educate potential consumers about competitive alternatives a good thing or a bad thing? What use was McGills entitled to make of Venture Tape's mark in order to inform consumers that McGills offered an alternative?

Were any consumers likely to be confused about the relationship between McGills and Venture Tape? Before any user clicks through to visit McGills, the user will see a search results page that contains a title, description and URL for each search result. As a result, users get a preview of what they are likely to find when they click on a link before they click, which makes their clicking decisions somewhat informed . *See* Eric Goldman, *Deregulating Relevancy in Internet Trademark Law*, 54 EMORY L.J. 507 (2005). If consumers thought it was worth checking out McGills' website after seeing the search results preview, isn't that a good thing? Or does the possibility that they might have thought McGills was a Venture Tape reseller still leave room for confusion?

*Remedies.* The court's damage award disgorged all of McGills' profits for a four-year period. Why was the court willing to impose such a harsh remedy?

*Keyword Metatags and Nominative Use. Playboy Enterprises, Inc. v. Welles,* 279 F.3d 796 (9th Cir. 2002) involved Terri Welles, who was *Playboy* magazine's Playmate of the Year 1981. She referenced this title in several ways in her website, including putting the words "Playboy" and "Playmate" in the keyword metatags of her website. The court rejected Playboy's trademark claims over the keyword metatags, concluding that Welles's references to "Playboy" and "Playmate" qualified as a protected nominative use because she had, in fact, been *Playboy*'s Playmate of the Year 1981 and was entitled to use that title in her self-promotion. In contrast, Welles's inclusion of the term "PMOY '81" as the web page's background (its "wallpaper") was not nominative use because such references were not necessary to identify Welles.

If a company references its competitor's trademark in a factually true statement (i.e., "our products compete with [third-party trademark]") in the keyword metatags, would that similarly qualify as nominative use? If the search engines will likely ignore the statement, would it matter?

*The Law Lags the Technology.* Courts properly educated about the demise of keyword metatags should find them legally immaterial. *See, e.g.*, Sazerac Brands LLC v. Peristyle LLC, 2017 WL 4558022 (E.D. Ky. 2017) ("Sazerac fails to explain why metatags should still form the basis for Lanham Act liability in light of major search engines' change in policy").

*Description Metatags.* Because search engines might publish the contents of description metatags verbatim, it makes sense to treat a description metatag's content as ad copy and run it through the same legal review as other ad copy. *See* North American Medical Corp. v. Axiom Worldwide, Inc., 522 F.3d 1211 (11th Cir. 2008).

### C.     Keyword Advertising

Keyword advertising has exploded into a $50+ billion/year industry. Google is by far the market leader, so we will focus on Google's practices. You are surely familiar with keyword advertisements on Google. They are presently displayed in the areas labeled "ads" at the top of the search results page and on the right-hand side when you enter search queries at Google, though Google routinely reconfigures various aspects of their presentation.

Google's main keyword advertising program is called AdWords. Generally, advertisers submit to Google a list of desired keywords, the associated ad copy, and an auction bid price for each keyword. When consumers enter a search query at Google, Google looks to see which advertisers have placed auction bids for the keywords in that query. If more than one advertiser has submitted a bid, Google conducts an auction to determine the display order for advertisers. When a person clicks on an ad, the advertiser pays Google for the click.*

However, the auction is not based solely on the advertisers' submitted bids. Google's revenue depends on click price multiplied by click quantity, so Google tries to estimate which ad ranking will maximize revenue. Google uses an "ad quality score" that acts as a proxy for consumers' propensity to click on a particular ad. Google displays keyword ads in an order determined by blending bid prices with ad quality scores.

Google runs another program called AdSense. AdSense allows third-party online publishers to display keyword advertising sourced by Google on their websites. Google then shares the revenues generated from this advertising with the publisher. When ads are displayed through AdSense, Google automatically analyzes the publisher's web page to isolate some keywords that describe the page's content. Google then auctions the keywords it has distilled from each page.

Some bids placed by advertisers are for keywords that contain third-party trademarks. For example, Volvo might place a bid to have its ad copy displayed when users search for the term "Mercedes."

---

* Google runs a "second price" auction, so the advertiser doesn't actually pay the amount it bid. Instead, the advertiser pays the next-highest amount bid by another advertiser.

Some trademark owners have objected to third-party advertisers appearing in response to "their" trademarks, especially competitors. This has led to numerous legal disputes.

In response to these disputes, and in an effort to reduce their own liability, the major search engines have voluntarily adopted policies about when they will permit advertising on keywords that contain third-party trademarks.

Google's *U.S. Trademark Policy* for AdWords does not restrict the bidding on any keywords due to trademark owner complaints, but it will restrict the appearance of the trademark in ad copy if requested by a trademark owner. However, even when requested, Google will not restrict the trademark in ad copy by "resellers," "informational sites," "authorized advertisers," and other specified situations.

Trademark owners routinely invoke search engine policies to limit third-party advertisers. Often, the search engine's remedies are sufficient to obviate any need for lawsuits.

Still, keyword advertising has spurred a substantial amount of litigation. Google and other search engines have been sued over two dozen times for *selling* trademarked keywords, but no court has definitively concluded that keyword sellers can be liable for trademark infringement. Given that in-court challenges to keyword selling have largely dried up, the practice appears de facto to be permitted.

*Buying* third-party trademarks for keyword advertising has also been the subject of countless lawsuits, but trademark owners rarely win those lawsuits. "[C]ourts have repeatedly found that the purchase of a competitor's marks as keywords alone, without additional behavior that confuses consumers, is not actionable." Alzheimer's Disease and Related Disorders Association, Inc. v. Alzheimer's Foundation of America, Inc., 2018 WL 1918618 (S.D.N.Y. 2018).

Advertisers may be more legally vulnerable when they include the third-party trademark in the keyword ad copy, but even in that case, advertisers routinely win. *See, e.g.*, Infostream Grp. Inc. v. Avid Life Media Inc., 2013 WL 6018030 (C.D. Cal. 2013) (granting motion to dismiss); Gen. Steel Domestic Sales, LLC v. Chumley, 2013 WL 1900562 (D. Colo. 2013) (defense win despite trademark use in ad copy).

The advertiser-favorable results can be substantially attributed to the following case, which wasn't a complete defense win but nevertheless eliminated a lot of doctrinal ambiguity that was giving hope to plaintiffs. The case illustrates the kinds of questions a court should ask in evaluating alleged consumer confusion from keyword advertising, and it shows a healthy skepticism towards the typical anti-technology and anti-consumer arguments advanced by trademark owners.

*Network Automation, Inc. v. Advanced System Concepts, Inc., 638 F.3d 1137 (9th Cir. 2011)*

"We must be acutely aware of excessive rigidity when applying the law in the Internet context; emerging technologies require a flexible approach."

501

Brookfield Commc'ns, Inc. v. West Coast Entm't Corp., 174 F.3d 1036, 1054 (9th Cir. 1999).

Network Automation ("Network") and Advanced Systems Concepts ("Systems") are both in the business of selling job scheduling and management software, and both advertise on the Internet. Network sells its software under the mark AutoMate, while Systems' product is sold under the registered trademark ActiveBatch. Network decided to advertise its product by purchasing certain keywords, such as "ActiveBatch," which when keyed into various search engines, most prominently Google and Microsoft Bing, produce a results page showing "www.NetworkAutomation.com" as a sponsored link. Systems' objection to Network's use of its trademark to interest viewers in Network's website gave rise to this trademark infringement action.

The district court was confronted with the question whether Network's use of ActiveBatch to advertise its products was a clever and legitimate use of readily available technology, such as Google's AdWords, or a likely violation of the Lanham Act, 15 U.S.C. § 1114. The court found a likelihood of initial interest confusion by applying the eight factors we established more than three decades ago in *AMF Inc. v. Sleekcraft Boats*, 599 F.2d 341 (9th Cir. 1979), and reasoning that the three most important factors in "cases involving the Internet" are (1) the similarity of the marks; (2) the relatedness of the goods; and (3) the marketing channel used. The court therefore issued a preliminary injunction against Network's use of the mark ActiveBatch.

Mindful that the sine qua non of trademark infringement is consumer confusion, and that the *Sleekcraft* factors are but a nonexhaustive list of factors relevant to determining the likelihood of consumer confusion, we conclude that Systems' showing of a likelihood of confusion was insufficient to support injunctive relief. Therefore, we vacate the injunction and reverse and remand.

I. FACTUAL AND PROCEDURAL BACKGROUND

Systems is a software engineering and consulting firm founded in 1981. It has used the ActiveBatch trademark since 2000, and it procured federal registration of the mark in 2001. Systems markets ActiveBatch software to businesses, which use the product to centralize and manage disparate tasks. Network is a software company founded in 1997 under the name Unisyn. Its signature product, AutoMate, also provides businesses with job scheduling, event monitoring, and related services. Network has approximately 15,000 total customers, and between 4,000 and 5,000 active customers, including Fortune 500 companies and mid-sized and small firms. The cost of a license to use AutoMate typically ranges from $995 to $10,995. There is no dispute that Network and Systems are direct competitors, or that ActiveBatch and AutoMate are directly competing products.

. . . Network purchased "ActiveBatch" as a keyword from Google AdWords and a comparable program offered by Microsoft's Bing search engine.

As a result, consumers searching for business software who enter "ActiveBatch" as a search term would locate a results page where the top objective results are links to Systems' own website and various articles about the product. In the "Sponsored Links" or "Sponsored Sites" section of the page, above or to the right of the regular results, users see Network's advertisement, either alone or alongside Systems' own sponsored link. The text of Network's advertisements begin with phrases such as "Job Scheduler," "Intuitive Job Scheduler," or "Batch Job Scheduling," and end with the company's web site address, www.NetworkAutomation.com. The middle line reads: "Windows Job Scheduling + Much More. Easy to Deploy, Scalable. D/L Trial." . . .

[Screenshot from the court's opinion]

[Screenshot taken March 17, 2011]

III. DISCUSSION . . .

To prevail on a claim of trademark infringement under the Lanham Act, 15 U.S.C. § 1114, a party "must prove: (1) that it has a protectible ownership interest in the mark; and (2) that the defendant's use of the mark is likely to cause consumer confusion."

Network does not contest the ownership or its use of the mark. . . .

This case, therefore, turns on whether Network's use of Systems' trademark is likely to cause consumer confusion. Network argues that its use of Systems' mark is legitimate "comparative, contextual advertising" which presents sophisticated consumers with clear choices. Systems characterizes Network's behavior differently, accusing it of misleading consumers by hijacking their attention with intentionally unclear advertisements. . . .

B.

Here we consider whether the use of another's trademark as a search engine keyword to trigger one's own product advertisement violates the Lanham Act. We begin by examining the *Sleekcraft* factors that are most relevant to the determination whether the use is likely to cause initial interest confusion.[4] While the district court analyzed each of the *Sleekcraft* factors, it identified the three most important factors as (1) the similarity of the marks, (2) the relatedness of the goods or services, and (3) the simultaneous use of the Web as a marketing channel, for any case addressing trademark infringement on the Internet. . . .

However, we did not intend *Brookfield* to be read so expansively as to forever enshrine these three factors—now often referred to as the "Internet trinity" or "Internet troika"—as the test for trademark infringement on the Internet. *Brookfield* was the first to present a claim of initial interest confusion on the Internet; we recognized at the time it would not be the last, and so emphasized flexibility over rigidity. Depending on the facts of each specific case arising on the Internet, other factors may emerge as more illuminating on the question of consumer confusion. . . .

The "troika" is a particularly poor fit for the question presented here. The potential infringement in this context arises from the risk that while using Systems' mark to search for information about its product, a consumer might be confused by a results page that shows a competitor's advertisement on the same screen, when that advertisement does not clearly identify the source or its product.

. . . [B]ecause the sine qua non of trademark infringement is consumer confusion, when we examine initial interest confusion, the owner of the mark must demonstrate likely confusion, not mere diversion. . . .

1. Strength of the Mark

---

[4] Systems' argument rests only on the theory of initial interest confusion. It does not argue source confusion.

"The stronger a mark—meaning the more likely it is to be remembered and associated in the public mind with the mark's owner—the greater the protection it is accorded by the trademark laws." . . .

This factor is probative of confusion here because a consumer searching for a generic term is more likely to be searching for a product category. *See* [*Brookfield*] at 1058 n. 19 ("Generic terms are those used by the public to refer generally to the product rather than a particular brand of the product."). That consumer is more likely to expect to encounter links and advertisements from a variety of sources. By contrast, a user searching for a distinctive term is more likely to be looking for a particular product, and therefore could be more susceptible to confusion when sponsored links appear that advertise a similar product from a different source. On the other hand, if the ordinary consumers of this particular product are particularly sophisticated and knowledgeable, they might also be aware that Systems is the source of ActiveBatch software and not be confused at all.

The district court acknowledged that the parties failed to address the strength of the mark, but it concluded that the factor favors Systems. It reasoned that ActiveBatch is a suggestive mark because it "requires a mental leap from the mark to the product," and as a registered trademark it is "inherently distinctive." We agree.† Because the mark is both Systems' product name and a suggestive federally registered trademark, consumers searching for the term are presumably looking for its specific product, and not a category of goods. Nonetheless, that may not be the end of the inquiry about this factor, as the sophistication of the consumers of the product may also play a role. . . .

2. Proximity of the Goods

"Related goods are generally more likely than unrelated goods to confuse the public as to the producers of the goods." "[T]he danger presented is that the public will mistakenly assume there is an association between the producers of the related goods, though no such association exists."

. . . However, the proximity of the goods would become less important if advertisements are clearly labeled or consumers exercise a high degree of care, because rather than being misled, the consumer would merely be confronted with choices among similar products. [*Playboy*] at 1035 (Berzon, J., concurring) ("[S]uch choices do not constitute trademark infringement off the internet, and I cannot understand why they should on the internet.").

Because the products at issue here are virtually interchangeable, this factor may be helpful, but it must be considered in conjunction with the labeling and appearance of the advertisements and the degree of care exercised by the consumers of the ActiveBatch software. By weighing this factor in

---

† [Editor's note: Unfortunately, the district court and the appeals court are wrong. A registered mark is presumed *distinctive*, that is, presumed to identify the source of a product or service; it is not necessarily *inherently* distinctive, automatically telling consumers that it identifies source. It might have *acquired* distinctiveness over time, so consumers learned that it identifies source, as with AMERICAN AIRLINES® or the shape of the Coca-Cola bottle. While this is not dispositive here, the error demonstrates some of the challenges courts face in applying trademark law.]

isolation and failing to consider whether the parties' status as direct competitors would actually lead to a likelihood of confusion, the district court allowed this factor to weigh too heavily in the analysis.

### 3. Similarity of the Marks

"[T]he more similar the marks in terms of appearance, sound, and meaning, the greater the likelihood of confusion." . . . "Similarity of the marks is tested on three levels: sight, sound, and meaning. Each must be considered as they are encountered in the marketplace."

In *Sleekcraft*, we concluded that the marks "Sleekcraft" and "Slickcraft" were similar in terms of sight, sound, and meaning by examining the actual situations in which consumers were likely to read, hear, and consider the meaning of the terms. Such an inquiry is impossible here where the consumer does not confront two distinct trademarks. . . . Again, however, because the consumer keys in Systems' trademark, which results in Network's sponsored link, depending on the labeling and appearance of the advertisement, including whether it identifies Network's own mark, and the degree of care and sophistication of the consumer, it could be helpful in determining initial interest confusion.

### 4. Evidence of Actual Confusion

"[A] showing of actual confusion among significant numbers of consumers provides strong support for the likelihood of confusion." However, "actual confusion is not necessary to a finding of likelihood of confusion under the Lanham Act." Indeed, "[p]roving actual confusion is difficult . . . and the courts have often discounted such evidence because it was unclear or insubstantial."

. . . As the district court noted, neither Network nor Systems provided evidence regarding actual confusion, which is not surprising given the procedural posture. Therefore, while this is a relevant factor for determining the likelihood of confusion in keyword advertising cases, its importance is diminished at the preliminary injunction stage of the proceedings. The district court correctly concluded that this factor should be accorded no weight.

### 5. Marketing Channels

"Convergent marketing channels increase the likelihood of confusion." In *Sleekcraft*, the two products were sold in niche marketplaces, including boat shows, specialty retail outlets, and trade magazines. However, this factor becomes less important when the marketing channel is less obscure. Today, it would be the rare commercial retailer that did not advertise online, and the shared use of a ubiquitous marketing channel does not shed much light on the likelihood of consumer confusion. *See Playboy*, 354 F.3d at 1028 ("Given the broad use of the Internet today, the same could be said for countless companies. Thus, this factor merits little weight.").

Therefore, the district court's determination that because both parties advertise on the Internet this factor weighed in favor of Systems was incorrect.

### 6. Type of Goods and Degree of Care

"Low consumer care . . . increases the likelihood of confusion." "In assessing the likelihood of confusion to the public, the standard used by the courts is the typical buyer exercising ordinary caution. . . . When the buyer has expertise in the field, a higher standard is proper though it will not preclude a finding that confusion is likely. Similarly, when the goods are expensive, the buyer can be expected to exercise greater care in his purchases; again, though, confusion may still be likely."

The nature of the goods and the type of consumer is highly relevant to determining the likelihood of confusion in the keyword advertising context. A sophisticated consumer of business software exercising a high degree of care is more likely to understand the mechanics of Internet search engines and the nature of sponsored links, whereas an un-savvy consumer exercising less care is more likely to be confused. The district court determined that this factor weighed in Systems' favor because "there is generally a low degree of care exercised by Internet consumers." However, the degree of care analysis cannot begin and end at the marketing channel. We still must consider the nature and cost of the goods, and whether "the products being sold are marketed primarily to expert buyers." . . .

We have recently acknowledged that the default degree of consumer care is becoming more heightened as the novelty of the Internet evaporates and online commerce becomes commonplace. In *Toyota Motor Sales v. Tabari*, 610 F.3d 1171 (9th Cir. 2010), we vacated a preliminary injunction that prohibited a pair of automobile brokers from using Toyota's "Lexus" mark in their domain names. We determined that it was unlikely that a reasonably prudent consumer would be confused into believing that a domain name that included a product name would necessarily have a formal affiliation with the maker of the product, as "[c]onsumers who use the internet for shopping are generally quite sophisticated about such matters." The *Tabari* panel reasoned,

> [I]n the age of FIOS, cable modems, DSL and T1 lines, reasonable, prudent and experienced internet consumers are accustomed to such exploration by trial and error. They skip from site to site, ready to hit the back button whenever they're not satisfied with a site's contents. They fully expect to find some sites that aren't what they imagine based on a glance at the domain name or search engine summary. Outside the special case of . . . domains that actively claim affiliation with the trademark holder, consumers don't form any firm expectations about the sponsorship of a website until they've seen the landing page—if then.

We further explained that we expect consumers searching for expensive products online to be even more sophisticated.

Therefore the district court improperly concluded that this factor weighed in Systems' favor based on a conclusion reached by our court more than a decade ago . . . that Internet users on the whole exercise a low degree of care. While the statement may have been accurate then, we suspect that there are many contexts in which it no longer holds true.

7. Defendant's Intent

"When the alleged infringer knowingly adopts a mark similar to another's, reviewing courts presume that the defendant can accomplish his purpose: that is, that the public will be deceived." Nevertheless, we have also "recognized that liability for infringement may not be imposed for using a registered trademark in connection with truthful comparative advertising."

Therefore, much like the proximity of the goods, the defendant's intent may be relevant here, but only insofar as it bolsters a finding that the use of the trademark serves to mislead consumers rather than truthfully inform them of their choice of products. The district court incorrectly considered the intent factor in isolation, and concluded that it weighed in Systems' favor without first determining that Network intended to deceive consumers rather than compare its product to ActiveBatch.

8. Likelihood of Expansion of the Product Lines

. . . Where two companies are direct competitors, this factor is unimportant. Therefore, the district court correctly declined to consider the likelihood of expansion.

9. Other Relevant Factors

The eight Sleekcraft factors are "not exhaustive. Other variables may come into play depending on the particular facts presented." In the keyword advertising context the "likelihood of confusion will ultimately turn on what the consumer saw on the screen and reasonably believed, given the context." Hearts on Fire Co. v. Blue Nile, Inc., 603 F. Supp. 2d 274, 289 (D. Mass. 2009).[6] In *Playboy*, we found it important that the consumers saw banner advertisements that were "confusingly labeled or not labeled at all." We noted that clear labeling "might eliminate the likelihood of initial interest confusion that exists in this case."

The appearance of the advertisements and their surrounding context on the user's screen are similarly important here. The district court correctly examined the text of Network's sponsored links, concluding that the advertisements did not clearly identify their source. However, the district court did not consider the surrounding context. In *Playboy*, we also found it important that Netscape's search engine did not clearly segregate the sponsored advertisements from the objective results. Here, even if Network has not clearly identified itself in the text of its ads, Google and Bing have partitioned their search results pages so that the advertisements appear in separately labeled sections for "sponsored" links. The labeling and appearance of the advertisements as they appear on the results page includes more than the text of the advertisement, and must be considered as a whole.

---

[6] The *Hearts on Fire* court identified a new seven-factor test to determine whether there is a likelihood of consumer confusion arising from a firm's use of a competitor's trademark as a search engine keyword triggering its own sponsored links. Network urges us to adopt the *Hearts on Fire* factors. While we agree that the decision's reasoning is useful, we decline to add another multi-factor test to the extant eight-factor *Sleekcraft* test.

## C.

Given the nature of the alleged infringement here, the most relevant factors to the analysis of the likelihood of confusion are: (1) the strength of the mark; (2) the evidence of actual confusion; (3) the type of goods and degree of care likely to be exercised by the purchaser; and (4) the labeling and appearance of the advertisements and the surrounding context on the screen displaying the results page.

The district court did not weigh the *Sleekcraft* factors flexibly to match the specific facts of this case. It relied on the Internet "troika," which is highly illuminating in the context of domain names, but which fails to discern whether there is a likelihood of confusion in a keywords case. Because the linchpin of trademark infringement is consumer confusion, the district court abused its discretion in issuing the injunction. . . .

*NOTES AND QUESTIONS*

*The Initial Interest Confusion Doctrine.* What is "initial interest confusion," and how does the doctrine enhance the court's analysis? If you did not fully understand the court's references to the doctrine, you are not alone. Courts have articulated dozens of different formulations of the doctrine; each circuit has its own articulation of the doctrine; and not infrequently, there are *intra*-circuit inconsistencies in the doctrine's articulation. *See* Eric Goldman, *Deregulating Relevancy in Internet Trademark Law*, 54 EMORY L.J. 507 (2005).

Although initial interest confusion cases date back to the early 1970s, the most famous statement of the initial interest confusion doctrine comes from the Ninth Circuit's *Brookfield* case:

> use of another's trademark in a manner reasonably calculated to capture initial consumer attention, even though no actual sale is finally completed as a result of the confusion.

However, as you saw in the *Network Automation* case, the Ninth Circuit does not apply the doctrine as broadly as that definition might imply.

Although trademark owners routinely claim initial interest confusion, and although it used to be a serious threat to the defense even when purchase confusion was obviously unlikely, the doctrine almost never helps the trademark owner win its case anymore.

In one particularly striking case, *1-800 Contacts, Inc. v. Lens.com, Inc.*, 722 F.3d 1229 (10th Cir. 2013), the court articulated a very broad definition of initial interest confusion, but then imposed an almost impossibly high evidentiary standard for proving it. The appeals court treated an ad's clickthrough rate as a dispositive proxy for a survey measuring consumer confusion. Since a 3% clickthrough rate for an online ad would be an astonishing success, while a plaintiff typically needs well over 10% confusion to prevail, an ad's low clickthrough rates will almost always indicate a *lack* of initial interest confusion. So while trademark owners will continue to assert initial interest confusion, their success rate with the doctrine will likely be trivial.

*Inferring Searcher Intent from Their Keywords.* The *Network Automation* court says:

> Because the mark is both Systems' product name and a suggestive federally registered
> trademark, consumers searching for the term are presumably looking for its specific product,
> and not a category of goods.

There are at least two problems with this statement. First, this is an appellate court making an
empirical presumption about consumer behavior. Notice that the court did not cite any research or
provide any other support for this presumption. How does this court know this to be true? Why is an
appellate court making this categorical statement without any support? What if the court is actually
wrong about consumer behavior?

Second, the court's presumption *is* almost certainly wrong. Can you think of circumstances where
consumers might use a trademark to search for a category of goods?

One circumstance: a category of goods where there is a strong market leader and few well-accepted
synonyms to describe the category. Consider, for example, the "Clapper" (some of you may remember
the advertisements "Clap On! Clap Off! The CLAPPER!!!" *See*
http://www.youtube.com/watch?v=cfgN5tUgjb8). How would you describe that category of goods? If
you can't think of a succinct but accurate term for the product category, you might consider doing a
keyword search for "the Clapper" and be delighted if you discovered multiple competitors in the
niche. Another infomercial example along these lines: the product advertised with the famous tagline
"I've fallen and I can't get up."

Another circumstance: a category of goods where there are multiple price points and quality levels,
and a consumer seeks to find products competing at a desired level of quality. For example, if a
consumer has a positive experience with a borrowed Nikon digital camera and is looking to acquire a
digital camera of like quality, the consumer might use the search term "Nikon" (or the specific
product name) as an entry point to discover all competitive options providing a similar quality.

Even if consumers aren't seeking a category of goods when they use a trademark, they still might be
looking for something other than the trademarked product. *See* Goldman, *Deregulating Relevancy*,
*supra* (giving examples of many possible searcher intents from a single trademark used as a search
term).

*What If the Advertiser Never Buys the Trademark at All?* Assume that BlueJet, an airline, buys the
keyword "airlines" and enables "broad matching," which causes the ad to appear for any search
query that contains the keyword, even if the query contains other words. For example, a search for
"United Airlines" or "Delta Airlines" may return ads for BlueJet because of the word "airlines," not
"united" or "delta." Is there a claim for trademark infringement even though BlueJet never
purchased the trademarks as keywords? *See, e.g.*, Rhino Sports, Inc. v. Sport Court, Inc., 2007 WL
1302745 (D. Ariz. 2007).

*Does Competitive Keyword Advertising Actually Hurt Trademark Owners?* David Franklyn & David
A. Hyman, *Trademarks as Keywords: Much Ado About Something?*, 26 HARV. J.L. & TECH. 481

(2013), showed how consumers adopt heterogeneous search tactics. While many use brand names to search for those brands, some don't, and even the ones initially interested in a particular brand are often interested in alternatives. Consumers aren't generally confused about the source or sponsorship of competitors' links in Google results pages. What they are often confused about, and what might be appropriately regulated by general consumer protection law, is which parts of the search results are "organic" and which parts are paid ads. However, this isn't a trademark concern.

*Publicity Rights Analogue* (see Chapter 13). *Habush v. Cannon*, 346 Wis.2d 709 (Wis. App. Ct. 2013), held that buying a person's name (in that case, a rival lawyer) as a keyword for competitive advertising didn't violate the person's publicity rights. *See generally* Eric Goldman & Angel Reyes III, *Regulation of Lawyers' Use of Competitive Keyword Advertising*, 2016 U. ILL. L. REV. 103.

CHAPTER 12: COMPETITIVE RESTRICTIONS

---

As the last two chapters illustrated, copyright and trademark law can restrict advertiser behavior. This chapter looks at three other ways—trade secrets, patents, and idea submission principles—that competitors and others can use intangible rights to limit advertiser behavior. This chapter concludes with a brief look at antitrust as another limit on anticompetitive behavior.

## 1.    Trade Secrets

### A.    An Overview of Trade Secret Law

A "trade secret" is information that derives value because it is secret. Think of a trade secret as information only one business knows that provides it some competitive advantage. So long as the business derives that advantage by keeping the information secret, the business can prevent others from misappropriating the information, which in turn helps preserve that competitive advantage.

Trade secrets last as long as the information is valuable and secret. As a result, it is possible for a trade secret to be protected perpetually. For example, the formula for making Coca-Cola soda has been protected as a trade secret for over 120 years (since 1886), with no end in sight.* In contrast, patents have a finite life of less than 20 years, after which everyone is free to replicate the invention and compete directly with the inventor. By keeping the formula a trade secret instead of patenting it, Coca-Cola has obtained over 100 extra years of protection (so far) from direct competition.

Although trade secrets are protected from misappropriation by corporate espionage or misuse by former employees, they are not protected from independent invention or reverse engineering. So if a competitor can figure out the trade secret independently or through reverse engineering, the trade secret "owner" can do nothing to stop the competitor from using that information to compete more effectively. No one has independently derived the exact recipe for Coca-Cola, but if someone did, trade secret law would be powerless to stop them from making soda tasting exactly like Coca-Cola.

In general, a trade secret loses its protection when it is no longer a secret. For example, published information is no longer a trade secret. A trade secret can also lose protection when the owner does not take reasonable efforts to ensure its secrecy. However, if a secret is inadvertently disclosed, or disseminated after being misappropriated despite the owner's reasonable efforts, the courts will often protect the information due to the owner's diligence.

---

\* *But see Original Recipe*, THIS AMERICAN LIFE (Feb. 11, 2011), http://www.thisamericanlife.org/radio-archives/episode/427/original-recipe, suggesting that the original Coca-Cola formula has in fact been disclosed.

Frequently, a trade secret owner wants or needs to share the trade secret with certain business partners, such as vendors or customers. To avoid losing trade secret status, the owner can share the information under a trade secret license that restricts the recipients' use and disclosure of the information. These trade secret licenses can take many forms, but usually the licenses are characterized as a non-disclosure agreements (NDAs) or confidentiality clauses in the parties' contracts. These confidentiality restrictions can extend to non-trade secret information (i.e., information that the discloser provides to the recipient even if the information does not qualify as a trade secret), although non-secret information is usually excluded from the license. Trade secret licenses are ubiquitous throughout the business world.

Trade secrets are protected by both state and federal law. Almost all states have adopted some version of the "Uniform Trade Secret Act," but adoptions are not entirely uniform. In partial response to this lack of uniformity, in 2016, Congress enacted the Defend Trade Secrets Act (DTSA). The DTSA does not preempt state laws, and trade secret owners routinely bring both state and DTSA claims simultaneously.

## B.    Future Marketing Plans as a Trade Secret

Future marketing plans—such as new products being developed and launched—frequently qualify as a trade secret. Premature disclosure of this information can tip off competitors about a company's plans, allowing the competitors to quickly mimic the plans (and thereby reduce or eliminate any first-mover advantage) or make countermoves. Therefore, trade secret protection can have significant value to marketers.

The following case involves an employee departing to a competitor. The former employer fights back to protect the employee's knowledge of future marketing plans. Pay close attention to what the court thinks is protectable as a trade secret and how the court fashions a legal tool to protect it. How does this employee's transition to a competitor differ from the ordinary movement of employees within an industry?

*PepsiCo, Inc. v. Redmond, 54 F.3d 1262 (7th Cir. 1995)*

. . . I.

The facts of this case lay [*sic*] against a backdrop of fierce beverage-industry competition between Quaker and PepsiCo, especially in "sports drinks" and "new age drinks." Quaker's sports drink, "Gatorade," is the dominant brand in its market niche. PepsiCo introduced its Gatorade rival, "All Sport," in March and April of 1994, but sales of All Sport lag far behind those of Gatorade. Quaker also has the lead in the new-age-drink category. Although PepsiCo has entered the market through joint ventures with the Thomas J. Lipton Company and Ocean Spray Cranberries, Inc., Quaker purchased Snapple Beverage Corp., a large new-age-drink maker, in late 1994. PepsiCo's products have about half of Snapple's market share. Both companies see 1995 as an important year for their products: PepsiCo has developed extensive plans to increase its market presence, while Quaker is trying to solidify its lead by integrating Gatorade and Snapple distribution. Meanwhile, PepsiCo and

Quaker each face strong competition from Coca Cola Co., which has its own sports drink, "PowerAde," and which introduced its own Snapple-rival, "Fruitopia," in 1994, as well as from independent beverage producers.

William Redmond, Jr., worked for PepsiCo in its Pepsi-Cola North America division ("PCNA") from 1984 to 1994. Redmond became the General Manager of the Northern California Business Unit in June, 1993, and was promoted one year later to General Manager of the business unit covering all of California, a unit having annual revenues of more than 500 million dollars and representing twenty percent of PCNA's profit for all of the United States.

Redmond's relatively high-level position at PCNA gave him access to inside information and trade secrets. Redmond, like other PepsiCo management employees, had signed a confidentiality agreement with PepsiCo. That agreement stated in relevant part that he

> w[ould] not disclose at any time, to anyone other than officers or employees of [PepsiCo], or make use of, confidential information relating to the business of [PepsiCo] . . . obtained while in the employ of [PepsiCo], which shall not be generally known or available to the public or recognized as standard practices.

Donald Uzzi, who had left PepsiCo in the beginning of 1994 to become the head of Quaker's Gatorade division, began courting Redmond for Quaker in May, 1994. Redmond met in Chicago with Quaker officers in August, 1994, and on October 20, 1994, Quaker, through Uzzi, offered Redmond the position of Vice President-On Premise Sales for Gatorade. Redmond did not then accept the offer but continued to negotiate for more money. Throughout this time, Redmond kept his dealings with Quaker secret from his employers at PCNA.

On November 8, 1994, Uzzi extended Redmond a written offer for the position of Vice President-Field Operations for Gatorade and Redmond accepted. . . .

On November 10, 1994, Redmond met with Barnes and told her that he had decided to accept the Quaker offer and was resigning from PCNA.

. . . PepsiCo filed this diversity suit on November 16, 1994, seeking a temporary restraining order to enjoin Redmond from assuming his duties at Quaker and to prevent him from disclosing trade secrets or confidential information to his new employer. The district court granted PepsiCo's request that same day but dissolved the order sua sponte two days later, after determining that PepsiCo had failed to meet its burden of establishing that it would suffer irreparable harm. The court found that PepsiCo's fears about Redmond were based upon a mistaken understanding of his new position at Quaker and that the likelihood that Redmond would improperly reveal any confidential information did not "rise above mere speculation."

From November 23, 1994, to December 1, 1994, the district court conducted a preliminary injunction hearing on the same matter. At the hearing, PepsiCo offered evidence of a number of trade secrets and confidential information it desired protected and to which Redmond was privy. First, it identified PCNA's "Strategic Plan," an annually revised document that contains PCNA's plans to compete, its financial goals, and its strategies for manufacturing, production, marketing, packaging, and distribution for the coming three years. Strategic Plans are developed by Weatherup and his staff with input from PCNA's general managers, including Redmond, and are considered highly confidential. The Strategic Plan derives much of its value from the fact that it is secret and competitors cannot anticipate PCNA's next moves. PCNA managers received the most recent Strategic Plan at a meeting in July, 1994, a meeting Redmond attended. PCNA also presented information at the meeting regarding its plans for Lipton ready-to-drink teas and for All Sport for 1995 and beyond, including new flavors and package sizes.

Second, PepsiCo pointed to PCNA's Annual Operating Plan ("AOP") as a trade secret. The AOP is a national plan for a given year and guides PCNA's financial goals, marketing plans, promotional event calendars, growth expectations, and operational changes in that year. The AOP, which is implemented by PCNA unit General Managers, including Redmond, contains specific information regarding all PCNA initiatives for the forthcoming year. The AOP bears a label that reads "Private and Confidential—Do Not Reproduce" and is considered highly confidential by PCNA managers.

In particular, the AOP contains important and sensitive information about "pricing architecture"— how PCNA prices its products in the marketplace. Pricing architecture covers both a national pricing approach and specific price points for given areas. Pricing architecture also encompasses PCNA's objectives for All Sport and its new age drinks with reference to trade channels, package sizes and other characteristics of both the products and the customers at which the products are aimed. Additionally, PCNA's pricing architecture outlines PCNA's customer development agreements. These agreements between PCNA and retailers provide for the retailer's participation in certain merchandising activities for PCNA products. As with other information contained in the AOP, pricing architecture is highly confidential and would be extremely valuable to a competitor. Knowing PCNA's pricing architecture would allow a competitor to anticipate PCNA's pricing moves and underbid PCNA strategically whenever and wherever the competitor so desired. PepsiCo introduced evidence that Redmond had detailed knowledge of PCNA's pricing architecture and that he was aware of and had been involved in preparing PCNA's customer development agreements with PCNA's California and California-based national customers. Indeed, PepsiCo showed that Redmond, as the General Manager for California, would have been responsible for implementing the pricing architecture guidelines for his business unit.

PepsiCo also showed that Redmond had intimate knowledge of PCNA "attack plans" for specific markets. Pursuant to these plans, PCNA dedicates extra funds to supporting its brands against other brands in selected markets. To use a hypothetical example, PCNA might budget an additional $500,000 to spend in Chicago at a particular time to help All Sport close its market gap with Gatorade. Testimony and documents demonstrated Redmond's awareness of these plans and his participation in drafting some of them.

Finally, PepsiCo offered evidence of PCNA trade secrets regarding innovations in its selling and delivery systems. Under this plan, PCNA is testing a new delivery system that could give PCNA an advantage over its competitors in negotiations with retailers over shelf space and merchandising. Redmond has knowledge of this secret because PCNA, which has invested over a million dollars in developing the system during the past two years, is testing the pilot program in California.

515

Having shown Redmond's intimate knowledge of PCNA's plans for 1995, PepsiCo argued that Redmond would inevitably disclose that information to Quaker in his new position, at which he would have substantial input as to Gatorade and Snapple pricing, costs, margins, distribution systems, products, packaging and marketing, and could give Quaker an unfair advantage in its upcoming skirmishes with PepsiCo. Redmond and Quaker countered that Redmond's primary initial duties at Quaker as Vice President-Field Operations would be to integrate Gatorade and Snapple distribution and then to manage that distribution as well as the promotion, marketing and sales of these products. Redmond asserted that the integration would be conducted according to a pre-existing plan and that his special knowledge of PCNA strategies would be irrelevant. This irrelevance would derive not only from the fact that Redmond would be implementing pre-existing plans but also from the fact that PCNA and Quaker distribute their products in entirely different ways: PCNA's distribution system is vertically integrated (i.e., PCNA owns the system) and delivers its product directly to retailers, while Quaker ships its product to wholesalers and customer warehouses and relies on independent distributors. The defendants also pointed out that Redmond had signed a confidentiality agreement with Quaker preventing him from disclosing "any confidential information belonging to others," as well as the Quaker Code of Ethics, which prohibits employees from engaging in "illegal or improper acts to acquire a competitor's trade secrets." Redmond additionally promised at the hearing that should he be faced with a situation at Quaker that might involve the use or disclosure of PCNA information, he would seek advice from Quaker's in-house counsel and would refrain from making the decision.

PepsiCo responded to the defendants' representations by pointing out that the evidence did not show that Redmond would simply be implementing a business plan already in place. On the contrary, as of November, 1994, the plan to integrate Gatorade and Snapple distribution consisted of a single distributorship agreement and a two-page "contract terms summary." Such a basic plan would not lend itself to widespread application among the over 300 independent Snapple distributors. Since the integration process would likely face resistance from Snapple distributors and Quaker had no scheme to deal with this probability, Redmond, as the person in charge of the integration, would likely have a great deal of influence on the process. PepsiCo further argued that Snapple's 1995 marketing and promotion plans had not necessarily been completed prior to Redmond's joining Quaker, that Uzzi disagreed with portions of the Snapple plans, and that the plans were open to re-evaluation. Uzzi testified that the plan for integrating Gatorade and Snapple distribution is something that would happen in the future. Redmond would therefore likely have input in remaking these plans, and if he did, he would inevitably be making decisions with PCNA's strategic plans and 1995 AOP in mind. Moreover, PepsiCo continued, diverging testimony made it difficult to know exactly what Redmond would be doing at Quaker. Redmond described his job as "managing the entire sales effort of Gatorade at the field level, possibly including strategic planning," and at least at one point considered his job to be equivalent to that of a Chief Operating Officer. Uzzi, on the other hand, characterized Redmond's position as "primarily and initially to restructure and integrate our—the distribution systems for Snapple and for Gatorade, as per our distribution plan" and then to "execute marketing, promotion and sales plans in the marketplace." Uzzi also denied having given Redmond detailed information about any business plans, while Redmond described such a plan in depth in an affidavit and said that he received the information from Uzzi. Thus, PepsiCo asserted, Redmond would have a high position in the Gatorade hierarchy, and PCNA trade secrets and confidential information would necessarily influence his decisions. Even if Redmond could somehow refrain from relying on this information, as he promised he would, his actions in leaving PCNA, Uzzi's actions in hiring Redmond, and the varying testimony regarding Redmond's new responsibilities, made Redmond's assurances to PepsiCo less than comforting.

On December 15, 1994, the district court issued an order enjoining Redmond from assuming his position at Quaker through May, 1995, and permanently from using or disclosing any PCNA trade secrets or confidential information. The court entered its findings of fact and conclusions of law on January 26, 1995, nunc pro tunc December 15, 1994. The court, which completely adopted PepsiCo's position, found that Redmond's new job posed a clear threat of misappropriation of trade secrets and confidential information that could be enjoined under Illinois statutory and common law. The court also emphasized Redmond's lack of forthrightness both in his activities before accepting his job with Quaker and in his testimony as factors leading the court to believe the threat of misappropriation was real. This appeal followed.

II. . . .

A.

The Illinois Trade Secrets Act ("ITSA"), which governs the trade secret issues in this case, provides that a court may enjoin the "actual or threatened misappropriation" of a trade secret. A party seeking an injunction must therefore prove both the existence of a trade secret and the misappropriation. The defendants' appeal focuses solely on misappropriation; although the defendants only reluctantly refer to PepsiCo's marketing and distribution plans as trade secrets, they do not seriously contest that this information falls under the ITSA.[5]

The question of threatened or inevitable misappropriation in this case lies at the heart of a basic tension in trade secret law. Trade secret law serves to protect "standards of commercial morality" and "encourage [ ] invention and innovation" while maintaining "the public interest in having free and open competition in the manufacture and sale of unpatented goods." Yet that same law should not prevent workers from pursuing their livelihoods when they leave their current positions. . . .

This tension is particularly exacerbated when a plaintiff sues to prevent not the actual misappropriation of trade secrets but the mere threat that it will occur. While the ITSA plainly permits a court to enjoin the threat of misappropriation of trade secrets, there is little law in Illinois or in this circuit establishing what constitutes threatened or inevitable misappropriation. . . . [Editor's note: The court then discussed two precedents, *Teradyne* and *AMP*].

---

[5] Under the ITSA, trade secret "means information, including but not limited to, technical or non-technical data, a formula, pattern, compilation, program, device, method, technique, drawing, process, financial data, or list of actual or potential customers that:
(1) is sufficiently secret to derive economic value, actual or potential, from not generally being known to other persons who can obtain economic value from its disclosure or use; and
(2) is the subject of efforts that are reasonable under the circumstances to maintain its secrecy or confidentiality." .
. .

. . . [A] plaintiff may prove a claim of trade secret misappropriation by demonstrating that defendant's new employment will inevitably lead him to rely on the plaintiff's trade secrets. The defendants are incorrect that Illinois law does not allow a court to enjoin the "inevitable" disclosure of trade secrets. Questions remain, however, as to what constitutes inevitable misappropriation and whether PepsiCo's submissions rise above those of the *Teradyne* and *AMP* plaintiffs and meet that standard. We hold that they do.

PepsiCo presented substantial evidence at the preliminary injunction hearing that Redmond possessed extensive and intimate knowledge about PCNA's strategic goals for 1995 in sports drinks and new age drinks. The district court concluded on the basis of that presentation that unless Redmond possessed an uncanny ability to compartmentalize information, he would necessarily be making decisions about Gatorade and Snapple by relying on his knowledge of PCNA trade secrets. It is not the "general skills and knowledge acquired during his tenure with" PepsiCo that PepsiCo seeks to keep from falling into Quaker's hands, but rather "the particularized plans or processes developed by [PCNA] and disclosed to him while the employer-employee relationship existed, which are unknown to others in the industry and which give the employer an advantage over his competitors." The *Teradyne* and *AMP* plaintiffs could do nothing more than assert that skilled employees were taking their skills elsewhere; PepsiCo has done much more.

Admittedly, PepsiCo has not brought a traditional trade secret case, in which a former employee has knowledge of a special manufacturing process or customer list and can give a competitor an unfair advantage by transferring the technology or customers to that competitor. PepsiCo has not contended that Quaker has stolen the All Sport formula or its list of distributors. Rather PepsiCo has asserted that Redmond cannot help but rely on PCNA trade secrets as he helps plot Gatorade and Snapple's new course, and that these secrets will enable Quaker to achieve a substantial advantage by knowing exactly how PCNA will price, distribute, and market its sports drinks and new age drinks and being able to respond strategically. This type of trade secret problem may arise less often, but it nevertheless falls within the realm of trade secret protection under the present circumstances.

Quaker and Redmond assert that they have not and do not intend to use whatever confidential information Redmond has by virtue of his former employment. They point out that Redmond has already signed an agreement with Quaker not to disclose any trade secrets or confidential information gleaned from his earlier employment. They also note with regard to distribution systems that even if Quaker wanted to steal information about PCNA's distribution plans, they would be completely useless in attempting to integrate the Gatorade and Snapple beverage lines.

The defendants' arguments fall somewhat short of the mark. Again, the danger of misappropriation in the present case is not that Quaker threatens to use PCNA's secrets to create distribution systems or co-opt PCNA's advertising and marketing ideas. Rather, PepsiCo believes that Quaker, unfairly armed with knowledge of PCNA's plans, will be able to anticipate its distribution, packaging, pricing, and marketing moves. Redmond and Quaker even concede that Redmond might be faced with a decision that could be influenced by certain confidential information that he obtained while at PepsiCo. In other words, PepsiCo finds itself in the position of a coach, one of whose players has left, playbook in hand, to join the opposing team before the big game. Quaker and Redmond's protestations that their distribution systems and plans are entirely different from PCNA's are thus not really responsive. . . .

For the foregoing reasons, we affirm the district court's order enjoining Redmond from assuming his responsibilities at Quaker through May, 1995, and preventing him forever from disclosing PCNA trade secrets and confidential information.

*NOTES AND QUESTIONS*

*The Inevitable Disclosure Doctrine.* The court defines the "inevitable disclosure" doctrine as occurring when "defendant's new employment will inevitably lead him to rely on the plaintiff's trade secrets." This case is a flagship example of the doctrine.

PepsiCo always could sue Redmond and Quaker for using any PepsiCo proprietary information if that actually happened. But, rather than waiting for ex post enforcement of a violation, the inevitable disclosure doctrine assumes that Redmond cannot avoid spilling the beans. An injunction keeps him from being put in a position where trade secrets inevitably will be disclosed.

By making a categorical assumption that trade secrets will be leaked regardless of the employee's and employer's efforts not to do so, the inevitable disclosure doctrine has significant effects on the labor market, both for employee mobility and for competitors recruiting experts from other industry players.

As a result, courts rarely accept inevitable disclosure arguments pursuant to state trade secret laws and usually only in situations involving high-level executives. The Defend Trade Secrets Act (DTSA) makes the inevitable disclosure doctrine unlikely under federal law. The DTSA says: "a court may grant an injunction to prevent any...threatened misappropriation...provided the order does not prevent a person from entering into an employment relationship, and that conditions placed on such employment shall be based on evidence of threatened misappropriation and not merely on the information the person knows."

*Scope of Injunctive Relief.* Because Redmond's knowledge about PepsiCo's 1995 marketing plans would become public information in relatively short order, the court upheld a six-month restriction on Redmond taking the Quaker job. What is Redmond supposed to do with his time in the interim?

*Marketing Plans as a Trade Secret.* What exactly did Redmond know that was verboten?

*Employee Raids.* An omitted part of the opinion said:

> The court also pointed out that Quaker, through Uzzi, seemed to express an unnatural interest in hiring PCNA employees: all three of the people interviewed for the position Redmond ultimately accepted worked at PCNA. Uzzi may well have focused on recruiting PCNA employees because he knew they were good and not because of their confidential knowledge.

This type of hiring pattern, sometimes called an "employee raid," is fairly common. A manager switches jobs and then cherry-picks his or her top-performing subordinates. PepsiCo's lawsuit against Redmond surely signaled PepsiCo's feelings about any future Quaker efforts to raid more PepsiCo employees.

*Denouement of the* PepsiCo v. Redmond *Lawsuit.* PepsiCo's All Sport drink never gained huge success. PepsiCo finally gave up trying to build its own product and in 2001 bought the entire Quaker company for over $13 billion. PepsiCo subsequently divested the All Sport brand, which still exists as an independent brand.

PepsiCo's acquisition of Quaker came despite Quaker's colossal mismanagement of Snapple. After buying the Snapple brand for $1.7 billion in 1994, Quaker resold it 27 months later for $300M—a staggering loss of $1.4 billion. James F. Peltz, *Quaker-Snapple: $1.4 Billion Is Down the Drain*, L.A. TIMES, Mar. 28, 1997. As a result, the Quaker-Snapple acquisition is often ranked as one of the biggest M&A flops of all time.

William Redmond left Quaker in 1996 and has since become a serial CEO, mostly in the consumer products space. See his *BusinessWeek biography*.

Donald R. Uzzi also left Quaker in 1996 and has gone on to various high-level corporate leadership roles. See his *BusinessWeek biography*. In 2003, he settled charges with the Securities & Exchange Commission regarding allegedly false financial statements made at his post-Quaker employer, Sunbeam. *See* SEC v. Albert Dunlap, et al., Civil Action No. 01-8437-CIV (Jan. 27, 2003), http://www.sec.gov/litigation/litreleases/lr17952.htm.

## C.    Customer Lists as a Trade Secret

Lists of actual or prospective customers are another traditional category of trade secrets that companies fiercely guard. The conventional wisdom is that it's easier and cheaper to make a new sale to an existing customer than to procure a new customer. After all, an existing customer already knows the company, has already chosen it, and is more likely to have a favorable first-hand experience. Therefore, companies derive significant value from their customer lists

Meanwhile, a company's list of existing customers would be a very useful list of prospective customers for a competitor that would simultaneously help build the rival's business and take away that business from the company.

The following case illustrates a trade secret battle between an employer and a departing employee who wants to compete. From a trade secret law standpoint, how much of the value of a "customer list" resides in the customers' identities (without any contact info), the salesperson's knowledge of the customer's unique preferences, or the personal relationship that the salesperson may have developed over the years with the customer?

*Gary Van Zeeland Talent, Inc. v. Sandas, 84 Wis. 2d 202 (1978)*

The appeal is from a summary judgment which dismissed the complaint of Gary Van Zeeland Talent, Inc., against its former employee, Edwin J. Sandas. Van Zeeland is a talent booking agency. Its principal business is placing musical groups in nightclubs and other places of entertainment.

Sandas, who had no previous experience in talent agency work, became an employee of Van Zeeland in 1972. Van Zeeland trained him in the methods of working with musical groups and clubs and the importance of matching musical talent to the needs of a club. Sandas was, however, a former band musician, and he was familiar with the procedures of booking bands through agents.

Sandas left the employment of Van Zeeland in 1975. Prior to the time he did so, he made copies of his employer's club or "customer" list. He admitted that he took the list because he was planning to start his own business in competition with Van Zeeland Talent, Inc. Shortly after termination of his employment, he commenced his own talent agency. . . .

We conclude that the customer list was not a trade secret. The list which Sandas took was prepared for the sole purpose of assuring that Christmas cards were sent to all Van Zeeland's customers. Because it did not contain street addresses, it was not used for actual mailing purposes, but only for the purpose of determining that Christmas cards had been sent to the customers on the list. It contained no street addresses, no telephone numbers, no business information in respect to the type of music preferred by the customer, no names of managers or owners, and no other information of any kind other than the club name, the city, and the state.

Van Zeeland kept far more extensive information about its customers than was contained in the list taken by Sandas. It kept billing records, the names of bands placed with various clubs, the dates of engagements, the individuals with whom the placements were made, the club name, the prices, the commissions, and credit information.

The defendant's affidavit in support of the motion for summary judgment established that it would be possible to compile or prepare a list like the one taken by Sandas from other sources. It was equally undisputed that it would take time and effort to prepare such a list.

Van Zeeland acknowledged that it would be relatively simple to prepare a customer list—the names of the clubs—in comparison to the more difficult task of matching appropriate talent with those clubs. There is no assertion that any list which matched bands with customers was taken. Van Zeeland admitted that a list of customers without detailed information about club preferences would be relatively useless.

Immediately after Sandas left Van Zeeland, he commenced a competing talent agency business. It is undisputed that, during the second month following the commencement of his own businesses, 80 percent of the telephone calls made by Sandas in placing bands were to clubs listed on the document taken from Van Zeeland.

Additionally, it is undisputed that, at the time that Sandas joined Van Zeeland, he signed an employment agreement which, among other provisions, contained the following:

> 7. Disclosure of information. The Employee recognizes and acknowledges that the list of the Employer's customers, as it may exist from time to time, is a valuable, special, and unique asset of the Employer's business. The Employee will not, during or after the term of his employment, disclose the list of the Employer's customers or any part thereof to any person, firm, corporation, association, or other entity for any reason or purpose whatsoever. In the event of a breach or threatened breach by the Employee of the provisions of this paragraph, the Employer shall be entitled to an injunction restraining the Employee from disclosing, in whole or in part, the list of the Employer's customers, or from rendering any services to any person, firm, corporation, association, or other entity to whom such list, in whole or in part, has been disclosed or is threatened to be disclosed. Nothing herein shall be construed as prohibiting the Employer from pursuing any other remedies available to the Employer for such breach or threatened breach, including the recovery of damages from the Employee.

Under these undisputed facts, then, the initial question is whether the customer list taken by Sandas was a trade secret entitled to legal protection.

Customer lists, in some circumstances, may be protected as trade secrets. Restatement of Torts, sec. 757, comment b at 5 (1939), defines a trade secret:

> A trade secret may consist of any formula, pattern, device or compilation of information which is used in one's business, and which gives him an opportunity to obtain an advantage over competitors who do not know or use it.

. . . [T]he general rule is that customer lists are not protected, and it is in the unusual case that such lists will be afforded the status of a trade secret. The difficulty in making this determination is capsulized in Alexander, *Commercial Torts*, sec. 3.4, p. 216 (1973), when he states:

> Perhaps more than any other area of trade-secret law, customer lists present problems of extreme commercial importance and of a close balancing of the interest of the employer and employee.

. . . It is apparent that what Van Zeeland seeks in this action is the restraint of competition, and it seeks to prevent Sandas from offering similar services to customers on the list which have previously been afforded musical booking services by Van Zeeland. The question basically, then, is whether such special protection contrary to the old and well established concepts of the common law should be afforded to Van Zeeland under the circumstances of this case.

A general statement of the relevant balancing factors which may be applied in determining whether a customer list should be protected under the trade secrets concept is contained in *Developments in the Law—Competitive Torts*, 77 Harv. L. Rev. 888, 955-56 (1964):

The use of customer lists and contacts by ex-employees stands on the periphery of trade secret law. Written customer lists generally have been regarded as trade secrets when the nature of the industry permits the list to be kept secret and the list cannot readily be duplicated by independent means. The size of the list and the type of information it contains about the customers may be relevant to the latter determination, as may the amount of time and effort which went into its composition.

Some economic considerations militate against protecting customer lists. Most are developed in the normal course of business and probably would be produced whether or not protected. The customer benefits from their promulgation, for more firms then compete for his order. Also, once someone has discovered a customer with particular preferences, it is wasted effort for other firms to have to discover him again. Incentive to compile lists may be strengthened by legal protection in a few cases; and without protection businesses will guard lists more closely, with resulting inefficiency and diversion of resources into industrial security. However, economic arguments for protecting customer lists are at best marginal and the case for protection rests almost entirely on the need to deter employee disloyalty. (footnotes omitted)

The philosophical position of this court has been set forth in two recent cases, *Abbott Laboratories v. Norse Chemical Corp.*, 33 Wis. 2d 445 (1967), and *American Welding & Engineering Co., Inc., v. Luebke*, 37 Wis. 2d 697 (1968). In both *Abbott* and *American Welding*, we considered the six factors mentioned in Restatement of Torts, sec. 757, comment b at 6 (1939), as being relevant in determining whether the material sought to be protected is a trade secret. That comment states:

Some factors to be considered in determining whether given information is one's trade secret are: (1) the extent to which the information is known outside of his business; (2) the extent to which it is known by employees and others involved in his business; (3) the extent of measures taken by him to guard the secrecy of the information; (4) the value of the information to him and to his competitors; (5) the amount of effort or money expended by him in developing the information; (6) the ease or difficulty with which the information could be properly acquired or duplicated by others.

. . . The Van Zeeland list was completely silent in respect to key personnel to be contacted and failed even to include street addresses. There was, indeed, complicated marketing data which was compiled by Van Zeeland which was included in its ordinary business records, which reflected the musical placements with individual customers, the individual dealt with, and the credit record of the customer. There is nothing in the record, however, to show that any attempt was made to keep this information secret, and such information was not taken by Sandas.

In *Abbott*, we pointed out that a customer list for artificial sweeteners was a matter of common knowledge and was available through trade journals throughout the industry. In the instant case, the evidence revealed that the customers for musical entertainment could be located easily through telephone directories, calls to chambers of commerce, and newspaper advertising. It is quite apparent then that the information contained on the list was readily available to anyone within or without the Van Zeeland business who wished to go through the routine of making inquiries from established sources. No special knowledge or expertise was required to gather this information. Moreover, the information on the list was only of marginal value to anyone. Van Zeeland's own testimony acknowledged that information merely in respect to the names and locations of the clubs was insufficient. Van Zeeland's testimony was capsulized in the plaintiff counsel's synopsis of testimony, "One must know the nature of each particular club with whom one deals. I procure this information by calling clubs."

It is apparent that the type of information which Van Zeeland considered important could not be contained in any listing or summary of club names and state and city addresses. . . .

The tenor of the Van Zeeland brief on this appeal reveals that much of Van Zeeland's concern is not over the utility of the customer list to Sandas or over the deprivation of the exclusive use of that list by Van Zeeland, but rather the concern that Sandas, in the course of his employment, had acquired such expertise and know-how in the placement of musical groups as to make him a significant competitor. Much of the Van Zeeland brief is concerned with the fact that Sandas came to Van Zeeland as a twenty-one-year-old impoverished cookware salesman but has now left the organization after having been trained by Van Zeeland to such an extent that he is an expert in talent placement. The law, however, does not protect against that type of unfairness, if unfairness it be. Rather, it encourages the mobility of workers; and so long as a departing employee takes with him no more than his experience and intellectual development that has ensued while being trained by another, and no trade secrets or processes are wrongfully appropriated, the law affords no recourse. . . .

We accordingly conclude, applying the general standards developed in *Abbott* and *American Welding* and the basic considerations of the Restatement of Torts, sec. 757, that the Van Zeeland customer list did not constitute a trade secret. . . .

Van Zeeland further contends that Sandas is estopped from denying that the club list is a trade secret, because, at the time of his employment, he signed an agreement which included paragraph 7, set forth in full *supra*. That portion of the agreement embodies the phrase:

> The Employee recognizes and acknowledges that the list of the Employer's customers, as it may exist from time to time, is a valuable, special, and unique asset of the Employer's business.

As a matter of public policy, we conclude that estoppel is not appropriate in a restraint-of-trade situation. As stated above, it is the public policy of the common law that there be unrestrained competition to further the welfare of the consumer and society in general. Matters of trade practices or information in respect to manufacturing processes will be afforded the status of trade secrets only when to do so furthers public policy. . . .

While a declaration that the customer list is of value may have some persuasiveness in showing that the employer attempted to keep the list a secret, it is the public's right to have reasonable competition, irrespective of what self-serving declarations the employer may insist upon. Merely stating or having the employee acknowledge that a customer list is secret does not make it a trade secret entitled to be protected by the law in derogation of freedom of commerce and trade. It would be contrary to public policy to permit the doctrine of estoppel to be applied in this case.

We also point out that paragraph 7 in its entirety constitutes an unreasonable restraint of trade. That paragraph provides that the employee will never, without time limitation, disclose the list of customers to any person. Even were this customer list a trade secret, subject to protection within a reasonable geographic area and for a reasonable period of time, this provision, which sets no limits with respect to either, is unreasonable and void. The unreasonable strictures upon the right of disclosure vitiate the entire agreement in accordance with the legislative policy of sec. 103.465, Stats., which provides in part:

> Any such restrictive covenant imposing an unreasonable restraint is illegal, void and unenforceable even as to so much of the covenant or performance as would be a reasonable restraint.

An additional factor should be noted. Where a restraint of trade is tolerated, it is permitted only to the extent absolutely necessary to afford reasonable protection. As indicated above, restraints may be unreasonable by a limitation that is overbroad in terms of geographic area or time. A facet of the time limitation which must be considered in determining its reasonableness is the extent to which the information is permanently valuable to the employer. Restatement (Second) of Contracts, sec. 330, comment d at 115 (Tent. Draft No. 12, 1977), provides in part:

> And if the restraint is to last longer than is required in light of those interests, taking account of such factors as the permanent or transitory nature of technology and information, it is unreasonable.

Van Zeeland's customer list was at best of only transitory value. Like the customer list in *American Welding*, it was probably partially obsolete at the time it came into Sandas' possession. The information contained in the Van Zeeland customer list is now, less than three years after Sandas left the employment, already of greatly diminished value. Exhibit 3, incorporated in the record, lists 1200 clubs. Of the 30 clubs listed in Milwaukee, only 16 are currently listed in the Milwaukee telephone directory, and of the 23 listed in Madison, only 11 are currently listed in the Madison telephone directory. It is apparent that this information was of only transitory significance, and any covenant in an employment agreement which would restrain the disclosure of this information for all time is patently unreasonable.

. . . Restatement of Contracts (Second), *supra*, comment g, at 119, states:

> Post-employment restraints are scrutinized with particular care because they are often the product of unequal bargaining power and because the employee is likely to give scant attention to the hardship he may later suffer through the loss of his livelihood.

. . . We take notice of paragraph 11 of the agreement which bound Sandas for a time period of five years and a radius of 300 miles from Van Zeeland's place of business not to operate or in any way be employed by or be connected with any business similar to Van Zeeland's. It is noteworthy also that, although Sandas' conduct clearly comes within the prohibitions of paragraph 11, no reliance is placed upon it. It is undoubtedly wise that Van Zeeland does not base its cause of action upon that restrictive covenant for, on its face, it appears to be an unreasonable restraint of trade. We call attention to paragraph 11 not because it poses a specific issue important in the decision of this appeal, but rather it demonstrates that the contract upon which Van Zeeland relies to estop Sandas is shot through with provisions that are contrary to public policy. Estoppel cannot be based upon a contract of that nature. . . .

*NOTES AND QUESTIONS*

*Was Sandas' Behavior Ethical?* The talent agency hired a youthful Sandas and taught him the business. Sandas contractually agreed not to take customer lists or to compete with the talent agency, and Sandas admitted that he could have recreated this list without taking it. Why did Sandas take the list instead of recreating it? Irrespective of the legal conclusion, was it right for him to do so? How would you counsel a new client who revealed that he had taken information from a previous employer to start his own business?

Even if you support Sandas' choices, you might nevertheless sympathize with the talent agency. What could the talent agency have done differently to successfully restrict Sandas' ability to leave the agency and go into competition with it after teaching him everything?

*Customer Lists vs. Customer Relationships.* In many sales-driven organizations, the customer list is not really valuable by itself. Instead, the real value lies in the personal relationships the salesperson forms with the customer contacts. Employers can have a difficult time maintaining these personal relationships when the salesperson leaves. Without an enforceable non-compete agreement from the salesperson (no easy feat), customers are likely to follow the salesperson to his or her new home.

*Non-Disclosure and Non-Compete Restrictions Compared.* As the case indicates, non-compete provisions are subject to significant public policy limits. Some states will enforce them when they are "reasonable." Other states won't even do that. For example, in California, non-compete provisions are categorically void for public policy except in certain situations involving business acquisitions.

Wisconsin treats non-disclosure restrictions as a type of non-compete restriction, which Wisconsin has statutorily restricted in scope and effect. Wisconsin's approach makes some sense, especially in the employment context where non-disclosure restrictions can, in fact, restrict employee mobility and competition with former employers. Nevertheless, in many other states, non-disclosure restrictions and non-compete restrictions are distinguished.

*Customer Lists in an Internet Era.* Given how the Internet has made it so much easier to compile factual information, including research on prospective customers, should we be less concerned about the taking of customer lists, especially if they do not contain any enhanced information uniquely added by the employer?

## 2.    Patents

*Overview of Patents*

The patent system is complex and full of arcane nuances, so this overview is necessarily simplified. Novel, useful and non-obvious ideas are eligible for patent protection.[*] To obtain a patent, the inventor (or the inventor's assignee) submits an application to the U.S. Patent & Trademark Office. Between filing fees and legal bills, a typical patent application costs more than $10,000 just to file with the government (in some cases substantially more). A patent examiner reviews the application, provides comments to the applicant and ultimately decides whether or not the patent should issue. It typically takes several years and at least $50,000 to get an issued patent.

An issued patent provides the owner with the exclusive right to make, use, sell, offer for sale, or import the invention for the patent's duration, which is typically twenty years from the filing date for the patent application. The patent does not grant the affirmative right to commercialize the invention. For example, biotech-related patents still require FDA approval before the invention can be commercialized. A patent owner also can decide not to exploit or license the patented idea at all.

Patent litigation is a high-stakes affair. Because patents effectively allow the patent owner to control a product market, alleged patent infringers are often fighting for the ability to continue their commercial activity—and they are willing to reinvest some of their expected profits to do so. Meanwhile, patent damages can be large—awards of hundreds of millions of dollars (or more) are possible—and sometimes a patent owner is trying to kick other companies out of a market to keep competitors from degrading prices and profits. Because of the big stakes and the arcane nature of both patent law and patented technology, both litigants often spend a lot of money. Many law firms quote a patent litigant (plaintiff or defendant) an anticipated price tag of $4-5 million to reach a trial.

To get a patent, the applicant must describe the patented invention well enough that other industry players could replicate the invention. This means that when a patent application becomes public (typically, eighteen months after filing), competitors can review the patent, learn from it, and use the patent application's ideas to spur new ones outside the patent's scope. Further, when the patent expires, everyone is free to use the invention with the help of the public disclosures made in the patent process. As discussed earlier, Coca-Cola has been able to get over 100 years (and counting) of extra protection for its distinctive soda formula by relying on trade secret protection instead of patents.

Meanwhile, once the application is published, a patent applicant cannot claim the information disclosed in the application as a trade secret—even if the application eventually is not granted.

---

[*] There are three types of patents: utility, design and plant patents. We will address only utility patents.

Finally, in industries with rapidly evolving technologies, lengthy time periods for getting issued patents (the 4+ year application period) degrades the patents' usefulness. In those cases, by the time the patent has issued, the industry has gone through one or two new generations of technology.

*Patents and the Advertising Industry*

Historically, most advertising lawyers spent very little time thinking about patents. However, that may be changing, and patents play an increasingly important role in the advertising industry. There are now patents on just about every corner of the advertising business, such as *Patent #6757661* (issued June 29, 2004) for "high-volume targeting of advertisements to user of online service," or *Patent #4024660* (issued May 24, 1977) for an "advertising pocket for shopping carts."

Many patents in the advertising industry protect a method of advertising (a "business method"); and many of those methods are performed by encoding the method in software. The Supreme Court has repeatedly cast doubt on the validity of business method and software patents, thought its opinions not quite rejected them outright. *See, e.g., Bilski v. Kappos*, 561 U.S. 593 (2010); *Alice Corporation Pty. Ltd v. CLS Bank Int'l*, 134 S. Ct. 2347 (2014). This leaves business methods and software patents, including those related to advertising, in an uncertain but precarious position.

Advertising lawyers should be aware of statutory time limits for filing patent applications. In the United States, patent applicants have a one-year grace period after they "offer" the invention for sale to file a patent application. Any later patent application for that invention will be time-barred. Advertising a patentable invention (even in a one-to-one sales pitch) often qualifies as an "offer" for sale. In foreign countries, there is no one-year grace period; an offer for sale in the United States may permanently forego the ability to file any further foreign patent applications on the advertised product. Therefore, when an advertiser initially begins advertising a new product, advertising counsel should double-check that the client has filed patent applications on the advertised product or is prepared to forego some or all patent protection for the product.

## 3.    Idea Submissions

There are a surprisingly large number of lawsuits—including advertising-related cases—over a company benefiting from a commercially valuable idea submitted by a third party. We refer to these cases as "idea submission" cases. Ideas can be submitted in a variety of ways, ranging from an oral "elevator pitch" to submission through postal mail or email.

Idea submission cases can implicate multiple legal doctrines. An idea might be protectable under patent or trade secret law; a written submission might be protectable under copyright law, although copyright does not protect the ideas as such; and there could be an express, implied-in-fact or quasi-contract between the discloser and the recipient governing the idea transmission. Occasionally, courts will find protection for a submitted idea even if none of these legal doctrines apply.

Although most idea submission lawsuits fail eventually, companies usually try to reduce their exposure to idea submission cases, such as refusing to open any unsolicited postal mail and putting legends on web feedback forms indicating that the feedback submitter waives any claims for the company's subsequent use of the feedback.

Try to figure out why the next two cases reach divergent conclusions. Pay attention to the specific role of contracts in each.

### Burgess v. Coca-Cola Co., 245 Ga. App. 206 (Ga. App. Ct. 2000)

Robert L. Burgess sued The Coca-Cola Company ("Coca-Cola") for allegedly taking his creative ideas and using them in a commercial that featured anthropomorphic polar bears drinking Coca-Cola. Burgess sought recovery under theories of misappropriation of ideas, breach of express and implied contract, breach of a confidential relationship, unjust enrichment, quantum meruit, and promissory estoppel. After two years of discovery during which over thirty-five people were deposed, Coca-Cola moved for summary judgment. Following a lengthy hearing, the trial court granted Coca-Cola's motion. For the following reasons, we affirm. . . .

. . . Burgess approached Coca-Cola in January 1989 to pitch a creative concept he referred to as "The Fantastic World of Coca-Cola." There is no evidence that Coca-Cola agreed to compensate Burgess for the disclosure of his idea prior to his pitching it for the first time to Coca-Cola executive John B. White. The presentation included seven storyboards which depicted various aspects of the concept. This "Fantastic World," as Burgess explained, was an imaginary world located inside a Coca-Cola vending machine and populated with a wide variety of Coca-Cola characters, including, as shown by one of the storyboards, a family of white teddy bear-like "cola bears" making ice to cool the Coca-Cola. Burgess also provided White with a written narrative of his concept. This first narrative did not mention bears. White told Burgess he was not in a position to help him. However, believing the concept might be suitable for a toy line, White introduced Burgess to Bruce Gilbert and Mike Ellison with Coca-Cola's Merchandise Licensing Division.

After hearing the "Fantastic World" pitch, Gilbert told Burgess he was intrigued by the idea of doing a line of Coca-Cola toys. However, Gilbert explained to Burgess that Coca-Cola was not in the business of manufacturing toys; rather, it licensed its trademark to companies for use on merchandise. Therefore, both Gilbert and Ellison told Burgess that before Coca-Cola could proceed any further, Burgess would have to interest a major toy company in his idea. Gilbert and Ellison informed Burgess orally and by letter dated January 12, 1989, that any compensation for the use of his idea would come only from the toy manufacturer. Coca-Cola then introduced Burgess to executives with Kenner Toys in Cincinnati, Ohio.

Burgess pitched his same "Fantastic World" idea to Kenner representatives in February 1989. Initially, they were impressed. The representatives were especially pleased with the cola bears and asked Burgess to develop his ideas further. On March 14, 1989, Kenner made a presentation to Coca-Cola using storyboards developed by Kenner and by Burgess. Coca-Cola liked the presentation, which focused on a line of plush toy teddy bears to be marketed to children between two and ten years of age. On June 14, 1989, the toy idea was again pitched to senior Coca-Cola executives who agreed that Kenner could move forward with its development of the toy line. However, because its products had never been marketed to such young children, Coca-Cola asked Kenner in a letter dated

August 18, 1989, to obtain a "seal of approval" from a reputable organization as well as a safety endorsement from an independent company before Coca-Cola would agree to licensing its trademark.

While it worked to satisfy Coca-Cola's conditions, Kenner began negotiations regarding the payment of royalties to Coca-Cola for use of its trademark and to Burgess for his creative efforts. While in the process of finalizing the deal, Kenner began test-marketing the sale of Coca-Cola plush toys, including a teddy bear. The results were surprisingly negative. Consequently, Kenner decided to abandon the project and to release Burgess to pitch his "Fantastic World" idea to other companies. Kenner paid Burgess $25,000 for his efforts on their behalf. There is no evidence that Burgess performed any consulting services for Coca-Cola. Further, Burgess admits that Coca-Cola never reached any agreement with him or with Kenner regarding the payment of royalties.

Burgess presented his "Fantastic World" toy idea to other companies, but they were not interested. From 1989 to 1992, Burgess also continued to contact different Coca-Cola executives, attempting to generate interest in various aspects of his idea, for example, a commercial about an evil character who steals the Coca-Cola recipe. The ideas were all related to the overall "Fantastic World" theme and involved many different characters, including "space aliens" and "cola kids." The evidence is undisputed that Coca-Cola never implemented, nor contracted with any licensee to implement, Burgess' "Fantastic World" concept.

In July 1991, Coca-Cola hired Creative Artists Agency ("CAA") of Hollywood, California, to develop new advertising. CAA was responsible for generating fresh advertising ideas for Coca-Cola's consideration. Coca-Cola executives did not participate in any aspect of CAA's creative process; they only reviewed the final submissions. One of the many concepts approved and ultimately made into a commercial was "Bears at the Theater." This commercial featured a family of anthropomorphic polar bears who were drinking Coca-Cola while they watched the aurora borealis. The commercial was the idea of Ken Stewart, the husband of a CAA executive. The evidence shows that Stewart came up with the idea on his own, free from any input from Coca-Cola personnel. He was unaware of any of Burgess' ideas. In fact, Stewart was inspired by his Labrador Retriever puppy, who apparently looked like a polar bear. Burgess presented no evidence from which a jury could reasonably infer that Stewart's idea for the "Bears at the Theater" commercial was created using Burgess' "Fantastic World" concept or any of its parts, including the cola bears.

The "Bears in the Theater" commercial, first broadcast in 1993, was one of twenty-seven commercial spots aired as part of Coca-Cola's "Always" campaign. Because "Bears in the Theater" was so well received by the public, Coca-Cola produced several more commercials focusing on the polar bear family. The success of these commercials prompted several companies to contact Coca-Cola for the rights to market plush and plastic Coca-Cola CAA polar bear figurines. Coca-Cola eventually agreed to license the CAA polar bear to several different companies.

Burgess claimed that the CAA polar bear, with its human attributes and family values, was taken from the cola bears he had envisioned in his Fantastic World. Not only did Coca-Cola adduce evidence showing that the CAA polar bear was independently created by Stewart, it introduced evidence showing that the use of a polar bear "spokescharacter" was not novel. First, Coca-Cola demonstrated a long history of various companies using animated anthropomorphic animals as product spokescharacters, including Kellogg's Tony the Tiger, Star Kist's Charlie the Tuna, and Nine Lives' Morris the Cat. Walter Maes, an advertising executive with 27 years of experience, explained that anthropomorphic characters have been used in the industry for decades and that there is nothing novel about such spokescharacters generally. Second, Robert Vianello, a professor of film and television, pointed out that anthropomorphic bears have been put to a number of commercial uses predating Burgess' disclosure of his idea to Coca-Cola. For example, the Icee Company has had an animated polar bear representing its frozen drink products since the 1960s. Such widespread use of anthropomorphic bears was further evidenced by the book, *Teddy Bears in Advertising Art*. Third and finally, Coca-Cola has used anthropomorphic bears, including polar bears, in its own advertising on many occasions since 1923. Coca-Cola used an anthropomorphic white bear called "Teddy Snow Crop" to market its Minute Maid frozen orange juice in 1961. It has also licensed the use of its "Enjoy Coke" logo on a variety of plush animals, including bears.

1. (a) To survive summary judgment on a claim for wrongful appropriation of or for conversion of an unpatented or unpatentable idea or product, a plaintiff must adduce some evidence from which a jury may infer the existence of each of these essential elements: "1) the idea must be novel; 2) the disclosure of the idea must be made in confidence; 3) the idea must be adopted and made use of by the defendant; and 4) the idea must be sufficiently concrete in its development to be usable." Burgess argues that the CAA anthropomorphic polar bear featured in Coca-Cola's "Always" campaign was an unauthorized use of the cola bears element of his "Fantastic World of Coca-Cola" concept. However, even if Coca-Cola had made use of Burgess' cola bears idea, which the evidence does not support,

Burgess' claim fails because using an anthropomorphic polar bear to sell a soft drink is not a novel idea.

As we have held:

> To be novel the concept must be peculiar and not generally available or known to others in the trade. To be protected, an idea must possess genuine novelty and invention, which it cannot have if it merely is an adaptation of existing knowledge, albeit a clever, useful, or sensible adaptation.

Coca-Cola demonstrated that anthropomorphic bears, including polar bears, had been used to sell a number of products, including its own, decades before Burgess ever pitched his "Fantastic World" concept. In short, it was simply a variation on an existing theme. That Burgess' cola bears were presented in a fresh or different setting does not constitute novelty because "creating a new and better way of doing something" already existent is not sufficient. "Without the element of novelty [Burgess] was deprived of an essential element entitling [him] to recover."

(b) Further, even if Burgess' concept was novel, he is not entitled to recover when the unrebutted evidence shows that Stewart and CAA created "Bears at the Theater" on their own initiative, by wholly independent means, and without any input or information from Coca-Cola or Burgess. Because Coca-Cola is entitled to the complete defense of "independent creation," the trial court properly granted summary judgment on this claim.

2. Each of Burgess' remaining claims depends upon his nonnovel idea acting either as consideration for a promise between Coca-Cola and himself or as a benefit conferred upon Coca-Cola. As we have held, however, under these circumstances, nonnovel ideas are insufficient "to serve as consideration for a promise of confidentiality[2] or as a basis for asserting unjust enrichment." Burgess' remaining claims fail as a matter of law because nonnovel ideas do not constitute protected property interests under Georgia law. Therefore, nonnovel ideas are inadequate as consideration, and "when one submits [such] an idea to another, no promise to pay for its use may be implied, and no asserted agreement enforced." Similarly, because a nonnovel idea confers no benefit upon the defendant, claims based upon quantum meruit and unjust enrichment for a defendant's alleged use of the idea must fail. And, because nonnovel ideas lack value sufficient to create a property interest, the unauthorized use of another's nonnovel idea would not result in an injustice, a necessary element in a promissory estoppel claim. Therefore, Burgess' claim for promissory estoppel must also fail. In fact, under these circumstances, "[l]ack of novelty in an idea is fatal to any cause of action for its unlawful use." Consequently, we find no error in the trial court's grant of summary judgment to Coca-Cola on Burgess' remaining claims.

---

[2] There is no evidence that a confidential relationship as defined in OCGA § 23-2-58 existed between Coca-Cola and Burgess prior to his disclosing his "Fantastic World" concept. As we have held, the mere fact that two persons have transacted business in the past based on oral commitments or understandings and that they have come to repose trust and confidence in each other as the result of such dealings is not sufficient, in and of itself, to warrant a finding that a confidential relationship exists between them within the contemplation of the Code section.

## Taco Bell Corp. v. TBWA Chiat/Day Inc., 552 F.3d 1137 (9th Cir. 2009)

Taco Bell Corp. ("Taco Bell") appeals the district court's summary judgment in favor of its former advertising agency, TBWA Worldwide, Inc. ("TBWA"), in Taco Bell's lawsuit seeking indemnification. This case follows a judgment issued against Taco Bell in the federal district court for the Western District of Michigan for breach by Taco Bell of an implied contract for using a third party's Chihuahua character in its advertising developed by TBWA. Taco Bell sought indemnification from TBWA on the ground that the liability Taco Bell incurred in favor of the third party was caused by TBWA. . . .

### I. Background

In June 1996, Ed Alfaro, a licensing manager at Taco Bell, attended a trade show in New York where he first discovered a cartoon depiction of a Chihuahua dog character ("Psycho Chihuahua") being marketed by its creators, Tom Rinks and Joe Shields of Wrench LLC, a Michigan corporation (collectively, "Wrench"). Alfaro told Rinks and Shields that he wanted to explore the use of Psycho Chihuahua by Taco Bell.

During the Summer and Fall of 1996, Wrench provided Taco Bell with goods bearing Psycho Chihuahua's image. From that time through June 1997, Alfaro tried to build support within Taco Bell for its use of Psycho Chihuahua in its advertising. He showed the goods to Taco Bell's senior managers and advertising agency at that time, Bozell Worldwide ("Bozell"). Taco Bell conducted a focus group study which included Psycho Chihuahua and several other designs. Alfaro reported to a senior Taco Bell executive that Psycho Chihuahua was the most popular out of all the designs.

In November 1996, Taco Bell and Wrench's licensing agent, Strategy Licensing, discussed the possible use of Psycho Chihuahua as Taco Bell's mascot and Taco Bell requested that Strategy Licensing submit a proposal on financial terms for the use of Psycho Chihuahua. On November 18, 1996, Strategy Licensing submitted a proposal but Taco Bell did not accept it. Discussions continued about Taco Bell's possible use of Psycho Chihuahua and Taco Bell understood that if it decided to use that character, Taco Bell would have to pay Wrench for such use.

In February 1997, Taco Bell's then-parent company, Pepsi Co., made a presentation to Taco Bell's marketing department regarding the possibility of using Psycho Chihuahua in a Taco Bell "Cinco de Mayo" promotion. Taco Bell then conducted additional focus group studies on Psycho Chihuahua which resulted in positive consumer response.

In March 1997, Taco Bell changed advertising agencies from Bozell to TBWA. Taco Bell commissioned TBWA to create a new advertising campaign for 1998.

Between February and April 1997, Alfaro continued to work with Wrench to develop possibilities for Taco Bell's use of Psycho Chihuahua.

In May 1997, TBWA presented approximately thirty advertising ideas to Taco Bell for its new campaign. One of the ideas involved a male Chihuahua dog passing a female Chihuahua dog to get to Taco Bell food. The executives to which the ideas were presented included Taco Bell's president, Peter Waller, and its chief marketing officer, Vada Hill. Waller and Hill selected TBWA's Chihuahua idea as one of the five advertisements that would be test-marketed during the Summer of 1997. Months later, market research demonstrated favorable results for the TBWA Chihuahua test advertisement and Waller and Hill chose that character as the center of its new advertising campaign starting in January 1998.

Meanwhile, Alfaro believed the character Wrench had created from the original Psycho Chihuahua closely resembled the TBWA Chihuahua to be used in Taco Bell commercials. He alerted Taco Bell's in-house counsel that Wrench would likely sue because of the similarities between the characters. Taco Bell sent a box of Psycho Chihuahua materials to TBWA at some point between June 27, 1997 and July 26, 1997. Alfaro drafted a memorandum that accompanied the materials, describing the parallel path he had taken with Wrench and their idea of using a Chihuahua to advertise Taco Bell food.

By January 1998, Taco Bell began using a Chihuahua to advertise its food. Wrench then sued Taco Bell, claiming that Taco Bell was using Psycho Chihuahua in its advertising without providing compensation to Wrench. Wrench LLC v. Taco Bell Corp., 51 F. Supp. 2d 840 (W.D. Mich. 1999).

In February 1998, Taco Bell and TBWA entered into a joint defense and confidentiality agreement ("Joint Defense Agreement"). They also executed a contract controlling their business relationship ("Agency Agreement"). The Agency Agreement was executed January 19, 1999 but the parties agreed to make the effective date retroactive to April 1, 1997 to include all of TBWA's services to Taco Bell from the beginning of their business relationship.

In its defense in *Wrench*, Taco Bell alleged there was no contract with Wrench because Alfaro had no authority to bind the company, the Chihuahua character used by Taco Bell was not Psycho Chihuahua, and the Chihuahua character used by Taco Bell was independently created by TBWA.

TBWA created and broadcast over forty more Chihuahua commercials between January 1998 and June 2000. In June 2003, the *Wrench* jury determined that Taco Bell had breached an implied contract by using Psycho Chihuahua without compensating Wrench. All copyright claims were disposed of prior to trial. A judgment was entered against Taco Bell in the amount of $30,174,031.00, and the court subsequently amended the judgment to account for pre-judgment and post-judgment interest, bringing the total to over $42,000,000.00.

Taco Bell requested full indemnification from TBWA for its liability to Wrench. Within weeks of the *Wrench* trial, Taco Bell filed this lawsuit against TBWA, suing it for breach of the Agency Agreement, express indemnification, and declaratory relief. Both sides moved for summary judgment. The district court denied Taco Bell's motion and granted TBWA's cross-motion. Summary judgment was entered in favor of TBWA, and this appeal followed.

II. Discussion . . .

A. *Wrench* Verdict

The first issue we consider is whether the *Wrench* jury findings are proof of TBWA's fault, obligating it to indemnify Taco Bell for the liability Taco Bell incurred.

A verdict sheet that was provided to the *Wrench* jury reflects what that jury found:

> Question Number 1: Did Wrench prove by a preponderance of the evidence that Wrench and Taco Bell had a mutual understanding that if Taco Bell used the Psycho Chihuahua character in its advertising and on products, Taco Bell would pay Wrench for this use?

> Question Number 2: Did Wrench prove by a preponderance of the evidence that Taco Bell used the Psycho Chihuahua character in its advertising from 1997 to 2000 and that the character used by Taco Bell was not independently created by [TWBA]?

> Question Number 3: Did Wrench prove by a preponderance of the evidence that it suffered damages because Taco Bell did not pay for its use of the Psycho Chihuahua character?

The *Wrench* jury answered all three questions affirmatively.

According to Taco Bell, these findings are proof of TBWA's fault. Because TBWA was involved in the creation of the TBWA Chihuahua character and TBWA had possession of the Psycho Chihuahua materials, Taco Bell argues the jury's findings that Psycho Chihuahua was used by Taco Bell and the character used was not independently created by TBWA confirms wrongdoing by TBWA. Taco Bell relies heavily on the second question in the verdict sheet submitted to the *Wrench* jury, but as to that question, the court in the *Wrench* trial instructed the jury:

> Let me give you some things to consider in determining whether the Taco Bell Chihuahua is the same character as the Psycho Chihuahua character. . . .

535

If you find that the Taco Bell Chihuahua is the same character as the Psycho Chihuahua character, then you must still consider whether, on the one hand, Taco Bell used Wrench's creation of the Psycho Chihuahua character or, on the other hand, whether Taco Bell and [TBWA] created the Taco Bell Chihuahua on an independent creative, but parallel path.

In answering this question, in addition to considering the differences and similarities—differences between and similarities of the two dogs, as I pointed out in the preceding paragraph, you should consider . . . the access or lack thereof to the Psycho Chihuahua character by people at Taco Bell and [TBWA].

Considering these instructions to the *Wrench* jury, no inference of fault by TBWA can be drawn from the jury's verdict. The instructions leave unclear what the *Wrench* jury determined on the issue of independent creation of the Chihuahua character. The jury was told to consider "whether Taco Bell and [TBWA] created the Taco Bell Chihuahua on an independent creative, but parallel path." The court also asked the jury to consider "the access or lack thereof to the Psycho Chihuahua character by people at Taco Bell and [TBWA]." The *Wrench* jury was never instructed to differentiate between Taco Bell and TBWA or determine which party was at fault for the liability to Wrench.

The undisputed facts do not support a finding of fault or negligence on the part of TBWA. TBWA was not a party to the implied contract between Taco Bell and Wrench and was unaware of its existence. TBWA had no knowledge of Psycho Chihuahua nor Taco Bell's contact with Wrench before proposing a Chihuahua character for Taco Bell advertising on June 2, 1997. The facts that Taco Bell did not have input on TBWA's creation of its advertising character and that a box of Psycho Chihuahua materials was sent to TBWA are of no consequence not only because TBWA created its own Chihuahua character before it received the Psycho Chihuahua materials, but also because Taco Bell was found liable for the use of Psycho Chihuahua without compensating Wrench, not copyright infringement. Taco Bell's arguments speak to copyright issues not pertinent to this case because those claims were disposed of before trial.

The Agency Agreement's indemnification provisions require TBWA to indemnify Taco Bell for liability incurred as a result of "(i) any materials created, produced, and/or furnished by [TBWA] for [Taco Bell] . . . (ii) [TBWA's] fault or negligence in the performance of its obligations hereunder; or (iii) [TBWA's] breach of its obligations under this Agreement." Even if liability arose from "materials created, produced, and/or furnished by [TBWA] for [Taco Bell]," Paragraph 7.1 includes an exception for claims covered by Paragraph 7.2, claims resulting from Taco Bell's fault. Although Taco Bell argues the *Wrench* jury finding warrants an inference that TBWA misappropriated Wrench's material, neither the verdict nor the undisputed facts allow a finding of TBWA's fault, but only Taco Bell's breach of a contract. The district court properly determined no obligation for TBWA to indemnify Taco Bell under the Agency Agreement arose from the verdict.

Furthermore, as properly decided by the district court, TBWA cannot be held at fault under the Agency Agreement which allows it to rely on the approval of Taco Bell. Taco Bell approved the Chihuahua character proposed by TBWA and continued to approve the Chihuahua advertisements for broadcasting after the *Wrench* lawsuit was initiated, despite the existence of its implied contractual commitment to Wrench. . . .

Taco Bell argues that its approval of advertising created by TBWA was only an approval of costs as provided for in Paragraph 4.1[2] of the Agency Agreement. This argument contradicts the statement of Taco Bell's counsel at oral argument of the summary judgment motions in the district court:

> So I would dispute strongly that there was an approval of the ads in the form of agreeing that they go forward and shifting the risk. I wouldn't dispute that there was approval in the sense of, Yes, let's run them. I think we'll sell some more tacos. That, I think there was an approval of.

In addition to the fact that the commercials were broadcast, the admission of Taco Bell's counsel confirmed that Taco Bell approved the Chihuahua commercials for airing. The district court correctly considered Taco Bell's approval to broadcast the Chihuahua commercials after Wrench filed its lawsuit a dispositive factor in Taco Bell's fault-based indemnification claim against TBWA. The admission confirmed that there was approval pursuant to the Agency Agreement's authorization section.

Paragraph 6.4 of the Agency Agreement states:

> 6.4 Authorization. [TBWA] will be entitled to rely and act upon any instruction, approval or authorization given by [Taco Bell] or by any of [Taco Bell's] representatives.

Under this paragraph, TBWA was permitted to rely on Taco Bell's approval of advertising TBWA created. The district court properly relied on the fact that Taco Bell approved for airing the Chihuahua commercials between January 1998 and June 2000 while denying the existence of its contractual obligation to Wrench. Under the Agency Agreement, TBWA cannot be found at fault for liability arising from advertisements approved by Taco Bell.

B. Agency Agreement

The next issue we consider is whether TBWA is at fault for breach of the Agency Agreement, leading to Taco Bell's liability in *Wrench*. Subparagraph 7.2(iii) provides that Taco Bell will indemnify TBWA for any liability resulting from "risks which have been brought to the attention of and discussed with [Taco Bell] and [Taco Bell] has nevertheless elected to proceed as evidenced in writing and signed by either the Vice President of Advertising or Senior Vice President-Marketing of [Taco Bell]."

---

[2] 4. Approvals and Billing Procedures.
4.1 Approvals. [TBWA] will obtain [Taco Bell's] prior approval for all work [TBWA] does on [Taco Bell's] behalf. If [TBWA] believes actual costs for production projects, subject to an estimate, will vary by more than 10%, [TBWA] will send [Taco Bell] a revised estimate for [Taco Bell's] approval. Variances under 10% will be deemed approved by [Taco Bell]. After a project is completed, [TBWA] will reconcile actual costs against the estimates and an appropriate adjustment will be made.

Taco Bell argues that the district court ignored material evidence of TBWA's breach of its obligations under Paragraph 7 to "exercise its best judgment in the preparation and placing of [Taco Bell's] advertising and publicity with a view to avoiding any claims, proceedings, or suits being made or instituted against Taco Bell." It is Taco Bell's position that it was TBWA's responsibility to make sure Taco Bell's advertising campaign did not misuse Psycho Chihuahua and TBWA breached its duty when it failed to do advertising copy clearance, uncover an application for a trademark, and bring risks of using a Chihuahua in advertising to Taco Bell's attention. Subparagraph 7.2(iii), speaking to Taco Bell's indemnification obligations to TBWA, does not require any copy clearance, trademark searches, or risk reporting by TBWA, but obligates Taco Bell to indemnify TBWA when Taco Bell elects to proceed in the event that risks are brought to its attention. Additionally, Taco Bell was the party aware of the potential risks of using a Chihuahua character in its advertising. It was Taco Bell that had an undisclosed contract with Wrench and denied the existence of that contract. Taco Bell's argument that TBWA failed to meet an obligation under the Agency Agreement by failing to do copyright and trademark searches is meritless not only because it is not supported by the language in the Agency Agreement, but also because the *Wrench* liability included neither copyright nor trademark damages. As discussed, the entire judgment was based on Taco Bell's breach of an implied contract to pay Wrench for use of Psycho Chihuahua. . . .

### III. Conclusion

The district court properly concluded there is evidence only of Taco Bell's fault in its liability to Wrench. As a result, no indemnification obligation from TBWA to Taco Bell arose.

*NOTES AND QUESTIONS*

*Idea Submission Protection and Copyright Preemption.* In the related ruling of *Wrench LLC v. Taco Bell Corp.*, 256 F.3d 446 (6th Cir. 2001), the court held that copyright law didn't preempt Wrench's implied contract claim. However, in other cases, copyright preemption can narrow or eliminate an idea submission claim. Courts sometimes (but inconsistently) find contract breach claims preempted by copyright law when the contract restrictions overlap with the exclusive rights of copyright owners. Some causes of action (such as conversion or unjust enrichment) are regularly preempted by copyright law when the subject material is a copyrighted work.

*Anthropomorphic Animals in Ads.* The *Burgess* case indicated that using anthropomorphic animals (in that case, polar bears) lacked sufficient novelty to satisfy the claim. The *Taco Bell* litigation also involved an anthropomorphic animal (in that case, a talking Chihuahua) but reached a contrary result. Why the difference?

One possibility is that jurisdictions are split on idea novelty as a prerequisite to the plaintiff's cause of action. Some jurisdictions, such as New York, typically require novelty for an idea submission case; other jurisdictions, such as California, take a more relaxed approach.

*Reliance on Ad Agency's Independent Development.* In both the *Burgess* and *Taco Bell* cases, the advertisers relied on independently created suggestions from their ad agencies. In the *Burgess* case, this independent development was sufficient to excuse the advertiser; in the *Taco Bell* case, it wasn't. Why the difference?

Coca-Cola's successful defense of independent development is actually quite remarkable. If you represented Coca-Cola or CAA, what kind of evidence would you try to present to demonstrate independent development?

Notice also the finger-pointing between the advertiser and the ad agency. Given the collaborative and iterative nature of developing an ad from concept to execution, such finger-pointing among the various players is fairly typical.

We will revisit the interactions between advertisers and ad agencies in Chapter 16.

*Damage Award.* The *Taco Bell* jury awarded the plaintiffs over $30 million, which with interest grew to $42 million. If Taco Bell had struck a deal with the plaintiffs before the ad campaign, how much do you think Taco Bell would have paid them? Why do you think Taco Bell decided not to pay? Did Taco Bell make a bad decision, or did they make a good decision with a bad outcome?

## 4.    Antitrust

Like patent law, antitrust law is another arcane corner of the law that warrants more in-depth coverage than this book can provide. In broad strokes, antitrust law seeks to promote competition. (A corollary: antitrust laws protect *competition*, not *competitors*.) By designating certain behaviors as impermissible, antitrust law can help the marketplace properly set prices and quantities.

Many antitrust cases involve a battle over the applicable standard of legal review. The two main ones are "rule of reason" and "per se," although numerous variations exist. The "rule of reason" standard evaluates the reasonableness of the anticompetitive behavior based on a consideration of all facts and circumstances. Because of its inclusive review process, "rule of reason" inquiry makes it hard to determine the legitimacy of a company's choices ex ante. The "per se" standard means the choice is presumptively illegal unless rebutted by a satisfactorily legitimate explanation. Examples of "per se" activities include agreements among competitors to fix prices or restrict production. In some cases, antitrust violations can be criminal.

Antitrust also restricts industry-dominant companies from taking advantage of their "market power." This often prompts a debate about what constitutes the "relevant market" to determine if the company in fact has market power in that market. Antitrust plaintiffs favor defining the relevant market as a small niche, while antitrust defendants favor defining the relevant market as a major industry. To resolve which market is the relevant market (and thus what share of the market the defendant has), economists are often used to argue about what prospective customers view as viable substitute offerings. Naturally, this sets up a battle among expert witnesses.

While advertisers must comply with antitrust law generally, the use of advertising usually does not raise specific antitrust concerns. For example, although monopolies often raise antitrust scrutiny, "monopolistic competition"—the process of developing consumer brand loyalty sufficient to allow commodity manufacturers to charge supra-competitive prices—does not inherently implicate antitrust law. In part, this reflects the prevailing views of economists (discussed in Chapter 2) that advertising is pro-competitive.

False advertising usually does not, by itself, support an antitrust claim. *See, e.g.*, Am. Prof'l Testing Serv., Inc. v. Harcourt Brace Jovanovich Legal and Prof'l Publ'ns, Inc., 108 F.3d 1147 (9th Cir. 1997) (no antitrust remedy for advertising disparaging a competitor).

For example, in *Retractable Technologies, Inc. v. Becton Dickinson & Co.*, 842 F.3d 883 (5th Cir. 2016), reversed a $340M damages award for false advertising-based antitrust claims. The court said the defendant's sales pitches "may have been wrong, misleading, or debatable," but those actions were "indicative of competition on the merits," as opposed to, say, bribes. The court added that its result was consistent with "traditional free speech principles": "If [a competitor's statements about another] should be false or misleading or incomplete or just plain mistaken, the remedy is not antitrust litigation but more speech—the marketplace of ideas."

Although false advertising isn't normally an antitrust issue, antitrust law does apply to advertising. For example, as the next case illustrates, antitrust problems may arise when competitors agree to restrict advertising.

Some factual background: the case involved two media conglomerates, PolyGram and Warner, and three operatic superstars called the Three Tenors, José Carreras, Plácido Domingo, and Luciano Pavarotti.

The Three Tenors created three recordings in association with the World Cup. A PolyGram subsidiary owned the first recording ("3T1"), created in 1990. Warner owned the second recording ("3T2"), created in 1994. Both recordings were very successful. 3T1 and 3T2 were both among the best-selling classical recordings in the United States in 1994, 1995, 1996, and 1997, and 3T1 became the best-selling classical record of all time. Nevertheless, PolyGram and Warner competed with each other in selling 3T1 and 3T2.

In 1998, the Three Tenors performed a third World Cup concert ("3T3"). PolyGram and Warner agreed that Warner would distribute 3T3 in the United States and PolyGram would distribute it in the rest of the world.

Subsequently, PolyGram and Warner worried that 3T1 and 3T2 would compete with 3T3 and thereby undercut their ability to recoup their substantial investments in 3T3, especially after they learned the Three Tenors' 1998 set list largely overlapped previous recordings. As a result, executives of PolyGram and Warner agreed to refrain from advertising or reducing prices of 3T1 or 3T2 audio or video products in all markets in the weeks surrounding the release of 3T3 (the "moratorium agreement"). PolyGram and Warner subsequently issued written instructions to their operating companies worldwide that forbade price discounting and advertising of 3T1 and 3T2 from August 1, 1998 through October 15, 1998. When the parties' legal departments learned of the moratorium agreement, they sent pretextual letters disavowing the agreement, but both parties nevertheless adhered to its terms.

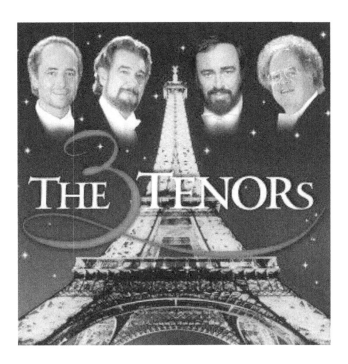

In 2001, the FTC brought an enforcement action under Section 5 of the FTC Act, which proceeded through the FTC's administrative adjudication process. For this purpose, the FTC Act Section 5 legal analysis effectively mirrors Section 1 of the Sherman Act.

### In the Matter of Polygram Holding, Inc., FTC Docket #9298 (2003)

MURIS, Chairman.

### INTRODUCTION . . .

Our story takes place not on the opera stage, but in the business world of operatic recordings. The drama is not so stirring, and no one loses his head, at least not literally. The story is troubling, nonetheless. Two recording companies agree to form a joint venture to market a new recording, by three of the world's foremost singers, and to split the costs and profits. By itself, such an agreement, even by competitors, is often beneficial, because it helps bring a new product to market. Here, however, the story turns dark when it becomes apparent that the new recording will repeat much of the repertoire of existing recordings, diminishing its marketing potential and worrying the recording companies. While other businesses might have worked harder to develop an improved or more distinctive product to attract greater consumer interest, our protagonists chose another route. They agreed to restrict their marketing of competing products that they respectively controlled—products that were clearly outside the joint venture they had formed. They imposed a moratorium on discounting and promotion of those recordings that might otherwise siphon off sales of the new product. We now consider whether such an agreement unreasonably restrains trade in violation of the antitrust laws. We conclude that it does. . . .

III. ANALYSIS OF THE CHALLENGED RESTRAINTS

. . . [W]e first must determine whether the agreement between PolyGram and Warner to forgo discounting and advertising of 3T1 and 3T2 falls within the category of restraints that are likely, absent countervailing procompetitive justifications, to have anticompetitive effects—i.e., to lead to higher prices or reduced output. In making this assessment, we consider what judicial experience and economic learning tell us about the likely competitive effects of such restrictions.

A. The Likely Anticompetitive Effects of the Moratorium

In keeping with the analytical structure detailed above, we start with an inquiry into whether the restraints at issue here—the agreement not to discount and the agreement not to advertise—are inherently suspect under the antitrust laws, in that they fall within a category of restraints that warrant summary condemnation because of their likely harm to competition. We find ample basis for concluding that they are....

2. The Agreement Not To Advertise

We also find that the agreement between PolyGram and Warner not to advertise their earlier Three Tenors products is presumptively anticompetitive. The Supreme Court in *CDA* [California Dental Ass'n. v. Federal Trade Commission, 526 U.S. 756 (1999)] indicated that, in ordinary commercial markets—like the one at issue here—complete bans on truthful advertising normally are likely to cause competitive harm. Indeed, the Court repeatedly has recognized that advertising facilitates competition. By informing consumers of the nature and prices of the goods or services available in a market, and thus creating an incentive for suppliers of the products and services to compete along these dimensions, advertising "performs an indispensable role in the allocation of resources in a free enterprise system." Restrictions on truthful and nondeceptive advertising harm competition, because they make it more difficult for consumers to discover information about the price and quality of goods or services, thereby reducing competitors' incentives to compete with each other with respect to such features. These principles apply not just to price advertising, but also to information about qualitative aspects of goods and services. "[A]ll elements of a bargain  quality, service, safety, and durability—and not just the immediate cost, are favorably affected by the free opportunity to select among alternative offers."

Complaint Counsel's economic expert testified that an agreement among competitors not to advertise is likely to harm consumers and competition by raising consumers' search costs and reducing sellers' incentives to lower prices. One reason a restriction on advertising may reduce a seller's incentives to lower prices is that, absent an ability to advertise, lower per-unit prices may not be sufficiently offset by higher volume. Dr. Stockum relied on several empirical studies that have found that advertising restrictions result in consumers' paying higher prices.[52] One of these studies, for example, showed

---

[52] .... *See* Lee Benham, *The Effect of Advertising on the Price of Eyeglasses*, 15 J.L. & ECON. 337 (1972) (restricting the advertising of eyeglasses raised the average retail price by $7.48); Lee Benham & Alexandra Benham, *Regulating Through the Professions: A Perspective on Information Control*, 18 J.L. & ECON. 421 (1975)

that even a short-lived restraint on advertising can lead to higher prices. On the basis of economic theory and empirical studies, Dr. Stockum concluded that, absent an efficiency justification, Respondents' agreement not to advertise or promote the catalog Three Tenors albums is very likely to be anticompetitive. Dr. Ordover, Respondents' economic expert, agreed in his deposition that a naked agreement among competitors not to advertise is likely to cause consumer harm. This testimony reinforces the general proposition that restrictions on advertising, such as those imposed here, are likely to reduce competition and harm consumers.

## B. Respondents' Justifications

Having concluded that both elements of Respondents' moratorium agreement were indeed inherently suspect restraints of trade because of their likely harm to competition, we turn to Respondents' proffered justifications. Respondents' sole argument in this regard is that the moratorium served a plausible procompetitive interest by preventing the PolyGram and Warner operating companies from using the promotional opportunity created by the 1998 Paris concert and the release of the new album to "free ride" on the joint venture. In particular, Respondents assert that PolyGram and

---

(prices were 25-40% higher in markets with greater professional information controls, including advertising restrictions); Ronald S. Bond et al., Staff Report on Effects of Restrictions on Advertising and Commercial Practice in the Professions: The Case of Optometry (Executive Summary), Bureau of Economics, Federal Trade Commission (Sept. 1980) (price for combined eye exam and glasses was $29 less in cities with least restrictive advertising regimes); John F. Cady, *An Estimate of the Price Effects of Restrictions on Drug Price Advertising*, 14 ECON. INQUIRY 493 (1976) (states restricting the advertising of prescription drugs have prices that are 2.9% higher than states that do not restrict advertising); Steven R. Cox et al., *Consumer Information and the Pricing of Legal Services*, 30 J. INDUS. ECON. 305 (1982) (attorneys who advertised had lower fees than those who did not advertise); Roger Feldman & James W. Begun, *The Welfare Cost of Quality Changes Due to Professional Regulation*, 34 J. INDUS. ECON. 17 (1985) (total loss of consumer welfare from state regulations governing optometrists that, inter alia, banned price advertising was $156 million); Roger Feldman & James W. Begun, *Does Advertising of Prices Reduce the Mean and Variance of Prices?*, 18 ECON. INQUIRY 487 (1980) (ban on advertising by optometrists and opticians increased prices by 11%); Roger Feldman & James W. Begun, The Effects of Advertising: Lessons from Optometry, 13 J. Hum. Resources 247 (1978) (price is 16% higher in states that ban optometric and optician price advertising); Amihai Glazer, *Advertising, Information and Prices—A Case Study*, 19 ECON. INQUIRY 661 (1981) (grocery prices rose because of newspaper strike in Queens County, NY, that eliminated large amounts of supermarket advertising, and fell after the strike ended); Deborah Haas-Wilson, *The Effect of Commercial Practice Restrictions: The Case of Optometry*, 29 J.L. & ECON. 165 (1986) (prices were 26–33% lower in markets in which price and non-price media advertising by optometrists occurred); William W. Jacobs et al., Staff Report on Improving Consumer Access to Legal Services: The Case for Removing Restrictions on Truthful Advertising (Executive Summary), Bureau of Economics, Federal Trade Commission (Nov. 1984) (restrictions on attorney advertising resulted in prices that were 5–10% higher); John E. Kwoka, Jr., *Advertising and the Price and Quality of Optometric Services*, 74 AM. ECON. REV. 211 (Mar. 1984) (prices of eye exams were $11–$12 lower in markets with advertising than in markets with advertising restrictions); James H. Love & Frank H. Stephen, *Advertising, Price and Quality in Self-Regulating Professions: A Survey*, 3 INT'L. J. ECON. BUS. 227 (1996) (reviewed 17 studies and found that restrictions on advertising generally have the effect of raising prices paid by consumers); Alex R. Maurizi et al., *Competing for Professional Control: Professional Mix in the Eyeglasses Industry*, 24 J.L. & ECON. 351 (1981) (advertisers charged approximately $7 less than non-advertisers); Robert H. Porter, *The Impact of Government Policy on the U.S. Cigarette Industry*, in EMPIRICAL APPROACHES TO CONSUMER PROTECTION ECONOMICS 446 (Pauline M. Ippolito & David T. Scheffman eds., 1986) (demand fell by 7.5% as result of 1971 ban on television and radio advertising in the cigarette industry; during the ban, prices increased from 3–6%); John R. Schroeter et al., *Advertising and Competition in Routine Legal Service Markets: An Empirical Investigation*, 36 J. INDUS. ECON. 49 (1987) (advertising made demand more elastic, meaning that consumers were more responsive to price differences); Robert L. Steiner, *Does Advertising Lower Consumer Prices?*, 37 J. MARKETING 19 (Oct. 1973) (advertising resulted in lower toy prices to the consumer).

Warner were concerned that aggressive promotion of 3T1 or 3T2 during the 3T3 release period would divert sales from 3T3, and that the prospect of such diversion could induce them to withhold promotional efforts in support of 3T3. They further assert that lack of success with 3T3 could have undermined the success of subsequent joint venture products—i.e., a proposed "Greatest Hits" album and a Boxed Set.

We reject these arguments as a matter of law because they go far beyond the range of justifications that are cognizable under the antitrust laws. Respondents are not asserting that restraints on the joint venture activities are reasonably necessary to achieve efficiencies in its operations, nor even that expansion of the joint venture is reasonably necessary to achieve such efficiencies. Rather, they are arguing that competitors may agree to restrict competition by products wholly outside a joint venture, to increase profits for the products of the joint venture itself. Such a claim is "nothing less than a frontal assault on the basic policy of the Sherman Act," for it displaces market-based outcomes regarding the mix of products to be offered with collusive determinations that certain new products will be offered under a shield from direct competition.

Preventing free-riding can be a legitimate efficiency. The most widely recognized application in antitrust of this efficiency is, as Respondents suggest, limiting intrabrand competition to improve interbrand competition. In such cases, the scope of the restraint is necessarily limited to products that are within the control (at least initially) of the entity that owns the restricted brand. Here, despite Respondents' invocation of a Three Tenors "brand," there is obviously no such thing, because one entity did not legally control all Three Tenors products. The marketing rights to 3T1 and 3T2 were held not by the joint venture but, rather, independently by the parties to the venture. . . .

The sort of behavior that Respondents disparage as "free-riding"—i.e., taking advantage of the interest in competing products that promotional efforts for one product may induce—is an essential part of the process of competition that occurs daily throughout our economy. For example, when General Motors ("GM") creates a new sport utility vehicle ("SUV") and promotes it, through price discounts, advertising, or both, other SUVs can "free ride" on the fact that GM's promotion inevitably stimulates consumer interest, not just in GM's SUV, but in the SUV category itself. Our antitrust laws exist to protect this response, because it is in reality the competition that drives a market economy to benefit consumers. There is no doubt that GM's SUV will likely be more profitable if its competitors do not respond. Promoting profitability, however, is not now, nor has it ever been, recognized as a basis to restrain interbrand competition under the antitrust laws . . .

Thus, we hold that the Respondents' "free-riding" argument is simply an attempt to shield themselves from legitimate interbrand competition. As such, the proffered justification is not cognizable under antitrust law. This conclusion, together with our previous conclusion that the restraints at issue are of the sort that are likely to harm competition, provides us with ample ground to condemn Respondents' actions as unlawful under Section 1, without further analysis. . . .

C. A More Detailed Factual Analysis...

2. Competitive Effect of Respondents' Advertising Restrictions

. . . Complaint Counsel's music industry marketing expert, Dr. Moore, explained that a record company's decisions regarding advertising and wholesale price are linked, and if there is no advertising, there is less incentive for the company to offer the recording at a significantly reduced price. Dr. Moore further testified—and Respondents' executives confirmed—that record companies advertise to increase their sales, and that such advertising generally results in lower retail prices for consumers.

Furthermore, before the moratorium, advertising was an important part of competition between 3T1 and 3T2. In 1994, when 3T2 was released, PolyGram advertised to inform consumers that 3T1 was the "original" Three Tenors recording, was still widely available, and indeed was often available at a discounted price. Largely as a result of its marketing campaign, PolyGram sold almost one million audio and video recordings of 3T1 in the second half of 1994, as compared with 377,000 in the same period in 1993. In turn, Warner used advertising to create a distinct identity for 3T2, suggesting to consumers that the newer release was the superior product. PolyGram and Warner again used advertising to highlight the advantages of their respective Three Tenors products during the Three Tenors' world concert tours in 1996 and 1997.

. . . The ban on advertising was intended to protect sales of 3T3 by withholding information from consumers about the nature and price of competing products. As one Warner executive explained at trial, the companies did not want consumers to "start comparing the repertoire along with the price and make a determination that, you know, the '94 concert is just fine for a few dollars less." We agree with the ALJ that the anticompetitive effect of this strategy is obvious. . . .

*NOTES AND QUESTIONS*

*Subsequent Proceeding.* Polygram appealed the FTC Commissioners' decision to the D.C. Circuit, which upheld the FTC's ruling. Polygram Holding Inc v. Federal Trade Commission, 416 F. 3d 29 (D.C. Cir. 2005).

*Advertising as Pro-Competitive.* Notice how much of the antitrust analysis mirrors the debates about the social benefits and costs of advertising we discussed in Chapter 2. In this case, the FTC decidedly viewed advertising as a pro-competition tool.

*Spillover Effects.* PolyGram and Warner defended their actions, in part, based on worries that promotion of 3T3 would stimulate demand for other works by the same artists. The FTC rejected that argument, saying that these spillover effects are part of ordinary economic activity. *See generally* Brett M. Frischmann & Mark A. Lemley, *Spillovers*, 107 COLUM. L. REV. 257 (2007); Eric Goldman, *Brand Spillovers*, 22 HARV. J. L. & TECH. 381 (2009). Reconsider this issue in light of what you read about ambush marketing in Chapter 11—was there anything unfair about advertising 3T1 to compete with 3T2?

*"Intrabrand" Competition.* To what extent do you think that different albums in a musical group's catalog compete with each other? Does a live album compete with a studio album? If this case were heard today, would the widespread availability of digital downloads and streaming of individual album tracks change the analysis?

*Keyword Advertising Restrictions.* Some trademark owners will contractually restrict business partners from bidding on their trademarks as online advertising keywords. In some cases, these business partners are marketing affiliates who are expected to generate new customers for the trademark owner. In other cases, however, the business partners may be the trademark owners' vendors, customers or even competitors. Would such contractual restrictions raise antitrust concerns? *See* In the Matter of 1-800 Contacts, Inc., F.T.C. Docket No. 9372 (Oct. 27, 2017). The administrative law judge found that agreements with competitors, purportedly settling trademark disputes, violated the antitrust laws where the agreements prohibited each party from bidding on each other's trademark terms as keywords and further required each party to implement negative keywords based on the other party's trademark terms, in order to prevent ads from displaying based on a generic keyword such as "contacts" when the searcher typed "1-800-contacts." The judge held that "displaying an ad in response to a search for 1-800 Contacts' trademark terms is an important method by which lower-priced online contact lens retailers compete with 1-800 Contacts for customers." See also Thompson v. 1-800 Contacts, Inc., 2018 WL 2271024 (D. Utah May 17, 2018) (denying motion to dismiss consumers' antitrust claim based on the same conduct).

*Price-setting as a Regulated Activity.* A company's price setting decisions can raise antitrust issues in multiple ways. Agreeing on prices with competitors typically violates antitrust laws (and can be criminal), but even independent pricing decisions can run into trouble. Setting prices too low can violate minimum pricing laws; and it may be considered predatory pricing and seen as an effort to drive out competitors. Further, charging customers different prices can be regulated by the Robinson-Patman Act, a Depression-era federal statute which prohibits certain types of price discrimination, and potentially by other laws. Nevertheless, many vendors are interested in price discrimination because it can help increase profits.

*Collusion on Advertising Restrictions.* If businesses collude to reduce advertising costs without restricting advertising quantity, antitrust law is still implicated.

In *Marker Völkl (International) GmbH & Tecnica Group S.p.A.*, F.T.C. File No. 1210004, 79 Fed. Reg. 30143 (May 27, 2014), the FTC alleged that well-known endorsers are the most effective (and costly) marketing tools in selling ski equipment. Ski equipment manufacturers usually compete for endorsers, and manufacturers may offer endorsers extra money to switch endorsements when their contracts end.

However, two manufacturers agreed not to recruit any skiers who'd previously endorsed the other or was otherwise "claimed" by the other, and they ultimately expanded that agreement to cover all their employees. The aim, naturally, was to avoid paying endorsers and employees more money. According to the FTC, "[a]greements between competitors not to compete for professional services, for employees, or for other inputs, are presumptively anticompetitive or inherently suspect, if not per se unlawful." The parties agreed to a consent order barring such conduct.

*Antitrust Scrutiny of Advertising Intermediaries.* Antitrust law typically focuses on manufacturers and retailers, including, in some cases, how they use advertising to advance their position. The

*Polygram* case involves manufacturers who impermissibly coordinated their actions. Sometimes, antitrust scrutiny can attach to other players in the advertising industry, such as publishers. For example, many major metropolitan newspapers benefited from the Newspaper Preservation Act of 1970, a statutory exception to antitrust law that allowed local competitors to work together. More recently, Google and Facebook have received considerable antitrust speculation for their role as advertising intermediaries due to their significant share of the online advertising market.

Advertisements routinely depict people—their image, name, voice, and other aspects of their personality. This chapter looks at the special legal issues that arise from depicting people in ads.

## 1. Overview of Publicity Rights

Publicity rights generally protect the use of people's names, images, voices or other personality attributes from unconsented commercialization.

Publicity rights evolved out of a person's privacy rights. In the United States, privacy rights generally trace back to the immensely influential privacy article by Samuel D. Warren and Louis D. Brandeis, *The Right to Privacy*, 4 HARV. L. REV. 193 (1890). Both Warren and Brandeis were lawyers at the time; Brandeis went on to become a celebrated U.S. Supreme Court justice.

The article reacted to improvements in camera technology. Initially, camera shutter speeds were so slow that people had to pose (i.e., stand still) for photographs. However, technological evolutions reduced shutter speeds, which allowed photographers to take photos of people without their consent. Warren and Brandeis argued that "the existing law affords a principle from which may be invoked to protect the privacy of the individual from invasion either by the too enterprising press, the photographer, or the possessor of any other modern device for rewording or reproducing scenes or sounds."

Recapping privacy law in the early 1960s, Dean William Prosser classified privacy legal claims over the intervening seventy years into four categories. *See* William L. Prosser, *Privacy*, 48 CAL. L. REV. 383 (1960) and RESTATEMENT (SECOND) OF TORTS (for which Prosser was the reporter). This included a category for "[a]ppropriation, for the defendant's advantage, of the plaintiff's name or likeness," which has evolved into the modern "publicity right."

Although the publicity rights doctrine is well-recognized, its legal implementation is a little chaotic. There is no federal publicity right. Currently, about half the states statutorily codify publicity rights, and some statutes explicitly provide that publicity rights survive beyond a person's death.* *See, e.g.*, CAL. CIVIL CODE § 3344.1 (surviving rights for seventy years post-mortem); INDIANA CODE 32–36 (surviving rights for 100 years post-mortem). In some states, publicity rights are protected by common law doctrines. In a few states, publicity rights are protected by both statute and common law.

---

* However, some statutes require pre-death commercialization of the name as a precondition of publicity rights descendibility.

Because many celebrities reside there, California and New York play particularly important roles in the development of publicity rights laws. However, publicity rights are not limited to celebrities, and they usually equally protect both famous and non-famous individuals.

Publicity rights generally govern two discrete activities: (1) "merchandising" by selling an item that incorporates some identifiable part of the person, such as the incorporation of a celebrity's image on a t-shirt or a videogame containing a character that resembles an actual person, and (2) the depiction of a person in ad copy.

This chapter focuses almost exclusively on the ad copy cases. Typically, ad copy publicity rights cases are doctrinally easier than merchandising cases, but both types of cases can create difficult line-drawing situations. In addition, the publicity rights doctrines have an uneasy fit with the First Amendment, especially in the merchandising context.

Publicity rights only protect individuals. Trademark law and related doctrines provide analogous protection for businesses' brand names and other identifiers. If a person's name develops secondary meaning in association with commercial offerings, people can develop trademark rights in their name or other attributes to complement their publicity rights (which exist automatically). When enforcing those rights, trademark law requires that the defendant's usage creates a likelihood of consumer confusion. In contrast, consumer confusion is unnecessary to succeed with a publicity rights claim.

## 2.      Publicity Rights and Ad Copy

With very limited exceptions, depicting a person in ad copy requires the person's consent. Even with this fairly clear rule, plenty of ambiguity remains. This part looks at the depiction of various personality attributes to explore the boundaries of the publicity rights doctrine.

### A.      A Person's Name

In reading this opinion, it may be helpful to know that a "Henley shirt" is a collarless polo shirt. It is named after Henley-on-Thames, England, whose rowers wore uniforms in this style.

*Henley v. Dillard Department Stores, 46 F. Supp. 2d 587 (N.D. Tex. 1999)*

. . . FACTS . . .

Plaintiff Donald Hugh Henley ("Henley" or "Plaintiff"), is a popular and critically acclaimed rock and roll musician. He began his music career in the 1970s as the founder and member of the band The Eagles. In the 1980s and 1990s, Henley maintained a successful solo career by continuing to produce platinum albums and perform on tour in concerts around the world.

On September 3 and 4, 1997, Defendant Dillard Department Stores ("Dillard" or "Defendant") ran a newspaper advertisement for a shirt known as a "henley." The ad features a photograph of a man wearing a henley shirt with the words, "This is Don" in large print, beside the picture, and an arrow pointing toward the man's head from the words. Underneath the words is the statement, "This is Don's henley" in the same size print, with a second arrow pointing to the shirt. The advertisement also included the name of the retailer, "Dillard's", general information about the sale price of the shirts, the name of the shirt's manufacturer, the available sizes and the following: "Sometimes Don tucks it in; other times he wears it loose—it looks great either way. Don loves his henley; you will too." The ad ran in newspapers throughout Texas and in Mexico.

DISCUSSION . . .

B. Right to Publicity

The right of publicity is often described as the "inherent right of every human being to control the commercial use of his or her identity." The right to publicity is considered an intellectual property right. It is a more expansive right than any common law or statutory trademark infringement right because it does not require a showing of likelihood of confusion.

The tort of misappropriation of one's name or likeness is generally referred to as the "Right of Publicity" and is based on section 652C of the Restatement of Torts which reads, "One who appropriates to his own use or benefit the name or likeness of another is subject to liability to the other for invasion of his privacy." The Fifth Circuit has specifically identified three elements a plaintiff must prove to recover for the tort of misappropriation of name and likeness in Texas: (1) the defendant appropriated the plaintiff's name or likeness for the value associated with it, and not in an incidental manner or for a newsworthy purpose; (2) the plaintiff can be identified from the publication; and (3) there was some advantage or benefit to the defendant.

The right of publicity is designed to protect the commercial interests of celebrities in their identities. It is intended to protect the value of a celebrity's notoriety or skill. Because a celebrity's identity can be valuable in the promotion of products, "the celebrity has an interest that may be protected from the unauthorized commercial exploitation of that identity." Such celebrities have an exclusive legal right to control and profit from the commercial use of their name, personality and identity. "If the celebrity's identity is commercially exploited, there has been an invasion of his right whether or not his 'name or likeness' is used." The tort does not protect the use of the celebrity's name per se, but rather the value associated with that name. . . .

1. Did Defendant Appropriate the Plaintiff's Name or Likeness for the Value Associated with it, and not in an Incidental Manner or for a Newsworthy Purpose?

The threshold issue to determine in analyzing this element is whether Defendant actually appropriated Defendant's name or likeness. . . .

While use of the expression "Don's henley" is arguably the use of Plaintiff's name, a genuine issue of fact exists as to whether that expression is, indeed, Plaintiff's name. However, Courts have recognized that a defendant may be held liable for using a phrase or image that clearly identifies the celebrity, in addition to finding liability for using a plaintiff's precise name. Because the use of the expression "Don's henley" is so clearly recognizable as a likeness of Plaintiff, the Court finds that no reasonable juror could conclude that the phrase "Don's henley" does not clearly identify the Plaintiff, Don Henley. . . .

The second issue the Court must resolve is whether Defendant appropriated Plaintiff's name or likeness for the value associated with it, and not in an incidental manner. Defendant argues that "there has been no evidence presented that Dillard chose to use the wording 'Don's henley' in order to capitalize on the alleged value of the name Don Henley." The Court disagrees, and in fact, finds that Defendant has presented no reasonable evidence to defeat Plaintiff's summary judgment motion. Plaintiff presents uncontroverted deposition testimony from Lisa M. Robertson, the creator of the print advertisement, admitting that use of Don Henley's 'name' was intended to make the ad more interesting. She . . . intended to use the expression as a "play on words" and intended consumers to recognize this advertisement as a "wordplay" on the name "Don Henley."[2] In other words, Defendant

---

[2] Q: Well, what prompted you to come up with the idea "This is Don. This is Don's Henley"?
A: Well, I was trying to find a play on words to use for the ad.
Q: And there's no doubt that when you were using the words "This is Don. This is Don's henley," the Don Henley wordplay meant Don Henley the recording artist, not some other person named Don Henley?
A: Well, obviously the name—yes, I mean I knew it was Don Henley; that was where it came from. But it wasn't, you know, to imply that he was a part of it.
Q: I think you said earlier that by using the word—by using the headline "This is Don. This is Don's henley," you intended a wordplay, correct?
A: Yes.
Q: And so it was your intention for consumers to recognize this advertisement as a wordplay.
A: Yes.
Q: And for the wordplay to work, the consumer had to recognize the name Don Henley, right?
A: Well, you'd have to know who he was to get it, yes.

admitted that she did not intend potential consumers to perceive the ad as depicting an anonymous man named "Don." She intended for them to associate the expression "Don's henley" with the Plaintiff Don Henley. Furthermore, Debra L. Green, the ad's designer, admitted that she believed the expression "Don's henley" would catch the consumers' eye because of its similarity to the name "Don Henley."[3] Therefore, Defendant admits Dillard used the play on words, "Don's henley" to attract consumers as they associated the expression and the ad with Plaintiff Don Henley. In other words, they used the value associated with Don Henley's identity and personality in order to attract consumers' attention.

Defendant presents testimony from Dillard's Vice President of Sales Promotion, William B. Warner, suggesting that the use of the words "Don's henley" adds no value to the advertisement.[4] Warner testified that he believes there is no value associated with the expression "Don's henley," and that the singular and sole purpose of choosing and printing that phrase was "fun." In fact, Defendant argues, the use of the expression, "Don's henley" was incidental to the primary focus of the advertisement. The portions of the ad that were of "chief importance" were the "handwritten text and arrows . . . the visual presentation of information." . . .

. . . The Court finds it unreasonable to draw the inference Defendant requests. Defendant's evidence could not lead a reasonable jury to conclude that the use of the words "Don's henley" was for any purpose other than to attract the attention of consumers.

... Defendant's use of the message "This is Don. This is Don's henley." in large letters, centered in the print ad was clearly and admittedly intended to attract the consumers' attention. The Court is hard pressed to believe that a reasonable jury could conclude that the size and style of the letters, rather than the message created with those letters, are the focus of the ad. No reasonable jury could conclude that the use of the word play was merely incidental to the advertisement.

2. Can the Plaintiff be Identified from the Publication?

The second element Plaintiff must satisfy to prove an infringement of the Right of Publicity, is that "plaintiff as a human being must be 'identifiable' from the total context of the defendant's use." While there are many ways a plaintiff can be identified in a defendant's use, the most obvious is use of a name that distinguishes the plaintiff. "Identifiability of plaintiff will probably not be a

---

Q: So for it to work or for them to get it, they must recognize the similarity between the words "This is Don. This is Don's henley" and the name of the recording artist Don Henley, correct?
A: Yes.
[3] Q: Do you think that the words "Don's," apostrophe "s," "henley" would catch a consumer's eye?
A: I think the sound of them reading it would repeat the sound of—I think that that would in some way associate with Don.
Q: Well, my question is would it have caught your average consumer's eye, the use of the words "Don's henley"?
A: I think so.

[4] Q: Did the words—in your opinion, do the words "Don" and "Don's henley" help make the ad more effective?
A: I think not. I think they make it fun, but not necessarily in any way that would actually make it more effective from the standpoint of achieving what a good ad is intended to achieve.
Q: Was it you [sic] opinion that the words "Don" and "Don's henley" add no value at all to the ad?
A: That's my basic opinion.

disputable issue in the majority of meritorious Right of Publicity cases." This is due to the fact that defendants will usually make the plaintiff's identity as identifiable as possible so as to draw the maximum amount of attention to the defendant's product. "The intent, state of mind and degree of knowledge of a defendant may shed light on the identifiability issue." "To establish liability, plaintiff need prove no more than that he or she is reasonably identifiable in defendant's use to more than a de [minimis] number of persons." . . .

The Court finds that the issue of identifiability is indisputable in this case because Defendant has offered no evidence to suggest that Plaintiff is not identifiable from the ad. Plaintiff's survey evidence indicates that sixty-five percent of survey respondents believed there was a spokesperson or endorser in the ad. Of those who said there was a spokesperson or endorser, twenty-three percent said the spokesperson or endorser was Don Henley.[8] In other words, fifteen percent of those asked believed Don Henley was a spokesman for or endorser of the ad, and thus, necessarily identified him from the ad. The results of this survey clearly prove that Don Henley was reasonably identifiable in Defendant's ad to more than a de [minimis] number of persons.

Further, in evaluating the intent and state of mind of Defendant, the evidence is undisputed that Defendant intended to appropriate Don Henley's identity and intended that consumers associate the ad with Don Henley. First, as stated *supra*, the creators of the ad admitted they intended consumers to associate Don Henley with the ad. Second, the Defendant intended to appropriate the image of performing artist Don Henley, not some other, anonymous person by that same name. This is proven by Plaintiff's evidence that the ad creators drafted an earlier version of the ad that added quotes or paraphrases from eight Don Henley song titles to the ad at issue.[9] The Court concludes that there is no fact issue from which a reasonable jury could conclude that Plaintiff was not identifiable from the ad.

3. Was there an Advantage or Benefit to Defendant?

Defendant insists that Plaintiff cannot prove a benefit inured to Dillard because the sales generated by the ad were not sufficient to cover the costs of running the ad. Plaintiff argues that the Court need consider no more than the fact that the ad was created with the belief that the use of the words "Don's henley" would help sell its product.

---

[8] It is arguable that, had the respondents been shown Defendant's ad and been asked "Who do you think is identified in this ad?" a different result would have occurred. In order to name Don Henley as the spokesperson or endorser of the ad (as the question was asked by the surveyor), the surveyees were required to believe the ad was, in fact, endorsed by Henley. Had the surveyees been asked the question "Who do you think is identified in this ad?" it is likely that the number responding "Don Henley" would have increased due to the fact that they would not have been required to believe he endorsed the product or gave his permission to have his name or likeness used in the ad. They would only have been required to believe he was identifiable from the ad.

[9] The ad, in draft form read, "If all you want to do is dance / pick up your witchy woman / take it to the limit in our cotton henley. We promise, you've spent your last worthless evening! Give her the best of your love, and when the party's over, toss our machine washable henley right in the dirty laundry. In the long run, you'll love the great colors and the super-sturdy construction. But hurry in, they may be already gone." [Editor's note: we underlined the song titles, which are a mixture of Eagles songs and Don Henley solo songs.]

. . . Comment d [of the Restatement (Second) of Torts § 652C] reads: "It is only when the publicity is given for the purpose of appropriating to the defendant's benefit the commercial or other values associated with the name or likeness that the right of privacy is invaded." Comment d further suggests that the notion that a benefit must inure to the defendant is intertwined with the factor requiring that the plaintiff prove the defendant appropriated the plaintiff's name or likeness for its value and not for an incidental use. The "benefit" element requires Plaintiff to prove that Defendant derived some commercial benefit from the use of plaintiff's name or likeness as opposed to deriving no commercial benefit due to the fact that the use was incidental. . . .

The plaintiff in a right to publicity action is not required to show that the defendant made money off the commercial use of the name or likeness, as Defendant suggests. It is immaterial that Defendant made little profit after the ad ran, only ran the advertisement once, and received no feedback on the ad. What Plaintiff must prove is that Defendant received a commercial benefit from use of Plaintiff's name or likeness that, without Plaintiff's image, he would not otherwise have received. Defendant's sophisticated and experienced ad creators described the benefit they received as being able to catch the eye of the consumer and make the ad more interesting. By appropriating Plaintiff's name or likeness, Defendant received the benefit of a celebrity endorsement without asking permission or paying a fee.

To reiterate an earlier point, the Right of Publicity cause of action exists to protect a celebrity's identity, which can be valuable in the promotion of products. Such celebrities have an exclusive legal right to control and profit from the commercial use of their name, personality and identity. . . . The Court, thus, refuses to require a plaintiff to prove that a defendant made a profit or secured a tangible benefit from use of the plaintiff's name or likeness.

. . . Defendant should not be shielded from liability because "the product promoted is undesirable, the ad [is] clumsy or somehow ineffective, or sales slump[ed] during the relevant time period." Rather, Dillard should be held liable because it received a benefit by getting to use a celebrity's name for free in its advertising. Whether or not the advertising worked for Dillard is wholly irrelevant. The Court concludes that there is no fact issue from which a reasonable jury could conclude that Defendant did not receive a benefit from its use of Plaintiff's likeness. . . .

*NOTES AND QUESTIONS*

*Celebrities v. Ordinary People.* This case emphasizes Don Henley's celebrity status. However, as illustrated by cases such as *Cohen* (discussed later), celebrity status is not required for a valid publicity rights claim.

*How Far Does a Name's Protection Extend?* Would the case's result have changed if Dillard had referenced "Donald's henley"? "Dawn's henley"? "Donny's henley"? "Dom's henley"? Once the court believed that Dillard was intentionally trying to evoke Don Henley, was Dillard liable no matter what variation of "Don Henley" they used? The ad derives value from the pun on Henley's name, but the court doesn't seem interested in the fact that it required extra mental effort for consumers to decode the pun.

554

*Consumer Surveys.* The case says "fifteen percent of those asked believed Don Henley was a spokesman for or endorser of the ad." Should the result change if all of the other 85% clearly understood that the ad was a joke? Should a small minority of consumers be able to create a veto on advertising where almost everyone the joke?

Consumer surveys are common in trademark and false advertising cases, but they are relatively rare in publicity rights cases.

*Celebrities on a First-Name Basis.* During the 2010 Super Bowl, the online brokerage E*Trade ran one of its "talking baby" commercials. In the commercial, the protagonist is explaining to his "girlfriend" (a baby girl) that he didn't call because he was taking advantage of E*Trade. The girlfriend accusatorily asks, "And that milkaholic Lindsay wasn't over?" After an awkward pause, the protagonist then replies "Lindsay?" in an unsure voice while a previously unseen baby girl in the protagonist's room—presumably, the "Lindsay" both babies are referencing—reveals herself to the camera and says "Milk-a-what?"

This ad prompted a $50 million lawsuit from Lindsay Lohan, a successful teen actress who battled highly publicized substance-addiction issues. Lohan v. E*Trade Secs. LLC, No. 10-004579 (N.Y. Sup. Ct. complaint filed March 8, 2010). Lohan claimed that the ad's "Lindsay" references were meant to be her. Among other things, she claimed that her first name is so well-known that ad viewers would have assumed it was her. Lohan and E*Trade subsequently settled the lawsuit on confidential terms.[*]

Lohan was born in 1986. In the 1980s, "Lindsay" was the 44th most popular girl name according to the Baby NameVoyager website (and the sound-alike "Lindsey" was the 42nd most popular). In 2010, "Lindsay" was the 596th most popular girl's name. Is either fact relevant?

---

[*] Lindsay Lohan has an expansive view of her publicity rights, and that has not fared well in court. *See, e.g.,* Lohan v Take-Two Interactive Software, Inc., 2018 NY Slip Op 02208 (N.Y. Ct. App. 2018).

No matter what first name E*Trade chose for the milkaholic character, does E*Trade face an unavoidable risk that some celebrity with the same name will claim the ad refers to him or her?

Does the following billboard, promoting tourism with the slogan "MORE RUSH THAN YOU GET FROM TALK RADIO," misappropriate anyone's personality rights? Does the capitalization matter?

Elroy Hirsch was a University of Wisconsin athlete who went on to become a successful and well-known pro football player. Hirsch received the nickname "Crazylegs" as described in *Hirsch v. S.C. Johnson & Son. Inc.*, 280 N.W.2d 129 (Wis. 1979):

> In the fourth game of his first season of play at Wisconsin, he acquired the name, "Crazylegs." In that game, Hirsch ran 62 yards for a touchdown, wobbling down the sideline looking as though he might step out of bounds at any moment. Hirsch's unique running style, which looked something like a whirling eggbeater, drew the attention of a sportswriter for the Chicago Daily News who tagged Hirsch with the nickname, "Crazylegs." It is undisputed that the name stuck, and Hirsch has been known as "Crazylegs" ever since.

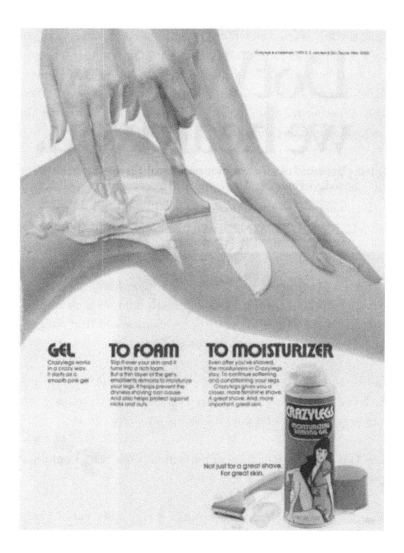

The court upheld Hirsch's claim against the product name. Are you surprised by that result? Why or why not?

*Using a Celebrity's "Abandoned" Name.* In *Abdul-Jabbar v. General Motors Corp.*, 85 F.3d 407 (9th Cir. 1996), the former basketball star Kareem Abdul-Jabbar alleged that the car manufacturer GMC violated the Lanham Act and California's statutory and common law right of publicity by using his former name, Lew Alcindor, without his consent, in a television ad aired during the 1993 NCAA men's basketball tournament. The court of appeals agreed that a jury could find GMC liable.

The ad involved a voiceover that asked, "Who holds the record for being voted the most outstanding player of this tournament?" The screen then displayed, "Lew Alcindor, UCLA, '67, '68, '69." The voiceover then asked, "Has any car made the 'Consumer Digest's Best Buy' list more than once? [and responds:] The Oldsmobile Eighty-Eight has." The ad also called the car "A Definite First Round Pick."

Abdul-Jabbar adopted his present name in 1971, and hadn't used "Lew Alcindor" for commercial purposes in over ten years at the time of decision. The court of appeals reasoned that, under

California common law, the key issue was whether his "identity" had been appropriated; California statutory law protected "name, voice, signature, photograph, or likeness." Using the former name could constitute use of his "identity," and the statute wasn't limited to presently used names. "To the extent GMC's use of the plaintiff's birth name attracted television viewers' attention, GMC gained a commercial advantage." Whether the name Lew Alcindor "equalled" Kareem Abdul-Jabbar in consumers' minds was a question for the jury.

In addition, Abdul-Jabbar provided sufficient evidence for a jury to find that he was injured "economically because the ad will make it difficult for him to endorse other automobiles, and emotionally because people may be led to believe he has abandoned his current name and assume he has renounced his religion." (Abdul-Jabbar changed his name as a result of his religious conversion to Islam).

While Lew Alcindor's "abandoned" name was famous, the more likely scenario is a celebrity's new stage name becomes more well-known than his or her birth name. For example, the real name of 50 Cent is Curtis Jackson. If ad copy referenced Curtis Jackson, would that violate his publicity rights if few consumers would realize that is the same person as 50 Cent?

*References to True Facts About Celebrities in Ad Copy.* Why can't GM's ad copy recite the true fact that Alcindor was the NCAA tournament MVP three times? What changes, if any, could GM make to its ad copy to reference Lew Alcindor and not violate his publicity rights?

In the discussion about GM's liability for false endorsement under the Lanham Act and the possibility of a nominative use defense, the court says:

> Had GMC limited itself to the "trivia" portion of its ad, GMC could likely defend the reference to Lew Alcindor as a nominative fair use. But by using Alcindor's record to make a claim for its car—like the basketball star, the Olds 88 won an "award" three years in a row, and like the star, the car is a "champ" and a "first round pick"—GMC has arguably attempted to "appropriate the cachet of one product for another," if not also to "capitalize on consumer confusion." We therefore hold that there is a question of fact as to whether GMC is entitled to a fair use defense.

This suggests GMC could have referenced Alcindor if it did not connect Alcindor's accomplishments to its product claims. But if GMC doesn't make that cognitive connection for the viewer, why would GMC invoke Alcindor's accomplishments? Worse, it might be even more suspicious if GMC invoked Alcindor's accomplishments without tying them to product claims; otherwise, it might look even more like an implied endorsement from Alcindor/Abdul-Jabbar. Given that GMC faces trouble either way, does this support an inference that GMC could not revamp the ad copy to reference Alcindor without triggering a violation of his publicity rights?

*The Boundaries of Commercial Speech. Jordan v. Jewel Food Stores, Inc.*, 743 F.3d 509 (7th Cir. 2014), held that an ad congratulating basketball legend Michael Jordan, run in a special issue of *Sports Illustrated* celebrating Jordan's career, was commercial speech, so the Lanham Act and right of publicity apply to it. Why did Jewel run this ad and use this particular ad copy?

558

*Tweeting about Celebrities.* A paparazzi photographed actress Katherine Heigl exiting a Duane Reade drugstore carrying two Duane Reade shopping bags. Duane Reade then tweeted the photo with the text "Love a quick #DuaneReade run? Even @KatieHeigl can't resist shopping #NYC's favorite drugstore."

Duane Reade
@DuaneReade                                      Follow

Love a quick #DuaneReade run? Even
@KatieHeigl can't resist shopping #NYC's
favorite drugstore bit.ly/1gLHctl
pic.twitter.com/uGTc3k1Mii

Reply   Retweet   Favorite   More

RETWEETS   FAVORITES
74         181

Assume that the tweet is factually correct, and assume Duane Reade properly procured any required copyright licenses to the photo. Does Katherine Heigl have a valid right of publicity claim against Duane Reade? Duane Reade removed the tweet and the case settled with Duane Reade making an unspecified payment to a charity associated with Heigl.

If you think Duane Reade went too far with this tweet, is there any way they could share this photo with their audiences without Heigl's permission? *See generally* Ashley Messenger, *Rethinking the Right of Publicity in the Context of Social Media*, 24 WIDENER L. REV. 259 (2018).

*Test Yourself*: In July 2014, NBA basketball player LeBron James, often nicknamed "King James," announced that he was re-signing with the Cleveland Cavaliers. This announcement sparked a flurry of tweets on Twitter. Which, if any, of the following do you think are legally problematic?

 Orbitz ✓
@Orbitz

 Follow

I guess traveling is allowed in Basketball #cominghome #imcominghome #thekingisback bit.ly/1mGI49B

9:58 AM - 11 Jul 2014

9 RETWEETS  1 FAVORITE                            ← ↻ ★

 **Barbasol**
@ShaveLikeAMan

 Follow

@KingJames As an Ohio-based company, we'd like to say... Welcome Home. #TheKingIsBack #barbasol

10:40 AM - 11 Jul 2014

1 RETWEET                                         ← ↻ ★

 **DiGiorno Pizza** ✓
@DiGiornoPizza

 Follow

lot of pizza getting eaten in Cleveland rn #WelcomeHomeLebron □□□

9:39 AM - 11 Jul 2014

40 RETWEETS  65 FAVORITES                         ← ↻ ★

Applebee's ✓
@Applebees

🕊 Follow

We are melting in anticipation @KingJames!!
#TheKingisBack

10:29 AM - 11 Jul 2014

26 RETWEETS 52 FAVORITES

Denny's ✓
@DennysDiner

🕊 Follow

if only you would have signed with *us*, king james, if
only. we coulda been a contender, we coulda been
somebody...

9:45 AM - 11 Jul 2014

198 RETWEETS 297 FAVORITES

Cottonelle ✓
@cottonelle

🕊 Follow

LeBron James is returning to Cleveland. Lesson: Stick with
what works, like Cottonelle TP and Flushable Wipes

9:33 AM - 11 Jul 2014

318 RETWEETS 141 FAVORITES

**Charmin** ☑      🐦 Follow
@Charmin

Looks like the king is returning his "throne" back to Cleveland. The internet is officially in meltdown & blowout mode. #tweetfromtheseat

9:56 AM - 11 Jul 2014

24 RETWEETS 13 FAVORITES      ↩ ↻ ★

*Product Reviews.* Later in this chapter, we'll discuss the special rules applicable to endorsements and testimonials. For now, let's just consider the publicity rights angle. Can an advertiser quote a favorable Yelp review or newspaper review in its ads and reference the author's name? If a celebrity mentions in an interview that she regularly uses the advertiser's product, can the advertiser mention this fact in future ads?

Although it seems like quoting or referencing truthful published endorsements or testimonials in ads (without the person's permission) should be OK, publicity rights make it a legally uncertain practice. Most advertisers take the conservative route and obtain permission before including these quotes or references with attribution. However, when it comes to Yelp reviews, sometimes advertisers include the quote without attributing it to the reviewer's name. And if a celebrity gives a shout-out to an advertiser, it may be too hard to obtain the celebrity's consent and yet too tempting not to spread the news.

*Press Releases.* Recall *Yeager v. Cingular Wireless LLC* from Chapter 2. The case found a publicity rights violation when a Cingular press release touting its disaster preparedness equipment—called MACH 1 and MACH 2—invoked legendary pilot Chuck Yeager's accomplishment of flying at Mach 1 speed.

*Ad Agency Liability.* In *Abdul-Jabbar*, the court treated the advertiser (GM) and its ad agency (Leo Burnett) as equally liable for the publicity rights violation. We'll revisit ad agency liability in Chapter 16.

*Personality Trademarks and Publicity Rights Compared.* In some cases, individuals may have protectable trademarks in addition to their publicity rights. Recall that getting a trademark requires making a "use in commerce" of the term, such as by affixing a person's name or likeness on goods or services available in the marketplace. Furthermore, to get a trademark in a personal name, the individual must show that their name has achieved secondary meaning, i.e., that when consumers see the name, they think of a single source of marketplace goods or services (e.g., Sears' Kardashian Kollection).

As a result of the "use in commerce" and secondary meaning requirements, non-celebrities rarely will have trademark rights protecting some aspect of their personality. Indeed, most celebrities will not have protectable trademark rights, either because they have not merchandized their personality or have not achieved the requisite secondary meaning.

Even when celebrities have trademark rights in their personalities, publicity rights claims are usually easier to win (in jurisdictions which have recognized publicity rights). Unlike trademark law, publicity rights do not require showing a likelihood of consumer confusion about product source. Also, as the *Henley* and *Abdul-Jabbar* cases indicate, courts will often apply publicity rights doctrines broadly, while they may not apply trademark doctrine so expansively.

Nevertheless, if their names or other personality attributes are eligible for trademark protection, celebrities may find value in securing federal trademark registration to complement their publicity rights. For example, federal trademark registration ensures access to federal courts (rather than state courts) and consistent minimum protectable rights across all jurisdictions. Also, trademark registrations can improve standing for certain types of actions, such as counterfeiting claims or domain-name enforcement actions.

*Keyword Advertising on Names.* Assume that an advertiser purchases a person's name as the trigger for its keyword advertising, i.e., when searchers use the search query "Joe Smith," a competitor's advertisement appears. Assume the plaintiff does not have any trademark rights in his or her name. Does the purchase of the keyword advertising trigger violate the person's publicity or privacy rights? Does it matter if the ad copy references the name? *See* Habush v. Cannon, 346 Wis. 2d 709 (Wis. App. Ct. 2013) (dismissing a Wisconsin publicity rights claim for one lawyer purchasing keyword ads on another lawyer's name); Eric Goldman & Angel Reyes III, *Regulation of Lawyers' Use of Competitive Keyword Advertising*, 2016 U. ILL. L. REV. 103.

*Incidental uses.* In general, advertising for a product that is itself fully First Amendment-protected speech—a book, movie, play, etc.—gets the same protection as the underlying speech, thus entitling it to an exception from the right of publicity, as long as the advertising accurately reflects the content of the promoted speech. Somewhat confusingly, courts sometimes call this "incidental" use, even though it can be quite central to the advertising the advertising itself is "incidental" to the protected speech. *See, e.g.*, Lerman v. Flynt Distrib. Co., 745 F.2d 123 (2d Cir. 1984); Namath v. Sports Illustrated, 48 A.D.2d 487, 371 N.Y.S.2d 10, (1st Dep't 1975), aff'd, 352 N.E.2d 584 (N.Y. 1976). This exception may apply even where the advertisement does not conform precisely to the content of the underlying publication. *See, e.g.*, Velez v. VV Publ'g Corp., 135 A.D.2d 47, 524 N.Y.S.2d 186, 189 (1st Dep't 1988) (rejecting Section 50 claim where picture of plaintiff in magazine was used in subsequent advertisement which added cartoon bubble containing text to photo of plaintiff). Indeed, one court found that the incidental use (and related public interest) exception covered an ad using the then-Mayor of New York's first name because the advertised magazine occasionally reported on the Mayor:

New York Magazine v. Metropolitan Transp. Authority, 987 F. Supp. 254 (S.D.N.Y. 1997), aff'd on other grounds, 136 F.3d 123 (2d Cir. 1998).

Is the special treatment of commercial advertising for protected media justified?

## B.    A Person's Voice

California's publicity rights statute expressly protects the use of a person's voice in ad copy. However, can an advertiser use a "sound-alike"?

### *Midler v. Ford Motor Co., 849 F.2d 460 (9th Cir. 1988)*

This case centers on the protectability of the voice of a celebrated chanteuse from commercial exploitation without her consent. Ford Motor Company and its advertising agency, Young & Rubicam, Inc., in 1985 advertised the Ford Lincoln Mercury with a series of nineteen 30 or 60 second television commercials in what the agency called "The Yuppie Campaign." The aim was to make an emotional connection with Yuppies,* bringing back memories of when they were in college. Different popular songs of the seventies were sung on each commercial. The agency tried to get "the original people," that is, the singers who had popularized the songs, to sing them. Failing in that endeavor in ten cases the agency had the songs sung by "sound-alikes." Bette Midler, the plaintiff and appellant here, was done by a sound-alike.

Midler is a nationally known actress and singer. She won a Grammy as early as 1973 as the Best New Artist of that year. Records made by her since then have gone Platinum and Gold. She was nominated in 1979 for an Academy award for Best Female Actress in *The Rose*, in which she portrayed a pop singer. Newsweek in its June 30, 1986 issue described her as an "outrageously original singer/comedian." Time hailed her in its March 2, 1987 issue as "a legend" and "the most dynamic and poignant singer-actress of her time."

When Young & Rubicam was preparing the Yuppie Campaign it presented the commercial to its client by playing an edited version of Midler singing "Do You Want To Dance," taken from the 1973 Midler album, "The Divine Miss M." After the client accepted the idea and form of the commercial, the agency contacted Midler's manager, Jerry Edelstein. The conversation went as follows: "Hello, I am Craig Hazen from Young and Rubicam. I am calling you to find out if Bette Midler would be interested in doing . . . ?" Edelstein: "Is it a commercial?" "Yes." "We are not interested."

Undeterred, Young & Rubicam sought out Ula Hedwig whom it knew to have been one of "the Harlettes," a backup singer for Midler for ten years. Hedwig was told by Young & Rubicam that "they wanted someone who could sound like Bette Midler's recording of [Do You Want To Dance]." She was asked to make a "demo" tape of the song if she was interested. She made an a capella demo and got the job.

At the direction of Young & Rubicam, Hedwig then made a record for the commercial. The Midler record of "Do You Want To Dance" was first played to her. She was told to "sound as much as

---

* [Editor's note: "Yuppie" is an acronym for "Young Urban Professional," an affluent segment of the Baby Boomer generation.]

possible like the Bette Midler record," leaving out only a few "aahs" unsuitable for the commercial. Hedwig imitated Midler to the best of her ability.

After the commercial was aired Midler was told by "a number of people" that it "sounded exactly" like her record of "Do You Want To Dance." Hedwig was told by "many personal friends" that they thought it was Midler singing the commercial. Ken Fritz, a personal manager in the entertainment business not associated with Midler, declares by affidavit that he heard the commercial on more than one occasion and thought Midler was doing the singing.

Neither the name nor the picture of Midler was used in the commercial; Young & Rubicam had a license from the copyright holder to use the song. At issue in this case is only the protection of Midler's voice. The district court described the defendants' conduct as that "of the average thief." They decided, "If we can't buy it, we'll take it." The court nonetheless believed there was no legal principle preventing imitation of Midler's voice and so gave summary judgment for the defendants. Midler appeals. . . .

California Civil Code section 3344 is ... of no aid to Midler. The statute affords damages to a person injured by another who uses the person's "name, voice, signature, photograph or likeness, in any manner." The defendants did not use Midler's name or anything else whose use is prohibited by the statute. The voice they used was Hedwig's, not hers. The term "likeness" refers to a visual image not a vocal imitation. The statute, however, does not preclude Midler from pursuing any cause of action she may have at common law; the statute itself implies that such common law causes of action do exist because it says its remedies are merely "cumulative."

The companion statute protecting the use of a deceased person's name, voice, signature, photograph or likeness states that the rights it recognizes are "property rights." By analogy the common law rights are also property rights. Appropriation of such common law rights is a tort in California. . . .

Why did the defendants ask Midler to sing if her voice was not of value to them? Why did they studiously acquire the services of a sound-alike and instruct her to imitate Midler if Midler's voice was not of value to them? What they sought was an attribute of Midler's identity. Its value was what the market would have paid for Midler to have sung the commercial in person.

. . . A voice is as distinctive and personal as a face. The human voice is one of the most palpable ways identity is manifested. We are all aware that a friend is at once known by a few words on the phone. At a philosophical level it has been observed that with the sound of a voice, "the other stands before me." A fortiori, these observations hold true of singing, especially singing by a singer of renown. The singer manifests herself in the song. To impersonate her voice is to pirate her identity.

We need not and do not go so far as to hold that every imitation of a voice to advertise merchandise is actionable. We hold only that when a distinctive voice of a professional singer is widely known and is deliberately imitated in order to sell a product, the sellers have appropriated what is not theirs and have committed a tort in California. Midler has made a showing, sufficient to defeat summary judgment, that the defendants here for their own profit in selling their product did appropriate part of her identity.

*NOTES AND QUESTIONS*

*Why Copyright Wasn't an Issue.* Bobby Freeman wrote the song "Do You Wanna Dance?" and recorded it in 1958. A 1965 cover version by the Beach Boys is perhaps the best known version. Midler herself covered the song, with a jazzier and much slower arrangement, under the title "Do You Want To Dance?" in 1973. Therefore, Midler did not own the copyright to the song, and her permission was not required for Ford to perform the copyrighted song in the advertisement. Because Ford did not use Midler's 1973 recording either, it did not need a copyright license for that recording.

*Damages.* On remand, a jury awarded Midler $400,000 from Ford's ad agency Young & Rubicam (Ford had already exited the case). Midler had asked for damages of $10 million. How should damages be computed in a sound-alike case?

*Waits v. Frito Lay, Inc.*, 978 F.2d 1093 (9th Cir. 1992), a sound-alike case involving raspy-voiced singer Tom Waits and a radio advertisement for "SalsaRio Doritos," explores that question. The jury awarded $2.6 million in compensatory and punitive damages and attorneys' fees against the manufacturer Frito-Lay and its advertising agency Tracy-Locke. The defendants appealed to the Ninth Circuit. That court upheld the award in its entirety, ruling that damages were not limited to economic injury (though the economic *value* of the use to the advertiser is important for liability). Injury to Waits' peace, happiness, and feelings was also compensable.

He was particularly embarrassed by the ad because it seemed to contradict his anti-commercial stance: "because of his outspoken public stance against doing commercial endorsements, the Doritos commercial humiliated Waits by making him an apparent hypocrite."

In addition, the jury could award him damages for injury to goodwill (his artistic reputation and reputation for refusing to endorse products). Further, the court upheld an award based on lost future publicity value. If Waits *did* do a commercial in the future, his asking price would be lowered because of the Doritos ad.

Moreover, the court upheld the punitive damages award, holding that the jury could have found the defendants' conduct "despicable because they knowingly impugned Waits' integrity in the public eye," and that defendants acted in conscious disregard of Waits's right of publicity.

*Asking Permission.* Businesspeople frequently believe that "it's better to ask for forgiveness than permission." Do the *Midler* and *Waits* cases provide supporting evidence for this maxim? When you are a practicing lawyer, will you prospectively ask IP rightsholders for their consent in ambiguous situations, or do these opinions make you a little gun-shy?

*Singers Closely Identified with Famous Songs.* Assume that ad copy includes a performance of a properly licensed song sung by a non-sound-alike. On publicity rights grounds, can a singer of that song nevertheless object to use of that song because the song is so closely identified with him or her? The answer appears to be no.

*Sinatra v. Goodyear Tire & Rubber Co.*, 435 F.2d 711 (9th Cir. 1970), involved Goodyear's radio and television ads promoting its "wide boots" tires. The ad copy included portions of the song "These Boots Are Made For Walkin'," a 1966 #1 hit for Nancy Sinatra (the daughter of Frank Sinatra). The ad agency properly secured licenses to the song's copyrights, owned by Criterion Music (not Sinatra). Sinatra alleged, among other things, "that the song has been so popularized by the plaintiff that her name is identified with it; [and] that she is best known by her connection with the song." Nevertheless, the Ninth Circuit concluded that her lawsuit was preempted by copyright law.

*Oliveria v. Frito-Lay, Inc.*, 251 F.3d 56 (2nd Cir. 2001), addresses a slightly different situation. Oliveria, who performs under the name "Astrud Gilberto," sang the well-known 1964 recording of the song "The Girl from Ipanema." Frito-Lay obtained the proper copyright licenses to use that recording in a television ad for its baked potato chips. Nevertheless, Oliveria claimed she had become known as the eponymous Girl from Ipanema due to the recording's success and her many subsequent performances of the song. The court rejected Oliveria's trademark claim because she did not cite "a single precedent throughout the history of trademark supporting the notion that a performing artist acquires a trademark or service mark signifying herself in a recording of her own famous performance." The court said that Oliveria's state law claims could be refiled in state court, but Oliveria never did so.

### C.    Recognizability: Lookalikes, Partial Views, and Implications of Presence

Visually depicting a person in ad copy is usually squarely covered by the person's publicity/privacy rights. It might also constitute an endorsement or testimonial, which is discussed later in this chapter. California's statute also protects against the use of "likenesses," which probably refers to drawings of people instead of photos or videos of them.

To get around this general rule, some advertisers have hired look-alike actors to portray famous celebrities. As with sound-alikes, courts generally have rejected this work-around.

For example, *Allen v. National Video, Inc.*, 610 F. Supp. 612 (S.D.N.Y. 1985), involved an ad depicting a look-alike of the famous director and actor Woody Allen:

> The present action arises from an advertisement, placed by National to promote its nationally franchised video rental chain, containing a photograph of defendant Boroff taken on September 2, 1983. The photograph portrays a customer in a National Video store, an individual in his forties, with a high forehead, tousled hair, and heavy black glasses. The customer's elbow is on the counter, and his face, bearing an expression at once quizzical and somewhat smug, is leaning on his hand. It is not disputed that, in general, the physical features and pose are characteristic of plaintiff.
>
> The staging of the photograph also evokes associations with plaintiff. Sitting on the counter are videotape cassettes of "Annie Hall" and "Bananas," two of plaintiff's best known films, as well as "Casablanca" and "The Maltese Falcon." The latter two are Humphrey Bogart films of the 1940's associated with plaintiff primarily because of his play and film "Play It Again, Sam," in which the spirit of Bogart appears to the character played by Allen and offers him

romantic advice. In addition, the title "Play It Again, Sam" is a famous, although inaccurate, quotation from "Casablanca."

The individual in the advertisement is holding up a National Video V.I.P. Card, which apparently entitles the bearer to favorable terms on movie rentals. The woman behind the counter is smiling at the customer and appears to be gasping in exaggerated excitement at the presence of a celebrity.

The photograph was used in an advertisement which appeared in the March 1984 issue of "Video Review," a magazine published in New York and distributed in the Southern District, and in the April 1984 issue of "Take One," an in-house publication which National distributes to its franchisees across the country. The headline on the advertisement reads "Become a V.I.P. at National Video. We'll Make You Feel Like a Star." The copy goes on to explain that holders of the V.I.P. card receive "hassle-free movie renting" and "special savings" and concludes that "you don't need a famous face to be treated to some pretty famous service."

The same photograph and headline were also used on countercards distributed to National's franchisees. Although the advertisement that ran in "Video Review" contained a disclaimer in small print reading "Celebrity double provided by Ron Smith's Celebrity Look-Alike's, Los Angeles, Calif.," no such disclaimer appeared in the other versions of the advertisement.

The defendants explained the look-alike's appearance in the ad copy this way:

Although defendants concede that they sought to evoke by reference plaintiff's general persona, they strenuously deny that they intended to imply that the person in the photograph was actually plaintiff or that plaintiff endorsed National. ... According to defendants, the idea of the advertisement is that even people who are not stars are treated

569

like stars at National Video. They insist that the advertisement depicts a "Woody Allen fan," so dedicated that he has adopted his idol's appearance and mannerisms, who is able to live out his fantasy by receiving star treatment at National Video. The knowing viewer is supposed to be amused that the counter person actually believes that the customer is Woody Allen.

Do you find that explanation credible?

Allen ultimately succeeded on his trademark claim of likely confusion over his endorsement, and the court did not definitively resolve his publicity/privacy rights claims because the New York statute covered only a portrait or picture, and the court was unsure that a look-alike could count as a portrait or picture. However, the court's discussion of those claims is nevertheless useful:

... New York has never recognized the right to privacy as part of its common law.

... [T]he New York legislature passed sections 50 and 51 of the Civil Rights Law in 1903. In its present form the statute provides that

> A person, firm or corporation that uses for advertising purposes, or for purposes of trade, the name, portrait or picture* of any living person without having first obtained the written consent of such person, is guilty of a misdemeanor.

Section 51 provides in addition that

> Any person whose name, portrait or picture is used within the state for advertising purposes or for purposes of trade without the written consent first obtained as above provided may maintain an equitable action in the supreme court of this state against the person, firm or corporation so using his name, portrait or picture, to prevent and restrain the use thereof; and may also sue and recover damages for any injuries sustained by reason of such use and if defendant shall have knowingly used such person's name, portrait or picture in such a manner as is forbidden or declared to be unlawful by the last section, the jury, in its discretion, may award exemplary damages. . . .

The right to privacy recognized by the Civil Rights law has been strictly construed, both because it is in derogation of New York common law and because of potential conflict with the First Amendment, particularly where public figures are involved. To make out a violation, a plaintiff must satisfy three distinct elements: 1) use of his or her name, portrait, or picture, 2) for commercial or trade purposes, 3) without written permission. Merely suggesting certain characteristics of the plaintiff, without literally using his or her name, portrait, or picture, is not actionable under the statute. Plaintiff here must therefore

---

* [Ed. note: The New York statute now covers voice as well.]

demonstrate, inter alia, that the advertisement in question appropriates his "portrait or picture."

In addition to the statutory right to privacy, plaintiff in this case argues that defendants have violated his "right of publicity," an analogous right recognized in the common law of many jurisdictions. ... Unlike the Civil Rights Law provision, which is primarily designed to compensate for the hurt feelings of private people who find their identities usurped for another's commercial gain, the right of publicity protects this property interest of the celebrity in his or her public identity. It is primarily this interest which Woody Allen seeks to vindicate in the case at bar.

The New York Court of Appeals, however, recently has held that no separate common law cause of action to vindicate the right of publicity exists in New York. Stephano v. News Grp. Publ'ns, Inc., 64 N.Y.2d 174 (1984). . . .

In examining the undisputed facts of this case with reference to plaintiff's summary judgment motion, it is immediately clear that two of the three prongs of the Civil Rights Law are satisfied. First, there is no question that the photograph said to be of plaintiff was used for commercial purposes, since it appeared in a magazine advertisement soliciting business for National Video franchisees. Second, defendants do not dispute that plaintiff never gave his consent to the use of the photograph, either orally or in writing. It therefore appears that the only element of plaintiff's case over which there is any serious dispute is whether the photograph is a "portrait or picture" of plaintiff.

Plaintiff argues that Boroff's physical resemblance to him, when viewed in conjunction with the undeniable attempt to evoke plaintiff's image through the selection of props and poses, makes the photograph in question a "portrait or picture" of plaintiff as a matter of law. Plaintiff notes that it is not necessary that all persons seeing the photograph actually identify him, only that he be identifiable from the photograph.....

More helpful are a line of cases holding that any recognizable likeness, not just an actual photograph, may qualify as a "portrait or picture." . . .

Therefore, if defendants had used, for example, a clearly recognizable painting or cartoon of plaintiff, it would certainly constitute a "portrait or picture" within the meaning of the statute. The case of a look-alike, however, is more problematic. A painting, drawing or manikin has no existence other than as a representation of something or someone; if the subject is recognizable, then the work is a "portrait." Defendant Boroff, however, is not a manikin. He is a person with a right to his own identity and his own face. Plaintiff's privacy claim therefore requires the court to answer the almost metaphysical question of when one person's face, presented in a certain context, becomes, as a matter of law, the face of another.

This question is not merely theoretical. The use in an advertisement of a drawing, which has no other purpose than to represent its subject, must give rise to a cause of action under the Civil Rights Law, because it raises the obvious implication that its subject has endorsed or is otherwise involved with the product being advertised. There is no question that this amounts to an appropriation of another's likeness for commercial advantage.

A living and breathing actor, however, has the right to exploit his or her own face for commercial gain. This right is itself protected by the Civil Rights Law. The privacy law does not prohibit one from evoking certain aspects of another's personality, but it does prohibit one from actually representing oneself as another person. The look-alike situation falls somewhere in between and therefore presents a difficult question.

As you can see, New York's approaches to publicity and privacy rights are both simpler and more complex than California's. California has overlapping statutory and common law publicity rights, while New York has only statutory privacy rights.

A more decisive New York look-alike case is *Onassis v. Christian Dior*, 472 N.Y.S.2d 254 (N.Y. Sup. Ct. 1984), which involved ad copy that included a look-alike of former First Lady Jacqueline Kennedy Onassis. The court harshly condemned the defendants:

Is the illusionist to be free to step aside, having reaped the benefits of his creation, and permitted to disclaim the very impression he sought to create? If we were to permit it, we would be sanctioning an obvious loophole to evade the statute. If a person is unwilling to give his or her endorsement to help sell a product, either at an offered price or at any price, no matter—hire a double and the same effect is achieved. The essential purpose of the statute must be carried out by giving it a common sense reading which bars easy evasion. ... Let the word go forth—there is no free ride. The commercial hitchhiker seeking to travel on the fame of another will have to learn to pay the fare or stand on his own two feet.

572

Another way that advertisers might try to work around the general prohibition against depicting people in ads is by showing only a seemingly unidentifiable portion of the person. For example, the following case addresses ad copy where the people's faces were not shown.

*Cohen v. Herbal Concepts, 63 N.Y.2d 379 (N.Y. 1984)*

Plaintiffs bring this action pursuant to section 51 of the Civil Rights Law seeking damages from defendants for publishing photographs of them for advertising purposes. It is conceded for purposes of this appeal that plaintiffs are the persons shown in the photographs and that defendants used the photographs as claimed without their consent. The legal issue submitted is whether a photograph of the nude plaintiffs, mother and child, which shows their bodies full length as viewed from a position behind and to the right of them, and which does not show their faces, reveals sufficiently identifiable likenesses to withstand defendants' motions for summary judgment. We hold that it does.

The action arises from these facts.

On the July 4th weekend in 1977, plaintiffs were visiting friends in Woodstock, New York, and Susan Cohen and her four-year-old daughter, Samantha, went bathing in a stream located on their friends' private property. Without their consent, defendant James Krieger took photographs of plaintiffs and subsequently sold them to defendant Herbal Concepts, Inc., a seller and advertiser of consumer products. Herbal Concepts used one of the photographs in an advertisement for Au Naturel, a product designed to help women eliminate body cellulite, those "fatty lumps and bumps that won't go away." The advertisement appeared in two editions of *House and Garden*, which is published by defendant Condé Nast Publications, Inc., and in single editions of *House Beautiful* and *Cosmopolitan*, which are published by defendant Hearst Corporation. Ira Cohen subsequently recognized his wife and daughter in the advertisements while reading one of the magazines and this action followed. . . .

. . . [I]n New York privacy claims are founded solely upon sections 50 and 51 of the Civil Rights Law. The statute protects against the appropriation of a plaintiff's name or likeness for defendants' benefit. Thus, it creates a cause of action in favor of "[a]ny person whose name, portrait or picture is used within this state for advertising purposes or for the purposes of trade without . . . written consent." The action may be brought to enjoin the prohibited use and may also seek damages for any injuries sustained including exemplary damages for a knowing violation of the statute. We are concerned in this case with the appropriation of plaintiffs' likenesses. Defendants claim that there has been no wrong because even if the photograph depicts plaintiffs, they are not identifiable from it.

The statute is designed to protect a person's identity, not merely a property interest in his or her "name", "portrait" or "picture", and thus it implicitly requires that plaintiff be capable of identification from the objectionable material itself. That is not to say that the action may only be maintained when plaintiff's face is visible in the advertising copy. Presumably, by using the term "portrait" the Legislature intended a representation which includes a facial reproduction, either artistically or by photograph, but if we are to give effect to all parts of the statute, it applies also to the improper use of a "picture" of plaintiff which does not show the face. Manifestly, there can be no appropriation of plaintiff's identity for commercial purposes if he or she is not recognizable from the picture and a privacy action could not be sustained, for example, because of the nonconsensual use of a photograph of a hand or a foot without identifying features. But assuming that the photograph depicts plaintiff, whether it presents a recognizable likeness is generally a jury question unless plaintiff cannot be identified because of the limited subject matter revealed in the photograph or the quality of the image. Before a jury may be permitted to decide the issue, to survive a motion for summary judgment, plaintiff must satisfy the court that the person in the photograph is capable of being identified from the advertisement alone and that plaintiff has been so identified.

The sufficiency of plaintiff's evidence for purposes of the motion will necessarily depend upon the court's determination of the quality and quantity of the identifiable characteristics displayed in the advertisement and this will require an assessment of the clarity of the photograph, the extent to which identifying features are visible, and the distinctiveness of those features. This picture depicts two nude persons, a woman and a child, standing in water a few inches deep. The picture quality is good and there are no obstructions to block the view of the subjects. The woman is carrying a small unidentified object in her left hand and is leading the child with her right hand. Neither person's face is visible but the backs and right sides of both mother and child are clearly presented and the mother's right breast can be seen. The identifying features of the subjects include their hair, bone structure, body contours and stature and their posture. Considering these factors, we conclude that a jury could find that someone familiar with the persons in the photograph could identify them by looking at the advertisement. Although we do not rely on the fact, it is also reasonable to assume that just as something in the advertising copy may aid recognition, identifiability may be enhanced also in photograph depicting two persons because observers may associate the two and thus more easily identify them when they are seen together.

The plaintiffs also submitted evidence that they were identified as the persons in defendants' advertisement by Ira Cohen's affidavit in which he stated that while leafing through one of defendants' magazines he "recognized [his] wife and daughter immediately." That was prima facie sufficient.

Defendants contend Mr. Cohen's affidavit is not probative on the issue of identification because he was present when the photograph was taken, as indeed he was. He was not only present, he was incensed by the photographer's intrusion and chased him away. Essentially, defendants' contention is that Mr. Cohen's identification is tainted by this independent knowledge that plaintiffs were photographed by defendant Krieger while bathing. Although Mr. Cohen's presence when the photograph was taken may have increased his ability to identify his wife and child, the motion court or the jury at trial could conclude that he also recognized them from the photograph and his presence when it was taken, standing alone, does not disqualify him from offering evidence that he did so. . . .

*NOTES AND QUESTIONS*

*Other Causes of Action?* Could the Cohens have sued the photographer for harassment or public disclosure of private facts (discussed in Chapter 14)? Would the property owner have a claim against the photographer for trespass? Could the advertisers be secondarily liable for that trespass? See the *Burgess* case discussed in Chapter 16 as well as California Civil Code § 1708.08 (California's "anti-paparazzi statute"), which says in part:

> (a) A person is liable for physical invasion of privacy when the defendant knowingly enters onto the land of another person without permission or otherwise committed a trespass in order to physically invade the privacy of the plaintiff with the intent to capture any type of visual image, sound recording, or other physical impression of the plaintiff engaging in a personal or familial activity and the physical invasion occurs in a manner that is offensive to a reasonable person . . .

> (f) (1) The transmission, publication, broadcast, sale, offer for sale, or other use of any visual image, sound recording, or other physical impression that was taken or captured in violation of subdivision (a) . . . shall not constitute a violation of this section unless the person, in the first transaction following the taking or capture of the visual image, sound recording, or other physical impression, publicly transmitted, published, broadcast, sold or offered for sale, the visual image, sound recording, or other physical impression with actual knowledge that it was taken or captured in violation of subdivision (a) . . . and provide[s] compensation, consideration, or remuneration, monetary or otherwise, for the rights to the unlawfully obtained visual image, sound recording, or other physical impression.

Under a statute like this, could Herbal Concepts have been liable for buying the photos from Krieger? How would this statute fare in a constitutional challenge?

*Test Yourself.* Look at the photo in the upper right of the following ad. Assume the woman on the left did not sign a proper publicity release. Does the photo violate her publicity rights?

The court said:

> Ms. Rosecrans' face is not visible in the photograph and the brochure does not identify her by
> name. To know that the person in the photograph is Ms. Rosecrans, the person would have to
> recognize Lisa Weeks (whose face is visible) as Ms. Rosecrans' daughter and extrapolate that
> the figure in the photograph must have been Ms. Weeks' mother, perhaps because the person
> knew that Ms. Rosecrans once worked as a flight nurse. For a person to arrive at these
> conclusions, he or she would have to have known Ms. Rosecrans extremely well and, given
> their familiarity with Ms. Rosecrans, would likely discount any negative implications from
> the photograph. By contrast, the average person would not be able to identify Ms. Rosecrans
> as the person in the photograph. Nor is there anything remotely pejorative or scandalous
> about the photograph and its context. To the contrary, in the brochure, Airamedic is praising
> the professionalism and dedication of its staff, including by implication Ms. Rosecrans.

As a result, the court awarded Rosecrans damages of only one dollar. *Rosecrans v. Airamedic, LLC,*
No. 1:16-cv-00452 (D. Me. March 30, 2017).

*Recreating the Cohen Photo.* If the advertiser and photographer liked the scene so much, could they
have freely recreated the scene with paid models and avoided all liability risks? Wouldn't that lesson
also apply to the Rosecrans photo?

*Identifiability.* Has the identifiability of people gone up over time? For example, automatic facial
recognition technology continues to improve, and many people now have distinctive tattoos that can
single-handedly identify them. *See* Yolanda M. King, *The Right-of-Publicity Challenges for Tattoo
Copyrights,* 16 NEV. L.J. 441 (2016). Furthermore, it has become fairly common for a seemingly
obscure person in a photograph to become uniquely identified when seen by millions of Internet

577

users. *See, e.g.*, Jonathan Krim, *Subway Fracas Escalates into Test of the Internet's Power to Shame*, WASH. POST, July 7, 2005 (discussing the naming and shaming of the South Korean "dog poop girl").

One possible inference is that it may be impossible to use an unconsented photograph of a person in ad copy, even if his or her face isn't shown, because anyone in ad copy can become personally identifiable if enough people see the photo; inevitably, someone will personally know the individual and be able to connect the identity.

*Identifiability When the Person Isn't Shown at All.* Because the photos depicted the individuals' backside, the Cohen case involves somewhat attenuated identifiability. But just how far can we push the identifiability concept? Could a person be visually identified if you couldn't see the person at all? Surprisingly, the answer is "yes" in some circumstances.

*Motschenbacher v. R.J. Reynolds Tobacco Co.*, 498 F.2d 821 (9th Cir. 1974) involved the following facts:

> Plaintiff Motschenbacher is a professional driver of racing cars, internationally known and recognized in racing circles and by racing fans. He derives part of his income from manufacturers of commercial products who pay him for endorsing their products.

> During the relevant time span, plaintiff has consistently "individualized" his cars to set them apart from those of other drivers and to make them more readily identifiable as his own. Since 1966, each of his cars has displayed a distinctive narrow white pinstripe appearing on no other car. This decoration has adorned the leading edges of the cars' bodies, which have uniformly been solid red. In addition, the white background for his racing number "11" has always been oval, in contrast to the circular backgrounds of all other cars.

> In 1970, defendants, R. J. Reynolds Tobacco Company and William Esty Company, produced and caused to be televised a commercial which utilized a "stock" color photograph depicting several racing cars on a racetrack. Plaintiff's car appears in the foreground, and although plaintiff is the driver, his facial features are not visible.

> In producing the commercial, defendants altered the photograph: they changed the numbers on all racing cars depicted, transforming plaintiff's number "11" into "71"; they "attached" a wing-like device known as a "spoiler" to plaintiff's car; they added the word "Winston," the name of their product, to that spoiler and removed advertisements for other products from the spoilers of other cars. However, they made no other changes, and the white pinstriping, the oval medallion, and the red color of plaintiff's car were retained. They then made a motion picture from the altered photograph, adding a series of comic strip-type "balloons" containing written messages of an advertising nature; one such balloon message, appearing to emanate from plaintiff, was: "Did you know that Winston tastes good, like a cigarette should?" They also added a sound track consisting in part of voices coordinated with, and echoing, the written messages. The commercial was subsequently broadcast nationally on network television and in color.

[screenshot from the ad.
Altered Motschenbacher car depicted in the lower left]

Several of plaintiff's affiants who had seen the commercial on television had immediately recognized plaintiff's car and had inferred that it was sponsored by Winston cigarettes.

On the question of identifiability, the court concluded:

[T]he "likeness" of plaintiff is itself unrecognizable; however, the [district] court's further conclusion of law to the effect that the driver is not identifiable as plaintiff is erroneous in that it wholly fails to attribute proper significance to the distinctive decorations appearing on the car. As pointed out earlier, these markings were not only peculiar to the plaintiff's cars but they caused some persons to think the car in question was plaintiff's and to infer that the person driving the car was the plaintiff.

As a result, the court said that Motschenbacher stated a cause of action for a publicity/privacy rights violation. In other words, the advertiser may have violated Motschenbacher's publicity/privacy rights by depicting a modified version of his car.

Compare *Roberts v. Bliss*, 229 F. Supp. 3d 240 (S.D.N.Y. 2017). Bliss produced a video called 10 Hours, showing Roberts walking around New York City and being subjected to repeated catcalls and sexual innuendo by strangers. Bliss retained the video's copyright. The video went viral and was viewed over 40 million times. Bliss licensed the video to TGI Friday's, which made advertisements where it completely replaced all depictions of Roberts with images of some of its appetizers, thus making it look like the strangers were directing the catcalls and innuendo to the food. Photos from the court's opinion (apologies for the low quality black-and-white images):

579

Anyone who had seen the original video would get TGI Friday's "joke," but you're not alone if you don't find it very funny.

Because the food replaced Roberts' image entirely, she had little chance with a publicity rights claim. Instead, Roberts sued for Lanham Act false endorsement. The court still rejects the claim:

> Although the ad may well call to a viewer's mind the 10 Hours video, and perhaps even Roberts because of her role in it, the ad does not use Roberts' image or persona, nor suggest in any way that Roberts herself endorsed the product advertised....

> While the advertisement does "call to mind" 10 Hours, the supplantation of Roberts with large gimmicky images of appetizers is an "obvious[] modification" of, and a "conscious

departure" from, the original work. This modification, moreover, is outlandish, not subtle….The ad replaces Roberts—the object of the harassing men's attention in the 10 Hours video—with the appetizers. They are now the subject of the men's desire. That, together with the play on words between "appcalling" and "catcalling," is what makes it a parody. And because the parody is obvious, the "risk of consumer confusion is at its lowest."… That Roberts, of course, looks nothing like the overblown images of walking food, and that an online video designed to highlight a societal ill and a chain restaurant attempting to promote its appetizers occupy distinct merchandising markets, reinforces the conclusion that it is implausible that a viewer of the ad would be confused about whether Roberts endorsed it.

*Getting Proper Consent.* Getting the depicted person's consent is essential to avoiding a publicity rights claim, but the advertiser must draft the consent properly and respect any limitations on the consent. *See, e.g.*, Sahoury v. Meredith Corp., 2012 WL 3185964 (D. N.J. Aug. 2, 2012) (breastfeeding mom had viable contract breach claims when she signed broad publicity consent but was orally told that the video footage would only appear in limited outlets and wouldn't use her or the baby's full name and those restrictions weren't followed).

Consider the following ad for a law firm:

The depicted firefighter, Robert Keiley, joined the FDNY in 2004—three years after 9/11. Therefore, he was not "there." Keiley signed a broad publicity consent, but he says he thought that his depiction would be used in a fire prevention ad and the 9/11 picture was photoshopped into his hands. *See* Reuven Fenton & Jennifer Fermino, *Law Firm's Ad Trick a 9/11 'Insult,'* N.Y. POST, March 28, 2011. Did the law firm or its ad agency do anything wrong?

*Labor Union Relations.* Many advertising agencies and some large advertisers have signed agreements with actors' labor unions, such as the Screen Actors Guild (SAG) and the American Federation of Television and Radio Artists (AFTRA). Each agreement should be reviewed carefully, but in general they (1) require that advertisers use only union members as actors in advertisements (with some exceptions, such as showing a company employee doing his or her normal job), and (2) specify minimum payments to actors, including payments for pensions and health benefits as well as "residuals" (ongoing payments for continued use of the ad copy).

## D.    Evoking a Persona

As we've seen, courts apply the publicity/privacy rights doctrines expansively when ad copy includes any potentially identifiable attribute of a person. But what if ad copy incorporates none of these personal attributes, and no one would think that a celebrity actually appeared in the ad (as viewers might have in *Motsenbacher*), and yet a celebrity persona is still recognizable? As the next case indicates, publicity rights can be stretched to cover that situation too.

*White v. Samsung Electronics America, Inc., 989 F.2d 1512 (9th Cir. 1993)*

KOZINSKI, Circuit Judge, dissenting from a request for an en banc rehearing.

. . . Concerned about what it sees as a wrong done to Vanna White, the panel majority erects a property right of remarkable and dangerous breadth: Under the majority's opinion, it's now a tort for advertisers to remind the public of a celebrity. Not to use a celebrity's name, voice, signature or likeness; not to imply the celebrity endorses a product; but simply to evoke the celebrity's image in the public's mind. This Orwellian notion withdraws far more from the public domain than prudence and common sense allow....

II

Samsung ran an ad campaign promoting its consumer electronics. Each ad depicted a Samsung product and a humorous prediction: One showed a raw steak with the caption "Revealed to be health food. 2010 A.D." Another showed Morton Downey, Jr. in front of an American flag with the caption "Presidential candidate. 2008 A.D." The ads were meant to convey—humorously—that Samsung products would still be in use twenty years from now.

The ad that spawned this litigation starred a robot dressed in a wig, gown and jewelry reminiscent of Vanna White's hair and dress; the robot was posed next to a Wheel-of-Fortune-like game board. The caption read "Longest-running game show. 2012 A.D." The gag here, I take it, was that Samsung would still be around when White had been replaced by a robot.*

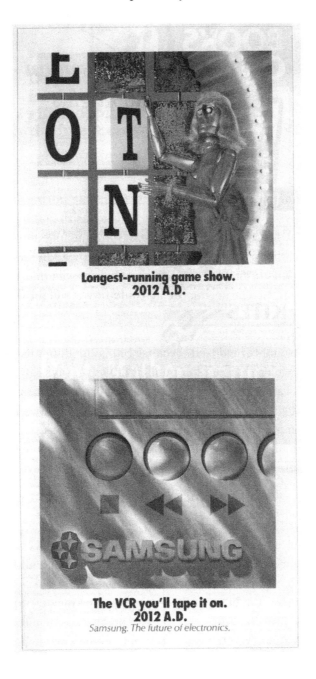

---

* [Editor's note: As of 2018, Vanna White still works on *Wheel of Fortune*, a position she has held since 1982, though she stopped physically turning letters in 1997. Steak became a central part of the Atkins Diet fad in the early 2000s. Morton Downey Jr. did not run for president in 2008, but actor Fred Thompson did, and many other actors and television personalities have won high office since the Samsung ad, including Donald Trump (president), Al Franken (U.S. senator from Massachusetts), Jesse Ventura (Minnesota governor) and Arnold Schwarzenegger (California governor).]

[photo of Vanna White (left) compared to close-up of Samsung ad (right)]

Perhaps failing to see the humor, White sued, alleging Samsung infringed her right of publicity by "appropriating" her "identity." Under California law, White has the exclusive right to use her name, likeness, signature and voice for commercial purposes. But Samsung didn't use her name, voice or signature, and it certainly didn't use her likeness. The ad just wouldn't have been funny had it depicted White or someone who resembled her—the whole joke was that the game show host(ess) was a robot, not a real person. No one seeing the ad could have thought this was supposed to be White in 2012.

The district judge quite reasonably held that, because Samsung didn't use White's name, likeness, voice or signature, it didn't violate her right of publicity. Not so, says the panel majority: The California right of publicity can't possibly be limited to name and likeness. If it were, the majority reasons, a "clever advertising strategist" could avoid using White's name or likeness but nevertheless remind people of her with impunity, "effectively eviscerat[ing]" her rights. To prevent this "evisceration," the panel majority holds that the right of publicity must extend beyond name and likeness, to any "appropriation" of White's "identity"—anything that "evoke[s]" her personality.

### III

But what does "evisceration" mean in intellectual property law? Intellectual property rights aren't like some constitutional rights, absolute guarantees protected against all kinds of interference, subtle as well as blatant. They cast no penumbras, emit no emanations: The very point of intellectual property laws is that they protect only against certain specific kinds of appropriation. I can't publish unauthorized copies of, say, *Presumed Innocent*; I can't make a movie out of it. But I'm perfectly free to write a book about an idealistic young prosecutor on trial for a crime he didn't commit. So what if I got the idea from *Presumed Innocent*? So what if it reminds readers of the original? Have I "eviscerated" Scott Turow's intellectual property rights? Certainly not. All creators draw in part on the work of those who came before, referring to it, building on it, poking fun at it; we call this creativity, not piracy.

The majority isn't, in fact, preventing the "evisceration" of Vanna White's existing rights; it's creating a new and much broader property right, a right unknown in California law. It's replacing the existing balance between the interests of the celebrity and those of the public by a different balance, one substantially more favorable to the celebrity. Instead of having an exclusive right in her name, likeness, signature or voice, every famous person now has an exclusive right to anything that reminds the viewer of her. After all, that's all Samsung did: It used an inanimate object to remind people of White, to "evoke [her identity]."

Consider how sweeping this new right is. What is it about the ad that makes people think of White? It's not the robot's wig, clothes or jewelry; there must be ten million blond women (many of them quasi-famous) who wear dresses and jewelry like White's. It's that the robot is posed near the "Wheel of Fortune" game board. Remove the game board from the ad, and no one would think of Vanna White. But once you include the game board, anybody standing beside it—a brunette woman, a man wearing women's clothes, a monkey in a wig and gown—would evoke White's image, precisely the way the robot did. It's the "Wheel of Fortune" set, not the robot's face or dress or jewelry that evokes White's image. The panel is giving White an exclusive right not in what she looks like or who she is, but in what she does for a living . . .

The intellectual property right created by the panel here has [no] essential limitations: No fair use exception; no right to parody; no idea-expression dichotomy. It impoverishes the public domain, to the detriment of future creators and the public at large. Instead of well-defined, limited characteristics such as name, likeness or voice, advertisers will now have to cope with vague claims of "appropriation of identity," claims often made by people with a wholly exaggerated sense of their own fame and significance. Future Vanna Whites might not get the chance to create their personae, because their employers may fear some celebrity will claim the persona is too similar to her own. The public will be robbed of parodies of celebrities, and our culture will be deprived of the valuable safety valve that parody and mockery create.

Moreover, consider the moral dimension, about which the panel majority seems to have gotten so exercised. Saying Samsung "appropriated" something of White's begs the question: Should White have the exclusive right to something as broad and amorphous as her "identity"? Samsung's ad didn't simply copy White's schtick—like all parody, it created something new. True, Samsung did it to make money, but White does whatever she does to make money, too; the majority talks of "the difference between fun and profit," but in the entertainment industry fun is profit. Why is Vanna White's right to exclusive for-profit use of her persona—a persona that might not even be her own creation, but that of a writer, director or producer—superior to Samsung's right to profit by creating its own inventions? Why should she have such absolute rights to control the conduct of others, unlimited by the idea-expression dichotomy or by the fair use doctrine? . . .

## VI

Finally, I can't see how giving White the power to keep others from evoking her image in the public's mind can be squared with the First Amendment. Where does White get this right to control our thoughts? The majority's creation goes way beyond the protection given a trademark or a copyrighted work, or a person's name or likeness. All those things control one particular way of expressing an idea, one way of referring to an object or a person. But not allowing any means of reminding people of someone? That's a speech restriction unparalleled in First Amendment law. . . .

The majority dismisses the First Amendment issue out of hand because Samsung's ad was commercial speech. So what? Commercial speech may be less protected by the First Amendment than noncommercial speech, but less protected means protected nonetheless. And there are very good reasons for this. Commercial speech has a profound effect on our culture and our attitudes. Neutral-seeming ads influence people's social and political attitudes, and themselves arouse political controversy. "Where's the Beef?" turned from an advertising catchphrase into the only really memorable thing about the 1984 presidential campaign. Four years later, Michael Dukakis called George Bush "the Joe Isuzu of American politics."

In our pop culture, where salesmanship must be entertaining and entertainment must sell, the line between the commercial and noncommercial has not merely blurred; it has disappeared. Is the Samsung parody any different from a parody on *Saturday Night Live* or in *Spy Magazine*? Both are equally profit-motivated. Both use a celebrity's identity to sell things—one to sell VCRs, the other to sell advertising. Both mock their subjects. Both try to make people laugh. Both add something, perhaps something worthwhile and memorable, perhaps not, to our culture. Both are things that the people being portrayed might dearly want to suppress.

Commercial speech is a significant, valuable part of our national discourse. The Supreme Court has recognized as much, and has insisted that lower courts carefully scrutinize commercial speech restrictions, but the panel totally fails to do this. . . .

## VII

... In the name of fostering creativity, the majority suppresses it. Vanna White and those like her have been given something they never had before, and they've been given it at our expense. I cannot agree.

*NOTES AND QUESTIONS*

*Denouement.* White ultimately won $403,000 in damages in the case.

*Who Owns the Right?* Let's assume that Samsung did, in fact, tortiously evoke White's role in its ads. Who is the proper plaintiff—White, the *Wheel of Fortune* producers, both, or neither?

In *Wendt v. Host International, Inc.*, 197 F.3d 1284 (9th Cir. 1999), Judge Kozinski again dissented from the denial of an en banc hearing, after a panel held that two actors who had portrayed characters on the TV show *Cheers* had publicity rights against the use of robots that vaguely resembled them in bars licensed by the copyright owner.*

---

* Host changed the robots' names to "Hank" and "Bob," though the characters on the TV show were Norm and Cliff.

The district court granted summary judgment for the defendants because it found that the robots didn't look like the plaintiffs: "[T]here is [no] similarity at all . . . except that one of the robots, like one of the plaintiffs, is heavier than the other. . . . The facial features are totally different." Nevertheless, the appeals court concluded that "material facts exist that might cause a reasonable jury to find [the robots] sufficiently 'like' [Wendt and Ratzenberger] to violate" their right of publicity.

After the case was remanded to the district court, the parties settled.

While *Wendt* is not an advertising law case per se, it does indicate that obtaining a copyright license to fictional characters may not be enough to use the fictional characters in ad copy. Where an actor may be publicly associated with the character, the actor's publicity rights mean consent also may be necessary. Ideally, the producers of the fictional work obtain permission from the actor to relicense his or her publicity rights as part of a copyright license. Otherwise, separate permissions from both the copyright holder and the actor may be required.

For more on the *White* case and its implications for the boundaries of publicity rights, see Stacey L. Dogan, *An Exclusive Right to Evoke*, 44 B.C. L. REV. 291 (2003).

Under this precedent, if ad copy depicts an empty Cleveland Cavaliers jersey with the number 23, has the advertiser violated LeBron James's publicity rights? (Ignore any trademark issues, and assume this is during the time when LeBron James is a member of the Cavaliers' team).

*Specificity.* In the *White* case, it was clear that the robot evoked Vanna White. In other cases, it may be less clear who is being evoked. If the evoking isn't clearly specific to the plaintiff, then that will give courts another reason to reject the expansion of publicity rights coverage.

For example, 5-Hour Energy drink ran a television ad in which an actor claims to have accomplished a series of seemingly impossible feats, including mastering origami "while beating the record for Hacky Sack," with the help of the drink. See the ad at
https://www.youtube.com/watch?v=aro0aTGBPUE.

Johannes "Ted" Martin "holds the world record for most consecutive kicks (no knees) in the footbag (i.e. hacky sack) singles category and has held that record since 1988 (with the exception of a brief period of 50 days in 1997)." Martin sued Living Essentials, makers of 5-Hour Energy. The courts rejected his claims. Martin v. Living Essentials, LLC, 160 F. Supp. 3d 1042 (N.D. Ill. 2016), *aff'd*, 653 Fed. Appx. 482 (7th Cir. 2016).

The appeals court explained: "we agree with the district court that the phrase 'the record for Hacky Sack' is too ambiguous to call an 'attribute' of Martin. . . . [N]o reasonable viewer would interpret the commercial for 5–hour ENERGY as referring to Martin, and because he does not plausibly allege that Living Essentials invoked his 'identity' through the actor's statement, Martin fails to state a claim" per Illinois' publicity rights statute.

In rejecting Martin's Lanham Act false endorsement claim, the appeals court amplified on Martin's non-identifiability:

> we cannot imagine how this ad would confuse anyone into thinking that Martin himself endorses 5–hour ENERGY or that his use of the caffeinated drink explains a record set before the product came to market. The mention of Hacky Sack, after all, is sandwiched between obviously absurd achievements (which fine print in the 30–second commercial disclaims as "not actual results," although who possibly would believe that the actor, with or without an energy shot, had disproved the theory of relativity or found the elusive Bigfoot?). And Martin's personal endorsement of 5–hour ENERGY cannot logically be inferred from the actor's claim that he "mastered origami while beating the record for Hacky Sack"; the actor cannot be accused of impersonating Martin, since he brags of besting, not holding for years, a footbag record. To eclipse Martin's record in five hours would require a superhuman effort of three to four kicks per second, but, that aside, why would a viewer assume that it was Martin's footbag record which had fallen? The actor is shown kicking two footbags, and Guinness World Records credits Finnish footbagger Juha–Matti Rytilahti, not Martin, with the most consecutive kicks of two footbags.

The district court reinforced the latter point, noting that there were 14 different hacky sack world records, so it's not clear which record (and record holder) the ad referred to.

A related case is Martin v. Wendy's International, Inc., 2017 WL 1545684 (N.D. Ill. April 28, 2017). Wendy's included a Guinness-branded footbag in its Kid's Meal along with various statements about footbag-related world records. The footbag instructions said that "Back in 1997, Ted Martin made his world record of 63,326 kicks in a little less than nine hours!" and encouraged customers to try to beat it. The court held that Wendy's did not violate Martin's publicity rights because "it would be nonsensical to hold that the law prohibits Guinness from reciting that bare fact in a promotional item but permits it to include the fact in the books it sells." It also held that Wendy's did not make a Lanham Act false endorsement because "mentioning plaintiff's record on the instructional card served only to offer a sample of the sort of world records Guinness publishes."

## 3.      Endorsements and Testimonials

In addition to the publicity rights and related doctrines that govern depicting people in ads, those ads must comply with the rules governing endorsements and testimonials. We discussed this issue a bit in Chapter 5 regarding distinguishing ads from editorial content, and you may wish to refamiliarize yourself with the discussion there.

The leading source of such rules is the FTC's Guides Concerning Use of Endorsements and Testimonials in Advertising.[3] *See* 16 C.F.R. §§ 255.0-255.5. The FTC defines an "endorsement" and "testimonial" (the FTC equates the two) as:

> any advertising message (including verbal statements, demonstrations, or depictions of the name, signature, likeness or other identifying personal characteristics of an individual or the name or seal of an organization) that consumers are likely to believe reflects the opinions, beliefs, findings, or experiences of a party other than the sponsoring advertiser, even if the views expressed by that party are identical to those of the sponsoring advertiser.

While this definition is not especially clear, it is intended to exclude the statements of people that consumers are likely to recognize as actors hired by the advertiser. A paradigmatic endorsement is when a celebrity personally vouches for the product's quality; a paradigmatic testimonial is when a person describes his or her experiences with the product (such as the amount of weight lost using a diet aid) or is depicted in before/after pictures. Actors playing out an obviously fictional or hypothetical scripted scene in an advertisement aren't making endorsements or testimonials.

---

[3] Other countries' regulators are expressing similar interest in these situations. The Canadian Code of Advertising Standards, for example, requires that any "material connection" between an influencer and a brand be "clearly and prominently disclosed in close proximity to the representation about the product or service," and also refers advertisers to the FTC Guidelines for examples to assist them in conforming to Canadian law. *See also* Influencer Marketing Steering Committee, Disclosure Guidelines, Apr. 19, 2018 (further Canadian guidance).

Some of the key requirements of the Endorsement and Testimonials Guidelines:

- endorsements must reflect the endorser's actual beliefs or experiences
- endorsers may not make representations that would be deceptive if made by the advertiser
- if the ad copy says an endorser uses the product, that must be true
- if the ad copy represents that the endorser is an expert, the endorser must have the requisite qualifications
- the advertiser must disclose any connections with the endorser that would affect the endorsement's credibility

Many of these guidelines are logical extensions of general false advertising principles and thus not controversial in the abstract. However, specific contexts can raise tricky issues.

*Example: Online Product Reviews.* In 2009, the FTC said the guidelines cover online product reviews. The FTC expressed concern about situations where an advertiser provides a financial benefit— including free product samples—to a blogger to write a blog post. Due to the benefit, the FTC believes the blog post becomes a paid endorsement or testimonial. As a result, the FTC expects the blogger to prominently disclose the benefit to avoid misleading the readers about the putative authenticity of the blogger's views.

The FTC's position treats traditional journalists, who the FTC thinks do not need to disclose receiving free product samples if they do so as part of their jobs, differently than identically situated bloggers, who should make such disclosures. The FTC has offered dubious justifications for this Internet exceptionalism. Furthermore, the FTC's guidelines regulate what many people would consider "editorial content" (the blog post), not obvious commercial speech or advertising.

*Example: Celebrity Interviews.* Consumers will recognize a celebrity appearing in a traditional thirty-second ad as a paid endorser. But what if the celebrity appears on a nighttime talk show and casually mentions how much better she's doing now that she's using a particular weight loss program?

The FTC's guidelines specify that, if it would not be obvious to most consumers that she was being paid as a spokesperson by the weight loss program, then her casual reference to the weight loss program would be a paid endorsement/testimonial—meaning she would need to disclose that fact when she drops the casual reference. And, because she is a spokesperson, what she says on the talk show is subject to the same substantiation requirements as an ordinary ad would be. As a reminder, the FTC interprets its substantiation obligation assuming that consumers usually understand a testimonial to reflect typical results—so the advertiser had better be prepared to substantiate typical results like those the celebrity achieved, or it will have to instruct the celebrity to disclose enough qualifiers so consumers wouldn't be misled about typicality. If you were writing a contract with an endorser who might appear on talk shows, how would you deal with this issue?

What about non-celebrities? Does it matter whether or not they are presented as experts? In one case, the security company ADT paid three people over $300,000 to appear on television shows, including the *Today Show* and local newscasts, and post content online, including on blogs. These

590

endorsers were touted as "The Safety Mom," a home security expert, or a tech expert. They reviewed products including ADT's security system, which they described as "amazing" or "incredible," and touted its capabilities, safety benefits, and cost. ADT set up these interviews through its PR firms and booking agents, providing reporters and anchors with suggested interview questions and background video. The experts never disclosed their payments from ADT.

The FTC brought an enforcement action against ADT. The resulting consent order prohibited ADT from misrepresenting that any discussion or demonstration of its products or services was an independent review by an impartial expert, required ADT to clearly and prominently disclose any material connections with the experts, and required ADT to remove existing reviews and endorsements that had been misrepresented as independent or that failed to disclose a material connection. *See In re* ADT LLC, F.T.C. File No. 122 3121 (Mar. 11, 2014). A connection is material, according to the FTC, when the connection might materially affect the weight or credibility a consumer gives the endorsement.

Why do you think the FTC is concerned with such situations? Without this rule, would advertisers be able to disseminate unsubstantiated claims by using paid endorsers, or are there other constraints on advertisers that might block abuse of this loophole? What do reasonable consumers expect when they see a celebrity or "expert" touting some product or service in an "interview" by a reporter associated with a TV station? If the interviewee makes only vague, general statements, would that be puffery? Even if consumers don't understand that she's a paid spokesperson, are they harmed if all she does is puff?

*Example: Celebrity Tweets.* Consider the following tweet (the FTC prepared this as a hypothetical example):

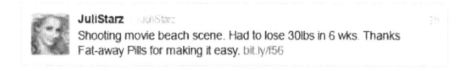

If Juli Starz is a paid endorser, and the bit.ly link in the tweet goes to disclosures that she is being paid by Fat-away and that typical weight loss is one pound per week, is this tweet acceptable? If not, can you rewrite the tweet within Twitter's 140-character limit to comply with the FTC's guidelines?

*Example: Celebrity Instagramming.* Kim Kardashian endorsed a prescription pharmaceutical on Instagram without disclosing her financial connection to the drugmaker:

591

Note the first substantive comment from "flawlessfashionstore": "[I don't know] if she's getting paid for this and do not care. But it is safe for mom & baby. I called my doctor because I couldn't even keep water down." Assume this comment is both true and being proffered by an ordinary consumer. If this speaker can make this statement without extensive disclosures, why can't Kardashian? Does Kardashian's celebrity status make her claims more believable? Does the fact that Kardashian is using her real name make her claims more believable?

The FDA issued a warning to the drugmaker, resulting in the following message, which required scrolling twice on an ordinary mobile device:

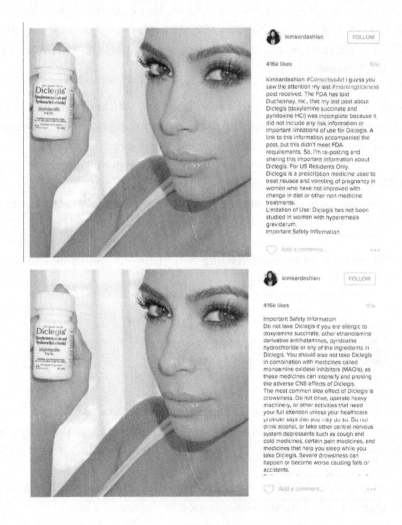

Was this an appropriate remedial action? Does the difficulty of after-the-fact corrective disclosure help justify the FTC's arguably overenthusiastic rules?

*Example: Pinterest.* The FTC issued a "closing letter" to Cole Haan, a shoe seller, indicating that it would take no further action based on the following situation. Cole Haan conducted a "Wandering Sole" contest on Pinterest, a social media site where users can save and organize images known as "pins" in collections called "boards." The contest rules instructed contestants to create Pinterest boards titled "Wandering Sole," which had to include five shoe images from Cole Haan's Wandering Sole Pinterest Board as well as five images of the contestants' "favorite places to wander." Contestants were told to use "#WanderingSole" in each pin description, and Cole Haan promised to award a $1,000 shopping spree to the contestant with the most creative entry.

Were contestants "endorsers" in the ordinary sense? The FTC stated that the pins featuring Cole Haan products were endorsements, and that the fact that the pins were incentivized by the contest "would not reasonably be expected by consumers who saw the pins." The FTC faulted Cole Haan for failing to instruct contestants to label their pins and Pinterest boards to make it clear that they had pinned Cole Haan products as part of a contest. The "#WanderingSole" hashtag was inadequate to disclose the financial incentive at issue. The FTC didn't take further action because it hadn't previously addressed whether contest entry was a material connection between advertiser and content disseminator that required disclosure, and because the contest was short and attracted few entrants. *Letter from Mary Engle,* Mar. 20, 2014. Despite the FTC's decision not to proceed, the letter clearly signaled the FTC's intent for similar contests going forward.

Is there any connection between advertiser and social media influencer that the FTC would consider too trivial to merit disclosure? How can the advertiser know for sure?

*Endorsers' Individual Liability.* The FTC initially represented that they would enforce the Endorsement and Testimonials Guidelines principally against advertisers, not individual bloggers or endorsers. Furthermore, the FTC has indicated that an advertiser can satisfy its obligations under the guidelines by prospectively telling endorsers to make the proper sponsorship disclosures and retrospectively monitoring the resulting online posts to ensure compliance (and taking corrective action where necessary). However, in 2017, the FTC sent warning letters to 21 social media influencers regarding their obligations to comply with the Endorsements & Testimonials Guidelines. Among other things, the FTC took the position that "tagging a brand in an Instagram picture is an endorsement of the brand and requires an appropriate disclosure." *See CSGO Lotto Owners Settle FTC's First-Ever Complaint Against Individual Social Media Influencers*, Federal Trade Commission, Sept. 7, 2017.

Should endorsers face individual liability for violating these guidelines? China's recently amended Advertising Law, effective as of September 1, 2015, provides that anyone who endorses a product may be jointly liable for any violation of the advertising law if he or she ought to have known of the violation, and may be banned from endorsing other products or services for a period of 3 years. Would such a rule be appropriate in the US? Would such a rule be constitutional? *Cf.* Luman v. Theismann, 647 Fed. Appx. 804 (9th Cir. 2016) (celebrity spokesperson wasn't liable for false advertising under California law because he was not the "seller" of the product).

*Showcasing Celebrity Activity.* In one NAD proceeding, eSalon had a Pinterest page called Hair Colors We Love with pictures of celebrities. The NAD found that the photos implied that the celebrities endorsed eSalon products, and recommended that eSalon only pin photos of celebrities who used eSalon. eSalon, NAD Case No. 5645 (Oct. 17, 2013).

Do you agree that pinning photos with the caption "Hair Colors We Love" implies endorsement? Separately, when a custom hair color producer pins photos with the caption "Hair Colors We Love," does that implicitly represent that the producer can replicate those hair colors on request? What sort of substantiation would you have asked eSalon for, as their counsel?

*Fabricated Endorsements*

Sometimes, advertisers simply fabricate endorsements, such as fake online consumer reviews touting the advertiser's offerings or bashing rivals' offerings. *See, e.g.*, Press Release, New York Office of the Attorney General, *A.G. Schneiderman Announces Agreement With 19 Companies To Stop Writing Fake Online Reviews And Pay More Than $350,000 In Fines*, Sept. 23, 2013 (announcing settlements with numerous companies that had written fake consumer reviews for themselves on websites such as Yelp, Google Local, and CitySearch).

Fake endorsements are not new to the Internet. Sony's David Manning incident provides a useful case study.

For about a year starting in 2000, Sony's Columbia Pictures ran advertisements for several movies containing laudatory comments from "David Manning," identified as a movie reviewer for the *Ridgefield (Conn.) Press*. While the *Ridgefield Press* is a real newspaper, David Manning was a fictitious person, and the quotes attributed to Manning were all fabricated. Why a Sony employee chose to engage in this artifice is baffling; as one journalist wrote, "[t]he shocking part is that practically every movie these days, good or bad, garners [a] poster-friendly blurb from some critic— even no-name hacks toiling for virtually unknown publications." Josh Grossberg, *Sony's Fake Critic Fallout*, E! ONLINE, June 6, 2001.

A *Newsweek* article on June 2, 2001, exposed Sony's ruse. Legal proceedings ensued.

Several private consumer class action lawsuits were brought against Sony for false advertising, unfair competition, and related claims. Sony tried to dismiss one such lawsuit on the grounds that its advertisements were protected by California's anti-SLAPP statute, which applies to certain types of speech. In *Rezec v. Sony Pictures Entertainment*, 116 Cal. App. 4th 135 (Cal. App. Ct. 2004), a divided California appellate court rejected Sony's dismissal attempt because the ads were commercial speech, which the court said is not protected by anti-SLAPP laws.

Sony subsequently settled the class action lawsuit for an announced value of $1.5 million, including $500,000 allocated to consumers who saw some of the movies advertised using the fake quotes. Perhaps not surprisingly, only 170 consumers' claims—totaling less than $5,100—were tendered. *See* William Booth, *Big Payday for Lawyers In Sony Fake-Blurb Deal*, WASH. POST, Sept. 10, 2005. Sony gave the remaining amount to charity.

Several attorneys general also explored actions against Sony. Sony settled with Connecticut's attorney general for $325,000, plus the promise to stop using fake quotes and showing ads depicting employees giving enthusiastic fake testimonials (a common practice among movie studios at the time).

*Are Celebrity Endorsements a Good Investment?*

The evidence is mixed about whether celebrity endorsements are a good deal for advertisers. *Compare* Peter Dabol, *Celebrities in Advertising Are Almost Always a Big Waste of Money*, AD. AGE, Jan. 12, 2011 ("[A] celebrity has little to no impact on an ad's effectiveness. In fact, regardless of gender or age, ads without celebrities out-performed ads with them"), *with* Anita Elberse & Jeroen Verleun, *The Economic Value of Celebrity Endorsements*, 52 J. ADVERTISING RES. 149 (2012) (finding that signing a celebrity athletic endorser was associated with a 4% increase in sales and higher stockholder returns, but that the sales benefits leveled off over time).

In contrast, there is general consensus that consumer "word-of-mouth" recommendations, also at issue in endorsement cases, have substantial selling power. *See, e.g.*, Jack Neff, *GE Study Proves Consumers Respond More to Shared Content Than to Paid Placements*, AD. AGE, Jan. 25, 2012; *cf.* Natasha T. Brison et al., *Facebook Likes and Sport Brand Image: An Empirical Examination of the National Advertising Division's Coastal Contacts' Decision*, 25 J. LEGAL ASPECTS SPORT 104 (2015) (Facebook "likes" increased favorable consumer perceptions of brands and likely purchase intentions). Do these results suggest that the FTC is correct to be concerned about new media endorsement situations?

If an advertising law course were taught fifty years ago, it almost certainly would not have discussed privacy issues. For decades, most members of the advertising community have been in denial about consumer privacy concerns. Many advertising professionals treat consumer data the way that journalists treat story tips: once they get the information—by whatever provenance—they feel it's fair game to use it without restriction.

This *laissez faire* attitude among advertising professionals is out-of-sync with anti-advertising sentiments among consumers and regulators. To many consumers, ads feel intrusive. Ads that target us based on our personal information (say, a recent bankruptcy or hospital stay) feel even more intrusive.

As a result, the advertising community constantly and increasingly clashes with those who seek to regulate it. Typically, regulators give advertisers a chance to self-regulate by developing industry standards that provide minimum levels of consumer protection. If a self-regulatory effort fails or takes too long, the regulators come in, crack down, and shake up the industry. This chapter will explore the detritus of several such crackdowns.

## 1. The Ambiguity of "Privacy"

The word "privacy" is so ubiquitous that it's easy to overlook the term's unavoidable semantic ambiguity. In fact, the word "privacy" means many different things, and it is easy for people to talk past each other in discussions about privacy. Privacy scholar Dan Solove notes,

> Lillian BeVier writes: "Privacy is a chameleon-like word, used denotatively to designate a wide range of wildly disparate interests from confidentiality of personal information to reproductive autonomy—and connotatively to generate goodwill on behalf of whatever interest is being asserted in its name." Other commentators have lamented that privacy is "vague and evanescent," "protean," and suffering from "an embarrassment of meanings." "Perhaps the most striking thing about the right to privacy," philosopher Judith Jarvis Thomson has observed, "is that nobody seems to have any very clear idea what it is."
>
> Often, privacy problems are merely stated in knee-jerk form: "That violates my privacy!" When we contemplate an invasion of privacy—such as having our personal information gathered by companies in databases—we instinctively recoil. Many discussions of privacy appeal to people's fears and anxieties. What commentators often fail to do, however, is translate those instincts into a reasoned, well-articulated account of why privacy problems

are harmful. When people claim that privacy should be protected, it is unclear precisely what they mean.

Daniel J. Solove, *A Taxonomy of Privacy*, 154 U. PENN. L. REV. 477 (2006). "Nearly every attempt to define privacy winds up being too specific to apply generally or too general to be useful." WOODROW HARTZOG, PRIVACY'S BLUEPRINT: THE BATTLE TO CONTROL THE DESIGN OF NEW TECHNOLOGIES 10 (2018).

This semantic ambiguity especially applies in the advertising context. Because the word "privacy" has so many disparate meanings, conversations about the intersection of advertising and privacy are usually irresolute and unfocused. If you hear people complain about "privacy" concerns regarding advertising, ask them exactly what they mean.

From a legal doctrine standpoint, "privacy" frequently has been equated with Prosser's privacy torts. As discussed in Chapter 13, Dean William Prosser taxonomized privacy legal claims into four types. *See* William L. Prosser, *Privacy*, 48 CAL. L. REV. 383 (1960) and RESTATEMENTS (SECOND) OF TORTS (for which Prosser was the reporter). Prosser's four privacy torts are:

1) Intrusion upon the plaintiff's seclusion or solitude, or into his private affairs
2) Public disclosure of embarrassing private facts about the plaintiff
3) Publicity which places the plaintiff in a false light in the public eye
4) Appropriation, for the defendant's advantage, of the plaintiff's name or likeness

We discussed the fourth tort, commercial appropriation, in Chapter 13 in our discussion about publicity rights. A few words about the other three:

*Intrusion into Seclusion*

This occurs when there is an offensive intrusion into a private place. For example, a homeowner enjoys nude sunbathing in his backyard, which is well screened by hedges to prevent people from ordinarily being able to see him. An intrusion into seclusion might occur if a photographer uses an unusually high-powered zoom lens to take photos of the nude sunbather from a distant skyscraper or hill.

*Public Disclosure of Private Facts*

This occurs when someone publicizes a true but private fact without a sufficient public interest. For example, publishing photos of a critically injured person as she is being wheeled from an ambulance into the emergency room can be a public disclosure of private facts. The facts are true (the accurate depiction of the victim's injuries) and they were visible in a public place (the ER), but there may be weak justifications for publishing the photos of a person in a medically vulnerable condition.

*False Light*

This occurs when someone offensively publishes a true fact that recklessly places someone else in a false light. For example, false light might occur if a newspaper publishes an article about sexually transmitted diseases in the pornography industry and includes a stock photo of a pornography actress with the story, even though the article does not state or imply the actress has an STD and she does not, in fact, have an STD. *Cf.* Manzari v. Associated Newspapers Ltd., 830 F.3d 881 (9th Cir. 2016). You might think of the relationship between false light and defamation as analogous to literal falsity and falsity by necessary implication. Defamation applies to false assertions of fact, while false light applies when everything said is true but the combination nevertheless creates a false impression.

The above examples are illustrative but not conclusive. Privacy plaintiffs have stretched these broadly worded and amorphous tort doctrines to cover a myriad of other circumstances. Plaintiffs frequently allege the common law privacy torts in advertising-related cases, though the claims routinely meet with little or no success. Instead, statutory or contract claims are more likely to succeed.

## 2.      Privacy Harms

Because privacy has so many definitions, it's hard to pin down exactly how advertising can cause privacy harms for consumers. After all, if consumers don't like the ads, they can just disregard them, right?

With the renewed legislative attention to advertising and privacy, this thinking is, at best, incomplete. Advertisers have to be sensitive to all the possible privacy harms they may contribute to, which can include:

- *Unwanted Intrusion.* Some consumers feel like telemarketing, door-to-door sales and junk mail are an invasion of their home. Some consumers feel that interruptive broadcast ads, such as TV and radio, and online ads like pop-ups or interstitial ads are also intrusive.
- *Out-of-Pocket Receiving Costs.* Consumers may resent any out-of-pocket costs that advertisers impose on them. For example, text messages may impose per-message costs; and junk mail or newspaper advertising inserts may have disposal costs.
- *Overly Personal Targeting.* Consumers can feel uncomfortable when an advertiser targets advertising based on "private" or embarrassing personal characteristics, such as ads for baby-related items targeted to women who have miscarried or hair restoration services targeted at middle-aged men.
- *Price/Service Discrimination.* When advertisers know their consumers better, they may try to ascertain the consumers' maximum willingness to pay and adjust pricing accordingly. Advertisers may also make distinctions between consumers, rewarding more loyal consumers and concomitantly disadvantaging less loyal consumers.

- *Unwanted Disclosures to the Government.* Advertisers who maintain databases containing personal information about consumers may be targeted by government entities seeking to learn more about consumers and their activities.

- *Unwanted Disclosures to Other Parties.* A personal information database also can result in unwanted data disclosures to various third parties, such as responses to litigants' discovery requests and unintentional disclosures to third parties, including acquisition by hackers. As just one example, Eli Lilly once sent an email regarding the antidepressant Prozac but made all of the recipients' email addresses visible to each other, thus inadvertently disclosing highly sensitive medical information. Federal Trade Comm'n, *Eli Lilly Settles FTC Charges Concerning Security Breach* (Jan. 18, 2002). As another example, ads can sometimes reveal personal or confidential information when seen by a family member. *E.g. How to Stop Facebook from Ruining Your Holiday Gift Surprises*, MONEY, Dec. 4, 2014. In the worst case, unintentional disclosures can lead to identity theft or physical or financial harm.

For more examples of privacy-related harms, *see* Daniel J. Solove, *A Taxonomy of Privacy*, 154 U. PENN. L. REV. 477 (2006).

Privacy harms can be difficult to measure because they may not occur immediately (or be recognized). For example, assume a hacker obtains a database of private consumer information. Some or all of the people in the database may experience identity theft, but it could take months or years for them to realize they are victims. Or it's possible that the stolen data is never used (or, in fact, was never actually stolen, or was never decrypted), in which case the purported victims will never actually suffer any financial losses at all. *See* In re Zappos.com, Inc., Customer Data Security Breach Litigation, MDL No. 2357 (D. Nev. June 1, 2015) ("Even if Plaintiffs' risk of identity theft and fraud was substantial and immediate in 2012, the passage of [3.5 years of litigation] without a single report from Plaintiffs that they in fact suffered the harm they fear must mean something.").

Privacy harms might also be so trivial that they may not warrant the heavy costs of judicial administration. For example, in *Harris v. Time*, 191 Cal.App.3d 449 (1987), a junk mail recipient claimed that the mailer induced him to open the envelope on false pretenses. The court rejected the claim, harshly, on the grounds of "de minimis non curat lex"—the law disregards trifles. Unfortunately for advertisers, there is no categorical "de minimis non curat lex" legal defense to privacy-related lawsuits, even if consumers in fact only suffered trifling harms.

Fortunately, courts have other ways to dispose of lawsuits involving minimal harm. The next two cases address whether the plaintiffs have adequately alleged any legally cognizable harm. As you read, try to identify the exact harms or risk of harms allegedly experienced by the plaintiffs. However, before we go through the facts, it is important to understand a bit about web tracking technologies.

*Cookies and Tracking Technologies.* Cookies are small datastrings that are stored on a user's computer and uniquely identify an individual or computer. In some cases, the cookies themselves do not contain any information supplied by the user. Instead, they act as a "key" to a database of profiles where the website stores information it wants to associate with the cookie. Thus, when a web user has a cookie on his or her computer, the website can check the cookie's unique identifier against its profile database, pull the information from the database, and proceed accordingly.

Cookies are especially valuable to ad networks that want to uniquely identify individuals as they travel across the Internet. The cookie's unique identifier lets the ad network know if it has seen the user before. This can help the ad network customize the ad shown to the user. Customization may be as targeted as an ad customized to the user's interest or as generic as imposing a "frequency cap" that prevents a specific ad from being shown too many times to the same person.

Advertisers and ad networks do not rely solely on the traditional form of cookies (the "HTTP cookie") to insert unique identifiers on a user's computer; they may use alternative identification methods such as the flash cookies at issue in that case. Consumers may be frustrated by non-HTTP cookies if they have undertaken technological efforts to manage their HTTP cookies (using tools available through their web browser or browser plug-ins) and those efforts are thwarted by bypassing HTTP cookies. At minimum, this suggests an ongoing cat-and-mouse game between users and advertisers; users undertake more efforts to suppress cookies, and advertisers use technological tricks to get around these suppression efforts.

With that cat-and-mouse game in mind, consider the harm theories in the following two cases.

**LaCourt v. Specific Media, Inc., 2011 WL 1661532 (C.D. Cal. 2011)**

I. Introduction

This case is one of a constellation of class action lawsuits pending before this Court which arise from the alleged use of Adobe Flash local shared objects ("LSOs" or "Flash Cookies") to track class members' use of the Internet without their knowledge or consent. . . .

II. Background

"Specific Media is an online third-party ad network that earns its revenue by delivering targeted advertisements." It uses HTTP cookies containing unique identifiers and browsing history information to track users in order to create behavioral profiles to target specific categories of ads at different users. Allegedly, Specific Media used LSOs in order to circumvent the privacy and security controls of users who had set their browsers' to block third-party HTTP cookies, block Specific Media's HTTP cookies, or who deleted Specific Media's HTTP cookies. In addition, it used LSOs to restore or "re-spawn" Specific Media HTTP cookies that were deleted by users.

Plaintiff Genevieve LaCourt and the six other plaintiffs (hereinafter, "Plaintiffs") purport to represent a class consisting of "[a]ll persons residing in the United States who, during the Class Period, used any web browsing program on any device to access web pages during which time and related to which Specific Media stored Adobe Flash local shared objects (LSOs) on such persons' computers." Each of the named plaintiffs allege that they "are persons who have set the privacy and security controls on their browsers to block third-party cookies and/or who periodically delete third-party cookies," and that they each had a "Flash cookie" installed on their computer by Specific Media without their notice or consent.

Plaintiffs allege that they sought to maintain the secrecy and confidentiality of the information obtained by Defendant through the use of LSOs. They further allege that "Defendant's conduct has caused economic loss to Plaintiffs and Class Members in that their personal information has discernable value, both to Defendant and to Plaintiffs and Class Members, and of which Defendant has deprived Plaintiffs and Class Members and, in addition, retained and used for its own economic benefit." . . .

## IV. Analysis

### A. Article III Standing

Defendant first argues that the Court lacks subject matter jurisdiction over this action because Plaintiffs have failed to allege "the irreducible constitutional minimum of standing" required by Article III of the Constitution, i.e., the existence of an actual case or controversy. In order to establish standing, a plaintiff must show: "(1) it has suffered an 'injury in fact' that is (a) concrete and particularized and (b) actual or imminent, not conjectural or hypothetical; (2) the injury is fairly traceable to the challenged action of the defendant; and (3) it is likely, as opposed to merely speculative, that the injury will be redressed by a favorable decision." Here, Specific Media challenges only Plaintiffs' ability to satisfy the first of these requirements, asserting that Plaintiffs have failed to plausibly allege an "injury in fact."

1. Plaintiffs have not alleged that any named Plaintiff was affected by Defendant's alleged conduct.

Specific Media argues that Plaintiffs, upon close reading of the Complaint, have not alleged that Specific Media ever actually tracked the online activity of any named plaintiff, or that Plaintiffs ever deleted any Specific Media browser cookies, or that Plaintiffs' browser cookies were ever "re-spawned" by Specific Media. Rather, the Complaint simply alleges that Specific Media installed Flash cookies on Plaintiffs' computers and then states that "Plaintiffs believe that, if they were to revisit the websites on which Specific Media [Flash cookies] were set, or were to visit other websites on which Specific Media served online advertisements, the tracking devices would be used as substitutes for HTTP cookies and to re-spawn previously deleted cookies." Thus, Specific Media argues, to the extent that Plaintiffs have alleged any injury at all, it is one that is entirely conjectural, hypothetical, or speculative.

Plaintiffs' mere use of the subjunctive does not mean that they have not alleged an injury that is "imminent." The threat that Plaintiffs' previously deleted cookies will be re-spawned when they visit websites in the Specific Media's network is, potentially, a threat of imminent harm sufficient to satisfy the "injury in fact" requirement of standing. However, it is not clear that Plaintiffs have even alleged this. . . .

2. Plaintiffs have not alleged an economic injury or harm to their computers.

601

Even assuming Plaintiffs can allege that they were affected by Specific Media's alleged practices regarding Flash Cookies, an even more difficult question is whether they can allege that they were injured by them. In this respect, Plaintiffs' Opposition is surprisingly tepid. . . .

The parties in their papers engage in a quasi-philosophical debate about the possible value of consumers' "personal information" on the Internet. Ultimately, the Court probably would decline to say that it is categorically impossible for Plaintiffs to allege some property interest that was compromised by Defendant's alleged practices.[1] The problem is, at this point they have not done so. Plaintiffs—who have more or less completely accepted Defendant's framing of the issue—make the problematic argument that "by taking and retaining [Plaintiffs'] personal information," i.e., their browsing history, Defendant has deprived Plaintiffs of this information's economic value. The theory underlying this assertion is presented by reference to a number of academic articles concerning the nature of "Internet business models . . . driven by consumers' willingness to supply data about themselves." While the Court would recognize the viability in the abstract of such concepts as "opportunity costs," "value-for-value exchanges," "consumer choice," and other concepts referred to in the Opposition, what Plaintiffs really need to do is to give some particularized example of their application in this case.

Defendant aptly notes that the Complaint does not identify a single individual who was foreclosed from entering into a "value-for-value exchange" as a result of Specific Media's alleged conduct. Furthermore, there are no facts in the FACC that indicate that the Plaintiffs themselves ascribed an economic value to their unspecified personal information. Finally, even assuming an opportunity to engage in a "value-for-value exchange," Plaintiffs do not explain how they were "deprived" of the economic value of their personal information simply because their unspecified personal information was purportedly collected by a third party.

In addition to the injury based on the supposed loss of their personal information, Plaintiffs also half-heartedly argue that they suffered harm to their computers "because Specific Media's installation of Flash LSOs circumvented and diminished the performance and capabilities of their computers." If the loss of the ability to delete cookies counts as harm to Plaintiffs' computers, then maybe Plaintiffs have alleged some de minimis injury, but probably not one that would give rise to Article III standing. If Plaintiffs are suggesting that their computers' performance was compromised in some other way—a claim that was made in the first iteration of the Complaint but all but abandoned in the FACC—then they need to allege facts showing that this is true.

3. *In re Doubleclick*

At least one case, *In re DoubleClick Privacy Litigation*, 154 F. Supp. 2d 497 (S.D.N.Y. 2001), has held—albeit not in the context of evaluating Article III standing—that website visitors do not suffer a cognizable "economic loss" from the collection of their data. In *Doubleclick*, the court rejected

---

[1] Or, for that matter, some type of privacy interest. It is noted that at ¶ 26 of the FACC Plaintiffs allege that "Plaintiffs consider information about their online activities to be in the nature of confidential information that they protect from disclosure, including by periodically deleting cookies."

plaintiffs' arguments that they suffered economic damages for the purpose of stating a claim under the Computer Fraud and Abuse Act based on both (1) the economic value of their attention to DoubleClick's advertisements (which is not an argument that Plaintiffs in this case make) and (2) the value of the demographic information compiled by it through the use of browser cookies (which basically is). In particular, the court wrote that "although demographic information is valued highly . . . the value of its collection has never been considered a [sic] economic loss to the subject." While Plaintiffs attempt to distinguish *DoubleClick* on the ground they have alleged that they were deprived not of "mere demographic information," but "of the value of their personal data," it is not clear what they mean by this. Defendant observes that, if anything, the Plaintiffs in *Doubleclick* alleged that the defendant collected much more information than Specific Media supposedly collected in this case, including "names, e-mail addresses, home and business addresses, telephone numbers, searches performed on the Internet, Web pages or sites visited on the Internet and other communications and information that users would not ordinarily expect advertisers to be able to collect."

*Doubleclick*, obviously, is not binding on this Court. Its reasoning at least suggests that the question of Plaintiffs' ability to allege standing is a serious one, however. It would be very difficult to conclude at this point that Plaintiffs have met their burden of establishing that this Court has subject matter jurisdiction. . . . It is not obvious that Plaintiffs cannot articulate some actual or imminent injury in fact. It is just that at this point they haven't offered a coherent and factually supported theory of what that injury might be. . . .

## Claridge v. RockYou, Inc., 2011 WL 1361588 (N.D. Cal. 2011)

### . . . BACKGROUND

Plaintiff brings the instant action against defendant for allegedly failing to secure and safeguard its users' sensitive personally identifiable information ("PII"), including email addresses, passwords, and login credentials for social networks like MySpace and Facebook.

Defendant RockYou is a publisher and developer of online services and applications for use with social networking sites such as Facebook, MySpace, hi5 and Bebo. Applications developed by RockYou include those that enable users to share photos, write special text on a friend's page, or play games with other users. Customers sign up to use RockYou's applications through rockyou.com, and they are asked to provide a valid e-mail address and registration password, which RockYou then stores in its database. Additionally, a customer may be required to provide RockYou with a username and password for accessing a particular social network. When users operate a RockYou application on a social networking site, RockYou utilizes the application as a platform to display paid advertisements. Defendant claims to be the leading provider of social networking application-based advertising services, with more than 130 million unique customers using its applications on a monthly basis.

Plaintiff Claridge was a registered account holder with RockYou during the relevant time period, having registered with RockYou on August 13, 2008. He signed up to utilize a photo sharing application offered by defendant, and submitted his e-mail address and password to defendant in order to do so.

Plaintiff alleges that RockYou promised through its website that it would safeguard its users' sensitive PII, through a written policy that stated: "RockYou! uses commercially reasonable physical, managerial, and technical safeguards to preserve the integrity and security of your personal information . . . " Despite this promise, plaintiff alleges that RockYou—which collects and stores millions of users' PII in a large-scale commercial database—stored all PII in "clear" or "plain" text, which means that RockYou utilized no form of encryption in order to prevent intruders from easily reading and removing users' PII. The PII was therefore readily accessible to anyone with access to the database.

Among the options available to protect its customers, plaintiff alleges that RockYou could have followed a commonly used method of protecting sensitive data that requires conversion and storage of a "hashed" form of a plain text password. Defendant failed, however, to use hashing, or any other common and reasonable method of data protection. Plaintiff alleges that, by failing to secure its users' PII, RockYou made email account and social networking account access available to even the least capable hacker. . . .

[B]ecause RockYou did not have proper security in place and failed to use commercially reasonable methods to prevent a well-known method of attack, its security flaw was being actively exploited and the contents of its database were known and being made public through underground hacker forums on or before November 29, 2009. . . .

Based on the foregoing allegations, plaintiff filed the instant suit against RockYou, on behalf of himself and a class of similarly situated individuals, defined as: "All individuals and entities in the United States who had RockYou accounts in 2009." . . .

As a preliminary matter, however, the court first turns its attention to the parties' standing arguments. Defendant, who challenges plaintiff's ability to adequately allege standing, appears to subsume within its arguments two different sub-arguments: plaintiff's ability to allege injury in fact standing (i.e., Article III standing); and plaintiff's ability to adequately allege the elements of injury in connection with the individual claims asserted against defendant.

To the extent the former is at issue, the parties dispute whether plaintiff has sufficiently alleged any actionable harm or concrete, tangible, non-speculative harm or loss. *See, e.g.,* Lujan v. Defenders of Wildlife, 504 U.S. 555, 560-61 (1992) ("Injury in fact" requires damage to "a legally protected interest which is (a) concrete and particularized, and (b) actual or imminent, not conjectural or hypothetical"). Plaintiff generally alleges that defendant's customers, including plaintiff, "pay" for the products and services they "buy" from defendant by providing their PII, and that the PII constitutes valuable property that is exchanged not only for defendant's products and services, but also in exchange for defendant's promise to employ commercially reasonable methods to safeguard the PII that is exchanged. As a result, defendant's role in allegedly contributing to the breach of plaintiff's PII caused plaintiff to lose the "value" of their PII, in the form of their breached personal data.

In the face of defendant's contention that these allegations are both insufficient and unprecedented in establishing either a concrete or non-speculative injury, plaintiff admits to advancing a novel theory of damages for which supporting case law is scarce. And indeed, the case law cited by the parties demonstrates no clearly established law regarding the sufficiency of allegations of injury in the context of the disclosure of online personal information.

On balance, the court declines to hold at this juncture that, as a matter of law, plaintiff has failed to allege an injury in fact sufficient to support Article III standing. Not only is there a paucity of controlling authority regarding the legal sufficiency of plaintiff's damages theory, but the court also takes note that the context in which plaintiff's theory arises—i.e., the unauthorized disclosure of personal information via the Internet—is itself relatively new, and therefore more likely to raise issues of law not yet settled in the courts. For that reason, and although the court has doubts about plaintiff's ultimate ability to prove his damages theory in this case, the court finds plaintiff's allegations of harm sufficient at this stage to allege a generalized injury in fact. If it becomes apparent, through discovery, that no basis exists upon which plaintiff could legally demonstrate tangible harm via the unauthorized disclosure of personal information, the court will dismiss plaintiff's claims for lack of standing at the dispositive motion stage.

Notwithstanding the court's conclusion that Article III standing has generally been adequately pled at this juncture, the court further concludes that plaintiff has nonetheless failed to allege the more particularized elements of injury with respect to several of plaintiff's numerous individual causes of action. . . .

Defendant here asserts plaintiff has failed to allege any loss of money or property as a result of defendant's allegedly unfair competition. The court agrees. . . .

Applying this heightened concept of injury under [California's Unfair Competition Law (UCL)], plaintiff's claim that his PII constitutes lost "money"—based on plaintiff's untested theory that PII constitutes "currency"—strains the acceptable boundaries of "injury" under the statute. Similarly, to the extent that plaintiff makes the equally untested claim that his PII constitutes "property," plaintiff makes no allegation—nor can he—that his PII was "lost" in the sense understood under the UCL. For as defendant points out, plaintiff's PII—e.g., his login and password information—did not cease to belong to him, or pass beyond his control. . . .

[Invoking its general discussion about harms, the court refused to dismiss the plaintiff's breach of contract and negligence claims, concluding that the plaintiff sufficiently pled enough harm to satisfy the prima facie elements and survive a motion to dismiss.]

*NOTES AND QUESTIONS*

*Denouements.* Following the dismissal, the plaintiffs in the *Specific Media* case filed another amended complaint, but they eventually dropped the case voluntarily.

Soon after the court's ruling above, the *RockYou* case settled with a $2,000 payment to the named plaintiff (no money for any other class members) and attorneys' fees of $290,000. Claridge v. RockYou, 09-CV-6032-PJH (N.D. Cal. Nov. 14, 2011).

*Article III Standing v. Prima Facie Elements.* Courts do not always carefully distinguish Article III standing from the claim's substantive prima facie elements. Article III standing acts as a threshold determinant over whether the case is appropriate for access to federal court (state courts may have similar standing requirements). As the *LaCourt* court lays out, Article III standing requires the plaintiff to show that: "(1) it has suffered an 'injury in fact' that is (a) concrete and particularized and (b) actual or imminent, not conjectural or hypothetical; (2) the injury is fairly traceable to the challenged action of the defendant; and (3) it is likely, as opposed to merely speculative, that the injury will be redressed by a favorable decision."

Article III standing has become a significant battleground in privacy-related litigation because plaintiffs cannot simply object to the defendant's conduct as the requisite injury. As the *LaCourt* opinion suggests, plaintiffs can get around the injury requirement through proper pleading and sufficient diligence before filing the complaint; but if the plaintiff truly has not suffered an injury from the privacy invasion, there may be no way to establish standing.

Even if the plaintiff can show an injury-in-fact sufficient to establish Article III standing, it may be further required to allege a damage or injury as part of the cause of action's prima facie elements. In the *Claridge* case, the court effectively collapsed the different injury inquiries for the contracts breach and negligence claims—saying that the same alleged injury-in-fact sufficed for both purposes. Even so, that alleged injury was insufficient to survive the California UCL claim.

*The* Spokeo *Ruling.* The Supreme Court has addressed Article III standing since the *LaCourt* and *Claridge* rulings, most notably in *Spokeo, Inc. v. Robins*, 578 U.S. ___ (2016). *Spokeo* addressed whether an alleged statutory violation (in the case, the Fair Credit Reporting Act) constituted a per se injury for Article III standing purposes, even if the plaintiff didn't allege any further injury.

Obviously, such a rule would help privacy plaintiffs a lot. If they claim a statutory violation, their case automatically can advance to the next step in litigation. In contrast, if statutory violations don't automatically confer an injury for Article III purposes, more privacy cases will fail—even where the defendant may have, in fact, violated the statute.

So what did the Supreme Court have to say on this vital topic? Well...

> Article III standing requires a concrete injury even in the context of a statutory violation. For that reason, Robins could not, for example, allege a bare procedural violation, divorced from any concrete harm, and satisfy the injury-in-fact requirement of Article III.

And...

> Robins cannot satisfy the demands of Article III by alleging a bare procedural violation. A violation of one of the FCRA's procedural requirements may result in no harm.

But then:

> the violation of a procedural right granted by statute can be sufficient in some circumstances to constitute injury in fact. In other words, a plaintiff in such a case need not allege any additional harm beyond the one Congress has identified.

The net result is that both plaintiffs and defendants can quote language from the Supreme Court opinion clearly supporting their position. This is not the sign of a well-drafted opinion and, not surprisingly, it has led to both defense- and plaintiff-favorable lower court rulings (though on balance, the plaintiffs have more to cheer about). *See* Hancock v. Urban Outfitters, Inc., 850 F.3d 511 (D.C. Cir. 2016) (defense win on Article III for inchoate privacy harm); Khan v. Children's National Health System, 2016 WL 2946155 (D. Md. May 19, 2016) (increased risk of identity theft from data breach insufficient harm for standing purposes).

*Explaining the Different Results.* Back to the *LaCourt* and *Claridge* opinions. Why did the courts reach different results on the adequacy of harm pleading? Some possible explanations:

- Claridge's lawyer did a better job than LaCourt's lawyer?
- The nature of the "invasion" differed?
- Names, email addresses, passwords and the like are more easily understood in privacy terms than browser history tracked by cookies, which a user is unlikely ever to consider "her own"?
- The defendants promised different things to their users?
- The judges just saw things differently?

*Personal Data as "Payment."* It has become popular in the privacy community to think of personal data as the person's commercially valuable "property." According to this logic, "free" Internet services aren't actually free; instead, they require people to "pay" by providing their personal data. *See, e.g.,* Chris J. Hoofnagle & Jay Whittington, *Free: Accounting for the Costs of the Internet's Most Popular Price*, 61 UCLA L. REV. 606 (2014).

This is the plaintiffs' basic contention in the *Claridge* case. Because consumers provided their commercially valuable personal data to RockYou, these consumers suffered a diminution in that commercial value when hackers took their personal data. Do you find this argument convincing? Think carefully about the assumptions embedded in this argument. Then again, do you think a celebrity should be able to recover if their personality is used in an ad, even if the celebrity would have refused consent for the ad irrespective of price?

Consider one judge's response in a lawsuit over Gmail:

> a plaintiff must allege how the defendant's use of the information deprived the plaintiff of the information's economic value. Put another way, a plaintiff must do more than point to the dollars in a defendant's pocket; he must sufficient [*sic*] allege that in the process he lost dollars of his own.

*In re* Google, Inc. Privacy Policy Litig., 2013 WL 6248499 (N.D. Cal. 2013). However, especially in the data breach context, courts are increasingly receptive to the idea that the unconsented exfiltration of personal data is a cognizable harm, at least for Article III standing purposes.

*Categories of Personal Data.* In the *Claridge* case, the misappropriated data was described as "sensitive personally identifiable information ("PII"), including email addresses, passwords, and login credentials for social networks like MySpace and Facebook." This statement implies different ways to classify data about people:

- "Sensitive" vs. "non-sensitive" data. Sensitive data can include personal health or financial information. People are more reluctant to share these types of information and are more easily embarrassed or harmed when others learn it.
- "Personally identifiable" vs. "non-personally identifiable" information. "Personally identifiable information" is typically referred to by the acronym "PII." PII can be used to uniquely identify a person. Unfortunately, there is no consensus about what constitutes PII. Many privacy statutes define PII using a laundry list of data items, but there is little analytical rigor to what specific data items are included or excluded in those definitions. We will revisit the differences between PII and non-PII shortly, in the *Pineda* case.

*Do Not Track: A Vain Hope?* Most browser software now contain a way for users to indicate that they do not want to be tracked, what's often called a "Do-Not-Track" setting. Websites can choose to honor the signal, or they can choose to ignore it. California law requires many websites now to disclose in their privacy policy if they honor a browser's Do-Not-Track signal. CAL. BUS. & PROFS. CODE § 22575(b)(5). However, several major websites have publicly disclosed that they ignore the Do-Not-Track signal. Why would they choose that?

There may be technological ways, such as "browser fingerprints," that let advertisers or ad networks uniquely identify users or computers without using cookies at all. *See, e.g., Web Browsers Leave 'Fingerprints' Behind as You Surf the Net*, EFF Press Release (May 17, 2010). Would such fingerprinting be actionable under the same theory that the plaintiffs offered in *Claridge*? Does it matter that consumers might not know about all the ways in which their information is being collected?

*Consuming a Device's Capacity.* Plaintiffs can get around Article III standing by claiming that the defendant consumed some of a mobile device's battery life. Yet power consumption as a harm does not create an injury-in-fact with respect to a desktop or laptop computer that's plugged into a charging source. Does this special treatment of mobile devices, compared to other computing devices, make sense?

**3.     Regulating the Lifecycle of Data**

*Who Enforces Privacy Violations?*

For the most part, the regulatory institutions for false advertising discussed in Chapter 3 also regulate privacy concerns, including federal government agencies (especially the Federal Trade Commission), state attorneys' general, and consumer class action lawyers. During President Obama's administration, the Federal Trade Commission played an unusually prominent role in the privacy enforcement community, repeatedly describing itself as "the nation's leading privacy enforcement agency." (All of the FTC Commissioners have turned over since Obama left office, so the FTC's future agenda remains to be seen). Also, California's attorney general office has a Privacy Enforcement & Protection Unit with dedicated prosecutors working the privacy beat, and class action law firms specializing in plaintiffs' privacy work have emerged.

However, competitors rarely sue each other over consumer privacy issues, often because competitors engage in similarly dicey practices and don't wish to indirectly implicate their own practices. Because competitor disputes over privacy are rare, the National Advertising Division (NAD) also does not play a major role.

In addition to formal enforcement mechanisms, many industry participants voluntarily adopt industry standards. For example, the Network Advertising Initiative's (NAI) Code of Conduct "is a set of self-regulatory principles that require NAI member companies to provide notice and choice with respect to Interest-Based Advertising (IBA), Cross-App Advertising (CAA), and Retargeting (collectively, Personalized Advertising) as well as Ad Delivery and Reporting (ADR) activities."

*Spotlight on the FTC Act.* The FTC Act Section 5 authorizes the FTC to enforce against "unfair or deceptive acts or practices in or affecting commerce." The FTC (like most serial plaintiffs) has a capacious view of what constitutes consumer deception. For example, the FTC has brought numerous deception-based enforcement actions against companies based on language in their privacy policies that many advertising lawyers would have considered puffery.

Even with the FTC's broad definition of deception, some privacy incidents still don't implicate any possible deception claims. In those cases, the FTC can rely on Section 5's "unfairness" prong, defined as acts that "cause or are likely to cause substantial injury to consumers that consumers themselves cannot reasonably avoid and that is not outweighed by countervailing benefits to consumers or competition." The FTC has used its unfairness authority to pursue dozens of enforcement actions against companies that suffered data security breaches, claiming lax security practices constitute an unfair trade practice. Thus far, the FTC has successfully defended its unfairness authority for data breach enforcements. *See In the Matter of LabMD, Inc.,* Docket No. 9357 (FTC July 29, 2016) (as of May 17, 2018, an appeal is still pending in the Eleventh Circuit); *FTC v. Wyndham Worldwide Corp.,* 799 F. 3d 236 (3d Cir. 2015).

*The Law of Advertising and Privacy*

Typically, privacy laws are analyzed on a law-by-law basis, in part because each privacy law has its own unique elements and jurisprudence. This section takes a different approach. It would be impossible for this book to cover the vast spectrum of privacy laws (and you should take a privacy law course if you can). Therefore, the book presents the topic in a more conceptual way, from an advertiser's perspective. As usual, this discussion focuses on US law, but later in the chapter, we'll discuss the implications of European privacy law.

As mentioned in Chapter 1, legendary retailing pioneer John Wanamaker reportedly said: "Half the money I spend on advertising is wasted; the trouble is I don't know which half." If that's true, advertisers would like to figure out which half of their ad dollars are being wasted and stop wasting them. By doing so, advertisers could improve the economic return from their advertising by getting their ads in front of the right consumers (and, naturally, not advertising to the wrong consumers) and delivering the right message for the audience. Consumer data—both personally identifiable and aggregate data—might help achieve these goals. Some marketers maintain that targeting specific consumers based on their data increases sales. Leslie K. John, Tami Kim & Kate Barasz, Ads That Don't Overstep, Harvard Bus. Rev., Jan-Feb. 2018, https://hbr.org/2018/01/ads-that-dont-overstep ("Research has shown that digital targeting meaningfully improves the response to advertisements and that ad performance declines when marketers' access to consumer data is reduced.... [W]hen a law that required websites to inform visitors of covert tracking started to be enforced in the Netherlands, in 2013, advertisement click-through rates dropped. Controlled experiments have found similar results.").

An advertiser goes through a three-stage process in trying to improve advertising efficacy using consumer data:

First, advertisers aggregate consumer data. Second, advertisers sort through the consumer data to determine or improve ad targeting. Third, advertisers use the consumer data to deliver their ads to the targeted consumers. (Which stages did the *LaCourt* and *Claridge* cases above concern?) This part will look at each of these three stages in turn.

### A.        Step 1: Aggregate Consumer Data

There are three main ways of acquiring consumer data. First, the advertiser can obtain the data directly from consumers themselves. Second, the advertiser can license data about consumers from third party databases. Third, the advertiser can aggregate data from other publicly available sources, ranging from government records (such as real property titles) to automatically gathering data posted on websites ("scraping" data). Let's look more closely at each of these three methods.

*Collecting Data from Users*

Advertisers can collect data from users simply by asking them for it. Consumers will often freely self-report data when asked.

Advertisers can also collect data passively by watching consumer behavior. For example, retail stores in physical space can monitor their shoppers moving around the store by seeing where their mobile device tries to establish a connection.

Data collection from users is subject to a wide variety of statutory restrictions under U.S. law. Some examples:

The Electronic Communications Privacy Act (the "ECPA") strongly protects private electronic communications such as telephone calls and email from real-time third-party interception, and it less strongly protects those communications (such as voicemails or emails sitting in an in-box) while in storage. When advertisers or their proxies (such as ad networks) try to gather information from users' online activities, the ECPA can come into play, and the ECPA is frequently alleged in Internet privacy lawsuits.

Another generally applicable statute is the Computer Fraud & Abuse Act (the "CFAA"), which (among other things) restricts accessing a networked computer without proper authorization and obtaining information from that computer. 18 U.S.C. § 1030(a)(2). Among other things, this prohibits surreptitious monitoring devices installed on computers or cellphones. While that may sound like common sense, many common Internet technologies such as cookies or unique IDs in URLs look like surreptitious monitoring devices to plaintiffs' lawyers.

When collecting information from users, a data collector can address the ECPA and CFAA by getting informed user consent through a properly formed privacy policy. This sounds easy enough in theory, but it raises plenty of challenges in practice. We discuss privacy policies later in this chapter.

Other statutory restrictions on data collection from users restrict particular industries or classes of users. For example, the Children's Online Privacy Protection Act ("COPPA") restricts online data collection from children under thirteen years of age without verifiable parental consent.

The following case involves a state statute that restricts businesses from asking users to voluntarily share their data. If you think you can guess what the term "personal identification information" means, the court's conclusion probably will surprise you.

### Pineda v. Williams-Sonoma Stores, Inc., 51 Cal. 4th 524 (Cal. 2011)

The Song-Beverly Credit Card Act of 1971 (Credit Card Act) is "designed to promote consumer protection." One of its provisions, section 1747.08, prohibits businesses from requesting that cardholders provide "personal identification information" during credit card transactions, and then recording that information. . . .

FACTS AND PROCEDURAL HISTORY . . .

The complaint alleged the following:

611

Plaintiff visited one of defendant's California stores and selected an item for purchase. She then went to the cashier to pay for the item with her credit card.

The cashier asked plaintiff for her ZIP code and, believing she was required to provide the requested information to complete the transaction, plaintiff provided it. The cashier entered plaintiff's ZIP code into the electronic cash register and then completed the transaction. At the end of the transaction, defendant had plaintiff's credit card number, name, and ZIP code recorded in its database.

Defendant subsequently used customized computer software to perform reverse searches from databases that contain millions of names, e-mail addresses, telephone numbers, and street addresses, and that are indexed in a manner resembling a reverse telephone book. The software matched plaintiff's name and ZIP code with plaintiff's previously undisclosed address, giving defendant the information, which it now maintains in its own database. Defendant uses its database to market products to customers and may also sell the information it has compiled to other businesses. . . .

DISCUSSION . . .

Section 1747.08, subdivision (a) provides, in pertinent part, "[N]o person, firm, partnership, association, or corporation that accepts credit cards for the transaction of business shall . . . : [¶] . . . [¶] (2) Request, or require as a condition to accepting the credit card as payment in full or in part for goods or services, the cardholder to provide *personal identification information*, which the person, firm, partnership, association, or corporation accepting the credit card writes, causes to be written, or otherwise records upon the credit card transaction form or otherwise." (italics added.)[6] Subdivision (b) defines personal identification information as "information concerning the cardholder, other than information set forth on the credit card, and including, but not limited to, the cardholder's address and telephone number." Because we must accept as true plaintiff's allegation that defendant requested and then recorded her ZIP code, the outcome of this case hinges on whether a cardholder's ZIP code, without more, constitutes personal identification information within the meaning of section 1747.08. We hold that it does.

Subdivision (b) defines personal identification information as "information *concerning* the cardholder . . . including, but not limited to, the cardholder's address and telephone number." (italics added.) "Concerning" is a broad term meaning "pertaining to; regarding; having relation to; [or] respecting . . . ." A cardholder's ZIP code, which refers to the area where a cardholder works or lives, is certainly information that pertains to or regards the cardholder.

In nonetheless concluding the Legislature did not intend for a ZIP code, without more, to constitute personal identification information, the Court of Appeal pointed to the enumerated examples of such

---

[6] Section 1747.08 contains some exceptions, including when a credit card is being used as a deposit or for cash advances, when the entity accepting the card is contractually required to provide the information to complete the transaction or is obligated to record the information under federal law or regulation, or when the information is required for a purpose incidental to but related to the transaction, such as for shipping, delivery, servicing, or installation.

information in subdivision (b), i.e., "the cardholder's address and telephone number." Invoking the doctrine *ejusdem generis*, whereby a "general term ordinarily is understood as being 'restricted to those things that are similar to those which are enumerated specifically' ", the Court of Appeal reasoned that an address and telephone number are "specific in nature regarding an individual." By contrast, the court continued, a ZIP code pertains to the *group* of individuals who live within the ZIP code. Thus, the Court of Appeal concluded, a ZIP code, without more, is unlike the other terms specifically identified in subdivision (b).

There are several problems with this reasoning. First, a ZIP code is readily understood to be part of an address; when one addresses a letter to another person, a ZIP code is always included. The question then is whether the Legislature, by providing that "personal identification information" includes "the cardholder's address", intended to include components of the address. The answer must be yes. Otherwise, a business could ask not just for a cardholder's ZIP code, but also for the cardholder's street and city in addition to the ZIP code, so long as it did not also ask for the house number. Such a construction would render the statute's protections hollow. Thus, the word "address" in the statute should be construed as encompassing not only a complete address, but also its components.

Second, the court's conclusion rests upon the assumption that a complete address and telephone number, unlike a ZIP code, are specific to an individual. That this assumption holds true in all, or even most, instances is doubtful. In the case of a cardholder's home address, for example, the information may pertain to a group of individuals living in the same household. Similarly, a home telephone number might well refer to more than one individual. The problem is even more evident in the case of a cardholder's *work* address or telephone number—such information could easily pertain to tens, hundreds, or even thousands of individuals. Of course, section 1747.08 explicitly provides that a cardholder's address and telephone number constitute personal identification information; that such information *might also* pertain to individuals other than the cardholder is immaterial. Similarly, that a cardholder's ZIP code pertains to individuals in addition to the cardholder does not render it dissimilar to an address or telephone number.

More significantly, the Court of Appeal ignores another reasonable interpretation of what the enumerated terms in section 1747.08, subdivision (b) have in common, that is, they both constitute information unnecessary to the sales transaction that, alone or together with other data such as a cardholder's name or credit card number, can be used for the retailer's business purposes. Under this reading, a cardholder's ZIP code is similar to his or her address or telephone number, in that a ZIP code is both unnecessary to the transaction and can be used, together with the cardholder's name, to locate his or her full address. The retailer can then, as plaintiff alleges defendant has done here, use the accumulated information for its own purposes or sell the information to other businesses.

There are several reasons to prefer this latter, broader interpretation over the one adopted by the Court of Appeal. First, the interpretation is more consistent with the rule that courts should liberally construe remedial statutes in favor of their protective purpose, which, in the case of section 1747.08, includes addressing "the misuse of personal identification information for, inter alia, marketing purposes." The Court of Appeal's interpretation, by contrast, would permit retailers to obtain indirectly what they are clearly prohibited from obtaining directly, "end-running" the statute's clear purpose. This is so because information that can be permissibly obtained under the Court of Appeal's construction could easily be used to locate the cardholder's complete address or telephone number. Such an interpretation would vitiate the statute's effectiveness. Moreover, that the Legislature intended a broad reading of section 1747.08 can be inferred from the expansive language it employed, e.g., "concerning" in subdivision (b) and "*any* personal identification information" in subdivision (a)(1). (Italics added.) The use of the broad word "any" suggests the Legislature did not want the category of information protected under the statute to be narrowly construed. . . .

Thus, in light of the statutory language, as well as the legislative history and evident purpose of the statute, we hold that personal identification information, as that term is used in section 1747.08, includes a cardholder's ZIP code. . . .

*NOTES AND QUESTIONS*

*Consequences.* In *Apple v. Superior Court ex rel Krescent*, 56 Cal. 4th 128 (2013), the California Supreme Court said the Song-Beverly requirements didn't apply to electronic downloads such as MP3 files from the iTunes store. Based on statutory exclusions, online retailers can ask for buyers' addresses (including zip codes), and gas stations may ask customers for their zip codes as part of authenticating the credit cards. Nevertheless, this ruling spurred many lawsuits against California retailers, and similar lawsuits proliferated in other states, including Massachusetts.

*Zip Codes as "Personal Identification Information."* On average, a zip code has over 7,000 people living in it. How does the court reach the counterintuitive result that a zip code is "personal identification information"? Following the court's logic, would a person's state or country also be "personal identification information"? After all, that is part of a person's address too.

*The Re-identification Problem and the Incoherence of Distinguishing PII.* Re-identification is a variant of a problem we discussed in Chapter 13: people might be identifiable even when their faces aren't shown. In this case, Williams-Sonoma could "re-identify" their customers by combining two pieces of information (name and zip code) with information from third-party databases. Merging these two databases allowed Williams-Sonoma to uniquely identify their customers and determine their customers' addresses even though the customers never told them this information. These types of re-identifications are more common than you might think. Unfortunately, the court's holding ("personal identification information, as that term is used in section 1747.08, includes a cardholder's ZIP code") doesn't reference or depend on Williams-Sonoma's re-identification, even though it was on the judges' minds.

As this case illustrates, bits of data, in combination, may uniquely identify a person, even if each bit (such as a zip code) standing alone is not very unique to a consumer. As a result, it's incoherent to regulate PII more heavily than non-PII because combining individual bits of non-PII can lead to the same consequences as PII. *See* Paul Ohm, *Broken Promises of Privacy: Responding to the Surprising Failure of Anonymization*, 57 UCLA L. REV. 1701 (2010).

One possible policy consequence is that every bit of consumer data, no matter how seemingly "anonymous," should be treated as PII. As the *Pineda* ruling demonstrated, this would be massively over-inclusive. Thus, we have a hodge-podge of privacy statutes, each with its own idiosyncratic definitions of PII, each of which advertisers need to review carefully for legal compliance.

*Offline Marketing.* The media tends to focus on online data collection, but offline data gathering practices for marketing purposes are pervasive and potentially legally problematic. *See, e.g.,* Kashmir Hill, *How Target Figured Out A Teen Girl Was Pregnant Before Her Father Did*, FORBES NOT-SO-PRIVATE-PARTS BLOG, Feb. 16, 2012.

*Voluntary Restrictions*

Even when not legally required to do so, advertisers may voluntarily choose to restrict data collection from consumers. Most commonly, an advertiser will publish a privacy policy that describes how the advertiser collects, uses and discloses consumer data—and often promises to restrict such activities more than the law requires.

Some statutes require companies to publish a privacy policy, even if the statutes don't dictate what (if any) privacy protections must be offered to the consumer. *See, e.g.,* CAL. CIVIL CODE § 1798.83; CAL. BUS. & PROF. CODE §§ 22575–79. Other statutes require companies to publish a privacy policy and regulate its contents. *See, e.g.,* the Gramm-Leach-Bliley Act (financial industry); the Health Insurance Portability & Accountability Act (HIPAA) (healthcare industry); and COPPA (with specific requirements for a privacy policy for preteen website users). Companies routinely use their privacy policy to get consumers' consent to the companies' practices—which may not be very protective of consumers' privacy interests at all. For that reason, privacy policies are sometimes derided as "lack-of-privacy" policies.

To prove that consumers agreed to a privacy policy's provisions, consumers should be required to affirmatively assent to its terms. Online, this is fairly easy to do by requiring users to "click through" the privacy policy—although many companies still rely on a privacy policy presented to users only as a link from their website's footer (to uncertain legal effect). Offline, it can be harder to obtain customer consent to a privacy policy when the company doesn't otherwise have a written contract with the customer. In those circumstances, companies may rely on legally dubious contract formation procedures.

As noted in *LaCourt*, the company's breach of the privacy policy does not lead to a successful contract breach claim if customers can't show legally cognizable harm. *See also In re* JetBlue Airways Corp. Privacy Litig., 79 F. Supp. 2d 299 (E.D.N.Y. 2005).

Even so, breaching a published privacy policy is never a good thing. Although the company might be able to defeat a contract breach claim, other legal theories may apply, and government regulators (including the FTC and state consumer protection agencies) do not look favorably upon such breaches. *See, e.g.,* United States v. ChoicePoint, Inc., F.T.C. File No. 052-3069 (2006) (a data broker that had numerous problems with the FTC, including alleged breaches of its privacy policy, settled for $15 million).

*Acquiring Data from Third-party Databases*

Once a company acquires consumer data, usually it can be licensed to other entities without any restrictions (other than those voluntarily imposed through a privacy policy during the data collection). Indeed, many companies license consumer data to third parties, some as 100% of their business and others as a complement to their core business.

There are a few statutory limits on consumer data licensing. For example, the Fair Credit Reporting Act restricts the licensing of consumer credit data for use in making credit decisions.

*Acquiring Data from Public Sources*

Advertisers can acquire data from public records generally without restriction. For example, advertisers can obtain real property titles, including mortgage information, from county records offices; and many state bars publish directories containing the names and addresses of licensed lawyers. In some cases, the government may charge a fee to provide the information in a more advertiser-friendly format, but the underlying data is in the public domain. The government also may choose to withhold selected information for good reason, such as privacy concerns, but those decisions are subject to First Amendment scrutiny and must be narrow in nature. *See, e.g.*, L.A. Police Dep't. v. United Reporting Publ'g Corp., 528 U.S. 32 (1999) (upholding a regulation preventing the release of arrestee mailing addresses from a facial challenge).

*Scraping*

In the Internet era, advertisers try to mine any available databases of consumer data. If the database publisher doesn't make the dataset available for downloading in a convenient way, advertisers or independent services may engage in a process sometimes called "scraping." Advertisers configure an automated tool (sometimes called a scraper, a robot or a spider) to access the database and automatically download its contents.

Although scraping may sound sinister, it is widely practiced on the Internet. Indeed, Google compiles its search index using the same basic technology. However, just because scraping is common doesn't mean it's legal. While scraping lawsuits are rare, they pose significant legal risk to the scraper—especially when the scraper competes with the scrapee. *See* Register.com, Inc. v. Verio, Inc., 356 F.3d 393 (2d Cir. 2004); Facebook Inc. v. Power Ventures, Inc., 844 F.3d 1058 (9th Cir. 2016).

## B.     Step 2: Ad Sorting and Targeting

The prior section looked at the legal restrictions on the acquisition of consumer data. This part looks at the legal restrictions on the advertiser's ability to use data to estimate consumer interest and target its advertising accordingly.

There are two primary ways to target ads: contextually and behaviorally.

In contextual targeting, a publisher publishes editorial content that attracts consumers and creates advertising inventory adjacent to the editorial content. For example, a print newspaper may contain several topically distinct sections—local news, sports, business, entertainment—and show different ads in the sections that might appeal to readers of that editorial content, i.e., tire ads in the sports section, insurance ads in the business section, movie ads in the entertainment section. Online, Google is the paradigmatic contextual targeter: it provides results keyed to particular search terms, and when it serves ads to other sites it targets them through contextual analysis of the surrounding material.

While contextual targeting isn't targeted on a per-person basis, it can be highly targeted. For example, there are many highly specialized niche magazines—say, *Golf Magazine*—where the readers' demographics and specific interests are so focused that advertisers have a pretty good idea of the type of consumer they are reaching. The publisher must compile statistics about its readers to sell advertisers. Although the publisher may not care about the personal information of any specific reader, it needs to aggregate enough information about the readers as a group to convince advertisers of its readers' likelihood to transact. Similarly, online contextual targeting does not require tracking the user's browsing history; the targeting reflects the user's online location at that moment.

In contrast, behavioral targeting develops targeting criteria based on a consumer's actions. So, for example, if a consumer searches for a flight to Hawaii, advertisers might develop a list of possible targetable criteria implicit in this search—the consumer may be looking for flights, but also hotels, rental cars, recreational activities in Hawaii, travel guides and perhaps travel gear like luggage. Furthermore, the search criteria reveal the intended dates of travel, so advertisers could also target seasonal offerings. The holy grail of behavioral advertising is to combine this piece of data (potential trip to Hawaii) with other facts gleaned from the consumer's prior behavior. So if the consumer elsewhere had visited vegetarian websites and booked a horseback riding tour on a previous vacation, advertisers could refine their pitches even more granularly to reflect those manifested interests. The search the consumer did three days ago on one website could then affect the results he or she would see on another, separately owned site.

The whole reason advertisers engage in ad targeting is to make more money. Otherwise, why would advertisers spend the time and money to aggregate the consumer data and determine targeting criteria? However, behavioral ad targeting does not guarantee an increase in advertiser profits. *See* Tanya Irwin, *MIT: Personalized Ads Don't Always Work*, MEDIAPOST MARKETINGDAILY, June 1, 2011 (researchers argue that ad targeting works better as consumers get closer to transacting).

Although most people associate ad targeting with the Internet and other direct marketing media such as direct mail or telemarketing, advertisers routinely try to engage in personalized ad targeting to the maximum extent permitted by a medium's technology. For example, as facial recognition has improved, companies have explored ways to deliver personalized billboard ads.

*Regulation of Behavioral Advertising*

Regulators have sought to curb behavioral ad targeting through various "do not track" initiatives. Unfortunately, that term is semantically ambiguous. Consumers generally think "do not track" means consumers can opt-out of having an advertiser collect any data at all from consumers, but regulatory efforts have generally focused on advertisers' ability to deliver personally targeted ads.

"Do Not Track" regulation baffles advertisers because its effects may be contrary to its purported objectives. If advertisers can't deliver personally targeted ads, then advertisers will, at the margins, reduce their total ad spend because some previously profitable ads will no longer be feasible—presumably a good outcome from some consumer advocates' perspectives. On the other hand, untracked consumers will still see ads, but they won't be targeted. In this situation, the ads will be less relevant to consumers and therefore less likely to actually help consumers. Thus, from the advertisers' perspective, "Do Not Track" efforts make things worse for consumers, not better.

Despite this, surveys routinely indicate that consumers strongly favor "Do Not Track" regulation. Why? One possibility: advertising can change consumer preferences—and the more targeted the ad, the more effective it may be at doing so. Consumers also may be concerned that ad targeting will lead to price discrimination, costing them money. Consumers may fear they will be subject to illegal discrimination such as redlining (basing the price of marketplace goods/services on the buyer's race).

Most frequently, the overwhelming concern about ad targeting seems to be an unshakable sense among consumers that it's "creepy." *See, e.g.*, Omer Tene & Jules Polonetsky, *A Theory of Creepy: Technology, Privacy and Shifting Social Norms*, 16 YALE J.L. & TECH. 59 (2013). It is easy to dismiss this sentiment as perhaps irrational—at most, the machines are watching, not individuals. *See* Eric Goldman, *Data Mining and Attention Consumption*, *in* PRIVACY AND TECHNOLOGIES OF IDENTITY: A CROSS-DISCIPLINARY CONVERSATION 225 (Katherine Strandburg & Daniela Raicu, eds. 2006). Nevertheless, consumers instinctively feel that ad targeting is surreptitious monitoring, which makes them uncomfortable, at least initially. Over time, if regulation doesn't ban ad targeting, advertisers may be able to prove that ad targeting benefits consumers if they deliver more relevant ads to consumers. *See* Posting of Eric Goldman to Technology & Marketing Law Blog, *Relevancy Trumps Creepiness, and Some Thoughts about Behavioral Targeting*, July 24, 2008. However, consumers might find contextually targeted ads relevant enough that the extra benefits of behavioral targeting aren't worth the creepiness.

It seems that first party targeting—targeting consumers based on their behavior on a website, e.g., "because you searched for X, you may also be interested in Y"—is more acceptable to consumers than third-party targeting, which involves acquiring and using data about the consumer from third parties, and explaining first-party targeting can even increase consumers' interest in the advertised products. Leslie K. John, Tami Kim & Kate Barasz, Ads That Don't Overstep, Harvard Bus. Rev., Jan-Feb. 2018, https://hbr.org/2018/01/ads-that-dont-overstep; Tami Kim, Kate Barasz, & Leslie K. John, Why Am I Seeing This Ad? The Effect of Ad Transparency on Ad Effectiveness, https://www.hbs.edu/faculty/Publication%20Files/KimBaraszJohn18_be5ba706-b8c3-4ac4-bb48-3cc462bb0e08.pdf.

*Other Targeting Restrictions*

There are numerous other laws restricting the criteria that marketers use for targeting, especially when it involves potential discrimination (e.g., redlining) or sensitive personal information like health or financial information, such as the Fair Credit Reporting Act's strict limits on using credit ratings for ad targeting.

## C.      Step 3: Ad Delivery

The prior subpart reviewed the legal restrictions on using data already in a database for ad targeting purposes. This subpart reviews the legal restrictions on delivering ads once the advertiser has determined who it would like to get them.

In general, advertisers have First Amendment-protected rights to disseminate their messages to consumers. As we discussed in Chapter 2, the First Amendment protections are partially diluted. Advertisers' messages are commercial speech, which receives only a medium level of protection. And while consumers have limited rights to control what content they consume, the First Amendment necessitates that listeners' rights have to give way sometimes.

A variety of legislative solutions try to balance these conflicting interests. Eric Goldman's *A Coasean Analysis of Marketing*, 2006 WIS. L. REV. 1151, offers a spectrum of consumers' rights to control their exposure and advertisers' rights to reach consumers:

## Entitlement Spectrum

| Opt In | Opt Out | Metadata Disclosure | No Delivery Restrictions |

Consumer Entitlement                                                     Marketer Entitlement

An *opt-in scheme* requires marketers to obtain consumer consent before disseminating marketing to them. Currently, the only marketing delivery media governed on an opt-in basis are fax marketing and certain text messages.

An *opt-out scheme* allows consumers to prevent future marketing exposures, on a medium-specific basis, across all marketers (such as a do-not-call registry) or from only particular marketers (such as marketer-specific opt-outs from future email marketing or telemarketing). Several direct marketing media, such as email marketing, telemarketing and (to a lesser extent) direct mail, are governed by opt-out regulatory schemes.

A *mandatory metadata* disclosure scheme requires marketers to make specified disclosures that help the consumer sort the marketing or assess its trustworthiness. Metadata can provide consumers with more information about the marketer, such as requiring telemarketers to display their phone numbers readable by Caller ID or requiring that marketing display the marketer's physical address. Metadata can also provide a summary or description of the marketing contents, such as a summary label that marketing is "advertising."

Some media have *no delivery restrictions* on marketing at all. In these situations, a consumer cannot avoid unwanted exposures to marketing in that medium (except, of course, by avoiding the medium altogether). Unrestricted media include most broadcasting (television, radio and cable) and print periodical marketing, as well as billboards and other physical signs.

Opt-ins represent one end of the allocative spectrum—the consumer has an entitlement to be free from marketing. At the other end of the spectrum, a marketer has entitlement to disseminate marketing to consumers in those media where the marketer's rights are unrestricted. In between these two end points are opt-outs and mandatory metadata schemes, where the entitlement is not absolute. Instead, each party shoulders some burden and, in effect, "shares" the entitlement. For example, with opt-outs, the marketer initially has the entitlement, but consumers can obtain the entitlement for themselves by communicating their preferences.

In general, to the extent statutes try to preference consumers over advertisers, the First Amendment imposes greater limits on the statute. This means that many restrictions on marketing delivery methods eventually get challenged under the First Amendment. Because typically those restrictions are subject to intermediate scrutiny, marketers win some cases; the government wins others.

*Example #1: Statutory Opt-out of Yellow Pages Distribution*

*Dex Media West, Inc. v. City of Seattle,* 793 F. Supp. 2d 1213 (W.D. Wash. 2011), *rev'd*, 696 F.3d 952 (9th Cir. 2012), involved a Seattle ordinance allowing consumers to opt out of yellow pages delivery and imposing certain licensing restrictions and fees on yellow pages publishers, along with a requirement that they prominently inform consumers of the opt-out option. As of May 12, 2011, city residents had made 136,651 opt-out requests through the city's opt-out system—averaging 17,081 new opt-outs per day—out of a total population of roughly 600,000.

The district court concluded that the yellow page directories constituted "commercial speech" because they contained ads for many different products, the ads referenced specific products, and the publisher had an economic interest to deliver the directories. The court distinguished yellow pages from ad-supported newspapers: "any noncommercial aspects of the speech at issue in yellow pages directories are merely tangential to Plaintiffs' predominantly commercial purpose. While the noncommercial aspects of the directories may render their receipt more welcome by some residents, these aspects of the directories are not at the core of their purpose."

The district court concluded that the ordinance satisfied *Central Hudson.* In support of that conclusion, the court cited the city's "substantial" interests in (1) waste reduction, (2) resident privacy, and (3) recovery of the costs of running the opt-out system. How does delivery of a yellow pages directory to a consumer constitute a "privacy invasion"?

The Ninth Circuit reversed. The court of appeals identified several components to the yellow pages: (1) business "white pages" sections, which provide names, addresses, and phone numbers of local businesses and professionals in alphabetical order; (2) traditional yellow pages, which list businesses by category of product or service; and (3) public interest material, which includes community information, maps, and government listings. Paid ads were mixed in with the listings, typically containing less than half of the content. "Display advertising comprised about 35% of the 2010 Dex Seattle Metro yellow pages."

Though many of the ads in the directories were commercial speech, the ordinance regulated the directories as a whole, and the directories weren't commercial speech. The directory did more than propose a commercial transaction, and "[t]here is no evidence that the editorial content is added as a mere sham to convert a pure advertising leaflet into noncommercial speech." The fact that the phone book companies depended on ads to pay for the directories didn't make them any different from the *New York Times* or broadcast television, which are also ad-dependent. Because the directories weren't commercial speech, strict scrutiny applied, and the ordinance failed.

*Example #2: Content Delivery to Private Property.*

Could Seattle have suppressed Yellow Pages distribution better if it had framed its regulation as an anti-trespass measure? The next case shows how "privacy" interests at home can trump other First Amendment considerations.

**Tillman v. Distribution Systems of America, Inc., 224 A.D.2d 79 (N.Y. App. Div. 1996)**

We hold that neither a publisher nor a distributor has any constitutional right to continue to throw a newspaper onto the property of an unwilling recipient after having been notified not to do so. "Traditionally the American law punishes persons who enter onto the property of another after having been warned by the owner to keep off . . . . [The State may leave] the decision as to whether distributers [*sic*] of literature may lawfully call at a home where it belongs—with the homeowner himself. [The State] can punish those who call at a home in defiance of the previously expressed will of the occupant." "[W]e perceive of no reason crucial to defendant's First Amendment rights that would require a householder to retrieve an unwanted paper from his lawn."

The plaintiffs reside in Jericho, New York. The defendant Distribution Systems of America, Inc., (hereinafter DSA) is a domestic corporation which is in the business of distributing newspapers and other publications. The defendant Newsday, Inc., (hereinafter Newsday) is a domestic corporation which is the parent of DSA and which is itself a wholly-owned subsidiary of the Times Mirror Company. Newsday admittedly avails itself of DSA's services in the making of deliveries. DSA is engaged in the distribution, on a saturation basis, of a publication known as "This Week."

According to the plaintiff Kenneth Tillman, the unsolicited newspapers, together with pull-out advertisements, were typically enclosed in a plastic bag and placed on Mr. Tillman's driveway; on other occasions, they were left on the front lawn or jammed in between the storm door and the front door of the house.

Beginning in 1990, Mr. and Mrs. Tillman made repeated requests to DSA, seeking to have these unwanted deliveries discontinued. According to Mr. Tillman, agents of DSA repeatedly promised to stop the deliveries. The Tillmans were eventually forced to resort to a lawyer, and the lawyer's requests were likewise met with assertions that the deliveries had been or would be stopped. Notwithstanding these assertions, it eventually became clear that DSA was either unwilling, as a matter of principle, or unable, as a matter of internal mismanagement, to comply with the Tillmans' request. . . .

"The ancient concept that 'a man's home is his castle' into which 'not even the king may enter' has lost none of its vitality, and none of the recognized exceptions includes any right to communicate offensively with another." "An individual's right to communicate must be balanced against the recipient's right 'to be let alone' in places in which the latter possesses a right of privacy." In accordance with this general principle, it has been held that a vendor has no right under the Constitution or otherwise to send unwanted material into the home of another, even if the flow of valid ideas is impeded by such prohibition. In *Rowan v. U.S. Post Office Dep't.*, 90 S.Ct. at 1490-91 (emphasis added) the court upheld a statute pursuant to which a person could require the removal of his name from a mailing list stating in relevant part:

> In today's complex society we are inescapably captive audiences for many purposes, but a sufficient measure of individual autonomy must survive to permit every householder to exercise control over unwanted mail. To make the householder the exclusive and final judge of what will cross his threshold undoubtedly has the effect of impeding the flow of ideas, information, and arguments that, ideally, he should receive and consider. Today's merchandising methods, the plethora of mass mailings subsidized by low postal rates, and the growth of the sale of large mailing lists as an industry in itself have changed the mailman from a carrier of primarily private communications, as he was in a more leisurely day, and have made him an adjunct of the mass mailer who sends unsolicited and often unwanted mail into every home. It places no strain on the doctrine of judicial notice to observe that whether measured by pieces or pounds, Everyman's mail today is made up overwhelmingly of material he did not seek from persons he does not know. And all too often it is matter he finds offensive. . . .

> The Court has traditionally respected the right of a householder to bar, by order or notice, solicitors, hawkers, and peddlers from his property. In this case the mailer's right to communicate is circumscribed only by an affirmative act of the addressee giving notice that he wishes no further mailings from that mailer.

> To hold less would tend to license a form of trespass and would make hardly more sense than to say that a radio or television viewer may not twist the dial to cut off an offensive or boring communication and thus bar its entering his home. Nothing in the Constitution compels us to listen to or view any unwanted communication, whatever its merit; we see no basis for according the printed word or pictures a different or more preferred status because they are sent by mail. . . .

[L]ocal governments have, on several occasions, attempted to come to the aid of those homeowners who find it increasingly difficult to hold out, as their "castles" are besieged by mail, by phone, or, as in this case, by paper bombardment. Several ordinances, which to some extent regulate unsolicited

622

distribution of written material, unsolicited mailings, unsolicited phone calls, or unsolicited commercial visits, have been challenged in the courts on First Amendment grounds. In general, the ordinances challenged have proved susceptible to constitutional attack, often because of the overbreadth of the particular ordinance's reach, or because a classification contained in the ordinance violates the equal protection clause. . . .

[W]e do not believe that, in extending constitutional protection to commercial speech, in general, the Supreme Court necessarily eroded the privacy protection afforded to a landowner who, as an individual, has knowingly decided to bar a certain type of speech, commercial or otherwise, from his or her property.

The most critical and fundamental distinction between the cases cited above, on the one hand, and the present case, on the other, is based on the fact that here we are not dealing with a government agency which seeks to preempt in some way the ability of a publisher to contact a potential reader; rather, we are dealing with a reader who is familiar with a publisher's product, and who is attempting to prevent the unwanted dumping of this product on his property. None of the cases cited by the defendants stands for the proposition that the Free Speech Clause prohibits such a landowner from resorting to his common-law remedies in order to prevent such unwanted dumping. There is, in our view, nothing in either the Federal or State Constitutions which requires a landowner to tolerate a trespass whenever the trespasser is a speaker, or the distributor of written speech, who is unsatisfied with the fora which may be available on public property, and who thus attempts to carry his message to private property against the will of the owner. . . .

The constitutional right of free speech does not correspond to the "right" to force others to listen to whatever one has to say. By the same token, the right to publish, distribute, and sell a newspaper does not correspond to the "right" to force others to buy or to read whatever one has written, or to spend their own time or money unwillingly participating in the distribution process by which a newspaper travels from the printing press to its ultimate destination, i.e., disposal. The state does all that it needs to do in order to protect the constitutional rights of a newspaper publisher when it refrains from censorship, and when it allows the distribution of the newspaper into the hands of the ultimate reader to proceed in accordance with the natural economic laws of a free market. The state need not, and in our opinion, should not, compel anyone to read, to buy, or even to touch, pick up, or handle a newspaper of which the individual in question wants to have no part. For these essential reasons, we affirm the order and judgment appealed from, which enjoined the defendants from continuing to deposit their newspaper on the plaintiffs' property.

*NOTES AND QUESTIONS*

As you can see, this court had a very strong view about the sanctity of one's home. In contrast, in Miller v. Distrib'n Sys. of Am., Inc., 175 Misc.2d 513 (N.Y. Sup. Ct. 1997), a court awarded nominal damages of $1 in a trespass case involving the same defendant.

If consumers could have claimed a trespass to real property claim for the unwanted deposit of yellow pages, did the Seattle ordinance simply protect a property owner's already-existing right to be free from trespass? Note the Seattle ordinance went beyond giving homeowners the right to opt-out of delivery.

If trespass protects the sanctity of one's home, does the rationale break down if a company asserts a trespass claim to stop unwanted advertising? If a user objects to a spammed email that they read on their laptop while at the local Starbucks?

*Aren't Opt-Outs Helpful to Advertisers?* In theory, opt-out notifications can provide useful information to advertisers and publishers. An opt-out tells the advertiser that the consumer isn't interested in hearing the pitch, so the advertiser can save the time and cost of trying to reach an uninterested prospect. In the case of the yellow pages, a consumer opt-out lets the publisher save the costs of manufacturing and delivering a directory that the consumer will likely toss in the recycle bin. Indeed, the *Dex* plaintiffs weren't opposed to an opt-out scheme; they were developing their own nationwide opt-out system for their companies (making city-by-city opt-out regulations annoying to the extent the procedures conflicted with their national solution).

Despite this attractive theoretical argument, opt-out systems create several problems in practice. First, opt-out systems are often not granular enough to depict a consumer's actual preferences. Take the Do-Not-Call registry as an example. Some consumers object to all telemarketing calls on principle, and other consumers might want to categorically block telemarketing calls to avoid the risk of making impulse decisions they might regret. However, many consumers would tolerate (or even welcome) a beneficial telemarketing call—say, a substantial discount offer on a product the consumer wants to buy. (Those same consumers would probably prefer the same offer to be delivered via a less intrusive medium than telemarketing, but the advertiser may have cost or efficacy reasons to use telemarketing as the offer delivery medium). Nevertheless, registering for the Do-Not-Call registry would block the beneficial calls along with the unwanted calls—a missed opportunity for both advertisers and consumers. *See* Ian Ayres & Matthew Funk, *Marketing Privacy*, 20 YALE J. ON REG. 77 (2003). As Ayres and Funk explain, the opt-out system could be designed more granularly to screen out the unwanted calls but facilitate calls that consumers want. However, a more granular system is more complicated and costly for everyone—consumers, advertisers and the government operating the system—and therefore it's rarely pursued as a policy option.

Second, the operators of opt-out registries charge advertisers to check the registry. For example, a nationwide license to access the FTC's Do-Not-Call registry costs over $16,000 a year. Advertisers also incur internal costs checking the registry. Effectively, these costs act like a tax to advertisers to communicating via media governed by opt-out schemes. In some cases, the costs overwhelm the advertisers' expected profits, making the ad campaign unprofitable to pursue.

## 4.    Privacy in the European Union (EU)

Thus far, we've discussed U.S. privacy law. The approaches to privacy regulation vary widely across the globe, and most developed countries have more stringent privacy laws than the U.S. does.

This part focuses on the European Union's General Data Protection Regulation, or GDPR, which came into effect in May 2018. The GDPR has many implications for advertising law both in Europe and internationally, not all of which are clear at the time of this writing (June 2018). The GDPR will affect the advertising community for the foreseeable future, so odds are high that you will have to navigate the GDPR—whether you want to or not.

This part gives you just a broad sketch of the GDPR. The actual text (https://eur-lex.europa.eu/legal-content/EN/TXT/PDF/?uri=CELEX:32016R0679&from=EN) is 88 pages of dense and impenetrable legalese (much of it in the passive voice), which has been supplemented substantially by official and unofficial guidance from the European Data Protection Board, national Supervisory Authorities, and others. You have zero chance of "intuiting" the right answer under the GDPR. If you're actually making a business decision governed by the GDPR, you'll need to consult with a GDPR expert.

In addition to the GDPR, European advertisers must comply with the ePrivacy Directive (Directive 2002/58/EC, as modified by Directive 2009/136/EC), sometimes called the "Cookie Directive." The ePrivacy Directive regulates communication privacy in numerous ways, including requiring consumer consent for:

- any direct marketing by phone, fax, email, text, or other electronic message. Consumers must affirmatively opt-in—i.e., the checkbox must be presented as unchecked—to receive these marketing materials (with limited exceptions).
- placing or reading cookies or other client-side persistent identifiers. Consumer consent usually can be obtained by displaying a web banner. This is why you often see websites asking for permission to place cookies.

As of June 2018, revisions to the ePrivacy Directive are being actively discussed, so you should check for updates.

*Who Must Comply with the GDPR?*

The GDPR applies to anyone who "processes" personal data, defined as "any operation or set of operations which is performed on personal data or on sets of personal data, whether or not by automated means."

The GDPR defines two roles: data "controllers" and "processors." The GDPR places a heavier compliance burden on controllers, so the distinction between the two is critical.

A controller "determines the purposes and means of processing personal data." A processor "processes personal data on behalf of a controller." In some cases, this will be fairly clear. An example:

> A brewery has many employees. It signs a contract with a payroll company to pay the wages. The brewery tells the payroll company when the wages should be paid, when an employee leaves or has a pay rise, and provides all other details for the salary slip and payment. The

payroll company provides the IT system and stores the employees' data. The brewery is the data controller and the payroll company is the data processor.

Typically, an advertiser who collects information directly from consumers would be the controller; and third party vendors who help the advertiser communicate with those consumers would be processors.

However, because the GDRP's definitions are flexible, it will not always be clear who is a controller and who is a processor. The GDPR also contemplates that entities working together can be "joint controllers," making the classification decision even more difficult. As one commentator wrote, "deciding who is a data controller and who a data processor in complicated areas like modern targeted advertising is maddeningly difficult." Lilian Edwards, *Data Protection: Enter the General Data Protection Regulation, in* LAW, POLICY AND THE INTERNET (2018).

*What Data Does the GDPR Cover?*

The GDPR defines "personal data" as "any information relating to an identified or identifiable natural person ('data subject'); an identifiable natural person is one who can be identified, directly or indirectly, in particular by reference to an identifier such as a name, an identification number, location data, an online identifier or to one or more factors specific to the physical, physiological, genetic, mental, economic, cultural or social identity of that natural person."

Like most privacy laws, this definition attempts to distinguish personal data from non-personal data, but as we discussed earlier in this chapter, even very general data about a person can become identifiable when combined with enough other data. Some items are categorically personal data, like names, telephone numbers and email addresses, and other items, like IP addresses or a unique identifier in a browser cookie, likely qualify as well.

However, the definition could be read much more broadly to cover virtually every scrap of data about any person. The GDPR only excludes truly "anonymous" data, if such a thing even exists.

The GDPR has extra protections for "sensitive" personal data. The GDPR prohibits processing data "revealing racial or ethnic origin, political opinions, religious or philosophical beliefs, or trade union membership, and the processing of genetic data, biometric data for the purpose of uniquely identifying a natural person, data concerning health or data concerning a natural person's sex life or sexual orientation," subject to many exclusions. There are also extra protections for information about criminal convictions and offenses.

*GDPR's Rights and Obligations*

The GDPR creates a wide range of rights for consumers and requirements on controllers and processors.

GDPR Article 5 enumerates six "principles" that apply to all processing of personal data:

- Lawfulness, Fairness and Transparency. Personal data shall be "processed lawfully, fairly and in a transparent manner."
- Purpose Limitation. Personal data shall be "collected for specified, explicit and legitimate purposes and not further processed in a manner that is incompatible with those purposes" (subject to some public interest exceptions).
- Data Minimization. Personal data shall be "adequate, relevant and limited to what is necessary in relation to the purposes for which they are processed."
- Accuracy. Personal data shall be "accurate and, where necessary, kept up to date."
- Storage Limitation. Personal data shall be "kept in a form which permits identification of data subjects for no longer than is necessary for the purposes for which the personal data are processed" (subject to some public interest exceptions).
- Integrity and Confidentiality (a/k/a Security). Personal data shall be "processed in a manner that ensures appropriate security of the personal data."

As you can see, these vaguely worded principles are more aspirational than prescriptive.* This reflects the GDPR's general regulatory approach. The GDPR wants companies to comply both with the letter of the law and its spirit, and it creates the possibility of enforcement when the spirit of the law isn't honored. The GDPR's aspirational approach to regulation conflicts with American jurisprudential norms that favor bright-line rules that provide more legal certainty.

The GDPR prohibits the processing of personal data unless permitted under one of six "lawful" bases, which includes consumer consent. However, the GDPR substantially raises the bar on when consent is properly given. The GDPR requires that "an indication of consent must be unambiguous and involve a clear affirmative action (an opt-in). It specifically bans pre-ticked opt-in boxes. It also requires distinct ('granular') consent options for distinct processing operations. Consent should be separate from other terms and conditions and should not generally be a precondition of signing up to a service." *Guide to the General Data Protection Regulation (GDPR)*, Information Commissioner's Office, Mar. 22, 2018. Because of the complexities associated with obtaining proper consent from consumers, controllers and processors often will find it more expedient or less risky to try to rely on one of the five other lawful bases for processing.

In addition to the Article 5 principles, Chapter III of the GDPR describes 8 consumer rights:

- Right to Be Informed. Consumers have the right to know when their data is being collected and why. Articles 13 and 14 enumerate minimum requirements of privacy disclosures.
- Right of Access. Consumers have the right to see their data.

---

* For example, what does it mean to process data "fairly"? A British regulatory agency, ICO, explains: "In general, fairness means that you should only handle personal data in ways that people would reasonably expect and not use it in ways that have unjustified adverse effects on them. You need to stop and think not just about how you can use personal data, but also about whether you should." *Guide to the General Data Protection Regulation (GDPR)*, Information Commissioner's Office, Mar. 22, 2018.

- Right to Rectification. Consumers have the right to correct erroneous information about them.
- Right of Erasure (also called the "right to be forgotten"). Consumers have the right to delete personal data about them in many circumstances.
- Right to Restrict Processing. Consumers have the right to suppress their personal data file or to restrict its processing in many circumstances.
- Right to Data Portability. Consumers have the right to obtain data about themselves and provide that data to others.
- Right to Object. Consumers have the right to object to and prevent their data from being used for specified purposes, including an absolute right to stop their data being used for direct marketing purposes.
- Rights Related to Automated Decision-Making. A decision with legal effects may be made solely by a machine, and consumers may be profiled, only with consumers' explicit consent, or where necessary for the contract, or as otherwise legally authorized.

The GDPR also requires various operational procedures that make companies more proactive about data protection and to treat it less like a "check-the-box" compliance function. For example, it expects companies to implement "data protection by design and by default," companies are required to conduct "data protection impact assessments" before undertaking significant actions, and some companies must designate a "Data Protection Officer." The GDPR also requires companies to report data breaches to government regulators and, in some cases, directly to consumers.

As mentioned earlier, data processors have fewer obligations than data controllers. A data processor must comply with its contracts with data controllers and:

- not use a sub-processor without the controller's permission;
- cooperate with regulators;
- ensure the security of its processing;
- keep records of processing activities;
- notify the data controller of any personal data breaches;
- employ a Data Protection Officer (in some cases); and
- appoint a representative within the European Union (if the processor isn't established in the EU).

*Remedies*

The GDPR authorizes direct consumer lawsuits for violations, either individually or through public interest organizations. Violations also can be enforced by government agencies, which can seek fines of up to €20M or 4% of a company's global annual revenue (and, in the case of a group of companies, 4% of the group's global annual revenue), whichever is greater.

*Jurisdictional Reach*

The GDPR applies to:

(1) Companies established in the EU, regardless of whether data processing takes place inside or outside the EU or the data relates to EU residents. Thus, a U.S. company with a physical presence in the EU will be subject to GDPR both for EU consumer data and non-EU consumer data.

(2) Companies not established in the EU that process EU residents' data where the processing is (a) related to offering goods or services to EU residents, or (b) related to monitoring EU residents' behavior within the EU. These companies must appoint a representative in the EU.

Thus, the GDPR purports to govern the processing of EU consumer data by companies that have no physical presence in the EU at all. So, a Silicon Valley-based Internet startup with a globally available website might need to comply with the GDPR from day one. However, the GDPR's potentially global reach raises many complex issues about transborder conflicts-of-laws and enforcements, so the GDPR's actual application to non-EU companies may not be as broad as the GDPR claims. As a practical matter, EU-based regulators will prioritize their enforcement efforts, and for the foreseeable future, the regulators are likely to have higher-value targets than small U.S. start-up companies with offices exclusively in the U.S. Still, E.U. regulators inevitably will bring cases that test this geographic issue.

So the legally conservative approach would be for everyone in the U.S. advertising community to comply with the GDPR unless they have no EU offices and never touch EU consumer data. Indeed, many U.S.-only companies have chosen to do just that. This is a reason why every advertising law professional must be familiar with the GDPR. However, compliance with the GDPR is quite expensive, and it goes far beyond what's required under U.S. law. Therefore, many other participants in the U.S. advertising industry will choose to ignore the GDPR unless/until they have physical offices in the EU. *See* Kurt Wimmer, *Free Expression and EU Privacy Regulation: Can the GDPR Reach U.S. Publishers?*, 68 SYR. L. REV. __ (2018).

Even if a U.S. company never directly collects EU consumer data, it might still encounter the GDPR if it receives transborder data transfers of EU consumer data from its business partners. For example, the GDPR regulates when a European company hires a U.S.-based advertising agency to help with ad buys, and the company wants to share consumer data with the agency. In this situation, the company is the data controller and the ad agency is a data processor; and the company must legally impose GDPR-based restrictions on the agency to satisfy its own GDPR obligations.[*]

---

[*] There is a separate issue about whether EU data can be transferred to the U.S. at all. Such transborder movements of data to non-EU countries are permitted only when adequate/appropriate safeguards are in place to protect consumer privacy. The U.S. as a country has not received an adequacy determination, but the self-certification mechanism known as "Privacy Shield" has. The Privacy Shield adequacy determination is currently being litigated in EU courts.

Thus, a U.S.-only company might still need to comply with the GDPR, at least in part, to facilitate such business arrangements.

*Implications for Advertising*

Nothing in the GDPR is good news for advertisers. Historically, American advertisers have earnestly swept up as much consumer data as possible, remixed it in infinite ways looking to optimize yields, and keep it forever. There is also rampant data brokering where consumer data is bought and sold without any notice to consumers or ability to opt-out. All of these activities run directly contrary to both the letter and the spirit of the GDPR. Something will have to give.

While the GDPR-and-advertising story mostly will be written over the next few years, the early data suggests that the GDPR will hit the advertising community hard. For example, immediately after the GDPR came into effect, online "programmatic" ads in Europe dropped 25-40%. Jessica Davies, *GDPR Mayhem: Programmatic Ad Buying Plummets in Europe*, DIGIDAY, May 25, 2018. A number of key U.S. publications, including the *Los Angeles Times* and the *Chicago Tribune*, blocked European readers from accessing their online editions, and the *Washington Post* launched a new ad-free online subscription for European readers that costs 50% more than online subscriptions that include ads.

One possible scenario is that the GDPR accelerates divergence between advertising privacy practices in the United States, which remain relatively lightly regulated, and the EU, where GDPR compliance make many forms of personalized advertising cost-prohibitive. Another possible scenario is that the United States eventually adopts pieces of the GDPR as domestic policy, which would have potentially dramatic consequences for the U.S. advertising industry. Even if U.S. law remains the same, aggressive transborder enforcement of the GDPR by EU regulators could impact the U.S. advertising industry.

The only certain things about the GDPR are that we will live with a cloud of uncertainty for quite some time, to the financial benefit of lots of lawyers and privacy consultants.

**5.      Case Studies for Review**

**A.      Practice Problem: Asylum626**

Asylum626 was a Doritos promotion targeted at young people in which they were inserted into a horror-movie plot. As the ad agency explained, "The more information you gave us at registration, the creepier the experience." Users could provide their names, email addresses, Twitter addresses, and Facebook accounts, which would allow Asylum626 to publish posts via their accounts (something disclosed at signup):

The campaign used Facebook Connect to choose two of the users' friends and "put" them in the asylum. The user could pick which friend to save; then the campaign invited the teens' entire social networks to try and "save" them, posting on their Facebook pages and Twitter feeds. Doritos promised to "use your webcam to bring you into the asylum in real time."

[A still from Asylum626:]

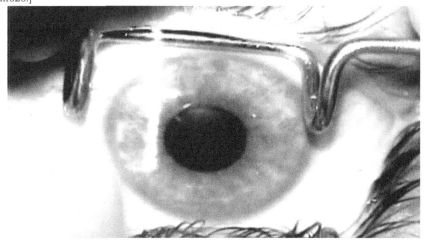

Users also had to take the position of torturer in order to finish the experience. In addition, they needed to buy Doritos to get special codes that unlocked the final level. The result was one-to-one tailoring of the campaign and intense engagement with the brand: users took responsibility for the ad content they were showing to others, using it as part of their social relationships.

One consumer group complained that the immersive, cross-platform nature of this game/ad was likely to put users in an accepting state of "flow," making them more inclined to accept the underlying brand message. *See* Supplemental materials to *Complaint and Request for Investigation of PepsiCo's Deceptive Practices in Marketing Doritos to Adolescents* filed with the Federal Trade Commission on Oct. 19, 2011, available at DigitalAds.org.

What concerns would you have as a lawyer asked to clear this campaign? As a parent who discovered (or failed to discover) that your child was participating? Are the privacy concerns here inherently entangled with other issues (promoting junk food, manipulating people who aren't adults), or can they be separately addressed?

### B.   FTC Enforcement Against Snapchat

This subpart takes a close look at an FTC enforcement action for deceptive marketing related to an online service. The FTC's enforcement target in this enforcement action is Snapchat, a service that allows users to send photos and videos to each other. (The service has since rebranded as "Snap," but we've retained the Snapchat moniker).

Historically, Snapchat's main point of competitive differentiation has been letting a photo sender "expire" the photo or video after a few seconds, which (in theory) lets the sender retain control over the photo's or video's future distribution. Despite the common assertions that younger generations don't value privacy, Snapchat usage exploded, especially among millennials, because it seemingly allowed young adults to express their true selves without risking lifetime consequences.

Unfortunately, Snapchat did not deliver on its basic promise of letting photo senders prevent photo or video recipients from keeping or republishing the materials.

This led to an FTC enforcement action. The following process is fairly typical for the FTC and investigated companies. The FTC notified Snapchat that it was launching an investigation, probably accompanied by requests for additional information. At that point, Snapchat could have dug in its heels for a fight. Instead, like most targets of an FTC investigation, Snapchat apparently chose to cooperate with the FTC investigation and explore settlement options.

When the parties reached a settlement, the matter was publicly announced by posting a draft complaint against Snapchat simultaneously with the settlement agreement. You will read both documents momentarily. Both documents are drafted under the threat of the FTC actually pursuing an expensive and debilitating enforcement case, so you shouldn't assume a judge would agree with the statements of either fact or law.

As part of the public announcement, the FTC also posted an "Analysis of Proposed Consent Order to Aid Public Comment" and a press release. The FTC then allowed public comment on the settlement for 30 days before submitting the settlement to a final approval. The commission received 40 public comments on the settlement, most of them trivial or nonsensical. *See* https://www.ftc.gov/system/files/documents/cases/141231snapchatletters.pdf. The FTC Commissioners granted final approval of the settlement in December 2014.

As you read the complaint and settlement agreement, think about which of the FTC's legal positions are straightforward and which represent an aggressive or possibly overreaching interpretation of the law.

Also consider the pros and cons of the FTC taking aggressive legal positions. Arguably, if regulators only pursue guaranteed victories, they tacitly encourage regulated entities to flirt with or go over the legal line. However, when regulators overzealously pursue cases where the defendant actually engaged in legally permissible behavior, they impose substantial costs on the defendant and make other industry participants fear that their legitimate behavior will be similarly targeted. Do you feel any differently about what constitutes the right enforcement balance in emerging technology fields? How should regulators handle innovative, but potentially risky to consumers, services such as Snapchat?

Why do you think the FTC chose to pursue the enforcement action against Snapchat as opposed to the thousands of other enforcement opportunities facing the FTC? Were there viable alternatives to FTC enforcement? Would those alternatives have resolved the issue as effectively as the FTC's action did?

### In the Matter of Snapchat, Inc., Docket **No. C-4501 (Complaint)**
December 23, 2014

. . . RESPONDENT'S BUSINESS PRACTICES

3. Snapchat provides a mobile application that allows consumers to send and receive photo and video messages known as "snaps." Before sending a snap, the application requires the sender to designate a period of time that the recipient will be allowed to view the snap. Snapchat markets the application as an "ephemeral" messaging application, having claimed that once the timer expires, the snap "disappears forever."

4. Snapchat launched its mobile application on Apple Inc.'s iOS operating system in September 2011 and on Google Inc.'s Android operating system in October 2012. Snapchat added video messaging to the iOS version of its application in December 2012 and to the Android version of its application in February 2013.

5. Both the iTunes App Store and the Google Play store list Snapchat among the top 15 free applications. As of September 2013, users transmit more than 350 million snaps daily.

SNAPCHAT'S "DISAPPEARING" MESSAGES (Counts 1 and 2)

6. Snapchat marketed its application as a service for sending "disappearing" photo and video messages, declaring that the message sender "control[s] how long your friends can view your

message." Before sending a snap, the application requires the sender to designate a period of time – with the default set to a maximum of 10 seconds – that the recipient will be allowed to view the snap, as depicted below:

7. Since the application's launch on iOS until May 2013, and since the application's launch on Android until June 2013, Snapchat disseminated, or caused to be disseminated, to consumers the following statements on its product description page on the iTunes App Store and Google Play:

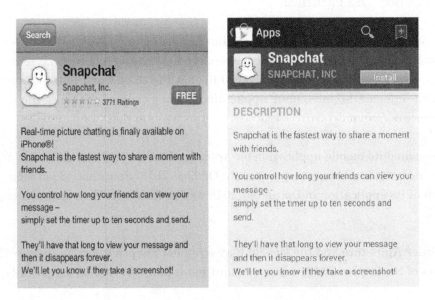

8. From October 2012 to October 2013, Snapchat disseminated, or caused to be disseminated, to consumers the following statement on the "FAQ" page on its website:

**Is there any way to view an image after the time has expired?**
No, snaps disappear after the timer runs out. ...

9. Despite these claims, several methods exist by which a recipient can use tools outside of the application to save both photo and video messages, allowing the recipient to access and view the photos or videos indefinitely.

10. For example, when a recipient receives a video message, the application stores the video file in a location outside of the application's "sandbox" (i.e., the application's private storage area on the device that other applications cannot access). Because the file is stored in this unrestricted area, until October 2013, a recipient could connect his or her mobile device to a computer and use simple file browsing tools to locate and save the video file. This method for saving video files sent through the application was widely publicized as early as December 2012. Snapchat did not mitigate this flaw until October 2013, when it began encrypting video files sent through the application.

11. Furthermore, third-party developers have built applications that can connect to Snapchat's application programming interface ("API"), thereby allowing recipients to log into the Snapchat service without using the official Snapchat application. Because the timer and related "deletion" functionality is dependent on the recipient's use of the official Snapchat application, recipients can instead simply use a third-party application to download and save both photo and video messages. As early as June 2012, a security researcher warned Snapchat that it would be "pretty easy to write a tool to download and save the images a user receives" due to the way the API functions. Indeed, beginning in spring 2013, third-party developers released several applications on the iTunes App Store and Google Play that recipients can use to save and view photo or video messages indefinitely. On Google Play alone, ten of these applications have been downloaded as many as 1.7 million times.

12. The file browsing tools and third-party applications described in paragraphs 10 and 11 are free or low cost and publicly available on the Internet. In order to download, install, and use these tools, a recipient need not make any modifications to the iOS or Android operating systems and would need little technical knowledge.

13. In addition to the methods described in paragraphs 10-12, a recipient can use the mobile device's screenshot capability to capture an image of a snap while it appears on the device screen.

14. Snapchat claimed that if a recipient took a screenshot of a snap, the sender would be notified. On its product description pages, as described in paragraph 7, Snapchat stated: "We'll let you know if [recipients] take a screenshot!" In addition, from October 2012 to February 2013, Snapchat disseminated, or caused to be disseminated, to consumers the following statement on the "FAQ" page on its website:

**What if I take a screenshot?**
Screenshots can be captured if you're quick. The sender will be notified immediately.

15. However, recipients can easily circumvent Snapchat's screenshot detection mechanism. For example, on versions of iOS prior to iOS 7, the recipient need only double press the device's Home

button in rapid succession to evade the detection mechanism and take a screenshot of any snap without the sender being notified. This method was widely publicized.

## Count 1

16. As described in Paragraphs 6, 7, and 8, Snapchat has represented, expressly or by implication, that when sending a message through its application, the message will disappear forever after the user-set time period expires.

17. In truth and in fact, as described in Paragraph 9-12, when sending a message through its application, the message may not disappear forever after the user-set time period expires. Therefore, the representation set forth in Paragraph 16 is false or misleading.

## Count 2

18. As described in Paragraphs 7 and 14, Snapchat has represented, expressly or by implication, that the sender will be notified if the recipient takes a screenshot of a snap.

19. In truth and in fact, as described in Paragraph 15, the sender may not be notified if the recipient takes a screenshot of a snap. Therefore, the representation set forth in Paragraph 18 is false or misleading.

## SNAPCHAT'S COLLECTION OF GEOLOCATION INFORMATION
### (Count 3)

20. From June 2011 to February 2013, Snapchat disseminated or caused to be disseminated to consumers the following statements in its privacy policy:

> We do not ask for, track, or access any location-specific information from your device at any time while you are using the Snapchat application.

21. In October 2012, Snapchat integrated an analytics tracking service in the Android version of its application that acted as its service provider. While the Android operating system provided notice to consumers that the application may access location information, Snapchat did not disclose that it would, in fact, access location information, and continued to represent that Snapchat did "not ask for, track, or access any location-specific information . . ."

22. Contrary to the representation in Snapchat's privacy policy, from October 2012 to February 2013, the Snapchat application on Android transmitted Wi-Fi-based and cell-based location information from users' mobile devices to its analytics tracking service provider.

## Count 3

23. As described in Paragraph 21, Snapchat has represented, expressly or by implication, that it does not collect users' location information.

24. In truth and in fact, as described in Paragraph 22, Snapchat did collect users' location information. Therefore, the representation set forth in Paragraph 23 is false or misleading.

## SNAPCHAT'S COLLECTION OF CONTACTS INFORMATION
### (Counts 4 and 5)

### Snapchat's Deceptive Find Friends User Interface

25. Snapchat provides its users with a feature to find friends on the service. During registration, the application prompts the user to "Enter your mobile number to find your friends on Snapchat!," implying – prior to September 2012 – through its user interface that the mobile phone number was the only information Snapchat collected to find the user's friends, as depicted below:

Users can also access this "Find Friends" feature at any time through the application's menu options.

26. However, when the user chooses to Find Friends, Snapchat collects not only the phone number a user enters, but also, without informing the user, the names and phone numbers of all the contacts in the user's mobile device address book.

27. Snapchat did not provide notice of, or receive user consent for, this collection until September 2012, at which time the iOS operating system was updated to provide a notification when an application accessed the user's address book.

### Count 4

28. As described in Paragraphs 25, through its user interface, Snapchat represented, expressly or by implication, that the only personal information Snapchat collected when the user chose to Find Friends was the mobile number that the user entered.

29. In truth and in fact, as described in Paragraph 26, the mobile number that the user entered was not the only personal information that Snapchat collected. Snapchat also collected the names and phone numbers of all contacts in the user's mobile device address book. Therefore, the representation set forth in Paragraph 28 is false or misleading.

### Snapchat's Deceptive Privacy Policy Statement Regarding the Find Friends Feature

30. From June 2011 to February 2013, Snapchat disseminated or caused to be disseminated to consumers the following statements, or similar statements, in its privacy policy regarding its Find Friends feature:

> Optional to the user, we also collect an email, *phone* number, and facebook id for purpose of finding friends on the service. (Emphasis in original).

31. As explained in Paragraph 26, the Snapchat application collected more than email, phone number, and Facebook ID for purpose of finding friends on the service. The application collected the names and phone numbers of all contacts in the user's mobile device address book.

### Count 5

32. As described in Paragraph 30, Snapchat, through its privacy policy, represented, expressly or by implication, that the only personal information Snapchat collected from a user for the purpose of finding friends on the service was email, phone number, and Facebook ID.

33. In truth and in fact, as described in Paragraph 31, email, phone number, and Facebook ID was not the only personal information that Snapchat collected for the purpose of finding friends on the service. Snapchat collected the names and phone numbers of all contacts in the user's mobile device address book when the user chose to Find Friends. Therefore, the representation set forth in Paragraph 32 is false or misleading.

### SNAPCHAT'S FAILURE TO SECURE ITS FIND FRIENDS FEATURE
### (Count 6)

34. Snapchat failed to securely design its Find Friends feature. As described in paragraph 25, Snapchat prompts the user to enter a mobile phone number that will be associated with the user's account. In addition, as described in paragraph 26, Snapchat collects the names and phone numbers of all the contacts in the user's address book. Snapchat's API uses this information to locate the user's friends on the service.

35. From September 2011 to December 2012, Snapchat failed to verify that the phone number that an iOS user entered into the application did, in fact, belong to the mobile device being used by that individual. Due to this failure, an individual could create an account using a phone number that belonged to another consumer, enabling the individual to send and receive snaps associated with another consumer's phone number.

36. Numerous consumers complained to Snapchat that individuals had created Snapchat accounts with phone numbers belonging to other consumers, leading to the misuse and unintentional disclosure of consumers' personal information. For example, consumers complained that they had sent snaps to accounts under the belief that they were communicating with a friend, when in fact they were not, resulting in the unintentional disclosure of photos containing personal information. In addition, consumers complained that accounts associated with their phone numbers had been used to send inappropriate or offensive snaps.

37. Snapchat could have prevented the misuse and unintentional disclosure of consumers' personal information by verifying phone numbers using common and readily available methods.

38. Indeed, in December 2012, Snapchat began performing short message-service ("SMS") verification to confirm that the entered phone number did in fact belong to the mobile device being used by that individual.

39. In addition, from September 2011 to December 2013, Snapchat failed to implement effective restrictions on the number of Find Friend requests that any one account could make to its API. Furthermore, Snapchat failed to implement any restrictions on serial and automated account creation. As a result of these failures, in December 2013, attackers were able to use multiple accounts to send millions of Find Friend requests using randomly generated phone numbers. The attackers were able to compile a database of 4.6 million Snapchat usernames and the associated mobile phone numbers. The exposure of usernames and mobile phone numbers could lead to costly spam, phishing, and other unsolicited communications.

40. From June 2011 to May 2012, Snapchat disseminated or caused to be disseminated to consumers the following statement in its privacy policy:

> The Toyopa Group, LLC is dedicated to securing customer data and, to that end, employs the best security practices to keep your data protected.

41. From May 2012 to February 2013, Snapchat disseminated or caused to be disseminated to consumers the following statement in its privacy policy:

> Snapchat takes reasonable steps to help protect your personal information in an effort to prevent loss, misuse, and unauthorized access, disclosure, alteration, and destruction.

42. From February 2013 to the present, Snapchat disseminated or caused to be disseminated to consumers the following statement in its privacy policy:

> We take reasonable measures to help protect information about you from loss, theft, misuse and unauthorized access, disclosure, alteration and destruction.

Count 6

43. As described in Paragraphs 40-42, Snapchat has represented, expressly or by implication, that it employs reasonable security measures to protect personal information from misuse and unauthorized disclosure.

44. In truth and in fact, as described in Paragraphs 34-39, in many instances, Snapchat did not employ reasonable security measures to protect personal information from misuse and unauthorized disclosure. Therefore, the representation set forth in Paragraph 43 is false or misleading.

45. The acts and practices of respondent as alleged in this complaint constitute deceptive acts or practices in or affecting commerce in violation of Section 5(a) of the Federal Trade Commission Act, 15 U.S.C. § 45(a).

### In the Matter of Snapchat, Inc., Docket No. C-4501 (Decision and Order)
December 23, 2014

### . . . DEFINITIONS

For purposes of this Order, the following definitions shall apply:...

3. "Covered information" shall mean information from or about an individual consumer, including but not limited to (a) a first and last name; (b) a home or other physical address, including street name and name of city or town; (c) an email address or other online contact information, such as an instant messaging user identifier or a screen name; (d) a telephone number; (e) a persistent identifier, such as a customer number held in a "cookie," a static Internet Protocol ("IP") address, a mobile device ID, or processor serial number; (f) precise geo-location data of an individual or mobile device, including GPS-based, Wi-Fi-based, or cell-based location information; (g) an authentication credential, such as a username or password; or (h) any communications or content that is transmitted or stored through respondent's products or services.

4. "Computor" shall mean any desktop, laptop computer, tablet, handheld device, telephone, or other electronic product or device that has a platform on which to download, install, or run any software program, code, script, or other content and to play any digital audio, visual, or audiovisual content.

I.

IT IS ORDERED that respondent and its officers, agents, representatives, and employees, directly or indirectly, shall not misrepresent in any manner, expressly or by implication, in or affecting commerce, the extent to which respondent or its products or services maintain and protect the privacy, security, or confidentiality of any covered information, including but not limited to: (1) the extent to which a message is deleted after being viewed by the recipient; (2) the extent to which respondent or its products or services are capable of detecting or notifying the sender when a recipient has captured a screenshot of, or otherwise saved, a message; (3) the categories of covered information collected; or (4) the steps taken to protect against misuse or unauthorized disclosure of covered information.

## II.

IT IS FURTHER ORDERED that respondent, in or affecting commerce, shall, no later than the date of service of this order, establish and implement, and thereafter maintain, a comprehensive privacy program that is reasonably designed to: (1) address privacy risks related to the development and management of new and existing products and services for consumers, and (2) protect the privacy and confidentiality of covered information, whether collected by respondent or input into, stored on, captured with, or accessed through a computer using respondent's products or services. Such program, the content and implementation of which must be fully documented in writing, shall contain privacy controls and procedures appropriate to respondent's size and complexity, the nature and scope of respondent's activities, and the sensitivity of the covered information, including:

A. the designation of an employee or employees to coordinate and be accountable for the privacy program;

B. the identification of reasonably foreseeable, material risks, both internal and external, that could result in the respondent's unauthorized collection, use, or disclosure of covered information, and assessment of the sufficiency of any safeguards in place to control these risks. At a minimum, this privacy risk assessment should include consideration of risks in each area of relevant operation, including, but not limited to: (1) employee training and management, including training on the requirements of this order; and (2) product design, development and research;

C. the design and implementation of reasonable privacy controls and procedures to address the risks identified through the privacy risk assessment, and regular testing or monitoring of the effectiveness of the privacy controls and procedures;

D. the development and use of reasonable steps to select and retain service providers capable of maintaining security practices consistent with this order, and requiring service providers by contract to implement and maintain appropriate safeguards;

E. the evaluation and adjustment of respondent's privacy program in light of the results of the testing and monitoring required by subpart C, any material changes to respondent's operations or business arrangements, or any other circumstances that respondent knows, or has reason to know, may have a material impact on the effectiveness of its privacy program.

## III.

IT IS FURTHER ORDERED that, in connection with its compliance with Part II of this order, respondent shall obtain initial and biennial assessments and reports ("Assessments") from a qualified, objective, independent third-party professional, who uses procedures and standards generally accepted in the profession. A person qualified to prepare such Assessments shall have a minimum of three (3) years of experience in the field of privacy and data protection. . . . The reporting period for the Assessments shall cover: (1) the first one hundred eighty (180) days after service of the order for the initial Assessment; and (2) each two (2) year period thereafter for twenty (20) years after service of the order for the biennial Assessments. Each Assessment shall:

A. set forth the specific privacy controls that respondent has implemented and maintained during the reporting period;

B. explain how such privacy controls are appropriate to respondent's size and complexity, the nature and scope of respondent's activities, and the sensitivity of the covered information;

C. explain how the safeguards that have been implemented meet or exceed the protections required by Part II of this order; and

D. certify that the privacy controls are operating with sufficient effectiveness to provide reasonable assurance to protect the privacy of covered information and that the controls have so operated throughout the reporting period.

Each Assessment shall be prepared and completed within sixty (60) days after the end of the reporting period to which the Assessment applies. . . .

IV.

IT IS FURTHER ORDERED that respondent shall maintain and upon request make available to the Federal Trade Commission for inspection and copying, unless respondent asserts a valid legal privilege, a print or electronic copy of:

A. for a period of five (5) years from the date of preparation or dissemination, whichever is later, statements disseminated to consumers that describe the extent to which respondent maintains and protects the privacy, security and confidentiality of any covered information, including, but not limited to, any statement related to a change in any website or service controlled by respondent that relates to the privacy, security, and confidentiality of covered information, with all materials relied upon in making or disseminating such statements;

B. for a period of five (5) years from the date received, all consumer complaints directed at respondent, or forwarded to respondent by a third party, that relate to the conduct prohibited by this order and any responses to such complaints;

C. for a period of five (5) years from the date received, any documents, whether prepared by or on behalf of respondent that contradict, qualify, or call into question respondent's compliance with this order; and

D. for a period of five (5) years after the date of preparation of each Assessment required under Part III of this order, all materials relied upon to prepare the Assessment, whether prepared by or on behalf of respondent including but not limited to all plans, reports, studies, reviews, audits, audit trails, policies, training materials, and assessments, for the compliance period covered by such Assessment. . . .

VIII.

This order will terminate on December 23, 2034, or twenty (20) years from the most recent date that the United States or the Commission files a complaint (with or without an accompanying consent decree) in federal court alleging any violation of the order, whichever comes later. . . .

*NOTES AND QUESTIONS*

The settlement terms are consistent with the FTC's typical terms in privacy cases, including "a comprehensive privacy program," biennial privacy audits, and recordkeeping—for the next 20 years.

The FTC alleged 6 counts against Snapchat. Do you think it would it have pursued the enforcement action if Snapchat had only committed one of the violations? Or was Snapchat's overall cluster of problems a key part of the FTC's decision to pursue the matter? Do you think it made a difference that Snapchat's defects affected the principal service differentiation it marketed to consumers?

Assume you are Snapchat's counsel when it is first developing its service, and you expect Snapchat will draw close attention from the FTC given the FTC's general interest in online services that advertise privacy features for their users. Anticipating the possibility of an FTC enforcement action, what would you tell Snapchat to do differently from the beginning to avoid the FTC's enforcement? Consider which problems relate to Snapchat's design from the outset.

Which, if any, of its problems could Snapchat have avoided through better disclosures to consumers? How exactly do you concisely explain to consumers that the product makes photos quickly disappear . . . except for the numerous ways that it doesn't?

The FTC's screenshots are often drawn from screens that consumers saw while using the product, not from advertising trying to persuade consumers to choose or download the product. Is the FTC taking the position that any improperly documented software constitutes a consumer deception? As a comparison example, if Microsoft Word's tutorial improperly described a feature of the software, would the FTC say that Microsoft engaged in a deceptive trade practice?

Is it fair to say that the FTC cracked down on Snapchat because Snapchat's software was buggy? Doesn't all software have bugs of some sort?

If you represented Snapchat and the FTC notifying you that it was investigating the facts enumerated in the complaint, would you choose to fight against the FTC? Why or why not? Does it affect your decision that the FTC's settlement included no cash payment from Snapchat?

Even though Snapchat didn't pay any money to the FTC as part of its settlement, how would you value the costs to Snapchat of this settlement? How much do you think the "comprehensive privacy program" and biennial audits cost? Consider the consent agreement's length (20 years, when

Snapchat had been in existence only for 2 years before the investigation started) and the "nuisance" factor as Snapchat tries to innovate with new services and compete against companies not similarly encumbered with FTC oversight. What do you think Snapchat will look like in 2034?

Think back to our discussion about "personal information" and the unexpected breadth of that concept in the Pineda case. Do you understand this definition from the FTC?

> "Covered information" shall mean information from or about an individual consumer, including but not limited to (a) a first and last name; (b) a home or other physical address, including street name and name of city or town; (c) an email address or other online contact information, such as an instant messaging user identifier or a screen name; (d) a telephone number; (e) a persistent identifier, such as a customer number held in a "cookie," a static Internet Protocol ("IP") address, a mobile device ID, or processor serial number; (f) precise geo-location data of an individual or mobile device, including GPS-based, Wi-Fi-based, or cell-based location information; (g) an authentication credential, such as a username or password; or (h) any communications or content that is transmitted or stored through respondent's products or services.

In particular, what pieces of data about consumers, no matter how obscure or minor, are clearly *excluded* from this definition?

In paragraph 11 of the complaint, the FTC notes the findings of a security researcher. This is not unusual. All privacy plaintiffs regularly keep up with technical discussions about security holes or bugs in software. These security researcher findings often become the foundation for an enforcement action.

Paragraph 37 of the complaint says "Snapchat could have prevented the misuse and unintentional disclosure of consumers' personal information by verifying phone numbers using common and readily available methods." Do you think Snapchat had failed to take adequate precautionary measures? Perhaps this reminds you of Judge Hand's negligence formula from *The T.J. Hooper* and *United States v. Carroll Towing*, both of which dealt with the adoption curves of new technological developments. In those cases, the "Hand Formula" defines negligence using the formula "$B > PxL$," where B = cost of preventing the injury and PxL is the cost of injury times the probability of injury occurring. Under that formula, was Snapchat "negligent"? What information would you need to know to make that determination?

In paragraph 39 of the complaint, the FTC recounts how "attackers" hacked Snapchat's database. Is this evidence that Snapchat committed deceptive practices on its consumers by promising more than it was prepared to deliver, or does it show Snapchat was a victim of possibly criminal behavior that deserved prosecutorial help from law enforcement? (Or both simultaneously?)

In paragraphs 40–42, the FTC cites the following language in Snapchat's privacy policy:

- The Toyopa Group, LLC is dedicated to securing customer data and, to that end, employs the best security practices to keep your data protected.

- Snapchat takes reasonable steps to help protect your personal information in an effort to prevent loss, misuse, and unauthorized access, disclosure, alteration, and destruction.
- We take reasonable measures to help protect information about you from loss, theft, misuse and unauthorized access, disclosure, alteration and destruction.

Do provisions of a privacy policy qualify as marketing claims? Do you think many consumers relied upon these statements when deciding to transact with Snapchat? What, if any, of these statements might be puffery? Did Snapchat actually fail to honor the statements? What evidence demonstrates that failing?

In paragraph 44, the FTC says Snapchat did not use "reasonable security procedures." What steps did Snapchat need to take to satisfy the FTC that it had reasonable security procedures? Or is the FTC's position that any corporation that suffers any security breach has per se demonstrated that it lacked reasonable security procedures?

*The Snappening.* In October 2014—after the settlement was announced but before the FTC finally approved it—hackers released tens of thousands of private photos that had been shared between individual Snapchat users. Mike Isaac, *A Look Behind the Snapchat Photo Leak Claims*, N.Y. TIMES, Oct. 17, 2014. (The release was colloquially referred to as the "Snappening," a portmanteau of "Snapchat" and a "happening"). Snapchat users had stored photos on an independent service called Snapsaved, which had been designed to demonstrate that Snapchat's disappearing-content claims were bogus. When Snapsaved was hacked, its photo archives were released to the wild. If a Snapchat user sent a photo to another Snapchat user who was also using Snapsaved, then the sender's photo may have been released even though the sender had never interacted with Snapsaved.

Should Snapchat be responsible for the hack of a third party service's database? Should Snapchat have done more to prevent Snapsaved from being able to obtain and save users' photos? Should the revelation of the hack-and-release have affected (or even scuttled) the in-process FTC settlement?

In 2015, Snapchat took several steps to block the possibility of third-party services like Snapsaved. Stephen Levy, *Snapchat's Non-Vanishing Message: You Can Trust Us*, Backchannel.com, Apr. 2, 2015.

This chapter addresses several types of promotional campaigns, including coupons, giveaways, sweepstakes and contests. Marketing people love these types of promotions because they pique consumer interest and get them to try new products or switch brands. Because of the extra consumer appeal of promotions, they are subject to special regulatory treatment, which this chapter explores.

## 1.    Coupons

In general, coupons must comply with the ordinary rules requiring ads to be truthful and non-misleading, with specific attention to price claims and, where necessary, to the regulation of the use of "free" by the FTC and state laws.*

In addition to heightened restrictions in certain industries, false advertising law constrains coupon offers, and the advertiser must disclose material conditions. In *Martin v. Coca-Cola Co.*, 785 F. Supp. 3 (D.D.C. 1992), Coca-Cola put an ad on bottles of Diet Coke: "Save 25 cents on your next purchase of a 2 or 3 liter bottle or multi-pack of Coca-Cola products with coupon on back of label." But the coupon was only good for twenty-five cents off Diet Sprite or Diet Minute Maid soda. The court deemed the plaintiff's argument that this was deceptive "preposterous." Do you agree? Would a reasonable consumer expect that "Coca-Cola products," without qualification, included Coke or Diet Coke—the very product on which the coupon appeared?

A more likely legal issue, however, is a coupon offer inadvertently gone wrong. Here's an example:

### In re Kentucky Grilled Chicken Coupon Marketing & Sales Practices Litigation, 2010 WL 2742310 (N.D. Ill. 2010)

On February 4, 2010, plaintiffs Christine Doering, James Asanuma, Veronica Mora, Kay Ready, and Daleen Brown (together "Plaintiffs"), on behalf of themselves and a purported class of over five million other people, filed a "Master Consolidated Class Action Complaint" in this multidistrict class action lawsuit. Plaintiffs allege claims for breach of contract (Count I), common law fraud (Count VI),

---

* Some specially regulated industries may have extra constraints on marketing techniques, including coupons. *Coldwell Banker Residential Real Estate Services, Inc. v. New Jersey Real Estate Commission*, 576 A.2d 938 (N.J. App. Div. 1990), upheld a ban on the use of coupons for furniture by real estate brokers against First Amendment and due process challenges. The targeted evil was "the capacity of extraneous inducements to distract the residential buyer and seller from the material elements of their decisions to list, sell and buy their homes. To many buyers and sellers, these are among the most significant financial decisions they face. Distracting gimmickry creates dangers which are the legitimate concern of the [regulators]." Indeed, the psychological/marketing literature generally agrees that coupons and similar offers may create a sense of obligation or otherwise undermine consumers' sales resistance. But is that a problem?

and violations of the consumer protection statutes of Illinois, Michigan, and California (Counts II–V & VII) in relation to a free product giveaway in May 2009. Pending before the court is defendant Yum! Brands, Inc. ("Yum!") and defendant KFC Corporation's ("KFC") (together "Defendants") motion to dismiss. For the reasons stated below, Defendants' motion is denied.

BACKGROUND . . .

Defendant KFC is the world's most popular chicken restaurant chain, and is a subsidiary of defendant Yum!. In April 2009, Defendants introduced a new product called "Kentucky Grilled Chicken." Defendants promoted "Kentucky Grilled Chicken" as a healthy fast-food menu option and incorporated the new menu item as part of their overall campaign to improve KFC's reputation for healthiness. Defendants' campaign included a "Kentucky Grilled Chicken" giveaway, which was announced by Oprah Winfrey on May 5, 2009, on her television talk show. Pursuant to the terms of the giveaway, any individual could obtain a free meal at KFC by first downloading a coupon from either unthinkfc.com or from Oprah Winfrey's website and then redeeming the coupon at a participating KFC franchise between May 5, 2009 and May 19, 2009, with the exception of May 10, 2009 (Mother's Day). When presented at a KFC restaurant, the coupon entitled the bearer to a free two-piece "Kentucky Grilled Chicken" meal, with two sides and a biscuit.

Defendants "began almost immediately to refuse to honor the coupons." At first they did so by "limit[ing] the promotion to the first 100 coupons presented at each KFC restaurant, per day." On May 7, 2009, Defendants "stopped the promotion altogether . . . [and] instructed franchises to stop honoring the coupons." Many of the KFC locations that refused to honor the coupon continued to offer "Kentucky Grilled Chicken" for purchase. From May 5 to May 7, 2009, at least 10.2 million coupons were downloaded from unthinkfc.com. Only 4.5 million coupons were actually redeemed at KFC franchises.

After stopping the coupon promotion, Defendants offered consumers the option of applying for a "rain check" for the promised free "Kentucky Grilled Chicken" meal. To apply for a "rain check," the consumer was required to fill out a form with the consumer's name and address, attach his or her coupon to the form, and mail the form to KFC or give it to a KFC team member. Defendants told consumers these procedures were necessary "so that KFC could verify the coupons' validity." Following receipt of the "rain check" application, KFC would then send the consumer a new coupon for a free meal at a later date, as well as an additional complimentary Pepsi product. . . .

ANALYSIS

. . .II. Count VI—Common Law Fraud

. . . Defendants argue that Plaintiffs' common law fraud claim must be dismissed because Plaintiffs have failed to allege facts "that plausibly give rise to an inference that KFC 'never intended to honor' the coupons."

Plaintiffs allege in their Master Complaint that "Defendants, in fact, never intended to honor the Coupons as represented." While Plaintiffs, of course, cannot know Defendants' state of mind, they have supported this general allegation with additional facts alleged in the Master Complaint. For example, Plaintiffs allege that, "[o]n information and belief, many of the KFC locations that refused to redeem the coupons had ample supplies of Kentucky Grilled Chicken on hand, and continued to make those supplies available for purchase." The "information and belief" on which this allegation rests includes the experiences of plaintiff Veronica Mora on May 5, 2009, who allegedly visited a KFC restaurant in Sylmar, California, where employees refused to honor the coupon while continuing to sell "Kentucky Grilled Chicken" to customers. It is also alleged that none of the four named plaintiffs who attempted to redeem the coupons in person were told that the specific KFC restaurant they visited had actually run out of "Kentucky Grilled Chicken."

Defendants argue that they could not have plausibly harbored an intention not to honor the coupons, when it is undisputed that Defendants honored 4.5 million coupons in the first two days of the promotion. However, Plaintiffs have also alleged that Defendants "began almost immediately to refuse to honor the coupons" and "stopped the promotion altogether on May 7, 2009—two days after it was announced," which left 5.7 million coupons unredeemed.

Based on the allegations of the Master Complaint, the court finds it plausible that Defendants never intended to honor the coupon as represented. It can be reasonably inferred from Defendants' choice to publicize their offer "on the highly popular 'Oprah' show" that Defendants hoped their promotion would reach millions of consumers. It is also reasonable to assume that Defendants contemplated the possibility that millions of consumers would seize the opportunity to obtain a free "Kentucky Grilled Chicken" meal, and that Defendants considered what would happen if individual KFC restaurants ran out of the advertised product. With these considerations in mind, the court finds that it is plausible Defendants intended all along to offer a "rain check" in place of the coupon, or otherwise limit redemption of the coupon beyond the terms stated on its face. Plaintiffs have alleged sufficient facts to comport with the pleading requirements of Rule 8 and state a plausible claim for common law fraud.

### III. Counts II, III, IV, V, & VII—Consumer Protection Statutes

. . . Plaintiffs contend that the Master Complaint's allegations are sufficient to support their statutory claims under the relevant state consumer protection statutes, because the allegations go beyond breach of contract to "implicate [ ] consumer protection concerns."

As discussed above, Plaintiffs have adequately alleged that Defendants "never intended to honor the Coupons." Based on this allegation, Plaintiffs characterize Defendants' actions as "a classic 'bait and switch' " and note that this type of conduct is actionable under the relevant state consumer protection statutes. . . .

Because Plaintiffs have alleged that Defendants never intended to honor their promotion from the outset, Plaintiffs' allegations "involve [ ] more than the mere fact that a defendant promised something and then failed to do it." Additionally, this court finds that the contract at issue in this litigation implicates an "inherent consumer interest" on its face, insofar as Defendants' offer was allegedly accepted by millions of consumers across the nation. For these reasons, the court declines to dismiss Plaintiffs' statutory claims as being redundant to the claim for breach of contract.

A.      Count II—Illinois

In Count II of their Master Complaint, Plaintiffs allege that Defendants' actions violate Section 2 and Section 2P of the Illinois Consumer Fraud and Deceptive Business Practices Act ("ICFA"), 815 ILCS 505/1, et seq. Relying on the language of the statute, Defendants argue that Plaintiffs' claims under the ICFA should be dismissed because "the offering of a free meal does not fall within the scope of the ICFA."

1. Section 2

Section 2 of the ICFA declares that it is unlawful to engage in:

> Unfair methods of competition and unfair or deceptive acts or practices, including but not limited to the use or employment of any deception, fraud, false pretense, false promise, misrepresentation or the concealment, suppression or omission of any material fact, with intent that others rely upon the concealment, suppression or omission of such material fact . . . in the conduct of any trade or commerce . . . whether any person has in fact been misled, deceived or damaged thereby.

815 ILCS 505/2. Defendants argue that Plaintiffs cannot state a cause of action under Section 2, because Defendants' alleged actions as set forth in the Master Complaint do not describe an act or practice that has taken place "in the conduct of any trade or commerce."

The ICFA defines the terms "trade" and "commerce" as "the advertising, offering for sale, sale, or distribution of any services and any property, . . . commodity, or thing of value." 815 ILCS 505/1(f). Defendants note that this definition "describe[s] four steps of a typical commercial sale" and argue that, because "the coupon did not involve any sale or offer of sale," the statute is inapplicable to the facts of this case. Defendants' interpretation ignores the plain language of the statute. This language is unambiguous, insofar as the use of the disjunctive "or" clearly signifies that allegations of unfair or deceptive acts or practices occurring at any one of the four stages in the life cycle of a typical consumer transaction ("advertising, offering for sale, sale, or distribution") will suffice to state a claim under Section 2. The court declines Defendant's invitation to read the disjunctive term "or" as though it means the conjunctive term "and" in this context.

The court further disagrees with Defendants' argument that the coupon did not constitute an "advertisement" because it was not "disseminated in connection with a 'commercial transaction.' " Plaintiffs have alleged that Defendants offered the coupon as part of their advertising campaign for their new line of chicken. . . . The allegations of the Master Complaint support the reasonable inference that the goal of Defendants' advertising campaign was to promote future sales of "Kentucky Grilled Chicken" and other KFC products, especially in light of the fact that the coupons were only redeemable in person at participating KFC restaurants. Because the "Kentucky Grilled Chicken" giveaway can reasonably be considered an attempt "to induce directly or indirectly any person to enter into any obligation or acquire any title or interest in any merchandise," the

"Kentucky Grilled Chicken" giveaway can be considered an "advertisement" for purposes of the ICFA.

2. Section 2P

Plaintiffs also allege that Defendants violated Section 2P of the ICFA, which states:

> It is an unlawful practice for any person to promote or advertise any business, product, utility service . . . or interest in property, by means of offering free prizes, gifts, or gratuities *to any consumer*, unless all material terms and conditions relating to the offer are clearly and conspicuously disclosed at the outset of the offer so as to leave no reasonable probability that the offering might be misunderstood.

815 ILCS 505/2P (emphasis added). Defendants argue that Plaintiffs' claims under Section 2P necessarily fail because (1) Plaintiffs are not "consumers" under the ICFA's definition of this term, and (2) Plaintiffs have not alleged any "unclear or inconspicuous disclosure."

The ICFA defines "consumer" as "any person who purchases or contracts for the purchase of merchandise not for resale in the ordinary course of his trade or business but for his use or that of a member of his household." Because "[n]one of the plaintiffs was required to purchase anything to receive a free meal," Defendants assert that Plaintiffs cannot state a claim for relief under Section 2P. The statutory definition of "consumer" is not as limited as Defendants contend. On its face, the ICFA definition does not require a "consumer" to have purchased merchandise from a named defendant. Nor does this reading make sense in the context of Section 2P. Section 2P applies to situations in which businesses promote their products by offering "free prizes, gifts, or gratuities to any consumer." Section 2P would be rendered meaningless if an individual must first purchase the "free" product to be considered a "consumer" for purposes of the protections set forth therein.

Defendants also argue that "[t]his case has nothing to do with the failure to clearly and conspicuously disclose the terms of the promotion." In response, Plaintiffs contend that the Master Complaint is "rife with allegations of after-the-fact conditions placed on the offer by Defendants and their employees." The conditions cited by Plaintiffs include (1) that redemption of the coupons would be limited "to the first 100 coupons presented at each KFC restaurant, per day, regardless of the supplies of 'Kentucky Grilled Chicken' on hand" and (2) that consumers would not be able to redeem the coupon after a certain date, at which point consumers would be required to provide their names and addresses before receiving a "rain check" good for a free meal at a later date. Section 2P requires disclosure of "all material terms and conditions relating to the offer . . . at the outset of the offer," for purposes of ensuring that the there is "no reasonable probability that the offering might be misunderstood." . . . Plaintiffs have set forth sufficient allegations in the Master Complaint to plausibly suggest that Defendants at some point made a decision to revise the terms of the offer and did not "clearly and conspicuously" disclose the new contract terms to Plaintiffs before Plaintiffs accepted the offer. . . .

[The court made similar rulings about plaintiffs' Michigan and California law claims, as well as defendants' contentions that they offered "rain checks" sufficient to satisfy relevant statutory safe harbors for sellers who run out of a product but offer consumers the same terms within a reasonable time once they've restocked. Given the allegations that, among other things, the supposed "rain checks" imposed additional requirements to provide personal information and that restaurants actually had the chicken in stock but still refused to honor the coupons, defendants hadn't shown that the complaint should be dismissed.]

*NOTES AND QUESTIONS*

How should Yum! have worded the coupon so that it clearly and conspicuously disclosed the limits on the offer? In response to surprisingly high demand for an offer, what should an advertiser do? Statutory safe harbors for rain checks do exist. However, as this case indicates, the rain checks must be as nearly equivalent to the initial offer as possible (other than the unavoidable delay in honoring the offer).

*Digital Distribution.* Distributing coupons electronically can cost less than other distribution methods, but electronic coupons may be harder to control. Among other things, coupon issuers should consider the possibility that a coupon will go viral and plan accordingly.

For example, in 2006, a Starbucks in Atlanta emailed a coupon for a free "iced grande beverage" to a relatively small number of employees and business partners and encouraged them to forward the email coupon to friends and family. The email got forwarded to millions of people nationwide, resulting in such large demand that Starbucks canceled the promotion (otherwise, Starbucks's losses could have been millions of dollars). What should Starbucks have done differently?

TRY YOUR COFFEE

ICED

Stop by your neighborhood Starbucks Coffee between noon and 9 pm for a complimentary iced grande beverage.

There are several types of coupon problems:

- *Redistributed coupons.* Often, coupons are meant to induce consumers to switch brands. If too many coupons end up in the hands of existing brand loyalists, their redemptions allow the loyalists to make their already-planned purchases at a lower cost. Thus, the advertiser may want to restrict coupon transferability to keep existing consumers from getting too many coupons.

- *Violation of redemption restrictions.* Coupons often restrict who can redeem them. Redemptions in violation of those terms—whether due to fraud or ignorance by the consumer or sloppy oversight by the person accepting the redeemed coupon—can undermine the coupon issuer's economic expectations.

- *Fraudulent coupons.* Some fraudsters make and redeem fake coupons. The person accepting redemption may not recognize the fake. Coupon counterfeiting may sound like a nickel-and-dime problem, but it can be a lucrative and sizable business. *See, e.g.,* Brad Tuttle, *The $40 Million Counterfeit Coupon Caper*, TIME.COM, July 19, 2012. An industry organization, the Coupon Information Center, attempts to combat fake coupons.

Because managing coupon redemptions can be complicated, advertisers and retailers often rely on third-party service providers to help with various administrative aspects.

*Counter-measures.* One tactic some retailers use to combat competitors' offers is the price or coupon match. By allowing a consumer who proves the existence of a cheaper price elsewhere to get the same deal at her usual store, the retailer avoids losing a customer. Or at least that's the theory.

Price match offers must be carefully drafted and enforced, as Wal-Mart discovered to its sorrow in 2014. Competitor Dollar General offered a $9.50 sale price for "all counts and sizes" of Pampers Swaddlers diapers, and $6.50 for packs of lower-end Luvs diapers. Because Dollar General typically stocks smaller packages, this equated to a discount of about 50 cents a pack. But Wal-Mart and other competitors stock much bigger packages with retail prices of up to $38. Relying on price match promises, consumers clogged understaffed Wal-Mart checkout lines, and some consumers received discounts of up to 75% until Wal-Mart stopped honoring the Dollar General offer. Wal-Mart now instructs cashiers that a price match requires that the item's size, quantity, brand, flavor and color are identical to the product carried by Wal-Mart. (Note that Wal-Mart often commissions manufacturers, even national brands, to supply unique product variants that are unavailable elsewhere). A Wal-Mart spokesperson ultimately said that the Dollar General offer was ineligible for the price match because it didn't specify "like for like item." One consumer's reaction to being denied a match was: "It said, 'any count, any size.' How much more specific do you have to get?" Serena Ng & Kelly Banjo, *Volatile Brew: Price-Matching and Social Media*, WALL ST. J., July 23, 2014.

If you were Wal-Mart's counsel, how would you draft the price match policy to avoid this problem in the future? How would you communicate it to consumers, remembering that long messages don't work well? For those consumers who were refused a match, do they have any potential legal claims? If Wal-Mart deliberately stocks "unmatchable" products, is the price match claim misleading?

*Retailer Issues.* What happens if the retailer misunderstands the manufacturer's coupon offer? *Renner v. Procter & Gamble Co.*, 54 Ohio App.3d 79, 561 N.E.2d 959 (1988), involved a coupon offering a free box of basic-size Luvs diapers "or equivalent off any larger size (up to $3.75)." "FREE" was the most prominent part of the coupon.

[coupon reproduced by court]

Renner took the coupon to a store where the basic size was priced at more than $3.75, and the cashier refused to give him the box for free, though he was able to redeem the coupon for a free box at a different store. Procter & Gamble ultimately explained to the first store that its intent was to provide a coupon for a free box of basic-size diapers *or* $3.75 off any larger size. Renner sued for violation of Ohio Administrative Code 109:4-3-02(A)(1), which provided that

> [i]t is a deceptive act or practice in connection with a consumer transaction for a supplier, in the sale or offering for sale of goods or services, to make any offer in written or printed advertising or promotional literature without stating clearly and conspicuously in close proximity to the words stating the offer any material exclusions, reservations, limitations, modifications, or conditions. Disclosure shall be easily legible to anyone reading the advertising or promotional literature and shall be sufficiently specific so as to leave no reasonable probability that the terms of the offer might be misunderstood.

The court of appeals found in P&G's favor: given that P&G intended to give consumers a free basic-size box, there were arguably no "material exclusions, reservations, limitations, modifications, or conditions" attached to the offer in the first place. "More importantly, however, we agree with the trial court that the $3.75 limitation was of sufficient clarity and conspicuousness so that it left 'no reasonable probability' that its terms would be misunderstood to apply such limitation to the free basic size disposable diaper offer, rather than merely to the alternative offer." The court suggested that the first store's misunderstanding didn't benefit P&G (since it was trying to get consumers to try the product) and that out of 2.5 billion similar coupons mailed, there had been very few complaints. Was there anything more that P&G could reasonably have done?

*Other Giveaways.* Perhaps even more than coupons, free samples or other "free" offers have excellent selling power, engendering warm feelings toward the "giver" and triggering reciprocity norms in consumers that may induce them to make a purchase. Gifts may also induce consumers to focus on

653

the short term—the immediate enjoyment of the gift—instead of the long-term consequences of a purchase decision.

But "free" gifts have implicit strings attached. Therefore, the 2009 CARD Act bars credit card issuers from offering "any tangible item," such as t-shirts or pizza, to students who sign up for a credit card. Issuers also can't offer any gifts "near the campus" or at an "event sponsored by or related to an institution of higher learning." Some people have proposed banning toys in "kids' meals" such as McDonald's Happy Meal in order to limit the consumption of junk food by kids.

Do such prohibitions reflect unjustified paternalism or reasonable regulation? These tactics are certainly promotional from the perspective of marketers; they build brand loyalty and generate consumer demand. Can you imagine any First Amendment argument against regulating the provision of free samples or gifts? *See* Discount Tobacco City & Lottery, Inc. v. U.S., 674 F.3d 509 (6th Cir. 2012) (holding that free tobacco samples and gifts with purchase of tobacco were protected by the First Amendment as "promotional methods that convey the twin messages of reinforcing brand loyalty and encouraging switching from competitors' brands"). There are multiple ways to generate sales, and they may be subject to different forms of regulation and different levels of First Amendment scrutiny.

Pure giveaways, like unrestricted coupon offers, can go very badly. In 2008, when the popular band Guns N' Roses had already delayed the release of its next album, *Chinese Democracy*, for a decade, Dr. Pepper offered to give every American a free can of Dr. Pepper soda if the album were released in the next year. Unfortunately for Dr. Pepper, Guns N' Roses did release the album that year. Dr. Pepper quickly set up a website allowing consumers to redeem their free can, but that website quickly crashed. In the end, very few consumers received their free cans, and Guns N' Roses lawyers threatened Dr. Pepper with a lawsuit. Dr. Pepper publicly claimed that it was just responding to an invitation from the band's managers. What sort of documentation would you want for such a promotion if you were Dr. Pepper's lawyers? How would you tell your clients to plan to implement a possible redemption?

## 2.    Sweepstakes and Contests

According to the FTC, "[a] recent research poll showed that more than half of all American adults entered sweepstakes within the past year. Most of these contests were run by reputable marketers and non-profit organizations to promote their products and services. Some lucky winners received millions of dollars or valuable prizes." FTC, *Facts for Consumers: Prize Offers: You Don't Have to Pay to Play!*.

Nonetheless, advertisers have a checkered history with sweepstakes and prizes. Certain advertisers engaged in repeated abuses, in which consumers—particularly elderly consumers—were induced to buy hundreds and even thousands of dollars' worth of magazine subscriptions, for example, in the mistaken belief that purchasing subscriptions would increase their chances of winning large prizes. Misleading sweepstakes advertising thus led to numerous lawsuits and legislative and regulatory responses. *See, e.g.*, Lesley Fair, *Strings Attached? Disclosing the Details of the Deal* (discussing

$650,000 of penalties for conduct such as running ads congratulating consumers on "winning" a TV, when trying to claim the prize resulted in a barrage of additional ads and "optional" offers, culminating in requirements that the consumers purchase some other third-party product or service); FTC, *FTC Sues to Stop Massive Sweepstakes Scam*, Sept. 23, 2013 (lawsuit alleging consumers were defrauded of more than $11 million by mass mailings that they'd "won" $2 million, which could be claimed by sending in a fee of $20 or $30; small print indicated that the fee was only paying for a list of others' sweepstakes). These sorts of practices, lacking the clear and conspicuous disclosure of the relevant terms, are unfair and deceptive and likely to bring significant trouble to advertisers who try them.

Because the rules governing sweepstakes and contests are so detailed and differ substantially from state to state, no lawyer should approve either without doing a careful review of all the relevant rules and regulations in all fifty states, plus U.S. territories. One multistate checklist may be found in DAVID H. BERNSTEIN & BRUCE P. KELLER, THE LAW OF ADVERTISING, MARKETING AND PROMOTIONS §7 (2017). By way of warning, it has thirty-two items on the basic checklist, and four more for Internet promotions. The Global Advertising Lawyers Alliance, an industry organization, also puts out a guide to sweepstakes regulations around the world. Often, sweepstakes and contest clearance is best handled by a lawyer who specializes in the field.

## A.    How Can a Contest or Sweepstakes Avoid Being an Illegal Lottery?

An illegal lottery has three components: (1) a prize, which can be anything of tangible value, (2) determined on the basis of chance, (3) where consideration is paid to participate.

A sweepstakes eliminates the third factor (consideration) so that it involves a prize awarded based on chance, but people may participate without payment.

A contest eliminates the second factor (chance) so that people are eligible for the prize if they provide the specified consideration, but there is no element of chance in the prize allocation. An example is a talent contest where the prize goes to the person who experts judge as the most talented (though, as we will discuss below, different states have different standards for determining when a contest is based on chance).

Advertisers need to be very careful about avoiding illegal lotteries (which can constitute crimes). Chance and consideration have a frustrating habit of creeping back into well-designed efforts to eliminate them.

Why are prizes such an attractive technique for advertisers? Psychologists suggest that the apparent "gift," whether from a coupon, a free sample, or a "free" chance to win something, triggers reciprocity norms among consumers, making them feel grateful and even creating a sense of obligation or debt to the advertiser. For extensive evidence on this point, see Robert Cialdini, *Influence: The Psychology of Persuasion* (rev. ed. 1998). Another possibility is that consumers overvalue the prize or overestimate their chance of winning, so consumers feel like they are getting more value from the advertiser than the advertiser is actually paying. Also, from an advertiser's standpoint, it's a way of providing a price discount or extra benefit to consumers without explicitly lowering prices, which the advertiser might want to avoid.

*Element One: Prize*

The Court of Appeals for the Seventh Circuit, in *George v. National Collegiate Athletic Ass'n*, 613 F.3d 658 (7th Cir. 2010), initially allowed a class action to proceed over the distribution of tickets to the popular NCAA Basketball Tournament. The complaint alleged this was an illegal lottery because it required applicants to submit a $6–$10 handling fee along with the face value of the tickets to get a chance to win tickets. If the applicants weren't selected, they would be reimbursed for the face value of the tickets, but not for the handling fee. Even though an applicant could only win one pair of tickets, many applicants bought multiple entries to maximize their chances of getting that pair, so both successful and unsuccessful applicants could incur multiple handling fees.

The Court of Appeals initially determined that plaintiffs sufficiently pled the elements of (1) prize, (2) chance, and (3) consideration, concluding that if the NCAA had set up its ticket distribution process so that the handling fee was refunded to non-winners, the process would have been legal. This opinion was then vacated, 623 F.3d 1135 (7th Cir. 2010), and the panel certified to the Indiana Supreme Court the state law questions.

In *George v. National Collegiate Athletic Ass'n*, 945 N.E.2d 150 (Ind. 2011), the Indiana Supreme Court concluded that the NCAA's ticket-allocation process was not an illegal lottery under Indiana law because winners (those who got tickets) received no "prize"—they got nothing more than losers did. Both winners and losers were out of pocket for the handling fee, and "[t]hose applicants whose offers to purchase tickets are accepted receive tickets for $150 per ticket, whereas those applicants whose offers are rejected receive $150 in cash per ticket." Did the NCAA successfully evade the prohibition on lotteries? Could other advertisers do the same thing, making their profits on "handling fees"? Would it matter if, at the time of allocation, the "street value" of the tickets was more than the face value?

Another issue about prizes does not relate to illegal lotteries, but to trademark owners' possible objection to the use of their marks in describing prizes. Apple issued guidelines stating its opposition to using iPads and other Apple products as prizes without Apple's authorization. Given the trademark doctrine of nominative use, does Apple have that right? Arguably, merely giving away an iTunes gift card shouldn't suggest a connection with Apple. What would you tell a client who wants to offer an Apple product as a prize?

*Element Two: Chance*

If the element of chance is absent, then the promotion is a contest of skill and not a game of chance. This is important because, in most states, it is legally permissible for contests of skill to require an entry fee or proof of purchase, though some states—including Arizona, Connecticut, Florida, Illinois, New Jersey, and Vermont—prohibit skill contests that require consideration.

Chance includes future events, such as the predicted winners of sports competitions—that is, even an educated guess may turn the contest into illegal gambling in some states, if consideration is required to enter. Fantasy sports leagues have generated substantial controversy on this point, though they are now generally tolerated. Most states allow consideration-based contests of skill as long as skill is the dominant factor in determining who wins, though a minority will allow such contests as long as winning isn't *purely* the result of chance.

Courts that apply the "dominant factor" test ask: (1) whether the contest is impossible to win without skill, and whether there is enough opportunity for entrants to make informed decisions; (2) whether the average player has enough skill to participate; (3) whether skill determines the actual result of the game, not just some element of the promotion; and (4) whether participants are aware of the skill and criteria that will be used to determine the winner.

However, courts that use this test still differ in results. Some courts have found Three Card Monte, video games that award free replays, and word puzzle games to be games of skill, whereas shell games, dice games and bingo are games of chance. Courts have divided on whether pinball and poker are games of chance or skill. Florida and South Carolina have split on whether a hole-in-one golf contest is skill-based: Florida's AG determined that it was skill, but South Carolina's AG believed that making a hole in one is so dependent on luck that the contest was fairly described as predominantly chance-based.

Contests of skill have to be judged based on specific, objective criteria by competent judges, and using random luck such as a coin flip to break ties isn't allowed, since it reintroduces chance. For trivia contests and the like, the correct answer must be ascertainable from authoritative reference works; the rules must clearly and conspicuously disclose this, and questions and answers with supporting data and judging procedures must be on file with an independent organization prior to the contest. F.T.C. Modifying Order, No. 8824, 52 F.R. 3221 (1987). Various states, including Connecticut and Florida, have other specific requirements for skill-based promotions. For an online contest, the participant's speed of response to a problem or puzzle might not be skill-based given that response times may depend on devices and services outside the entrant's control.

What if chance is eliminated because "everyone wins"? Many states, including California, have special requirements when every participant is a winner or when everyone who makes a purchase or a visit to a location wins. There's an obvious interaction here with the rules on "free" offers—among other things, the price of the underlying good must not be raised to account for the cost of the prize.

*Element Three: Consideration*

Be aware: the cases on this element vary a lot from state to state. A national advertiser should be very conservative; a local advertiser should be very precise.

In *Levin v. Jordan's Furniture, Inc.*, 944 N.E.2d 1096 (Table), 2011 WL 1450357 (Mass. App. Ct. 2011), Jordan's promised that customers who bought certain items of furniture during the promotional period would get those items free if the Boston Red Sox swept the 2008 World Series. In

2007, Jordan's had run a similar promotion, and an estimated 30,000 customers received free furniture after the Red Sox won the 2007 World Series. (Note that Jordan's changed the terms a bit the second time around!) In 2008, however, the Phillies won the World Series. A disappointed customer sued. Massachusetts law bars illegal lotteries, which as noted above require (1) a prize, (2) some element of chance, and (3) consideration, or the payment of a price. It was undisputed that the free furniture was a prize and that there was an element of chance. However, the plaintiff failed to plead that any part of the purchase price of the furniture was paid for the chance to win the prize, and there was therefore no illegal lottery. Thus, the chance of winning may be conditioned on purchase, so long as no part of the price is paid for the chance to win. What would you advise a business that wants to run such a promotion? What sort of evidence would you keep on hand to substantiate that no part of the price covered the chance to win? What happens if a consumer does properly allege that the price reflects the cost of the prize, as, in a profit-seeking business, one might imagine it did?

Currently, all states permit sweepstakes in connection with advertising products and services as long as no consideration is required. In this context, consideration means something different than its definition in the contract formation sense. Consideration includes buying a product, even when the price is the standard price. If the prize is merely a discount coupon, some states will view that as a consideration issue, because a winner must spend some of her own money to obtain the prize.

The majority view is that any substantial expenditure of effort, such as taking a long survey or making multiple visits to a store, constitutes consideration. In the minority view, any effort that provides commercial value to the advertiser, such as "refer a friend" promotions, will be consideration.

In some states, requiring the consumer to visit a store constitutes consideration. *State ex rel. Schillberg v. Safeway Stores*, 450 P.2d 949 (Wash. 1969), held that consideration sufficient to support a contract is enough to constitute consideration for a lottery. "[O]ne need not part with something of value, tangible or intangible, to supply the essential consideration for a lottery." According to the Washington Supreme Court, the time, thought, attention and energy expended by members of the public in studying Safeway's advertising and journeying to a Safeway store to procure a prize slip, as well as the actual increase in patronage that resulted from the contest, amounted to consideration Other states have disagreed.

In most states, filling out an entry form, taking a short survey, or mailing or phoning in an entry don't qualify as consideration. However, the more effort is required, the more likely it is to constitute consideration. Would giving your name and address to the advertiser and consenting to receive further targeted promotions count as consideration? What about giving your friends' names? What about "liking" the advertiser's Facebook page?

"Post consideration"—some type of payment before the winner can claim the prize—is also illegal in many states. Thus, some states specifically ban "notifying" people that they've won a prize if they have to buy something, pay money, or submit to a sales presentation to claim the prize. Other states allow certain conditions, such as attending a sales presentation or paying shipping and handling fees, provided that all the advertising clearly and conspicuously discloses these limits.

**B.      Alternate Means of Entry**

Sweepstakes usually provide at least two different methods of entering the sweepstakes. The first entry method requires the consumer to do something valuable for the advertiser, such as buying something from the advertiser. That entry method will qualify as consideration, creating an apparent illegal lottery.

To avoid an illegal lottery, the advertiser must provide a second entry method that doesn't require any consideration. This is typically called an "alternate means of entry" or "AMOE." The chances of winning through the alternate means of entry must be equal to the chances of winning through purchase.

Because the alternate means of entry is the key to negating any consideration in the sweepstakes and avoiding an illegal lottery, advertisers relying on it must structure it properly. A sweepstakes can provide multiple alternate entry methods, even if some methods create consideration, so long as there always remains one consideration-free entry method.

A typical alternate means of entry is to let the consumer enter the sweepstakes by mailing in a postcard. Although the postcard imposes some costs on consumers—postage, the costs of the postcard, and the time required to fill it out—typically those costs aren't treated as "consideration" (except in South Carolina and Vermont).

In order to ensure that consumers understand that no consideration is required, a sweepstakes must prominently disclose that no purchase is necessary and explain the alternate means of entry. One implication of this rule is that, if a product contains a sweepstakes piece, the package must disclose the alternate means of entry—that information can't just be confined to ads or displays.

Some states enforce these requirements vigorously. In 2013, A&P Supermarkets paid $102,000 to settle the New York Attorney General's charge that A&P violated state law with its "Frozen Food Month Sweepstakes," in which any customer who purchased more than $50 in frozen food products at an A&P store was automatically entered in a sweepstakes. Though the official rules disclosed a free alternate method of entry, the AG considered this insufficient. Along with the monetary payment, A&P promised to advertise the free method of entry with larger signs, to include copies of the official rules in the stores, and to advertise the free method with "equal prominence" to the paid entry. Seth Heyman, *Recent Sweepstakes Enforcement Actions Illustrate Legal Pitfalls*, Oct. 18, 2013.

Online-only alternate means of entry may not be sufficient because some states believe that not all eligible potential participants have free access to the Internet. Does this represent a discrimination against a new medium? It's true that not everyone has easy Internet access, but not everyone has easy access to a stamped, self-addressed envelope either. New York does not allow online-only alternate means of entry for store-based contests on a theory that the elderly may be excluded, but this discomfort may change with time.

For those advertisers committed to running an online contest, one solution is to limit eligibility to those United States residents who already have Internet access to avoid consideration problems. Rules should also cover Internet security issues such as hacking and technical glitches, and the Internet-only nature of the contest should be prominently disclosed. Asking entrants for personal information or to watch an online ad raises consideration issues, which in turn may be averted by providing an offline alternate means of entry, or at least some way to avoid submitting the information or watching the ad.

What about other new methods of communication? The following case involves the use of text messages, which are faster than traditional mail, but raise special questions because carriers charge extra fees for messages to particular numbers. If the advertiser gets a cut of those fees, consideration problems arise.

*Couch v. Telescope Inc., 2:07-cv-03916-JHN-VBK (C.D. Cal. 2007), appeal dismissed, Couch v. Telescope Inc., 611 F.3d 629 (9th Cir. 2010)*

. . . These four cases all involve games conducted in conjunction with four popular television programs: *American Idol, Deal or No Deal, 1 vs. 100,* and *The Apprentice.* The Defendants in all four cases have brought motions to dismiss. As these motions present identical legal issues and involve similar facts, the goal of judicial economy warrants their joint resolution. Except as noted, this Order applies equally to all parties in each of the four presented cases.

A.      Couch v. Telescope: The *American Idol* Challenge

*American Idol* is a televised singing competition that has been broadcast by Defendant Fox Broadcasting Company since 2002. During airings of the program, promotions invite viewers to participate in the "American Idol Challenge," a trivia game. A trivia question is posed, along with three possible answers. Viewers then have 24 hours to answer the question, either by sending a text message to 51555 or by registering on the program's website. Although entering online is free, viewers who enter by sending text messages incur a 99 cent fee, in addition to standard text messaging rates charged by their wireless carriers. Each week, winners are selected at random from among those entries with correct answers. There is a $10,000 weekly prize and $100,000 grand prize. . . . Plaintiff Darlene Couch, a Georgia resident, has entered the American Idol Challenge via text message, paid the 99 cent fee, and has not won a prize. She alleges that the American Idol Challenge is an illegal lottery. She now seeks relief under California Business and Professions Code § 17200 (the Unfair Competition Law, or "UCL") and Connecticut General Statute § 52-554. Defendants move to dismiss both claims for relief. . . .

[The other TV shows involved essentially the same setup for prizes.]

III. Discussion

A.      Plaintiffs' First Claims for Relief: Unfair Competition

. . . Here, Plaintiffs allege that Defendants violated California Penal Code § 319 by running an illegal lottery; this is the "unlawful practice" for which they seek remedy under § 17200. Defendants argue that Plaintiffs fail to state a claim for three reasons: first, American Idol Challenge, the Lucky Case Game, [1] vs. 100, and Get Rich with Trump (collectively, "the Games") are not illegal lotteries under California Penal Code § 319; second, Plaintiffs lack standing to pursue relief under the UCL, and; third, the doctrine of in pari delicto bars their claims. The Court considers each of these arguments in turn.

1. Illegal Lottery

Defendants first argue that [the promotions] are not illegal lotteries under California law because they provide free alternative methods of entry. Consequently, Defendants argue that Plaintiffs' UCL claims, predicated on violation of the lottery law, must fail as a matter of law. The Court disagrees. Article IV § 19 of the California Constitution prohibits lotteries (with the notable exception of the official state lottery). This reflects a long-standing public policy against lotteries. *See, e.g.*, Phalen v. Virginia, 49 U.S. 163, 168 (1850) (describing lotteries as a "wide-spread pestilence" that "infests the whole community: it enters every dwelling; it reaches every class; it preys upon the hard earnings of the poor; it plunders the ignorant and simple."). The chief evil to be remedied by anti-lottery laws is "to prevent people from giving up money or money's worth in the hope that chance will make their investment profitable."

State law defines a lottery as: any scheme for the disposal of property by chance, among persons who have paid or promised to pay any valuable consideration for the chance of obtaining such property . . . upon any agreement, understanding or expectation that it is to be distributed or disposed of by lot or chance. CAL. PEN. CODE § 319. The essential elements of a lottery, therefore, are chance, consideration, and the prize.[4] If any one of the three elements is missing, the game or scheme at issue is not a lottery. Conducting a lottery or selling lottery tickets is a misdemeanor under state law.

Defendants concede that the elements of chance and prize are met. They argue instead that there is an absence of consideration: because they offer viewers a free alternative method of entry (that is, because viewers can enter online for free, rather than pay 99 cents per text message), there is no consideration and thus no lottery. Plaintiffs counter that because some viewers paid for the privilege of entering, the game is a lottery as to them, notwithstanding that other viewers entered for free.

Summarizing the "implicit holdings" of the leading lottery cases specifically on the question of consideration, the court in *People v. Shira* explained, in order for a promotional giveaway scheme to be legal any and all persons must be given a ticket free of charge and without any of them paying for the opportunity of a chance to win a prize. Conversely, a promotional scheme is illegal where any

---

[4] The three-element definition of lotteries is firmly established. Notwithstanding this well-worn definition, the Court is mindful of Chief Justice Warren's pertinent admonition: "So varied have been the techniques used by promoters to conceal the joint factors of prize, chance, and consideration, and so clever have they been in applying these techniques to feigned as well as legitimate business activities, that it has often been difficult to apply the decision of one case to the facts of another."

and all persons cannot participate in a chance for the prize and some of the participants who want a chance to win must pay for it. 62 Cal. App. 3d 442, 459 (1976). The critical factual distinction between cases in which a lottery was not found and those in which a lottery was found is that the former "involved promotional schemes by using prize tickets to increase the purchases of legitimate goods and services in the free market place" whereas in the latter "the game itself is the product being merchandised." *Id*; *see also* Haskell, 965 F. Supp at 1404 (stating the broad principle that "business promotions are not lotteries so long as tickets to enter are not conditioned upon a purchase."). The presence of a free alternative method of entry in the leading cases made it clear that the money customers paid was for the products purchased (gasoline or movie tickets), and not for the chance of winning a prize. The relevant question here, therefore, is whether the Games were nothing more than "organized scheme[s] of chance," in which payment was induced by the chance of winning a prize.

The relevant question is not, as Defendants contend, whether some people could enter for free. In [other cases], the courts concluded that those who made payments purchased something of equivalent value. The indiscriminate distribution of tickets to purchasers and non-purchasers alike was evidence thereof. Here, however, Defendants' offers of free alternative methods of entry do not alter the basic fact that viewers who sent in text messages paid only for the privilege of entering the Games. They received nothing of equivalent economic value in return. Accordingly, the Court finds that Plaintiffs have sufficiently alleged that Defendants conducted illegal lotteries as defined by California law.

2. Standing

[The court found that plaintiffs sufficiently alleged that the wrongful conduct took place in California.]

3. In Pari Delicto

Finally, Defendants argue that Plaintiffs' cases must be dismissed because of the doctrine of in pari delicto, which holds that "a plaintiff who has participated in wrongdoing may not recover damages from the wrongdoing." California courts, citing the long-standing public policy against gambling, have thus refused to adjudicate disputes arising out of "gambling contracts or transactions." In the instant case, however, Defendants and Plaintiffs are not in pari delicto, or "equally at fault."

Defendants are alleged to have violated the UCL by conducting lotteries, an activity expressly forbidden by California law. There is no equivalent legal wrong under California law of playing a lottery. Under state law, and as alleged in the Complaints, Defendants may be in delicto but there is no pari: Plaintiffs have committed no legal wrong by sending in their text message entries. Nor is this a case, like the long line of California cases establishing the doctrine, in which a wronged player seeks to recover a gaming debt. Instead, Plaintiffs seek declaratory judgments that the Games are illegal lotteries, injunctive relief against the continued operation of the Games, and restitution for amounts unlawfully collected. Rather than asking the Court to accept the legitimacy of a gaming activity by deciding a dispute arising out of the activity, Plaintiffs seek to stop the Games themselves. Accordingly, the Court finds that the doctrine of in pari delicto does not bar Plaintiffs' claims. . . .

[Claims under other states' consumer protection laws also survived.]

*NOTES AND QUESTIONS*

The problem here is that the producers added the ninety-nine cent fee to the text messages and pocketed that cash. If viewers' text message entries had only incurred whatever fees were charged by the consumer's wireless carrier and not also involved fees that went to the TV show's producers, then the defendants would have been in the clear because that would be analogous to requiring a self-addressed stamped envelope (which, after all, involves a payment to the U.S. Postal Service). Is this result consistent with the Indiana case earlier in this chapter absolving the NCAA of running an illegal lottery? The Indiana Supreme Court found that there were no real "winners" of the ticket distribution system, just some people who got tickets and other people who were refunded an equivalent amount of cash. Here, however, there were winners and losers—is that enough of a difference?

Do you agree with the court's reasoning that as long as some consumers are paying just for the chance to win, it is an illegal lottery, even though they could have avoided paying by going online? *See* Hardin v. NBC Universal, 283 Ga. 477 (2008) (text messaging fee was not consideration when there was an online alternate method of entry, and the evidence was that most people entered online). Note that in *Couch*, the court didn't discuss what the TV shows did to disclose the various means of entry and their disparate costs. Would disclosure alone be enough to protect consumers?

The parties ultimately settled the case. Consumers could obtain a refund of their text messaging fees, and the defendants agreed for five years not to "create, sponsor or operate any contest or sweepstakes, for which entrants are offered the possibility of winning a prize, in which people who enter via premium text message do not receive something of comparable value to the premium text message charge in addition to the entry." The class lawyers received over $5 million. *See* Couch v. Telescope Inc., et al., "American Idol Challenge" Settlement Website.

*Loot Boxes.* Many video games offer "loot boxes," where players pay real-world money (directly, or through the purchase of in-game virtual currency) to buy a randomized package of virtual items that may help with gameplay. The loot box purchase contains an element of surprise: some loot boxes will contain rare and valuable items, but others will contain items of lesser value. Players and regulators have claimed that such loot boxes constitute a "game of chance," while gamemakers have tried to sidestep such allegations by enhancing their disclosures and analogizing to other variable-value purchases like baseball trading cards.

### C.    Other Rules about Sweepstakes and Contests

*How To Formulate and Communicate the Sweepstakes or Contest Rules.* Advertising that allows consumers to enter a sweepstakes or contest must include the material terms or a cost-free means of obtaining the rules. Those rules must be fairly detailed: they should specify the entry method; the free alternate method of entry and that payment will not increase the chance of winning; how the winner will be selected; who is eligible (which can be based on classes of likely customers, including occupation or residency, and which should exclude those connected to the sponsor) and what they must do to claim prizes; key dates, including the dates for using an alternate means of entry; limits on entry (e.g., one per household, five entries per day); odds of winning (it's acceptable to say that those depend on the number of eligible entries, as long as that's true); other conditions ("while supplies last," "void where prohibited by law," and so on, including anything required by state law); total value of prizes; the sponsor's name and address; and the availability of a list of winners.

Though abbreviated disclosures are allowed in certain forms of advertising as long as the full rules are readily available, the short form description of the contest can't be materially misleading. For example, the Federal Communications Commission fined a Boston radio station $4,000 for promoting a contest as a chance to win a choice of one of three cars. The on-air announcements didn't explain that the winner only won a two-year lease, not full ownership. Moreover, the "winner" only got the lease if she passed a credit check. The fact that the official rules on the promotion's website disclosed all these terms was insufficient because these serious limits weren't broadcast. *In re Greater Boston Radio, Inc.*, FCC File No.: EB-08-IH-5305 (Feb. 28, 2013). However, in general, broadcasters can disclose material contest terms online rather than in their broadcasts, as long as the terms don't differ substantively from what's announced. *See* Amendment of Section 73.1216 of the Commission's Rules Related to Broadcast Licensee-Conducted Contests, 80 Fed. Reg. 64354 (2015).

Is this Twitter disclosure successful? What other information, if any, would you need to evaluate it?

Similar to other disclosures, less significant matters can be disclosed in the full rules. Among other things, the rules should specify what happens if something goes wrong—for example, if more prizes are won than the specified odds (which might happen if a printer makes an error in printing game pieces). The rules should also contemplate what happens if the promised prize isn't available, although advertisers often procure the prize before the sweepstakes or contest starts to ensure its availability to the winner.

Even if people exploit gaps in the official rules, the advertiser must honor its own rules. Food company Beatrice ran a sweepstakes that was "cracked" by one player who submitted 4,018 winning entries with a face value of more than $16 million. Beatrice ended the sweepstakes early when the player informed it of the vulnerability. The company ended up paying a settlement totaling $2 million to 2,400 sweepstakes players, plus an additional sum to the individual player, after a lawsuit for breach of contract. *Beatrice Mails First Checks from Game-Contest Lawsuit*, ASSOC. PRESS, Apr. 28, 1988.

If the advertiser plans to publicize the winners, then it should specify that entry constitutes consent to such publicity (see the section on the right of publicity in Chapter 13 for discussion of when written consent is required). It's fairly typical for advertisers to require a winner to sign documentation—including a publicity consent—after being chosen but before the prize is awarded, but such additional hurdles to receiving the prize should be disclosed in the rules. Some states also specifically regulate contests in which the winner's name or likeness will be publicized, and Tennessee expressly bans prizes contingent on publicity releases.

Various states have particular requirements for what must be in the rules and how they must be displayed, including such major markets as Florida, Massachusetts, New York, and Texas. Checking to ensure compliance with every state in which the contest is valid is therefore vital. Rules may need to be posted in retail outlets, or specific elements such as a description or value of the prizes or the geographic area of the contest must be posted. In order to make nationally acceptable materials, the advertiser may simply create point-of-sale displays with the full rules including every piece of information required anywhere. But there are still risks: Washington limits how often and for how long grocery stores may use sweepstakes, and Connecticut bans sweepstakes in certain stores.

Broadcast ads should include "no purchase necessary," information on where to obtain the full rules and an alternate means of entry, end date, any eligibility restrictions, and of course the ubiquitous "void where prohibited." Is this last requirement worth anything in avoiding deception? How are consumers to know where the contest is prohibited?

*Subject-Matter Specific Restrictions.* There are often specific restrictions for sweepstakes tied to specific products or services: 900 numbers (see the FTC publication Complying with the 900 Number Rule), alcoholic beverages, banking, dairy products, food retailers, insurance, gasoline and tobacco. Why do you think regulators targeted banking for specific restrictions? Perhaps it's reasonable to be concerned about encouraging consumers to use irrelevant reasons to choose financial products, but why worry about dairy products?

Many states also have extremely detailed regulations for promotions that require consumers to sit through a sales presentation to win or to have a chance to win. *See, e.g.*, TEX. BUS. & COMMERCE CODE, Title 13, ch. 621. Why would states conclude that consumers are particularly vulnerable in these circumstances?

Moreover, many states regulate specific types of prizes such as live animals and lottery tickets, or promotions in which all prizes might not be won. The IRS requires sponsors to report prizes worth a fair market value of $600 or more. 26 U.S.C. § 6041. Anti-gambling statutes may make a sweepstakes illegal if the number of prizes is dependent on the number of entrants, so the prizes should be fixed before the promotion begins.

Florida, New York, and Rhode Island (if local retail stores are involved) require advertisers to register the sweepstakes and submit the rules to the state in advance, and to post security when the total prize exceeds a low dollar value threshold. These are easy rules for marketers to miss! A list of winners must be filed to release the security; many other states also require lists of winners to be published and made available on request. Other states may require registration depending on the circumstances; for example, Arizona mandates it when proof of purchase is required for a skill contest. Several states have record retention requirements, and some treat the failure to award prizes—even if unclaimed—as unlawful. Some states allow the rules to state that "unclaimed prizes will not be awarded," but others explicitly require "second chance" random drawings.

Sweepstakes targeted at children raise additional issues. CARU, the children's arm of the Better Business Bureau that reviews children's advertising (performing the same function for such advertising as its sister the NAD does for general advertising), told Discovery Girls Magazine to change its advertising for a sweepstakes. The magazine, which is directed to children ages eight and up, required entrants to provide an email address and complete a survey with over 50 questions, many "personal in nature," in exchange for a chance to win an iPod Nano. The sweepstakes therefore collected personally identifiable information from children without first obtaining prior verifiable parental consent, in violation of COPPA (the Children's Online Privacy Protection Act) and of CARU's guidelines. In addition, the sweepstakes didn't clearly disclose the odds of winning. Discovery Girls Magazine agreed to modify its sweepstakes and advertising going forward. ASRC Press Release, *CARU Recommends Discovery Girls Magazine Modify Sweepstakes Advertising; Company Agrees to Do So*, Sept. 18, 2013.

Likewise, CARU acted against the Boy Scouts of America (now "Scouts BSA"), when its Boy's Life Magazine failed to include its "Many Will Enter, Five Will Win" odds statement in the magazine's ad announcing the contest. Even though the odds were disclosed prominently on the magazine's website, which was the only method of entry, CARU was concerned that a child looking at the magazine ad could develop an unrealistic expectation of winning the sweepstakes. Since the ad is usually the child's first contact with the sweepstakes, it was not sufficient to clear up confusion later on. As advertising lawyers commenting on the case observed, this result "emphasizes the importance for marketers and advertisers of properly drafting an abbreviated rules statement and including it in the promotional materials for the sweepstakes. Many companies fail to put an odds statement in abbreviated rules targeting child and adult audiences, even though many state laws (not just the CARU guidelines) specifically require the disclosure of this information in advertising." Maura Marcheski & Melissa Landau Steinman, *The Sweepstakes Games You Can't Afford to Lose*, ALL ABOUT ADVERT. L., Oct. 16, 2013.

And note that this discussion only applies to U.S. rules—an international contest would of course require compliance with still more rules. Canada, for example, technically prohibits sweepstakes, but allows promotions in which the winner is chosen at random but then required to demonstrate a skill. Thus, American sweepstakes that extend to Canada often impose an extra requirement that Canadian winners correctly answer a simple math question. Quebec requires the rules to be in French and that the sponsor have a local presence; many contests exclude Quebecois residents.

Other countries, such as India and Sweden, consider sweepstakes to be the same as lotteries and ban them unconditionally. A number of countries, including Argentina, France, Mexico, and Poland, require translation into a local language—even if the contest is run online from the U.S. Many countries specify the form and content of required disclosures, and may additionally regulate what kinds of personal information the marketer can ask for or what uses may be made of that information. Some common U.S. provisions—including publicity or liability releases, limitations on liability and forum selection clauses—may be unenforceable. Even including them in the rules may give rise to liability for unfair practices. Some countries (including the U.S.) tax prizes, while other countries, including Brazil, Mexico, and Spain, impose the taxes on the promoters themselves. Some require preregistration with local authorities, a local drawing and posting of security.

Illegal sweepstakes can subject marketers to civil and criminal liability, so it is worth taking the time to get this right. A lawyer should consider the countries important to the advertiser's strategy, as well as its appetite for risk.

*After the Contest Ends.* When the contest ends, the legal work is not yet over. The sponsor must give away all the prizes. Ideally, every winner should sign an affirmation of eligibility, publicity release, and release of liability before receiving a prize, a requirement which of course should previously have been disclosed in the official rules. The sponsor must file a 1099-MISC tax form for anyone receiving prizes worth at least $600. The sponsor should publish a winners list on its website and send the list to any states in which it was registered. The winners list and related records should be retained for at least 90 days, though two years is a better practice.

### D.    Direct Mail Advertising of Sweepstakes and Contests

The Deceptive Mail Prevention and Enforcement Act of 1999 governs solicitations sent through the mail. 39 U.S.C. 3001 et seq. It requires clear and conspicuous disclosure of the estimated odds of winning; the quantity, estimated retail value, and nature of each prize; the schedule of prize payments if payments are made over time; and the name and address of the sweepstakes sponsor. Official contest rules and entry procedures must also be included. In addition, a statement that no purchase is necessary and a statement that making a purchase won't increase the odds of winning must be foregrounded further: they must be disclosed clearly and conspicuously in the mailing itself, in the rules that are the part of the mailing, and on the order or entry form. The mailing may not claim that individuals who don't make a purchase may be disqualified from receiving further sweepstakes mailings or that the individual is a winner unless that's true. The Act also requires a name removal notification system by which anyone's name and address can be removed from the mailing list by request through a toll-free number or address within forty-five days of the request.

The Act prohibits, among other things: claims that people are winners unless they've actually won prizes; purchase requirements; the use of fake checks that don't clearly state that they are non-negotiable and have no cash value; and seals, names or terms that imply an affiliation with or endorsement by the federal government. For skill contests, the Act also requires clear and conspicuous disclosure of the rules and conditions, including the judging methods and identity of judges, the value of the prizes, the maximum cost to enter all rounds or levels, how many rounds of the contest are required to win the grand prize, the number or percentage of entrants correctly solving the sponsor's past three skill contests, and the time frame for the winner to be determined.

Consider the following ad:

Does it adequately disclose that the recipient is not yet a winner? The FTC considered that the small print disclaimers about the odds were irrelevant because the larger print was a message that person actually won. Indeed, many consumers sought to claim their prize at Fowlerville Ford, only to be met with a sales pitch.

The Deceptive Mail Prevention and Enforcement Act does not apply to sweepstakes and skill contests which are not directed to a specific named individual or which do not include an opportunity to order a product or service (e.g., magazine subscriptions). Numerous states also regulate sweepstakes and contest disclosures, in much the same vein.

The Telemarketing Sales Rule covers prize promotions made on the phone, requiring disclosure of the odds, the fact that purchase is not required, and other conditions on receiving the prize.

Despite the extensive, contest-specific regulation, general consumer protection laws still apply. In the following case, the plaintiff had standing under California's consumer protection laws.

*Haskell v. Time, Inc., 965 F. Supp. 1398 (E.D. Cal. 1997)*

Plaintiff Eben Haskell, on behalf of himself and the general public of California, seeks to enjoin various statements made by defendants in their magazine sweepstakes solicitations. . . .

I. Factual and Procedural Background. . . .

The facts are largely undisputed. Defendants are in the business of selling magazine and book subscriptions. Each company sends out millions of mailings containing product offers and sweepstakes opportunities to households across the United States. Each defendant's sweepstakes bulletins are similar in content and format. The bulletins proclaim enthusiastically, but tautologically, that the recipient is the winner, if the recipient has and returns the winning entry. The official rules of the sweepstakes accompany each bulletin. The majority of recipients do not respond to the mailings; of those who do respond, only a minority purchase any products.

The defendants readily agree to plaintiff's claim that they send additional bulletins to recipients who have responded to earlier mailings by purchasing products. Defendants assert that this is no more than common sense marketing. Repeat customers receive multiple bulletins that contain further sweepstakes opportunities and product offers. These bulletins may also include an announcement that the customer has qualified for membership into a "V.I.P. Club" or other preferred-customer group. Whether addressed to customers who have purchased in the past or to prospective customers, follow-up mailings may also contain a reminder that failure to enter results in forfeiture of the opportunity to win the sweepstakes, and a reminder that because mailing costs are high, a failure to enter the sweepstakes or purchase products may result in the customer's name being dropped from the mailing list.

Plaintiff argues that these practices—particularly the repeat mailings to customers—violate State lottery and unfair business practices laws by leading customers to believe that they must purchase products to enter the sweepstakes, obtain additional entries, or receive preferred-customer benefits. Plaintiff recognizes that none of the defendants conditions sweepstakes entry on a purchase and none of the defendants promises that a purchase will lead to additional mailings, entries, or other opportunities or benefits. Undaunted, plaintiff advances a new theory in the amended complaint, a theory developed particularly to fit the case of recipients who become obsessed with playing the sweepstakes. According to plaintiff, repeat customers come to learn that if they order, they will receive further mailings, with additional entries and preferred-customer opportunities. Once they realize this cause and effect relationship, plaintiff contends that repeat customers in effect are in the same position as if defendants conditioned entry, chances, or preferred-customer opportunities on a purchase.

II. Illegal Lotteries . . .

Plaintiff claims that defendants' sweepstakes violate criminal statutes outlawing certain lotteries. . . .

B. Are the Sweepstakes Illegal Lotteries?

Three elements must be present to constitute a lottery: prize, chance, and consideration. If any of these elements is missing, the game is not an illegal lottery. It is undisputed that defendants' sweepstakes contain an element of chance and that prizes are awarded. The issue presented in this case is whether defendants' repeat mailings amount to a requirement that consumers pay valuable consideration to obtain entries for the contests.

1. Purchase required to receive "extra" chances.

Plaintiff contends that by sending more sweepstakes entries—with solicitations to subscribe—to past customers, defendants lead these customers to believe that they can "purchase" more entries by purchasing more magazines.[9] Plaintiff argues for a theory of what may be termed de facto consideration based on consumer experience. The consideration is "de facto" because there is no promise by the sweepstakes operator to send an entry upon a further magazine order and there is no right in the recipient to insist on a further entry. There is simply a subjective expectation based on past practice.

Plaintiff's theory of de facto consideration is not part of California law, certainly not California criminal law. . . .

A penal statute is strictly construed. The lottery statute makes it a crime if the operator of the lottery promises a chance in return for some benefit. Absent a promise, whether explicit or implicit, there is no consideration. Without such a promise by the lottery operator, the player has not paid "any valuable consideration for the chance." To adopt plaintiff's theory of de facto consideration would be to criminalize the widespread and fairly unremarkable marketing practice of targeting for repeat future mailings those recipients who have ordered in the past. . . .

Here, each defendant's official rules state that no purchase is necessary to enter or win. There is no insinuation that a purchase will enhance one's chances of winning. . . . Plaintiff admits that only a minority of people who receive sweepstakes bulletins even enter the contest, and that of this group of entrants, only a much smaller minority of entrants purchase a product when they enter the contest. Recipients understand that no purchase is required to enter.
Furthermore, plaintiff's theory also stumbles because the purchase of a product is not the only way a recipient can obtain additional chances. [The defendants offered alternate means of entry, and targeted those who entered without ordering for future mailings.] . . .

Finally, the factual setting here is significant. Defendants operate nationwide sweepstakes involving literally hundreds of millions of mailings and entries. The entries are widely distributed. Multiple entries also are widely available. In these circumstances the sweepstakes at issue here do not fit within the scope of the lottery statute merely because some customers come to believe that they may enhance their chances of receiving further solicitations if they purchase a product. . . .

### D. AFP's "Prompt-Pay" Sweepstakes

In Count 9 of the amended complaint against AFP, plaintiff alleges that AFP's "Prompt-Pay" sweepstakes, another customer-only contest, is an illegal lottery because payment by a certain date is a requirement for eligibility. Customers receive an entry invitation for the Prompt-Pay sweepstakes with their invoices for AFP subscriptions. The invitation explains that if the customer

---

[9] It is undisputed that defendants particularly target past customers for further mailings. . . .

pays the bill by a certain date, the customer will be automatically entered into a special $100,000 sweepstakes. The invitation also includes the official rules for the Prompt-Pay sweepstakes. The rules state that "[n]o new purchase is required to enter. You are eligible only if you have subscribed and agreed to pay prior to the date you received this sweepstakes offer."

AFP's order forms do not indicate a payment deadline but do offer a "4-step easy pay plan" by which a customer need only "pay 1/4 each month." It appears that AFP may intend that customers will begin to pay for their subscriptions one month after ordering a magazine. If the invoice's request for payment by a certain date is for an earlier date than the one-month time frame, then the invoice could create a new obligation such that the recipients' prompt payment could constitute consideration for entry into the prompt pay sweepstakes. If, however, the payment deadline is sometime after one month has passed, then AFP is only asking that customers fulfill their pre-existing obligations to AFP. Acceding to this request would not constitute consideration.

It is unclear from the record whether the requested payment date is less than one month from the date of order. On the current record, the court cannot determine whether the Prompt-Pay sweepstakes imposes a new obligation on potential entrants and requires contestants to pay something to enter. Summary judgment is denied.

### III. Unfair Business Practices Act Claims

A. Reasonable Consumer Standard

Plaintiff's remaining claims are brought under the Business and Professions Code. To survive summary judgment, plaintiff must prove that defendants' statements are misleading to a reasonable consumer. . . .

Furthermore, anecdotal evidence alone is insufficient to prove that the public is likely to be misled. Thus, to prevail, plaintiff must demonstrate by extrinsic evidence, such as consumer survey evidence, that the challenged statements tend to mislead consumers. *See* Johnson & Johnson-Merck Consumer Pharmaceuticals Co. v. Smithkline Beecham Corp., 960 F.2d 294, 297, 298 (2d Cir.1992). In *Merck*, the court concluded that a plaintiff must demonstrate that "a statistically significant part of the commercial audience holds the false belief allegedly communicated by the challenged advertisement" to state a cognizable claim. As discussed below, plaintiff fails to meet this evidentiary burden.

*The Allegations*

Plaintiff's main allegations under §§ 17200 and 17500 relate to defendants' "threats" of forfeiture of sweepstakes entries and defendants' statements that customers receive "extra" chances.

The forfeiture statements warn potential sweepstakes participants that unless the entry is returned on time, the holder of the numbers contained in that entry cannot claim the prize should one of those numbers turn out to be the winning number. Plaintiff claims that defendants mislead consumers by implying that if a participant does not return an entry, all previous entries will also be forfeited. Plaintiff relies on statements such as:

> [Y]our life will be filled with exciting new possibilities if you return the grand prize winning entry. But let me give you fair warning: if you fail to return an entry, there is no way you can win the $1,666,675.00. In fact if you hold the Grand Prize winning entry and fail to respond, you will FORFEIT the $1,666,675.00! And then, we'll have no choice but to award the prize money to someone else! so return your entry as soon as possible.

> As you can see from the enclosed NOTICE OF FORFEITURE made out to [recipient's name], if your entry doesn't make it on time we'll have no choice but to void the assigned numbers— and that means you'll automatically forfeit all prize money any of your Guaranteed Finalist numbers may have won. And as much as we'd like to, we can't make any exceptions even for folks like you who enter regularly. . . .

Neither of these bulletins ever refers to past entries. They are not reasonably understood as suggesting that past entries will be forfeited should the consumer choose not to return the current entries. Even if it were possible to interpret the language as plaintiff suggests, plaintiff has failed to meet his evidentiary burden.

Plaintiff relies only on the declarations of a few sweepstakes customers and the declaration of one professor of rhetoric. Plaintiff provides no consumer survey evidence indicating that a significant portion of the population has been misled by defendants' bulletins. Indeed, plaintiff does not dispute that a majority of recipients neither respond to defendants' bulletins nor purchase any of defendants' products. Plaintiff has therefore failed to prove that defendants' statements mislead the reasonable consumer. Summary judgment on the forfeiture claims is therefore appropriate.

Plaintiff also claims that defendant AFP's "drop notices" mistakenly lead customers to believe that they must purchase products in order to avoid being dropped from defendants' mailing lists. Plaintiff relies on statements such as:

> We really regret it but we simply cannot afford to keep on writing to groups of people who never buy magazines. If you do not order now, or write to stay on our list, you may be among the first to go. Those who are dropped now will miss out—there's no guarantee of another chance for them.

> Mailing costs have skyrocketed. . . . Names must be cut from our regular mailing list. Groups of people who do not order will be the first to go.

> With costs rising as they are we must restrict our best offerings to groups of people who buy magazines. We're sorry to have to say so, but—if you do not order this time or write to stay on our list, you may find yourself excluded from the most rewarding opportunities in our history. Don't let your name be dropped. An order right now will keep your name on our regular mailing list.

A reasonable consumer would not conclude from these statements that a purchase is required to continue receiving AFP's mailings. Both examples clearly state that a consumer may write to AFP and request to remain on the mailing list. And again, even if it were possible to conclude that one's name will be dropped from the mailing list if one does not purchase a product, plaintiff has provided insufficient evidence that reasonable consumers would be misled by the statements.

Finally, plaintiff also claims that defendants' statements that repeat customers receive "preferences" and "extra" chances are misleading in that they lead customers to believe that by purchasing products, they are increasing their chances of winning the sweepstakes. This is an argument in the alternative to plaintiff's claim that defendants' sweepstakes are illegal lotteries because customers in fact are treated preferentially by receiving repeat mailings. Plaintiff here relies on statements such as:

> . . . Because you've been loyal to the company and displayed a faith and trust in our products through the years, we want to show our loyalty to you. As a way of expressing our thanks, we gave preference to [your] name to pass through the initial stages of the Sweepstakes.

The next page of this bulletin states that the odds of winning the Grand Prize in this sweepstakes are approximately one in 213,500,000. The statement's reference to "preference" is entirely vague. Nothing specific is offered. The statement as to preference is a meaningless form of puffing. Given the remote odds of winning, no reasonable person would rely on this vacuous language to conclude that by purchasing products, one may substantially increase one's odds of winning the sweepstakes.

Plaintiff also relies on statements such as:

> And thanks to your recent entry, you're getting this extra opportunity for a better-than-most shot at winning. With this FINAL ROUND ENTRY, you can activate not 1 . . . not 10 . . . but 20 SuperPrize Numbers to DOUBLE YOUR CHANCES to win $10,000,000.00 from this Bulletin!

> All it takes to instantly Double Your Chances is a timely entry. When you select any of our un beatable [sic] deals, affix the special seal to your Double Your Chances Order Certificate and we'll immediately double your 10 SuperPrize Numbers to 20—giving you double the chance of winning! Of course, no purchase is ever necessary to enter or win. So if not ordering this time, be sure to follow the directions on the Non-Order Entry Certificate to get all 20 of your SuperPrize Numbers in the running.

This statement states only that the recipient of the bulletin has received an "extra opportunity" to enter because of a prior entry, not a prior purchase. Furthermore, the bulletin expressly states that no purchase is necessary to activate all 20 SuperPrize Numbers. Thus, no reasonable person would conclude that a purchase is a required prerequisite for receiving "extra" chances. And, again, plaintiff has provided insufficient evidence to prevail under the reasonable consumer standard.

For the reasons given above, defendants' motions for summary judgment on plaintiffs' claims under Sections 17200 and 17500 of the California Unfair Business Practices Act are therefore granted.

C. Defendants' Distribution of Entries

. . . [P]laintiff's claim that defendants' statements that "No Purchase Is Necessary" to win are misleading is wholly unsupported by the evidence. Plaintiff has failed to provide any evidence that reasonable consumers are misled by the statement that "No Purchase Is Necessary" to win and has also failed to provide any evidence that defendants' statement is false. Indeed, as discussed in section II.B. above, no one is required to purchase any of defendants' products in order to win any sweepstakes prize.[15] Defendants' motions for summary judgment on plaintiff's eighth cause of action are therefore granted. . . .

*NOTES AND QUESTIONS*

The influence of years of lawsuits and regulations can be seen in the wording of the promotions at issue here. Is this a sign that the regulations have finally produced non-misleading contests? Note that the court did refuse to dismiss the complaint with respect to one of the promotions at issue. Even an experienced advertiser has to be very careful to comply with all of the rules put in place to deter abuses.

As the opinion notes, customer-only sweepstakes are generally legal, but they must be clearly restricted to people who are already paying customers as of the date the promotion is first advertised. If the promotion stays open, then people might pay in order to participate—unlawful consideration.

Even if the promotion is clear that no consideration is required, it might still be misleading for other reasons. In *Freeman v. Time, Inc.*, 68 F.3d 285 (9th Cir. 1995), Freeman received computer-personalized mailers announcing the "Million Dollar Dream Sweepstakes" as part of ads for various Time publications. The mailers had statements in large type that Freeman had won the sweepstakes, qualified by language in smaller type indicating that Freeman would win only if he returned a winning prize number, for example: "If you return the grand prize winning number, we'll officially announce that MICHAEL FREEMAN HAS WON $1,666,675.00 AND PAYMENT IS SCHEDULED TO BEGIN." It continued, "If you return the grand prize winning entry, we'll say $1,666,675.00 WINNER MICHAEL FREEMAN OF ENCINO, CALIFORNIA IS OUR LARGEST MAJOR PRIZE WINNER!" And then: "We are now scheduled to begin payment of the third and largest prize—the $1,666,675 listed next to the name MICHAEL FREEMAN! In fact, arrangements have already been made which make it possible to begin payment of the $1,666,675 DIRECTLY to MICHAEL FREEMAN if one of your numbers is the grand prize winner." Finally: "[i]f you return your entry with the Validation Seal attached and your entry includes the grand prize winning number, MICHAEL FREEMAN IS GUARANTEED TO BE PAID THE ENTIRE $1,666,675.00!" . . .

---

[15] The winners of million-dollar prizes of defendants' sweepstakes are often not purchasers. *E.g.*, Time Undisputed Fact 32; PCH Mem. at 10 (eighteen of twenty-three $1 million prizes since 1986 have been awarded to people whose entries were not accompanied by an order).

The question was whether members of the public would be likely to be deceived by these mailings. Here, "the mailings were sent to millions of persons and there is no allegation that a particularly vulnerable group was targeted." Freeman argued that readers were likely to read only the large print, but the court was not persuaded. "The promotions expressly and repeatedly state the conditions which must be met in order to win. None of the qualifying language is hidden or unreadably small. The qualifying language appears immediately next to the representations it qualifies and no reasonable reader could ignore it. Any persons who thought that they had won the sweepstakes would be put on notice that this was not guaranteed simply by doing sufficient reading to comply with the instructions for entering the sweepstakes." In addition, with respect to Freeman's Consumer Legal Remedies Act claim, which has as an element that the plaintiff must have suffered damage, the court expressed doubt that he qualified: the only possible damage was "a de minimis 29¢ for postage to mail in his entry."

If Freeman approached you, would you have represented him in this claim? In other words, was the disclosure here obviously sufficient to avoid deceiving a reasonable consumer?

Have major advertisers sufficiently absorbed the relevant principles about proper disclosure? State attorneys general in recent years have reached some major settlements, including with the successful defendants above. In 2000, Time settled lawsuits by the AGs of forty-eight states and the District of Columbia, agreeing to pay over $4.9 million for past conduct and to include clear and conspicuous disclosures of the odds of winning its contests, the fact that no purchase is necessary, and the fact that purchase will not improve the odds of winning. A year later, Publishers Clearinghouse agreed to a $34 million multistate settlement incorporating similar provisions and, in addition, requiring it to create safeguards to protect especially vulnerable consumers. Publishers Clearinghouse was required to review the accounts of consumers who made frequent purchases and eliminate from its mailing list those who were determined to be confused or disoriented or to make excessive purchases. *See* State of Connecticut Attorney General's Office, *Ct. Reaches Unprecedented $34 Million Settlement with Publishers Clearinghouse*. Why might the AGs have brought the suits if the disclosures were already in the form described in the previous cases? Who has the right idea about what a "reasonable consumer" would be thinking?

Consider also the following case, where the advertiser relied on the inattention and inaction of consumers and the state stepped in.

*State v. Imperial Marketing, 203 W.Va. 203 (1998)*

. . . I. PROCEDURAL HISTORY

Suarez Corporation Industries, located in Canton, Ohio, and its affiliated enterprises are in the business of selling consumer goods, such as simulated jewelry, through the use of direct mail marketing solicitations. Many solicitations were sent by Suarez to West Virginia residents prior to the institution of this action in 1994. . . .

Specifically, the Attorney General instituted this action in the Circuit Court of Kanawha County against numerous defendants, including Suarez, alleging that the solicitation activities of the defendants constituted multiple transgressions of the West Virginia Consumer Credit and Protection Act and, particularly, the Prizes and Gifts Act contained therein. . . . Ultimately, the litigation focused upon three specific marketing efforts of Suarez involving several thousand West Virginia consumers. [Editor's note: We omit discussion of two of the promotions.]

. . . With regard to the second solicitation, consumers were notified that they had been awarded a cash prize of "as much as $1,000." The consumers were also told, however, that the prize had been placed in a five-piece clutch purse ensemble which could be purchased for $12, plus $2 for special packaging and insurance. The solicitation indicated that "priority handling" would be afforded to consumers purchasing the purse ensemble. If consumers desired the cash prize without purchasing the purse ensemble, consumers were required to follow a [convoluted] claim procedure . . . .[6]

. . . Subsequently, on April 25, 1997, the circuit court entered the final order permanently enjoining Suarez from violating the West Virginia Consumer Credit and Protection Act and the Prizes and Gifts Act. . . . As the final order stated, the evidence established that the solicitations "were actually misleading by virtue of material misrepresentations made, and that they exceed acceptable standards and practices allowing a certain degree of puffing in respect to sales transactions." . . .

This appeal followed. . . .

III. THE PERMANENT INJUNCTION

. . . "The West Virginia Prizes and Gifts Act, was designed by the West Virginia Legislature to assist in protecting West Virginia citizens from being victimized by misleading and deceptive practices when a seller is attempting to market a product using a prize or gift as an inducement."

. . . As W. Va. Code, 46A-6D-3(a) [1992], concerning having won a prize or gift, provides in part:

> [A] person may not, in connection with the sale or lease or solicitation for the sale or lease of goods, property or service, represent that another person has won anything of value or is the winner of a contest, unless all of the following conditions are met:

---

[6] The record contains the following instructions for claiming the cash prize without purchasing the five-piece clutch purse ensemble:

> If not ordering and to claim your cash prize only, cut out and affix the prize confirmation code located on the front [of] the Declaration of Cash Prize form to a 3-1/2 x 5-1/2 inch index card with your name, address and phone number and insert all into your own # 10 white envelope. Failure to follow these instructions will cause forfeiture of your cash prize. Mail to Bulk-Sort Center . . . to claim your cash prize. Do not use the enclosed envelope that is for ordering only, or your cash prize and status as an eligible finalist will be waived. Since we will be required to remove your check from the purse if not ordering, we are required to give priority handling to those who accept the purse.

The record indicates that in almost no circumstances did the cash prize exceed a nominal amount.

(1) The recipient of the prize, gift or item of value is given the prize, gift or item of value without obligation; and

(2) The prize, gift or item of value is delivered to the recipient at no expense to him or her, within ten days of the representation.

Moreover, as W. Va. Code, 46A-6D-4(a) [1992], concerning eligibility to receive a prize or gift, provides:

A person may not represent that another person is eligible or has a chance to win or to receive a prize, gift or item of value without clearly and conspicuously disclosing on whose behalf the contest or promotion is conducted, as well as all material conditions which a participant must satisfy. In an oral solicitation all material conditions shall be disclosed prior to requesting the consumer to enter into the sale or lease. Additionally, in any written material covered by this section, each of the following shall be clearly and prominently disclosed:

(1) Immediately adjacent to the first identification of the prize, gift or item of value to which it relates; or

(2) In a separate section entitled "Consumer Disclosure" which title shall be printed in no less than ten-point bold-face type and which section shall contain only a description of the prize, gift or item of value and the disclosures outlined in paragraphs (i), (ii) and (iii) of this subdivision:

(i) The true retail value of each item or prize;

(ii) The actual number of each item, gift or prize to be awarded; and

(iii) The odds of receiving each item, gift or prize.

. . . Although ostensibly requiring no purchase or obligation, the solicitations under consideration, while suggesting a certain mutability on the surface, possess a persistent deceptive quality beneath. . . .

[C]onsumers were notified that they had been awarded a cash prize of "as much as $1,000." The consumers were also told, however, that the prize had been placed in a five-piece clutch purse ensemble which could be purchased for $12, plus $2 for special packaging and insurance. The solicitation indicated that "priority handling" would be afforded to consumers purchasing the purse ensemble. If consumers desired the cash prize without purchasing the purse ensemble, consumers were required to follow a [convoluted] claim procedure . . . . Thus, the violation of W. Va. Code, 46A-6D-3(a) [1992], i.e., that the recipient of a prize or gift must be given the prize or gift "without obligation" and that it be delivered to the recipient "at no expense," is evidenced by the following language of the clutch purse solicitation:

As a guaranteed cash prize winner, the 5 piece Givone Clutch Purse Ensemble holding your check will be transferred to you when you cover the sponsor's special publicity discount fee of just $12, plus $2 for special packaging and insurance. * * * Remember, since the checks will already be in the purses, we are required by the sponsor's rules to give priority handling to those who are able to accept entitlement to their purse by submitting the minimum fee.

. . . During the course of this litigation, both the Attorney General and Suarez elicited the testimony of various consumers before the circuit court concerning the solicitations. Whereas the witnesses for the State indicated that the true import of the solicitations was difficult to grasp and that they had experienced a certain degree of bureaucratic hubris in their communications with Suarez, the witnesses called by Suarez suggested that the solicitations were quite clear and that their dealings with Suarez were satisfactory. The futility of that type of extrinsic evidence in cases of this nature, however, is evidenced by the fact that, during a one year period only, more than 17,000 West Virginia consumers received solicitations from Suarez or its affiliated enterprises. Rather, under the circumstances of this action, and in view of the solicitations described above, this Court is of the opinion that the testimony of the consumers failed to establish a genuine issue of material fact within the meaning of Rule 56. As the final order of April 25, 1997, stated: "It is irrelevant, however, that there are some West Virginia consumers who are satisfied with their merchandise. The issue is: whether defendant, in its solicitation efforts in West Virginia . . . engaged in conduct which is calculated to or likely to, deceive and misrepresent the offer, and thereby violate [West Virginia law]." . . .

[The court upheld a requirement that defendant offer refunds to customers without requiring them to return the merchandise they had received, but set aside a $500,000 penalty that would be imposed if defendants didn't comply. The concurring opinion, directly below, suggested that given the facts it recited, such a penalty would be appropriate if the district court explained its award more clearly.]

STARCHER, Justice, concurring:

. . . I write to make clear that the permanent injunction against Suarez and the award of relief to West Virginia consumers is warranted, not only because of these three solicitations, but also because of the dozens of other solicitations entered into the record by the Attorney General. Seventeen Suarez solicitations were attached to one pleading alone.

Simply put, each of these solicitations contains language clearly violating the Consumer Credit and Protection Act and the Prizes and Gifts Act. I was unable to count the number of times the phrases "Official Prize Claim Notice," "Winners Certification Claim Form," or "Cash Prize Release Document" were used. Each solicitation began by telling the consumer that he or she was a winner— but buried in the fine print, or on another letter in the envelope, was the hint they really weren't a big winner after all. Therefore, many of the solicitations violate W. Va. Code, 46A-6D-3 [1992], which prohibits persons from making representations that someone has won a prize unless that prize is awarded to the consumer without obligation and delivered within 10 days of the representation.

Another problem with the solicitations in the record is that, while every solicitation carried the disclaimer "no purchase necessary," every solicitation also carried the suggestion the recipient was more likely to be a winner or would get their prize faster if they first bought some merchandise. W. Va. Code, 46A-6D-4(c) [1992] prohibits persons from making representations that as a condition of receiving a prize, the consumer must pay money or purchase, lease or rent goods or services.

Another example is a solicitation that tells the consumer that they have won a "4-Door Chevrolet Caprice, Model Year 1995 if your Vehicle Award Claim is confirmed as a winning claim"—and attached is a note entitling the consumer to three "Bonus Awards" "worth up to $300." As discussed in the majority opinion, the use of the vague language "worth up to" is a clear violation of the Consumer Credit and Protection Act. *See* W. Va. Code, 46A-6D-4(a)(2)(i) [1992] (written sweepstakes materials must contain "[t]he true retail value of each item or prize").

The record also contains a solicitation from the "tie-breaker supervisor" of the "Payables Desk, Department of Sweepstakes Administration" which tells the recipient that he or she is "tied" with other individuals to win a cash prize—without telling the reader the odds of winning, that is, how many other people the reader was "tied" with. This solicitation was likely drafted by someone who full-well knew the language was misleading, but thought it could later be argued that it "technically" was within the bounds of every consumer protection statute in the country. On the contrary, because the solicitation is misleading on its face, and because it fails to state the odds the consumer has of winning the sweepstakes, it violates West Virginia's consumer protection laws. *See* W. Va. Code, 46A-6D-4(a)(2)(iii) [1992] (written sweepstakes materials must contain "[t]he odds of receiving each item, gift or prize"). . . .

*NOTES AND QUESTIONS*

Among other problems with the advertiser's conduct, the Federal Trade Commission has done some research indicating that consumers generally ignore the "up to" part of an "up to X" claim. *See FTC Report: Many Consumers Believe "Up To" Claims Promise Maximum Results*, June 29, 2012.

Go back and review the earlier cases finding that no reasonable consumer would misunderstand the defendants' solicitations. What are the key differences between the solicitations in this case and those found acceptable in the previous California cases? The acceptable solicitations used all-caps and other attention-getting mechanisms to suggest that recipients were already winners or would get more chances to win by buying—how much more did they do to correct any potential misunderstandings than the defendants in the West Virginia case?

Note also the multiple provisions of the law at issue. Each type of offer triggers specific disclosure requirements, and as the concurrence emphasizes, conduct that pushes multiple legal boundaries can collectively add up to convince a court of an advertiser's deceptive intent.

E.     **Externalities of Contests**

Promotions can occasionally run the risk of generating claims for ordinary negligence. In *Weirum v. RKO General, Inc.*, 539 P.2d 36 (Cal. 1975), a radio station "with an extensive teenage audience" held a contest where prizes went to the first person to locate a mobile disc jockey driving a conspicuous car and then fulfill another condition such as answering a question. The radio station periodically broadcast information about his location and intended destination. Two minors in separate cars failed to win the prize in one location and then tried to follow the DJ's car to the next location, jockeying for position at speeds up to 80 miles per hour. One of them (it wasn't clear which one) negligently forced a car off the highway, killing the driver. While one stopped to report the accident, the other stopped only momentarily, kept up the pursuit, and collected a cash prize from the DJ.

The jury found that the radio station was liable for the death, and the California Supreme Court affirmed the verdict. The court emphasized the excitement the station tried to generate with announcements such as "9:30 and The Real Don Steele is back on his feet again with some money and he is headed for the Valley. Thought I would give you a warning so that you can get your kids out of the street." The key question was whether the station owed any duty to the driver from broadcasting the contest, and the answer was found in the principle that people must use ordinary care to prevent others from being injured as a result of their conduct. Foreseeability was the essential factual question, and the record supported the jury's finding:

> These tragic events unfolded in the middle of a Los Angeles summer, a time when young people were free from the constraints of school and responsive to relief from vacation tedium. Seeking to attract new listeners, [the station] devised an "exciting" promotion. Money and a small measure of momentary notoriety awaited the swiftest response. It was foreseeable that defendant's youthful listeners, finding the prize had eluded them at one location, would race to arrive first at the next site and in their haste would disregard the demands of highway safety.

> Indeed, [the DJ] testified that he had in the past noticed vehicles following him from location to location. He was further aware that the same contestants sometimes appeared at consecutive stops.

The intervening negligence of the contestants didn't preclude liability for the station: the likelihood that contestants would react in this way was exactly what made the station's actions negligent. The court rejected the argument that imposing liability on the station would lead to advertisers' liability to people who were trampled in a rush to get to a sale (something that has, more recently, occurred numerous times at post-Thanksgiving Black Friday sales). The court said that

> [t]he giveaway contest was no commonplace invitation to an attraction available on a limited basis. It was a competitive scramble in which the thrill of the chase to be the one and only victor was intensified by the live broadcasts which accompanied the pursuit. In the assertedly analogous situations described by defendant, any haste involved in the purchase of the commodity is an incidental and unavoidable result of the scarcity of the commodity itself. In such situations there is no attempt, as here, to generate a competitive pursuit on public streets, accelerated by repeated importuning by radio to be the very first to arrive at a particular destination. Manifestly the "spectacular" bears little resemblance to daily commercial activities.

The court further commented that the station "could have accomplished its objectives of entertaining its listeners and increasing advertising revenues by adopting a contest format which would have avoided danger to the motoring public."

*NOTES AND QUESTIONS*

What kinds of contest formats would generate similar excitement and entertainment without creating the same risks?

Suppose your client wants to hold a Black Friday sale that includes live tweeting by salespeople and a Twitter hashtag for shoppers to use as well in order to generate "buzz" for the sale. Would this be the kind of "live broadcast" that risked liability under *Weirum*? In an age in which it seems that almost everyone records themselves and reports their activities in real time, is it foreseeable that people will behave badly in pursuit of *any* highly desirable good that's only available in limited quantities and for a short time?

*Publishers' House Rules.*

In addition to the legal requirements, promotions must also satisfy any house rules set by publishers. For example, all the major television networks have their own disclosure policies, though these house rules largely track the legal requirements for contests. Facebook has a well-known restriction that "Personal Timelines and friend connections must not be used to administer promotions (ex: 'share on your Timeline to enter' or 'share on your friend's Timeline to get additional entries', and 'tag your friends in this post to enter' are not permitted)."

How do contests differ from other forms of promotion using social media? Consider the following picture, showing an offer of free food for various social media–related activities:

[photo by Will Bachman, 2012]

681

How would the FTC analyze this under the endorsement guidelines discussed in Chapter 13? What about trademark law: suppose Twitter wants to charge a licensing fee for the use of its name in this way and claims that unauthorized uses cause confusion?

When we think about the advertising industry, we usually focus on advertisers and consumers. After
all, the whole point of advertising is for advertisers to change consumer behavior.

However, the advertising industry comprises numerous intermediaries who facilitate
communications between advertisers and consumers. Consider how a broadcast advertisement
reaches a consumer:

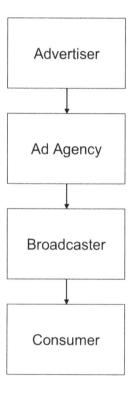

In this situation, an advertiser retains an advertising agency to help the advertiser prepare the
advertisement. On the advertiser's behalf, the advertising agency then enters into contracts with
broadcasters (such as TV or radio stations) to run the ad. After delivering the ad to the broadcaster,
the broadcaster airs the ad to its audience.

Not infrequently, an ad campaign involves many more intermediaries. Consider, for example, a
newspaper coupon distribution:

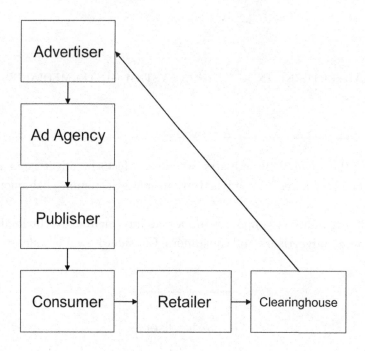

The advertiser and ad agency prepare the ad copy, place it with a newspaper or other coupon distributor, and then a consumer will clip it. A consumer redeems the coupon at a retailer, who typically tenders the coupon to a clearinghouse that will verify the coupon's authenticity (and police for coupon fraud) and pay retailers on behalf of the advertiser. The advertiser then settles up with the clearinghouse.

Or consider the possible intermediaries involved in an email campaign:

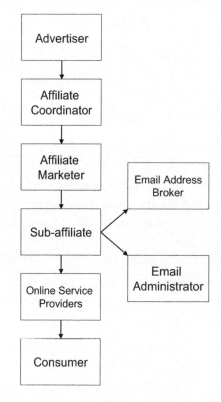

An advertiser may want to generate new registrants for the advertiser's website. The advertiser may approach an intermediate service provider who coordinates promotional opportunities for affiliate marketers seeking payment opportunities. The service provider can notify these affiliate marketers of the advertiser's opportunity. Participating affiliate marketers may send emails to promote the advertiser or run ads through different websites. The ads may be using copy supplied by the advertiser, or the copy may be prepared by the affiliate marketer. The affiliate marketers may have their own service providers, such as vendors who sell lists of email addresses or who help send large volumes of email. The affiliate marketers may also solicit the help of "sub-affiliates"—other marketers who would be willing to help out (for a cut of the action), such as websites that host ad-supported content.

With so many layers of service providers, the advertiser may not know the identity of the affiliate marketer or the identity or presence of any sub-affiliates, since the advertiser only has a relationship with the coordinating service provider. The advertiser also may not know the contents of the emails used to promote it; who received the emails; how the email recipients were identified and selected; and if the sender complied with applicable laws (such as CAN-SPAM).

As you can imagine, the presence of intermediaries between the advertiser and consumer increases the costs of advertising. After all, each player wants to make a profit, and each profit margin adds to the advertiser's overall cost.

Why do advertisers incur these extra expenses? In theory, each intermediary brings specialized expertise to the process. An affiliate marketer may have low-cost ways to access a community of like-minded individuals. For example, imagine someone who knows how to communicate and sell to a community of very active knitters—a community that is probably poorly understood by most outsiders. It may be too costly for any individual advertiser or ad agency to learn how to reach and effectively persuade that micro-community. Therefore, it may be cheaper to outsource the outreach to experts who already know that audience.

At the same time, a complex web of outsourced relationships can diffuse responsibility for any problems. If the ultimate ad is illegal, who bears responsibility? Often, each participant can point the finger at the others, effectively saying that legal compliance was someone else's responsibility. For example, when "kid-tracking" apps touted their ability to track possibly cheating spouses—a feature that can also be used by abusers, and can enable stalking and be illegal if the user installs an app surreptitiously—some of the app makers blamed various affiliates for the relevant ads. Jennifer Valentino-DeVries, *Hundreds of Apps Can Empower Stalkers to Track Their Victims*, N.Y. TIMES, May 19, 2018, https://www.nytimes.com/2018/05/19/technology/phone-apps-stalking.html.

This chapter will explore some of the legal and regulatory issues various intermediaries face. It will look at when advertising agencies are liable for their advertisers' ads (answer: sometimes), when advertisers are responsible for the acts of their affiliate marketers (answer: occasionally), and when publishers are liable for the ads they run (answer: usually for offline publishers, usually not for online publishers). The chapter also looks at when publishers can be forced to run third-party ads (answer: never). The chapter will conclude with some discussion about payment disputes between publishers and advertisers.

## 1. Advertising Agencies

In general, agents and principals are equally liable for any tortious behavior within the agency's scope. Therefore, advertisers are generally responsible for the acts of their advertising agencies.

Agencies also may be liable for the ad copy they help prepare and disseminate, as the following case illustrates.

### Doherty, Clifford, Steers & Shenfield, Inc. v. Federal Trade Commission, 392 F.2d 921 (6th Cir. 1968)

[The FTC determined that certain ads for Sucrets and Children's Sucrets cough medicine, manufactured by Merck, constituted false advertising. The FTC issued a cease-and-desist order against both Merck and its advertising agency, Doherty. The court discussed the order against Doherty:]

The Commission held that the advertising agency was an active participant in the preparation of the advertisements and that the agency knew or had reason to know that Merck's claims were false or deceptive.

Doherty urges that it acted only as agent for its client, relying in good faith on the information furnished by Merck. Doherty asserts that having used every available source to assure itself of the accuracy of Merck's claims, there was nothing else the advertising agency could have done. In substance, Doherty contends that there is no substantial evidence from which the Commission could have found that the agency knew or should have known that Merck's claims were false or deceptive. For these reasons Doherty seeks to have the Commission's order set aside and the complaint dismissed as to the agency.

The proper criterion in deciding in a case of this kind as to whether a cease and desist order should issue against the advertising agency is "the extent to which the advertising agency actually participated in the deception. This is essentially a problem of fact for the Commission." In order to be held to be a participant in such deception, the agency must know or have reason to know of the falsity of the advertising. Carter Products, Inc. v. F. T. C., 323 F.2d 523, 534 (5th Cir.).

The Commission held that among the obligations of Doherty as an advertising agency under its agreement with Merck, Doherty was to "offer general marketing consultation for both new and existing products," "formulate advertising Plans" and "prepare layouts and copy for advertisements;" that Doherty's function was to "originate advertising ideas;" that "the advertising at issue, therefore, is the product of both respondents jointly"; that the advertising agency "developed and put into final form the commercials involved in this proceeding"; and that "it is the final form of these commercials from which the falsity of the advertising may reasonably be imputed." We hold that the record in this case demonstrates that the advertising agency participated actively in the deception; and the Commission's findings of fact to this effect are supported by substantial evidence.

To be aware of the true extent of the therapeutic qualities of Sucrets and Children's Sucrets, the advertising agency needed to do nothing more than to read the packaging labels and instructions for use. . . . The advertising prepared by Doherty went far beyond the more modest claim appearing on the labels and instructions.

The protestations of innocence on the part of the advertising agency are refuted convincingly by a document in the record described as "Proposed 1962 Marketing Plan Sucrets Antiseptic Lozenges" prepared by Doherty. This document outlines an ambitious advertising program aimed at selling Sucrets directly to the "self-medicating" market, described as "the middle-lower socio-economic group," and designed to encourage mothers to buy Children's Sucrets for their children. . . . [T]he advertising agency [had an affirmative role] in promoting a program to create in the minds of the "self-medicating" consumer the impression that Sucrets will kill germs, cure sore throat, including "strep" throat, and alleviate "fiery" throat pain.

We find substantial evidence in the record to support the Commission's conclusion that the advertising agency knew or should have known the falsity of these claims. . . .

*NOTES AND QUESTIONS*

*Agencies' Liability under the FTC Act.* The FTC has held numerous ad agencies liable for FTC Act violations. However, the scienter standards for agency liability are higher than for the advertiser's liability; the agency will be liable only if it committed a knowing violation, while the advertiser may be liable with less scienter. What are the arguments for strict liability, and why might they be more persuasive for advertisers than for ad agencies?

If you worked at an ad agency, what steps would you take to satisfy the FTC requirements? Must the agency get substantiation from the advertiser where the information is not on the product label? How many questions should the agency ask? Can the agency satisfy its obligations simply by reciting in its form contract that the advertiser must provide it with truthful information and must correct anything untrue or misleading in the ads the advertiser approves? Could the agency simply accept an advertiser's word that the advertiser has substantiation? Does it matter whether the substantiation is so technical that a layperson may have difficulty interpreting it?

*Agencies' Liability under the Lanham Act.* The limited case law suggests that agencies may be held jointly liable with their clients under the Lanham Act. In *Nestlé Purina Petcare Co. v. Blue Buffalo Co.*, 2015 WL 1782661 (E.D. Mo. Apr. 20, 2015), the court allowed counterclaims against agencies to proceed when (1) one agency allegedly "designed and built" the website focused on the allegedly false claims, and (2) another agency allegedly "developed the content" of allegedly false ads on the advertiser's Facebook & Twitter accounts and "arranged for these links to [the challenged website] to appear when Google.com users search for terms related to Blue Buffalo"); *cf.* Duty Free Americas, Inc. v. Estee Lauder Companies, Inc., 797 F.3d 1248 (11th Cir. 2015) (recognizing the existence of contributory liability under the Lanham Act's false advertising provision; liability requires material contribution to the false advertising "either by knowingly inducing or causing the conduct, or by materially participating in it").

*Agencies' Liability under Other Legal Doctrines.* Courts routinely treat advertising agencies as jointly and severally liable for other types of claims. For example, in *Waits v. Frito Lay*, 978 F.2d 1093 (9th Cir. 1992), Frito Lay's advertising agency helped recruit a Tom Waits sound-alike singer for an ad it produced for Frito Lay. The agency was jointly liable for the $2.6 million jury verdict.

Statutes may also expressly make advertising agencies liable for legal violations. For example, D.C. Code § 22-1511 (a criminal false advertising statute) expressly references advertising agencies as one of the regulated entities.

*Interagency Conflicts. In re Diamond Mortg. Corp. of Illinois*, 118 B.R. 583 (Bkrtcy. N.D. Ill. 1989) involved a financial Ponzi scheme. The first ad agency (Molner) helped the advertiser prepare fraudulent ad copy; a second ad agency (Yaffe) helped place the ads with television broadcasters. The court had no sympathy for the second ad agency's lack of involvement in developing the ad copy:

> [L]ogic dictates that neither the producer of the commercial nor the agency responsible for airing it should be able to escape liability by blaming the other. The fact that these plaintiffs did not sue Molner is irrelevant. When Yaffe chose to put Molner's product on the air, it in effect adopted it as its own. It was the airing of those commercials that arguably led to these plaintiffs' losses. It follows that if Yaffe was going to air Molner's product, it acquired Molner's duty to ascertain that they were accurate. Molner may have written the [fraudulent] ads, but if Yaffe hadn't put them on the air, this lawsuit would not now be pending.

*What to Do in Practice?* Concerned about the risks of false advertising or other claims, advertising agencies routinely have their lawyers review the ad copy they produce for their advertisers. Whom do these lawyers represent? If the lawyer, ad agency and advertiser have a three-way conference call to discuss the lawyer's liability concerns, is that conversation subject to the attorney–client evidentiary privilege? (With respect to an advertiser's disclosure of potentially privileged information to an ad agency, *compare In re* Jenny Craig, Inc., 1994 WL 16774903 (F.T.C. 1994) *with* LG Electronics U.S.A., Inc. v. Whirlpool Corp., 661 F. Supp. 2d 958 (N.D. Ill. 2009)). If the lawyer doesn't represent the advertiser, does that mean the advertiser should have its own independent counsel review the ads as well?

Often, the agency will bill the full costs of this lawyer to the advertiser, plus any expense mark-up. Does this change your analysis about who the lawyer represents? If you are a lawyer retained by an advertising agency in this circumstance, consider what (if any) duties you have under *Model Rules of Professional Conduct* Rule 1.8(f), which says: "A lawyer shall not accept compensation for representing a client from one other than the client unless: (1) the client gives informed consent; (2) there is no interference with the lawyer's independence of professional judgment or with the client–lawyer relationship; and (3) information relating to representation of a client is protected as required by Rule 1.6."

A contract between the advertising agency and advertiser typically has an indemnity clause requiring one party to defend the other against certain types of claims and pay any losses caused by those claims. Even if a court awards damages jointly and severally, the indemnity allows the parties to shift the financial exposure between each other. With respect to liability for false advertising, how would you draft the indemnity clause if you represented the ad agency? The advertiser? *See* Richard Pollet, *The Agency–Client Contract and Ethical Considerations in the Agency–Client Relationship*, PLI Advertising Law in the New Media Age 2000, 808 PLI/Comm 405 (Oct. 2000). Both sides can ameliorate some risk through insurance.

*Other Vendors.* In *FTC v. Chapman*, 714 F.3d 1211 (10th Cir. 2013), the court upheld an FTC judgment against a grant writer whose materials were sold through a grant-related telemarketing program. She was found to have violated a portion of the Telemarketing Sales Rule which provides that "[i]t is a deceptive telemarketing act or practice and a violation of this Rule for a person to provide substantial assistance or support to any seller or telemarketer when that person knows or consciously avoids knowing that the seller or telemarketer is engaged in any act or practice that violates [other portions] of this Rule." 16 C.F.R. § 310.3(b).

Though she claimed that she had no role in the misleading marketing, she was aware the state attorney general had investigated the business and requested that it change its marketing, but she never asked to see the marketing materials; she knew that a success rate claim for one of her products was not substantiated; and she'd been advised by a former employee of the telemarketing company to be vigilant about monitoring its marketing. This was enough to establish her actual or constructive knowledge. As for "substantial assistance," it was "sufficient that Ms. Chapman played an integral part in the . . . scheme by providing the services and products they marketed to consumers" even if she was uninvolved in the marketing itself.

The FTC also pursues payment processors—entities that process credit card transactions for individual merchants—for violations of the Rule. The FTC takes the position that telemarketing in general, and certain high-risk services such as debt relief, weight loss, and business opportunities in particular, are well-known for fraudulent seller conduct. Thus, the FTC believes there is a duty of inquiry for those providing substantial assistance to anyone engaging in telemarketing.

Is liability for content developers and payment processors justified for the same reasons as liability for ad agencies? Or is the FTC overreaching?

## 2. Affiliates

As illustrated in the chapter's introduction, advertising campaigns often involve multiple intermediaries between the advertiser and consumer, including marketing affiliates or sub-affiliates. This part looks at advertisers' potential liability for the actions of affiliates.

For example, the federal anti-spam law, CAN-SPAM, has a provision holding advertisers liable for illegal spam sent by marketing affiliates. 15 U.S.C. § 7705 says:

(a) In general. It is unlawful for a person to promote, or allow the promotion of, that person's trade or business, or goods, products, property, or services sold, offered for sale, leased or offered for lease, or otherwise made available through that trade or business, in a commercial electronic mail message the transmission of which is in violation of section 7704(a)(1) of this title if that person—

(1) knows, or should have known in the ordinary course of that person's trade or business, that the goods, products, property, or services sold, offered for sale, leased or offered for lease, or otherwise made available through that trade or business were being promoted in such a message;

(2) received or expected to receive an economic benefit from such promotion; and

(3) took no reasonable action—
(A) to prevent the transmission; or
(B) to detect the transmission and report it to the [Federal Trade] Commission.

(b) Limited enforcement against third parties

(1) In general. Except as provided in paragraph (2), a person (hereinafter referred to as the "third party") that provides goods, products, property, or services to another person that violates subsection (a) shall not be held liable for such violation.

(2) Exception. Liability for a violation of subsection (a) shall be imputed to a third party that provides goods, products, property, or services to another person that violates subsection (a) if that third party—

(A) owns, or has a greater than 50 percent ownership or economic interest in, the trade or business of the person that violated subsection (a); or

(B)(i) has actual knowledge that goods, products, property, or services are promoted in a commercial electronic mail message the transmission of which is in violation of section 7704(a)(1) of this title; and (ii) receives, or expects to receive, an economic benefit from such promotion.

Some state anti-spam laws have analogous advertiser liability provisions. However, with respect to most types of marketing other than spam, advertiser liability is not statutorily codified and thus depends on common law interpretations.

Either way, plaintiffs have not found it easy to hold advertisers accountable for their affiliates' illegal activities. The next case shows how easy it was for an advertiser to avoid liability for its affiliates' actions.

**Fenn v. Redmond Venture, Inc., 2004 UT App 355 (Utah Ct. App. 2004)**

. . . In September of 2002, Fenn, Garriott, and Johnson all received unsolicited email messages advertising various RedV computer software products. Prior to receiving the email advertisements, Fenn, Garriott, and Johnson had no contact or relationship with RedV. After receiving the unsolicited email messages, Fenn, Garriott, and Johnson filed separate actions alleging that RedV had violated the [Unsolicited Commercial and Sexually Explicit Email Act, Utah Code Ann. §§ 13-36-101–105 (the "Act")] by sending email messages that did not comply with the Act's requirements. . . .

Fenn, Garriott, and Johnson contend that the district court erred by interpreting the Act to absolve RedV of liability for its promoters' alleged email violations. The Act requires a sender of unsolicited commercial email to include certain information in the subject line and body of each email message. A person "who sends or causes to be sent" a noncompliant unsolicited commercial email is subject to civil liability. Thus, the Act clearly imposes liability upon a company that causes its independent contractors to send unsolicited commercial email messages in violation of the Act. Because "we view the facts and all reasonable inferences drawn therefrom in the light most favorable to the nonmoving part[ies]," we assume that RedV's promoters sent noncompliant email to Fenn, Garriott, and Johnson. Hence, our inquiry focuses on whether the district court erred in concluding, on undisputed facts, that RedV did not cause its promoters to send the noncompliant email.

Crucial to our inquiry is an understanding of the contractual relationship between RedV and its promoters. RedV submitted an affidavit stating that it requires all promoters to adhere to the terms of a marketing contract. The marketing contract requires promoters to comply with RedV's "Anti-Spam Agreement," which provides: "RedV takes appropriate steps to ensure that any promotion of its products is NOT accomplished via unsolicited business electronic communications ("SPAM"). Promoter hereby agrees not to use SPAM in its promotion of RedV's products."

Examining the four corners of the Anti-Spam Agreement, we conclude that it unambiguously prohibits RedV promoters from using unsolicited email messages as a marketing tool. Thus, RedV's affidavit, if undisputed, establishes that RedV did not "cause" illegal email to be sent within the meaning of [the Act]. As the district court observed: "If [the email messages were] sent by RedV [p]romoters, the actions of those . . . [p]romoters were clearly unauthorized under the explicit terms of RedV's policies." . . .

In response to RedV's motion for summary judgment, Fenn, Garriott, and Johnson submitted the affidavits of Garriott and Johnson. Both affidavits stated that the unsolicited email messages were sent "by or at the behest of [RedV]." However, this assertion merely echoes, without providing any support for, the complaint's allegation that "[d]efendant[ ] sent or caused to be sent . . . unsolicited [email messages]." The affidavits, as such, rest upon the mere allegations found in the complaint and fail to raise factual issues.

Fenn, Garriott, and Johnson also argue that the existence of two different versions of the RedV Anti-Spam Agreement leads to the reasonable inference that RedV fabricated the agreements solely for the purpose of this litigation. Fenn, Garriott, and Johnson point out that the second version of the agreement, attached to RedV's affidavit, is far more detailed than the first. However, the provisions of the agreements that ban the use of unsolicited email are practically identical.[3] That RedV produced two slightly different versions of the same agreement does not, by itself, support an inference of fabrication.

Finally, Fenn, Garriott, and Johnson contend that because the email messages advertised RedV products, we must infer that RedV's Anti-Spam Agreement was a sham. This inference is not reasonable based on the record. Although we can properly infer that the email messages were sent by RedV promoters, we cannot, absent additional evidence, infer that RedV encouraged or required its promoters to send the unsolicited email.

In short, Fenn, Garriott, and Johnson presented no evidence suggesting that RedV encouraged or required its promoters to send unsolicited email, or that the Anti-Spam Agreement was a sham. Because no genuine issues of material fact remained, and RedV was entitled to summary judgment as a matter of law, we conclude that the district court did not err in granting judgment in RedV's favor. . . .

*NOTES AND QUESTIONS*

*Analogous Cases.* Other cases have held advertisers not liable for the spam sent by affiliates, such as *Hypertouch, Inc. v. Kennedy-Western University*, 2006 WL 648688 (N.D. Cal. 2006) (advertiser isn't responsible for affiliates' alleged violation of CAN-SPAM when plaintiff "failed to provide any evidence that [advertiser] had actual knowledge or consciously avoided knowledge of a current or future violation of the CAN-SPAM Act by anyone who sent the e-mails at issue") and *United States v. Impulse Media*, 2008 WL 1968307 (W.D. Wash. 2008) (jury rejected CAN-SPAM claim that advertiser caused its affiliates to send spam).

Courts have also absolved affiliates for email sent by downstream sub-affiliates. *See* Ferron v. Echostar Satellite LLC, 2008 WL 4377309 (S.D. Ohio 2008) (no liability under state consumer protection law for spam sent by sub-affiliates); ASIS Internet Servs., v. Optin Glob., Inc., 2008 WL 1902217 (N.D. Cal. 2008) (no CAN-SPAM liability).

For more on this topic, see Jean Noonan & Michael Goodman, *Third-Party Liability for Federal Law Violations in Direct-to-Consumer Marketing: Telemarketing, Fax, and E-mail*, 63 BUS. LAW. 585 (2008).

*Anti-Spam Agreements.* Does the *Fenn* case mean that an advertiser can avoid liability under the anti-spam statute simply by including an anti-spam clause in its contract with affiliates? It's easy for advertisers to adopt policies saying they don't want any business generated by spam, but the

---

[3] The first version of the agreement states that "RedV network ("RedV") takes maximum steps to ensure that any promotion of its products is NOT accomplished via the Unsolicited Business Email ("SPAM"). As a result, RedV and the Promoter enter into an agreement that the Promoter shall not use SPAM in the promotion of RedV's products." The second version reads, "RedV takes appropriate steps to ensure that any promotion of its products is NOT accomplished via unsolicited business electronic communications ("SPAM"). Promoter hereby agrees not to use SPAM in its promotion of RedV's products."

advertiser might look the other way if spam-procured customers are profitable. Thus, advertisers might rationally choose to articulate anti-spam policies—thereby cutting off potential liability—but never enforce the policies unless the law imposes a monitoring duty. Contrast how (as discussed earlier in this chapter) ad agencies have some duty to police their advertisers' words.

Even if the advertiser isn't legally required to police its anti-spam policies, should the advertiser voluntarily choose to do so?

If an advertiser's campaign includes multiple levels of affiliates and sub-affiliates, how does the advertiser communicate its anti-spam policy to affiliates it does not directly contract with?

*Affiliate Liability Issues in Other Contexts.* Plaintiffs often look to hold companies responsible for the acts of their affiliates. There are a few other areas where this issue arises:

- *Collection of Sales Taxes.* Some states have passed laws to treat online affiliates as the equivalent of traveling salespeople, thus giving states the requisite physical nexus to impose sales tax collection obligations on those companies. *See* Overstock.com, Inc. v N.Y. State Dep't. of Taxation & Fin., 20 N.Y.3d 586 (N.Y. Ct. App. 2013) (upholding the tax).
- *Trademarks.* Trademark owners occasionally sue companies when affiliates bid on the trademark owner's trademark as keywords for search engine advertising. Most courts, but not all, have rejected these arguments. *Compare* Sellify Inc. v. Amazon.com, Inc., 2010 WL 4455830 (S.D.N.Y. 2010) *with* 1-800 Contacts, Inc. v. Lens.com, Inc., 722 F.3d 1229 (10th Cir. 2013); *but cf.* Duty Free Americas, Inc. v. Estee Lauder Companies, Inc., 797 F.3d 1248 (11th Cir. 2015) (direct control or monitoring of a third party's false advertising could create contributory liability under the Lanham Act).
- *FTC Act.* The FTC takes the position that advertisers can be responsible if their affiliates write fake reviews. *See In re* Legacy Learning Systems, Inc., F.T.C. File No. 102 3055 (2011) (a $250,000 settlement because affiliates wrote fake reviews that pretended to be the authentic views of consumers); FTC v. LeadClick Media, LLC, 838 F.3d 158 (2d Cir. 2016) (affiliate coordinator was liable for fake "news" written by affiliates; affiliate coordinator knew about fake sites and had authority to control the affiliates, and also participated in the deception by buying ad space on genuine news sites and selling the space to affiliates who advertised with fake news).
- The *Telephone Consumer Protection Act (TCPA).* The TCPA restricts telemarketing, including unsolicited text messages. In *Chutich v. Papa John's Int'l, Inc.*, No. C10-1139 (W.D. Wash. 2012), a court certified a class action against Papa John's for the marketing practices of an affiliate hired by some of Papa John's franchisees (note the layering of potential liability given the franchising arrangement). Papa John's eventually settled the case for $16.5 million.

## 3.  Publishers

### A.  Publisher Liability for Advertisements (Offline)

Subject to some exceptions, publishers generally are liable for the contents of ads they publish. In other words, the law generally does not distinguish between advertisers who developed ad copy and the publishers who run the ad copy, although in some cases the scienter prerequisite for liability is higher for publishers than advertisers. In a sense, the legal rules deputize publishers to act as gatekeepers and "police" the ads they publish—at peril of assuming liability for the ads they accept.

The following case is a landmark Supreme Court case on defamation liability, but many people overlook that the allegedly defamatory content was in a third-party ad provided to the publisher. Pay close attention to how the court analyzes the newspaper's liability for publishing third-party ads.

*New York Times v. Sullivan, 376 U.S. 254 (1964)*

. . . Respondent L. B. Sullivan is one of the three elected Commissioners of the City of Montgomery, Alabama. He testified that he was

> Commissioner of Public Affairs, and the duties are supervision of the Police Department, Fire Department, Department of Cemetery and Department of Scales.

He brought this civil libel action against the four individual petitioners, who are Negroes and Alabama clergymen, and against petitioner the New York Times Company, a New York corporation which publishes the *New York Times*, a daily newspaper. A jury in the Circuit Court of Montgomery County awarded him damages of $500,000, the full amount claimed, against all the petitioners, and the Supreme Court of Alabama affirmed.

Respondent's complaint alleged that he had been libeled by statements in a full-page advertisement that was carried in the *New York Times* on March 29, 1960. Entitled "Heed Their Rising Voices," the advertisement began by stating that,

> As the whole world knows by now, thousands of Southern Negro students are engaged in widespread nonviolent demonstrations in positive affirmation of the right to live in human dignity as guaranteed by the U.S. Constitution and the Bill of Rights.

It went on to charge that,

> in their efforts to uphold these guarantees, they are being met by an unprecedented wave of terror by those who would deny and negate that document which the whole world looks upon as setting the pattern for modern freedom. . . .

Succeeding paragraphs purported to illustrate the "wave of terror" by describing certain alleged events. The text concluded with an appeal for funds for three purposes: support of the student movement, "the struggle for the right to vote," and the legal defense of Dr. Martin Luther King, Jr., leader of the movement, against a perjury indictment then pending in Montgomery.

The text appeared over the names of 64 persons, many widely known for their activities in public affairs, religion, trade unions, and the performing arts. Below these names, and under a line reading "We in the south who are struggling daily for dignity and freedom warmly endorse this appeal," appeared the names of the four individual petitioners and of 16 other persons, all but two of whom were identified as clergymen in various Southern cities. The advertisement was signed at the bottom of the page by the "Committee to Defend Martin Luther King and the Struggle for Freedom in the South," and the officers of the Committee were listed.

Of the 10 paragraphs of text in the advertisement, the third and a portion of the sixth were the basis of respondent's claim of libel. They read as follows:

Third paragraph:

> In Montgomery, Alabama, after students sang "My Country, 'Tis of Thee" on the State Capitol steps, their leaders were expelled from school, and truckloads of police armed with shotguns and tear-gas ringed the Alabama State College Campus. When the entire student body protested to state authorities by refusing to reregister, their dining hall was padlocked in an attempt to starve them into submission.

Sixth paragraph:

> Again and again, the Southern violators have answered Dr. King's peaceful protests with intimidation and violence. They have bombed his home, almost killing his wife and child. They have assaulted his person. They have arrested him seven times—for "speeding," "loitering" and similar "offenses." And now they have charged him with "perjury"—a felony under which they could imprison him for ten years. . . .

# Heed Their Rising Voices

> "The growing movement of peaceful mass demonstrations by Negroes is something new in the South, something understandable.... Let Congress heed their rising voices, for they will be heard."
>
> —*New York Times* editorial
> Saturday, March 19, 1960

## Your Help Is Urgently Needed . . . . NOW!!

*We in the south who are struggling daily for dignity and freedom warmly endorse this appeal*

**COMMITTEE TO DEFEND MARTIN LUTHER KING AND THE STRUGGLE FOR FREEDOM IN THE SOUTH**
312 West 125th Street, New York 27, N. Y. UNiversity 6-1700

*Please mail this coupon TODAY!*

. . . It is uncontroverted that some of the statements contained in the two paragraphs were not accurate descriptions of events which occurred in Montgomery. [The court then described the various errors.]

. . . The cost of the advertisement was approximately $4800, and it was published by the Times upon an order from a New York advertising agency acting for the signatory Committee. The agency submitted the advertisement with a letter from A. Philip Randolph, Chairman of the Committee, certifying that the persons whose names appeared on the advertisement had given their permission. Mr. Randolph was known to the Times' Advertising Acceptability Department as a responsible person, and, in accepting the letter as sufficient proof of authorization, it followed its established practice. There was testimony that the copy of the advertisement which accompanied the letter listed

696

only the 64 names appearing under the text, and that the statement, "We in the south . . . warmly endorse this appeal," and the list of names thereunder, which included those of the individual petitioners, were subsequently added when the first proof of the advertisement was received. Each of the individual petitioners testified that he had not authorized the use of his name, and that he had been unaware of its use until receipt of respondent's demand for a retraction. The manager of the Advertising Acceptability Department testified that he had approved the advertisement for publication because he knew nothing to cause him to believe that anything in it was false, and because it bore the endorsement of "a number of people who are well known and whose reputation" he "had no reason to question." Neither he nor anyone else at the Times made an effort to confirm the accuracy of the advertisement, either by checking it against recent Times news stories relating to some of the described events or by any other means.

Alabama law denies a public officer recovery of punitive damages in a libel action brought on account of a publication concerning his official conduct unless he first makes a written demand for a public retraction and the defendant fails or refuses to comply. Respondent served such a demand upon each of the petitioners. . . . The Times did not publish a retraction in response to the demand, but wrote respondent a letter stating, among other things, that "we . . . are somewhat puzzled as to how you think the statements in any way reflect on you," and "you might, if you desire, let us know in what respect you claim that the statements in the advertisement reflect on you." Respondent filed this suit a few days later without answering the letter. The Times did, however, subsequently publish a retraction of the advertisement upon the demand of Governor John Patterson of Alabama, who asserted that the publication charged him with

> grave misconduct and . . . improper actions and omissions as Governor of Alabama and Ex-Officio Chairman of the State Board of Education of Alabama.

When asked to explain why there had been a retraction for the Governor but not for respondent, the Secretary of the Times testified:

> We did that because we didn't want anything that was published by The Times to be a reflection on the State of Alabama, and the Governor was, as far as we could see, the embodiment of the State of Alabama and the proper representative of the State, and, furthermore, we had by that time learned more of the actual facts which the and [sic] purported to recite and, finally, the ad did refer to the action of the State authorities and the Board of Education, presumably of which the Governor is the ex-officio chairman. . . .

On the other hand, he testified that he did not think that "any of the language in there referred to Mr. Sullivan." . . .

## I.

We may dispose at the outset of two grounds asserted to insulate the judgment of the Alabama courts from constitutional scrutiny. . . . [Editor's note: The first was lack of state action.]

The second contention is that the constitutional guarantees of freedom of speech and of the press are inapplicable here, at least so far as the Times is concerned, because the allegedly libelous statements were published as part of a paid, "commercial" advertisement. The argument relies on *Valentine v. Chrestensen*, 316 U.S. 52, where the Court held that a city ordinance forbidding street distribution of commercial and business advertising matter did not abridge the First Amendment freedoms, even as applied to a handbill having a commercial message on one side but a protest against certain official action, on the other. The reliance is wholly misplaced. The Court in *Chrestensen* reaffirmed the constitutional protection for "the freedom of communicating information and disseminating opinion"; its holding was based upon the factual conclusions that the handbill was "purely commercial advertising" and that the protest against official action had been added only to evade the ordinance.

The publication here was not a "commercial" advertisement in the sense in which the word was used in *Chrestensen*. It communicated information, expressed opinion, recited grievances, protested claimed abuses, and sought financial support on behalf of a movement whose existence and objectives are matters of the highest public interest and concern. That the Times was paid for publishing the advertisement is as immaterial in this connection as is the fact that newspapers and books are sold. Any other conclusion would discourage newspapers from carrying "editorial advertisements" of this type, and so might shut off an important outlet for the promulgation of information and ideas by persons who do not themselves have access to publishing facilities—who wish to exercise their freedom of speech even though they are not members of the press. The effect would be to shackle the First Amendment in its attempt to secure "the widest possible dissemination of information from diverse and antagonistic sources." To avoid placing such a handicap upon the freedoms of expression, we hold that, if the allegedly libelous statements would otherwise be constitutionally protected from the present judgment, they do not forfeit that protection because they were published in the form of a paid advertisement. . . .

III

. . . As to the Times, we similarly conclude that the facts do not support a finding of actual malice. The statement by the Times' Secretary that, apart from the padlocking allegation, he thought the advertisement was "substantially correct," affords no constitutional warrant for the Alabama Supreme Court's conclusion that it was a

> cavalier ignoring of the falsity of the advertisement [from which] the jury could not have but been impressed with the bad faith of The Times, and its maliciousness inferable therefrom.

The statement does not indicate malice at the time of the publication; even if the advertisement was not "substantially correct"—although respondent's own proofs tend to show that it was—that opinion was at least a reasonable one, and there was no evidence to impeach the witness' good faith in holding it. The Times' failure to retract upon respondent's demand, although it later retracted upon the demand of Governor Patterson, is likewise not adequate evidence of malice for constitutional purposes. Whether or not a failure to retract may ever constitute such evidence, there are two reasons why it does not here. First, the letter written by the Times reflected a reasonable doubt on its part as to whether the advertisement could reasonably be taken to refer to respondent at all. Second, it was not a final refusal, since it asked for an explanation on this point—a request that respondent chose to ignore. Nor does the retraction upon the demand of the Governor supply the necessary proof. It may be doubted that a failure to retract, which is not itself evidence of malice, can retroactively become such by virtue of a retraction subsequently made to another party. But, in any event, that did not happen here, since the explanation given by the Times' Secretary for the distinction drawn between respondent and the Governor was a reasonable one, the good faith of which was not impeached.

Finally, there is evidence that the Times published the advertisement without checking its accuracy against the news stories in the Times' own files. The mere presence of the stories in the files does not, of course, establish that the Times "knew" the advertisement was false, since the state of mind required for actual malice would have to be brought home to the persons in the Times' organization having responsibility for the publication of the advertisement. With respect to the failure of those persons to make the check, the record shows that they relied upon their knowledge of the good reputation of many of those whose names were listed as sponsors of the advertisement, and upon the letter from A. Philip Randolph, known to them as a responsible individual, certifying that the use of the names was authorized. There was testimony that the persons handling the advertisement saw nothing in it that would render it unacceptable under the Times' policy of rejecting advertisements containing "attacks of a personal character"; their failure to reject it on this ground was not unreasonable. We think the evidence against the Times supports, at most, a finding of negligence in failing to discover the misstatements, and is constitutionally insufficient to show the recklessness that is required for a finding of actual malice. . . .

[Justices Black and Goldberg filed concurrences.]

*NOTES AND QUESTIONS*

*Newspaper Responsibility for Ads.* Notice that the court treats the New York Times as legally responsible for the third-party ad copy without discussing the issue. This is consistent with general tort doctrines. By making the editorial decision to publish the ad, the New York Times took equal responsibility for the ad's legality along with the advertiser.

*Publisher Standards.* Many publishers voluntarily adopt internal guidelines about the ads they will accept for publication. These standards vary widely and are often vague and highly subjective. For example, the New York Times' Standards of Digital Advertising (revised January 2015) says,

> Advertisements that are, in the opinion of The Times, indecent, vulgar, suggestive or otherwise offensive to good taste are unacceptable. Taste is judgment in which time, place and context make vital differences. Each advertisement must, therefore, be judged on its own merits.

The Times's standards enumerate its current policy about the ads at issue in the *Sullivan* case:

> We believe that the broad principles of freedom of the press confer on us an obligation to keep our advertising columns open to all points of view. Therefore, The New York Times accepts advertisements in which groups or individuals comment on public or controversial

issues. We make no judgments on an advertiser's arguments, factual assertions or conclusions. We accept advocacy/opinion advertisements regardless of our editorial position on any given subject.

We do not, however, accept advocacy advertisements that are attacks of a personal nature, that seek to comment on private disputes or that contain vulgar or indecent language.

We do not accept advertisements that are gratuitously offensive on racial, religious or ethnic grounds or that are considered to be in poor taste. We do not verify, nor do we vouch for, statements of purported fact in advocacy/opinion advertisements. We reserve the right, however, to require documentation of factual claims when it is deemed necessary.

In addition, we do not accept advocacy advertisements that promote illegal activities or actions. We do not accept ads that are libelous or might be legally actionable. We also do not accept an advocacy ad that accused an entire country, race or religion as being guilty of a crime. And conversely we will not accept advertising that denies or trivializes great human tragedies such as the Armenian Genocide or World Trade Center bombing.

Advertisements that include photographs of individuals or the names of individuals as signatories, or which state or imply that named individuals support or endorse the messages, must be accompanied by a signed release wherein the sponsors certify that no one's name or photograph has been used in the advertisements without his or her consent. If affiliations of signatories are included in the opinion advertisement, then a line of copy which reads "Affiliations listed for identification purposes only" must appear in the advertisement.

The sponsor's name must be in the advertisement. If the advertiser is not known to our readers, the sponsor's mailing address or telephone number, email address or Web site address (that leads to direct contact with the advertiser) must appear in the advertisement.

Some publisher standards are driven by liability concerns (i.e., no defamatory ads); some are designed to prevent advertisers from making their ads appear like editorial content; and others may reflect idiosyncratic normative decisions. *See, e.g.*, Sarah Kershaw, *Google Tells Sites for 'Cougars' to Go Prowl Elsewhere*, N.Y. TIMES, May 14, 2010 (Google banned ads promoting "cougar sites," i.e., sites for older women seeking to date younger men, though Google accepts similar ads for other dating sites).

Why might publishers adopt voluntary standards to prevent ads that are legal? In some cases, the publisher is worried that its audience will think less of the publication based on the ads it runs. Think of the times you've changed the television or radio station because the content of an advertisement annoyed you or left a website because of some irritatingly animated or flashing ad. Or sometimes it's a bona fide effort to protect readers/viewers from scams or other harms.

Do these voluntary standards reduce or increase a publisher's liability exposure? On the one hand, by preemptively screening out risky ads, the publisher publishes fewer legally risky ads. On the other hand, plaintiffs may cite the standards against the publisher in a variety of ways, such as by arguing that the publisher's exercise of control over the ads should increase its liability for the ads it accepts. *See* the *Goddard* and *Langdon* cases below.

*Publisher Investigation.* Why didn't the New York Times undertake any effort to verify the ad's assertions? How much investigation of ads should publishers do?

*Statutory Duties.* Publishers may have statutory duties to police or reject ads, such as discriminatory real estate ads.

*Publisher Liability for Personal Injuries.* The following case provides an illustration of how a publisher (the Yellow Pages) can become responsible for its advertisers' misconduct.

*Knepper v. Brown, 345 Or. 320 (2008)*

In this common-law fraud action, plaintiffs obtained a $1.5 million jury verdict against Dex Media, Inc. (Dex), based on Dex's involvement in creating and publishing a Yellow Pages advertisement that misrepresented a doctor's qualifications. On appeal, Dex argued that plaintiffs presented no evidence that the misrepresentation caused the injuries that plaintiffs claimed (pain and physical deformities resulting from a botched liposuction procedure) and that it therefore was entitled to a directed verdict or to a judgment notwithstanding the jury's verdict. The Court of Appeals disagreed and affirmed the judgment for plaintiffs. We allowed Dex's petition for review and, for the reasons that follow, now affirm the decision of the Court of Appeals and the judgment of the trial court. . . .

Dr. Timothy Brown is a licensed medical doctor who holds certifications from the American Board of Medical Specialties in dermatology and anatomic and clinical pathology. Brown started a dermatology practice in Oregon in 1985 and thereafter maintained an advertisement in Dex's Yellow Pages directory, under the heading "Physicians and Surgeons" and the subheading "Dermatology (skin)." The advertisement listed various services and prominently noted that Brown was "Certified by the American Board of Dermatology."

In 1993, Brown began to offer "tumescent" liposuction in his office, after receiving some limited informal training in how to perform that procedure. He mentioned the new service in his 1993/94 Yellow Pages advertisement, which still appeared under the "Dermatology" subheading and which still referred to his board certification in dermatology.

In 1996, Brown placed a second advertisement in Dex's Yellow Pages—this time under the subheading "Surgery, Plastic and Reconstructive." The new advertisement stated that Brown performed liposuction, wrinkle treatments, and sclerotherapy. It also stated that Brown was "Board Certified"—without specifying any area of certification.

The new advertisements were added at the urging of a Dex sales representative, Mueller. Brown's office manager, Newman, told Mueller that Brown was interested in attracting more liposuction patients. Mueller met with Newman to help her "mock up" a new advertisement. Mueller told Newman that the "plastic and reconstruction surgery" subheading in the Yellow Pages would be the best place to reach that target market. Mueller also told Newman that the advertisement should identify Brown as "board certified," because "patients were expecting a [board certified] plastic surgeon to do these techniques." Newman repeatedly told Mueller that she was concerned that such an advertisement would be misleading, because Brown's board certification was in dermatology, not plastic and reconstructive surgery. Mueller continued to push for a nonspecific "board certified" designation under the "Surgery, Plastic and Reconstructive" subheading, and Brown, who had the final say, acceded to Mueller's advice.

Early in 1997, plaintiff M. M. Knepper was considering cosmetic liposuction surgery. She knew that she wanted to be treated by a plastic surgeon. She consulted the "Surgery, Plastic and Reconstructive" subheading in the Yellow Pages and compiled a list of doctors and medical facilities that performed liposuction. Knepper saw Brown's advertisement and included his name and telephone number on her list, believing him to be a plastic surgeon because of the location of his ad and the "board certified" designation that appeared after his name. Knepper did not call Brown's office at the time, however.

Some months later, Knepper attended a Women's Show and stopped at a booth offering information about Brown's cosmetic surgery practice. Knepper recognized Brown's name from her list of potential plastic surgeons. She picked up a brochure, which stated that Brown was board certified in, among other things, "Dermatologic Surgery." One of Brown's employees, who was manning the booth, told Knepper that Brown was a board-certified plastic surgeon. Knepper thereafter made an appointment to discuss liposuction with Brown. At the consultation, Brown also told Knepper that he was board certified in plastic surgery.

Knepper decided to retain Brown, and he performed a liposuction procedure on her in December 1997. After the procedure, Knepper contacted Brown's office to report continuing pain and "misshapenness," and Brown performed two more liposuction procedures in an unsuccessful attempt to repair the damage. Plaintiffs eventually filed the present action against Brown and Dex, alleging claims of medical malpractice, fraud, conspiracy to commit fraud, and loss of consortium. Brown later settled with plaintiffs, leaving plaintiffs' fraud claim (and the derivative conspiracy and loss of consortium claims) against Dex to be decided at trial. Plaintiffs' fraud claim alleged that (1) Dex knew that Brown was not board certified in plastic and reconstructive surgery; (2) Dex and Brown together designed and developed an advertisement that falsely implied that Brown was a board-certified plastic surgeon; (3) Knepper wanted a board-certified plastic surgeon to perform liposuction surgery on her; (4) Knepper relied in part on the misleading Dex advertisement and retained Brown to perform liposuction surgery; (5) if Knepper had known the truth about Brown's credentials, she would not have consented to surgery by him; and (6) Brown performed the liposuction negligently, causing injury to plaintiffs. . . .

. . . Plaintiffs also presented the testimony of Dr. Lloyd Hale, a plastic surgeon, regarding the nature and extent of Knepper's injuries and whether Knepper's three liposuction procedures were performed in a manner that met the applicable standard of care. Hale also testified about the qualifications of dermatologists, as opposed to those of plastic surgeons, to perform surgical procedures. He observed that dermatologists usually do not receive formalized surgical training, while plastic surgeons receive extensive surgical training over a period of many years. Hale further observed that surgical knowledge, training, and experience are important for obtaining good results from liposuction. Hale acknowledged that plastic surgeons do not always meet the standard of care for liposuction or other surgical procedures, but he stated that he had never seen an injury like Knepper's—which he described as an "uncorrectable disaster"—at the hands of a doctor who had gone through formalized surgical training. . . .

Dex's initial argument is that, to hold Dex liable for fraud, plaintiffs were required, but failed, to present evidence establishing that Brown's negligent treatment of Knepper was a reasonably foreseeable consequence of Dex's publication of Brown's advertisement. . . . Dex argues that plaintiffs were required to prove that the particular type of injury that Knepper suffered—a botched medical procedure at the hands of a third party (Brown)—was a reasonably foreseeable consequence of Dex's publication of Brown's misleading advertisement. . . .

Courts have noted that, when an intentional tort is involved, the range of legal causation can be quite broad: "'For an intended injury, the law is astute to discover even very remote causation.'" W. Page Keeton, Prosser and Keeton on Torts § 43, 293 n.6 (5th ed. 1984). Still, the historical references to "proximate injury" as an element of fraud indicates that courts also recognize that there is some limitation on the consequences for which a perpetrator of an intentional fraud may be held liable. A requirement that any claimed damages be foreseeable appropriately recognizes that the scope of liability for an intentional, fraudulent misrepresentation depends on the nature of the misrepresentation, the audience to whom the misrepresentation was directed, and the nature of the action or forbearance, intended or negligent, that the misrepresentation justifiably induced. Restatement (Second) of Torts § 548A (1977) incorporates that requirement:

> "A fraudulent misrepresentation is a legal cause of a pecuniary loss resulting from action or inaction in reliance upon it if, but only if, the loss might reasonably be expected to result from the reliance." . . .

When we apply that foreseeability principle in the present case, it is clear that plaintiffs' damages reasonably might be expected to result from their reliance on Dex's misrepresentation. An advertisement that misrepresents a medical provider's qualifications self-evidently creates a risk that a consumer who seeks treatment from the provider in reliance on that misrepresentation will suffer an adverse result that would not have occurred if the provider's qualifications had been as represented. The testimony at trial showed that Knepper's injuries fell precisely within the foreseeable risk of harm that the misrepresentation created: Knepper testified that she wanted to have a board-certified plastic surgeon perform the liposuction, and a juror could infer from that testimony that Knepper believed that she was more likely to suffer an adverse result from being treated by a medical provider who was not board certified in plastic surgery. Further, plaintiffs' medical expert testified that he had never seen adverse results like the ones that Knepper experienced from a medical provider who was certified in plastic surgery. A juror could infer from that testimony that plaintiffs' injuries probably would not have occurred if Knepper had received treatment from a board-certified plastic surgeon (as she believed Brown to be). Stated in terms of the applicable legal standard, Dex had reason to expect that Knepper would act in justifiable reliance on Dex's misrepresentation by retaining Brown for the surgery, and that an adverse result was more likely if Brown, rather than a board-certified plastic surgeon, performed liposuction surgery. There is no additional requirement that plaintiffs also prove that Dex in fact did foresee that Knepper would suffer the particular adverse results of the medical services that Brown performed. It follows that plaintiffs' injuries were foreseeable as a result of Dex's intentional misrepresentation, and that is all that plaintiffs had to show. Dex must respond in damages accordingly.

We turn to Dex's next argument . . . Dex contends that, to prevent an unconstitutional chilling effect on the free flow of information, Oregon courts must recognize that publishers require some additional protection from claims arising out of false or misleading advertisements, and cannot be held liable for the publication of such advertisements unless the publication is done maliciously or with intent to harm another or in reckless disregard of that possibility.

We think that Dex's argument demands too much. This is not a case of the unwitting publication of an advertisement that turns out to be false. It is, instead, a case in which the publisher took a knowing and active part in the perpetration of the fraud. Punishing fraud has no impermissible "chilling" effect on the right to express views on "any subject whatever." *See* Article I, section 8, of the Oregon Constitution (protecting such a right of expression). Fraud is excepted from that constitutional protection. What Dex argues would extend constitutional protection to fraud, and we reject that argument.

As we have explained, plaintiffs' evidence permitted the jury to infer that the fraudulent misrepresentation by Dex and Brown was designed to mislead potential patients into believing that Brown was a board-certified plastic surgeon, thereby luring them into accepting surgery by Brown that he was not specially trained to perform. The misrepresentation created the risk that those who relied on it would be harmed as a particular result of Brown's lack of expertise as a plastic surgeon, and that is what happened to plaintiffs. The trial judge did not err in refusing to grant Dex's motions for directed verdict and judgment notwithstanding the jury's verdict. . . .

*NOTES AND QUESTIONS*

*Advertiser Misconduct Doesn't Necessarily Relieve the Publishers.* According to the court, Dr. Brown made several misrepresentations directly to Mrs. Knepper after she saw the ad, and Dr. Brown's negligence in surgery is the most direct cause of Mrs. Knepper's injuries. Why didn't Dr. Brown's subsequent misconduct cut off Dex's liability?

*The "Empty Chair" Problem.* Dr. Brown settled before trial, leaving Dex as the only defendant in front of the jury. This created a situation sometimes called the "empty chair" phenomenon. The jury may have had sympathy toward Mrs. Knepper and ire toward Dr. Brown, but Dr. Brown wasn't around to punish. The jury could only direct that ire toward the remaining defendant, Dex. At minimum, it was a risky decision for Dex to proceed to a jury as the only defendant.

We might criticize Dex's decision to proceed to trial rather than settle after Dr. Brown settled. However, defendants' desire to avoid being the only defendant in front of a jury can set up a "race" among defendants to settle, which can allow the plaintiff to conduct an auction where the settlement price for each remaining defendant goes up as prior defendants settle.

*Commissions and Rogue Salespeople.* Often, advertising salespeople are paid on commission. In theory, commission compensation aligns the salesperson's interests with the company's interests. In practice, salespeople may be willing to stretch the truth to generate a sale, knowing that any repercussions from their misstatements will come long after they have spent their commission check. For example, it took a dozen years to get a final determination that Dex salesperson Mueller's sale was illegitimate. For this reason and others, commission compensation may not ensure salespeople act in the publisher's best interest. What could/should Dex have done differently to dissuade Mueller from overselling Dr. Brown?

## B.    Publisher Liability for Advertisements (Online)

The general rule, exemplified by *New York Times v. Sullivan*, is that publishers are liable for the ads they run. However, this rule does not apply to online publishers. In 1996, Congress enacted 47 U.S.C. § 230 as part of the Communications Decency Act (CDA), which in turn was part of the Telecommunications Act of 1996 (the provision is commonly misidentified as "Section 230 of the CDA" but it was actually Section 509 of the CDA). 230(c)(1) reads:

> No provider or user of an interactive computer service shall be treated as the publisher or speaker of any information provided by another information content provider.

A successful 230(c)(1) defense has three elements:

1)  It applies to "providers or users of interactive computer services." With very limited exceptions, all online publishers are covered by this term.

2)  The plaintiff's claims must try to treat the defendant as a "publisher or speaker" of content. Courts have interpreted this language to apply to virtually all types of claims. However, the statute (230(e)) expressly excludes four types of claims from 230(c)'s coverage:

    - Prosecutions of federal crimes, although prosecutions of state crimes are preempted.
    - "Intellectual property claims." This clearly means that federal copyright and federal trademark claims are not preempted by 230. In most jurisdictions, state law IP claims, such as state trade secret or publicity rights claims, also are not preempted by 230. However, in the Ninth Circuit, state IP claims *are* preempted by 230. Perfect 10 v. ccBill, 488 F.3d 1102 (9th Cir 2007). Due to a quirk in the law, federal trade secret claims pursuant to the Defend Trade Secrets Act *are* covered by 230.
    - Claims under the federal Electronic Communications Privacy Act (an anti-wiretapping law) or analogous state laws.
    - Certain claims related to the promotion of sex trafficking.

    If the plaintiff's claim does not fit in one of these statutory exclusions, 230 presumptively applies to the claim.

3)  The claim must be based on "information provided by another information content provider." In general, this requirement distinguishes between first-party content (content originated by

the publisher) and third-party content (someone else's content). If the plaintiff's claim relates to third-party content, as opposed to first-party content, 230 applies. The division between first-party content and third-party content is not always crystal-clear, however. As a result, 230 litigation often explores this ambiguous division.

In effect, Section 230(c)(1) says that online publishers are categorically not liable for claims based on third-party content unless the claims are federal criminal prosecutions, IP claims (but only federal IP claims in the Ninth Circuit), sex trafficking promotions, or the Electronic Communications Privacy Act. The United States is the only country that has adopted such an intermediary-favorable rule.

Case law interpreting 230(c)(1) has virtually uniformly held that online publishers can claim 230(c)(1) protection for claims related to third-party advertisements. It does not matter that the publisher profits from the advertisement, even if its profits vary with user activity such as clicks or purchases. *See, e.g.*, Cisneros v. Yahoo!, Inc., CGC-04-433518 (Cal. Superior Ct. 2008) (addressing a case over search engines' display of gambling ads paid on a CPC basis: "the fact that defendants made money from selling internet access to sponsored sites [is] irrelevant to the application of Section 230").

This next case illustrates a sophisticated but unsuccessful effort to undermine 230(c)(1)'s protection of a publisher (Google) for allegedly tortious third-party ads (mobile services). Why did Google accept these ads, and is it fair that Google has no responsibility for them? And does it make sense that the same ads might have generated liability for offline publishers?

*Goddard v. Google, Inc., 640 F. Supp. 2d 1193 (N. D. Cal. 2009)*

I. BACKGROUND

Plaintiff Jenna Goddard ("Plaintiff") alleges that she and a class of similarly situated individuals were harmed as a result of clicking on allegedly fraudulent web-based advertisements for mobile subscription services.* She alleges that Defendant Google, Inc. ("Google") illegally furthered this scheme. . . . Google asserted that each of Plaintiff's claims was barred by § 230(c)(1) of the Communications Decency Act ("CDA"), which prevents a website from being treated as the "publisher or speaker" of third-party content, and thus typically immunizes website operators from liability arising from the transmission of such content. As Google argued, claims that seek to impose liability on a website operator as the speaker or publisher of third-party content—or to impose liability that is "merely a rephrasing of" such speaker or publisher liability, Barnes v. Yahoo!, Inc., 570 F.3d 1096, 1106 (9th Cir. 2009)—are barred by the CDA unless the website also is an "information content provider," meaning that it "is 'responsible, in whole or in part, for the creation or development of' the offending content." Fair Housing Council of San Fernando Valley v.

---

* [Editor's note: among other things at issue, the case involved advertisements for "free" ringtones that unexpectedly subscribed downloaders to subscription services charged through their cellphone bills.]

Roommates.Com, LLC (Roommates), 521 F.3d 1157, 1162 (9th Cir. 2008) (en banc) (quoting 47 U.S.C. § 230(f)(3)).

Faced with the implications of this clear analytic framework, which was articulated in the Ninth Circuit's 2008 en banc decision in *Roommates*, Plaintiff resorted to creative argument in an attempt to show that her claims did not seek to hold Google liable for the dissemination of online content at all. The Court rejected Plaintiff's artful pleading and dismissed the complaint. Plaintiff was granted leave to amend, with express instructions that she attempt to "establish Google's involvement in 'creating or developing' the AdWords, either 'in whole or in part,' " so as to avoid CDA immunity.

In her amended complaint, Plaintiff now alleges that "Google's involvement [in creating the allegedly fraudulent advertisements] was so pervasive that the company controlled much of the underlying commercial activity engaged in by the third-party advertisers." Plaintiff alleges that Google "not only encourages illegal conduct, [but] collaborates in the development of the illegal content and, effectively, requires its advertiser customers to engage in it." These allegations, if supported by other specific allegations of fact, clearly would remove Plaintiff's action from the scope of CDA immunity. The quoted allegations, however, are mere "labels and conclusions" amounting to a "formulaic recitation of the elements" of CDA developer liability, and as such, they "will not do." Bell Atl. Corp. v. Twombly, 550 U.S. 544, 555 (2007). Rather, the Court must examine the pleading to determine whether Plaintiff alleges mechanisms that plausibly suggest the collaboration, control, or compulsion that she ascribes to Google's role in the creation of the offending AdWords. Having undertaken such an examination, the Court concludes that Plaintiff has not come close to substantiating the "labels and conclusions" by which she attempts to evade the reach of the CDA. Accordingly, her complaint once again must be dismissed. . . .

## III. DISCUSSION

As explained at length in this Court's earlier order, the CDA has been interpreted to provide a "robust" immunity for internet service providers and websites, with courts "adopting a relatively expansive definition of 'interactive computer service' and a relatively restrictive definition of 'information content provider.'" Carafano v. Metrosplash.com, Inc., 339 F.3d 1119, 1123 (9th Cir. 2003). Thus, a website operator does not become liable as an "information content provider" merely by "augmenting the content [of online material] generally." *Roommates*, 521 F.3d at 1167–68. Rather, the website must contribute "materially . . . to its alleged unlawfulness." *Id.* at 1167–68. A website does not so "contribute" when it merely provides third parties with neutral tools to create web content, even if the website knows that the third parties are using such tools to create illegal content. *See, e.g., id.* at 1169 & n. 24 (noting that where a plaintiff brings a claim "based on a website operator's passive acquiescence in the misconduct of its users," the website operator generally will be immune "even if the users committed their misconduct using tools of general availability provided by the website operator"); *see also* Zeran v. Am. Online, Inc., 129 F.3d 327, 333 (4th Cir. 1997) (holding that provider is shielded from liability despite receiving notification of objectionable content on its website and failing to remove it).

A. Developer liability

Plaintiff identifies several mechanisms by which Google allegedly contributes to the illegality of the offending advertisements, or even "requires" the inclusion of illegal content in such advertisements. Each of these mechanisms involves Google's "Keyword Tool," which Plaintiff describes as a "suggestion tool" employing an algorithm to suggest specific keywords to advertisers.[3] To demonstrate that the Keyword Tool is not a "neutral tool" of the kind uniformly permitted within the scope of CDA immunity, Plaintiff alleges that when a potential advertiser enters the word "ringtone" into Google's Keyword Tool, the tool suggests the phrase "free ringtone," and that this suggestion is more prevalent than others that may appear. Plaintiff contends that the suggestion of the word "free," when combined with Google's knowledge "of the mobile content industry's unauthorized charge problems," makes the Keyword Tool "neither innocuous nor neutral." Plaintiff also alleges that Google disproportionately suggests the use of the term "free ringtone" to ordinary users of Google's web search function, causing them to view the allegedly fraudulent MSSPs' [Editor's note: this is an acronym for "mobile subscription service provider"] AdWords with greater frequency.

Even assuming that Google is aware of fraud in the mobile subscription service industry and yet disproportionately suggests the term "free ringtone" in response to an advertiser's entry of the term "ringtone," Plaintiff's argument that the Keyword Tool "materially contributes" to the alleged illegality does not establish developer liability. The argument is nearly identical to that rejected by the Ninth Circuit in *Carafano v. Metrosplash*, 339 F.3d 1119 (9th Cir. 2003). There, the defendant website provided its users with a "detailed questionnaire" that included multiple-choice questions wherein "members select[ed] answers . . . from menus providing between four and nineteen options." Although they included sexually suggestive phrases that might facilitate the development of libelous profiles, the menus of pre-prepared responses were considered neutral tools because "the selection of the content was left exclusively to the user."

Under *Carafano*, even if a particular tool "facilitate[s] the expression of information," it generally will be considered "neutral" so long as users ultimately determine what content to post, such that the tool merely provides "a framework that could be utilized for proper or improper purposes." Indeed, as already noted, the provision of neutral tools generally will not affect the availability of CDA immunity "even if a service provider knows that third parties are using such tools to create illegal content." As a result, a plaintiff may not establish developer liability merely by alleging that the operator of a website should have known that the availability of certain tools might facilitate the posting of improper content. Substantially greater involvement is required, such as the situation in which the website "elicits the allegedly illegal content and makes aggressive use of it in conducting its business."

Like the menus in *Carafano*, Google's Keyword Tool is a neutral tool. It does nothing more than provide options that advertisers may adopt or reject at their discretion. "[T]he selection of the content [is] left exclusively to the user." While a website clearly will not "automatically [enjoy] immun[ity] so long as the content originated with another information content provider," Plaintiff's

---

[3] Plaintiff also alleges that Google representatives meet with certain advertisers in order to assist them with the creation of AdWords, but she does not allege that these representatives have contributed in any way to the allegedly illegal MSSP AdWords that give rise to this action.

allegations, if true, would not establish that Google did anything to encourage the posting of false or misleading AdWords, much less that Google "elicit[ed] . . . [or] ma[de] aggressive use of [them] in conducting its business." As in *Carafano*, where the dating website easily could have been expected to know that the inclusion of sexually suggestive options in its "pre-prepared" user profile responses might well encourage libelous impersonations or pranks, Plaintiff's suggestion that Google should have been aware of the danger of combining the words "free" and "ringtone" does not make Google a co-developer of the offending AdWords. Indeed, "the [allegedly misleading] posting[s] w[ere] contrary to [Google's] express polic[y]," which warns advertisers that they "are responsible for the keywords [they] select and for ensuring that [their] use of the keywords does not violate any applicable laws." . . .

. . . Plaintiff alleges that Google effectively "requires" advertisers to engage in illegal conduct. Yet Plaintiff's use of the word "requires" is inconsistent with the facts that Plaintiff herself alleges. The purported "requirement" flows from Google's alleged "suggestion" of the phrase "free ringtone" through its Keyword Tool, and from the MSSPs' purported knowledge that only "free ringtones" generate substantial revenue-producing internet traffic. According to Plaintiff, MSSPs "[f]acing the Hobson's choice of accepting either Google's 'suggestions' or drastically reduced revenue . . . have accepted Google's 'suggestions' to include the keyword 'free' along with the keyword 'ringtone' in order to advertise to the majority of 'ringtone' searches, whether their products are free or not."

In Google's apt paraphrase, Plaintiff is alleging "that Google's mathematical algorithm 'suggests' the use of the word 'free' in relation to 'ringtone' as a means of attracting more visitors to [the MSSPs'] sites, and that MSSPs whose offerings are not actually free are literally powerless to resist." This reasoning fails to disclose a "requirement" of any kind, nor does it suggest the type of "direct and palpable" involvement that otherwise is required to avoid CDA immunity. Such involvement might occur where a website "remov[es] the word 'not' from a user's message reading '[Name] did not steal the artwork' in order to transform an innocent message into a libelous one." Even accepting Plaintiff's factual allegations as true, the allegations do not come close to suggesting involvement at such a level, or, indeed, that Google's AdWords program was anything other than "a framework that could be utilized for proper or improper purposes."

B. Contract claims in light of *Barnes v. Yahoo!*

As in her original complaint, Plaintiff alleges that she and similarly situated individuals were intended third-party beneficiaries of Google's Advertising Terms, which in turn incorporate a Content Policy requiring that mobile subscription service advertisers display certain information about their products, including whether downloading the products will result in charges to the consumer. Plaintiff alleges that Google "breached" its Content Policy. . . .

Read as broadly as possible, [the 2009 Ninth Circuit opinion in *Barnes v. Yahoo!*] stands for the proposition that when a party engages in conduct giving rise to an independent and enforceable contractual obligation, that party may be "h[eld] . . . liable [not] as a publisher or speaker of third-party content, but rather as a counter-party to a contract, as a promisor who has breached." Theoretically, intended third-party beneficiaries—whose rights under a contract are different from those of the contracting parties but still are legally cognizable—could invoke the distinction drawn in

709

*Barnes* between liability for acts that are coextensive with publishing or speaking and liability for breach of an independent contractual duty. In a third-party-beneficiary case, "as in any other contract case, the duty the defendant allegedly violated [would] spring [ ] from a contract—an enforceable promise—not from any non-contractual conduct or capacity of the defendant." A court thus would be able to infer that the defendant had "implicitly agreed to an alteration" in the baseline rule that there is "no liability for publishing or speaking the content of other information service providers."

In the instant case, there is no allegation that Google ever promised Plaintiff or anyone else, in any form or manner, that it would enforce its Content Policy. Under California law, "[i]f a contract is to be a basis of liability for the [defendant's] violation of [its own terms and conditions] . . . [,] it must be a contract in which the [defendant] promises to abide by [these terms]." Google's Advertising Terms and incorporated Content Policy constituted a promise by Google's advertising customers to Google in exchange for participation in Google's advertising service. Neither agreement contains any promise by Google to enforce its terms of use or otherwise to remove noncompliant advertisements. *Cf.* Green v. America Online, 318 F.3d 465, 472 (3d Cir. 2003) (holding that "Green failed to state a claim for breach of contract because . . . by their terms, the Member Agreement and Community Guidelines were not intended to confer any rights on Green and AOL did not promise to protect Green from the acts of other subscribers").

Moreover, even if Google had promised to enforce its Advertising Terms and incorporated Content Policy—and it did not—Plaintiff would not be a third-party beneficiary of that promise. In that scenario, Google would be the promisor under the agreement and each allegedly fraudulent MSSP would be a promisee. But a third party is not an intended beneficiary of an agreement unless the promisee intends the agreement to benefit the third party. For Plaintiff to be an intended third-party beneficiary of Google's alleged promise, the Advertising Terms would have to reflect an intent by each allegedly fraudulent MSSP to benefit Plaintiff. That proposition simply is illogical, and this Court . . . is "aware of no case in which a third-party-beneficiary contract was formed when a promisee bargained for and obtained a promisor's engagement to force the promisee to satisfy its own obligation to the third party."

Undoubtedly, the allegedly fraudulent MSSPs did promise to abide by the Content Policy, and Plaintiff might well sue them as an intended third-party beneficiary of their contract with Google. But Plaintiff's claim against Google rests not on any promise, but on a "general [content] policy . . . on the part of [Google]," a theory of liability that *Barnes* expressly precludes. Plaintiff's inability to point to any promise by Google, and her ultimate reliance on Google's Content Policy, reveals that unlike the claim in *Barnes*, which rested on a promise that scarcely could have been clearer or more direct, Plaintiff's contract claim alleges liability that "is [not] different from, and [is] merely a rephrasing of, liability for negligent undertaking." This Court already has rejected Plaintiff's contract claim on that very ground . . . and now does so again.

## IV. CONCLUSION

As in the original complaint, each of Plaintiff's claims would treat Google as the publisher or speaker of third-party content. Yet Plaintiff has failed to allege facts that plausibly would support a conclusion that Google created or developed, in whole or in part, any of the allegedly fraudulent AdWords advertisements. Plaintiff offers numerous theories of such involvement, but these theories merely lend truth to the Ninth Circuit's observation that there almost always will be some "argu[ment] that something the website operator did encouraged the illegality." As the en banc court cautioned in *Roommates*, only

> [w]here it is *very clear* that the website directly participates in developing the alleged illegality . . . [will] immunity . . . be lost. . . . [I]n cases of enhancement by implication or development by inference[,] . . . section 230 must be interpreted to protect websites not merely from ultimate liability, but from having to fight costly and protracted legal battles.

(emphasis added). Here, Plaintiff's theory is at best one of "enhancement by implication or development by inference." These "implications" and "inferences" fall well short of making it "very clear" that Google contributed to any alleged illegality, and Plaintiff's complaint clearly must be dismissed. . . .

[The court then declined to give the plaintiff a chance to file another amended complaint:] [T]he Ninth Circuit implicitly has identified a special form of "prejudice" to defendants who improperly are denied early dismissal of claims falling within the zone of CDA immunity. As the court stated in *Roommates*, "close cases . . . . must be resolved in favor of immunity, lest we cut the heart out of section 230 by forcing websites to . . . fight[ ] off claims that they promoted or encouraged—or at least tacitly assented to—the illegality of third parties." Because the CDA "must be interpreted to protect websites not merely from ultimate liability, but from having to fight costly and protracted legal battles," this Court's conclusion that Plaintiff almost certainly will be unable to state a claim compels the additional conclusion that Google must be extricated from this lawsuit now lest the CDA's "robust" protections be eroded by further litigation. For these reasons, Plaintiff's complaint will be dismissed without leave to amend.

*NOTES AND QUESTIONS*

*Internet Exceptionalism.* 230(c)(1) strikes many people as counterintuitive because it makes legal distinctions between the online and offline worlds. It exposes online publishers to far less liability for third-party ads than offline publishers face, because offline publishers can be held liable for editorial decisions such as the decision to publish a particular ad, while the online publisher can't be.

For example, assume an advertiser runs the same ad in both an offline newspaper and a website. If the ad copy is defamatory, the offline newspaper shares equal liability for the ad, while the website would be immune—even though advertiser's identity and the content of the ad copy is identical! The medium of publication determines the liability result.

Would 230(c)(1) change the results in the *Sullivan* or *Knepper* cases if its legal principle applied to offline advertising?

*Dismissal on a Motion to Dismiss.* The court granted Google's 12(b)(6) motion to dismiss. This means that Google never had to answer the complaint, respond to discovery requests, file a summary judgment motion, or convince a jury. If 230(c)(1) applies to a case, usually the result is a fairly cheap and early end to the lawsuit. As the opinion indicated, quick resolution of 230(c)(1)–immunized lawsuits advances the immunity's underlying policy.

*How Far Can a Publisher Go in Helping an Advertiser Prepare Ad Copy and Still Remain Eligible for 230 Protection?* The line between first-party content and third-party content can be ambiguous when online publishers help advertisers prepare ad copy. In the *Goddard* case, for example, Google suggested that advertisers buy certain terms as keyword ad triggers. The ultimate decision of which terms to purchase might ultimately rest with the advertiser, but Google's involvement could be influential. Does Google's persuasion differ from Mueller's influence of Dr. Brown's choices in the *Knepper* case? If Google's keyword suggestion tool recommended that Dr. Brown purchase the keyword phrase "board certified plastic and reconstructive surgery" for his advertisements, should Google be liable for any resulting personal injury?

eBay structures the ad creation process further. Advertisers creating auction listings must fill out specific forms, in some cases using structured pull-down menus that limit the words advertisers can choose. As the *Goddard* case indicates, Ninth Circuit case law, including the *Carafano* and *Roommates.com* cases briefly discussed in *Goddard*, is ambiguous about whether an advertiser's selection of options from a pull-down menu is properly characterized as third-party content (the advertiser chose the words) or first-party content (the publisher chose the words). If the advertiser's use of words in the pull-down menu contribute to the third-party lawsuit, should the publisher still be able to claim 230(c)(1) immunity?

While it's not clear just how much a publisher can help advertisers structure illegal ads, Section 230 definitely has limits. For example, in FTC v. LeadClick Media, LLC, 838 F.3d 158 (2d Cir. 2016), LeadClick ran an affiliate network that provided ads to third party websites, including fake news websites, i.e., the articles about the advertiser's products looked like legitimate news articles and had consumer comments providing (also fake) testimonials. The Second Circuit held LeadClick had directly violated the FTC Act by committing deceptive acts, which the court tautologically said was "allowing" third parties to commit wrongful acts. In turn, LeadClick didn't qualify for Section 230 because the FTC Act violation was based on LeadClick's own conduct. Furthermore, LeadClick partially helped the websites develop their wrongful content by, for example, occasionally suggesting edits to the fake news websites.

*Illegal Ads and the Federal Criminal Prosecution Exception.* By its terms, Section 230 does not apply to federal criminal prosecutions. Google found out the hard way what happens when Section 230 isn't available. In 2011, the Department of Justice and Google settled allegations that Google had illegally accepted third-party advertisements for illicit pharmaceuticals (such as cheap Canadian pharmaceuticals). Google paid a civil forfeiture of $500 million, an amount comprising both Google's ad revenues from the illegal ads *plus* the profits made by the pharmaceutical retailers running those ads.

*Liability for Linking.* Some government agencies believe that a company is liable for third-party content it links to, as if the linked third-party content were the company's own advertising. *See, e.g.*, SEC Release Nos. 34-58288, IC-28351; File No. S7-23-08 (Aug. 7, 2008).

The SEC proposed (Sec. II(B)(2)) that a securities issuer is responsible under securities laws for third-party web content it links to if "the context of the hyperlink and the hyperlinked information together create a reasonable inference that the company has approved or endorsed the hyperlinked information." Thus, if the linked content makes factual claims the issuer itself couldn't lawfully make, the guidance says linking to the content would violate the securities laws. But this would make the issuer (the company establishing the link) liable for third-party content on a remote website—exactly what 230 seems to prevent.

For a different result, *see* In re Gemtronics, Inc., Docket No. 9330, Initial Decision (F.T.C. A.L.J. Sept. 16, 2009) (a dietary supplement seller was not liable for comments on a website that it did not own or control but (among other things) it had linked to).

## C.    Publisher "Must Carry" Obligations

With limited exceptions, publishers may freely refuse to publish ads for any reason. Stated differently, publishers cannot be required to publish ads against their will; such requirements violate the First Amendment's Freedom of the Press clause. The following Supreme Court case reinforced that expansive First Amendment interpretation.

*Miami Herald Publishing Co. v. Tornillo, 418 U.S. 241 (1974)*

I

The issue in this case is whether a state statute granting a political candidate a right to equal space to reply to criticism and attacks on his record by a newspaper violates the guarantees of a free press.

In the fall of 1972, appellee, Executive Director of the Classroom Teachers Association, apparently a teachers' collective bargaining agent, was a candidate for the Florida House of Representatives. On September 20, 1972, and again on September 29, 1972, appellant printed editorials critical of appellee's candidacy. In response to these editorials, appellee demanded that appellant print verbatim his replies, defending the role of the Classroom Teachers Association and the organization's accomplishments for the citizens of Dade County. Appellant declined to print the appellee's replies, and appellee brought suit in Circuit Court, Dade County, seeking declaratory and injunctive relief and actual and punitive damages in excess of $5,000. The action was premised on Florida Statute § 104.38 (1973), a "right of reply" statute which provides that, if a candidate for nomination or election is assailed regarding his personal character or official record by any newspaper, the candidate has the right to demand that the newspaper print, free of cost to the candidate, any reply the candidate may make to the newspaper's charges. The reply must appear in as conspicuous a place and in the same kind of type as the charges which prompted the reply, provided it does not take up more space than the charges. Failure to comply with the statute constitutes a first-degree misdemeanor. . . .

III

A

The challenged statute creates a right to reply to press criticism of a candidate for nomination or election. The statute was enacted in 1913, and this is only the second recorded case decided under its provisions.

Appellant contends the statute is void on its face because it purports to regulate the content of a newspaper in violation of the First Amendment. Alternatively it is urged that the statute is void for vagueness, since no editor could know exactly what words would call the statute into operation. It is also contended that the statute fails to distinguish between critical comment which is, and which is not, defamatory.

B

The appellee and supporting advocates of an enforceable right of access to the press vigorously argue that government has an obligation to ensure that a wide variety of views reach the public. The contentions of access proponents will be set out in some detail. It is urged that, at the time the First Amendment to the Constitution was ratified in 1791 as part of our Bill of Rights, the press was broadly representative of the people it was serving. While many of the newspapers were intensely partisan and narrow in their views, the press collectively presented a broad range of opinions to readers. Entry into publishing was inexpensive; pamphlets and books provided meaningful alternatives to the organized press for the expression of unpopular ideas, and often treated events and expressed views not covered by conventional newspapers. A true marketplace of ideas existed in which there was relatively easy access to the channels of communication.

Access advocates submit that, although newspapers of the present are superficially similar to those of 1791, the press of today is in reality very different from that known in the early years of our national existence. In the past half century, a communications revolution has seen the introduction of radio and television into our lives, the promise of a global community through the use of communications satellites, and the specter of a "wired" nation by means of an expanding cable television network with two-way capabilities. The printed press, it is said, has not escaped the effects of this revolution. Newspapers have become big business, and there are far fewer of them to serve a larger literate population. Chains of newspapers, national newspapers, national wire and news services, and one-newspaper towns[13] are the dominant features of a press that has become noncompetitive and enormously powerful and influential in its capacity to manipulate popular opinion and change the course of events. Major metropolitan newspapers have collaborated to establish news services national in scope. Such national news organizations provide syndicated "interpretive reporting" as well as syndicated features and commentary, all of which can serve as part of the new school of "advocacy journalism."

---

[13] "Nearly half of U.S. daily newspapers, representing some three-fifths of daily and Sunday circulation, are owned by newspaper groups and chains, including diversified business conglomerates. One-newspaper towns have become the rule, with effective competition operating in only 4 percent of our large cities." Background Paper by Alfred Balk in Twentieth Century Fund Task Force Report for a National News Council, A Free and Responsive Press 18 (1973).

The elimination of competing newspapers in most of our large cities, and the concentration of control of media that results from the only newspaper's [sic] being owned by the same interests which own a television station and a radio station, are important components of this trend toward concentration of control of outlets to inform the public. The result of these vast changes has been to place in a few hands the power to inform the American people and shape public opinion.[15] Much of the editorial opinion and commentary that is printed is that of syndicated columnists distributed nationwide and, as a result, we are told, on national and world issues there tends to be a homogeneity of editorial opinion, commentary, and interpretive analysis. The abuses of bias and manipulative reportage are, likewise, said to be the result of the vast accumulations of unreviewable power in the modern media empires. In effect, it is claimed, the public has lost any ability to respond or to contribute in a meaningful way to the debate on issues. The monopoly of the means of communication allows for little or no critical analysis of the media except in professional journals of very limited readership.

> This concentration of nationwide news organizations—like other large institutions—has grown increasingly remote from and unresponsive to the popular constituencies on which they depend and which depend on them.

Report of the Task Force in Twentieth Century Fund Task Force Report for a National News Council, A Free and Responsive Press 4 (1973). Appellee cites the report of the Commission on Freedom of the Press, chaired by Robert M. Hutchins, in which it was stated, as long ago as 1947, that "[t]he right of free public expression has . . . lost its earlier reality."

The obvious solution, which was available to dissidents at an earlier time when entry into publishing was relatively inexpensive, today would be to have additional newspapers. But the same economic factors which have caused the disappearance of vast numbers of metropolitan newspapers, have made entry into the marketplace of ideas served by the print media almost impossible. It is urged that the claim of newspapers to be "surrogates for the public" carries with it a concomitant fiduciary obligation to account for that stewardship. From this premise, it is reasoned that the only effective way to insure fairness and accuracy and to provide for some accountability is for government to take affirmative action. The First Amendment interest of the public in being informed is said to be in peril because the "marketplace of ideas" is today a monopoly controlled by the owners of the market. . . .

IV

However much validity may be found in these arguments, at each point the implementation of a remedy such as an enforceable right of access necessarily calls for some mechanism, either governmental or consensual. If it is governmental coercion, this at once brings about a confrontation

---

[15] "Local monopoly in printed news raises serious questions of diversity of information and opinion. What a local newspaper does not print about local affairs does not see general print at all. And, having the power to take initiative in reporting and enunciation of opinions, it has extraordinary power to set the atmosphere and determine the terms of local consideration of public issues." B. Bagdikian, The Information Machines 127 (1971).

with the express provisions of the First Amendment and the judicial gloss on that Amendment developed over the years. . . .

We see that . . . the Court has expressed sensitivity as to whether a restriction or requirement constituted the compulsion exerted by government on a newspaper to print that which it would not otherwise print. The clear implication has been that any such a compulsion to publish that which "'reason' tells them should not be published" is unconstitutional. A responsible press is an undoubtedly desirable goal, but press responsibility is not mandated by the Constitution, and, like many other virtues, it cannot be legislated.

Appellee's argument that the Florida statute does not amount to a restriction of appellant's right to speak, because "the statute in question here has not prevented the Miami Herald from saying anything it wished," begs the core question. Compelling editors or publishers to publish that which "'reason' tells them should not be published" is what is at issue in this case. The Florida statute operates as a command in the same sense as a statute or regulation forbidding appellant to publish specified matter. Governmental restraint on publishing need not fall into familiar or traditional patterns to be subject to constitutional limitations on governmental powers. The Florida statute exacts a penalty on the basis of the content of a newspaper. The first phase of the penalty resulting from the compelled printing of a reply is exacted in terms of the cost in printing and composing time and materials and in taking up space that could be devoted to other material the newspaper may have preferred to print. It is correct, as appellee contends, that a newspaper is not subject to the finite technological limitations of time that confront a broadcaster, but it is not correct to say that, as an economic reality, a newspaper can proceed to infinite expansion of its column space to accommodate the replies that a government agency determines or a statute commands the readers should have available.

Faced with the penalties that would accrue to any newspaper that published news or commentary arguably within the reach of the right-of-access statute, editors might well conclude that the safe course is to avoid controversy. Therefore, under the operation of the Florida statute, political and electoral coverage would be blunted or reduced. . . .

Even if a newspaper would face no additional costs to comply with a compulsory access law and would not be forced to forgo publication of news or opinion by the inclusion of a reply, the Florida statute fails to clear the barriers of the First Amendment because of its intrusion into the function of editors. A newspaper is more than a passive receptacle or conduit for news, comment, and advertising. The choice of material to go into a new paper, and the decisions made as to limitations on the size and content of the paper, and treatment of public issues and public official—whether fair or unfair—constitute the exercise of editorial control and judgment. It has yet to be demonstrated how governmental regulation of this crucial process can be exercised consistent with First Amendment guarantees of a free press as they have evolved to this time. . . .

[Justices Brennan and White filed concurrences. Justice White's concurrence observed that Florida's "law runs afoul of the elementary First Amendment proposition that government may not force a newspaper to print copy which, in its journalistic discretion, it chooses to leave on the newsroom floor."]

*NOTES AND QUESTIONS*

*The 1970s Media Industry.* As the case indicates, the 1970s saw a lot of media industry consolidation. At the time of the case, many communities had a small number of publishers who could reach an appreciable percentage of the local community—one daily newspaper, up to three broadcast television stations and some radio stations. If, for whatever reason, one of those publishers exhibited bias or made an error and wasn't willing to correct it, there were very few alternative channels to reach the local community.

Today's media industry is very different. Industry segmentation and fragmentation has created a different problem: it's now hard to find a single publisher who can reach an appreciable percentage of the local community. At the same time, anyone who has a problem with a publisher's bias or errors can easily find multiple publishers to proffer an alternative perspective—or can self-publish through websites, blogs, message boards or email lists.

The 1970s media consolidation makes the *Miami Herald* case even more remarkable. The court effectively says that, even if a single publisher has a de facto monopoly on the ability to effectively communicate with the local community, it still cannot be forced to carry unwanted content. Presumably, in the modern media ecosystem with multitudinous publication alternatives, there would be even less need to impose must-carry obligations on publishers.

Even so, media consolidation still exists. For example, Google has a supra-majority share of both the search market and the search advertising market, spurring objections when Google removes a website from its search index or restricts a search advertiser. We will revisit objections to Google's marketplace power in the *Langdon* case below.

*Exception: Broadcasting.* Unlike other publishers, broadcasters licensed by the Federal Communications Commission (FCC) can be subject to must-carry obligations. Consider the "Equal Time Rule," 47 U.S.C. § 315. The rule requires broadcasters to provide political candidates with equal broadcasting opportunities. As a result, if a broadcaster sells a one-minute ad to one candidate, it must allow that candidate's opponents to buy a one-minute ad at favorable prices. Broadcaster must-carry obligations are premised, in part, on the perception that broadcast spectrum is scarce, which necessitates regulatory restriction on entry to the broadcast market. Other media do not have the same legal restrictions on marketplace entry, which reduces the importance of must-carry obligations for those media.

*Exception: Discrimination.* In *Pittsburgh Press Co. v. Pittsburgh Commission on Human Relations*, 413 U.S. 376 (1973), the Supreme Court held that the First Amendment did not protect a newspaper's classified ad headings titled "help wanted—male" and "help wanted—female" because the headings facilitated illegal sex-based job discrimination.

*Exception: Government as Advertising Venue Provider.* When the government is the "publisher" or otherwise provides advertising inventory, must-carry rules take on a different perspective. Because the government's rejection of advertisements constitutes state action restricting the advertiser's speech, the advertiser can challenge the rejection as a Constitutional violation.

In *Perry Education Ass'n v. Perry Local Educators' Ass'n*, 460 U.S. 37 (1983), a school district gave the teachers' union a preferential right to distribute materials through the interschool mail system. A rival union complained that this preferential distribution right violated its First Amendment rights. The U.S. Supreme Court ultimately rejected the complaint, saying that the mail system did not qualify as a "public forum" or "limited public forum," in which the government would not be allowed to discriminate on the basis of content or viewpoint. The court then determined that the school district's restrictions were reasonable:

> [W]hen government property is not dedicated to open communication, the government may—without further justification—restrict use to those who participate in the forum's official business. Finally, the reasonableness of the limitations on PLEA's access to the school mail system is also supported by the substantial alternative channels that remain open for union-teacher communication to take place. These means range from bulletin boards to meeting facilities to the United States mail. . . . There is no showing here that PLEA's ability to communicate with teachers is seriously impinged by the restricted access to the internal mail system. The variety and type of alternative modes of access present here compare favorably with those in other nonpublic forum cases where we have upheld restrictions on access.

Courts have divided on how to treat advertising allowed by public authorities on property open to the public. *Compare, e.g.*, Seattle Mideast Awareness Campaign v. King County, 781 F. 3d 489 (9th Cir. 2015) (finding public transit advertising to be a limited public forum and that transit authorities could impose restrictions on false or misleading speech), *with, e.g.*, AFDI v. Suburban Mobility Auth. for Regional Transp., 698 F. 3d 885 (6th Cir. 2012) (finding that, by allowing political advertising, transit authority created a designated public forum and could not further restrict content without satisfying strict scrutiny) *and* Christ's Bride Ministries, Inc. v. Southeastern Pennsylvania Transportation Authority, 148 F.3d 242 (3d Cir. 1998) (transit authority's decision to remove anti-abortion ads would not have satisfied rational basis review).

*Distinctions between Publishers and Advertisers.* While the First Amendment lets publishers decide what to publish, the government sometimes can require advertisers to include mandatory disclosures without violating the First Amendment. Cigarette label warnings are one obvious example, but "disclosure + disclaimer" laws are pervasive, as Chapter 5 covers in greater detail. Is the difference between an advertiser and a publisher—both of which may be profit-seeking entities—sufficient to justify this different treatment?

*Statutory Protection for Refusing Ads.* In addition to the First Amendment, 47 U.S.C. § 230(c)(2)—another section of the Communications Decency Act that complements 230(c)(1) discussed above—provides online publishers with a statutory safe harbor for refusing ads. It states:

> No provider or user of an interactive computer service shall be held liable on account of (A) any action voluntarily taken in good faith to restrict access to or availability of material that the provider or user considers to be obscene, lewd, lascivious, filthy, excessively violent,

harassing, or otherwise objectionable, whether or not such material is constitutionally protected. . . .

The next case shows how Section 230 supplements the First Amendment to give publishers the discretion to reject unwanted ads.

*Langdon v. Google, Inc., 474 F. Supp. 2d 622 (D. Del. 2007)*

. . . Plaintiff has two internet websites; www.NCJusticeFraud.com ("NCJustice") and www.ChinaIsEvil.com ("China"). The Amended Complaint alleges that the NCJustice website exposes fraud perpetrated by various North Carolina government officials and employees, including Roy Cooper ("Cooper"), the North Carolina Attorney General, and that the China website delineates atrocities committed by the Chinese government. The Amended Complaint alleges that Defendants refused to run ads on the two websites, specifically two Cooper ads on the NCJustice website and one ad on the China website.

More particularly, Plaintiff alleges that Google gave a fraudulent excuse for not running the Cooper ads, that the reasons for refusal do not appear in its website or in its ad content policy, and that Google gave no reason for not running the China ad. . . .

Plaintiff's allegations against Microsoft are that he applied for and was accepted into Microsoft's pilot ad program, submitted his China ad, but never received a response. Plaintiff alleges that ignoring him resulted in a de facto refusal to run his ad. He alleges that Microsoft is using fraud to breach its contract.

Plaintiff's allegations against Yahoo are that he attempted to advertise on Yahoo's search engine, but was told by a Yahoo representative that it does not accept advertising for websites it does not host. Plaintiff alleges he wrote to Yahoo regarding the matter but received no response. . . .

Plaintiff alleges that he has no viable alternative other than to advertise on Defendants' search engines. He seeks declaratory and injunctive relief and compensatory and punitive damages. . . .

3. Defendants' First Amendment Rights

Google and Microsoft argue that Plaintiff's claims are barred as a matter of law, and that the relief sought by him is precluded by their First Amendment Rights. Google points to the relief sought by Plaintiff that Google, Yahoo, and Microsoft place Plaintiff's ads for his websites in prominent places on their search engine results and that Defendants "honestly" rank Plaintiff's websites.

Google argues that such relief would compel it to speak in a manner deemed appropriate by Plaintiff and would prevent Google from speaking in ways that Plaintiff dislikes. It contends such relief contravenes the First Amendment. Plaintiff did not respond to this issue.

The First Amendment guarantees an individual the right to free speech, "a term necessarily comprising the decision of both what to say and what not to say." Defendants are correct in their position that the injunctive relief sought by Plaintiff contravenes Defendants' First Amendment rights. *See* Miami Herald Publ'g Co. v. Tornillo, 418 U.S. 241 (1974) (forcing newspapers to print candidates' replies to editorials is an impermissible burden on editorial control and judgment); Sinn v. The Daily Nebraskan, 829 F.2d 662 (8th Cir. 1987) (University newspaper's rejection of roommate advertisements in which advertisers stated their gay or lesbian orientation was a constitutionally protected editorial decision); Associates & Aldrich Co. v. Times Mirror Co., 440 F.2d 133 (9th Cir. 1971) (Court cannot compel the publisher of a private daily newspaper to accept and print advertising in the exact form submitted based upon the freedom to exercise subjective editorial discretion in rejecting a proffered article). Accordingly, the Court will grant Google's and Microsoft's Motion To Dismiss the Amended Complaint on the basis that Plaintiff seeks relief precluded by their First Amendment rights.

4. Communications Decency Act

Google and Microsoft argue that the Communications Decency Act, 47 U.S.C. § 230(c)(2)(A), provides them immunity from suit from claims grounded upon their exercise of editorial discretion over internet content and editorial decisions regarding screening and deletion of content from their services. . . .

Plaintiff argues that § 230 is inapplicable because none of the Defendants refused to run the Cooper ads because they were obscene or that the websites were harassing. He also argues that neither Google nor Microsoft offered a reason for not running the China ads and that Yahoo provided a false reason for not running the ads. Plaintiff argues that Defendants cannot create "purported reasons" for not running the ads. . . .

It is evident from the allegations in the Amended Complaint that Plaintiff attempts to hold Defendants liable for decisions relating to the monitoring, screening, and deletion of content from their network. As noted by the *Green* Court, these actions are "quintessentially related to a publisher's role" and "§ 230 'specifically proscribes liability' in such circumstances."

Plaintiff's position that § 230 is inapplicable is not well-taken. Plaintiff argues there was no refusal to run his ads on the basis they were obscene or harassing, and that Defendants cannot create "purported reasons for not running his ads." He omits, however, reference to that portion of § 230 which provides immunity from suit for restricting material that is "otherwise objectionable."

Section 230 provides Google, Yahoo, and Microsoft immunity for their editorial decisions regarding screening and deletion from their network. Therefore, the Court will grant the Motions To Dismiss all such claims as raised by Plaintiff.

5. Plaintiff's First Amendment Rights

Defendants argue that Plaintiff cannot state a claim for violation of his right to free speech under either the United States or Delaware Constitution because they are not state actors. Particularly,

720

Google contends that the Amended Complaint makes clear that it is a for-profit company as it is identified as a corporation and there are allegations of Google's for-profit AdWords program.

Plaintiff alleges that internet search engines are public forums, and that private property opened to the public may be subject to the First Amendment. Plaintiff compares internet search engines to malls and/or shopping centers and contends that Google has dedicated its private property as a public forum. Plaintiff relies upon several U.S. Supreme Court cases to support his position. He also posits that Google works with private and public universities and that this government entwinement with a private entity results in state action as required by 42 U.S.C. § 1983.

When bringing a § 1983 claim, a plaintiff must allege that some person has deprived him of a federal right, and that the person who caused the deprivation acted under color of state law. To act under "color of state law" a defendant must be "clothed with the authority of state law."

Plaintiff has failed to state a claim that Defendants violated his First Amendment right to free speech. Defendants are private, for profit companies, not subject to constitutional free speech guarantees. They are internet search engines that use the internet as a medium to conduct business. . . .

Plaintiff's analogy of Defendants' private networks to shopping centers and his position that since they are open to the public they become public forums is not supported by case law. The Supreme Court has consistently held that a private shopping center is not a public forum for speech purposes. The Court has routinely rejected the assumption that people who want to express their views in a private facility, such as a shopping center, have a constitutional right to do so. Private property does not "lose its private character merely because the public is generally invited to use it for designated purposes." Similarly, the Court finds unavailing Plaintiff's argument that he has no reasonable alternative to advertising on Defendants' search engines. *See* Cyber Promotions, Inc. v. American Online, Inc., 948 F.Supp. 436, 443 (E.D. Pa. 1996) (private company had numerous alternatives for reaching customers including mail, television, cable, newspapers, magazines, and competing commercial online services).

Defendants are not state actors. Plaintiff has failed to state a § 1983 claim, and therefore, the Court will grant the Motions To Dismiss the First Amendment Claims. . . .

*NOTES AND QUESTIONS*

Courts routinely conclude that search engines have virtually unrestricted discretion to decide what content to carry and how to order it, relying on First Amendment and Section 230 grounds. *See, e.g.,* Zhang v. Baidu.com, Inc., 10 F.Supp.3d 433 (S.D.N.Y. 2014); O'Kroley v. Fastcase, Inc., 831 F.3d 352 (6th Cir. 2016); *see also* Prager University v. Google LLC, 2018 WL 1471939 (N.D. Cal. March 26, 2018) (YouTube isn't a "company town" and therefore is not obligated to follow the First Amendment for its users).

If all of the major search engines independently decide not to carry Langdon's search ads, what cost-effective advertising alternatives does Langdon have in practice? Note that search advertising is usually charged on a cost-per-click basis, meaning that Langdon does not have to pay for running the ads unless someone clicks on them. Therefore, unlike many forms of advertising which require an upfront payment, search advertising can be extremely low-cost for highly targeted, lightly clicked ads. Then again, due to Google's ad quality score, Langdon's ads will not necessarily show to consumers regardless of what bids Langdon placed for his ads.

**4.    Measuring Advertising Activity and Fraud**

*Payment Methods for Advertising*

Publishers typically charge advertisers using one of the following methods:

- *Fixed fee.* The advertiser pays a fixed amount for the advertising services, such as a set monthly fee, regardless of how many people actually see the ad copy. Roadside billboards and consumer classified advertisements in print periodicals are typically charged on this basis.

- *Per impression.* The advertiser pays based on the number of consumers who are exposed to the ad copy, typically priced in blocks of 1,000 consumers. As a result, it is often called "CPM" advertising (cost per thousand impressions, where M is the Roman numeral for 1,000). Broadcast advertising and online display advertising is often sold on a CPM basis.

- *Per click/per call.* The advertiser pays based on the number of consumers who directly respond to the advertiser. For example, online keyword advertising is typically charged on a cost-per-click ("CPC") basis. Each time a consumer clicks on the link in the keyword ad, the advertiser pays the agreed-upon CPC amount. A variation is to charge per-call for the number of phone calls to a unique telephone number in the ad copy (*see, e.g.,* Google AdWords' bid-per-call option).

- *Per action.* Sometimes, the advertiser wants consumers to take a specified action beyond just clicking or calling, such as filling out an online form or creating an online account. An ad may be charged on a cost-per-action ("CPA") basis when consumers take the desired action. A variation is when advertisers pay for every new customer attributable to the publisher, regardless of how much the customer spends with the advertiser. These ads may be described as cost-per-acquisition (also "CPA").

- *Revenue share.* An advertiser can pay the publisher by sharing incremental revenues generated by ads disseminated by the publisher. For example, many online retailers pay independent contractors ("affiliates") a percentage of all new sales directly attributable to the affiliate's promotional efforts. *Note:* In some industries, such as real estate, travel, medical and legal services, getting paid a commission may require the publisher to have the requisite state-issued license or may be an illegal referral scheme.

How do publishers and advertisers decide which payment method is best? In a perfectly efficient market, it shouldn't matter. Assume that an advertiser is running a direct-response advertisement for a widget it makes that will generate $1.00 of gross profit per unit, and the advertiser is willing to share half of that profit ($0.50 per unit) with the publisher. Assume a print publisher has an audience of 1,000,000 readers, 1% of the readers will contact the advertiser in response to the ad (10,000 readers), and 2.5% of those will actually buy an average of one widget (resulting in 250 buyers and 250 widgets sold). In this case, the advertisement will generate $250 of gross profit for the advertiser. The advertiser should be willing to pay:

- on a fixed-fee basis: $125 (50% of the advertiser's expected profits)
- on a CPM basis: 12.5 cents CPM (1 million, or 1,000 M, readers x $0.125 CPM = $125)
- on a CPC basis: 1.25 cents (10,000 reader contacts x $0.0125 = $125)
- using a revenue share: if the product price is $10, then gross revenue would be $2,500 (gross profit, as noted above, is $250), and the revenue share would be 5%.

As you can see, the advertiser and publisher could set prices so that they are equally happy with any of the pricing options.

In reality, the parties often won't know how well the ad will actually perform. Unless the publisher and advertiser have a solid track record of experience with each other, neither party may know how the publisher's audience will respond to the advertiser's offering.

As a result, the different pricing options effectively shift risk between the advertiser and the publisher. With the fixed-fee option, the publisher knows exactly how much it will be paid, and the advertiser assumes all of the risk about the audience's propensity to buy its offering.

In contrast, with a revenue share, the advertiser takes no risk—it only pays if it gets new incremental sales—while the publisher assumes all of the risk of performance. Thus, with the revenue share, the publisher might get paid zero dollars for its advertising services, even if the poor performance is due solely to how the advertiser handles interested consumers and not due to the publisher's failure to deliver interested consumers.

Ad pricing options can be placed on a risk continuum:

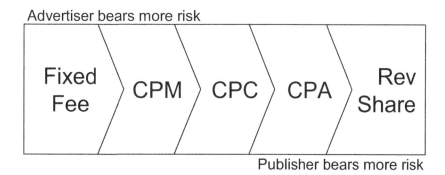

As you can see, CPC advertising fits in the middle of the risk continuum. The publisher takes some risk that it can deliver consumers to the advertiser's doorstep, but once there, the advertiser has the onus to convert those consumers into buyers. Meanwhile, the advertiser does not pay the publisher anything until the publisher delivers a consumer to the advertiser's doorstep. This compromise in risk-sharing may help explain the massive success of CPC pricing for online keyword advertising. At minimum, it gives one good explanation for why many advertisers prefer CPC keyword advertising over fixed-fee ads like Yellow Pages, where advertisers bears all of the performance risk.

The risk continuum is less relevant to brand advertising, which does not seek to generate immediate sales anyway. Instead, for mass-market consumer goods, brand advertisers often want widespread exposure to as many consumers as possible. This partially explains why brand advertisers frequently accept CPM advertising for broadcast ads—broadcasters can deliver big audiences, and the risks to advertisers inherent in CPM advertising matter less. (Also, broadcast may be more effective at communicating brand messages to consumers than print or text.)

*Tracking and Measuring Activity*

With CPM, CPC and CPA advertising, the compensated activity must be tracked by someone. For, example, who determines how many ad impressions were delivered? Advertisers are reluctant to rely on publisher self-reporting of impressions. After all, publishers—and their commissioned salespeople—have financial incentives to lie.

As a result, in some sectors of the advertising industry, third-party service providers measure publisher activity. For example, the Nielsen service measures the number of TV broadcast viewers and radio listeners. Its measurement methodologies can vary, but often the measurement vendors use population sampling to measure the media consumption of a small but statistically significant subgroup. Vendors can then extrapolate those numbers to the larger community.

In the print publishing business, the Alliance for Audited Media (AAM), formerly known as the Audit Bureau of Circulations (ABC), is a leading service provider. The AAM promulgates general rules for counting the number of copies circulated by publishers (such as how to count paid subscriptions and freely distributed copies) and audits individual publishers to verify their counts.

Despite the AAM, print publishers are caught overstating their circulation numbers to advertisers with disquieting frequency. For example, in the early 2000s, major newspapers such as *Newsday*, the *Chicago Sun-Times* and the *Dallas Morning News* were all embroiled in circulation inflation scandals. *See, e.g.*, Frank Ahrens, *Circulation Fraud Contained, Audit Group Says*, WASH. POST, Nov. 12, 2004, at E4.

*In re Newsday Litigation*, 2008 WL 2884784 (E.D.N.Y. 2008) gives some perspective of the financial and criminal repercussions of circulation measurement fraud. The court says:

> The fraud was massive, resulting in losses affecting tens of thousands of victim advertisers in an amount originally estimated by Tribune itself as exceeding eighty million dollars. The charging documents generally allege that the fraud continued for almost four years, from January of 2000 through July of 2004.

Nine individuals were prosecuted as part of the fraud. In addition, *Newsday* and its sibling publication *Hoy* entered into an agreement with the federal government. According to the court:

> In the agreement, Newsday and Hoy each admit that they
>
> > violated federal criminal law by engaging in schemes that defrauded their advertisers, by systematically inflating paid circulation numbers reported in their books and records and falsely representing the accuracy of the inflated numbers to the Audit Bureau of Circulations ("ABC"), an industry organization.
>
> > Newsday and Hoy further acknowledge in the agreement that they have made payments "of approximately $83 million, to date, to entities that placed ads in Newsday and Hoy in settlement of pending or potential claims" related to the circulation fraud. In addition, both Newsday and Hoy have agreed to pay $15 million to settle a civil forfeiture action commenced by the United States....

Measurement service providers for online activities generally have not yet gained the degree of recognition that providers like Nielsen and AAM have garnered offline. Accordingly, it is still fairly common for online publishers to self-report the number of ad impressions or clicks they deliver to advertisers. When online advertisers pay on a "cost per action" or "revenue share" basis, the advertisers measure the actions or revenues and report back to publishers. Reports of online activities are not easily verified by third parties, so online publishers and advertisers often disagree with each other about the measurements.

The parties may also dispute the definition of the measured activity in the advertising contract. The following case shows a fairly typical dispute over how to count the number of ad "impressions" delivered by the publisher. How could the parties have avoided this dispute?

### Go2Net, Inc. v. C.I. Host, Inc., 60 P.3d 1245 (Wash. Ct. App. 2003)

This lawsuit involves a dispute over the meaning of "impressions," a key term in Internet advertising. C I Host twice contracted with Go2Net to post advertisements on its website. The agreements provided that Go2Net would charge C I Host based on the number of "impressions" recorded by Go2Net's ad engine count. C I Host refused to pay for the service, purportedly because it suspected that Go2Net was including visits by search engines and other "artificial intelligence" agents, as well as human viewers, in its count of impressions. Go2Net filed suit against C I Host to enforce the agreements, arguing that the agreements unambiguously allowed Go2Net to count impressions in this manner. The trial court granted summary judgment to Go2Net, and denied C I Host's motion for reconsideration based on what C I Host argued was newly discovered evidence. C I Host appeals. We affirm.

FACTS

C I Host, Inc., is a Texas-based provider of web hosting and electronic commerce consulting services. Go2Net, Inc., d/b/a Infospace, is a Seattle-based Internet service company that owns and manages a variety of websites and provides advertising services on the web. On May 15 and July 7, 2000, respectively, C I Host entered into separate advertising agreements with Go2Net, Inc., under which Go2Net agreed to display advertisements for C I Host on websites within the Go2Net network, including a website called HyperMart.

Both advertising agreements provided that Go2Net would deliver C I Host a certain number of "impressions." The parties dispute the precise meaning of this term. A *Wall Street Journal* article dated November 16, 2001, discusses problems in the Internet ad industry arising from the fact that Internet publishers "use many different methods to measure ad impressions." Some count the number of times an ad is sent to a computer screen, while others count only the number of times it actually shows up on the screen. And some companies count visits by automated web crawlers and search engines as ad impressions, even though the "visits" were not made by actual human consumers. The article stated that several Internet companies were in the process of developing a standardized "single method for counting online ad 'impressions.'" The Interactive Advertising Bureau, a group of online publishers that rely on ad revenue, recently defined the term "impression" as follows:

> 1) an ad which is served to a user's browser. Ads can be requested by the user's browser (referred to as pulled ads) or they can be pushed, such as emailed ads; 2) a measurement of responses from an ad delivery system to an ad request from the user's browser, which is filtered from robotic activity and is recorded at a point as late as possible in the process of delivery of the creative material to the user's browser—therefore closest to the actual opportunity to see by the user.

The May advertising agreement contemplated a one-month advertising campaign commencing on May 30, 2000, in which Go2Net would deliver approximately 385,000 "total impressions" for $4,820. The July agreement contemplated a twelve-month campaign, commencing July 13, 2000, in which Go2Net would deliver 30,000,000 "total impressions" for $286,100. The agreements provided that Go2Net's equipment would count the number of impressions and would bill accordingly:

> All impressions billed are based on Go2Net's ad engine count of impressions. In the event of a conflict between the number of impressions reported by Go2Net, Inc. and any remote server, the Go2Net, Inc. count stands. All payments will be based on Go2Net, Inc. ad server counts.

The agreements did not guarantee or provide for payment based on the number of "click-throughs," or times a viewer clicks on a banner advertisement and is routed to the advertiser's website. Rather, the agreements provided that:

> Go2Net makes no representations or warranties relating to the results of Advertiser's advertising by means of the Internet, including without limitation, the number of page views or click-thrus such advertising will receive and any promotional effect thereof.

The term "impressions" was not explicitly defined in either agreement. . . .

726

C I Host's computer network system possesses the capability to automatically track and monitor all persons visiting C I Host websites. Therefore, C I Host is able to create daily, weekly, and monthly reports that reveal the number of persons that have visited a C I Host website by clicking on a particular ad carried by a particular website. However, C I Host's monitoring system does not monitor or track visits by non-human entities such as web crawlers or search engines, also known as "artificial intelligence." At some point during the advertising campaign, C I Host audited its traffic activity reports and discovered that the number of persons who had accessed the C I Host website by "clicking through" from ads on Go2Net websites was lower than its typical average for this type of advertising. This purportedly caused C I Host to believe that Go2Net was not delivering the number of impressions for which C I Host was being billed. . . .

## ANALYSIS

. . . Although it may seem counterintuitive in light of undisputed evidence in the record that there is no single industry-wide accepted definition of "impressions," so that the term would seem to be inherently ambiguous, C I Host's arguments are ultimately unpersuasive. This is because the agreements plainly provide that "[a]ll impressions billed are based on Go2Net's ad engine count of impressions," and that "[i]n the event of a conflict between the numbers of impressions reported by Go2Net, Inc. and any remote server, the Go2Net, Inc. count stands." This language shows an objective mutual intent to allow Go2Net's method of counting impressions to prevail, and it effectively preempts any arguments over the definition of "impressions." Go2Net did exactly what the agreement said it could do: it billed C I Host based on Go2Net's ad engine count of impressions. Had C I Host wished to ensure that Go2Net's ad engine was counting only the number of times a human actually viewed the ad, it should have contracted to count the number of impressions itself, or specified its own definition of "impressions" in the agreements. C I Host is effectively asking the court to alter the plain language of the agreement to read that "all impressions billed are based on Go2Net's ad engine count of impressions, and Go2Net's ad engine shall count only the number of times a C I Host ad is actually sent to a computer screen." This is not a reasonable reading of the agreements, because it is based on a definition of "impressions" that the parties did not express, and it contradicts the plain meaning of the clause providing that Go2Net's count of impressions will stand. . . .

The fact that Faulkner canceled the ad campaign after discovering an unexpectedly low click-through rate is not objective evidence of the parties' alleged intent to count only visits from human viewers as "impressions." Rather, it simply indicates C I Host's intent not to spend any more money on an unsuccessful ad campaign. The *Wall Street Journal* article submitted by C I Host demonstrates that, at the time the parties entered into the advertising agreements, there was no universally agreed-upon definition of impressions in the Internet advertising industry. However, that does not render these particular agreements ambiguous; it merely indicates that there is more than one way to count impressions, including the method employed by Go2Net. This only serves to emphasize the importance of specifying in the contract how impressions are to be counted. Here, the parties agreed to bill based on Go2Net's ad engine count of impressions. . . . The agreement is not ambiguous. . . .

*NOTES AND QUESTIONS*

*Non-Performance as a Defense to a Collections Action*. Frequently, when a publisher sues an advertiser for non-payment, the advertiser will disparage the publisher's performance as a defense or counterclaim. By getting advertisers to prepay for advertising, publishers can avoid having to sue their customers for non-payment and avoid the associated risk of non-performance counterclaims.

*Whose Numbers Control?* The publisher's contract included a provision that its impression counts were determinative. Not every court would honor such a self-serving clause; at minimum, most courts would apply a duty of good faith and fair dealing to the clause.

*Counting Robotic Activity*. The publisher was in the uncomfortable position of arguing that the advertiser should pay for impressions generated automatically by third-party activity. In many situations, publishers would automatically screen out those impressions and not attempt to charge for them. Some disputes arise when the publisher is less conservative about discounting automated activity than the advertiser would like the publisher to be.

*Performance Assumptions*. The advertiser made certain assumptions about the number of clicks the advertisements would generate, and the advertiser canceled the ad campaign when the publisher failed to meet those assumptions. If the advertiser really cared about click-throughs, why did the parties agree to measure the publisher's performance based on impressions?

"Bad traffic" (i.e., poorly performing referrals from a publisher) is a common complaint by advertisers. To overcome this advertiser fear, Meredith, a major print publisher that charged for ads per impression, nevertheless contractually promised to deliver a minimum sales "lift" (i.e., new incremental sales) for its largest advertisers. *See* Nat Ives, *Meredith Guarantees Top Advertisers Sales Gains*, AD. AGE, July 25, 2011.

*Industry Standards*. An industry group, the Internet Advertising Bureau (IAB), has developed guidelines for defining impressions that many publishers and advertisers now refer to. IAB, *Ad Impression Measurement Guidelines*, https://www.iab.com/guidelines/iab-measurement-guidelines/.

*Underdelivery*. When publishers fail to deliver a promised number of impressions, they often fix this problem by giving the advertiser "make-goods," which are subsequent additional ads provided at no additional cost to reach the contracted quantity. For example, if a TV broadcaster promises that an upcoming TV series episode will deliver 5,000,000 viewers but the episode actually only attracts 3,000,000 viewers, the broadcaster may promise to "make good" the unrealized 2,000,000 viewers through subsequent additional advertising. A make-good remedy means the publisher doesn't have to refund money to advertisers for underperformance.

*What is a "Click"?* A lot of the online advertising in the 1990s was sold on a per-impression basis. Although some online advertising is still sold per-impression, CPC advertising has eclipsed it in importance.

However, measuring activity on a "per-click" basis does not eliminate definitional ambiguity. In the mid-2000s, advertisers brought class action lawsuits against both Google and Yahoo claiming that the search engines charged for illegitimate clicks on the advertisers' CPC ads—a phenomenon called "click fraud," although the "fraud" reference may be a misnomer (or at least overly dramatic). Click fraud can occur in a variety of ways, including:

- Outright overstatement of activity.
- Charging for clicks produced by automated behavior, such as by robots automatically following online links.
- Charging for clicks that are made for illegitimate purposes. For example, competitor A may click on competitor B's ads to drain competitor B's advertising budget; or if the search engine "syndicates" the ad to a third-party website and shares some of the revenue with the website, the website operator has a financial incentive to click on the ad.

Both search engines ultimately entered into multi-million dollar settlements with advertisers over these claims.

*What is a "Visitor"?* In *WebMD, LLC v. RDA International, Inc.*, 22 Misc. 3d 1114 (N.Y. Sup. Ct. 2009), the parties contracted for the publisher to deliver "36,000 visitors" to a specified website. The advertiser subsequently contended that the contract meant 36,000 *unique* visitors. The difference could be substantial; visitors who visited the specified website more than once would be counted as one unique visitor, under the advertiser's interpretation, and as a visitor each time they arrived at the specified website, under the publisher's interpretation. Like the advertiser's arguments in *Go2Net*, the advertiser's argument went nowhere:

> [A]lthough undefined, the term "visitors" is unambiguous. The definitions advanced by the organizations quoted by [advertiser] refer to "unique visitors," and do not define the term "visitor" to mean "unique visitor." If [advertiser] wished to be guaranteed "unique visitors" to the site, it should have specified such in the agreement.

*Contract Drafting Tips.* Publishers should be very precise in their contracts about what they are delivering to advertisers. They should also include, as the publisher in *Go2Net* did, a provision saying that their measurements are determinative.

Advertisers also should precisely define what they are buying. If the advertiser wants *unique* visitors, it should say so. Or, if impressions are just a proxy for some other desired behavior (like clicks), the advertiser should make its performance assumptions explicit in the contract. Of course, this may be easier said than done. For example, unless you are a major advertiser, good luck negotiating with Google over its AdWords contract.

## 1.     The Food and Drug Administration (FDA)

Food and drugs are regulated the FTC and the FDA, and they have overlapping jurisdiction. In 1971, the agencies issued a memorandum of understanding under which the FDA assumed primary responsibility for drug labeling and the FTC assumed primary responsibility for the advertising of food, medical devices and cosmetics. The FDA is responsible for ads for prescription drugs, and the FTC covers ads for over-the-counter drugs.

### A.     Prescription Drugs and Medical Devices

The FDA's authority to regulate prescription drug and medical device advertising arises from the 1938 Federal Food, Drug, and Cosmetic Act (FDCA), which authorizes the agency to comprehensively regulate drugs and medical devices in the United States.

As part of its mandate, the FDA regulates all forms of prescription drug advertising, including direct-to-consumer advertising. It generally defines advertising expansively to include any information, other than labeling, that promotes a drug product and is sponsored by a manufacturer.

Labeling, which is subject to more stringent regulations, includes "brochures, booklets, mailing pieces, detailing pieces, file cards, bulletins, calendars, price lists, catalogs, house organs, letters, motion picture films, film strips, lantern slides, sound recordings, exhibits, literature," and other matter directed toward medical professionals. *See* 21 C.F.R. 202.1(1)(2) (2000). Pharmaceutical companies are not allowed to market drugs for "off-label," non-approved uses. However, doctors may prescribe drugs off-label, and billions of dollars of revenue come from such use. In the past decade, numerous companies paid multi-million dollar fines for unlawful off-label marketing to doctors.

More recently still, pharmaceutical companies have increasingly succeeded in arguing that restrictions on truthful, nonmisleading marketing of off-label uses to doctors violate the First Amendment. In *United States v. Caronia*, 703 F.3d 149 (2d Cir. 2012), the court of appeals vacated a pharmaceutical sales representative's conviction for conspiring to introduce a misbranded drug into interstate commerce. The conviction was based on Caronia's having promoted a drug for "off-label use," i.e., a use other than the one approved by the FDA. The court held that, to survive the First Amendment, the misbranding provisions of the FDCA must be construed "as not prohibiting and criminalizing the truthful off-label promotion of FDA-approved prescription drugs." *Amarin Pharma, Inc. v. U.S. Food & Drug Admin.*, 119 F. Supp. 3d 196 (S.D.N.Y. 2015), held that the drug company could make the same statements to doctors about off-label uses to promote prescriptions for those unapproved uses, so long as the statements were truthful and nonmisleading. Because off-label use of drugs is lawful, penalizing truthful statements promoting an off-label use "'paternalistically' interferes with the ability of physicians and patients to receive potentially relevant treatment information."

The health care industry spent $14 billion on advertising in 2014, an increase of nearly 20 percent since 2011; much of that is direct-to-consumer (DTC) prescription drug advertising. There is a vigorous debate about whether DTC advertising benefits consumers more than it harms them. Opponents argue that treating drugs like ice cream inevitably leads to drugmakers promoting the creation and/or overdiagnosis of various conditions, pathologizing everyday life (the advent of "restless leg syndrome" is a typical example), and leading consumers to spend billions on treatments that tend to have significant side effects and risks attached. *Cf., e.g.,* L.B. Vater et al., *What Are Cancer Centers Advertising to the Public? A Content Analysis*, 160 ANNALS INTERNAL MED. 813 (2014) (finding that cancer center ads generally appeal to emotion rather than presenting data on treatment response, side effects, costs, and alternatives). Proponents argue that consumers who identify problems that can be treated are better off, even if previous generations accepted conditions such as erectile dysfunction as inevitable.

Research suggests that drug ads do communicate important information about benefits and risks to the public, but imperfectly so. Ads for Lipitor, for example, didn't tell many consumers more than they already knew about the existence of cholesterol-lowering medicines, but they did inform 34% of ad viewers that Lipitor hasn't been shown to prevent heart attacks, compared to 5% who knew that without seeing the ad. On the other hand, that percentage demonstrates that most people who saw the Lipitor ad didn't understand the limitation. Ads were best at communicating basic information such as the medicine's name and what it treats, with mixed effectiveness communicating about side effects and where to get more information. Viewers were more likely than non-viewers to perceive side effects as serious, but viewers were also not very good at remembering which side effects were mentioned; they often focused on just one out of a list. Over 60% of viewers said they trusted the information they'd seen in a specific ad shown to them, while a substantially lower percentage of those who weren't shown a specific ad but were asked about ads in general said so. Ads do lead many people to talk to their doctors, and a "small but significant minority" said they received prescriptions for the drugs as a result. *See* The Henry J. Kaiser Family Foundation, *Understanding the Effects of Direct-to-Consumer Prescription Drug Advertising*, Nov. 2001.

Advertisements for prescription drugs must include a true statement of: (1) the drug's generic name, in letters at least half as large as the letters in the brand name and as prominently placed as the brand name; (2) the drug's formula (for drugs with a single active ingredient, this means the generic name and quantity of that ingredient); and (3) a brief true summary of the drug's side-effects, contraindications, warnings, and precautions, as well as the indications for use, providing a "fair balance" of the risks and effectiveness of the drug such that side effects and contraindications are featured with comparable prominence to the benefits. Consumer-directed ads must have fair balance information in language that they can understand. *See* F.D.A. Notice, *Direct to Consumer Promotion*, 60 F.R. 42,581, 42,583 (Aug. 16, 1995).

A prescription drug advertisement that violates the FDCA or an FDA regulation is considered "misbranded" and may lead to seizure, an injunction, and criminal penalties. *See* 21 U.S.C. §§ 331, 332, 334.

Because it may be impractical to include all the "brief summary" information in very short ads, there is an exception to the brief summary requirement if "adequate provision" is made for distribution of the approved product labeling to as many people as possible. Adequate provision might include: (1) a toll free number in the ad; (2) print advertisements appearing contemporaneously in publications directed at the same audience, where the broadcast ad refers to at least one publication; (3) a URL in the ad; *and* (4) disclosure in the ad that healthcare providers may have more information. *See* FDA, *Guidance for Industry, Consumer-Directed Broadcast Advertisements*.

The most commonly used exception to the "brief summary" requirement is for "reminder advertisements," which highlight the name of the drug and drug company, but don't communicate anything about the drug's indication or dosage recommendations. Even implicit representations about the drug's effects will remove the ad from the reminder category. Thus, when a Celebrex TV ad depicted a woman playing a guitar accompanied by the statement "With Celebrex, I will play the longer version," the FDA concluded that this was a full product ad because the statement made representations about the drug's indication and benefits, and so the company violated the rules by failing to include risk, side effect and contraindication information. The FDA also asked Pfizer to pull several ads for Viagra because they "ma[d]e clear that Viagra is intended for sex" but did not make the required disclosures.

What would an acceptable ad for Viagra look like? Is the "brief summary" requirement consistent with the First Amendment?

Help-seeking or "see your doctor" ads describe the symptoms of a disease or condition, and encourage consumers to consult their physician to discuss treatment options, but do not mention the drug's name. Because no drug is mentioned, the FDA doesn't consider these to be drug ads at all. *See* 21 C.F.R. § 202.1(e)(1).

Because "brief summaries" are often too lengthy and technical to effectively communicate risk information to consumers, and exhaustive lists of minor risks can distract and confuse consumers about the most important risk, in 2004 the FDA issued a draft guidance—which does not have the force of law, but describes the FDA's current thinking—allowing more consumer-friendly presentation of information. *See* FDA, *Draft Guidance for Industry, Brief Summary: Disclosing Risk Information in Consumer-Directed Print Advertisements* (Feb. 2004). Under this draft guidance, which is still the most recent statement from the FDA, advertisers have the option of using the "Highlights of Prescribing Information" category from the label, which includes only the most common and most serious risks.

As consumers and drug companies embraced the Internet for disseminating health information and drug advertising, the FDA did not issue Internet-specific guidance, preferring instead to use warning letters to indicate when a drug company had gone too far. In Fall 2009, the FDA sent fourteen warning letters over sponsored links, stating that the links were misleading because they made representations about the efficacy of the named drugs but failed to communicate risk information and/or inadequately communicated the drugs' proper indication. Online, ads don't *need* to be short; they could in theory include full prescribing information—but then companies couldn't use short messaging services like Twitter, and in any event consumers are unlikely to read all that information. The FDA has so far focused on ensuring that risk communication occurs in the consumer's initial encounter with a benefit claim, but how that will work is up for debate.

Recently, the FDA issued three new draft guidance documents. The first focused on "interactive promotional media," including "blogs, microblogs, social networking sites, online communities, and live podcasts." *See* FDA, *Guidance for Industry Fulfilling Regulatory Requirements for Postmarketing Submissions of Interactive Promotional Media for Prescription Human and Animal Drugs and Biologics* (Jan. 2014). This guidance addresses the requirement that drugmaking firms must submit all promotional labeling and advertising at the time of initial dissemination or publication, and indicates that the FDA will exercise enforcement discretion—not claim that a company has violated this requirement of the FDCA—in certain circumstances, "due to the high volume of information that may be posted within short periods of time using interactive promotional media that allow for real-time communication." In other respects, the FDA intends to hold companies responsible for promotional communications on "sites that are owned, controlled, created, influenced, or operated by, or on behalf of, the firm. . . . Thus, a firm is responsible if it exerts influence over a site in any particular, even if the influence is limited in scope. For example, if the firm collaborates on or has editorial, preview, or review privilege over the content provided, then it is responsible for that content." The FDA also considers a firm responsible for content on third-party sites "if the firm has any control or influence on the third-party site, even if that influence is limited in scope." When a firm does control the placement of its promotional content on a site, it will have to submit both its content and the surrounding pages to the FDA to give context to its marketing. Finally, a company is responsible for content generated by an employee or agent acting on its behalf. In addition, if access is restricted (e.g., members only), the company must submit all its content for the FDA's review; for unrestricted sites such as public Twitter feeds, more limited submissions are sufficient.

By contrast, "a firm generally is not responsible for UGC [user-generated content] that is truly independent of the firm (i.e., is not produced by, or on behalf of, or prompted by the firm in any particular). FDA will not ordinarily view UGC on firm-owned or firm-controlled venues such as blogs, message boards, and chat rooms as promotional content on behalf of the firm as long as the user has no affiliation with the firm and the firm had no influence on the UGC." Consider whether this guidance is consistent with 47 U.S.C. §230, discussed in Chapter 16—are there cases where even "influence" on content is rendered non-actionable by §230?

The second draft document, "Guidance for Industry: Internet/Social Media Platforms with Character Space Limitations—Presenting Risk and Benefit Information for Prescription Drugs and Medical Devices" (June 2014), gives short shrift to character limits on Twitter and similar services. Important risk information is required within the same tweet as promotion of a drug's indication, plus a link to more information. If it won't fit, the FDA doesn't want the tweet to exist. Should drugs be promoted on Twitter?

The third draft document, "Guidance for Industry: Internet/Social Media Platforms: Correcting Independent Third-Party Misinformation About Prescription Drugs and Medical Devices" (June 2014), provides some leeway for manufacturers to act swiftly to correct misinformation disseminated by unrelated sources. If a company voluntarily corrects such misinformation in a truthful and non-misleading manner, disclosing that the correction comes from the company and linking to more information, the FDA won't object even if the corrective information does not satisfy other regulations of labeling and advertising.

*Devices*

The regulatory regime for medical devices is substantially different in some ways from that of regulating drugs. Where advertising is concerned, however, the issues are often similar. In 2013, the FDA sent a warning letter to genetic testing company 23andMe, informing the company that it was violating the FDCA by marketing its testing kit in ways that made it an unapproved device (an article intended for "the diagnosis of disease or other conditions, or in the cure, mitigation, treatment, or prevention of disease" or "intended to affect the structure or any function of the body," 21 U.S.C. §321(h)). 23andMe claimed that its test would provide "health reports on 254 diseases and conditions," including categories such as "carrier status," "health risks," and "drug response," and also that its test provided a "first step in prevention" that enabled users to "take steps toward mitigating serious diseases" such as diabetes, coronary heart disease, and breast cancer. While 23andMe garnered substantial press attention for its contention that it was being unfairly targeted by the FDA, the company's claims illustrate why the FDCA provides for extensive regulation of medical devices. As the FDA pointed out, the results of the test could have serious health implications—a false positive for a breast cancer-associated gene, for example, could lead to prophylactic surgery, while a false negative could lead a consumer to ignore a real risk. Self-diagnosing drug response, likewise, presents real dangers.

Despite numerous opportunities, 23andMe failed to submit data showing its efficacy for the claimed purposes. "[T]he main purpose of compliance with FDA's regulatory requirements is to ensure that the tests work," but the company had apparently not conducted the studies that it had long promised the FDA. Instead, it launched new marketing campaigns, including TV ads. Thus, the FDA ordered the company to immediately discontinue marketing the test. *FDA Warning Letter*, Nov. 22, 2013. As you should see, advertising regulation and substantive regulation of safety and efficacy go hand in hand: the advertising often determines what it is that must be proved safe and effective.

*Enforcement*

During the administration of George W. Bush, the FDA's chief counsel believed that the First Amendment precluded many of the FDA's traditional regulatory measures, and required top-level approval before issuing any warning letter (the first step in enforcement). In 2003, the FDA initiated only twenty-four enforcement actions in response to false or misleading advertisements from drug manufacturers. This was a 75% drop from the number of actions in 1999–2000. In addition, the FDA's responses to false and misleading advertisements slowed, with the average delay between ad placement and FDA action reaching almost six months. Under the Obama administration, the FDA returned to a somewhat more active role. In 2017, the Division of Drug Marketing, Advertising and Communications (DDMAC), which oversees prescription drug advertising, issued five warning letters, so the pace has slowed again.

Although the FDA does not require pre-clearance of promotional pieces except in "extraordinary circumstances," manufacturers are required to submit a copy of their advertising to the FDA at the time of its initial dissemination and may also submit it for subsequent disseminations. There has historically been a high rate of prepublication submission due in significant part to the high cost of developing corrective materials or campaigns, should the advertisement later be found objectionable.

Failure to submit advertising, however, takes a back seat to more substantive concerns in DDMAC warning letters. DDMAC targets minimization, omission, or inappropriate display of risk information and unsubstantiated efficacy and safety claims. (See the Seasonale example in the section on disclosures in Chapter 5.)

## B.    Food Advertising

The FTC regulates food advertising under its statutory authority to prohibit deceptive acts or practices under Sections 5 and 12 of the Federal Trade Commission Act (FTC Act). Section 5 of the FTC Act prohibits "unfair or deceptive acts or practices," and, in the case of food products, sections 12 and 15 prohibit "any false advertisement" that is "misleading in a material respect."

To ensure consistency in the treatment of nutritional and health claims in food advertising and labeling, the FTC has taken steps to harmonize its enforcement with the FDA's food labeling regulations. The FTC would not be likely to question a company's use of a health claim or a nutrient content claim if the FDA explicitly has approved the claim. *See* 59 Fed. Reg. 28,388, 28,390–96 (June 1, 1994). In addition, the FDA's imprimatur will generally be sufficient to satisfy the FTC substantiation requirements.

Food advertising was significantly affected by the Nutrition Labeling and Education Act of 1990 (NLEA). *See* Pub. L. No. 101-535, 104 Stat. 2353 (codified in part at 21 U.S.C. § 343(i), (q) and (r)). In addition to requiring nutrition information on virtually all food products, the NLEA directed the FDA to standardize and limit the terms permitted on labels, and allows only FDA-approved nutrient content claims and health claims to appear on food labels.

The NLEA defines a health claim as "any claim that characterizes the relationship of any nutrient to a disease or health-related condition." *See* 21 C.F.R. § 101.14(a)(1). Current health claims recognized by the FDA include: calcium for osteoporosis; sodium for hypertension; fat and cholesterol for coronary disease; dietary fat for cancer; fiber and antioxidants found in fruits, vegetables and grains for cancer and heart disease; and soluble fiber for heart disease.

A nutrient claim, on the other hand, is one that expressly or by implication "characterizes the level of any nutrient." *See* 21 U.S.C. 343 (r)(1)(A). As mandated by the NLEA, the FDA's regulations define certain absolute and comparative terms that can be used to characterize the level of a nutrient in a food. Absolute terms (*e.g.*, "low," "high," "lean") describe the amount of nutrient in one serving of a food. Relative or comparative terms (*e.g.*, "less," "reduced," "more") compare the amount of a nutrient in one food with the amount of the same nutrient in another food. Examples of approved "low" claims include "low cholesterol;" "low sodium;" "low fat;" and "low calorie." For "less" or "reduced" claims, the product must show 25% less caloric content, total fat, saturated fat, cholesterol, sodium or sugar than the comparative product.

*The EU's Approach*

Regulation (EC) No 1924/2006 of the European Parliament and of the Council of 20 December, 2006, governs nutrition and health claims made on foods. Whereas the U.S. approach generally allows sellers to make non-disease claims such as "supports healthy liver function" without preapproval as long as they are properly substantiated, the EU does not distinguish between disease and function claims.

Health claims are only allowed "after a scientific assessment of the highest possible standard" carried out by the European Food Safety Authority (EFSA). Nutrition and health claims are not allowed, among other things, to "give rise to doubt about the safety and/or the nutritional adequacy of other foods," imply "that a balanced and varied diet cannot provide appropriate quantities of nutrients in general," or "refer to changes in bodily functions which could give rise to or exploit fear in the consumer, either textually or through pictorial, graphic or symbolic representations." Claims are only permitted if "the average consumer can be expected to understand the beneficial effects as expressed in the claim"; there are other disclosure requirements as well, along with bans on references to rate or amount of weight loss or use of recommendations of individual doctors.

Most notably from an American perspective, health and nutrition claims in the EU are only permitted if they are specifically contained on lists developed pursuant to the regulation. In addition, "[r]eference to general, non-specific benefits of the nutrient or food for overall good health or health-related well-being may only be made if accompanied by a specific health claim included in the lists provided for [by the regulation]." Advertisers can reword authorized claims as long as the rewording is likely to have the same meaning for consumers and the rewording aimed to increase the understanding of the targeted consumers. "Vitamin A contributes to the maintenance of normal vision" could therefore not be rephrased as "Vitamin A . . . helps keep your vision in tip-top condition"; "helps keep" was fine, but "tip-top" would be understood to mean "very best" or "optimum," rather than as "normal" as in the authorized claim. ASA Adjudication on GlaxoSmithKline UK Ltd., Complaint No. A13-242431 (May 7, 2014).

Producers can apply to member states to authorize their health claims; member states then forward appropriate claims to the EFSA, which has five months to give its opinion. Member states submitted an unexpectedly high number of 44,000 health claims by the initial deadline of January 31, 2008. The EFSA submits claims it deems potentially acceptable to the European Commission, which then may ask the EFSA to evaluate those claims. This ultimately results in a list of approved or rejected health claims, with conditions of use or reasons for rejection. The EFSA passed 4,637 to the European Commission between July 2008 and March 2010, of which the European Commission asked the EFSA to evaluate 2,758. The EFSA then published the first series of its opinions on October 1, 2009, and estimated that that the assessment of all submitted health claims would require at least two more years. As of June 2011, the EFSA had published five series of opinions covering 2,723 claims. As this experience indicates, the U.S. model leads to many more health claims on the market. What are the costs and benefits of the two approaches?

## C.     Nutritional Supplement Advertising

The FTC regulates advertising claims for dietary and nutritional supplements using the same general principles it uses to regulate all other advertising: 1) whether the advertisement is truthful and not misleading; and 2) whether the advertiser has adequate substantiation for all objective product claims. As with food advertising, the FTC attempts to harmonize its advertising enforcement program with the FDA's labeling regulations and gives great deference to FDA scientific determinations.

The Dietary Supplement Health and Education Act (DSHEA) of 1994 requires that supplement labeling containing certain health claims must bear the mandatory disclaimer, "this statement has not been evaluated by the Food and Drug Administration. This product is not intended to diagnose, treat, cure or prevent any disease." *See* 21 U.S.C. §§ 343(r)(6)(C). If products bear the disclaimer, they are exempt from FDA pre-authorization of "structure/function" claims (such as "Calcium builds strong bones"). DSHEA allows supplements to (1) "claim[ ] a benefit related to a classical nutrient deficiency disease and disclose[ ] the prevalence of such disease in the United States"; (2) "describe[ ] the role of a nutrient or dietary ingredient intended to affect the structure or function in humans"; (3) "characterize[ ] the documented mechanism by which a nutrient or dietary ingredient acts to maintain such structure or function"; and (4) "describe[ ] general well-being from consumption of a nutrient or dietary ingredient." *See* 21 U.S.C. § 343(r)(6). Whereas prescription drugs can only make claims supported by at least two adequate and well-controlled studies, supplements can make claims that the FDA has not determined to be false or misleading: the default is reversed. Consumers decidedly do not understand the different regulatory regimes at work. *See* Arthur P. Goldman, *Unregulated Herbal Remedies—an Accident Waiting to Happen*, CHI. TRIB., Dec. 24, 2002, at C19 (most Americans are unaware that dietary supplements do not receive premarket testing).

DSHEA made it difficult for the FDA to regulate supplement claims, but both the FDA and the FTC continue to monitor the market. The FTC has devoted considerable attention to false and misleading supplement claims, which remain an important part of its docket, since the attraction of making such claims apparently outweighs fear of the FTC's enforcement authority. *See, e.g.,* Debra D. Burke & Anderson P. Page, *Regulating the Dietary Supplements Industry: Something Still Needs to Change*, 1 HASTINGS BUS. L.J. 121 (2005). Consumers who are hopeful, or desperate, are willing to believe unsubstantiated claims, and advertisers are willing to make unproven claims supposedly based on science. The combination leads to great deception and inefficiency, with concomitant risks to consumers who see supplements as cheaper than expensive doctor visits and prescription drugs. *See, e.g.,* Michael A. McCann, *Dietary Supplement Labeling: Cognitive Biases, Market Manipulation & Consumer Choice*, 31 AM. J.L. & MED. 215 (2005).

In recent research, DNA tests revealed that many herbal supplements, including popular supplements such as echinacea and St. John's wort, did not contain the advertised ingredients (one third of the 44 tested), or contained far less than advertised; some also contained undisclosed allergens such as black walnut, soy, and rice, and undisclosed glutens. Steven G. Newmaster et al., *DNA Barcoding Detects Contamination and Substitution in North American Herbal Products*, 11 BMC MED. 222 (2013). "This suggests that the problems are widespread and that quality control for many companies, whether through ignorance, incompetence or dishonesty, is unacceptable," said David Schardt, a senior nutritionist at the Center for Science in the Public Interest, an advocacy group. "Given these results, it's hard to recommend any herbal supplements to consumers." Do you agree? A professor who'd conducted a similar study called the state of supplement regulation "the Wild West," and said most consumers had no idea how few safeguards were in place. "If you had a child who was sick and 3 out of 10 penicillin pills were fake, everybody would be up in arms," he said. "But it's O.K. to buy a supplement where 3 out of 10 pills are fake." Anahad O'Connor, _Herbal Supplements Are Often Not What They Seem_, N.Y. TIMES, Nov. 3, 2013.

In contrast to pharmaceutical companies, supplement manufacturers have been extremely active in resisting remaining FDA regulation of advertising claims on First Amendment grounds. Consider why supplement manufacturers, who face relatively limited regulation compared to pharmaceutical companies, have been so willing to litigate to get to say even more. (The pharmaceutical companies have resisted certain limits on pharmaco-sponsored continuing medical education and the distribution of studies that discuss off-label uses of drugs on First Amendment grounds, but they have not challenged the basic standards the FDA uses to determine what claims a drug may make on its label.) Industry size, industry structure, and federal preemption of state-law torts when the FDA has formally approved a claim all play a role.

We will therefore spend most of the balance of this section on preemption or preclusion of private causes of action in areas regulated by the FDA and on First Amendment issues.

### D. The FDCA's Interaction with Consumer Protection/Unfair Competition Laws

The Supreme Court has recently spoken on the relationship between the Lanham Act and the FDCA/FDA regulations. While it seems to articulate a broad rule, there are many remaining questions. As you read the following case, keep in mind the difference between food regulation and drug/supplement regulation.

### POM Wonderful LLC v. Coca-Cola Co., 573 U.S. – (2014)

Kennedy, J.

POM Wonderful LLC makes and sells pomegranate juice products, including a pomegranate-blueberry juice blend. One of POM's competitors is the CocaCola Company. Coca-Cola's Minute Maid Division makes a juice blend sold with a label that, in describing the contents, displays the words "pomegranate blueberry" with far more prominence than other words on the label that show the juice to be a blend of five juices. In truth, the Coca-Cola product contains but 0.3% pomegranate juice and 0.2% blueberry juice.

Alleging that the use of that label is deceptive and misleading, POM sued Coca-Cola under §43 of the Lanham Act. That provision allows one competitor to sue another if it alleges unfair competition arising from false or misleading product descriptions. The Court of Appeals for the Ninth Circuit held that, in the realm of labeling for food and beverages, a Lanham Act claim like POM's is precluded by a second federal statute. The second statute is the Federal Food, Drug, and Cosmetic

CHAPTER 17: CASE STUDIES IN FOOD AND DRUGS

Act (FDCA), which forbids the misbranding of food, including by means of false or misleading labeling. The ruling that POM's Lanham Act cause of action is precluded by the FDCA was incorrect. There is no statutory text or established interpretive principle to support the contention that the FDCA precludes Lanham Act suits like the one brought by POM in this case. Nothing in the text, history, or structure of the FDCA or the Lanham Act shows the congressional purpose or design to forbid these suits. Quite to the contrary, the FDCA and the Lanham Act complement each other in the federal regulation of misleading food and beverage labels. Competitors, in their own interest, may bring Lanham Act claims like POM's that challenge food and beverage labels that are regulated by the FDCA.

I A

This case concerns the intersection and complementarity of these two federal laws. A proper beginning point is a description of the statutes.

. . . Section 45 of the Lanham Act provides:

> The intent of this chapter is to regulate commerce within the control of Congress by making actionable the deceptive and misleading use of marks in such commerce; to protect registered marks used in such commerce from interference by State, or territorial legislation; to protect persons engaged in such commerce against unfair competition; to prevent fraud and deception in such commerce by the use of reproductions, copies, counterfeits, or colorable imitations of registered marks; and to provide rights and remedies stipulated by treaties and conventions respecting trademarks, trade names, and unfair competition entered into between the United States and foreign nations.

15 U. S. C. §1127.

. . . The Lanham Act creates a cause of action for unfair competition through misleading advertising or labeling. Though in the end consumers also benefit from the Act's proper enforcement, the cause of action is for competitors, not consumers.

The term "competitor" is used in this opinion to indicate all those within the class of persons and entities protected by the Lanham Act. Competitors are within the class that may invoke the Lanham Act because they may suffer "an injury to a commercial interest in sales or business reputation proximately caused by [a] defendant's misrepresentations." The petitioner here asserts injury as a competitor.

The cause of action the Act creates imposes civil liability on any person who "uses in commerce any word, term, name, symbol, or device, or any combination thereof, or any false designation of origin, false or misleading description of fact, or false or misleading representation of fact, which . . . misrepresents the nature, characteristics, qualities, or geographic origin of his or her or another person's goods, services, or commercial activities." . . . This principle reflects the Lanham Act's purpose of " 'protect[ing] persons engaged in [commerce within the control of Congress] against unfair competition.' " POM's cause of action would be straightforward enough but for Coca-Cola's contention that a separate federal statutory regime, the FDCA, allows it to use the label in question and in fact precludes the Lanham Act claim.

So the FDCA is the second statute to be discussed. The FDCA statutory regime is designed primarily to protect the health and safety of the public at large. The FDCA prohibits the misbranding of food and drink. A food or drink is deemed misbranded if, inter alia, "its labeling is false or misleading," information required to appear on its label "is not prominently placed thereon," or a label does not bear "the common or usual name of the food, if any there be." To implement these provisions, the Food and Drug Administration (FDA) promulgated regulations regarding food and beverage labeling, including the labeling of mixes of different types of juice into one juice blend. One provision of those regulations is particularly relevant to this case: If a juice blend does not name all the juices it contains and mentions only juices that are not predominant in the blend, then it must either declare the percentage content of the named juice or "[i]ndicate that the named juice is present as a flavor or flavoring," e.g., "raspberry and cranberry flavored juice drink." The Government represents that the FDA does not preapprove juice labels under these regulations. That contrasts with the FDA's regulation of other types of labels, such as drug labels, and is consistent with the less extensive role the FDA plays in the regulation of food than in the regulation of drugs.

Unlike the Lanham Act, which relies in substantial part for its enforcement on private suits brought by injured competitors, the FDCA and its regulations provide the United States with nearly exclusive enforcement authority, including the authority to seek criminal sanctions in some circumstances. Private parties may not bring enforcement suits. Also unlike the Lanham Act, the FDCA contains a provision pre-empting certain state laws on misbranding. That provision, which Congress added to the FDCA in the Nutrition Labeling and Education Act of 1990, forecloses a "State or political subdivision of a State" from establishing requirements that are of the type but "not identical to" the requirements in some of the misbranding provisions of the FDCA. It does not address, or refer to, other federal statutes or the preclusion thereof.

B

POM Wonderful LLC is a grower of pomegranates and a distributor of pomegranate juices. Through its POM Wonderful brand, POM produces, markets, and sells a variety of pomegranate products, including a pomegranate blueberry juice blend.

POM competes in the pomegranate-blueberry juice market with the Coca-Cola Company. Coca-Cola, under its Minute Maid brand, created a juice blend containing 99.4% apple and grape juices, 0.3% pomegranate juice, 0.2% blueberry juice, and 0.1% raspberry juice. Despite the minuscule amount of pomegranate and blueberry juices in the blend, the front label of the Coca-Cola product displays the words "pomegranate blueberry" in all capital letters, on two separate lines. Below those words, Coca-Cola placed the phrase "flavored blend of 5 juices" in much smaller type. And below that phrase, in still smaller type, were the words "from concentrate with added ingredients"—and, with a line break before the final phrase— "and other natural flavors." The product's front label also displays a vignette of blueberries, grapes, and raspberries in front of a halved pomegranate and a halved apple.

Claiming that Coca-Cola's label tricks and deceives consumers, all to POM's injury as a competitor, POM brought suit under the Lanham Act. POM alleged that the name, label, marketing, and advertising of Coca-Cola's juice blend mislead consumers into believing the product consists predominantly of pomegranate and blueberry juice when it in fact consists predominantly of less expensive apple and grape juices. That confusion, POM complained, causes it to lose sales. POM sought damages and injunctive relief.

The District Court granted partial summary judgment to Coca-Cola on POM's Lanham Act claim, ruling that the FDCA and its regulations preclude challenges to the name and label of Coca-Cola's juice blend. . . .

The Court of Appeals for the Ninth Circuit affirmed in relevant part. Like the District Court, the Court of Appeals reasoned that Congress decided "to entrust matters of juice beverage labeling to the FDA"; the FDA has promulgated "comprehensive regulation of that labeling"; and the FDA "apparently" has not imposed the requirements on Coca-Cola's label that are sought by POM. "[U]nder [Circuit] precedent," the Court of Appeals explained, "for a court to act when the FDA has not—despite regulating extensively in this area— would risk undercutting the FDA's expert judgments and authority." For these reasons, and "[o]ut of respect for the statutory and regulatory scheme," the Court of Appeals barred POM's Lanham Act claim.

## II A

... First, this is not a pre-emption case. In pre-emption cases, the question is whether state law is pre-empted by a federal statute, or in some instances, a federal agency action. This case, however, concerns the alleged preclusion of a cause of action under one federal statute by the provisions of another federal statute. So the state–federal balance does not frame the inquiry. Because this is a preclusion case, any "presumption against pre-emption," has no force. In addition, the preclusion analysis is not governed by the Court's complex categorization of the types of pre-emption. Although the Court's pre-emption precedent does not govern preclusion analysis in this case, its principles are instructive insofar as they are designed to assess the interaction of laws that bear on the same subject.

Second, this is a statutory interpretation case, and the Court relies on traditional rules of statutory interpretation. That does not change because the case involves multiple federal statutes. Nor does it change because an agency is involved. Analysis of the statutory text, aided by established principles of interpretation, controls.

... POM argues that this case concerns whether one statute, the FDCA as amended, is an "implied repeal" in part of another statute, i.e., the Lanham Act. POM contends that in such cases courts must give full effect to both statutes unless they are in "irreconcilable conflict," and that this high standard is not satisfied here. Coca-Cola resists this canon and its high standard. Coca-Cola argues that the case concerns whether a more specific law, the FDCA, clarifies or narrows the scope of a more general law, the Lanham Act. The Court's task, it claims, is to "reconcil[e]" the laws, and it says the best reconciliation is that the more specific provisions of the FDCA bar certain causes of action authorized in a general manner by the Lanham Act.

The Court does not need to resolve this dispute. Even assuming that Coca-Cola is correct that the Court's task is to reconcile or harmonize the statutes and not, as POM urges, to enforce both statutes in full unless there is a genuinely irreconcilable conflict, Coca-Cola is incorrect that the best way to harmonize the statutes is to bar POM's Lanham Act claim.

## B

Beginning with the text of the two statutes, it must be observed that neither the Lanham Act nor the FDCA, in express terms, forbids or limits Lanham Act claims challenging labels that are regulated by the FDCA. By its terms, the Lanham Act subjects to suit any person who "misrepresents the nature, characteristics, qualities, or geographic origin" of goods or services. This comprehensive imposition of liability extends, by its own terms, to misrepresentations on labels, including food and beverage labels. No other provision in the Lanham Act limits that understanding or purports to govern the relevant interaction between the Lanham Act and the FDCA. And the FDCA, by its terms, does not preclude Lanham Act suits. In consequence, food and beverage labels regulated by the FDCA are not, under the terms of either statute, off limits to Lanham Act claims. No textual provision in either statute discloses a purpose to bar unfair competition claims like POM's.

This absence is of special significance because the Lanham Act and the FDCA have coexisted since the passage of the Lanham Act in 1946. If Congress had concluded, in light of experience, that Lanham Act suits could interfere with the FDCA, it might well have enacted a provision addressing the issue during these 70 years. Congress enacted amendments to the FDCA and the Lanham Act, *see, e.g.*, Nutrition Labeling and Education Act of 1990; Trademark Law Revision Act of 1988, including an amendment that added to the FDCA an express pre-emption provision with respect to state laws addressing food and beverage misbranding. Yet Congress did not enact a provision addressing the preclusion of other federal laws that might bear on food and beverage labeling. This is "powerful evidence that Congress did not intend FDA oversight to be the exclusive means" of ensuring proper food and beverage labeling. Perhaps the closest the statutes come to addressing the preclusion of the Lanham Act claim at issue here is the pre-emption provision added to the FDCA in 1990 as part of the Nutrition Labeling and Education Act. But, far from expressly precluding suits arising under other federal laws, the provision if anything suggests that Lanham Act suits are not precluded.

This pre-emption provision forbids a "State or political subdivision of a State" from imposing requirements that are of the type but "not identical to" corresponding FDCA requirements for food and beverage labeling. It is significant that the complex pre-emption provision distinguishes among different FDCA requirements. It forbids state-law requirements that are of the type but not identical to only certain FDCA provisions with respect to food and beverage labeling. Just as significant, the provision does not refer to requirements imposed by other sources of law, such as federal statutes. For purposes of deciding whether the FDCA displaces a regulatory or liability scheme in another statute, it makes a substantial difference whether that other statute is state or federal. By taking care to mandate express pre-emption of some state laws, Congress if anything indicated it did not intend the FDCA to preclude requirements arising from other sources. Pre-emption of some state requirements does not suggest an intent to preclude federal claims.

The structures of the FDCA and the Lanham Act reinforce the conclusion drawn from the text. When two statutes complement each other, it would show disregard for the congressional design to hold that Congress nonetheless intended one federal statute to preclude the operation of the other. The Lanham Act and the FDCA complement each other in major respects, for each has its own scope and purpose. Although both statutes touch on food and beverage labeling, the Lanham Act protects commercial interests against unfair competition, while the FDCA protects public health and safety. The two statutes impose "different requirements and protections."

The two statutes complement each other with respect to remedies in a more fundamental respect. Enforcement of the FDCA and the detailed prescriptions of its implementing regulations is largely committed to the FDA. The FDA, however, does not have the same perspective or expertise in assessing market dynamics that day-to-day competitors possess. Competitors who manufacture or distribute products have detailed knowledge regarding how consumers rely upon certain sales and marketing strategies. Their awareness of unfair competition practices may be far more immediate and accurate than that of agency rulemakers and regulators. Lanham Act suits draw upon this market expertise by empowering private parties to sue competitors to protect their interests on a case-by-case basis. By "serv[ing] a distinct compensatory function that may motivate injured persons to come forward," Lanham Act suits, to the extent they touch on the same subject matter as the FDCA, "provide incentives" for manufacturers to behave well. Allowing Lanham Act suits takes advantage of synergies among multiple methods of regulation. This is quite consistent with the congressional design to enact two different statutes, each with its own mechanisms to enhance the protection of competitors and consumers.

A holding that the FDCA precludes Lanham Act claims challenging food and beverage labels would not only ignore the distinct functional aspects of the FDCA and the Lanham Act but also would lead to a result that Congress likely did not intend. Unlike other types of labels regulated by the FDA, such as drug labels, it would appear the FDA does not preapprove food and beverage labels under its regulations and instead relies on enforcement actions, warning letters, and other measures. Because the FDA acknowledges that it does not necessarily pursue enforcement measures regarding all objectionable labels, if Lanham Act claims were to be precluded then commercial interests—and indirectly the public at large—could be left with less effective protection in the food and beverage labeling realm than in many other, less regulated industries. It is unlikely that Congress intended the FDCA's protection of health and safety to result in less policing of misleading food and beverage labels than in competitive markets for other products.

C

Coca-Cola argues the FDCA precludes POM's Lanham Act claim because Congress intended national uniformity in food and beverage labeling. Coca-Cola notes three aspects of the FDCA to support that position: delegation of enforcement authority to the Federal Government rather than private parties; express pre-emption with respect to state laws; and the specificity of the FDCA and its implementing regulations. But these details of the FDCA do not establish an intent or design to preclude Lanham Act claims.

Coca-Cola says that the FDCA's delegation of enforcement authority to the Federal Government shows Congress' intent to achieve national uniformity in labeling. But POM seeks to enforce the Lanham Act, not the FDCA or its regulations. The centralization of FDCA enforcement authority in the Federal Government does not indicate that Congress intended to foreclose private enforcement of other federal statutes.

. . . Although the application of a federal statute such as the Lanham Act by judges and juries in courts throughout the country may give rise to some variation in outcome, this is the means Congress chose to enforce a national policy to ensure fair competition. It is quite different from the disuniformity that would arise from the multitude of state laws, state regulations, state administrative agency rulings, and state-court decisions that are partially forbidden by the FDCA's pre-emption provision. Congress not infrequently permits a certain amount of variability by authorizing a federal cause of action even in areas of law where national uniformity is important. The Lanham Act itself is an example of this design: Despite Coca-Cola's protestations, the Act is uniform in extending its protection against unfair competition to the whole class it describes. It is variable only to the extent that those rights are enforced on a case-by-case basis. The variability about which Coca-Cola complains is no different than the variability that any industry covered by the Lanham Act faces. And, as noted, Lanham Act actions are a means to implement a uniform policy to prohibit unfair competition in all covered markets.

Finally, Coca-Cola urges that the FDCA, and particularly its implementing regulations, addresses food and beverage labeling with much more specificity than is found in the provisions of the Lanham Act. That is true. The pages of FDA rulemakings devoted only to juice-blend labeling attest to the level of detail with which the FDA has examined the subject. *E.g.*, Food Labeling; Declaration of Ingredients; Common or Usual Name for Nonstandardized Foods; Diluted Juice Beverages, 58 Fed. Reg. 2897–2926 (1993). Because, as we have explained, the FDCA and the Lanham Act are complementary and have separate scopes and purposes, this greater specificity would matter only if the Lanham Act and the FDCA cannot be implemented in full at the same time. But neither the statutory structure nor the empirical evidence of which the Court is aware indicates there will be any difficulty in fully enforcing each statute according to its terms....

\* \* \*

Coca-Cola and the United States ask the Court to elevate the FDCA and the FDA's regulations over the private cause of action authorized by the Lanham Act. But the FDCA and the Lanham Act complement each other in the federal regulation of misleading labels. Congress did not intend the FDCA to preclude Lanham Act suits like POM's. The position Coca-Cola takes in this Court that because food and beverage labeling is involved it has no Lanham Act liability here for practices that allegedly mislead and trick consumers, all to the injury of competitors, finds no support in precedent or the statutes. The judgment of the Court of Appeals for the Ninth Circuit is reversed, and the case is remanded for further proceedings consistent with this opinion.

*NOTES AND QUESTIONS*

In early 2016, a jury found against Pom on its false advertising claims against Coca-Cola.

After *POM Wonderful*, what should happen when private litigants argue that the defendant has engaged in false or misleading advertising that also violates the FDCA or FDA regulations? Before *POM Wonderful*, courts had attempted to draw a line between cases that required the *interpretation* of the FDCA or of FDA regulations—these were the sole province of the FDA—and cases that involved alleged falsity independent of the FDA. In the latter set of cases, courts could evaluate falsity, a traditional area of judicial competence, and could even use FDA rules as evidence of the meaning of certain terms, but the theory was that the cause of action would exist even in the absence of the FDCA. These cases seem relatively unaffected by *POM Wonderful*.

Consider, for example, the following highly influential case.

*Sandoz Pharmaceuticals Corporation v. Richardson-Vicks, Inc., 902 F.2d 222 (3d Cir. 1990)*

This appeal, from an order of the district court denying plaintiff/appellant Sandoz Pharmaceuticals Corp.'s request for a preliminary injunction against defendant/appellee Richardson-Vicks, Inc., is another installment in the cough syrup marketing wars. Sandoz alleges that Vicks's representations about its product, Vicks Pediatric Formula 44 ("Pediatric 44"), constituted false and deceptive advertising in violation of section 43(a) of the Lanham Act.

At the nub of the controversy is Vicks's assertion that Pediatric 44 starts to work the instant it is swallowed. Sandoz alleges that the representations about the instant action of the product are false. It also alleges that such representations constitute per se violations of the Lanham Act, given Vicks's failure to disclose, on Pediatric 44's label, that the demulcents which theoretically effectuate the immediate relief are intended to be active[1] yet are not approved by the Food and Drug Administration ("FDA"). . . .

Vicks's advertising claims with regard to Pediatric 44 are based on the effect of certain locally-acting, inert sugary liquids known as "demulcents," which operate directly on cough receptors in the recipient's throat and respiratory passages. Demulcents are topically acting antitussives, in contrast to centrally acting antitussives, which are the traditional cough antidotes. Because these demulcents work on contact, Vicks claims that Pediatric 44 begins to reduce coughs as soon as it is swallowed.

Vicks performed various tests to support this conclusion. The record contains test results which support, if only marginally, Vicks's arguments that Pediatric 44 starts to work right away, that there is a scientific basis for this claim, and that Pediatrics 44 is superior to its competitors. However, the FDA has never approved any "demulcents" as effective for the relief of coughs, and whether Vicks's level of testing could meet the high standards for drug approval set by the FDA is far from certain. . . . [The court explained that if the demulcent was "active" according to the FDA, it would require extensive testing.]

Sandoz has presented no evidence showing that Pediatric 44's "inactive" label is misleading to the consuming public, and Sandoz did not actively pursue the argument, either here or in the district court, that the "inactive" label in question was deceptive. Instead, it alleges that the label contains a literally false description of the product. In essence, Sandoz states that if Vicks claims that its demulcents enable Pediatric 44 to begin to work as soon as it is swallowed, then these demulcents are "active" ingredients within the meaning of 21 C.F.R. § 210.3(b)(7). . . .

The Lanham Act is primarily intended to protect commercial interests. . . . The FD & C Act, in contrast, is not focused on the truth or falsity of advertising claims. It requires the FDA to protect the public interest by "pass[ing] on the safety and efficacy of all new drugs and . . . promulgat[ing] regulations concerning the conditions under which various categories of OTC drugs . . . are safe, effective and not misbranded."

---

[1] Demulcents have not been classified as inactive or active by the Food and Drug Administration, *see* 41 Fed.Reg. 38,354 (1976) (panel report listing demulcents in FDA category III, which covers ingredients for which "the available data are insufficient to classify" the ingredient, 21 C.F.R. § 330.10(a)(5)(iii) (1988)), but Sandoz argues that they are clearly active ingredients insofar as Vicks claims that they make its product effective.

. . . . Sandoz's counsel argued to the district court that "[i]f [the demulcents] relieve coughs they're active. That's true as a matter of common sense and normal English." Such an interpretation of FDA regulations, absent direct guidance from the promulgating agency, is not as simple as Sandoz proposes.

The FDA has not found conclusively that demulcents must be labelled as active or inactive ingredients within the meaning of 21 C.F.R. § 210.3(b)(7).[10] We decline to find and do not believe that the district court had to find, either "as a matter of common sense" or "normal English," that which the FDA, with all of its scientific expertise, has yet to determine. Because "agency decisions are frequently of a discretionary nature or frequently require expertise, the agency should be given the first chance to exercise that discretion or to apply that expertise." Thus, we are unable to conclude that Vicks's labeling of Pediatric 44's demulcents as inactive is literally false, even if Vicks concurrently claims that these ingredients enable its medicine to work the instant it is swallowed.

Sandoz's position would require us to usurp administrative agencies' responsibility for interpreting and enforcing potentially ambiguous regulations. Jurisdiction for the regulation of OTC drug marketing is vested jointly and exhaustively in the FDA and the FTC, and is divided between them by agreement. Neither of these agencies' constituent statutes creates an express or implied private right of action, and what the FD & C Act and the FTC Act do not create directly, the Lanham Act does not create indirectly, at least not in cases requiring original interpretation of these Acts or their accompanying regulations. . . .

*NOTES AND QUESTIONS*

If the FDA didn't exist, could the plaintiff have claimed that the defendant's label was false or misleading? On the other hand, given that the FDA does exist, if everyone else follows the FDA's rules for labeling active ingredients, isn't the defendant's use "false" according to the definition used by the market? Isn't the real problem here materiality?

Now examine another influential pre-*POM Wonderful* case, this one allowing a claim to proceed. Does *POM Wonderful* affect the court's reasoning?

*Solvay Pharmaceuticals, Inc. v. Ethex Corp., 2004 WL 742033 (D. Minn. 2004)*

. . . Both Solvay and Ethex produce and market competing prescription pancreatic enzyme supplements used in the treatment of cystic fibrosis. Solvay's products are marketed under the trademark Creon, while Ethex's products are marketed under the trademark Pangestyme. Specifically at issue in this case are Creon 10 and 20 and Pagnestyme CN-10 and CN-20.

Solvay contends that Ethex has falsely and misleadingly promoted and advertised Pangestyme CN-10 and CN-20 as substitutes for Creon 10 and 20. According to Solvay, Ethex markets the

---

[10] Sandoz is free to petition the FDA to investigate these alleged labeling violations. Sandoz represents that it has embarked upon this path already. The fact that it has been unable to get a quick response from the FDA, however, does not create a claim for Sandoz under the Lanham Act.

Pangestyme products either expressly or by implication as "equivalent," "comparable," and "generic" versions of Creon, despite the fact that the two products are not, in fact, equivalent. Such false and misleading advertising and promotion has allegedly harmed Creon's sales and reputation, and puts cystic fibrosis patients at risk of receiving different treatment than that prescribed by their doctors.

[Solvay alleged violation of the Lanham Act and state unfair and deceptive trade practices laws.] . . .

Ethex objects that counts one through six are impermissible attempts to enforce the Federal Drug and Cosmetic Act ("FDCA"), which is only enforceable by the federal government. . . .

Solvay maintains that it is alleging in this case that Creon and Pangestyme are factually not "equivalent," "substitutable," "generic," "comparable," and "alternative," and that Ethex's representations are therefore factually false. Solvay has specifically disclaimed any FDA related allegation.

A. The FDCA and FDA

The primary regulatory system covering prescription drugs was created by the Food, Drug and Cosmetic Act ("FDCA"). The FDCA requires FDA approval, through a "new drug application" ("NDA"), before a new drug may be put on the market. A product similar to an NDA approved drug may be approved and marketed based on an "abbreviated new drug application" ("ANDA"). An ANDA requires the manufacturer of the similar drug to demonstrate that the two drugs are therapeutically equivalent, that is pharmaceutically equivalent[3] and bioequivalent.[4] Each year the FDA publishes Approved Drug Products with Therapeutic Equivalence Evaluations, commonly known as the "Orange Book," listing all NDA approved drugs along with therapeutic equivalence determinations. Enforcement of the FDCA is permitted exclusively "by and in the name of the United States" or, in certain circumstances by a state.

Prescription pancreatic enzyme supplements are, like any other drug, subject to FDA regulation. In 1995 the FDA declared that all pancreatic enzyme drugs would require NDA or ANDA approval, but permitted such drugs to remain on the market while the FDA fleshed out the approval process. Thus, neither Creon nor Pangestyme has been tested, approved, compared or otherwise passed on by the FDA, and neither is listed in the Orange Book.

. . . Courts have come to the general conclusion that the FDA's enforcement of the FDCA is primarily concerned with the safety and efficacy of new drugs, while the Lanham Act is focused on the truth or falsity of advertising claims. More specifically, where a claim requires interpretation of a matter that is exclusively within the jurisdiction and expertise of the FDA and FDCA, plaintiffs cannot use the Lanham Act as a backdoor to private enforcement. However, "false statements are actionable under

---

[3] Two drugs sharing the same active ingredients, strength, and dosage are considered "pharmaceutically equivalent."

[4] Two drugs that do not have significantly different rates and extent of absorption in the body are considered "bioequivalent."

the Lanham Act, even if their truth may be generally within the purview of the FDA," where the truth or falsity of the statements in question can be resolved through reference to standards other than those of the FDA.

. . . Solvay is not relying on either explicit or implicit FDA endorsement or terms that only the FDA can define. Solvay alleges that any statement or representation that Pangestyme is "equivalent," "substitutable," "generic," "comparable," and "alternative" to Creon is literally false. Similar to the plaintiff in *Grove Fresh,* Solvay may use the FDA regulations listing definitions of bioequivalence, pharmaceutical equivalence, and therapeutic equivalence to establish the appropriate standard by which to judge the literal falsity of Ethex's advertisements. However, "[e]ven without the FDA regulation . . . [plaintiff] could attempt to establish a violation of section 43(a) . . . . [by] provid[ing] other evidence establishing the proper market definition" of generic, equivalent, comparable, or substitutable. As Ethex acknowledges, an FDA determination is not necessarily required in order for two drugs to be properly considered equivalent.

The Court is thus satisfied that Solvay could, based on the allegations in the complaint, prove that Pangestyme and Creon are not substitutable, alternatives, equivalent, or comparable, and that any advertisement to the contrary is literally false. Such a claim does not require the Court to determine anything within the particular jurisdiction of the FDA and is within the purview of the Lanham Act. Plaintiff's claims will therefore not be dismissed on this basis. . . .

*NOTES AND QUESTIONS*

*Consumer Confusion over FDA Approval.* Suppose a plaintiff submits credible evidence that a substantial number of the relevant consumers believe that the mere presence on the market of a drug implies FDA approval of that drug, even though in that particular instance the FDA has not approved the drug (this is the case for a number of drugs that were grandfathered into the current scheme). Should the plaintiff's implied falsity claim survive? *See Mutual Pharmaceutical Company, Inc. v. Watson Pharmaceuticals, Inc.*, 2010 WL 446132 (D.N.J. 2010) (allegations that inclusion of drug on price lists and wholesaler ordering systems constituted implicit misrepresentation of FDA approval stated claim against grandfathered drug).

*State Law Claims.* As *POM Wonderful* mentioned, the FDCA preempts certain state law claims, but does preserve some in the area of food and supplement labeling where the state law is "identical" to the rules adopted by the FDA. Preemption is broader with respect to pharmaceuticals—perhaps justified by the extensive and individualized approval process for pharmaceuticals and the generally tighter rules on their advertising.

Compliance with FDA regulations will insulate a defendant from state-law claims regarding prescription drugs. *See* Pa. Emp. Benefit Tr. Fund v. Zeneca, Inc., 2005 WL 2993937 (D. Del. 2005) ("By approving information to be included in the drug labeling, the FDA has determined that the information complies with its rules and regulations. Therefore, if the FDA labeling supports the statements made in advertising for an FDA-approved drug, the statements are not actionable under [Delaware law.]"). In addition, even after *Pom Wonderful*, some courts find that statements specifically approved by the FDA can't be the basis of Lanham Act claims. *See* Apotex Inc. v. Acorda

Therapeutics, Inc., 823 F.3d 51 (2d Cir. 2016) ("representations that are wholly consistent with an FDA label" aren't subject to Lanham Act liability, though "Lanham Act liability might arise if an advertisement uses information contained in an FDA-approved label that does not correspond substantially to the label, or otherwise renders the advertisement literally or implicitly false"; "in order to avoid chilling speech that ought to be protected, Acorda's advertisements cannot form the basis for Apotex's claims to the extent they were in line with the FDA-approved label").

How do we know that the defendant is in compliance with the FDA's rules? The FDA rarely issues pronouncements that a specific advertiser is doing something correctly. If a court evaluates compliance, then might it risk disagreement with the FDA itself were the FDA to examine the ad at issue, since after all there is often room for judgment calls in applying regulations. On the other hand, the FDA is as resource-constrained and short-staffed as any federal agency, and it doesn't go after every violation of its regulations itself, so additional help from plaintiffs and courts might further the purposes of the statutory scheme.

Based on the FDCA's explicit preemption provision, which preempts non-identical state requirements, courts generally allow consumer claims to proceed when they enforce state standards for foods or supplements "identical" to those set out in the FDCA and FDA regulations. *See, e.g.,* Consumer Justice Ctr. v. Olympian Labs, Inc., 121 Cal. Rptr. 2d 749 (Cal. App. Ct. 2002) (finding it "clear" that the explicit preemption provisions of the FDCA do not bar states from allowing consumers to sue to enforce labeling rules that are identical to federal rules). Thus, the states can create a privately enforceable cause of action identical to the FDCA, even though the FDCA itself expressly rejects a private cause of action based on violation of the FDCA. California in particular has taken up this invitation, as has its plaintiff's bar. Why would Congress do this?

Are there any reasons to treat consumer lawsuits differently from competitor lawsuits when it comes to preemption by the FDCA and FDA regulations? *POM Wonderful* didn't apply the "identical" standard, because in the Court's analysis it just didn't matter whether the Lanham Act imposed "identical" requirements on Coca-Cola to the FDA's rules, as long as there was no conflict with a label the FDA had *mandated*. After *POM Wonderful*, it may thus be easier for competitors to sue for false advertising than for directly deceived consumers, who can't take advantage of the Lanham Act. Is this the right balance?

Consider the popular food labeling term "natural." "Natural" is a useful selling term for many producers, but it lacks a coherent definition. Because the FDA has repeatedly declined to regulate "natural" claims in most circumstances, some courts have allowed state-law consumer protection claims to proceed, while others have barred them for the same reason. Recently, the FDA has sought comments on whether it ought to formulate a definition of "natural." Its existing policy is that "natural" means that "nothing artificial or synthetic (including all color additives regardless of source) has been included in, or has been added to, a food that would not normally be expected to be in the food." 58 Fed. Reg. 2302, 2407 (1993). Any changes or additions to this policy would likely require notice and comment rulemaking, and would involve many other issues besides the role of bioengineering, including the characterization of methods of food processing such as pasteurization and irradiation.

Given the FDA's position, should consumer protection litigation be allowed to fill the regulatory gap, if consumers do have expectations about what "natural" means? Or should courts refuse to decide such cases because the FDA has declined to act? Does it matter if consumers' expectations are incoherent or unreasonable? Fifty percent of consumers surveyed in 2009 said the "natural" label was important or very important to them, while only 35% said the same of "organic," even though only the latter has a clear regulatory definition and is held to much more stringent standards than the FDA concept of "natural." CONTEXT MARKETING, BEYOND ORGANIC: HOW EVOLVING CONSUMER CONCERNS INFLUENCE FOOD PURCHASES 4 (2009). "Natural" is more strongly associated than "organic" with the absence of artificial flavors, colors, and preservatives. *Where Organic Ends and Natural Begins*, Hartman Group (Mar. 23, 2010).

For comparison purposes, USDA's Food Safety and Inspection Service says all fresh meat qualifies as "natural," but meat that carries a "natural" label cannot contain any artificial flavors or flavorings, coloring ingredients, chemical preservatives or other artificial or synthetic ingredients and must not be more than "minimally processed." In one study, consumers who were unfamiliar with USDA natural labels were willing to pay $1.26 per pound more for steaks labeled natural, but those provided the definition of natural were unwilling to pay more for those steaks; they were willing to pay $3.07 per pound more for steak labeled natural *and* no growth hormones. Konstantinos G. Syrengelas, Karen Lewis DeLong, Carola Grebitus, & Rodolfo M. Nayga, Jr., *Is the Natural Label Misleading? Examining Consumer Preferences for Natural Beef, Applied Economic Perspectives and Policy*, ppx042, https://doi.org/10.1093/aepp/ppx042 (Oct. 26, 2017). Does this suggest anything about whether "natural" is misleading for other foods?

*The NAD and the FDA.* The NAD distinguishes between general labeling requirements and certain specific FDA decisions. If a government agency mandates, or even approves for use, general language for all industry participants to use, the NAD will not contradict that. But the NAD will exercise its own judgment about specific claims.

In one case, Novartis claimed that its transdermal patch is "clinically proven more effective than Dramamine." The NARB upheld an NAD finding that this claim was not substantiated when used in ads, despite the fact that in 1979 the FDA approved labeling that supported this claim. The NARB was influenced by several factors: (1) a subsequent 1985 study cast doubt on the superiority claim, and the NAD was not confident that the FDA would reach the same result if it reevaluated the issue; (2) in 1979, there was no direct-to-consumer advertising, and in general the NAD was not confident that "the same rigor and review that would likely be afforded today was present"; (3) the support relied on pooling study results rather than a true head-to-head comparison, and it was not clear why the FDA (unusually) had allowed a comparative claim under these circumstances. The NAD panel was also "troubled by the fact that 183 of the 194 study participants in the three studies were employees of the advertiser, an unorthodox procedure at best."

The NARB noted that "there are many sound reasons for giving great, perhaps under appropriate circumstances even decisive, weight to federal agency decisions regarding advertising claims. However, such deference is not automatic, and it never completely replaces the obligation of the self-regulation system to exercise its own sound discretion." *See* Novartis Consumer Health, Report of

NARB Panel 110 (NARB July 25, 2000). How does this compare to how the courts in the previous cases treated FDA decisions?

Novartis agreed to modify the ads, but not to change the labeling (which would have required FDA approval).

### E.    The First Amendment

In recent years, the FDA has faced significant First Amendment constraints on its ability to regulate as the courts give more weight to commercial speakers' interests in disseminating the information of their choice. The following case is of interest because of the scrutiny it gives to the FDA's evaluation of the clinical evidence, where one might think the FDA had a comparative advantage over a generalist judge.

*Alliance for Natural Health U.S. v. Sebelius, 714 F. Supp. 2d 48 (D.D.C. 2010)*

Plaintiffs Alliance for Natural Health U.S., Durk Pearson, Sandy Shaw, and Coalition to End FDA and FTC Censorship have sued the Food and Drug Administration ("FDA" or "Agency") and other defendants, seeking review of the Agency's decision to deny plaintiffs' petition for authorization of qualified health claims regarding selenium-containing dietary supplements. Invoking both circuit and district court opinions that have addressed similar claims, plaintiffs seek a declaratory judgment that the FDA's final order denying plaintiffs' petition is invalid and a permanent injunction enjoining the Agency from "taking any action that would preclude [plaintiffs] from placing [their proposed selenium] health claims on [dietary supplement] labels." . . .

BACKGROUND

I. STATUTORY AND REGULATORY FRAMEWORK

A "dietary supplement" is a "product (other than tobacco) intended to supplement the diet that bears or contains" one or more of certain dietary ingredients, including vitamins, minerals, herbs or botanicals, amino acids, concentrates, metabolites, constituents, or extracts. A dietary supplement is deemed to be "food," which is defined in part as "articles used for food or drink for man or other animals," except when it meets the definition of a "drug," which is defined in part as "articles intended for use in the diagnosis, cure, mitigation, treatment, or prevention of disease in man or other animals." A "health claim" is "any claim made on the label or in labeling of a food, including a dietary supplement, that expressly or by implication . . . characterizes the relationship of any substance to a disease or health-related condition."

Under the Federal Food, Drug, and Cosmetic Act ("FFDCA"), manufacturers wishing to market a new drug must undergo a "strict and demanding" process designed to ensure consumer safety and product efficacy in order to obtain FDA approval before introducing the product into interstate commerce. "Prior to 1984, the FDA took the position that a statement that consumption of a food could prevent a particular disease was 'tantamount to a claim that the food was a drug . . . and therefore that its sale was prohibited until a new drug application had been approved.'" But in the mid-1980s, companies began making health claims on foods without seeking new drug approval, a practice the FDA supported. Congress subsequently enacted the Nutrition Labeling and Education Act of 1990 ("NLEA"), amending the FFDCA to provide the FDA with authority to regulate health claims on food.

The NLEA created a "safe harbor" from the "drug" designation for foods and dietary supplements labeled with health claims. Under the Act, a manufacturer may make a health claim on a food without FDA new drug approval if the FDA determines that "significant scientific agreement," based on the "totality of publicly available scientific evidence," supports the claim. For dietary supplement health claims, however, Congress declined to establish an authorization process and instead left the creation of an approval "procedure and standard" to the FDA. The FDA subsequently promulgated a regulation adopting the NLEA's standard for food health claims (i.e., "significant scientific agreement") for dietary supplement health claims. The FDA may consider a dietary supplement labeled with an unauthorized health claim to be a misbranded food; a misbranded drug; and/or an unapproved new drug. A dietary supplement labeled with such a claim, or a claim that is false or misleading, is subject to seizure, and the Agency may enjoin the product's distribution or seek criminal penalties against its manufacturer.

## II. *PEARSON V. SHALALA* AND SUBSEQUENT CASE LAW

### A. Introduction

Plaintiffs' lawsuit is the latest in a series of disputes between dietary supplement designers and the FDA regarding the Agency's regulation of health claims regarding dietary supplements after the passage of the NLEA. Pearson, Shaw, and other individuals and groups affiliated with the production, sale, and use of dietary supplements have, since 1995, sought judicial review of FDA decisions denying a variety of proposed health claims. The first of these lawsuits, challenging the FDA's rejection of the plaintiffs' proposed claims on First Amendment grounds, resulted in an invalidation of the Agency's regulations regarding health claim review by the D.C. Circuit. Since then, the FDA has struggled to balance its concerns for consumer protection and dietary supplement manufacturers' First Amendment commercial speech rights as defined by *Pearson I*. An abbreviated summary of these cases follows.

### B. *Pearson I*

In 1995, a group of dietary supplement manufacturers filed suit against the FDA and other defendants under the First Amendment, challenging the FDA's rejection of four health claims that the manufacturers sought to include on certain dietary supplements. The claims characterized a relationship between dietary supplements and the risk of particular diseases. The Agency, applying the "significant scientific agreement" standard set forth in 21 C.F.R. § 101.14, determined that the evidence concerning the supplements "was inconclusive . . . and thus failed to give rise to 'significant scientific agreement.'" The Agency therefore declined to authorize the claims, finding them to be "inherently misleading and thus entirely outside the protection of the First Amendment" as commercial speech. The FDA also declined to consider the proposed alternative of "permitting the claim[s] while requiring . . . corrective disclaimer[s]," arguing that even if the proposed claims were only "potentially misleading," it had no obligation under the First Amendment to consider a "disclaimer approach," as opposed to suppression, where the claims at issue lacked significant scientific agreement. The manufacturers sued, arguing that the FDA's "significant scientific agreement" standard was unconstitutionally vague and was tantamount to a blanket ban on commercial speech in violation of the manufacturers' First Amendment rights.

After the district court denied the manufacturers' motion for summary judgment, the D.C. Circuit reversed. The Court, applying the commercial speech test set forth in *Central Hudson Gas & Electric Corporation v. Public Service Commission of New York*, 447 U.S. 557 (1980),[5] held that there was not a "reasonable fit between the government's goals" of protecting public health and preventing consumer fraud and "the means chosen to advance those goals," namely, the rejection of plaintiffs' proposed health claims without consideration of disclaimers. Specifically, the Court held that under the First Amendment commercial speech doctrine, there is a "preference for disclosure over outright suppression" and for "less restrictive and more precise means" of regulating commercial speech. The Agency's rejection of disclaimers without a showing that they were insufficient to meet the government's goal of avoiding consumer confusion demonstrated a disregard for "less restrictive" means of speech regulation that violated the First Amendment. The Court remanded the case to the district court with instructions to remand it to the Agency to consider whether disclaimers could sufficiently prevent consumer confusion and, if so, the content of those disclaimers. . . .

In requiring the Agency to consider the adequacy of possible disclaimers accompanying the manufacturers' proposed health claims, the Court recognized that "where evidence in support of a claim is outweighed by evidence against the claim, the FDA could deem it incurable by a disclaimer and ban it outright." Similarly, the Court "s[aw] no problem with the FDA imposing an outright ban on a claim where evidence in support of the claim is qualitatively weaker than evidence against the claim." However, the Court stated that the Agency "must still meet its burden of justifying a restriction on speech," and a "conclusory assertion" as to misleadingness is inadequate.

## C. *Pearson II*

In late 2000, several of the plaintiffs from *Pearson I* and other dietary supplement designers, sellers, and manufacturers filed a second lawsuit to challenge the Agency's decision prohibiting plaintiffs from including on their dietary supplements' labels a health claim concerning folic acid.[7] After the

---

[5] The *Central Hudson* analysis, as clarified by the Supreme Court in *Thompson v. Western States Medical Center*, 535 U.S. 357 (2002), consists of four parts: 1) "whether 'the speech concerns lawful activity and is not misleading;' " 2) if the speech is protected, "whether the asserted government interest [in regulation] is substantial;" 3) "whether the regulation directly advances the governmental interest asserted;" and 4) "whether [the regulation] is not more extensive than is necessary to serve that interest."

[7] The folic acid health claim at issue in *Pearson II* was the same folic acid claim at issue in *Pearson I*, which stated that ".8 mg of folic acid in a dietary supplement is more effective in reducing the risk of neural tube defects than a lower amount in foods in common form." With respect to this claim, the Court of Appeals in *Pearson I* "strongly suggested, without declaring so explicitly" that the claim "was only 'potentially misleading,' not 'inherently misleading,' and therefore the FDA's refusal to authorize [the claim] (or to propose a disclaimer to accompany the [c]laim) violated the First Amendment." Pearson II, 130 F.Supp.2d at 110; *see also* Pearson I, 164 F.3d at 659 ("[I]t appears that credible evidence did support [the folic acid claim], and we suspect that a

decision in *Pearson I*, the FDA published a notice requesting submission of scientific data concerning the four health claims at issue in that case, including the folic acid claim. . . . [T]he Agency issued a decision stating that it would not authorize the manufacturers' folic acid claim, even with clarifying disclaimers, because it found the claim to be inherently misleading. . . .

The district court agreed with the plaintiffs, finding that the FDA "failed to comply with the constitutional guidelines outlined in *Pearson [I]* " when it concluded, without explanation, that the "weight of the evidence is against . . . the proposed [folic acid] claim" and that the claim was therefore "inherently misleading" and not susceptible to correction by disclaimer. . . . [The court] disagreed with the FDA's weighing of the scientific data and found "as a matter of law that [the folic acid claim] is not 'inherently misleading.' " In coming to this conclusion, the court analyzed the scientific data regarding folic acid and concluded that "[t]he mere absence of significant affirmative evidence in support of a particular claim . . . does not translate into negative evidence 'against' it." Moreover, the court held that the "question which must be answered under *Pearson [I]* is whether there is any 'credible evidence' " in support of the claim. If so, unless that evidence is "outweighed by evidence against the claim" or is "qualitatively weaker" than evidence against the claim, the claim "may not be absolutely prohibited."

Because the court found that there was credible evidence to support the folic acid claim, it held that the FDA's determination that the folic acid claim was "inherently misleading" and could not be cured by disclaimers was "arbitrary and capricious" under the APA and that the FDA had not "undertake[n] the necessary analysis required by *Pearson [I]*." The court granted the plaintiffs' motion for a preliminary injunction and remanded the case to the FDA to "draft one or more appropriately short, succinct, and accurate disclaimers."

D. *Pearson III*

After the preliminary injunction was entered in *Pearson II*, the FDA filed a motion for reconsideration . . . . The district court . . . restated the holdings in *Pearson I*, which included 1) the obligation of the Agency to "demonstrate with empirical evidence that disclaimers . . . would bewilder consumers and fail to correct for deceptiveness," and 2) the establishment of "a very heavy burden which Defendants must satisfy if they wish to totally suppress a particular health claim."

E. *Whitaker v. Thompson*

In June 2001, the plaintiffs filed another lawsuit to challenge the Agency's decision not to authorize the antioxidant claim at issue in *Pearson I*.[12]

---

clarifying disclaimer could be added to the effect that 'The evidence in support of this claim is inconclusive.' " (citation omitted)).

[12] The claim at issue was that "Consumption of antioxidant vitamins may reduce the risk of certain kinds of cancers."

. . . [T]he court reviewed the Agency's analysis of the claim in light of *Pearson I*, noting that "[t]he deference due to an agency's expert evaluation of scientific data does not negate 'the duty of the court to ensure that an agency . . . conduct a process of reasoned decision-making." As such, the court reviewed over 150 intervention and observational studies regarding the relationship between antioxidant vitamins and cancer relied upon by the FDA in reaching its conclusions and found that nearly one-third of the studies "supported" the antioxidant/cancer relationship. The court determined that the FDA had "failed to follow its own [Guidance] Report and give appropriate weight" to these studies. . . . The court then found that the circumstances under which the Agency might ban a claim as misleading, described in *Pearson I*, were not present because 1) one-third of the evidence examined supported the claim; and 2) the FDA failed to provide "empirical evidence that an appropriate disclaimer would confuse customers and fail to correct for deceptiveness." As a result, the court granted a preliminary injunction after concluding that the Agency's decision to suppress the claim did not "comport with the First Amendment's clear preference for disclosure over suppression of commercial speech."

### III. FACTUAL AND PROCEDURAL HISTORY

In July 2002, Wellness Lifestyles, Inc., one of the plaintiffs in *Whitaker*, submitted to the FDA two proposed health claims regarding the relationship between selenium and cancer risk. On February 21, 2003, the FDA exercised enforcement discretion with respect to two "qualified"[13] versions of the health claims.[14] In December 2007, the FDA, in response to an Agency for Healthcare Research and Quality ("AHRQ") study, announced its intention to "reevaluate the scientific evidence on these two qualified health claims and determine if the scientific evidence continues to support the qualified health claim, and if so, whether the qualified health claim language should be modified to reflect a stronger or weaker relationship." The Agency commenced a public comment period on this issue, and plaintiffs filed extensive comments in opposition to the FDA's proposed re-evaluation of the two selenium claims.

In addition to opposing the FDA's planned re-evaluation of the qualified selenium health claims, plaintiffs submitted a health claim petition seeking authorization of ten new qualified health claims (collectively, "qualified selenium health claims")[16] concerning the purported relationship between

---

[13] "Qualified health claims" are health claims that include one or more disclaimers designed to eliminate potentially misleading assertions. They were created in response to the D.C. Circuit's holding in *Pearson I*.

[14] The original proposed health claims were 1) "Selenium may reduce the risk of certain cancers;" and 2) "Selenium may produce anticarcinogenic effects in the body." The FDA concluded that the petition "d[id] not meet the 'significant scientific agreement standard' " but ultimately exercised enforcement discretion with respect to qualified versions of the claims that stated as follows: 1) "Selenium may reduce the risk of certain cancers. Some scientific evidence suggests that consumption of selenium may reduce the risk of certain forms of cancer. However, FDA has determined that this evidence is limited and not conclusive;" and 2) "Selenium may produce anticarcinogenic effects in the body. Some scientific evidence suggests that consumption of selenium may produce anticarcinogenic effects in the body. However, FDA has determined that this evidence is limited and not conclusive."

[16] Plaintiffs proposed the following claims:

selenium and cancer. Plaintiffs' submission included over 150 scientific articles purporting to examine one or more aspects of the relationship between selenium and cancer, which supplemented the 17 articles previously submitted to the FDA during the public comment period.

. . . The FDA concluded that while scientific evidence supports qualified health claims concerning the relationship between selenium intake and a reduced risk of bladder, prostate, and thyroid cancer, no such evidence exists to support a relationship between selenium intake and a reduced risk of urinary tract (other than bladder), lung and other respiratory tract, colon and other digestive tract, brain, liver, and breast cancers. The Agency also concluded that proposed Claims 1 and 2, regarding selenium intake and certain cancers and anticarcinogenic effects, "are misleading because they are overbroad, fail to disclose material information, and are not supported by the scientific evidence the agency reviewed. . . . " [The FDA denied most claims and said it would not take action against certain modified claims.][19]

Plaintiffs filed the instant lawsuit on August 4, 2009, claiming a violation of the First Amendment as a result of the FDA's denial of Claims 1 ("certain cancers claim"); 2 ("anticarcinogenic effects claim"); 5 ("lung/respiratory tract claim"); and 6 ("colon/digestive tract claim"). Plaintiffs also maintain that the FDA's modification of Claim 3 ("prostate claim") violates their First Amendment rights because it "constructively suppress[es] [this] claim with the imposition of an onerous, value laden set of qualifications that only allow Plaintiffs to propound a false, negatively value-laden, and inaccurate claim to the public." Plaintiffs also oppose the FDA's proposed qualifications of Claim 3 as being "unreasonably long and burdensome for Plaintiffs and other industry members to include on their dietary supplement labels," thereby violating *Central Hudson*'s requirement that the government's means of accomplishing its goals be reasonable. . . .

ANALYSIS

I. LEGAL STANDARD

A. Scope of Review

---

1. Selenium may reduce the risk of certain cancers. Scientific evidence supporting this claim is convincing but not yet conclusive.

2. Selenium may produce anticarcinogenic effects in the body. Scientific evidence supporting this claim is convincing but not yet conclusive.

[Plaintiffs proposed identical claims for specific forms of cancer.] . . . .

[19] The Agency stated that it would consider the exercise of its enforcement discretion for the following qualified health claims: 1) "One study suggests that selenium intake may reduce the risk of bladder cancer in women. However, one smaller study showed no reduction in risk. Based on these studies, FDA concludes that it is highly uncertain that selenium supplements reduce the risk of bladder cancer in women;" 2) "Two weak studies suggest that selenium intake may reduce the risk of prostate cancer. However, four stronger studies and three weak studies showed no reduction in risk. Based on these studies, FDA concludes that it is highly unlikely that selenium supplements reduce the risk of prostate cancer;" and 3) "One weak, small study suggests that selenium intake may reduce the risk of thyroid cancer. Based on this study, FDA concludes that it is highly uncertain that selenium supplements reduce the risk of thyroid cancer."

Plaintiffs raise their claims under the First Amendment to the United States Constitution. "[A] Court's review of 'constitutional challenges to agency actions . . . is de novo.' " The Court shall make "an independent assessment of [the plaintiffs'] claim of constitutional right when reviewing agency decision-making," and it need not accord deference to the agency's "pronouncement on a constitutional question."

. . . The Agency contends that because "this case does not involve a challenge to a regulation broadly prohibiting an entire category of misleading speech" and instead involves "particularized findings concerning the scientific evidence relating to plaintiffs' specific health claims," the "APA's deferential [arbitrary and capricious] standard applies here." . . .

The Court concludes that it is obligated to conduct an independent review of the record and must do so without reliance on the Agency's determinations as to constitutional questions. But it would be inconsistent with binding precedent and wholly inappropriate to evaluate the voluminous scientific studies at issue in this case without some deference to the FDA's assessment of that technical data. Moreover, deference to the Agency's interpretation of scientific information, provided such interpretation is reasoned and not arbitrary or capricious, is consistent with the test set forth in *Pearson I*. By instructing the FDA to employ less restrictive means of regulating speech and to provide greater empirical support for its regulatory decisions, the D.C. Circuit did not purport to tell the Agency how to assess scientific data. Rather, it provided the Agency with guidelines for developing regulations once it had evaluated the evidence before it.

This is not, however, to say that where the FDA's conclusions are contrary to its purported evaluation standards or are otherwise arbitrary, as the court concluded they were in *Pearson II* and *Whitaker*, a reviewing court should not overturn the Agency. But "[t]he enforced education into the intricacies of the problem before the agency is not designed to enable the court to become a superagency that can supplant the agency's expert decision-maker. To the contrary, the court must give due deference to the agency's ability to rely on its own developed expertise."

B. Regulation of Commercial Speech

. . . The Supreme Court has "rejected the 'highly paternalistic' view that government has complete power to suppress or regulate commercial speech." Moreover, it has distinguished between "inherently misleading" speech and "potentially misleading" speech. "[Actually or inherently m]isleading advertising may be prohibited entirely." "But the States may not place an absolute prohibition on certain types of potentially misleading information . . . if the information also may be presented in a way that is not deceptive." Moreover, "[t]he First Amendment does not allow the FDA to simply assert that [a plaintiff's c]laim is misleading in order to 'supplant its burden to demonstrate that the harms it recites are real and that its restriction will in fact alleviate them to a material degree.' " Indeed, in *Pearson I*, the D.C. Circuit rejected the FDA's contention that health claims lacking "significant scientific agreement" are inherently misleading as "almost frivolous." Even when it finds "that speech is misleading, the government must consider that 'people will perceive their own best interests if only they are well enough informed, and . . . the best means to that end is to open the channels of communication rather than to close them.' "

*Central Hudson* established a multi-step analysis of speech regulation. "As a threshold matter," the Court must determine "whether the commercial speech [being regulated] concerns unlawful activity or is misleading." If so, the speech is not protected. But if the speech is lawful and not misleading, or is only potentially misleading, the Court must ask "whether the asserted governmental interest in regulating the speech is substantial." If it is, the Court then ascertains "whether the regulation [at issue] directly advances the governmental interest asserted" and "whether [the regulation] is not more extensive than is necessary to serve that interest." This last step requires the Court to evaluate "whether the fit between the government's ends and the means chosen to accomplish those ends is . . . reasonable."

The government has the burden of showing that the regulations on speech that it seeks to impose are "not more extensive than is necessary to serve" the interests it attempts to advance. Therefore, the Court in *Pearson I* noted that disclaimers are "constitutionally preferable to outright suppression," and that generally, "the preferred remedy is more disclosure, rather than less." For this reason, the Court in *Pearson I* concluded that "when government chooses a policy of suppression over disclosure—at least where there is no showing that disclosure would not suffice to cure misleadingness—the government disregards a far less restrictive means."

## II. FDA's COMPLETE BAN OF PLAINTIFFS' CLAIMS

In its response to plaintiffs' petition, the Agency denied four of the proffered claims outright. Under *Central Hudson* and *Pearson I*, the FDA may refuse to consider disclaimers for health claims (i.e., prohibit their use completely) only if such health claims are inherently misleading, or are potentially misleading but the Agency has deemed the claim "incurable by disclaimer." The court in *Whitaker* arguably went even further than *Pearson I*, holding that "any complete ban of a claim would be approved only under narrow circumstances, i.e., when there was almost no qualitative evidence in support of the claim and where the government provided empirical evidence proving that the public would still be deceived even if the claim was qualified by a disclaimer." The Court considers each of plaintiffs' claims to determine whether the FDA has met its burden with respect to those claims it has banned outright.[22]

## A. Plaintiffs' "Certain Cancers" and "Anticarcinogenic Effects" Claims

The FDA asserts that claims that selenium may reduce the risk of certain cancers and may produce anticarcinogenic effects are "misleading on their face," "independent of the proffered scientific

---

[22] The Court considers only the first sentence of each of plaintiffs' proposed claims, not the suggested disclaimer in the second sentence (i.e., that the "[s]cientific evidence supporting this claim is convincing but not yet conclusive"). To the extent the FDA denied these claims outright, it did so on the basis of the claimed relationship between selenium dietary supplements and various cancers, not because of the disclaimer. Specifically, where the FDA banned a claim entirely because it found "no credible evidence of a risk reduction relationship" or believed the claim was inherently misleading, it concluded that the proposed disclaimer was "clearly false" without further assessment of its merits. To the extent the Court overturns the Agency's findings as to the substance of the health claims, it must allow the FDA to consider plaintiffs' proposed disclaimer and/or alternate disclaimers in the first instance.

evidence." Specifically, the Agency concluded that the certain cancers claim "is incomplete and misleading because it fails to reveal the individual cancer(s) that selenium may have an effect on," thus leading a consumer to purchase selenium in hopes of preventing a cancer for which there is no evidence of risk reduction from selenium intake. The FDA also argues that by "referring in general terms to 'certain cancers,' the requested claim language . . . suggests that cancers at different sites are essentially the same disease and that it is not important to distinguish between them." Similarly, the anticarcinogenic effects claim "falsely implies that [selenium] can protect against all cancers," when in fact cancer "is not a single disease" but a "collective term for a large number of individual diseases that differ with respect to risk factors, etiology, methods of diagnosis and treatment, and mortality risk." Moreover, the Agency argues that the phrase "anticarcinogenic effects" is ambiguous because "anticarcinogenic" might mean both the "treatment and mitigation of existing cancer as well as the reduction of risk of getting cancer in the first place." Since "[c]laims about treatment or mitigation of disease are classified as drug claims, not health claims," the FDA "believes that no qualified claim based on that phrase would be truthful and non-misleading."

The Court concludes that the FDA's position fails under *Pearson I*. The Agency has not provided any empirical evidence, such as "studies" or "anecdotal evidence," that consumers would be misled by either of plaintiffs' claims were they accompanied by qualifications. Moreover, the explanation the FDA offers to demonstrate that plaintiffs' claims are misleading—that the claims leave out pertinent information—is not support for banning the claims entirely, but rather favors the approach of remedying any potential misleadingness by the disclosure of additional information.

The FDA's position is particularly troubling in light of its admission that plaintiffs' certain cancers claim "is literally true . . . in that there is credible evidence that selenium may reduce the risk of at least three cancers" and that the anticarcinogenic effects claim "is true to the extent that it refers to reducing the risk of . . . three cancers[.]" As the Circuit Court in *Pearson I* made clear, "the government's interest in preventing the use of labels that are true but do not mention [material information] would seem to be satisfied—at least ordinarily—by inclusion of a prominent disclaimer setting forth [that information]." Here, the FDA has not provided any evidence that completing plaintiffs' certain cancers claim by "reveal[ing] the individual cancer(s) that selenium may have an effect on" and explaining that cancers at different sites are different diseases and respond differently to treatments would not eliminate the consumer confusion it fears. And, the FDA's argument that "disclaimer language defining 'anticarcinogenic' as reducing the risk of, rather than treating or mitigating, cancer would not cure the misleading nature" of the claim because it "would still fail to specify the disease at issue" begs the question why an additional disclaimer, specifying the disease[s], would not remedy the purported problem.

Supreme Court precedent and *Pearson I* obligate the FDA to, at a minimum, consider "less restrictive" means of correcting that misleadingness before it turns to suppression. Because the Agency has not done so here, the Court will remand the claims relating to certain cancers and anticarcinogenic effects to the FDA for the purpose of drafting one or more disclaimers or, alternatively, setting forth empirical evidence that any disclaimer would fail to correct the claims' purported misleadingness.

B. Plaintiffs' Lung and Respiratory Tract Claim

In contrast to the certain cancers and anticarcinogenic effects claims, the FDA considered the scientific evidence proffered by plaintiffs and concluded that it could draw scientific conclusions from only four of those studies concerning plaintiffs' lung/respiratory tract claim. Because all of those studies reported "no significant difference in mean serum levels" between control cases and lung cancer cases, the Agency concluded that "there is no credible evidence for a claim about selenium supplements and reduced risk of lung cancer or other respiratory tract cancers." Plaintiffs contend that a number of the studies discounted by the FDA provide sufficient credible evidence of a positive relationship between selenium intake and a lowered risk of lung and respiratory tract cancers.

As an initial matter, the FDA's determination regarding the lung and respiratory tract claim is not inconsistent with *Pearson I*, in which the Court allowed for the possibility that "where evidence in support of a claim is outweighed by evidence against the claim, the FDA could deem it incurable by a disclaimer and ban it outright." Here, the Agency claims that there is no evidence in support of the proposed claim and cites studies suggesting that there is no relationship between selenium intake and reduced lung cancer risk. However, the Court in *Pearson I* also suggested that when " 'credible evidence' supports a claim, that claim may not be absolutely prohibited." Therefore, the proper inquiry is what qualifies as "credible evidence" and is there any such evidence to support the lung and respiratory tract claim?

In its latest Guidance Document, the FDA states that it uses an "evidence-based review system" to evaluate the strength of the evidence in support of a statement. . . .

For example, it states that "[r]andomized, controlled trials offer the best assessment of a causal relationship between a substance and a disease." In contrast, "research synthesis studies" and "review articles" "do not provide sufficient information on the individual studies reviewed" to determine critical elements of the studies and/or whether those elements were flawed. The FDA also explains the questions it considers in determining whether scientific conclusions can be drawn from an intervention or observational study, such as where the studies were conducted (i.e., on what type of population); what type of information was collected; and what type of biomarker of disease risk was measured. If the FDA concludes that the elements of a study are flawed such that it is impossible to draw scientific conclusions from the study, it eliminates that study from further review.

Using the above procedure, the FDA disregarded the studies plaintiffs cite as "credible evidence" in support of their proposed lung/respiratory tract claim . . . . The Agency states that it eliminated the van den Brandt and Knekt studies because they were conducted on Dutch and Finnish populations whose average baseline selenium levels . . . are significantly lower than the levels observed in the "vast majority of the U.S. population." . . . As such, the FDA's decision not to extrapolate from these studies to the U.S. population is both rational based on the studies' conclusions and consistent with the Agency's evaluation criteria. . . .

Finally, the Agency rejected the SU.VI.MAX study because the study "did not confirm that all subjects were free of the cancers of interest prior to the intervention" and therefore may have involved subjects who already had cancer at the time the study began. Because of this omission, the

FDA stated that it could not draw scientific conclusions from the study. However, the SU.VI.MAX study states that one of the criteria for participation in the study was "lack of disease likely to hinder active participation or threatened [*sic*] 5-year survival." . . . The Agency also appears to have overlooked a later report on the SU.VI.MAX study population concerning prostate cancer, which noted that three participants were excluded at the start of the study because they had prostate cancer, indicating that some sort of cancer screening process was conducted at the study's outset. As such, the Agency's stated reason for its disregard of the study is unsupported by the record. And the FDA provided no response to the plaintiffs' argument regarding the results of the study, namely that "in men, the incidence of respiratory cancers was reduced from 88 per 100,000 for the control group to 37 per 100,000 for the supplemented group," while in women, the "incidence of respiratory tract cancers was reduced from 21 per 100,000 in the control group to only 12 per 100,000 in the supplemented group."

. . . To the extent that the FDA is concerned about possible limitations of the SU.VI.MAX study protocol and/or results, it must remedy such limitations with disclaimers. Accordingly, the Court remands the lung/respiratory tract claim to the Agency to determine an appropriate disclaimer in light of the SU.VI.MAX study.

C. Plaintiffs' Colon and Digestive Tract Claim

[The court reached similar conclusions with respect to the FDA's exclusion of certain studies from its analysis.]

### III. FDA'S QUALIFICATION OF PLAINTIFFS' PROSTATE CLAIM

After reviewing the scientific literature submitted with plaintiffs' petition, the FDA concluded that it could draw scientific conclusions regarding plaintiffs' prostate claim from eight observational studies and one intervention study. Of these, the Agency determined that two nested case-control studies suggested that selenium may reduce the risk of prostate cancer. However, the FDA rejected plaintiffs' proposed claim because it found the characterization of the evidence in support of the claim as "convincing but not yet conclusive" to be false and misleading. Instead, the Agency stated that it would exercise enforcement discretion with respect to the following qualified health claim: "Two weak studies suggest that selenium intake may reduce the risk of prostate cancer. However, four stronger studies and three weak studies showed no reduction in risk. Based on these studies, FDA concludes that it is highly unlikely that selenium supplements reduce the risk of prostate cancer."

The Court agrees with plaintiffs' contention that the FDA's proposed claim is at odds with the Supreme Court's mandate that there be a "reasonable fit" between the government's goal and the restrictions it imposes on commercial speech. The Agency has not drafted a "precise disclaimer" designed to qualify plaintiffs' claim while adhering to the "First Amendment preference for disclosure over suppression," as mandated. Rather, it has replaced plaintiffs' claim entirely. And the Agency's "qualification" effectively negates any relationship between prostate cancer risk and selenium intake. Indeed, the FDA's language is an example of a "disclaimer" that "contradict[s] the claim and defeats the purpose of making [it] in the first place." While such language might be

CHAPTER 17: CASE STUDIES IN FOOD AND DRUGS

appropriate were there no credible evidence in support of a positive relationship between prostate cancer risk and selenium intake, the Agency concedes that there is such evidence. As such, the FDA is obligated to at least consider the possibility of approving plaintiffs' proposed language with the addition of "short, succinct, and accurate disclaimers." Here, the FDA has completely eviscerated plaintiffs' claim, with no explanation as to why a less restrictive approach would not be effective. For instance, to the extent that the FDA takes issue with the proposed "convincing but not yet conclusive" claim, the Agency makes no attempt to demonstrate that this concern would not be accommodated by altering this portion of the claim with language that more accurately reflects the strength of the scientific evidence at issue. Such qualification would be a "far less restrictive means" than negation of plaintiffs' claim.

Moreover, in light of its review of the scientific literature, the Court finds that the Agency's "disclaimer" is inaccurate. . . . Even if the FDA determines the study evidences only a limited reduction in risk in certain subgroups, the Court concludes that the Agency erred in finding that the study "show[s] no reduction in [prostate cancer] risk."

. . . [T]he Court will remand plaintiffs' prostate claim to the FDA for the purpose of reconsidering the scientific literature and drafting one or more short, succinct, and accurate disclaimers in light of that review. . . .

*NOTES AND QUESTIONS*

*Resolution.* In October 2010, the FDA revised the qualified health claims at issue. The prostate claim can now reads: "Selenium may reduce the risk of prostate cancer. Scientific evidence concerning this claim is inconclusive. Based on its review, FDA does not agree that selenium may reduce the risk of prostate cancer." From the advertiser's perspective, is this a better disclaimer? Are consumers likely to understand it?

*Affirmative Efficacy Claims vs. Claims of Uncertain Efficacy. Pearson I* resolved an important predicate question against the FDA. Before allowing a claim, the FDA wanted significant scientific agreement as to the ultimate conclusion: "this product reduces the risk of heart disease." The *Pearson I* court was concerned that the FDA therefore banned some truthful claims that could meet the "significant scientific agreement" standard in another way: claims for which it was true to say that "there is inconclusive evidence that this product may reduce the risk of heart disease" or that "this product may improve heart health, but there is no significant scientific agreement that this is true." The standard for testing the statements is formally the same, but the substance of the claim is very different—"it is true that this product works" as opposed to "it is true that this product might work, and it is also true that we don't really know." The FDA did not want to allow this kind of regression, but the court agreed that it was truthful and non-misleading to say, in appropriate cases, that preliminary results suggest a nutrient/disease relationship and that further studies are needed. Which position on the appropriate application of "significant scientific agreement" is more convincing, the FDA's or the court's?

Consider the district court's description of *Pearson II*, in which the district court "disagreed with the FDA's weighing of the scientific data." Is this an appropriate job for a court? Can it be avoided if the

764

First Amendment is to have any force in the FDA context? Later, the court states that "it would be inconsistent with binding precedent and wholly inappropriate to evaluate the voluminous scientific studies at issue in this case without *some* deference to the FDA's assessment of that technical data" (emphasis added), citing, among others, *Serono Labs., Inc. v. Shalala*, 158 F.3d 1313, 1320 (D.C.Cir.1998) (agency "evaluations of scientific data within its area of expertise" are "entitled to a *high* level of deference") (emphasis added). Should the court have deferred further, or do the First Amendment interests at stake justify a higher level of judicial review?

Consider next the court's statement: "[t]he mere absence of significant affirmative evidence in support of a particular claim . . . does not translate into negative evidence 'against' it." How seriously should we take this claim? Does this mean that an advertiser can claim "selenium protects against Alzheimer's" until the FDA produces convincing evidence to disprove the claim? Is this statement consistent with the FTC's substantiation requirement?

Now turn to the lung and respiratory tract claim. The existence of one positive study apparently means that plaintiffs can make their claims, no matter how many other studies produce negative results. Many statisticians would identify this conclusion as erroneous: if we were 95% certain that selenium does not protect against lung cancer, we would not be surprised if 5 out of 100 studies found a protective effect. In fact, we would *expect* 5% of trials, or one in twenty, to produce false positives.

The following cartoon shows this feature of scientific studies, as well as popular misunderstandings thereof:

WE FOUND NO LINK BETWEEN PURPLE JELLY BEANS AND ACNE ($p > 0.05$).

WE FOUND NO LINK BETWEEN BROWN JELLY BEANS AND ACNE ($p > 0.05$).

WE FOUND NO LINK BETWEEN PINK JELLY BEANS AND ACNE ($p > 0.05$).

WE FOUND NO LINK BETWEEN BLUE JELLY BEANS AND ACNE ($p > 0.05$).

WE FOUND NO LINK BETWEEN TEAL JELLY BEANS AND ACNE ($p > 0.05$).

WE FOUND NO LINK BETWEEN SALMON JELLY BEANS AND ACNE ($p > 0.05$).

WE FOUND NO LINK BETWEEN RED JELLY BEANS AND ACNE ($p > 0.05$).

WE FOUND NO LINK BETWEEN TURQUOISE JELLY BEANS AND ACNE ($p > 0.05$).

WE FOUND NO LINK BETWEEN MAGENTA JELLY BEANS AND ACNE ($p > 0.05$).

WE FOUND NO LINK BETWEEN YELLOW JELLY BEANS AND ACNE ($p > 0.05$).

WE FOUND NO LINK BETWEEN GREY JELLY BEANS AND ACNE ($p > 0.05$).

WE FOUND NO LINK BETWEEN TAN JELLY BEANS AND ACNE ($p > 0.05$).

WE FOUND NO LINK BETWEEN CYAN JELLY BEANS AND ACNE ($p > 0.05$).

WE FOUND A LINK BETWEEN GREEN JELLY BEANS AND ACNE ($p < 0.05$).

WHOA!

WE FOUND NO LINK BETWEEN MAUVE JELLY BEANS AND ACNE ($p > 0.05$).

WE FOUND NO LINK BETWEEN BEIGE JELLY BEANS AND ACNE ($p > 0.05$).

WE FOUND NO LINK BETWEEN LILAC JELLY BEANS AND ACNE ($p > 0.05$).

WE FOUND NO LINK BETWEEN BLACK JELLY BEANS AND ACNE ($p > 0.05$).

WE FOUND NO LINK BETWEEN PEACH JELLY BEANS AND ACNE ($p > 0.05$).

WE FOUND NO LINK BETWEEN ORANGE JELLY BEANS AND ACNE ($p > 0.05$).

Under the standard set forth by the district court, how many negative studies would be required before the FDA could conclude that the single positive study reflected random variation rather than an actual protective effect?

Finally, consider the disclaimer issue in light of what you have learned about disclosures and disclaimers. Are disclaimers likely to effectively qualify the claims at issue? If the FDA determines that disclaimers won't work, what sort of empirical evidence will it have to submit to satisfy a reviewing court of this conclusion? Would general evidence that consumers simply don't process technical disclaimers suffice?

Here are some examples of the disclaimers approved by the *Pearson* court:

> 0.8 mg folic acid in a dietary supplement is more effective in reducing the risk of neural tube defects than a lower amount in foods in common form. FDA does not endorse this claim. Public health authorities recommend that women consume 0.4 mg folic [acid] daily from fortified foods or dietary supplements or both to reduce the risk of neural tube defects.

> As part of a well-balanced diet that is low in saturated fat and cholesterol, Folic Acid, Vitamin B6 and Vitamin B-12 may reduce the risk of vascular disease. FDA evaluated the above claim and found that, while it is known that diets low in saturated fat and cholesterol reduce the risk of heart disease and other vascular diseases, the evidence in support of the above claim is inconclusive.

---

[4] "Significant," https://www.xkcd.com/882/ (alternative text reads: "'So, uh, we did the green study again and got no link. It was probably a—' 'RESEARCH CONFLICTED ON GREEN JELLY BEAN/ACNE LINK; MORE STUDY RECOMMENDED!'").

How well will these work? A study evaluating the DSHEA disclaimer and the *Pearson* disclaimer ("the scientific evidence is suggestive, but not conclusive") showed that they did not affect consumers' beliefs. Their presence on a supplement label had *no* significant effect on consumer reactions. Notably, the disclaimers were worthless at decreasing consumers' confidence in the health benefit claim, and worthless at decreasing consumers' belief that the FDA evaluated and approved that claim. *See* Paula Fitzgerald Bone & Karen Russo France, *Assessing Consumer Perceptions of Health Claims*, Nov. 17, 2005.

Could the FDA rely on the Bone and France study to argue that the same or similar disclaimers applied to different health claims would be just as ineffective? That is, the court's dissection of specific studies about selenium was quite particularized, but consumer perception of the disclaimer might be a separate issue, since it is not about the science but about how consumers interpret claims about science. Under the First Amendment, how specific does the FDA's evidence about the effectiveness of disclaimers have to be?

The FTC weighed in on this issue in response to the FDA's request for comments. Comments of the Staff of the Bureau of Economics, the Bureau of Consumer Protection, and the Office of Policy Planning of the Federal Trade Commission, *In the Matter of Assessing Consumer Perceptions of Health Claims*, Docket No. 2005N-0413 (Jan. 17, 2006). The FTC staff concluded, based on consumer testing, that current FDA language for qualified and unqualified claims didn't communicate the intended levels of scientific certainty to consumers. Indeed, consumers routinely perceived statements that were supposed to indicate uncertainty as indicating more scientific consensus than statements that were supposed to indicate consensus. On the flip side, and to advertisers' detriment, the current language used to communicate that there was significant scientific agreement on a claim didn't actually indicate strong scientific certainty to consumers.

One worrying feature of the current language was the wide range of interpretations consumers gave it—"a qualified claim that, on average, communicates the correct level of scientific certainty may still mislead a substantial number of consumers." However, other language did exist that could communicate levels of certainty; "report card" formats showing where a particular claim fell on a spectrum consistently performed well in testing. Would a report card or similar ranking system (for example, one to five stars indicating the level of scientific consensus about a claim) satisfy the *Pearson* court?

## 2.     "Organic" Claims: From the Wild West to the Walled Garden?

In the 1970s and 1980s, growing interest in traditional and less chemically dependent methods of cultivation led to a rise in "organic" agriculture and "organic" claims on food. Unfortunately, the meaning of "organic" was unclear. Dozens of private and state organic certification bodies provided varying third-party organic certifications, and not all "organic" foods were certified. The 1990 Organic Foods Production Act (OFPA) established a national organic standard. Why didn't the government wait for the market to converge on a definition?

Under OFPA, the U.S. Department of Agriculture (USDA) is responsible for regulating the use of "organic" on agricultural products. Only agricultural products that meet USDA standards can be labeled "organic" and use the USDA Organic seal. Under OFPA, the National Organic Standards Board (NOSB), which includes representatives from famers, retailers, consumers, environmental groups and food processors, makes recommendations to the USDA to define and regulate the organic label. In 1997, the USDA released the first proposed national organic standard, but did not follow NOSB recommendations in that its standard would have allowed food to be labeled organic even if it had undergone genetic modification or irradiation, had been fertilized with processed sewage sludge, or (for livestock) had been treated with antibiotics. After significant consumer protest, a more stringent revised standard was finalized in 2001. *See* Elaine Marie Lipson, *One Nation, Organically Grown*.

The organic label does not have any relationship to the producer's size. In fact, small farmers may find it harder to comply with the certification and recordkeeping requirements. Nor does organic mean local. Many organic foods are imported from other countries.

Among other things, the organic standard prohibits synthetic pesticides; prohibits genetic modification; prohibits irradiation; requires livestock to be given access to pasture; bans giving livestock growth hormones or antibiotics (sick animals are to be treated, but removed from the herd and not sold as organic); requires livestock to get organically grown feed; requires land to be free of chemical applications for three years before its crops can be considered organic; and requires written farm plans and audit trails. All growers and food processors who label their food organic, except those who make $5,000 or less per year from an organic enterprise, must be certified by a USDA-accredited, independent third-party agent. Knowing misuse of the organic label violates the law and may incur a civil penalty.

Under the rules, there are four categories for organic labeling. "100% organic" is just that. "Organic" requires 95% of the ingredients to be certified organic. Only these two categories can use the USDA Organic seal.

"Made with organic" requires 70% of the non-water, non-salt ingredients to be certified organic, and there are other requirements, including a rule that "made with organic ingredients" is not allowed. Instead, the claim must specify the organic ingredients or food categories, i.e., "Made with Organic [specify ingredients and or food categories]," but it may not list more than three ingredients or food categories. *See* United States Dep't of Agriculture, *Guidance: Products in the "Made with Organic \*\*\*" Labeling Category* (May 2, 2014); *see also* United States Dep't of Agriculture, *"Made with" Organic Labeling Examples* (Apr. 2014) (offering examples of allowed and non-allowed claims).

When the product is made with less than 70% organic ingredients, "organic" can be listed on the side panel only. The law also specifies display of the certifier's name and address and certain restrictions on permissible non-organic ingredients.

Is this scheme consistent with the First Amendment?

*The Standard's History.* Maine organic blueberry farmer and National Organic Program inspector Arthur Harvey successfully challenged several aspects of the rule initially adopted by the USDA. *See* Harvey v. Veneman, 396 F. 3d 28 (1st Cir. 2005). The rule initially could be read to allow the use of any non-organic ingredients "not commercially available in organic form" for multi-ingredient products labeled "organic." The court of appeals held that the OPFA didn't authorize a blanket exemption, but ingredients such as corn starch could be reviewed individually and allowed onto a list of acceptable nonorganic ingredients. Likewise, the rule improperly allowed the use of synthetic substances such as ascorbic acid and potassium hydroxide in processing organic-labeled items (though allowing this for "made with organic" labeled items was acceptable), and improperly permitted the use of up to 20% conventional feed in the first nine months of a dairy herd's year-long conversion to organic.

Proponents of the rule's initial version argued that these three provisions made producing organic products economically feasible, especially for smaller family farms. According to the CEO of Organic Valley Family of Farms, for example, "we realize, after this many years of experience, that synthetics are pretty necessary for a lot of different processes." Dan Sullivan, *Organics in the News*, March 31, 2005. Without synthetics, he argued, producers would abandon the "organic" label and move to the "made with organic" category, thus decreasing the amount of organic food available. By some estimates, more than 90% of multi-ingredient organic foods on the market, including many dairy products, would be disqualified from "organic" status under *Harvey*.

Congress responded to *Harvey* by amending OPFA to restore most of the initial rule. The Secretary of Agriculture could designate agricultural products that are commercially unavailable in organic form for short-term placement on a list of approved ingredients for organic-labeled products. For example, organic vanilla is grown in Madagascar, which is subject to major storms that interrupt supply. Processed organic products could be allowed to substitute small amounts of conventional vanilla when organic vanilla is commercially unavailable. Reversing the First Circuit, synthetic substances on the approved list may also be used in handling or processing an organic product. The law also allows more flexibility in the last year of transition of dairy herds to organic.

*What Do Consumers Think "Organic" Means?* Consumers Union surveyed consumers around the time of *Harvey* and found that 74% did not expect food labeled "made with organic" to contain artificial ingredients, despite the fact that synthetic ingredients are allowed in the 30% non-organic portion of the product. Eighty-five percent didn't expect food labeled "organic" to contain artificial ingredients (recall that the law requires only 95% organic content). The USDA is still working on standards for "organic" fish, but so far allows the use of the label on fish that would not meet the standards applied to other food. Consumers Union found 93% agreement that organic fish should be produced with 100% organic feed like all other animals. *See* Urvashi Rangan, *Comment to National Organic Standards Board on Aquaculture Recommendations*, November 18, 2008.

To what extent should consumer perception control the regulatory definition of "organic"? If consumers knew more about the difficulties of producing 100% organic multi-ingredient/processed foods, would they be more forgiving, and should that make a difference?

**Rebecca Tushnet, It Depends on What the Meaning of "False" Is: Falsity and Misleadingness in Commercial Speech Doctrine, 41 Loyola L.A. L. Rev. 101 (2008) (excerpt)**

The overall effects of the organic regulations are hard to predict. One effect is to decrease producers' incentives to make processed food with organic content below the threshold, because they can't truthfully advertise the organic content and organic food is more expensive. At the same time, the "made with organic" rules may also encourage producers to make more products with 70 percent or greater organic content, even if they cost more than a 60 percent organic product, and discourage them from adding a tiny bit of organic material to a conventional product. Consumers may well benefit from a fairly high threshold, since a 10 percent organic product may not satisfy consumer expectations for "organic." Moreover, in the absence of a uniform definition, many people would find it too difficult to sort through varying claims and would either mistakenly discount all such claims or mistakenly accept them. In other words, the "market for lemons" problem can be avoided in the market for organic lemons, but only if each consumer doesn't have to parse the definition of organic.

Separately, the ability to use a small percentage of non-organic ingredients may encourage more makers of multi-ingredient, processed food to enter the organic market. However, it also risks confusing consumers who, for example, expect that their organic sausages will be made entirely from organic meat and not include inorganic casings. Another specific example from the USDA's proposed list of exempt ingredients is hops. Exempting hops may make it more difficult for small producers of fully organic beer to compete against large firms that use the maximum amount of nonorganic hops, which cost half as much as organic hops, even as it encourages the production of more "organic" beers. Because both sets of producers can advertise "organic" beer, the regulation may either aid consumers or deceive them, depending on what they think organic means.

The issue of consumer response to standard-setting is worth further discussion to show just how hard the problem is. By setting a standard, the government establishes what "organic" means. If people misunderstand the term—in other words, if they continue to give a different meaning to it—there is an information problem that leads to inefficient results. If people do not understand the term but nonetheless rely on it, then a key question is whether the government has gotten the social policy producing the underlying definition right. Moreover, the correctness of the government's definition has to be compared to the situation without regulation, in which producers could give the term multiple meanings as long as they were not intentionally fraudulent. If consumers still relied on the term without understanding it or understanding that different producers were using different definitions, the welfare effects would change, but not obviously in any particular direction. To this must be added the likelihood that consumers would discount the term "organic" if they believed it to be self-defined, moderating both the harms and benefits of varying definitions. Only if consumers carefully research multiple meanings of unregulated terms—and only if they do this again and again, for each term that makes a difference to them—can we expect the unregulated market to beat the government systematically in shaping meaning.

### FTC, Green Guides Statement of Basis and Purpose (2012)

. . . The final [Green] Guides do not include a section on organic claims for two reasons. First, the USDA's NOP already addresses organic claims for agricultural products. Second, the Commission continues to lack sufficient evidence upon which to base generally applicable guidance for organic claims.

. . . [The] Commission also declines to issue general guidance on claims for products outside the NOP's jurisdiction. The record is simply too thin to support general guidance. Moreover, any advice the Commission promulgated for non-agricultural products could lead to general confusion or a perceived conflict with current or future NOP guidelines. In response to commenters concerned that the absence of guidance may result in fraud, the Commission reminds marketers they remain subject to the FTC Act's general proscriptions against unfair or deceptive marketing. As with any deceptive marketing claim, the Commission may bring an enforcement action against a marketer for deceptive organic claims.

Finally, some commenters requested a definition for "organic." The Commission, however, does not define terms. Instead, it examines how consumers interpret claims. At this time, the Commission lacks sufficient evidence regarding how consumers perceive organic claims to provide generally applicable advice.

### Letter from Consumers Union to David Vladeck, Director, FTC Bureau of Consumer Protection, Mar. 12, 2010

. . . We would like to take this opportunity to request that the Commission investigate the widespread, misleading use of "organic" claims on personal care products.

In particular, we have repeatedly asked the USDA to require that "organic" personal care products meet the same standards as "organic" food and to prohibit any use of the organic claim on products that don't meet the requirements of the NOP, such as seafood, fish and the subject of this particular complaint, personal care products. The USDA is superimposing a different labeling structure for "organic" personal care products and one that deviates from that required by the NOP. As a result, an extremely confusing marketplace exists for consumers shopping for "organic" personal care products. . . . USDA is not requiring that all "organic" claims on personal care products, including those that do not bear the "USDA-organic" seal, be NOP compliant, which is required for food. . . .

Personal care products tend to contain many synthetic ingredients, and many consumers are willing to pay more to buy "organic" personal care products in order to avoid these synthetic ingredients. . . .

Organic personal care products that are not compliant with the NOP can contain many petroleum-derived ingredients, conventional agricultural ingredients (those that have been treated with pesticides, etc.), preservatives, colorings and fragrances which may use or contain chemicals of concern in the production or final product. For example, phthalates, some of which have been banned by the Consumer Product Safety Commission in children's products for reproductive health effect concerns, may be lurking in many of the fragrances that could be used in organic personal care products. Parabens, EDTA, PEGs, coal tar colors (FD&C), ethanolamines—are just a few examples of synthetic materials that should certainly be reviewed and approved before being used in an organic personal care product. We believe many of those materials would not be approved after review by the NOSB. Finally, water and salt are required to be exempt from organic certification and the final calculation of organic content in a given product. However, we have noted several cases where "organic waters" are listed on ingredient panels. This would not be allowed for "organic" food and should not be allowed for "organic" personal care products. These so-called "organic" products can mislead and deceive consumers into paying more for something they did not expect.

. . . [Consumers Union also highlighted that there was no percentage requirement for "made with organic" claims on personal care products, as there is for food. As a result, personal products with minimal organic content can make "organic" label claims with apparent impunity.]

In the absence of USDA enforcement against unsubstantiated organic claims, the cosmetics industry has launched competing "organic" certifications. There are several different industry-based organic certification programs including Organic and Sustainable Industry Standards (OASIS), National Sanitation Foundation (NSF) International certification, and another mark called ECOCERT, which only add to the marketplace confusion.

While we appreciate industry efforts to standardize the meaning of claims used on products, it is entirely inappropriate for industry to be defining the meaning of "organic" since the meaning of that word, especially for products that fall under the scope of the independent NOP, must adhere to the requirements outlined in the OFPA and NOP. . . . Marketing activities of these industry groups only result in additional confusing messages to consumers about what organic means, what the USDA role is in organic certification of personal care products, and what is available to consumers.

For example, OASIS claims to be "the first organic standard for the U.S. beauty and personal care market, bringing clarity to consumer confusion around organic product claims—with a certification seal that will become the internationally accepted seal representing verified Organic standards for personal care. The only 'industry consensus' standard with the support of 30 founding members." Even though there are many certified USDA Organic personal care brands and products, OASIS tells consumers: "Until today, the USA has not had a dedicated organic standard for the beauty and personal care industry. In absence of a true industry standard, companies attempted to apply the USDA NOP (National Organic Program) Organic food standard for beauty and personal care ingredients and products. But the USDA's food standards were never designed for this industry, and limit certain types of 'green chemistry' posing significant challenges for those seeking to create certified organic products."

. . . In response to the question, "What is the difference between ECOCERT® and the USDA?" Organic wear® tells consumers: "ECOCERT® is the only organic certification for color cosmetics. USDA guidelines are for food products and they have no jurisdiction over color cosmetics." . . .

773

*NOTES AND QUESTIONS*

Is the Consumers Union position persuasive? Are the competing certifications evidence that the market is correcting the problem?

*A Remaining Role for State Law? In re Aurora Dairy Corp. Organic Milk Marketing and Sales Practices Litigation*, 621 F.3d 781 (8th Cir. 2010), considered whether the OFPA preempted state consumer protection law. As noted above, the OFPA creates a certification program through which agricultural producers may become certified to produce organic products. The OFPA also provides for the accreditation of certification agents, who inspect producers and make recommendations to the USDA regarding certification. Pursuant to the OFPA, the USDA promulgated regulations, known as the National Organic Program (NOP), 7 C.F.R. pt. 205, defining which agricultural products qualify as organic.

One certifying agent, QAI, Inc., certified Aurora Dairy Corporation's dairy farm to produce organic milk. Aurora was never decertified, though the USDA proposed revoking its certification in 2007 due to willful violations of the OFPA, including multiple cases of using nonorganic cows to produce "organic" milk, failure to produce and handle milk in accordance with regulations, and recordkeeping failures. Aurora and the USDA eventually entered into a consent agreement pursuant to which Aurora agreed to improve its practices and submit to further review.

Aurora sold its milk to the retailer defendants. Class plaintiffs sued Aurora, the retailers, and QAI, alleging that the defendants failed to comply with the OFPA and NOP and that Aurora's milk violated the law by claiming to be organic when it wasn't. In addition, plaintiffs alleged that Aurora and the retailers made other false statements:

> [S]everal of the cartons featured depictions of pastoral scenes with cows grazing in pastures, and advertised the idyllic conditions under which the dairy cows lived. Aurora advertised, "As producers of organic milk, our motto is 'Cows First,'" and, "We believe that animal welfare and cow comfort are the most important measures in organic dairy." Wal-Mart represented its milk was produced without the use of antibiotics or pesticides, and [that] organic farmers are committed to the humane treatment of animals. Safeway asserted its dairy cows "enjoy a healthy mix of fresh air, plenty of exercise, clean drinking water and a wholesome, 100% certified organic diet." Target declared, "Our milk comes from healthy cows that graze in organic pastures and eat wholesome organic feed."

The plaintiffs also alleged false advertising off the carton, such as Costco's *Costco Connection* magazine, which contained an article about Costco's house brand (for which Aurora was a supplier) claiming that "The cows on the farm have quite the life. They feed on a balanced organic vegan diet and have access to organic pastures for grazing." The cases around the nation were consolidated, and the district court granted the motion to dismiss.

The court of appeals affirmed the dismissal of all claims against QAI. Congress meant to replace the "patchwork" of existing state regulations with a national standard defining organic food, which included the certification scheme under which QAI is an accredited certifying agent. Thus, all claims against QAI were preempted. Aurora's certification also allows it to sell or label products using the OFPA-regulated terms without penalty. There is an administrative procedure for appeals of a certification agent's decisions. "[T]o the extent state law permits outside parties, including consumers, to interfere with or second guess the certification process, the state law is an 'obstacle to the accomplishment of congressional objectives' of the OFPA" and was preempted. QAI couldn't comply with the OFPA and its regulations detailing the process for revoking certifications and also comply with any additional state law duty to revoke certifications.

For the same reasons, claims attacking Aurora's certification were preempted. Class plaintiffs argued that defendants must be both certified and compliant with the underlying requirements to comply with the OFPA, but in light of the statute's structure and purpose, compliance and certification couldn't be viewed separately. The goal of establishing national standards would be undermined by an inevitable divergence in application by numerous court systems. Not only different legal interpretations, but also "different enforcement strategies and priorities" could fragment uniformity. (Note the difference in this analysis from other courts which find that state enforcement of a federal scheme such as the FDCA does not conflict with the scheme, just increases the incentives to comply.) "[A]ny attempt to hold Aurora or the retailers liable under state law based upon its products supposedly not being organic directly conflicts with the role of the certifying agent . . . ." Thus, claims based on Aurora's and the retailers' selling milk as organic when it was not were preempted.

Other claims, however, remained. State law challenges to the certification determination were preempted, but not state law challenges to the "facts underlying certification." The defendants argued that, if OFPA certification is to mean anything, it must mean the certified products have met all the statutory and regulatory requirements. The court of appeals disagreed. Certification requires, among other things, preventive livestock healthcare practices, including sufficiently nutritional feed. Congress, the court felt confident, didn't intend to prevent states from enforcing animal cruelty laws if a producer was neglecting its animals, especially given the states' historic roles in the area of consumer protection, fraud, and tort claims. Notably, "[c]ertification relies upon inspection and observation of only a portion of a producer's operations, and thus, the evidence which supported certification could, and very likely would, be different from the evidence which supports a state cause of action."

Preempting state law claims unrelated to certification and certification compliance doesn't advance the purpose of establishing national standards for organic foods. In fact, preemption of consumer protection law might diminish consumer confidence if consumers become aware that the certifying agent didn't suspend certification in spite of clear facts to the contrary and that there wasn't anything that anyone else could do. Furthermore, "although broad factual preemption may increase organic production in the short term, consumers may well elect to avoid paying the premium for organic products upon realizing preemption grants organic producers a de facto license to violate state fraud, consumer protection, and false advertising laws with relative impunity . . . ." *See also* Quesada v. Herb Thyme Farms, 323 P.3d 1 (Cal. 2014) (claim that a grower intentionally mislabeled conventionally grown produce as organic wasn't preempted; reasoning similarly).

*A Role for the Lanham Act?* In *All One God Faith, Inc. v. The Hain Celestial Group, Inc.*, 2010 WL 2133209 (N.D. Cal. 2010), the plaintiff sued multiple defendants for falsely advertising their cosmetics as organic, alleging that consumers expect that personal care products labeled as organic won't contain synthetic compounds such as preservatives, cleansing agents, or moisturizing agents derived from conventionally produced agricultural materials, or petrochemicals. These expectations may well be causally connected to the federal "organic" standards for food, to which they conform, though plaintiff's amended complaint alleged that consumer research surveys established their existence.

In such cases, should the Lanham Act apply, which might functionally expand the scope of USDA regulation beyond what Congress or the USDA intended?

The court dismissed the complaint based on the primary jurisdiction doctrine, which allocates matters to relevant agencies first where Congress has given the agency comprehensive authority that requires expertise or uniformity. Defendants argued that deciding the case would force the court to evaluate how consumer understandings line up with existing regulations and potentially impose standards in conflict with those Congress mandated (for example, statutes and regulations allow some use of synthetic ingredients in products labeled organic, while the complaint alleged that reasonable consumers expect that organic products have no synthetic ingredients). The court agreed that it would have to interpret and apply USDA regulations to determine what "organically produced," "nonagricultural" and "synthetic" mean. The court stayed the case pending further USDA action.

Was this the right result? Compare it to the FDA preemption cases in Section 1. If the plaintiff could prove that consumers were being deceived, why wait for the USDA to act?

*The Halo Effect.* In a recent study, participants were asked to sample pairs of identical foods. One was labeled "organic" and the other "regular," though they were actually both organic. Participants estimated the "organic" foods to be lower in calories, higher in nutritional value, and worth paying more for than the "regular" foods, though people who typically read nutrition labels and who often bought organic foods did somewhat better at estimating calories. Wan-chen Jenny Lee et al., *You Taste What You See: Do Organic Labels Bias Taste Perceptions?*, 29 FOOD QUALITY & PREFERENCE 33 (2013). Does "organic" mislead calorie-conscious consumers? Is that misleadingness justified by the other (truthful) information conveyed by the term?

## 3.    Green Marketing

"Green" marketing often covers the same types of goods that the FDA and USDA regulate, although it can be used far more broadly. The regulations, such as they are, on "green" claims provide a contrast to the more rule-based regulations covered in the first parts of this chapter. Think about whether the essentially reactive approach of "green" marketing regulation would be more appropriate for these other fields; whether "green" claims ought to get the same kind of detailed instructions as drugs or "organic" foods; or whether these differing types of regulation have been implemented appropriately given the different topics.

In 1992, in response to growing consumer interest in the environment, growing advertiser response to this interest, and growing confusion about what environmental-type claims meant, the FTC issued its first Green Guides, providing specific criteria for using terms such as biodegradable, recyclable, and recycled, as well as more general guidance. The Guides have been revised three times as environmental concerns changed and experience with green marketing claims improved. We will examine portions of the 2012 revisions, and the FTC's commentary on them.

**FTC, Statement of Basis and Purpose (2012) (opening commentary)**

The Commission issued the Green Guides, 16 CFR Part 260, to help marketers avoid deceptive environmental claims under Section 5 of the FTC Act, 15 U.S.C. 45.

Industry guides, such as these, are administrative interpretations of the law. Therefore, they do not have the force and effect of law and are not independently enforceable. The Commission, however, can take action under the FTC Act if a marketer makes an environmental claim inconsistent with the Guides. In any such enforcement action, the Commission must prove that the challenged act or practice is unfair or deceptive.

The Green Guides outline general principles that apply to all environmental marketing claims and provide guidance regarding many specific environmental benefit claims. The Guides explain how reasonable consumers likely interpret each such claim, describe the basic elements necessary to substantiate it, and present options for qualifying it to avoid deception.[5]

Illustrative qualifications provide guidance for marketers who want assurance about how to make non-deceptive environmental claims, but are not the only permissible approaches to qualifying a claim. As discussed below, although the Guides assist marketers in making non-deceptive environmental claims, the Guides cannot always anticipate which specific claims will, or will not, be deceptive because of incomplete consumer perception evidence and because perception often depends on context. . . .

[B]ecause the Guides are based on consumer understanding of environmental claims, consumer perception research provides the best evidence upon which to formulate guidance. The Commission therefore conducted its own study in July and August of 2009.

The study presented 3,777 participants with questions calculated to determine how they understood certain environmental claims. The first portion of the study examined general environmental benefit claims ("green" and "eco-friendly"), as well as "sustainable," "made with renewable materials," "made with renewable energy," and "made with recycled materials" claims. To examine whether consumers' understanding of these claims differed depending on the

---

[5] The Guides, however, neither establish standards for environmental performance nor prescribe testing protocols.

product being advertised, the study tested the claims as they appeared on three different products: wrapping paper, a laundry basket, and kitchen flooring.[6]

I.     General Issues

. . . . [T]he Commission agrees that enforcement is a key component of greater compliance. Therefore, in recent years it has stepped up enforcement against companies making deceptive environmental claims. For example, the Commission sued a company for providing environmental certifications to any businesses willing to pay a fee without considering their products' environmental attributes. Additionally, the Commission announced three actions charging marketers with making false and unsubstantiated claims that their products were biodegradable. The Commission also charged four sellers of clothing and other textile products with deceptively labeling and advertising these items as made of bamboo fiber, manufactured using an environmentally friendly process, and/or biodegradable. . . .

**16 CFR Part 260: Guides for the Use of Environmental Marketing Claims**

§ 260.1 Purpose, Scope, and Structure of the Guides.

. . . (d) The guides consist of general principles, specific guidance on the use of particular environmental claims, and examples. Claims may raise issues that are addressed by more than one example and in more than one section of the guides. The examples provide the Commission's views on how reasonable consumers likely interpret certain claims. . . . In addition, although many examples present specific claims and options for qualifying claims, the examples do not illustrate all permissible claims or qualifications under Section 5 of the FTC Act. Nor do they illustrate the only ways to comply with the guides. Marketers can use an alternative approach if the approach satisfies the requirements of Section 5 of the FTC Act....

§ 260.3 General Principles.

. . . (b) Distinction between benefits of product, package, and service: Unless it is clear from the context, an environmental marketing claim should specify whether it refers to the product, the product's packaging, a service, or just to a portion of the product, package, or service. In general, if the environmental attribute applies to all but minor, incidental components of a product or package, the marketer need not qualify the claim to identify that fact. However, there may be exceptions to this general principle. For example, if a marketer makes an unqualified recyclable claim, and the presence of the incidental component significantly limits the ability to recycle the product, the claim would be deceptive.

Example 1: A plastic package containing a new shower curtain is labeled "recyclable" without further elaboration. Because the context of the claim does not make clear whether it refers to the plastic

---

[6] The study results support the 1998 Guides' approach of providing general, rather than product-specific, guidance because consumers generally viewed the tested claims similarly for the three tested products. . . .

package or the shower curtain, the claim is deceptive if any part of either the package or the curtain, other than minor, incidental components, cannot be recycled.

Example 2: A soft drink bottle is labeled "recycled." The bottle is made entirely from recycled materials, but the bottle cap is not. Because the bottle cap is a minor, incidental component of the package, the claim is not deceptive.

(c) Overstatement of environmental attribute: An environmental marketing claim should not overstate, directly or by implication, an environmental attribute or benefit. Marketers should not state or imply environmental benefits if the benefits are negligible.

Example 1: An area rug is labeled "50% more recycled content than before." The manufacturer increased the recycled content of its rug from 2% recycled fiber to 3%. Although the claim is technically true, it likely conveys the false impression that the manufacturer has increased significantly the use of recycled fiber.

Example 2: A trash bag is labeled "recyclable" without qualification. Because trash bags ordinarily are not separated from other trash at the landfill or incinerator for recycling, they are highly unlikely to be used again for any purpose. Even if the bag is technically capable of being recycled, the claim is deceptive since it asserts an environmental benefit where no meaningful benefit exists.

(d) Comparative claims: Comparative environmental marketing claims should be clear to avoid consumer confusion about the comparison. Marketers should have substantiation for the comparison.

Example 1: An advertiser notes that its glass bathroom tiles contain "20% more recycled content." Depending on the context, the claim could be a comparison either to the advertiser's immediately preceding product or to its competitors' products. The advertiser should have substantiation for both interpretations. Otherwise, the advertiser should make the basis for comparison clear, for example, by saying "20% more recycled content than our previous bathroom tiles." . . .

§ 260.4 General Environmental Benefit Claims.

(a) It is deceptive to misrepresent, directly or by implication, that a product, package, or service offers a general environmental benefit.

(b) Unqualified general environmental benefit claims are difficult to interpret and likely convey a wide range of meanings. In many cases, such claims likely convey that the product, package, or service has specific and far-reaching environmental benefits and may convey that the item or service has no negative environmental impact. Because it is highly unlikely that marketers can substantiate all reasonable interpretations of these claims, marketers should not make unqualified general environmental benefit claims.

(c) Marketers can qualify general environmental benefit claims to prevent deception about the nature of the environmental benefit being asserted. To avoid deception, marketers should use clear and prominent qualifying language that limits the claim to a specific benefit or benefits. Marketers should not imply that any specific benefit is significant if it is, in fact, negligible. If a qualified general claim conveys that a product is more environmentally beneficial overall because of the particular touted benefit(s), marketers should analyze trade-offs resulting from the benefit(s) to determine if they can substantiate this claim.[7] . . .

Example 1: The brand name "Eco-friendly" likely conveys that the product has far-reaching environmental benefits and may convey that the product has no negative environmental impact. Because it is highly unlikely that the marketer can substantiate these claims, the use of such a brand name is deceptive. A claim, such as "Eco-friendly: made with recycled materials," would not be deceptive if: (1) the statement "made with recycled materials" is clear and prominent; (2) the marketer can substantiate that the entire product or package, excluding minor, incidental components, is made from recycled material; (3) making the product with recycled materials makes the product more environmentally beneficial overall; and (4) the advertisement's context does not imply other deceptive claims.

Example 2: A marketer states that its packaging is now "Greener than our previous packaging." The packaging weighs 15% less than previous packaging, but it is not recyclable nor has it been improved in any other material respect. The claim is deceptive because reasonable consumers likely would interpret "Greener" in this context to mean that other significant environmental aspects of the packaging also are improved over previous packaging. A claim stating "Greener than our previous packaging" accompanied by clear and prominent language such as, "We've reduced the weight of our packaging by 15%," would not be deceptive, provided that reducing the packaging's weight makes the product more environmentally beneficial overall and the advertisement's context does not imply other deceptive claims.

Example 3: A marketer's advertisement features a picture of a laser printer in a bird's nest balancing on a tree branch, surrounded by a dense forest. In green type, the marketer states, "Buy our printer. Make a change." Although the advertisement does not expressly claim that the product has environmental benefits, the featured images, in combination with the text, likely convey that the product has far-reaching environmental benefits and may convey that the product has no negative environmental impact. Because it is highly unlikely that the marketer can substantiate these claims, this advertisement is deceptive.

Example 5: A marketer reduces the weight of its plastic beverage bottles. The bottles' labels state: "Environmentally-friendly improvement. 25% less plastic than our previous packaging." The plastic bottles are 25 percent lighter but otherwise are no different. The advertisement conveys that the bottles are more environmentally beneficial overall because of the source reduction. To substantiate this claim, the marketer likely can analyze the impacts of the source reduction without evaluating environmental impacts throughout the packaging's life cycle. If, however, manufacturing the new

---

[7] [Editor's note: Some have contended that this statement requires companies to engage in "life-cycle analysis," a complicated and often hotly contested effort to measure the total environmental impact of a product from cradle to tomb. The FTC declined to explicitly require life-cycle analysis as a precondition for making an environmental benefit claim. As you read the examples, consider whether you agree that the FTC's reasoning covertly requires a life-cycle analysis.]

bottles significantly alters environmental attributes earlier or later in the bottles' life cycle, i.e., manufacturing the bottles requires more energy or a different kind of plastic, then a more comprehensive analysis may be appropriate.

[The FTC found that its consumer studies supported its recommendation against making general, unqualified environmental benefit claims. From its Statement of Basis and Purpose:] Specifically, on average, approximately half of the respondents viewing general, unqualified "green" and "eco-friendly" claims inferred specific, unstated environmental benefits. Moreover, 27 percent of respondents interpreted the unqualified claims "green" and "eco-friendly" as suggesting the product has no negative environmental impact.

. . . The Commission designed its questionnaire to be as non-suggestive and non-leading as possible. Thus, before asking any closed-ended questions about specific environmental attributes, the study asked open-ended questions about what, if anything, a claim suggested or implied about a product. The responses to these non-suggestive, open-ended questions show that a large percentage of the participants took particular environmental attribute claims from an unqualified claim. Fifty-three percent of respondents indicated, in this unprompted format, that the product had one or more implied specific environmental characteristics. For example, of those who were told that the product was "Green" or "Eco-Friendly," 33 percent indicated that the claim suggested that the product was made with recycled materials. . . .

As administrative interpretations of Section 5, the Guides do not create an obligation that does not already exist under Section 5. Rather, they clarify this obligation, cautioning marketers that unqualified general environmental benefit claims are difficult, if not impossible, to substantiate and reminding marketers not to make claims they cannot substantiate. . . .

Finally, although some commenters asked the Commission to include an example illustrating a non-deceptive, unqualified general environmental benefit claim, the Commission declines to do so. As discussed above, it is highly unlikely that marketers can substantiate all reasonable interpretations of such a claim. In fact, even the scenarios commenters described as meriting unqualified general environmental benefit claims illustrate the difficulty in substantiating such claims. For instance, one commenter suggested including an example about a local nursery selling organically grown, indigenous species of trees for local planting. Here, however, there may be negative environmental impacts depending on, among other things, the nursery's irrigation systems, waste disposal practices, and vehicle and machinery use. It also is highly unlikely that the nursery could substantiate all the specific claims reasonable consumers take away from a general "green" claim. For example, consumers may incorrectly assume that the nursery uses only renewable energy. Moreover, even if one could postulate an example where a product has no negative impact and has every implied environmental benefit, similar factual scenarios would be so rare that the example would have limited applicability and may lead to more confusion than benefit. Nevertheless, because the Guides are simply guidance, they do not foreclose the possibility that a marketer could create an advertisement for a particular product with general environmental claims that only implies claims the marketer can substantiate. . . .

§ 260.6 Certifications and Seals of Approval.

(a) It is deceptive to misrepresent, directly or by implication, that a product, package, or service has been endorsed or certified by an independent third-party.

(b) A marketer's use of the name, logo, or seal of approval of a third-party certifier or organization may be an endorsement, which should meet the criteria for endorsements provided in the FTC's Endorsement Guides, 16 C.F.R. Part 255 . . . .

(c) Third-party certification does not eliminate a marketer's obligation to ensure that it has substantiation for all claims reasonably communicated by the certification.

(d) A marketer's use of an environmental certification or seal of approval likely conveys that the product offers a general environmental benefit (see § 260.4) if the certification or seal does not convey the basis for the certification or seal, either through the name or some other means. Because it is highly unlikely that marketers can substantiate general environmental benefit claims, marketers should not use environmental certifications or seals that do not convey the basis for the certification.

(e) Marketers can qualify general environmental benefit claims conveyed by environmental certifications and seals of approval to prevent deception about the nature of the environmental benefit being asserted. To avoid deception, marketers should use clear and prominent qualifying language that clearly conveys that the certification or seal refers only to specific and limited benefits.

Example 1: An advertisement for paint features a "GreenLogo" seal and the statement "GreenLogo for Environmental Excellence." This advertisement likely conveys that: (1) the GreenLogo seal is awarded by an independent, third-party certifier with appropriate expertise in evaluating the environmental attributes of paint; and (2) the product has far-reaching environmental benefits. If the paint manufacturer awarded the seal to its own product, and no independent, third-party certifier objectively evaluated the paint using independent standards, the claim would be deceptive. The claim would not be deceptive if the marketer accompanied the seal with clear and prominent language: (1) indicating that the marketer awarded the GreenLogo seal to its own product; and (2) clearly conveying that the award refers only to specific and limited benefits.

Example 2: A manufacturer advertises its product as "certified by the American Institute of Degradable Materials." Because the advertisement does not mention that the American Institute of Degradable Materials ("AIDM") is an industry trade association, the certification likely conveys that it was awarded by an independent certifier. To be certified, marketers must meet standards that have been developed and maintained by a voluntary consensus standard body. An independent auditor applies these standards objectively. This advertisement likely is not deceptive if the manufacturer complies with § 260.8 of the Guides (Degradable Claims) because the certification is based on independently-developed and -maintained standards and an independent auditor applies the standards objectively.

Example 3: A product features a seal of approval from "The Forest Products Industry Association," an industry certifier with appropriate expertise in evaluating the environmental attributes of paper products. Because it is clear from the certifier's name that the product has been certified by an industry certifier, the certification likely does not convey that it was awarded by an independent certifier. The use of the seal likely is not deceptive provided that the advertisement does not imply other deceptive claims.

Example 4: A marketer's package features a seal of approval with the text "Certified Non-Toxic." The seal is awarded by a certifier with appropriate expertise in evaluating ingredient safety and potential toxicity. It applies standards developed by a voluntary consensus standard body. Although non-industry members comprise a majority of the certifier's board, an industry veto could override any proposed changes to the standards. This certification likely conveys that the product is certified by an independent organization. This claim would be deceptive because industry members can veto any proposed changes to the standards.

Example 5: A marketer's industry sales brochure for overhead lighting features a seal with the text "EcoFriendly Building Association" to show that the marketer is a member of that organization. Although the lighting manufacturer is, in fact, a member, this association has not evaluated the environmental attributes of the marketer's product. This advertisement would be deceptive because it likely conveys that the EcoFriendly Building Association evaluated the product through testing or other objective standards. It also is likely to convey that the lighting has far-reaching environmental benefits. The use of the seal would not be deceptive if the manufacturer accompanies it with clear and prominent qualifying language: (1) indicating that the seal refers to the company's membership only and that the association did not evaluate the product's environmental attributes; and (2) limiting the general environmental benefit representations, both express and implied, to the particular product attributes for which the marketer has substantiation. For example, the marketer could state: "Although we are a member of the EcoFriendly Building Association, it has not evaluated this product. Our lighting is made from 100 percent recycled metal and uses energy efficient LED technology."

Example 6: A product label contains an environmental seal, either in the form of a globe icon or a globe icon with the text "EarthSmart." EarthSmart is an independent, third-party certifier with appropriate expertise in evaluating chemical emissions of products. While the marketer meets EarthSmart's standards for reduced chemical emissions during product usage, the product has no other specific environmental benefits. Either seal likely conveys that the product has far-reaching environmental benefits, and that EarthSmart certified the product for all of these benefits. If the marketer cannot substantiate these claims, the use of the seal would be deceptive. The seal would not be deceptive if the marketer accompanied it with clear and prominent language clearly conveying that the certification refers only to specific and limited benefits. For example, the marketer could state next to the globe icon: "EarthSmart certifies that this product meets EarthSmart standards for reduced chemical emissions during product usage." Alternatively, the claim would not be deceptive if the EarthSmart environmental seal itself stated: "EarthSmart Certified for reduced chemical emissions during product usage."

Example 7: A one-quart bottle of window cleaner features a seal with the text "Environment Approved," granted by an independent, third-party certifier with appropriate expertise. The certifier granted the seal after evaluating 35 environmental attributes. This seal likely conveys that the product has far-reaching environmental benefits and that Environment Approved certified the product for all of these benefits and therefore is likely deceptive. The seal would likely not be deceptive if the marketer accompanied it with clear and prominent language clearly conveying that the seal refers only to specific and limited benefits. For example, the seal could state: "Virtually all products impact the environment. For details on which attributes we evaluated, go to [a website that discusses this product]." The referenced webpage provides a detailed summary of the examined environmental attributes. A reference to a website is appropriate because the additional information provided on the website is not necessary to prevent the advertisement from being misleading. As always, the marketer also should ensure that the advertisement does not imply other deceptive claims, and that the certifier's criteria are sufficiently rigorous to substantiate all material claims reasonably communicated by the certification.

Example 8: Great Paper Company sells photocopy paper with packaging that has a seal of approval from the No Chlorine Products Association, a non-profit third-party association. Great Paper Company paid the No Chlorine Products Association a reasonable fee for the certification. Consumers would reasonably expect that marketers have to pay for certification. Therefore, there are no material connections between Great Paper Company and the No Chlorine Products Association. The claim would not be deceptive.

§ 260.7 Compostable Claims.

(a) It is deceptive to misrepresent, directly or by implication, that a product or package is compostable. [Editor's note: For this, as with degradability and recyclability claims, the FTC takes the position that a scientific definition of "compostable" is not controlling. Rather, the question is whether consumers will get what they expect, and if a theoretically compostable/biodegradable/recyclable product is not practically so in the consumer's area, the FTC will consider the claim deceptive unless it is sufficiently qualified to make the risks clear. So, for example, if recycling facilities are available to at least 60% of consumers or communities where products are sold, marketers can make unqualified recyclability claims. But below that, the lower the level of access to appropriate facilities, the more a marketer should emphasize the limited availability of recycling for the product.]

Example 1: A manufacturer indicates that its unbleached coffee filter is compostable. The unqualified claim is not deceptive, provided the manufacturer has substantiation that the filter can be converted safely to usable compost in a timely manner in a home compost pile or device. If so, the extent of local municipal or institutional composting facilities is irrelevant. . . .

Example 3: A manufacturer makes an unqualified claim that its package is compostable. Although municipal or institutional composting facilities exist where the product is sold, the package will not break down into usable compost in a home compost pile or device. To avoid deception, the manufacturer should clearly and prominently disclose that the package is not suitable for home composting.

Example 4: Nationally marketed lawn and leaf bags state "compostable" on each bag. The bags also feature text disclosing that the bag is not designed for use in home compost piles. Yard trimmings programs in many communities compost these bags, but such programs are not available to a substantial majority of consumers or communities where the bag is sold. The claim is deceptive because it likely conveys that composting facilities are available to a substantial majority of consumers or communities. To avoid deception, the marketer should clearly and prominently indicate the limited availability of such programs. A marketer could state "Appropriate facilities may not exist in your area," or provide the approximate percentage of communities or consumers for which such programs are available. . . .

§ 260.8 Degradable Claims.

. . . (c) It is deceptive to make an unqualified degradable claim for items entering the solid waste stream if the items do not completely decompose within one year after customary disposal. Unqualified degradable claims for items that are customarily disposed in landfills, incinerators, and recycling facilities are deceptive because these locations do not present conditions in which complete decomposition will occur within one year . . .

*NOTES AND QUESTIONS*

The FTC continues to engage in enforcement actions related to the Green Guides. Problematic claims often travel together. For example, *In re Down to Earth Designs, Inc.*, File No. 122 3268 (settlement order, Jan. 17, 2014), involved biodegradability, compostability and other environmental claims.

Flush.
Compost.
Toss.

gDiapers. No garbage.

785

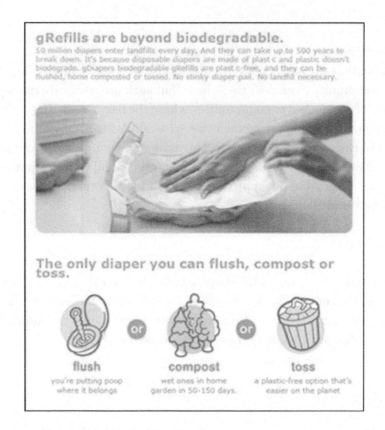

Among the problems: The biodegradability claims violated the FTC Act because the advertiser couldn't substantiate that the products would completely break down and decompose into elements found in nature within one year after customary disposal in the trash; it was misleading to claim products would offer an environmental benefit when flushed; it was misleading to claim that diaper liners and wipes were compostable when they couldn't be composted if they were soiled with solid human waste; and it was misleading to advertise the diapers as plastic-free because one component of the system included plastic.

Are the Guides specific enough to provide useful rules for marketers? Are they consistent with the First Amendment? (Compare the limits on the FDA imposed by *Pearson* and subsequent cases.)

In one recent administrative proceeding, the ALJ rejected the FTC's position on "biodegradable" claims in the Guides. The ALJ found that the consumer meaning survey relied on by the FTC was too poorly designed to support the FTC's interpretation that an unqualified "biodegradable" claim meant that the product would "completely decompose within one year after customary disposal," which in most cases meant landfill disposal. However, even the more reasonable interpretation that the products would biodegrade in a period between 9 months and 5 years after customary disposal was unsubstantiated. FTC v. ECM BioFilms, No. 9358 (Jan. 28, 2015).

How should advertisers proceed when the truth of the matter is uncertain? In 1988, the National Association of Diaper Services ("NADS") commissioned a study that concluded that disposable diapers significantly contribute to America's solid waste output, which some called a crisis. The disposable diaper industry responded with its own life-cycle analyses concluding that the effects were mixed, but that the evidence arguably favored disposable diapers, given factors such as the energy required to heat water to clean cloth diapers. NADS then commissioned another study, which found that cloth diapers, when laundered by a diaper service, were better for the environment than disposables, though that study omitted the energy use and environmental impact of transporting the diapers to consumers. The different studies used completely incompatible assumptions about how many diaper users of each kind flushed fecal matter before disposal, so that the disposable-funded study concluded that cloth services used more than four times as much water as the NADS study concluded they did. One disposable maker's study found that cloth diaper usage consumed three times more energy than disposable usage, while the NADS study found that disposables used 70% more energy than cloth. The divergence came in part from the disposable-funded study counting co-generation (simultaneously generating electricity and usable heat) as an environmental benefit, while the cloth-funded study assumed that co-generation caused pollution.

What kind of claims could cloth diaper services make under the Green Guides? What kind of claims could disposable diaper manufacturers make? If they should both be allowed to make environmental claims, is that a strength or a weakness of the Guides? *See* John M. Church, *A Market Solution to Green Marketing: Some Lessons from the Economics of Information*, 79 MINN. L. REV. 245 (1994) (arguing that, in the absence of scientific consensus on measuring environmental impacts, consumer confusion and distrust of marketers' environmental claims indicates that the market for information is functioning efficiently).

*Remaining State Regulations.* Because the FTC took a while to act, states enacted a patchwork of regulations. California, New York, and Rhode Island defined many terms also covered by the Green Guides. California enacted a qualified ban on generic terms such as "ecologically safe," "earth friendly," and "green," while Rhode Island banned certain terms such as "biodegradable" and "environmentally safe" outright. California prohibits representing a product as recyclable unless it can be "conveniently recycled" in every county with a population over 300,000. Some states, including California, make compliance with FTC rules a defense, but not all do (and some lawyers will be willing to argue that the Green Guides aren't "rules"). In states that adopted the FTC Guides as state law, such as Indiana and Wisconsin, the Guides have independent force, which they do not under federal law because they are merely interpretations of § 5 of the FTCA. *See* E. Howard Barnett, *Green with Envy: The FTC, the EPA, the States, and the Regulation of Environmental Marketing*, 1 ENVTL. LAW. 491 (1995).

*International Trade Barriers to Regulation of Green Marketing.* NAFTA and GATT prohibit "technical barriers to trade." Labeling requirements and other regulations that make it difficult or impossible for importers to market their products may be invalidated by WTO panels if insufficiently justified. In a potentially unsettling development for those in favor of greener production processes, the U.S. ban on importing tuna whose producers engaged in processes deemed unsafe for dolphins was found to violate GATT. *See* United States—Restrictions on Import of Tuna, GATT DOC. DS21/R (Sept. 1991); *see generally* Douglas A. Kysar, *Preferences for Processes: The Process–Product Distinction and the Regulation of Consumer Choice*, 118 HARV. L. REV. 525 (2004). In what circumstances are U.S. advertising regulations justified, even if that keeps certain products out of the country?

CHAPTER 17: CASE STUDIES IN FOOD AND DRUGS

*The NAD and Environmental Claims.* The NAD has devoted substantial attention to green claims. It has followed the lead of the FTC in disapproving general environmental benefit claims. In *Panasonic Corporation of North America*, NAD Case #4697 (7/16/2007), for example, claims for large-screen plasma televisions included: "Panasonic Plasmas are environmentally friendly. No lead. No mercury. No worries. Most LCD TVs have mercury." The NAD recommended discontinuing the general "environmentally friendly" claim, because large-screen plasma TVs consume large amounts of power, more than comparably sized LCDs, though the advertiser remained free to tout the absence of lead or mercury.

In *Seventh Generation, Inc.*, NAD Case #4488 (5/8/2006), by contrast, the NAD held that the claim that Seventh Generation cleaning products are "as gentle on the planet as they are on people" was puffery. In *Tom's of Maine*, NAD Case # 3470 (6/1/1998), the label of Tom's of Maine Natural Mouthwash stated that it was "pure and natural" and contained "pure, simple ingredients from nature." But the product contained a polymer not sourced from nature, and thus the NAD held the advertising needed to be modified to avoid any claim, direct or by implication, that the product was 100% natural.

*The Lanham Act and Environmental Claims. Static Control Components, Inc. v. Lexmark International, Inc.*, 487 F. Supp. 2d 861 (E.D. Ky. 2007), concerned Lexmark's sale of refillable printer toner cartridges. Lexmark didn't remanufacture all the cartridges or parts it collected. Hundreds of thousands of cartridges were incinerated, with their ash going to a landfill, which Lexmark called "thermally recycling."

Lexmark's prebate cartridges had a label about Lexmark's "Environmental Program": "We manage resources today to ensure a beautiful tomorrow. Small steps can have big rewards. Thank you for your ongoing support, together we have recycled millions of toner cartridges, one cartridge at a time. See details inside about how you can continue to participate in this important environmental initiative." Lexmark's website claimed, "Return Prebate cartridges are a great choice for the environment." It further stated: "Lexmark Return Prebate Program Cartridges are sold at a discount in exchange for the customer's agreement to use the cartridge only once and return it only to Lexmark for remanufacturing or recycling," and that "Lexmark recycles Return Program Cartridges, keeping them out of the waste stream."

Lexmark conducted market research among people responsible for purchasing printers and physically replacing used cartridges with new or remanufactured cartridges. Responses to the "environmentally friendly message" included:

> The green environmental label gives you a better conscience.

> You want it to be green. You don't want this stuff out in the street. You want it to be recycled; you want it to be treated properly.

Focus groups asked to create their own names for the prebate program suggested names such as "Save the Toner Tree," "Responsible Use of Resources," "Environmental Express (so that people get the impression that it speeds up the process)," "Envirosave," and "Save $ and the Environment."

The court denied summary judgment on a competitor's false advertising claims. Statements such as "Lexmark recycles Return Program Cartridges, keeping them out of the waste stream" were unambiguous, but the court found that there were significant disputed facts about whether "thermal recycling" could count as recycling under certain definitions.

What would have been the result under the Green Guides as set forth above? Should the court have required Lexmark to submit evidence that consumers subscribe to the definitions Lexmark wanted to use?

Made in the USA
Las Vegas, NV
14 December 2023

82777862R00227